4th Workshop on Knowledge-Augmented Methods for Natural Language Processing (KnowledgeNLP 2025)

Albuquerque, New Mexico, USA
3 May 2025

ISBN: 979-8-3313-1920-5

Printed from e-media with permission by:

Curran Associates, Inc.
57 Morehouse Lane
Red Hook, NY 12571

Some format issues inherent in the e-media version may also appear in this print version.

Printed with permission by Curran Associates, Inc. (2025)

For permission requests, please contact the Association for Computational Linguistics at the address below.

Association for Computational Linguistics
209 N. Eighth Street
Stroudsburg, Pennsylvania 18360

Phone: 1-570-476-8006
Fax: 1-570-476-0860

acl@aclweb.org

Additional copies of this publication are available from:

Curran Associates, Inc.
57 Morehouse Lane
Red Hook, NY 12571 USA
Phone: 845-758-0400
Fax: 845-758-2633
Email: curran@proceedings.com
Web: www.proceedings.com

KnowledgeNLP'25 2025

The 4th International Workshop on Knowledge-Augmented Methods for Natural Language Processing

Proceedings of the Workshop

May 3, 2025

Order copies of this and other ACL proceedings from:

Association for Computational Linguistics (ACL)
317 Sidney Baker St. S
Suite 400 - 134
Kerrville, TX 78028
USA
Tel: +1-855-225-1962
acl@aclweb.org

Introduction

Welcome to the 4th International Workshop on Knowledge-Augmented Methods for Natural Language Processing (KnowledgeNLP'25), held in conjunction with NAACL 2025. KnowledgeNLP will take place on May 3rd, 2025, allowing for both virtual and in-person attendance in New Mexico, USA.

Recent progress in large-scale models like ChatGPT has significantly advanced NLP capabilities. However, these models face limitations in memorizing rare information, are prone to hallucinations, and cannot access up-to-date information. Additionally, their fixed parameter size prevents them from fully encapsulating the continuously evolving world knowledge.

The field of knowledge-augmented NLP spans a wide array of techniques and applications. Acquiring relevant knowledge is challenging due to its diversity and distribution across numerous sources. Once acquired, effectively representing and utilizing this knowledge to support model predictions presents another major challenge. This workshop seeks to bring researchers together to share their insights and progress in this domain, aiming to highlight the importance of knowledge-augmented NLP.

In response to our call for papers, we received 48 submissions. Each submission was rigorously reviewed by at least three Program Committee members selected for their expertise. Based on the reviewers' feedback, we accepted 28 papers, including 6 oral presentations and 22 poster presentations. We are honored to invite five keynote speakers: Prof. Doug Downey (Allen Institute for AI and Professor Northwestern University), Prof. Graham Neubig (Carnegie Mellon University), Dr. Yunyao Li (Adobe), Prof. Yu Su (Ohio State University), Prof. Manling Li (Northwestern University).

We hope you find the workshop papers insightful and inspiring. We express our gratitude to the keynote speakers for their engaging talks, the authors for their valuable contributions, and the Program Committee members for their thorough reviews. Special thanks to the emergency reviewers for their expertise and to the NAACL 2025 workshop chairs for their support during the organization process.

Organizing Committee

Program Chairs

Weijia Shi, University of Washington
Wenhao Yu, Tencent AI Seattle Lab
Akari Asai, University of Washington
Meng Jiang, University of Notre Dame
Greg Durrett, University of Texas at Austin
Hannaneh Hajishirzi, University of Washington
Luke Zettlemoyer, University of Washington

Program Committee

Reviewers

Amit Agarwal, Oracle
Neelima Agarwal, Microsoft
Ashutosh Ahuja, Starbucks
Abhinav Balasubramanian, NVIDIA
Mithil Bangera, University Of New Haven
Yeshil Bangera
Vibha Belavadi, Adobe Systems
Zeyi Chen, University of Washington
Shristi Drolia, Novocure
Ritam Dutt, Carnegie Mellon University
Krupa Galiya
Mohammad Hasan, Indiana University Indianapolis
Yebowen Hu, University of Central Florida
Chao-Wei Huang, National Taiwan University
Zhehui Huang, University of Southern California
Shruti Jalan, Amazon
Amit Jaspal, Facebook
Bhargava Kumar, TD Securities
Yoonsang Lee, Seoul National University
Pengwei Li, Meta
Bryan Li, University of Pennsylvania
Su Liu, Amazon
Zefang Liu, J.P. Morgan Chase and Georgia Institute of Technology
Xiao Liu, University of California, Davis
Maochuan Lu, University of California, Berkeley
Elan Sopher Markowitz, University of Southern California
Bang Nguyen, University of Notre Dame
Garima Panwar, Amazon
Hitesh Laxmichand Patel, Oracle
Priyaranjan Pattnayak, Oracle
Meghana Puvvadi, NVIDIA
Yinzhu Quan, Georgia Institute of Technology
Arina Razmyslovich, DNI
Aaditya Shukla, NVIDIA
Ishneet Sukhvinder Singh, Algoverse AI Research
Dewang Sultania, Adobe Systems
Shounak Sural, Adobe
Suhas Suresha, Adobe Systems
Jiaxiang Tang, HKUST
Van-Hien Tran, NICT
Takehito Utsuro, University of Tsukuba
Ishita Verma, Adobe Systems
Qingyun Wang, University of Illinois, Urbana Champaign
Di Wu, University of California, Los Angeles
Zhenyu Wu, Xi'an Jiaotong University
Paul Youssef, Marburg University

Mengxia Yu, University of Notre Dame
Yuwei Zhang, University of California, San Diego
Andrea Zugarini, Expert.ai Srl

Table of Contents

Program

Saturday, May 3, 2025

09:00 - 09:10	*Opening Remarks*
09:10 - 09:50	*Invited Talk 1*
09:50 - 10:30	*Invited Talk 2*
10:30 - 11:00	*Coffee Break*
10:30 - 11:50	*Poster Session*
11:50 - 12:30	*Invited Talk 3*
12:30 - 14:00	*Lunch Break*
14:00 - 14:40	*Invited Talk 4*
14:40 - 15:30	*Oral Presentations 1*
15:30 - 16:00	*Coffee Break*
16:00 - 16:40	*Invited Talk 5*
16:40 - 17:20	*Oral Presentations 2*
17:20 - 17:30	*Closing Remarks*

Entity Retrieval for Answering Entity-Centric Questions

Hassan S. Shavarani
School of Computing Science
Simon Fraser University
BC, Canada
sshavara@sfu.ca

Anoop Sarkar
School of Computing Science
Simon Fraser University
BC, Canada
anoop@sfu.ca

Abstract

The similarity between the question and indexed documents is a crucial factor in document retrieval for retrieval-augmented question answering. Although this is typically the only method for obtaining the relevant documents, it is not the sole approach when dealing with entity-centric questions. In this study, we propose *Entity Retrieval*, a novel retrieval method which rather than relying on question-document similarity, depends on the salient entities within the question to identify the retrieval documents. We conduct an in-depth analysis of the performance of both dense and sparse retrieval methods in comparison to *Entity Retrieval*. Our findings reveal that our method not only leads to more accurate answers to entity-centric questions but also operates more efficiently.

https://github.com/shavarani/EntityRetrieval

1 Introduction

Information retrieval has significantly enhanced the factual reliability of large language model (LLM) generated responses (Shuster et al., 2021) in question answering (Zhu et al., 2021; Zhang et al., 2023). This improvement is particularly evident in Retrieval-Augmented Generation (RAG; Lewis et al., 2020b; Izacard and Grave, 2021b; Singh et al., 2021), which typically employs the Retriever-Reader architecture (Chen et al., 2017). RAG retrievers can be sparse (Peng et al., 2023), dense (Karpukhin et al., 2020), or hybrid (Glass et al., 2022), while the readers are usually generative language models[1] such as BART (Lewis et al., 2020a), T5 (Raffel et al., 2020), or GPT-4 (OpenAI, 2023) that generate answers based on the documents identified by the retriever. Recent RAG methodologies leverage the in-context learning capabilities of LLMs to incorporate retrieved documents into the prompt (Shi et al., 2023; Peng et al., 2023; Yu et al., 2023).

Entity-centric questions seek concise factual answers about the real world, typically in the form of single words or short phrases. These answers often reference or directly stem from a knowledge base entity (Ranjan and Balabantaray, 2016), and Retrieval-Augmentation enhances LLM performance in answering such questions, particularly for rare entities that appear infrequently in LLM training and fine-tuning data (Kandpal et al., 2023).

But is there a correlation between the quality of the retrieved documents and the generated response quality? Sciavolino et al. (2021) found that dense retrievers retrieve less relevant documents for answering entity-centric questions than simpler sparse retrievers. Additionally, Cuconasu et al. (2024) show that the presence of irrelevant documents leads to worse answers. These findings underscore the crucial role of the retrieval module, particularly for entity-centric questions.

In this paper, we propose *Entity Retrieval* (Figure 1b), which uses salient entities in the question to lookup knowledge base (e.g., Wikipedia) articles that correspond to each entity. Each article is truncated to the first W words to form a document set that augments the question passed to the LLM.

Our contributions are as follows: (1) we propose *Entity Retrieval*, a novel method of acquiring augmentation documents using salient entities in the questions, (2) we compare the retrieval performance quality of several retrieval techniques (both dense and sparse) to *Entity Retrieval* for questions within two entity-centric question answering datasets, (3) we study the Retrieval-Augmentation quality of the compared techniques and *Entity Retrieval*, using salient entity annotations of the questions, and (4) we examine the application of a recent state-of-the-art entity linking method for *Entity Retrieval* in the absence of entity annotations in entity-centric questions.

[1]The readers in the original architecture were designed to extract answer spans rather than generate answers.

Proceedings of the 4th International Workshop on Knowledge-Augmented Methods for Natural Language Processing (KnowledgeNLP'25), pages 1–17
May 3, 2025 ©2025 Association for Computational Linguistics

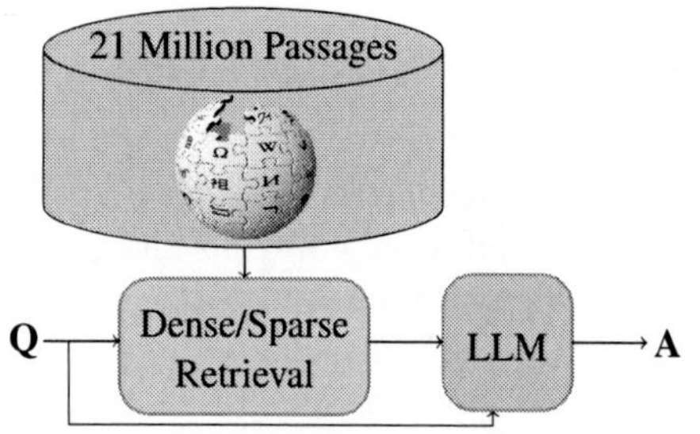

(a) Retrieval-Augmented QA with Dense/Sparse Retrieval

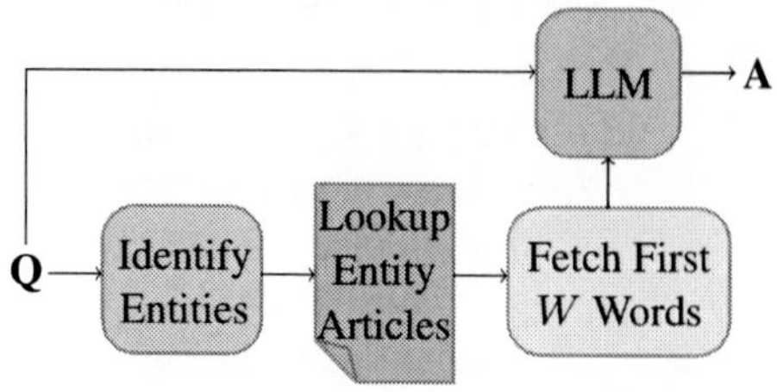

(b) Retrieval-Augmented QA with *Entity Retrieval*

Figure 1: *Entity Retrieval* simplifies the process of obtaining augmentation documents by replacing the need to search through large indexed passages with a straightforward lookup. For **Q**: `What is the capital of Seine-Saint-Denis`? *Entity Retrieval* considers the first few sentences of `Seine-Saint-Denis` Wikipedia article which states "`Its prefecture is` **`Bobigny`**`.`" and returns **A = Bobigny** where the other retrieval methods return **A = Saint-Denis** or **A = Paris**.

2 Retrieval for Retrieval-Augmentation

Retrieval-Augmentation (Lewis et al., 2020b) can be employed as a method of converting Closed-book question answering[2] (Roberts et al., 2020) into extractive question answering (Abney et al., 2000; Rajpurkar et al., 2016), where the answers can be directly extracted from the retrieved documents. Despite the abundance of effective retrieval techniques for Retrieval-Augmented Question Answering in existing literature (Zhan et al., 2020a,b; Yamada et al., 2021; Chen et al., 2022; Izacard et al., 2022; Santhanam et al., 2022; Ni et al., 2022, *inter alia.*), this section will concentrate on a select few methods[3] utilized to study answering entity-centric questions in this paper.

BM25 (Robertson et al., 1994, 2009) is a probabilistic retrieval method that ranks documents based on the frequency of query terms appearing in each document, adjusted by the length of the document and overall term frequency in the collection. It operates in the sparse vector space, relying on precomputed term frequencies and inverse document frequencies to retrieve documents based on keyword matching.

DPR (Dense Passage Retrieval; Karpukhin et al., 2020) leverages a bi-encoder architecture, wherein the initial encoder processes the question and the subsequent encoder handles the passages to be retrieved. The similarity scores between the two encoded representations are computed using a dot product. Typically, the encoded representations of the second encoder are fixed and indexed in FAISS (Johnson et al., 2019), while the first encoder is optimized to maximize the dot-product scores based on positive and negative examples.

ANCE (Xiong et al., 2021) is another dense retrieval technique similar to DPR[4]. It employs one encoder to transform both the questions and passages into dense representations. The key distinction from DPR is that ANCE uses hard negatives generated by periodically updating the passage embeddings during training, which helps the model learn more discriminative features, thereby enhancing retrieval performance over time.

3 Entity Retrieval for Question Answering

While quite powerful, most Retrieval-Augmented systems are notably time and resource-intensive, necessitating the storage of extensive lookup indices and the need to attend to all retrieved documents to generate the response (see Section 4.7). This attribute renders such methods less desirable, particularly given the drive to run LLMs locally and on mobile phones (Alizadeh et al., 2023).

Entity recognition has been an integral component of statistical question answering systems (Aghaebrahimian and Jurčíček, 2016, *inter alia*). Additionally, the extensively studied field of Knowledge Base Question Answering (Cui et al., 2017, *inter alia*) has underscored the significance of entity information from knowledge bases in question answering (Salnikov et al., 2023). A traditional neural question answering pipeline may

[2]Closed-book QA focuses on answering questions without additional context during inference.

[3]We selected the methods supported by `pyserini.io` for the similarity between the underlying modules, minimizing discrepancies across different implementations.

[4]We have also implemented DKRR (Izacard and Grave, 2021a), however, due to its significantly poorer performance compared to other methods, we exclude it from our analysis.

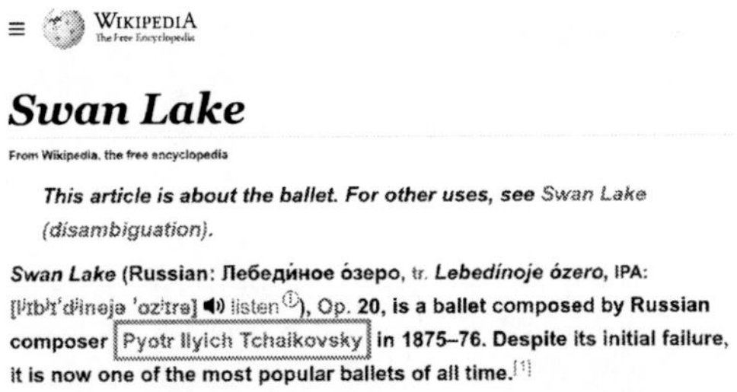

Figure 2: The first paragraph of the Wikipedia article typically provides an informative summary for the entity. For example, the first paragraph of `Swan Lake` Wikipedia article contains the answer to "`Who is the composer of The Swan Lake ballet?`"

contain entity detection, entity linking, relation prediction, and evidence integration (Mohammed et al., 2018; Lukovnikov et al., 2019), where entity detection can employ LSTM-based (Hochreiter and Schmidhuber, 1997) or BERT-based (Devlin et al., 2019) encoders. Inspired by this body of work, we investigate the relevance of retrieval based on entity information as an alternative strategy to the proposed retrieval methods of Section 2, especially for answering entity-centric questions with LLMs.

Our proposed method, *Entity Retrieval*, leverages the salient entities within the questions to identify and retrieve their corresponding knowledge base articles. We will then truncate these articles to the first W words[5] to form the list of the documents augmenting entity-centric questions when prompting LLMs. Figure 1 presents a schematic comparison between *Entity Retrieval* and other retrieval methods in identifying retrieval documents to enhance question answering with LLMs. Figure 2 provides an intuitive example to motivate the effectiveness of *Entity Retrieval*.

4 Experiments and Analysis

4.1 Setup

We focus on Wikipedia as the knowledge base and utilize the pre-existing BM25, DPR, and ANCE retrieval indexes in Pyserini (Lin et al., 2021). These indexes, follow established practices (Chen et al., 2017; Karpukhin et al., 2020) and segments the articles into non-overlapping text blocks of 100 words, resulting in 21,015,300 passages. For dense retrievers, the passages are processed with a pre-trained context encoder, generating fixed embedding vectors stored in a FAISS index (Douze et al., 2024). Our experimental entity-centric questions are encoded using the question encoder, and the top k relevant passages to the encoded question are retrieved from the FAISS index. For BM25 sparse retriever, the passages are stored in a Lucene index and the questions are keyword-matched to this index.

As outlined in Section 3, the document retrieval process will require loading the entire index (as well as the question encoder for dense retrieval) into memory which entails significant time and memory consumption. To address this challenge, following Ram et al. (2023), we treat document retrieval as a pre-processing step, caching the most relevant passages for each question before conducting the question answering experiments.

For *Entity Retrieval*, similar to BM25, DPR, and ANCE, we maintain document lengths at 100 words. However, our approach diverges in sourcing documents: rather than drawing from a large index of 21 million passages, we employ the salient entities within the question and retrieve their corresponding Wikipedia articles, which we then truncate to the initial 100 words.

We conduct our Retrieval-Augmented Question Answering experiments using LLaMA 3 model[6], and in all such experiments[7], we prevent it from generating sequences longer than 10 subwords.

We do not use any instructional question-answer pairs in the prompts of our models[8]. In the Closed-book setting, the prompt includes only the question, along with a simple instruction to answer it. In Retrieval-Augmented settings using BM25, DPR, and ANCE, the prompt incorporates pre-fetched retrieved documents from the corresponding retrieval index alongside the question and the instruction. Similarly, in the *Entity Retrieval* settings, the prompt consists of the first W words of the Wikipedia articles corresponding to the salient entities in the question. We follow Ram et al. (2023) for question normalization and prompt formulation. Appendix A provides the prompts, and example retrieved documents for each setting.

[5]The first sentences of Wikipedia articles have been proven informative for document classification (Shavarani and Sekine, 2020) as well as question answering (Choi et al., 2018).

[6]`https://llama.meta.com/llama3/`.

[7]We run our experiments on one server containing 2 RTX A6000s with 49GB GPU memory each.

[8]Further exploration into few-shot experimental setups involving additional (context, question, answer) in-context examples is left for future investigation.

4.2 Data

We use the following datasets in our experiments[9]:

EntityQuestions (Sciavolino et al., 2021) is created by collecting 24 common relations (e.g., 'author of' and 'located in') and transforming fact triples (subject, relation, object) that contain these relations, into natural language questions using predefined templates. The dataset comprises 176,560 train, 22,068 dev, and 22,075 test question-answer pairs. To expedite our analytical experiments in this paper, given the extensive size of the dev and test sets, we constrain the question-answer pairs in these subsets to those featuring salient entities within the top 500K most linked Wikipedia pages, as suggested by Shavarani and Sarkar (2023). Thus, the dev and test subsets of EntityQuestions considered in our experiments consist of 4,710 and 4,741 questions, respectively.

FactoidQA (Smith et al., 2008) contains 2,203 hand crafted question-answer pairs derived from Wikipedia articles, with each pair accompanied by its corresponding Wikipedia source article included in the dataset.

StrategyQA (Geva et al., 2021) is a complex boolean question answering dataset, constructed by presenting individual terms from Wikipedia to annotators. Its questions contain references to more than one Wikipedia entity, and necessitate implicit reasoning for binary (Yes/No) responses. The dataset comprises 5,111 answered questions initially intended for training question answering systems, with the system later tested on test set questions with unreleased answers. This training set is split into two subsets resulting in `train` and `train_filtered` subsets containing 2,290 and 2,821 questions, respectively.

4.3 Evaluation

We evaluate the performance of the retrieval methods using the following metrics; in each of which a document is considered *relevant* if it contains a normalized form of the expected answer to the question:

- nDCG@k (normalized Discounted Cumulative Gain at rank k; Järvelin and Kekäläinen, 2002) evaluates the quality of a ranking system by considering both the relevance and the position of documents in the top k results. Mathematically, it is represented as

$$\text{nDCG@}k = \frac{\sum_{i=1}^{k} \frac{2^{r_i}-1}{\log_2(i+1)}}{\sum_{i=1}^{|REL_k|} \frac{2^{r_i}-1}{\log_2(i+1)}}$$

  Where, r_i denotes the relevance score of a document at the ith position for a question, with relevance score $r_i = 1$ if the document is *relevant*, and $r_i = 0$, otherwise. REL_k refers to the *relevant* subset of the retrieved documents. nDCG@k scores range between 0 and 1, where a score of 1 signifies an optimal ranking with the most *relevant* documents positioned at the top.

- MRR (Mean Reciprocal Rank; Voorhees and Harman, 1999) is the average of the reciprocal ranks of the first *relevant* document for each question. Mathematically, it is represented as

$$\text{MRR} = \frac{1}{|Q|}\sum_{j=1}^{|Q|}\frac{1}{r_j}$$

  where $|Q|$ represents the total number of questions and r_j denotes the rank of the first *relevant* document for the j-th question.

- Top-k Retrieval Accuracy, as reported by Sciavolino et al. (2021), is calculated as the number of questions with at least one *relevant* document in the top k retrieved documents divided by the total number of questions in the dataset.

We evaluate the performance of the Retrieval-Augmented Question Answering models with each retrieval method as follows:

- For FactoidQA and EntityQuestions datasets, we use `OpenQA-eval` (Kamalloo et al., 2023) scripts to evaluate model performance, and report exact match (EM) and F1 scores by comparing expected answers to normalized model responses.

- For StrategyQA, we present accuracy scores by comparing model responses to the expected boolean answers in the dataset. As well, to assess model comprehension of the task, we count the number of answers that deviate from Yes or No and report this count in a distinct column labeled "`Inv #`" for each experiment.

[9]Please note that since *Entity Retrieval* does not involve training, all mentioned dataset subsets (e.g., train, dev, or test) will be used for evaluation regardless of their names.

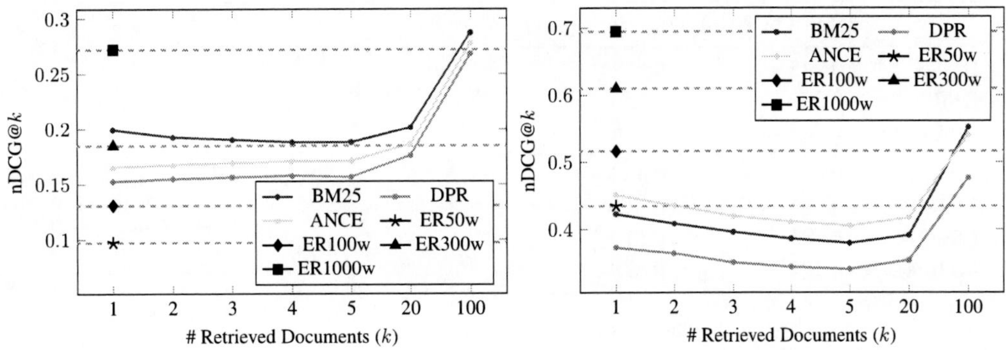

(a) FactoidQA

(b) EntityQuestions (dev)

Figure 3: nDCG@k scores evaluate the quality of BM25, DPR, ANCE, and *Entity Retrieval* by considering both the relevance and the position of documents in the top k retrieved passages for each question. Note that *Entity Retrieval* typically results in k=1 document since the datasets under study often have one salient entity. The horizontal lines aid in visually comparing the performance of *Entity Retrieval*, which averages one document, to other methods retrieving k>1 documents.

4.4 Entity Retrieval Performance using Question Entity Annotations

We begin our analysis by comparing *Entity Retrieval* performance to BM25, DPR, and ANCE. For this experiment, we calculate nDCG with various retrieved document sets of size k = 1, 2, 3, 4, 5, 20, and 100. We use the entity annotations provided with the questions from FactoidQA and the dev set of EntityQuestions to fetch their corresponding Wikipedia articles, excluding StrategyQA from our analysis as it does not include entity annotations. On average, FactoidQA and EntityQuestions datasets contain one salient entity per question.

Apart from a few questions, the majority of FactoidQA questions, and all questions in the EntityQuestions dataset, contain only one entity annotation (leading to one augmentation document). This puts *Entity Retrieval* at a disadvantage. To address this, we consider truncating the *Entity Retrieval* documents to varying lengths. We compare *Entity Retrieval* using the first 100 words (equivalent to the size of documents returned by BM25, DPR, and ANCE, noted as *ER100w*) and also consider the first 50, 300, and 1000 words of the retrieved Wikipedia articles (noted as *ER50w*, *ER300w*, and *ER1000w*). A 300-word *Entity Retrieval* document matches the word count of three documents returned by BM25 or DPR.

Figure 3 presents the computed nDCG@k scores across varying document sizes, highlighting the superior performance of *Entity Retrieval* over other retrieval methods in the context of the entity-centric datasets under study. Notably, *ER1000w*, which corresponds to ten BM25 retrieved passages in terms of word count, exhibits a retrieval performance on par with 100 retrieved documents in FactoidQA and surpasses BM25, the top-performing retriever on EntityQuestions, by 25%. This impressive performance by *Entity Retrieval* can be attributed to its ability to retrieve fewer, yet more relevant, documents. This observation aligns with the conclusion drawn by Cuconasu et al. (2024), which emphasizes that the retrieval of irrelevant documents can negatively impact performance. *Entity Retrieval* effectively minimizes the retrieval of such documents. Further insights can be gleaned from the comparison of nDCG scores along the x-axis of the plots in Figure 3. As the number of retrieved documents increases, the likelihood of retrieving irrelevant documents also rises, leading to a decline in retrieval performance when moving from 1 to 5 retrieved documents.

Table 1 showcases the calculated MRR scores, emphasizing the quicker attainment of relevant retrieval documents in *Entity Retrieval* compared to other retrieval methods. Concurrently, Figure 4 illustrates the impact of incrementing the number of retrieved documents on the expansion of the expected answers' coverage for the EntityQuestions dev subset.

While it may be appealing to consider 100 or more documents to simultaneously enhance both nDCG and Retrieval Accuracy, it is important to note that 100 retrieved documents would comprise 10,000 words. This could potentially overwhelm the model with excessive noise (irrelevant documents), and as well, could make it extremely costly

	FactoidQA	EntityQuestions (dev)
BM25	0.245	0.522
DPR	0.209	0.456
ANCE	0.222	0.536
ER50w	0.097	0.435
ER100w	0.131	0.516
ER300w	0.185	0.610
ER1000w	**0.272**	**0.695**

Table 1: MRR scores comparing the retrieval quality of BM25, DPR, ANCE, and *Entity Retrieval* through the average of the reciprocal ranks of the first relevant document for each question.

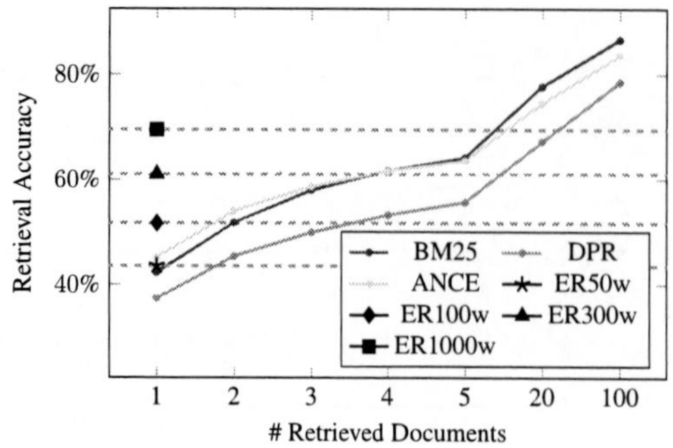

Figure 4: Retrieval Accuracy scores showcasing the correlation between the number of retrieved documents and the expected answers' coverage in EntityQuestions (dev) subset.

to execute Retrieval-Augmented Question Answering, especially when the cost of API calls is calculated per token. We would need at least 10,000 tokens (optimistically, assuming each word equates to only one token) in addition to the tokens in the question. These factors suggest that retrieving a few documents for each question is more beneficial.

Taking these considerations into account, along with the nDCG@k, MRR, and Retrieval Accuracy results from this section, we gain a comprehensive understanding of the trade-off between the quality of the retrieved documents, which diminishes as we consider more documents, and the answer coverage, which increases as the model has a higher chance of encountering the right document with the correct hint for the answer. Consequently, we opt for $k = 4$ as a default, and we will always retrieve the top-4 documents in our Retrieval-Augmented Question Answering experiments.

4.5 Retrieval-Augmented Question Answering

Next, we examine the effectiveness of our proposed *Entity Retrieval* method compared to other retrieval methods in improving the quality of responses to entity-centric questions. We explore three settings: Closed-book, Retrieval-Augmented, and *Entity Retrieval* with question entity annotations (Section 4.1). The primary purpose of using question entity annotations is to demonstrate their ability to accurately identify relevant augmentation documents. These experiments establish an expected performance ceiling for *Entity Retrieval* and can inspire future research to meet or exceed this threshold.

The initial eight rows of Table 2 present the results of our experiments using LLaMA 3 (8B) model. Upon examining these results, it is evident that *ER100w*, the most analogous *Entity Retrieval* setting to other retrieval methods, outperforms in terms of both EM and F1 scores. This setting, like the other retrieval methods, returns 100-word documents. However, as we noted earlier, *Entity Retrieval* generally retrieves fewer documents overall, making it both more accurate and more efficient.

Our dense retrieval results align with the observations of Sciavolino et al. (2021), asserting that entity-centric questions indeed challenge dense retrievers. Although the BM25 method proves successful in enhancing the results compared to the Closed-book setting, it is noteworthy that even *Entity Retrieval* with the initial 50 words of the articles corresponding to the salient entities within questions yields superior results. This is particularly significant when compared to other retrieval methods which necessitate indexing the entire knowledge base on disk and loading the index into memory; a process required in inference time where caching is not an option.

4.6 Entity Retrieval in absence of Question Entity Annotations

Section 4.5 establishes *Entity Retrieval* as a viable augmentation method for entity-centric questions. Next, we aim to reach the established performance ceiling in the absence of question entity annotations. Here, we examine the potential of entity linking as an automated method to provide these annotations. Our primary research question is: how effectively can current entity linking methods help *Entity Retrieval* achieve optimal performance?

Ideally, we would like to evaluate all recent entity linking methods to identify the most effective one. However, due to time and budget limitations,

LLaMA3 (8B)	FactoidQA		EntityQuestions			
			dev		test	
	EM	**F1**	**EM**	**F1**	**EM**	**F1**
Closed-book	30.5±0.4	39.3±0.0	22.9±0.5	37.9±0.7	22.9±0.2	38.3±0.5
Retrieval-Augmented QA						
BM25	32.4±0.8	42.6±0.3	23.7±0.3	38.5±0.6	23.4±0.2	38.7±0.3
DPR	29.8±1.0	38.9±1.1	21.9±0.3	36.2±0.2	20.7±0.6	35.4±0.4
ANCE	30.4±0.4	39.9±0.3	23.1±0.5	37.9±0.4	22.7±0.5	37.9±0.6
Entity Retrieval w/ Question Entity Annotations						
ER50w	34.4±0.5	43.7±0.5	24.9±0.1	41.2±0.1	24.1±0.6	41.1±0.3
ER100w	33.6±0.3	42.9±0.4	**26.3**±0.2	**42.8**±0.1	**25.7**±0.1	**42.4**±0.0
ER300w	33.7±0.9	43.0±1.1	26.2±0.3	42.7±0.1	25.5±0.7	**42.4**±0.8
ER1000w	**35.0**±0.3	**44.9**±0.5	25.1±0.4	41.9±0.4	24.2±0.9	41.1±0.6
Entity Retrieval w/ SpEL Entity Annotations						
ERSp50w	29.6±0.3	38.6±0.5	24.1±0.5	39.1±0.2	23.6±0.8	39.4±0.5
ERSp100w	28.7±0.9	37.7±1.0	24.8±0.5	40.0±0.2	24.4±0.3	39.9±0.2
ERSp300w	26.9±0.4	35.6±0.5	24.5±0.3	39.9±0.4	24.4±0.5	40.2±0.3
ERSp1000w	21.7±0.7	30.8±1.0	24.2±0.2	39.6±0.3	22.9±0.5	39.0±0.7

Table 2: Question answering efficacy comparison between Closed-book and Retrieval-Augmentation using BM25, DPR, ANCE, and *Entity Retrieval*. EM refers to the exact match between predicted and expected answers, disregarding punctuation and articles (a, an, the).
* Results represent the average of three runs, accompanied by a margin of error based on a 99% confidence interval.

we depend on the recent benchmarking studies by Ong et al. (2024) to choose a method. They examine the latest entity linking methods in terms of performance against unseen data and endorse SpEL (Shavarani and Sarkar, 2023) as the top performer. Consequently, we investigate *Entity Retrieval* using entities identified with SpEL, while reserving the examination of other entity linking techniques for *Entity Retrieval* for future research.

We maintain the *Entity Retrieval* settings as before, defining *ERSp50w*, *ERSp100w*, *ERSp300w*, and *ERSp1000w* for performing entity linking with SpEL, then retrieving the Wikipedia articles corresponding to the SpEL identified entities, and using the first 50, 100, 300, and 1000 words of these articles as documents to augment the question when prompting the LLM. Table 3 presents the aggregated entity identification statistics of SpEL across various subsets of each dataset under study.

The final four rows of Table 2 showcase the comparative results of utilizing entities identified by SpEL for *Entity Retrieval*. Given that one-third of EntityQuestions and approximately half of FactoidQA lack identified annotations, the exact match scores reveal that *Entity Retrieval* performs robustly and surpasses BM25, the top-performing competitor, for EntityQuestions while approaching DPR's performance for FactoidQA. This underscores the potential of *Entity Retrieval* within this paradigm. In addition, the disparity between the results with and without question entity annotations strongly indicates the necessity for further research in Entity Linking, which could enhance

	Max.	Avg.	Linked %
FactoidQA	8	0.8	56.5%
EntityQuestions	3	0.7	65.6%
StrategyQA	4	1.1	74.9%

Table 3: Maximum and Average SpEL identified entity count as well as the total percentage of questions with at least one identified entity in each dataset. SpEL successfully identifies and links entities in 1,244 FactoidQA, 3,108 EntityQuestions (dev), 3,095 EntityQuestions (test), 1,735 StrategyQA (train), and 2,094 StrategyQA (train_filtered) questions. For the remaining questions in each dataset where no entities are identified, they will be introduced to the LLM without any augmented documents in the *Entity Retrieval* settings.

Question	Who performed Alexis Colby?	What is the capital of Seine-Saint-Denis?
Answer	Joan Collins	Bobigny
Closed-Book	Diana Ross	Paris
BM25	Linda Evans	Saint-Denis
DPR	Alexis Cohen	Saint-Denis
ANCE	Nicollette Sheridan performed Alexis Colby.	Saint-Denis
ERSp100w	Joan Collins	Bobigny
Question	**Where did John Snetzler die?**	**Where was Brigita Bukovec born?**
Answer	Schaffhausen	Ljubljana
Closed-Book	He died in London, England, in 178	Brigita Bukovec was born in Slovenia
BM25	John Snetzler died in London.	Slovenia
DPR	John Snetzler died in London	in Slovakia
ANCE	in England	Rîbnița
ERSp100w	Schaffhausen	Ljubljana

Table 4: Example questions from EntityQuestions (dev) to demonstrate the performance of *Entity Retrieval*.

LLaMA3 (8B)	**train**		**train_filtered**	
	Acc.	**Inv #**	**Acc.**	**Inv #**
BM25	43.5±0.6	608±14	48.9±0.7	673±12
ANCE	46.6±1.3	552±11	51.8±0.7	647±35
ERSp50w	50.1±1.1	370±28	**56.3**±0.9	417±21
ERSp100w	**50.3**±1.4	**369**±15	56.2±0.8	**384**±9
ERSp300w	46.2±1.3	504±17	53.5±1.5	546±20
ERSp1000w	39.5±1.4	775±6	43.4±0.5	919±14

Table 5: Comparison of *Entity Retrieval* using SpEL identified entities to the best-performing dense and sparse retrieval methods of Table 2 on the StrategyQA dataset. Given the expected boolean results for StrategyQA questions, we restricted LLaMA 3 to generate only one token. *Acc.* indicates the fraction of answers that correctly match the expected Yes or No responses in the dataset, while *Inv #* represents the count of labels that are neither Yes nor No, but another invalid answer.
* Results represent the average of three runs, accompanied by a margin of error based on a 99% confidence interval.

entity-centric question answering as a downstream task. Table 4 provides some example questions where *Entity Retrieval* has led to better answers.

Table 5 compares of the performance of *Entity Retrieval* using SpEL identified entities against other retrieval methods on the StrategyQA dataset. The results clearly demonstrate the superior performance of *Entity Retrieval* over the top-performing retrieval methods of Table 2. It is important to note that the 100-word setting (*ERSp100w*) is the most analogous to other retrieval methods. Interestingly, the results from the 1000-word setting suggest that longer documents do not necessarily enhance the model's recall. In fact, beyond a certain length, the model may become overwhelmed by the sheer volume of noise, leading to confusion. Lastly, the invalid count values suggest that *Entity Retrieval* is more effective in assisting the model to comprehend the boolean nature of expected responses, eliminating the need to rely on retrieval from millions of passages.

4.7 Real-time Efficiency Analysis

Our analysis thus far has primarily focused on the retrieval performance, without consideration for the time and memory efficiency; crucial factors in retrieval method selection. In this section, we shift our focus to these aspects.

We begin by replacing our pre-built retrieval cache document sets with the original retrieval modules that were used in creating the cached sets. We load the indexes and the necessary models for fetching the retrieval documents. We then record the peak main memory requirement of each method during the experiment. It is important to note that all retrieval methods primarily rely on main memory, with minimal differences in GPU memory requirements. Therefore, we report an average GPU memory requirement of 35GB for LLaMA 3 (8B) and exclude it from our results ta-

	Total Time	Disk Storage	Main Memory
BM25	45min	11GB	2.3GB
ANCE	960min	61.5GB	64.2GB
ERSp100w	34min	9.4GB	6.3GB

Table 6: Comparison of the required resources for each retrieval method in real-time execution. The reported total time values exclude the time taken to load the indexes and models, focusing solely on the time used to answer the questions.

ble. We then feed all 2,203 FactoidQA questions into the BM25, ANCE, and *Entity Retrieval* (using SPEL identified entities) to fetch the top-4 documents. We report the total time taken to generate answers to all the questions, which includes the time for querying the BM25 or ANCE indexes in the Retrieval-Augmented settings, or the time for performing on-the-fly entity linking and fetching the Wikipedia articles from disk in the *Entity Retrieval* setting. Additionally, we keep track of all the pre-built models and indexes that each method requires for download and storage. We report the total size of all downloaded files to disk.

Table 6 presents our findings on time and memory requirements. It is evident that ANCE requires significantly more time to fetch and provide documents, six times more disk space to store its indexes, and over ten times higher main memory demands to load its dense representations[10]. In contrast, BM25 and *Entity Retrieval* are more resource-friendly. Notably, *Entity Retrieval* is 25% faster than BM25 in response generation while demanding the total memory and disk space of a standard personal computer. Future research can be directed towards reducing the memory requirements of *Entity Retrieval*; a direction which we find quit promising.

5 Related Work

Similar to our studies, Kandpal et al. (2023) investigate the impact of salient entities on question answering, and propose constructing oracle retrieval documents as the 300-word segment surrounding the ground-truth answer from the Wikipedia page that contains the answer (entity name). Our approach leverages salient entities from questions without directly involving answers. Additionally, they primarily use entities to classify questions into those concerning frequent knowledge base entries versus those about rare entries on the long-tail, whereas our approach assigns a more substantial role to entities, treating them as pointers guiding the retrieval of relevant documents to augment questions.

Sciavolino et al. (2021) compare DPR and BM25 retrievers for entity-centric questions, and demonstrate that DPR greatly underperforms BM25. They attribute this to dense retrievers' difficulty with infrequent entities, which are less represented in training data. In contrast, BM25's frequency-based retrieval is not sensitive to entity frequency. We take a parallel approach and propose a simple yet effective method that leverages salient entities in the question for identifying augmentation documents.

Similar to our studies, Dhingra et al. (2020); Asai et al. (2020) focus on answering questions with minimal lexical overlap between the retrieved documents and the question text. However, they emphasize multi-hop question answering, using entity linking to extract entities from the question and leveraging knowledge base articles to guide the multi-hop process. In contrast, we utilize entity links to directly identify augmentation documents. Sun et al. (2018) employ entity linking to identify entities in the question, generating a set of seed entities, which are then expanded using the PPR algorithm to create a subgraph of the knowledge base containing relevant entities. A graph propagation algorithm subsequently learns representations for each node in the subgraph, and each representation is binary classified to determine if it answers the question. Our approach differs as we focus on using LLMs, employing entity linking in a Retrieval-Augmented setting without relying on graph propagation.

6 Conclusion

In this study, we focused on Retrieval-Augmented Question Answering, and explored various retrieval methods that rely on the similarity between the question and the content of the passages to be retrieved. We introduced a novel approach, *Entity Retrieval*, which deviates from the conventional textual similarity-based mechanism. Instead, it capitalizes on the salient entities within the question to identify retrieval documents. Our findings indicate that our proposed method is not only more accurate but also faster in the context of entity-centric question answering.

[10]Our empirical results demonstrate that DPR follows the same trend.

Limitations and Ethical Considerations

Our proposed *Entity Retrieval* method is specifically tailored for answering entity-centric questions, with its performance heavily reliant on the presence of question entities. In scenarios where entity annotations are absent, the method's effectiveness is directly tied to the performance of external entity linking methods. We acknowledge that our exploration of potential entity linking methods has not been exhaustive, and further investigation may yield insights that could enhance the *Entity Retrieval* method, even in the absence of question entity annotations.

Furthermore, we recognize that entity linking can occasionally result in ambiguous entities. Our research has not delved into the impact of such ambiguities on the *Entity Retrieval* method, and we propose that future studies should focus on ensuring the selection of the most contextually appropriate entities for retrieval.

Our research is primarily centered on Wikipedia as the knowledge base, a choice heavily influenced by previous studies for the sake of comparability. However, we acknowledge the importance of exploring other knowledge bases and ontologies, particularly in different domains, such as UMLS (Bodenreider, 2004) in the medical field.

In terms of benchmarking, we have compared the *Entity Retrieval* method against a limited selection of existing retrieval methods, guided by our judgement, experience, and considerations of implementation availability. We concede that our comparison has not been exhaustive, and this reasoning extends to our comparison using different LLMs and their available sizes.

Our research is on English only, and we acknowledge that entity-centric question answering in other languages is also relevant and important. We hope to extend our work to cover multiple languages in the future. We inherit the biases that exist in the data used in this project, and we do not explicitly de-bias the data. We are providing our code to the research community and we trust that those who use the model will do so ethically and responsibly.

References

Steven Abney, Michael Collins, and Amit Singhal. 2000. Answer extraction. In *Sixth Applied Natural Language Processing Conference*, pages 296–301, Seattle, Washington, USA. Association for Computational Linguistics.

Ahmad Aghaebrahimian and Filip Jurčíček. 2016. Open-domain factoid question answering via knowledge graph search. In *Proceedings of the Workshop on Human-Computer Question Answering*, pages 22–28, San Diego, California. Association for Computational Linguistics.

Keivan Alizadeh, Iman Mirzadeh, Dmitry Belenko, Karen Khatamifard, Minsik Cho, Carlo C Del Mundo, Mohammad Rastegari, and Mehrdad Farajtabar. 2023. Llm in a flash: Efficient large language model inference with limited memory. *arXiv preprint arXiv:2312.11514*.

Akari Asai, Kazuma Hashimoto, Hannaneh Hajishirzi, Richard Socher, and Caiming Xiong. 2020. Learning to retrieve reasoning paths over wikipedia graph for question answering. In *International Conference on Learning Representations*.

Olivier Bodenreider. 2004. The unified medical language system (umls): integrating biomedical terminology. *Nucleic acids research*, 32(suppl_1):D267–D270.

Danqi Chen, Adam Fisch, Jason Weston, and Antoine Bordes. 2017. Reading Wikipedia to answer open-domain questions. In *Proceedings of the 55th Annual Meeting of the Association for Computational Linguistics (Volume 1: Long Papers)*, pages 1870–1879, Vancouver, Canada. Association for Computational Linguistics.

Xilun Chen, Kushal Lakhotia, Barlas Oguz, Anchit Gupta, Patrick Lewis, Stan Peshterliev, Yashar Mehdad, Sonal Gupta, and Wen-tau Yih. 2022. Salient phrase aware dense retrieval: Can a dense retriever imitate a sparse one? In *Findings of the Association for Computational Linguistics: EMNLP 2022*, pages 250–262, Abu Dhabi, United Arab Emirates. Association for Computational Linguistics.

Eunsol Choi, He He, Mohit Iyyer, Mark Yatskar, Wen-tau Yih, Yejin Choi, Percy Liang, and Luke Zettlemoyer. 2018. QuAC: Question answering in context. In *Proceedings of the 2018 Conference on Empirical Methods in Natural Language Processing*, pages 2174–2184, Brussels, Belgium. Association for Computational Linguistics.

Florin Cuconasu, Giovanni Trappolini, Federico Siciliano, Simone Filice, Cesare Campagnano, Yoelle Maarek, Nicola Tonellotto, and Fabrizio Silvestri. 2024. The power of noise: Redefining retrieval for rag systems. *arXiv preprint arXiv:2401.14887*.

Wanyun Cui, Yanghua Xiao, Haixun Wang, Yangqiu Song, Seung-won Hwang, and Wei Wang. 2017. Kbqa: Learning question answering over qa corpora and knowledge bases. *Proceedings of the VLDB Endowment*, 10(5).

Jacob Devlin, Ming-Wei Chang, Kenton Lee, and Kristina Toutanova. 2019. BERT: Pre-training of deep bidirectional transformers for language understanding. In *Proceedings of the 2019 Conference of* the North American Chapter of the Association for Computational Linguistics: Human Language Technologies, Volume 1 (Long and Short Papers), pages 4171–4186, Minneapolis, Minnesota. Association for Computational Linguistics.

Bhuwan Dhingra, Manzil Zaheer, Vidhisha Balachandran, Graham Neubig, Ruslan Salakhutdinov, and William W. Cohen. 2020. Differentiable reasoning over a virtual knowledge base. In *International Conference on Learning Representations*.

Matthijs Douze, Alexandr Guzhva, Chengqi Deng, Jeff Johnson, Gergely Szilvasy, Pierre-Emmanuel Mazaré, Maria Lomeli, Lucas Hosseini, and Hervé Jégou. 2024. The faiss library. *arXiv preprint arXiv:2401.08281*.

Mor Geva, Daniel Khashabi, Elad Segal, Tushar Khot, Dan Roth, and Jonathan Berant. 2021. Did aristotle use a laptop? a question answering benchmark with implicit reasoning strategies. *Transactions of the Association for Computational Linguistics*, 9:346–361.

Michael Glass, Gaetano Rossiello, Md Faisal Mahbub Chowdhury, Ankita Naik, Pengshan Cai, and Alfio Gliozzo. 2022. Re2G: Retrieve, rerank, generate. In *Proceedings of the 2022 Conference of the North American Chapter of the Association for Computational Linguistics: Human Language Technologies*, pages 2701–2715, Seattle, United States. Association for Computational Linguistics.

Sepp Hochreiter and Jürgen Schmidhuber. 1997. Long short-term memory. *Neural computation*, 9(8):1735–1780.

Gautier Izacard, Mathilde Caron, Lucas Hosseini, Sebastian Riedel, Piotr Bojanowski, Armand Joulin, and Edouard Grave. 2022. Unsupervised dense information retrieval with contrastive learning. *Transactions on Machine Learning Research*.

Gautier Izacard and Edouard Grave. 2021a. Distilling knowledge from reader to retriever for question answering. In *International Conference on Learning Representations*.

Gautier Izacard and Edouard Grave. 2021b. Leveraging passage retrieval with generative models for open domain question answering. In *Proceedings of the 16th Conference of the European Chapter of the Association for Computational Linguistics: Main Volume*, pages 874–880, Online. Association for Computational Linguistics.

Kalervo Järvelin and Jaana Kekäläinen. 2002. Cumulated gain-based evaluation of ir techniques. *ACM Transactions on Information Systems (TOIS)*, 20(4):422–446.

Jeff Johnson, Matthijs Douze, and Hervé Jégou. 2019. Billion-scale similarity search with gpus. *IEEE Transactions on Big Data*, 7(3):535–547.

Ehsan Kamalloo, Nouha Dziri, Charles Clarke, and Davood Rafiei. 2023. Evaluating open-domain question answering in the era of large language models. In *Proceedings of the 61st Annual Meeting of the Association for Computational Linguistics (Volume 1: Long Papers)*, pages 5591–5606, Toronto, Canada. Association for Computational Linguistics.

Nikhil Kandpal, Haikang Deng, Adam Roberts, Eric Wallace, and Colin Raffel. 2023. Large language models struggle to learn long-tail knowledge. In *International Conference on Machine Learning*, pages 15696–15707. PMLR.

Vladimir Karpukhin, Barlas Oguz, Sewon Min, Patrick Lewis, Ledell Wu, Sergey Edunov, Danqi Chen, and Wen-tau Yih. 2020. Dense passage retrieval for open-domain question answering. In *Proceedings of the 2020 Conference on Empirical Methods in Natural Language Processing (EMNLP)*, pages 6769–6781, Online. Association for Computational Linguistics.

Mike Lewis, Yinhan Liu, Naman Goyal, Marjan Ghazvininejad, Abdelrahman Mohamed, Omer Levy, Veselin Stoyanov, and Luke Zettlemoyer. 2020a. BART: Denoising sequence-to-sequence pre-training for natural language generation, translation, and comprehension. In *Proceedings of the 58th Annual Meeting of the Association for Computational Linguistics*, pages 7871–7880, Online. Association for Computational Linguistics.

Patrick Lewis, Ethan Perez, Aleksandra Piktus, Fabio Petroni, Vladimir Karpukhin, Naman Goyal, Heinrich Küttler, Mike Lewis, Wen-tau Yih, Tim Rocktäschel, et al. 2020b. Retrieval-augmented generation for knowledge-intensive nlp tasks. *Advances in Neural Information Processing Systems*, 33:9459–9474.

Jimmy Lin, Xueguang Ma, Sheng-Chieh Lin, Jheng-Hong Yang, Ronak Pradeep, and Rodrigo Nogueira. 2021. Pyserini: A Python toolkit for reproducible information retrieval research with sparse and dense representations. In *Proceedings of the 44th Annual International ACM SIGIR Conference on Research and Development in Information Retrieval (SIGIR 2021)*, pages 2356–2362.

Denis Lukovnikov, Asja Fischer, and Jens Lehmann. 2019. Pretrained transformers for simple question answering over knowledge graphs. In *The Semantic Web–ISWC 2019: 18th International Semantic Web Conference, Auckland, New Zealand, October 26–30, 2019, Proceedings, Part I 18*, pages 470–486. Springer.

Salman Mohammed, Peng Shi, and Jimmy Lin. 2018. Strong baselines for simple question answering over knowledge graphs with and without neural networks. In *Proceedings of the 2018 Conference of the North American Chapter of the Association for Computational Linguistics: Human Language Technologies, Volume 2 (Short Papers)*, pages 291–296, New Orleans, Louisiana. Association for Computational Linguistics.

Jianmo Ni, Chen Qu, Jing Lu, Zhuyun Dai, Gustavo Hernandez Abrego, Ji Ma, Vincent Zhao, Yi Luan, Keith Hall, Ming-Wei Chang, and Yinfei Yang. 2022. Large dual encoders are generalizable retrievers. In *Proceedings of the 2022 Conference on Empirical Methods in Natural Language Processing*, pages 9844–9855, Abu Dhabi, United Arab Emirates. Association for Computational Linguistics.

Nicolas Ong, Hassan S. Shavarani, and Anoop Sarkar. 2024. Unified examination of entity linking in absence of candidate sets. In *Proceedings of the 2024 Conference of the North American Chapter of the Association for Computational Linguistics: Human Language Technologies*, Mexico. Association for Computational Linguistics.

OpenAI. 2023. Gpt-4 technical report.

Baolin Peng, Michel Galley, Pengcheng He, Hao Cheng, Yujia Xie, Yu Hu, Qiuyuan Huang, Lars Liden, Zhou Yu, Weizhu Chen, et al. 2023. Check your facts and try again: Improving large language models with external knowledge and automated feedback. *arXiv preprint arXiv:2302.12813*.

Colin Raffel, Noam Shazeer, Adam Roberts, Katherine Lee, Sharan Narang, Michael Matena, Yanqi Zhou, Wei Li, and Peter J Liu. 2020. Exploring the limits of transfer learning with a unified text-to-text transformer. *The Journal of Machine Learning Research*, 21(1):5485–5551.

Pranav Rajpurkar, Jian Zhang, Konstantin Lopyrev, and Percy Liang. 2016. SQuAD: 100,000+ questions for machine comprehension of text. In *Proceedings of the 2016 Conference on Empirical Methods in Natural Language Processing*, pages 2383–2392, Austin, Texas. Association for Computational Linguistics.

Ori Ram, Yoav Levine, Itay Dalmedigos, Dor Muhlgay, Amnon Shashua, Kevin Leyton-Brown, and Yoav Shoham. 2023. In-context retrieval-augmented language models. *Transactions of the Association for Computational Linguistics*, 11:1316–1331.

Prakash Ranjan and Rakesh Chandra Balabantaray. 2016. Question answering system for factoid based question. In *2016 2nd International Conference on Contemporary Computing and Informatics (IC3I)*, pages 221–224. IEEE.

Adam Roberts, Colin Raffel, and Noam Shazeer. 2020. How much knowledge can you pack into the parameters of a language model? In *Proceedings of the 2020 Conference on Empirical Methods in Natural Language Processing (EMNLP)*, pages 5418–5426, Online. Association for Computational Linguistics.

Stephen Robertson, Hugo Zaragoza, et al. 2009. The probabilistic relevance framework: Bm25 and beyond. *Foundations and Trends® in Information Retrieval*, 3(4):333–389.

Stephen E. Robertson, Steve Walker, Susan Jones, Micheline Hancock-Beaulieu, and Mike Gatford. 1994. Okapi at trec-3. In *Text Retrieval Conference*.

Mikhail Salnikov, Hai Le, Prateek Rajput, Irina Nikishina, Pavel Braslavski, Valentin Malykh, and Alexander Panchenko. 2023. Large language models meet knowledge graphs to answer factoid questions. In *Proceedings of the 37th Pacific Asia Conference on Language, Information and Computation*, pages 635–644, Hong Kong, China. Association for Computational Linguistics.

Keshav Santhanam, Omar Khattab, Jon Saad-Falcon, Christopher Potts, and Matei Zaharia. 2022. ColBERTv2: Effective and efficient retrieval via lightweight late interaction. In *Proceedings of the 2022 Conference of the North American Chapter of the Association for Computational Linguistics: Human Language Technologies*, pages 3715–3734, Seattle, United States. Association for Computational Linguistics.

Christopher Sciavolino, Zexuan Zhong, Jinhyuk Lee, and Danqi Chen. 2021. Simple entity-centric questions challenge dense retrievers. In *Proceedings of the 2021 Conference on Empirical Methods in Natural Language Processing*, pages 6138–6148, Online and Punta Cana, Dominican Republic. Association for Computational Linguistics.

Hassan S. Shavarani and Anoop Sarkar. 2023. SpEL: Structured prediction for entity linking. In *Proceedings of the 2023 Conference on Empirical Methods in Natural Language Processing*, pages 11123–11137, Singapore. Association for Computational Linguistics.

Hassan S. Shavarani and Satoshi Sekine. 2020. Multiclass multilingual classification of Wikipedia articles using extended named entity tag set. In *Proceedings of the Twelfth Language Resources and Evaluation Conference*, pages 1197–1201, Marseille, France. European Language Resources Association.

Weijia Shi, Sewon Min, Michihiro Yasunaga, Minjoon Seo, Rich James, Mike Lewis, Luke Zettlemoyer, and Wen-tau Yih. 2023. Replug: Retrieval-augmented black-box language models. *arXiv preprint arXiv:2301.12652*.

Kurt Shuster, Spencer Poff, Moya Chen, Douwe Kiela, and Jason Weston. 2021. Retrieval augmentation reduces hallucination in conversation. In *Findings of the Association for Computational Linguistics: EMNLP 2021*, pages 3784–3803, Punta Cana, Dominican Republic. Association for Computational Linguistics.

Devendra Singh, Siva Reddy, Will Hamilton, Chris Dyer, and Dani Yogatama. 2021. End-to-end training of multi-document reader and retriever for open-domain question answering. *Advances in Neural Information Processing Systems*, 34:25968–25981.

Noah A Smith, Michael Heilman, and Rebecca Hwa. 2008. Question generation as a competitive undergraduate course project. In *Proceedings of the NSF Workshop on the Question Generation Shared Task and Evaluation Challenge*, volume 9.

Haitian Sun, Bhuwan Dhingra, Manzil Zaheer, Kathryn Mazaitis, Ruslan Salakhutdinov, and William Cohen. 2018. Open domain question answering using early fusion of knowledge bases and text. In *Proceedings of the 2018 Conference on Empirical Methods in Natural Language Processing*, pages 4231–4242, Brussels, Belgium. Association for Computational Linguistics.

Ellen M Voorhees and Donna Harman. 1999. Overview of the eighth text retrieval conference (trec-8). In *Proceedings of the Eighth Text REtrieval Conference (TREC-8), NIST Special Publication.*

Lee Xiong, Chenyan Xiong, Ye Li, Kwok-Fung Tang, Jialin Liu, Paul N. Bennett, Junaid Ahmed, and Arnold Overwijk. 2021. Approximate nearest neighbor negative contrastive learning for dense text retrieval. In *International Conference on Learning Representations*.

Ikuya Yamada, Akari Asai, and Hannaneh Hajishirzi. 2021. Efficient passage retrieval with hashing for open-domain question answering. In *Proceedings of the 59th Annual Meeting of the Association for Computational Linguistics and the 11th International Joint Conference on Natural Language Processing (Volume 2: Short Papers)*, pages 979–986, Online. Association for Computational Linguistics.

Wenhao Yu, Zhihan Zhang, Zhenwen Liang, Meng Jiang, and Ashish Sabharwal. 2023. Improving language models via plug-and-play retrieval feedback. *arXiv preprint arXiv:2305.14002*.

Jingtao Zhan, Jiaxin Mao, Yiqun Liu, Min Zhang, and Shaoping Ma. 2020a. Learning to retrieve: How to train a dense retrieval model effectively and efficiently. *arXiv preprint arXiv:2010.10469*.

Jingtao Zhan, Jiaxin Mao, Yiqun Liu, Min Zhang, and Shaoping Ma. 2020b. Repbert: Contextualized text embeddings for first-stage retrieval. *arXiv preprint arXiv:2006.15498*.

Qin Zhang, Shangsi Chen, Dongkuan Xu, Qingqing Cao, Xiaojun Chen, Trevor Cohn, and Meng Fang. 2023. A survey for efficient open domain question answering. In *Proceedings of the 61st Annual Meeting of the Association for Computational Linguistics (Volume 1: Long Papers)*, pages 14447–14465, Toronto, Canada. Association for Computational Linguistics.

Fengbin Zhu, Wenqiang Lei, Chao Wang, Jianming Zheng, Soujanya Poria, and Tat-Seng Chua. 2021. Retrieving and reading: A comprehensive survey on open-domain question answering. *arXiv preprint arXiv:2101.00774*.

A Example Prompts for Different Experimental Settings

In this section, we present the prompts used in our experimental settings. For each setting, we provide the prompt template, and explain the processes needed to obtain the augmentation documents if a Retrieval-Augmented setting is being discussed.

A.1 Closed-book Setting

In this setting, we do not have any augmentation documents, so the prompt contains the instruction, followed by the question:

```
Answer this question:
Q: {question}
A:
```

Here is an example prompt with the question mentioned in Figure 1 and Table 4:

```
Answer this question:
Q: What is the capital of Seine-Saint
  -Denis?
A:
```

A.2 Retrieval-Augmented Settings

In this setting, we examine two variations of prompts based on the number of available augmented documents. For a single document, the prompt is as follows:

```
{document}

Based on this text, answer this
question:
Q: {question}
A:
```

When multiple documents are available, they are presented sequentially, followed by the instruction and question:

```
{document1}

{document2}

...

{documentN}

Based on these texts, answer this
question:
Q: {question}
A:
```

Doc#	Content
1	Pierrefitte-sur-Seine<newline>Pierrefitte-sur-Seine Pierrefitte-sur-Seine is a commune in the Seine-Saint-Denis department and Ile-de-France region of France. Today forming part of the northern suburbs of Paris, Pierrefitte lies from the centre of the French capital. The town is served by Pierrefitte - Stains railway station on line D of the RER regional suburban rail network. The south of the commune, where the National Archives of France relocated in 2013, is also served by Saint-Denis - Universite station on Paris Metro Line 13. This station lies on the border between the communes of Pierrefitte-sur-Seine and Saint-Denis. Primary and secondary schools in the commune include:
2	"Saint-Ouen, Seine-Saint-Denis"<newline>Saint-Ouen, Seine-Saint-Denis Saint-Ouen () is a commune in the Seine-Saint-Denis department. It is located in the northern suburbs of Paris, France, from the centre of Paris. The communes neighbouring Saint-Ouen are Paris, to the south, Clichy, to the west, Asnieres-sur-Seine and L'Ile-Saint-Denis, to the north, and Saint-Denis to the east. The commune of Saint-Ouen is part of the canton of Saint-Ouen, which also includes L'Ile-Saint-Denis and part of Epinay-sur-Seine. Saint-Ouen also includes the Cimetiere de Saint-Ouen. On 1 January 1860, the city of Paris was enlarged by annexing neighbouring communes. On that occasion, a part of the commune of Saint-Ouen
3	"Ile-de-France"<newline>of France. The population of immigrants is more widely distributed throughout the region than it was in the early 2000s, though the concentrations remain high in certain areas, particularly Paris and the department of Seine-Saint-Denis. The proportion of residents born outside of Metropolitan France has dropped since the 1999 census (19.7 percent) and the 2010 census (23 percent). . The Petite Couronne (Little Crown, i.e. ""Inner Ring"") is formed by the 3 departments of Ile-de-France bordering with the French capital and forming a geographical ""crown"" around it. The departments, until 1968 part of the disbanded Seine department, are Hauts-de-Seine, Seine-Saint-Denis
4	"Saint-Denis, Seine-Saint-Denis"<newline>Saint-Denis, Seine-Saint-Denis Saint-Denis () is a commune in the northern suburbs of Paris, France. It is located from the centre of Paris. Saint-Denis is a subprefecture () of the department of Seine-Saint-Denis, being the seat of the arrondissement of Saint-Denis. Saint-Denis is home to the royal necropolis of the Basilica of Saint Denis and was also the location of the associated abbey. It is also home to France's national football and rugby stadium, the Stade de France, built for the 1998 FIFA World Cup. Saint-Denis is a formerly industrial suburb currently changing its economic base. Inhabitants of Saint-Denis are called

Table 7: Top 4 documents retrieved from the BM25 Lucene index for the question `What is the capital of Seine-Saint-Denis?` from the EntityQuestions (dev) dataset.

Next, we examine the various Retrieval-Augmentation techniques studied in this paper: BM25, DPR, and ANCE, showcasing their top four retrieved documents for `What is the capital of Seine-Saint-Denis?`. Tables 7, 8, and 9 present these retrieved documents. The finalized prompt template will include the four retrieved documents alongside the question, as previously discussed.

In analyzing the retrieved documents, you can verify the originating Wikipedia articles mentioned in the beginning of each passage. Notably, passages are drawn from three or four different articles, and given the entity-centric nature of the question, relying on multiple sources could mislead the LLM, as suggested by Cuconasu et al. (2024). Additionally, these methods primarily focus on lexical similarity, particularly the presence of `capital`, `Seine`, `Saint`, and `Denis`. However, this focus has not consistently led to retrieval of passages containing the correct answer: `Bobigny`.

A.3 *Entity Retrieval* Settings

For *Entity Retrieval*, we utilize an entity linker to identify entities within the question. In this

Doc#	Content
1	"L'Ile-Saint-Denis"<newline>L'Ile-Saint-Denis L'Ile-Saint-Denis (the island of Saint Denis) is a commune in the northern suburbs of Paris, France. It is located from the center of Paris. The commune is entirely contained on an island of the Seine River, hence its name. Several transit connections are located nearby. The closest station to L'Ile-Saint-Denis is Saint-Denis station, which is an interchange station on Paris RER line D and on the Transilien Paris - Nord suburban rail line. This station is located in the neighboring commune of Saint-Denis, from the town center of L'Ile-Saint-Denis. Tram T1 stops near Ile-Saint-Denis's town hall. Bus route 237
2	"15th arrondissement of Paris"<newline>15th arrondissement of Paris The 15th arrondissement of Paris (""XV arrondissement"") is one of the 20 arrondissements of the capital city of France. In spoken French, this arrondissement is referred to as ""quinzieme"". The arrondissement, called Vaugirard, is situated on the left bank of the River Seine. Sharing the Montparnasse district with the 6th and 14th arrondissements, it is the city's most populous arrondissement. The ""Tour Montparnasse"" - the tallest skyscraper in Paris - and the neighbouring Gare Montparnasse are both located in the 15th arrondissement, at its border with the 14th. It is also home to the convention center
3	"L'Ile-Saint-Denis"<newline>few of the students were White. There are three primary schools in the commune: Ecole Samira Bellil, Ecole Paul Langevin, and Ecole Jean Lurcat. College Alfred Sisley, a junior high school, is on the island. L'Ile-Saint-Denis L'Ile-Saint-Denis (the island of Saint Denis) is a commune in the northern suburbs of Paris, France. It is located from the center of Paris. The commune is entirely contained on an island of the Seine River, hence its name. Several transit connections are located nearby. The closest station to L'Ile-Saint-Denis is Saint-Denis station, which is an interchange station on Paris RER line D and
4	"2nd arrondissement of Paris"<newline>2nd arrondissement of Paris The 2nd arrondissement of Paris (""II arrondissement"") is one of the 20 arrondissements of the capital city of France. In spoken French, this arrondissement is colloquially referred to as ""deuxieme"" (second/the second). Also known as Bourse, this arrondissement is located on the right bank of the River Seine. The 2nd arrondissement, together with the adjacent 8th and 9th arrondissements, hosts an important business district, centred on the Paris Opera, which houses the city's most dense concentration of business activities. The arrondissement contains the former Paris Bourse (stock exchange) and a large number of banking headquarters, as

Table 8: Top 4 documents retrieved from the DPR index for the question `What is the capital of Seine-Saint-Denis?` from the EntityQuestions (dev) dataset.

study, we employed SpEL, though any suitable entity linking method can be used. The primary requirement is that the linker accepts a string (the question) as input and returns a list containing (`begin character`, `end character`, `identified entity`) tuples. The `begin character` and `end character` values help determine the order of entity annotations in the text, ensuring proper sequence if the returned list is unordered.

The `identified entity` values are then used to search the Wikipedia dump on disk, fetching articles corresponding to the identified entities. Efficient implementation of this lookup process is crucial for the method's performance. Our approach involves a two-step indexing and lookup process. First, we index the file bytes marking the beginning of each Wikipedia article in the dump file. When an article is needed, we use this index to locate the byte number and employ the seek method to navigate to the correct position in the file and read the article.

After gathering the relevant articles, we truncate each one to the first W words (suffixed with the Wikipedia identifier, as per convention) to create a list of augmentation documents to accompany the question when querying the LLM.

To prompt the LLM, we use the same prompts previously mentioned. If no entities are found in

Doc#	Content
1	"L'Ile-Saint-Denis"<newline>L'Ile-Saint-Denis L'Ile-Saint-Denis (the island of Saint Denis) is a commune in the northern suburbs of Paris, France. It is located from the center of Paris. The commune is entirely contained on an island of the Seine River, hence its name. Several transit connections are located nearby. The closest station to L'Ile-Saint-Denis is Saint-Denis station, which is an interchange station on Paris RER line D and on the Transilien Paris - Nord suburban rail line. This station is located in the neighboring commune of Saint-Denis, from the town center of L'Ile-Saint-Denis. Tram T1 stops near Ile-Saint-Denis's town hall. Bus route 237
2	"L'Ile-Saint-Denis"<newline>few of the students were White. There are three primary schools in the commune: Ecole Samira Bellil, Ecole Paul Langevin, and Ecole Jean Lurcat. College Alfred Sisley, a junior high school, is on the island. L'Ile-Saint-Denis L'Ile-Saint-Denis (the island of Saint Denis) is a commune in the northern suburbs of Paris, France. It is located from the center of Paris. The commune is entirely contained on an island of the Seine River, hence its name. Several transit connections are located nearby. The closest station to L'Ile-Saint-Denis is Saint-Denis station, which is an interchange station on Paris RER line D and
3	"Saint-Denis, Seine-Saint-Denis"<newline>one private elementary, middle, and high school (""Ensemble Scolaire Jean-Baptiste de la Salle-Notre Dame de la Compassion"") and one private middle and high school (""College et lycee Saint-Vincent-de-Paul""). Saint-Denis is twinned with: Saint-Denis, Seine-Saint-Denis Saint-Denis () is a commune in the northern suburbs of Paris, France. It is located from the centre of Paris. Saint-Denis is a subprefecture () of the department of Seine-Saint-Denis, being the seat of the arrondissement of Saint-Denis. Saint-Denis is home to the royal necropolis of the Basilica of Saint Denis and was also the location of the associated abbey. It is also home to France's
4	"Saint-Ouen, Seine-Saint-Denis"<newline>Saint-Ouen, Seine-Saint-Denis Saint-Ouen () is a commune in the Seine-Saint-Denis department. It is located in the northern suburbs of Paris, France, from the centre of Paris. The communes neighbouring Saint-Ouen are Paris, to the south, Clichy, to the west, Asnieres-sur-Seine and L'Ile-Saint-Denis, to the north, and Saint-Denis to the east. The commune of Saint-Ouen is part of the canton of Saint-Ouen, which also includes L'Ile-Saint-Denis and part of Epinay-sur-Seine. Saint-Ouen also includes the Cimetiere de Saint-Ouen. On 1 January 1860, the city of Paris was enlarged by annexing neighbouring communes. On that occasion, a part of the commune of Saint-Ouen

Table 9: Top 4 documents retrieved from the ANCE index for the question `What is the capital of Seine-Saint-Denis?` from the EntityQuestions (dev) dataset.

the question, we refer to the prompt in Appendix A.1. If one entity is recognized, resulting in one augmentation document, we use the first prompt from Appendix A.2. If multiple entities are identified, we use the second prompt from the same appendix section. In rare cases where the number of identified entities exceeds k (the expected number of documents to retrieve), we simply consider the first k unique entities to form the list of augmentation documents.

Table 10 presents the single document retrieved for `What is the capital of Seine-Saint-Denis?`, which contains the answer: `Bobigny`. Examining the lexical distribution in this document, we observe that unlike the BM25 method, *Entity Retrieval* treats the salient entity `Seine-Saint-Denis` as an atomic term rather than emphasizing each word in the question. This focused approach, coupled with the retrieval of fewer documents, allows the model to concentrate on the relevant information, reducing noise and potential confusion.

However, the effectiveness of *Entity Retrieval* in real-world scenarios, where question entity annotations are not available, largely depends on the quality of the entity linker used to identify salient entities in the question. Therefore, further research into developing more accurate entity linking mod-

Doc#	Content
1	Seine-Saint-Denis<newline>Seine-Saint-Denis In 2019, it had a population of 1,644,903 across 40 communes. In French, the learned but rarely used demonym for the inhabitants of Seine-Saint-Denis is ; more common is . The department is surrounded by the departments of Hauts-de-Seine, Val-de-Marne, Paris, Val-d'Oise, and Seine-et-Marne. It is thus the only one of the five French departments surrounded entirely by other departments of the same region. Image:Petite couronne.png The most populous commune is Saint-Denis; the prefecture Bobigny is the eleventh-most populous. As of 2019, there are 5 communes with more than 70,000 inhabitants: is made up of three departmental and 40

Table 10: The only document retrieved by *Entity Retrieval* using SPEL annotations for the question `What is the capital of Seine-Saint-Denis?` from the EntityQuestions (dev) dataset. SPEL identifies only one entity in the question: `Seine-Saint-Denis` and returns the first 100 words (considering W=100) of its Wikipedia article as the retrieved document. The answer to the question: `Bobigny` is highlighted for ease of verification.

els could enhance *Entity Retrieval* performance.

ELECTRA and GPT-4o: Cost-Effective Partners for Sentiment Analysis

James P. Beno
Stanford Engineering CGOE
jim@jimbeno.net

Abstract

Bidirectional transformers excel at sentiment analysis, and Large Language Models (LLM) are effective zero-shot learners. Might they perform better as a team? This paper explores collaborative approaches between ELECTRA and GPT-4o for three-way sentiment classification. We fine-tuned (FT) four models (ELECTRA Base/Large, GPT-4o/4o-mini) using a mix of reviews from Stanford Sentiment Treebank (SST) and DynaSent. We provided input from ELECTRA to GPT as: predicted label, probabilities, and retrieved examples. Sharing ELECTRA Base FT predictions with GPT-4o-mini significantly improved performance over either model alone (82.50 macro F1 vs. 79.14 ELECTRA Base FT, 79.41 GPT-4o-mini) and yielded the lowest cost/performance ratio ($0.12/F1 point). However, when GPT models were fine-tuned, including predictions decreased performance. GPT-4o FT-M was the top performer (86.99), with GPT-4o-mini FT close behind (86.70) at much less cost ($0.38 vs. $1.59/F1 point). Our results show that augmenting prompts with predictions from fine-tuned encoders is an efficient way to boost performance, and a fine-tuned GPT-4o-mini is nearly as good as GPT-4o FT at 76% less cost. Both are affordable options for projects with limited resources.

1 Introduction

Sentiment analysis—the computational study of opinions, attitudes, and emotions in text (Medhat et al., 2014)—has seen major advances from transformer architectures (Vaswani et al., 2017). Bidirectional encoders like BERT (Devlin et al., 2019), RoBERTa (Liu et al., 2019), and ELECTRA (Clark et al., 2020) excel at sentiment analysis when fine-tuned, and Large Language Models (LLM) like GPT (Radford et al., 2018) are strong zero-shot and few-shot learners (Kheiri and Karimi, 2023).

Recent work has explored collaboration between these models, such as using GPT to augment data of minority classes before fine-tuning with RoBERTa (Kok-Shun et al., 2023), using GPT for aspect extraction and RoBERTa for sentiment scoring (Qian et al., 2024), and escalating to LLMs when RoBERTa classification confidence was low (Andrade et al., 2024). However, leveraging external knowledge of sentiment from fine-tuned encoders to enhance LLMs remains under-explored.

This research investigates collaborative approaches between ELECTRA and GPT-4o models (OpenAI, 2024b,c) for three-way sentiment classification (negative, neutral, positive) of reviews. Our research focused on the following hypotheses: Providing predictions from a fine-tuned ELECTRA as context to a GPT model will improve classification performance (**H1**). The improvement in performance will be less for a fine-tuned GPT (**H2**). The format of predictions in the prompt will affect performance (**H3**). Including similar examples in the prompt will improve performance (**H4**).

These hypotheses build on ELECTRA's strength in capturing nuanced sentiment patterns when fine-tuned (Clark et al., 2020; Potts et al., 2021; B et al., 2023), and GPT's versatility through in-context learning (Radford et al., 2019; Liu et al., 2019; Kocoń et al., 2023; OpenAI, 2024a)—they can perform well across diverse tasks when given the appropriate context through prompting (Liu et al., 2023; Khattab et al., 2024). Although they may struggle with emotion and nuance (Kocoń et al., 2023), retrieved examples can improve performance (Zhang et al., 2023).

To test these hypotheses, we established four baselines and conducted 28 experiments across three sentiment classification datasets: Stanford Sentiment Treebank (SST), and DynaSent Rounds 1 and 2. We used ELECTRA Base/Large and GPT-4o/4o-mini, each of which were fine-tuned (FT) on a merge of SST and DynaSent reviews.

We investigated the effects of different prompt augmentation scenarios using Declarative Self-improving Python (DSPy) (Khattab et al., 2024),

Proceedings of the 4th International Workshop on Knowledge-Augmented Methods for Natural Language Processing (KnowledgeNLP'25), pages 18–36
May 3, 2025 ©2025 Association for Computational Linguistics

a framework for programming language models. We started with a prompt to classify a review, and augmented it with knowledge from ELECTRA in the form of: the predicted class label, the probabilities of each class, similar reviews with their class labels, and combinations. We evaluated classification performance with the macro average F1 score, and cost-effectiveness by dividing total fine-tuning costs by the F1. Our key insights are the following.

Sharing predictions boosted performance. Augmenting GPT-4o-mini (not fine-tuned) with predictions from ELECTRA Base FT significantly improved performance over either model alone. It also yielded the lowest cost/performance ratio.

Adding probabilities or examples did not help. Using probabilities, or including few-shot examples, did not improve performance more than the predicted label alone for both GPT models.

Fine-tuned GPTs performed best. GPT-4o FT-M alone achieved the highest overall performance on the merged test set, with GPT-4o-mini FT closely following at significantly lower cost.

Sharing predictions hurt fine-tuned GPTs. When GPT models were fine-tuned, including ELECTRA predictions decreased performance—even when fine-tuned with the same inference-time prompt that included the ELECTRA prediction. Fine-tuning with the prediction for more epochs allowed GPT to discriminate better. Performance improved, but the cost grew significantly.

Fine-tuned ELECTRA Large outperformed base GPTs. ELECTRA Large fine-tuned was the best performing encoder model, and was better than both GPT-4o and GPT-4o-mini base models.

These findings offer affordable options for projects with limited resources. If fine-tuning via API is an option, a fine-tuned GPT-4o-mini is nearly as good as GPT-4o FT at 76% less cost. Alternatively, augmenting LLM prompts with predictions from fine-tuned encoder models is an efficient way to boost performance. For projects that want to stay local, a fine-tuned ELECTRA Large model is quite capable, and better than default GPTs.

The key contributions of this research are:

- Proposes a novel collaboration where fine-tuned bidirectional encoders assist GPT models with the task of sentiment classification.
- Demonstrates that augmenting GPT prompts (not fine-tuned) with predictions from fine-tuned encoders significantly improves classification performance and reduces costs, achieving the lowest cost/performance ratio.
- Evaluates various formats for incorporating encoder output into GPT prompts, and offers practical guidelines to maximize performance.

2 Prior Literature

2.1 MLMs and ELECTRA

Masked Language Models (MLM) like BERT (Bidirectional Encoder Representations from Transformers) (Devlin et al., 2019) employed bidirectional encoding to obtain holistic representations of text. RoBERTa (Robustly Optimized BERT Pretraining Approach) (Liu et al., 2019) optimized the pre-training approach, but both models were inefficient because learning only occurred in about 15% of the tokens that were masked.

This led to the development of ELECTRA (Efficiently Learning an Encoder that Classifies Token Replacements Accurately) (Clark et al., 2020). ELECTRA was pre-trained with two models using replaced token detection. As a result, it learned from all tokens and had comparable or better performance in a variety of tasks with less compute.

ELECTRA was found to be a top performer in sentiment classification on datasets such as SST (Clark et al., 2020), DynaSent (Potts et al., 2021), and IMDB movie reviews (B et al., 2023). It was also found to be better suited for prompt-based learning due to its use of a discrimnator (Xia et al., 2022). We chose to use ELECTRA for these reasons, in addition to observing a performance gain relative to RoBERTa in early trials.

2.2 GPT Models

Bidrectional transformers seemed to have an edge over early autoregressive models like GPT (Radford et al., 2018) for sentiment analysis. But that edge is being whittled away by the successors of GPT pre-trained at a massive scale: GPT-3, GPT-3.5, GPT-4, and GPT-4o (OpenAI, 2024a,b,c).

For sentiment analysis of social media posts, Kheiri and Karimi (2023) found that GPT models significantly outperformed a number of prior models on the SemEval 2017 dataset. In contrast, Kocoń et al. (2023) found that, although ChatGPT is versatile and competent across a wide range of tasks, it did not perform as well as RoBERTa—especially for pragmatic tasks involving detection of emotional and contextual nuances. They pro-

Table 1: Examples of Merged Training Dataset

Index	Sentence	Label	Source
0	Those 2 drinks are part of the HK culture and has years of history. It is so bad.	negative	dynasent_r2
1	I was told by the repair company that was doing the car repair that fixing the rim was "impossible" and to replace it.	negative	dynasent_r1
2	It is there to give them a good time .	neutral	sst_local
3	Like leafing through an album of photos accompanied by the sketchiest of captions .	negative	sst_local
4	Johnny was a talker and liked to have fun.	positive	dynasent_r1

pose that fine-tuning ChatGPT may be necessary, which we explore in this research.

2.3 Collaborative Approaches

Recent work has revealed several promising approaches for collaboration between these models.

Kok-Shun et al. (2023) explored a unique framework that chains GPT and RoBERTa for emotion detection. They used GPT's generative capabilities to augment training data for minority classes. The augmented dataset is then used to fine-tune RoBERTa on emotion detection.

Qian et al. (2024) tapped the strengths of different models in a Natural Language Processing (NLP) pipeline to analyze stadium reviews. One GPT-3.5 model was fine-tuned to extract experience aspects, while another classified these aspects into categories. A RoBERTa model then performed sentiment scoring on the extracted aspects. We are chaining ELECTRA and GPT-4o in a similar manner here, but in a different order.

Andrade et al. (2024) investigated the benefits of collaboration between MLMs and open LLMs for sentiment classification, similar to the current research. In their "Call-My-Big-Sibling" (CMBS) approach, the initial classification is done with a calibrated RoBERTa model. If RoBERTa has low confidence on the classification, an open LLM like Llama 2 (Touvron et al., 2023) is invoked to perform the classification task instead.

In CMBS, the final prediction is either made by RoBERTa or Llama 2—it's a decision tree. In contrast, our approach always passes the ELECTRA prediction to the LLM. If we had to come up with a similar analogy, it would be "Show-Me-Your-Answers" (SMYA). And then it's up to the LLM to decide if it follows the ELECTRA prediction, or decides to classify the review differently.

Most recently, Charpentier and Samuel (2024) created GPT-BERT, a hybrid model that learns bidirectional representations like an MLM, but is also generative like a GPT. By shifting the prediction of masked tokens one position to the right, GPT-BERT can be trained on both MLM and autoregressive objectives without changing architecture. In the BabyLM Challenge 2024 benchmark, it outperformed models trained on only one objective, showing there is potential in this combined approach.

Table 2: Label Distribution for the Merged Dataset

Split	Negative	Neutral	Positive
Train	21,910	49,148	31,039
Validation	1,868	1,669	1,884
Test	2,352	1,829	2,349

Table 3: Contribution of Sources to the Merged Dataset

Dataset	Samples	Percent (%)
DynaSent R1 Train	80,488	78.83
DynaSent R2 Train	13,065	12.80
SST-3 Train	8,544	8.37
Total	102,097	100.00

3 Data

Models were trained and evaluated in English on a merge of movie reviews from the Stanford Sentiment Treebank (SST) (Socher et al., 2013) and business reviews from DynaSent Rounds 1 and 2 (Potts et al., 2021), licensed under Apache 2.0 and Creative Commons Attribution 4.0 respectively. See Table 1 for examples. By default, SST is a five-way classification (positive, somewhat positive, neutral, somewhat negative, negative). The positive and negative classes were combined to produce SST-3 (positive, neutral, negative).

The SST-3, DynaSent R1, and DynaSent R2 datasets were randomly mixed to form a Merged dataset with 102,097 Train examples, 5,421 Validation examples, and 6,530 Test examples. See Table 2 for the distribution of labels, and Table 3 for a

Table 4: Models Used in Research

Model	Provider	Access	Identifier
ELECTRA Base	Hugging Face	Local	google/electra-base-discriminator
ELECTRA Large	Hugging Face	Local	google/electra-large-discriminator
GPT-4o	OpenAI	API	gpt-4o-2024-08-06
GPT-4o-mini	OpenAI	API	gpt-4o-mini-2024-07-18

breakdown of sources. It's worth noting that the source datasets all have class imbalances. Merging the data helps mitigate this imbalance, but there is still a majority of neutral examples in the training split. Another potential issue is that the models will learn the dominant dataset, which is DynaSent R1. As a test, the minority classes were over-sampled to create a new balanced dataset. When this was evaluated, the performance did not improve.

4 Models

Four models were fine-tuned and evaluated in this research, both individually and in collaboration with each other: ELECTRA Base and Large, and GPT-4o and 4o-mini. See Table 4 for details.

ELECTRA (Clark et al., 2020), released with an Apache 2.0 license, was chosen as the bidirectional transformer because its pre-training architecture gives it an advantage over MLMs. It also outperformed RoBERTa in early trials. We evaluated both the Base (110M parameters) and Large (335M parameters) variants.

To function as a classifier, ELECTRA's output is sent through a mean pooling layer. A classifier head is appended with 2 hidden layers of dimension 1024, and a final output dimension of 3. Swish GLU (Shazeer, 2020) was used as the hidden activation function, and dropout layers were added with a rate of 0.3. See Appendix B for more details on the model architecture and hyper-parameters.

For comparison and collaboration, two GPT models were used via OpenAI's API: GPT-4o (OpenAI, 2024b) and GPT-4o-mini (OpenAI, 2024c). Although the full specifications are not public, they are state-of-the-art autoregressive language models with strong zero-shot capabilities. GPT-4o is described as a "high-intelligence flagship model for complex, multi-step tasks." GPT-4o-mini is described as an "affordable and intelligent small model for fast, lightweight tasks."

5 Methods

Our research progressed through the following stages. Code and datasets are available at: `https://github.com/jbeno/sentiment`.

5.1 ELECTRA Baseline & Fine-tuning

We first developed a training pipeline to support interactivity and distributed training across multiple GPUs. Training progress was tracked through Weights and Biases so we could monitor train/validation metrics (loss, macro F1, accuracy) across epochs. The final models were selected from checkpoints at convergence, or just before train/validation metrics started to diverge.

Two baseline models were established by training only classifier heads for ELECTRA Base and Large. Hyper-parameters were consistent with the fully fine-tuned versions. The fine-tuning process involved a number of trials on Lambda Labs multi-GPU instances to identify the best hyper-parameters, optimizer, and learning rate schedule. See Appendix B for the final configuration.

We also explored alternative approaches including an ensemble of binary classifiers, and additional fine-tuning on DynaSent R2 and SST-3, but these did not outperform our initial approach.

5.2 GPT Data Preparation & Fine-tuning

To use OpenAI's fine-tuning API, we converted the Merged training data to JSONL format that defined the System, User, and Assistant roles. We noticed that if the context at inference time varied even slightly from the fine-tuning context, performance would suffer. So we created three templates to enable better comparisons between fine-tuned and default models using the same DSPy signatures (see Appendix D):

- **Minimal (FT-M):** No prompt other than System role. User role only contained the review sentence.
- **Prompt (FT):** Default fine-tuning. User role included full DSPy prompt.

- **Prompt with Label (FT-L):** User role included DSPy prompt with ELECTRA predicted label.

We included the ELECTRA predictions in the third template to align the fine-tuning context with the inference time context, but also to provide an opportunity for the GPT models to learn from the ELECTRA predictions. In total there were 9 fine-tuning jobs (see Table 5, and Appendix C for GPT fine-tuning details).

Table 5: Fine-Tuning Job Details

Model	Code	Format	Epochs
4o-mini	FT-M	Minimal	1
4o-mini	FT	Prompt	1
4o-mini	FT-L	Prompt w/Base Label	1
4o-mini	FT-L	Prompt w/Base Label	5
4o-mini	FT-L	Prompt w/Large Label	1
4o-mini	FT-L	Prompt w/Large Label	5
4o	FT-M	Minimal	1
4o	FT	Prompt	1
4o	FT-L	Prompt w/Large Label	1

5.3 DSPy Signatures & Modules

With DSPy, you create modules (ex: Classify, ClassifyWithExamples), signatures (input/output templates, ex: review + examples → classification), define metrics (ex: classification_match) and evaluators of data, and use optimizers to find the best performing prompt or module parameters.

We explored a variety of approaches to integrating ELECTRA's output into GPT's decision-making process. Each approach was implemented as a custom DSPy signature and module (see Appendix E for the full examples).

Classification Prompt. Prompt to "Classify the sentiment of a review as either 'negative', 'neutral', or 'positive'." One input field 'review' described as "The review text to classify." and one output field 'classification' described as "One word representing the sentiment classification: 'negative', 'neutral', or 'positive' (do not repeat the field name, do not use 'mixed')".

Predicted Label. Classification prompt with an additional input field 'classifier_decision' described as "The sentiment classification proposed by a model fine-tuned on sentiment." During evaluation, the DSPy module first sends the review through the ELECTRA model to obtain its prediction. This output is then inserted into the signature.

Probabilities. Classification prompt, but instead of 'classifier_decision' it featured three input fields for the probabilities of each class as obtained from the ELECTRA model. For example: 'negative_probability' was described as "Probability the review is negative from a model fine-tuned on sentiment". The float is converted to a percent to make it easier for the model to interpret.

Prediction & Probabilities. Same as Probabilities, but it also included the 'classifier_decision' to emphasize the final decision made by ELECTRA.

Top Examples. A custom retriever was created from 300 reviews in the Validation split. During inference, input text is run through the fine-tuned ELECTRA Large model to extract the output representations (prior to the classifier head). The top five matches and class labels based on cosine similarity are shown as few-shot examples. This signature had 'classifier_decision' plus an 'examples' field described as "A list of examples that demonstrate different sentiment classes."

Balanced Examples. If ELECTRA was wrong, and the Top Examples were all of the same class, it might be hard for GPT to make an independent decision. To compensate, in Balanced Examples, a different retriever was used that retrieved a total of six examples (the top two examples from each class) to ensure the few-shot examples with true labels did not bias the answer toward a particular class—although that might be desirable sometimes.

All of the Above. And lastly, a final DSPy signature had all of the above context from ELECTRA included: classification prompt, predicted label, probabilities, and top five examples (not balanced). It was unclear if providing all this information would help GPT make a decision, or if the large number of tokens would dilute the signal.

We then conducted two of the four baselines, and 26 of the 28 experiments (see Table 6) using these DSPy signatures and modules. The fine-tuned ELECTRA models and retriever were instantiated locally for inference, and the GPT models were accessed via OpenaAI API. To address single-run concerns, each baseline and experiment was run a second time with a different random seed (123 vs. 42) and temperature (0.1 vs. 0.0).

6 Results

Our experiments revealed significant differences in performance across baseline, fine-tuning, and collaborative scenarios. See Table 6 for the mean macro average F1 between the two runs. Appendix A has the raw data of each run.

Table 6: Summary of Model Configuration, Test Set Performance, and Cost

ID[1]	GPT[2]	ELECTRA	Description	Merged[3] Macro F1[4]	DynaSent R1 Macro F1[4]	DynaSent R2 Macro F1[4]	SST-3 Macro F1[4]	Cost ($)[5] FT	Cost ($)[5] /F1
B1	—	Base	Baseline, Classifier head	69.51 ± 0.20	70.86 ± 0.15	61.39 ± 0.28	60.60 ± 0.36	0.65	0.01
B2	—	Large	Baseline, Classifier head	67.94 ± 0.08	69.70 ± 0.04	59.78 ± 0.00	57.95 ± 0.37	2.51	0.04
B3	4o-mini	—	Baseline (Zero shot)	†79.41 ± 0.16	81.16 ± 0.05	77.02 ± 0.47	69.99 ± 0.97	—	—
B4	4o	—	Baseline (Zero shot)	79.97 ± 0.24	80.95 ± 0.25	80.14 ± 0.12	72.08 ± 0.17	—	—
E1	—	Base FT	Fine-tune all layers	†79.14 ± 0.22	82.12 ± 0.02	70.67 ± 1.64	69.04 ± 1.29	9.73	0.12
E2	—	Large FT	Fine-tune all layers	82.76 ± 0.57	86.22 ± 0.44	77.33 ± 1.46	71.77 ± 1.22	53.26	0.65
E3	4o-mini	Base FT	Prompt, Label	†82.50 ± 0.34	86.40 ± 0.15	75.33 ± 1.22	70.88 ± 1.20	**9.73**	**0.12**
E4	4o-mini	Large FT	Prompt, Label	83.80 ± 0.43	87.71 ± 0.27	78.73 ± 1.12	71.77 ± 1.10	53.26	0.64
E5	4o-mini	Large FT	Prompt, Label, Examples (Few shot)	83.42 ± 0.30	86.94 ± 0.28	79.50 ± 1.12	72.33 ± 0.49	53.26	0.64
E6	4o-mini	Large FT	Prompt, Label, Balanced Ex. (Few shot)	82.98 ± 0.42	86.28 ± 0.62	79.87 ± 0.36	71.98 ± 0.75	53.26	0.64
E7	4o-mini	Large FT	Prompt, Probs	83.27 ± 0.37	86.60 ± 0.23	79.41 ± 0.69	72.26 ± 1.03	53.26	0.64
E8	4o-mini	Large FT	Prompt, Label, Probs	83.66 ± 0.32	87.22 ± 0.28	79.98 ± 0.36	71.78 ± 1.06	53.26	0.64
E9	4o-mini	Large FT	Prompt, Label, Probs, Examples	83.19 ± 0.39	86.58 ± 0.60	78.99 ± 0.42	71.94 ± 0.64	53.26	0.64
E10	4o-mini FT	—	Fine-tune w/prompt	86.70 ± 0.11	89.65 ± 0.30	87.00 ± 0.13	**75.83 ± 0.21**	33.15	0.38
E11	4o-mini FT 5	—	Fine-tune w/prompt (5 epochs)	84.86 ± 0.13	87.74 ± 0.13	86.22 ± 0.40	75.38 ± 0.32	165.75	1.95
E12	4o-mini FT-M	—	Minimal fine-tune	86.51 ± 0.06	89.57 ± 0.18	87.13 ± 0.22	75.74 ± 0.17	16.60	0.19
E13	4o-mini FT	Base FT	Prompt, Label, FT w/prompt	81.06 ± 0.52	84.67 ± 0.14	73.06 ± 2.03	69.70 ± 1.77	42.88	0.53
E14	4o-mini FT-L	Base FT	Prompt, Label, FT w/prompt, label	81.84 ± 0.26	85.20 ± 0.06	77.29 ± 1.22	70.70 ± 1.39	49.31	0.60
E15	4o-mini FT-L 5	Base FT	Prompt, Label, FT w/prompt, label (5 epochs)	83.67 ± 0.30	86.38 ± 0.51	81.19 ± 0.62	75.02 ± 0.03	207.64	2.48
E16	4o-mini FT	Large FT	Fine-tune w/prompt	83.94 ± 0.09	87.57 ± 0.11	80.17 ± 0.28	72.46 ± 0.00	86.41	1.03
E17	4o-mini FT-L	Large FT	Fine-tune w/prompt, label	84.12 ± 0.06	87.58 ± 0.10	80.75 ± 0.20	73.34 ± 0.06	92.84	1.10
E18	4o-mini FT-L 5	Large FT	Fine-tune w/prompt, label (5 epochs)	84.83 ± 0.06	87.75 ± 0.17	84.37 ± 0.81	75.59 ± 0.01	251.17	2.96
E19	4o	Large FT	Prompt, Label	83.19 ± 0.01	85.71 ± 0.00	82.06 ± 0.11	73.48 ± 0.06	53.26	0.64
E20	4o	Large FT	Prompt, Label, Examples (Few shot)	83.29 ± 0.28	86.11 ± 0.14	81.48 ± 0.07	72.96 ± 1.27	53.26	0.64
E21	4o	Large FT	Prompt, Label, Balanced Ex. (Few shot)	83.19 ± 0.28	86.01 ± 0.19	81.04 ± 0.21	72.88 ± 1.03	53.26	0.64
E22	4o	Large FT	Prompt, Probs	82.99 ± 0.47	86.37 ± 0.45	78.42 ± 1.05	71.90 ± 1.04	53.26	0.64
E23	4o	Large FT	Prompt, Label, Probs	83.31 ± 0.33	86.69 ± 0.35	79.46 ± 0.33	72.17 ± 0.97	53.26	0.64
E24	4o	Large FT	Prompt, Label, Probs, Examples	83.04 ± 0.42	86.53 ± 0.29	78.47 ± 1.00	71.83 ± 1.20	53.26	0.64
E25	4o FT	—	Fine-tune w/prompt	86.79 ± 0.06	90.46 ± 0.03	88.14 ± 0.28	73.09 ± 0.01	276.24	3.18
E26	4o FT-M	—	Minimal fine-tune	**86.99 ± 0.00**	**90.57 ± 0.00**	**89.00 ± 0.00**	73.99 ± 0.00	138.37	1.59
E27	4o FT	Large FT	Fine-tune w/prompt	84.03 ± 0.30	87.90 ± 0.13	80.01 ± 0.73	72.00 ± 1.15	329.50	3.93
E28	4o FT-L	Large FT	Fine-tune w/prompt, label	84.37 ± 0.19	87.81 ± 0.09	81.28 ± 1.03	73.10 ± 0.66	383.10	4.55

Bold = best overall, highlighted = best in section

† Scores relevant to Hypothesis 1 (ELECTRA prediction improving non-fine-tuned GPT performance)

1 Some ID numbers changed from their original ID in the research repo.

2 GPT fine-tuning types: FT = fine-tune with prompt, FT-M = minimal without prompt, FT-L = with prompt including ELECTRA label, FT 5 = 5 epochs vs. 1

3 Merged dataset: Combination of test splits from DynaSent R1/R2 and SST-3

4 Each experiment was run twice with different random seeds (42, 123) and temperature (0.0, 0.1); values reported are means ± standard deviations. Standard deviations are based on two runs (n=2) and should be interpreted with caution.

5 Cost: FT = Fine-tuning cost, no inference-time API charges. Ratio is FT cost divided by F1 score.

Baselines. Regarding baselines, both GPT models outperformed the ELECTRA classifiers, with GPT-4o achieving a 79.97 mean macro F1 and GPT-4o-mini scoring 79.41, compared to ELECTRA Base (69.51) and Large (67.94). This demonstrates the strong zero-shot capabilities of GPT models.

Fine-tuning. Fine-tuning improved performance across all models. ELECTRA Base's mean macro F1 increased from 69.51 to 79.14, while ELECTRA Large showed greater gains, improving from 67.94 to 82.76. This improvement is the result of fine-tuning all layers—the baselines had the same classifier head. Fine-tuned GPT models had the highest scores (see Figure 2), with GPT-4o-mini FT rising from 79.41 to 86.70, and GPT-4o FT-M achieving 86.99 with the minimal template.

Sharing Predictions. The effect of adding ELECTRA predictions to GPT prompts depended on if the GPT model was fine-tuned (see Figure 1 for the differences in mean F1). Sharing ELECTRA Base predictions with GPT-4o-mini (not fine-tuned) significantly improved the macro F1 in round one from 79.52 to 82.74 ($p < 0.0001$, McNemar's test and bootstrap analysis), a +3.22 gain. There was an even greater gain of +3.97 points

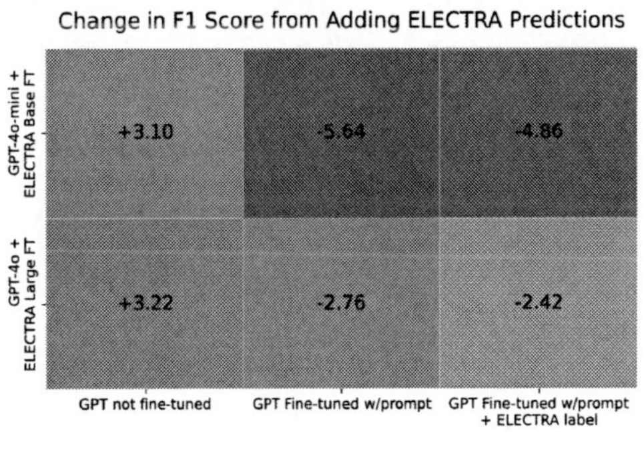

Figure 1: Change in Mean F1 from Adding Predictions

when ELECTRA Large predictions were shared (from 79.52 to 83.49, $p < 0.0001$). Similarly, including ELECTRA Large predictions with GPT-4o improved the macro F1 from 80.14 to 83.18 ($p < 0.001$) in round one, a +3.04 gain.

However, sharing ELECTRA predictions with fine-tuned GPT models actually decreased performance. GPT-4o-mini FT's mean macro F1 dropped from 86.70 to 81.06 when including ELECTRA Base predictions, and to 81.84 when fine-tuned with the predictions included in the prompt. Similarly, GPT-4o FT's mean F1 fell from 86.79 to 84.03 when including ELECTRA Large predictions, and to 84.37 when fine-tuned with them.

Few-shot Examples. Some contexts performed better than others for specific model combinations (see Figure 3). Providing few-shot examples in addition to the predicted label was mostly the same or worse than using the label alone. However, when looking at the more challenging DynaSent Round 2 dataset, GPT-4o-mini saw some benefit. Including just the ELECTRA Large predicted label produced a mean macro F1 of 78.73. Adding examples increased the mean macro F1 to 79.50 (+0.77), and balanced examples increased it to 79.87 (+1.14).

Sharing Probabilities. Using probabilities instead of (or in addition to) the predicted label was mostly the same or worse than using the label alone. However, similar to using examples, the more challenging datasets saw some benefit. For DynaSent Round 2, GPT-4o-mini had a mean macro F1 of 78.73 with just the ELECTRA Large predicted label. Using probabilities instead changed it to 79.41, and using the label with probabilities increased it to 79.98. A similar minor improvement was seen with SST on this dataset.

Datasets. Performance also varied across datasets. GPT-4o FT-M achieved the top scores on DynaSent R1 (90.57 mean macro F1) and DynaSent R2 (89.00). Surprisingly, GPT-4o-mini FT—the smaller model—performed best on SST-3 with a 75.83 mean macro F1, exceeding even GPT-4o FT's performance of 73.99.

Cost. The most cost-effective approach was ELECTRA Base FT with GPT-4o-mini (not fine-tuned) at $0.12 per F1 point. GPT-4o-mini FT provided a good compromise at $0.38 per F1 point, while GPT-4o FT-L with ELECTRA Large FT proved most expensive at $4.55 per F1 point.

7 Analysis

H1. Sharing predictions would boost performance. The significant improvement in GPT-4o-mini's performance when augmented with ELECTRA Base FT or Large FT predictions strongly supports H1. We also saw a similar boost for GPT-4o with ELECTRA Large FT predictions.

However, following ELECTRA's predictions had mixed results. When GPT-4o-mini changed its decision and followed ELECTRA Base FT in round one, it was correct 548 times and wrong 412 times (+136 net improvement, 57.08% success rate). When GPT-4o changed its decision and followed ELECTRA Large FT, it was correct 521 times and wrong 481 times (+40 net improvement, 52% success rate).

Most of the improvement was in the neutral and positive classes (see Figure 4). There was barely any improvement in the negative class, but importantly—it didn't worsen. ELECTRA Base FT had more than double the incorrect negative predictions, but GPT-4o-mini did not follow them. The negative class was 21.46% of the Merged dataset, so ELECTRA may not have learned it well. Conversely, GPT-4o followed more of the negative predictions, and performance suffered.

DynaSent R1 was the dominant source of the Merged dataset (80,488 samples, or 78.83%), and saw the most improvement. It could be that ELECTRA learned this dataset the most, but it also represented less challenging reviews.

H2. Improvement would be less for fine-tuned GPTs. H2 was supported more strongly than anticipated. For a fine-tuned GPT model, including the ELECTRA prediction actually decreased performance (see Figure 1). Initially, we thought this was because the fine-tuning context did not include the ELECTRA prediction in the prompt. But we still saw a decrease in performance (although less) when it was included.

GPT was trained to be a helpful chat assistant that thinks through problems, evaluates information critically, and synthesizes knowledge. When presented with an ELECTRA prediction, it can decide when to follow the prediction and when to rely on its own judgment. In contrast, when fine-tuned specifically for sentiment classification, the model is optimized to map directly from input text to sentiment labels, potentially bypassing the critical thinking that made the base model effective at filtering ELECTRA's suggestions.

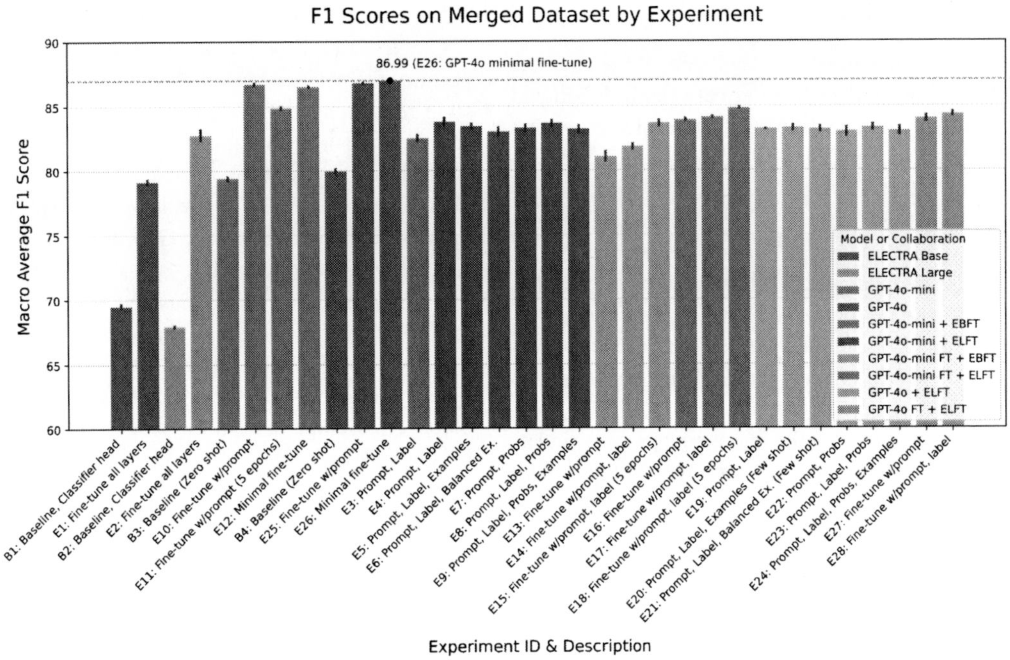

Figure 2: Mean Macro F1 Scores on Merged Dataset by Experiment

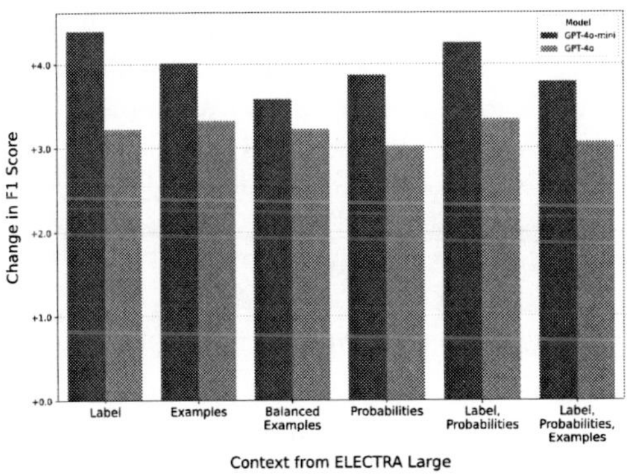

Figure 3: Impact of Context on Mean F1 Score

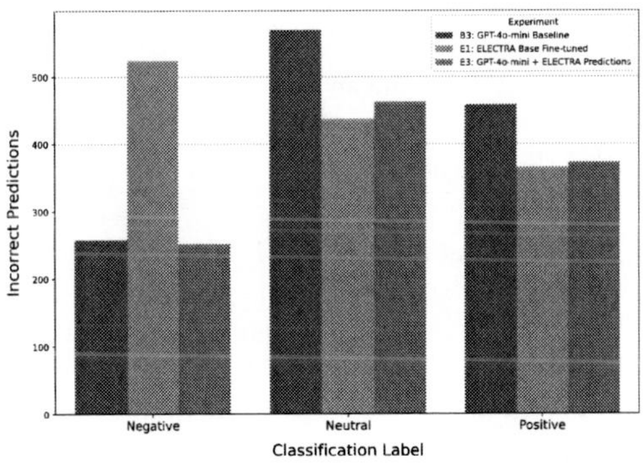

Figure 4: Incorrect Predictions by Label (Round 1)

It may also be that it takes more time to learn the nuances of when ELECTRA is right vs. wrong. When we extended fine-tuning from 1 to 5 epochs, GPT was better able to discriminate ELECTRA's predictions. The follow rate decreased from 96.34% to 89.66%, and the discrimination gap—the difference between following correct and incorrect predictions—went from 16.89% to 35.95%. Although additional epochs improved performance, it comes with a significant increase to the cost: \$207.64 to \$251.17 vs. only \$33.15 to just fine-tune GPT-4o-mini—with better performance.

H3. Format of prediction would impact performance. Although using the predicted label alone was best, GPT-4o-mini saw more variability in performance between the different contexts, as shown in Figure 3. However, for GPT-4o, there was not much of a difference when looking at the mean change in F1 score.

H4. Including examples would improve performance. Contrary to this hypothesis, including examples did not improve performance for either GPT-4o-mini or GPT-4o when looking at the mean change in F1 score. It either had no effect (GPT-4o) or actually decreased performance (GPT-4o-mini).

8 Conclusion

This research investigated collaborative approaches to sentiment classification between bidirectional transformers and LLMs. Our results show that augmenting prompts with predictions from a fine-tuned ELECTRA can significantly improve performance when the GPT model is not fine-tuned—up to +4.39 points of gain in the mean macro F1 score. Including probabilities or similar examples improved performance slightly on the more challenging datasets. However, this collaborative benefit disappeared when the GPT models were fine-tuned.

It is possible that the fine-tuning process hinders the critical thinking that's present in the default GPT models. Fine-tuning over more epochs improves the situation—GPT gets smarter about when to follow ELECTRA vs. when to ignore it. However, this comes at a significant cost increase—six to seven times the cost of fine-tuning GPT-4o-mini alone, and the performance is still not comparable.

Our findings offer several cost-effective paths for sentiment analysis projects. For organizations that can fine-tune via API, GPT-4o-mini FT offers nearly equivalent performance to GPT-4o FT-M (86.70 vs 86.99 mean macro F1) at 76% lower cost ($0.38 vs $1.59/F1 point). For those with data privacy concerns or resource constraints, GPT-4o-mini with ELECTRA Base FT had the best cost/performance ratio ($0.12/F1 point). Projects that need to stay completely local can fine-tune ELECTRA Large, which outperformed both base GPT models.

Future work could explore optimization of inference-time prompts through DSPy, and alternate System role instructions during fine-tuning. In addition, this collaborative approach could be extended to different datasets/domains, classification tasks, and model pairings. There may also be potential for including multiple predictions from an ensemble of models. A new collaborative scenario would be fine-tuning GPTs on the ELECTRA output representations.

9 Limitations

The cost/performance evaluation only considered the fine-tuning costs to achieve the reported macro F1 on the test set. In practice, there may be ongoing costs for inference time API calls for hosted GPT models. The time and cost required to fine-tune different datasets will vary, and this will affect the relative cost/performance differences.

Our research was limited to GPT-4o and GPT-4o-mini from OpenAI, but there are many GPT-style models available. Some of these are open source and can be fine-tuned locally or on hosted compute resources, such as Llama 2 or 3 from Meta (Touvron et al., 2023; Dubey et al., 2024). The cost of fine-tuning an open source GPT model without API fees was not evaluated.

Resource and time constraints prevented us from exploring every possible collaborative scenario. Once we saw ELECTRA Large FT performed better than ELECTRA Base FT, we only evaluated the output from Large in the different prompt contexts for both GPT-4o and GPT-4o-mini.

Many experimental runs involved prompting the GPT models, and these prompts could be further optimized with frameworks like DSPy. Some of the prompts are verbose, and these additional tokens could dilute the signal of the ELECTRA context.

Although we quantified changes in GPT classification decisions before and after ELECTRA predictions were included, we did not have time to thoroughly explore *why* the ELECTRA prediction was ignored in some cases, but followed in others. Future research could prompt the model to explain their decision, and the responses could be analyzed. This additional instruction would likely affect the classification decision—similar to Chain of Thought (Wei et al., 2022)—and would be a new experimental scenario.

We tried to give the GPT models a chance to learn when ELECTRA was right or wrong during fine-tuning (GPT-4o FT-L, GPT-4o-mini FT-L). There may be a more direct way of fine-tuning GPT so that it learns when to trust ELECTRA's prediction, and when to decide for itself.

The data used for this research was a merge of movie and business reviews from SST-3 and DynaSent R1/R2. The majority of the reviews were written in English and relatively short in length. Assessing generalization to other domains, languages and longer lengths would require future research.

10 Acknowledgments

Thank you to the Stanford Engineering Center for Global and Online Education (CGOE) for the opportunity to conduct this research as part of the Natural Language Understanding class (XCS224U), and to Professor Christopher Potts, Insop Song, and Petra Parikova for your support and guidance.

References

Claudio M. V. de Andrade, Washington Cunha, Davi Reis, et al. 2024. A strategy to combine 1st gen transformers and open LLMs for automatic text classification. *arXiv preprint arXiv:2408.09629*.

Mala J B, Anisha Angel S J, Alex Raj S M, and Rajeev Rajan. 2023. Efficacy of ELECTRA-based language model in sentiment analysis. In *2023 International Conference on Intelligent Systems for Communication, IoT and Security (ICISCoIS)*, pages 682–687.

Lucas Georges Gabriel Charpentier and David Samuel. 2024. GPT or BERT: why not both? *arXiv preprint arXiv:2410.24159*.

Kevin Clark, Minh-Thang Luong, Quoc V Le, and Christopher D Manning. 2020. ELECTRA: Pre-training text encoders as discriminators rather than generators. *arXiv preprint arXiv:2003.10555*.

Jacob Devlin, Ming-Wei Chang, Kenton Lee, and Kristina Toutanova. 2019. BERT: Pre-training of deep bidirectional transformers for language understanding. In *Proceedings of the 2019 Conference of the North American Chapter of the Association for Computational Linguistics: Human Language Technologies, Volume 1 (Long and Short Papers)*, pages 4171–4186, Minneapolis, Minnesota. Association for Computational Linguistics.

Abhimanyu Dubey, Abhinav Jauhri, Abhinav Pandey, Abhishek Kadian, Ahmad Al-Dahle, Aiesha Letman, Akhil Mathur, Alan Schelten, Amy Yang, Angela Fan, et al. 2024. The Llama 3 herd of models. *arXiv preprint arXiv:2407.21783*.

Omar Khattab, Arnav Singhvi, Paridhi Maheshwari, Zhiyuan Zhang, Keshav Santhanam, Sri Vardhamanan A, Saiful Haq, Ashutosh Sharma, Thomas T. Joshi, Hanna Moazam, Heather Miller, Matei Zaharia, and Christopher Potts. 2024. DSPy: Compiling declarative language model calls into state-of-the-art pipelines. In *The Twelfth International Conference on Learning Representations*.

Kiana Kheiri and Hamid Karimi. 2023. SentimentGPT: Exploiting GPT for advanced sentiment analysis and its departure from current machine learning. *arXiv preprint arXiv:2307.10234*.

Jan Kocoń, Ireneusz Cichecki, Oliwier Kaszyca, et al. 2023. ChatGPT: Jack of all trades, master of none. *Information Fusion*, 99:101861.

Brice Valentin Kok-Shun, Johnny Chan, Gabrielle Peko, and David Sundaram. 2023. Intertwining two artificial minds: Chaining GPT and RoBERTa for emotion detection. In *2023 IEEE Asia-Pacific Conference on Computer Science and Data Engineering (CSDE)*, pages 1–6.

Pengfei Liu, Weizhe Yuan, Jinlan Fu, et al. 2023. Pre-train, prompt, and predict: A systematic survey of prompting methods in natural language processing. *ACM Computing Surveys*, 55(9):1–35.

Yinhan Liu, Myle Ott, Naman Goyal, Jingfei Du, Mandar Joshi, Danqi Chen, Omer Levy, Mike Lewis, Luke Zettlemoyer, and Veselin Stoyanov. 2019. RoBERTa: A robustly optimized BERT pretraining approach. *arXiv preprint arXiv:1907.11692*.

Walaa Medhat, Ahmed Hassan, and Hoda Korashy. 2014. Sentiment analysis algorithms and applications: A survey. *Ain Shams Engineering Journal*, 5(4):1093–1113.

OpenAI. 2024a. GPT-4 technical report. *OpenAI Web Site*.

OpenAI. 2024b. Hello GPT-4o. *OpenAI Web Site*.

OpenAI. 2024c. GPT-4o mini: advancing cost-efficient intelligence. *OpenAI Web Site*.

Christopher Potts, Zhengxuan Wu, Atticus Geiger, and Douwe Kiela. 2021. DynaSent: A dynamic benchmark for sentiment analysis. In *Proceedings of the 59th Annual Meeting of the Association for Computational Linguistics and the 11th International Joint Conference on Natural Language Processing (Volume 1: Long Papers)*, pages 2388–2404, Online. Association for Computational Linguistics.

Tyreal Yizhou Qian, Weizhe Li, Hua Gong, Chad Seifried, and Chenglong Xu. 2024. Experience is all you need: a large language model application of fine-tuned GPT-3.5 and RoBERTa for aspect-based sentiment analysis of college football stadium reviews. *Sport Management Review*, 0(0):1–25.

Alec Radford, Karthik Narasimhan, Tim Salimans, and Ilya Sutskever. 2018. Improving language understanding by generative pre-training. *OpenAI Blog*.

Alec Radford, Jeff Wu, Rewon Child, David Luan, Dario Amodei, and Ilya Sutskever. 2019. Language models are unsupervised multitask learners. *OpenAI Blog*.

Noam Shazeer. 2020. GLU variants improve transformer. *arXiv preprint arXiv:2002.05202*.

Richard Socher, Alex Perelygin, Jean Wu, Jason Chuang, Christopher D. Manning, Andrew Ng, and Christopher Potts. 2013. Recursive deep models for semantic compositionality over a sentiment treebank. In *Proceedings of the 2013 Conference on Empirical Methods in Natural Language Processing*, pages 1631–1642, Seattle, Washington, USA. Association for Computational Linguistics.

Hugo Touvron, Louis Martin, Kevin Stone, Peter Albert, Amjad Almahairi, Yasmine Babaei, Nikolay Bashlykov, Soumya Batra, Prajjwal Bhargava, Shruti Bhosale, Dan Bikel, Lukas Blecher, Cristian Canton Ferrer, Moya Chen, Guillem Cucurull, David Esiobu, Jude Fernandes, Jeremy Fu, Wenyin Fu, Brian Fuller, Cynthia Gao, Vedanuj Goswami, Naman Goyal, Anthony Hartshorn, Saghar Hosseini, Rui Hou, Hakan Inan, Marcin Kardas, Viktor Kerkez, Madian Khabsa, Isabel Kloumann, Artem Korenev, Punit Singh Koura,

Marie-Anne Lachaux, Thibaut Lavril, Jenya Lee, Diana Liskovich, Yinghai Lu, Yuning Mao, Xavier Martinet, Todor Mihaylov, Pushkar Mishra, Igor Molybog, Yixin Nie, Andrew Poulton, Jeremy Reizenstein, Rashi Rungta, Kalyan Saladi, Alan Schelten, Ruan Silva, Eric Michael Smith, Ranjan Subramanian, Xiaoqing Ellen Tan, Binh Tang, Ross Taylor, Adina Williams, Jian Xiang Kuan, Puxin Xu, Zheng Yan, Iliyan Zarov, Yuchen Zhang, Angela Fan, Melanie Kambadur, Sharan Narang, Aurelien Rodriguez, Robert Stojnic, Sergey Edunov, and Thomas Scialom. 2023. Llama 2: Open foundation and fine-tuned chat models. *arXiv preprint arXiv:2307.09288*.

Ashish Vaswani, Noam Shazeer, Niki Parmar, Jakob Uszkoreit, Llion Jones, Aidan N Gomez, Ł ukasz Kaiser, and Illia Polosukhin. 2017. Attention is all you need. In *Advances in Neural Information Processing Systems*, volume 30. Curran Associates, Inc.

Jason Wei, Xuezhi Wang, Dale Schuurmans, Maarten Bosma, Fei Xia, Ed Chi, Quoc V Le, Denny Zhou, et al. 2022. Chain-of-thought prompting elicits reasoning in large language models. *Advances in neural information processing systems*, 35:24824–24837.

Mengzhou Xia, Mikel Artetxe, Jingfei Du, Danqi Chen, and Veselin Stoyanov. 2022. Prompting ELECTRA: Few-shot learning with discriminative pre-trained models. In *Proceedings of the 2022 Conference on Empirical Methods in Natural Language Processing*, pages 11351–11361. Association for Computational Linguistics.

Boyu Zhang, Hongyang Yang, Tianyu Zhou, Muhammad Ali Babar, and Xiao-Yang Liu. 2023. Enhancing financial sentiment analysis via retrieval augmented large language models. In *Proceedings of the Fourth ACM International Conference on AI in Finance*, ICAIF '23, page 349–356, New York, NY, USA. Association for Computing Machinery.

A Results of Individual Runs

Table 7: Round 1 Results

				Merged		DynaSent R1		DynaSent R2		SST-3		Cost ($)	
ID	GPT[1]	ELECTRA	Description	F1	Acc	F1	Acc	F1	Acc	F1	Acc	FT	/F1
B1	—	Base	Baseline, Classifier head	69.65	69.83	70.96	71.28	61.59	61.67	60.85	70.14	0.65	0.01
B2	—	Large	Baseline, Classifier head	67.88	68.06	69.72	70.06	59.78	59.72	57.68	67.51	2.51	0.04
B3	4o-mini	—	Baseline (Zero shot)	79.52	80.34	81.12	81.00	77.35	77.92	70.67	80.05	—	—
B4	4o	—	Baseline (Zero shot)	80.14	80.74	81.12	80.94	80.22	80.56	72.20	80.45	—	—
E1	—	Base FT	Fine-tune all layers	79.29	79.69	82.10	82.14	71.83	71.94	69.95	78.24	9.73	0.12
E2	—	Large FT	Fine-tune all layers	82.36	82.96	85.91	85.83	76.29	76.53	70.90	80.36	53.26	0.65
E3	4o-mini	Base FT	Prompt, Label	82.74	83.35	86.50	86.44	76.19	76.53	71.72	80.54	**9.73**	**0.12**
E4	4o-mini	Large FT	Prompt, Label	83.49	84.21	87.52	87.47	77.94	78.47	70.99	80.77	53.26	0.64
E5	4o-mini	Large FT	Prompt, Label, Examples (Few shot)	83.20	83.80	86.74	86.64	78.71	79.03	71.98	80.72	53.26	0.64
E6	4o-mini	Large FT	Prompt, Label, Balanced Ex. (Few shot)	82.68	83.28	85.84	85.69	79.61	80.00	71.45	80.41	53.26	0.64
E7	4o-mini	Large FT	Prompt, Probs	83.01	83.60	86.44	86.36	78.92	79.17	71.53	80.54	53.26	0.64
E8	4o-mini	Large FT	Prompt, Label, Probs	83.43	84.12	87.02	86.94	79.72	80.14	71.03	80.81	53.26	0.64
E9	4o-mini	Large FT	Prompt, Label, Probs, Examples	82.91	83.54	86.15	86.06	78.69	79.03	71.49	80.90	53.26	0.64
E10	4o-mini FT	—	Fine-tune w/prompt	86.77	87.26	89.86	89.75	86.90	87.08	**75.68**	**83.26**	33.15	0.38
E11	4o-mini FT 5	—	Fine-tune w/prompt (5 epochs)	84.95	85.27	87.83	87.67	85.93	85.97	75.60	81.13	165.75	1.95
E12	4o-mini FT-M	—	Minimal fine-tune	86.55	87.00	89.70	89.58	86.97	87.08	75.62	82.76	16.60	0.19
E13	4o-mini FT	Base FT	Prompt, Label, FT w/prompt	81.42	81.90	84.77	84.78	74.49	74.72	70.95	79.55	42.88	0.53
E14	4o-mini FT-L	Base FT	Prompt, Label, FT w/prompt, label	82.02	82.53	85.24	85.11	78.15	78.47	71.68	79.64	49.31	0.60
E15	4o-mini FT-L 5	Base FT	Prompt, Label, FT w/prompt, label (5 epochs)	83.88	84.27	86.74	86.61	81.62	81.81	75.00	81.27	207.64	2.48
E16	4o-mini FT	Large FT	Fine-tune w/prompt	84.00	84.58	87.65	87.58	80.37	80.69	72.46	80.95	86.41	1.03
E17	4o-mini FT-L	Large FT	Fine-tune w/prompt, label	84.16	84.70	87.65	87.56	80.89	81.11	73.29	81.22	92.84	1.10
E18	4o-mini FT-L 5	Large FT	Fine-tune w/prompt, label (5 epochs)	84.87	85.25	87.87	87.75	83.80	83.89	75.58	81.63	251.17	2.96
E19	4o	Large FT	Prompt, Label	83.18	83.68	85.71	85.56	81.98	82.22	73.44	81.09	**53.26**	**0.64**
E20	4o	Large FT	Prompt, Label, Examples (Few shot)	83.09	83.66	86.01	85.86	81.53	81.81	72.06	80.68	53.26	0.64
E21	4o	Large FT	Prompt, Label, Balanced Ex. (Few shot)	82.99	83.55	85.87	85.69	80.89	81.11	72.15	80.86	53.26	0.64
E22	4o	Large FT	Prompt, Probs	82.65	83.25	86.05	85.97	77.67	77.92	71.16	80.54	53.26	0.64
E23	4o	Large FT	Prompt, Label, Probs	83.08	83.71	86.44	86.33	79.23	79.58	71.48	80.77	53.26	0.64
E24	4o	Large FT	Prompt, Label, Probs, Examples	82.74	83.35	86.32	86.22	77.76	78.06	70.98	80.41	53.26	0.64
E25	4o FT	—	Fine-tune w/prompt	86.83	87.43	90.44	90.36	88.34	88.47	73.08	82.31	276.24	3.18
E26	4o FT-M	—	Minimal fine-tune	**86.99**	**87.57**	**90.57**	**90.50**	**89.00**	**89.17**	73.99	82.26	138.37	1.59
E27	4o FT	Large FT	Fine-tune w/prompt	83.82	84.47	87.80	87.72	79.49	79.86	71.18	80.68	329.50	3.93
E28	4o FT-L	Large FT	Fine-tune w/prompt, label	84.23	84.82	87.74	87.64	80.55	80.83	72.63	81.54	383.10	4.55

Table 8: Round 2 Results

				Merged		DynaSent R1		DynaSent R2		SST-3		Cost ($)	
ID	GPT[1]	ELECTRA	Description	F1	Acc	F1	Acc	F1	Acc	F1	Acc	FT	/F1
B1	—	Base	Baseline, Classifier head	69.37	69.57	70.75	71.11	61.19	61.25	60.34	69.77	0.65	0.01
B2	—	Large	Baseline, Classifier head	67.99	68.15	69.67	70.03	59.78	59.72	58.21	67.83	2.51	0.04
B3	4o-mini	—	Baseline (Zero shot)	79.29	80.15	81.19	81.08	76.69	77.36	69.30	79.55	—	—
B4	4o	—	Baseline (Zero shot)	79.80	80.47	80.77	80.61	80.05	80.42	71.96	80.27	—	—
E1	—	Base FT	Fine-tune all layers	78.98	79.46	82.13	82.19	69.51	69.72	68.13	78.19	9.73	0.12
E2	—	Large FT	Fine-tune all layers	83.16	83.71	86.53	86.44	78.36	78.61	72.63	80.91	53.26	0.64
E3	4o-mini	Base FT	Prompt, Label	82.26	82.92	86.29	86.25	74.47	74.86	70.03	80.14	9.73	0.12
E4	4o-mini	Large FT	Prompt, Label	84.10	84.73	87.90	87.83	79.52	79.86	72.54	81.27	53.26	0.63
E5	4o-mini	Large FT	Prompt, Label, Examples (Few shot)	83.63	84.18	87.13	87.03	80.29	80.56	72.68	80.72	53.26	0.64
E6	4o-mini	Large FT	Prompt, Label, Balanced Ex. (Few shot)	83.28	83.81	86.71	86.58	80.12	80.42	72.51	80.41	53.26	0.64
E7	4o-mini	Large FT	Prompt, Probs	83.53	84.07	86.76	86.67	79.89	80.14	72.98	81.13	53.26	0.64
E8	4o-mini	Large FT	Prompt, Label, Probs	83.88	84.47	87.41	87.33	80.23	80.56	72.53	81.09	53.26	0.64
E9	4o-mini	Large FT	Prompt, Label, Probs, Examples	83.46	84.03	87.00	86.89	79.28	79.58	72.39	80.81	53.26	0.64
E10	4o-mini FT	—	Fine-tune w/prompt	86.62	87.09	89.44	89.33	87.08	87.22	**75.98**	**83.39**	33.15	0.38
E11	4o-mini FT 5	—	Fine-tune w/prompt (5 epochs)	84.76	85.07	87.64	87.47	86.50	86.53	75.15	80.68	165.75	1.96
E12	4o-mini FT-M	—	Minimal fine-tune	86.47	86.89	89.44	89.31	87.28	87.36	75.86	82.81	16.60	0.19
E13	4o-mini FT	Base FT	Prompt, Label, FT w/prompt	80.69	81.24	84.57	84.58	71.62	71.94	68.45	78.82	42.88	0.53
E14	4o-mini FT-L	Base FT	Prompt, Label, FT w/prompt, label	81.65	82.25	85.15	85.03	76.43	76.81	69.71	79.50	49.31	0.60
E15	4o-mini FT-L 5	Base FT	Prompt, Label, FT w/prompt, label (5 epochs)	83.46	83.89	86.02	85.89	80.75	80.97	75.04	81.58	207.64	2.49
E16	4o-mini FT	Large FT	Fine-tune w/prompt	83.87	84.44	87.49	87.42	79.97	80.28	72.46	80.95	86.41	1.03
E17	4o-mini FT-L	Large FT	Fine-tune w/prompt, label	84.07	84.59	87.51	87.42	80.61	80.83	73.38	81.22	92.84	1.10
E18	4o-mini FT-L 5	Large FT	Fine-tune w/prompt, label (5 epochs)	84.79	85.15	87.63	87.50	84.94	85.00	75.59	81.36	251.17	2.96
E19	4o	Large FT	Prompt, Label	83.20	83.69	85.71	85.56	82.13	82.36	73.52	81.09	53.26	0.64
E20	4o	Large FT	Prompt, Label, Examples (Few shot)	83.48	84.00	86.21	86.06	81.43	81.67	73.85	81.40	53.26	0.64
E21	4o	Large FT	Prompt, Label, Balanced Ex. (Few shot)	83.38	83.89	86.14	85.97	81.18	81.39	73.61	81.31	53.26	0.64
E22	4o	Large FT	Prompt, Probs	83.32	83.87	86.68	86.58	79.16	79.44	72.63	80.90	53.26	0.64
E23	4o	Large FT	Prompt, Label, Probs	83.54	84.10	86.93	86.81	79.69	80.00	72.85	81.04	53.26	0.64
E24	4o	Large FT	Prompt, Label, Probs, Examples	83.34	83.89	86.73	86.61	79.18	79.44	72.68	80.90	53.26	0.64
E25	4o FT	—	Fine-tune w/prompt	86.74	87.32	90.48	90.42	87.94	88.06	73.09	82.04	276.24	3.18
E26	4o FT-M	—	Minimal fine-tune	**86.99**	**87.57**	**90.57**	**90.50**	**89.00**	**89.17**	73.99	82.26	138.37	1.59
E27	4o FT	Large FT	Fine-tune w/prompt	84.24	84.84	87.99	87.89	80.52	80.83	72.81	81.18	329.50	3.91
E28	4o FT-L	Large FT	Fine-tune w/prompt, label	84.50	85.04	87.87	87.75	82.01	82.22	73.56	81.54	383.10	4.53

Bold = best overall, highlighted = best in section

[1] GPT fine-tuning types: FT = fine-tune all layers with prompt, FT-M = minimal fine-tune format without prompt, FT-L = fine-tune with prompt including ELECTRA label, FT 5 = fine-tune for 5 epochs

B ELECTRA Fine-tuning Details

Table 9: ELECTRA Fine-Tune Configuration

Setting	ELECTRA Base FT	ELECTRA Large FT
Source	Hugging Face	Hugging Face
Source Model ID	google/electra-base-discriminator	google/electra-large-discriminator
Encoder Blocks	12	24
Embedding Dimension	768	1024
Attention Heads	12	16
Feedforward Size	3072	4096
Parameters	110 Million	335 Million
Custom Pooling Layer Method	Mean	Mean
Classifier Head Hidden Layers	2	2
Classifier Head Hidden Dimension	1024	1024
Classifier Head Hidden Activation	SwishGLU	SwishGLU
Finetuned Encoder Blocks	12	24
Total Layers	104	200
Total Parameters	112,830,979	338,293,763
Trainable Parameters	100%	100%
Learning Rate	$1e^{-5}$	$1e^{-5}$
Learning Rate Decay	0.95	0.95
Batch Size	16	16
Accumulation Steps	2	2
Target Epochs	50	50
Actual Epochs	20	23
Selected Best Epoch	14	13
Dropout Rate	0.30	0.30
L2 Strength	0.01	0.01
Optimizer	AdamW	AdamW
Zero Redundancy	Yes	Yes
Scheduler	CosineAnnealingWarmRestarts	CosineAnnealingWarmRestarts
Scheduler: T_0	5	5
Scheduler: T_mult	1	1
Scheduler: eta_min	$1e^{-7}$	$1e^{-7}$
Early Stop	Validation F1 Score	Validation F1 Score
N Iterations No Change	10	10
Dataset	Merged (Dyn R1, Dyn R2, SST-3)	Merged (Dyn R1, Dyn R2, SST-3)
Train Size	102,097	102,097
Train Label Distribution	Neu: 49,148, Pos: 31,039, Neg: 21,910	Neu: 49,148, Pos: 31,039, Neg: 21,910
Validation Size	5,421	5,421
Validation Label Distribution	Neu: 1,669, Pos: 1,884, Neg: 1,868	Neu: 1,669, Pos: 1,884, Neg: 1,868
Hosting Provider	Lambda Labs	Lambda Labs
GPU Type	Tesla V100	A100
GPU Memory	16 GB	40 GB
GPU Quantity	8	8
Rate	$4.40/hour	$10.32/hour
Training Time (Up to Selected Epoch)	02:12:44	05:09:23
Training Time (Total)	03:09:40	09:23:29
Cost (Up to Selected Epoch)	$9.73	$53.26
Cost (Total)	$13.91	$96.92

C GPT Fine-tuning Details

Table 10: GPT Fine-Tune Configuration

Setting	4o-mini FT-M	4o-mini FT	4o-mini FT-L Base 1	4o-mini FT-L Base 5	4o-mini FT-L Large 1	4o-mini FT-L Large 5	4o FT-M	4o FT	4o FT-L Large 1
GPT Model	4o-mini	4o-mini	4o-mini	4o-mini	4o-mini	4o-mini	4o	4o	4o
ELECTRA Model	None	None	Base FT	Base FT	Base FT	Base FT	None	None	Large FT
Code	FT-M	FT	FT-L	FT-L	FT-L	FT-L	FT-M	FT	FT-L
Code Meaning	Minimal Format	Fine-Tune	Fine-Tune w/Label	Fine-Tune w/Label	Fine-Tune w/Label	Fine-Tune w/Label	Minimal Format	Fine-Tune	Fine-Tune w/Label
Format	JSON (No Prompt)	DSPy Prompt	DSPy Prompt + Label	DSPy Prompt + Label	DSPy Prompt + Label	DSPy Prompt + Label	JSON (No Prompt)	DSPy Prompt	DSPy Prompt + Label
Source	OpenAI	OpenAI	OpenAI	OpenAI	OpenAI	OpenAI	OpenAI	OpenAI	OpenAI
Source Model ID	gpt-4o-mini-2024-07-18	gpt-4o-mini-2024-07-18	gpt-4o-mini-2024-07-18	gpt-4o-mini-2024-07-18	gpt-4o-mini-2024-07-18	gpt-4o-mini-2024-07-18	gpt-4o-2024-08-06	gpt-4o-2024-08-06	gpt-4o-2024-08-06
Dataset	Merged	Merged	Merged	Merged	Merged	Merged	Merged	Merged	Merged
Train Size	102,097	102,097	102,097	102,097	102,097	102,097	102,097	102,097	102,097
Validation Size	5,421	5,421	5,421	5,421	5,421	5,421	5,421	5,421	5,421
Fine-Tuning Date	2024-10-23								
Total Job Time	01:17:07	01:07:05	01:09:00	01:09:00	01:09:00	01:09:00	01:31:06	01:43:43	01:47:49
LR Multiplier	1.8	1.8	1.8	1.8	1.8	1.8	2.0	2.0	2.0
Seed	42	42	42	42	42	42	42	42	42
Batch Size	68	68	68	68	68	68	68	68	68
Epochs	1	1	1	1	1	1	1	1	1
Train Loss	0.1250	0.1383	0.1286	0.1286	0.1286	0.1286	0.1185	0.1150	0.1075
Validation Loss	0.1112	0.1114	0.1429	0.1429	0.1429	0.1429	0.1054	0.1056	0.1242
Trained Tokens	5,534,849	11,049,720	13,193,757	13,193,757	13,193,757	13,193,757	5,534,849	11,049,720	13,193,757
Rate	$3/1M tokens	$3/1M tokens	$3/1M tokens	$3/1M tokens	$3/1M tokens	$3/1M tokens	$25/1M tokens	$25/1M tokens	$25/1M tokens
Cost	$16.60	$33.15	$39.58	$39.58	$39.58	$39.58	$138.37	$276.24	$329.84

D OpenAI Fine-tuning Templates

Table 11: FT-M: Minimal Template for Fine-tuning

Role	Content
System	"You are a model that classifies the sentiment of a review as either 'positive', 'neutral', or 'negative'."
User	"Those 2 drinks are part of the HK culture and has years of history. It is so bad."
Assistant	"negative"

Table 12: FT: Prompt Template for Fine-tuning

Role	Content
System	"You are a sentiment analysis assistant."
User	**"Classify the sentiment of a review as either 'negative', 'neutral', or 'positive'.\n—\n\nFollow the following format.\n\nReview: The review text to classify.\nClassification: One word representing the sentiment classification: 'negative', 'neutral', or 'positive' (do not repeat the field name, do not use 'mixed')\n\n—\n\nReview:** Those 2 drinks are part of the HK culture and has years of history. It is so bad.**\nClassification:**"
Assistant	"negative"

Table 13: FT-L: Prompt with Predicted Label Template for Fine-tuning

Role	Content
System	"You are a sentiment analysis assistant."
User	"Classify the sentiment of a review as either 'negative', 'neutral', or 'positive'.\n—\n\nFollow the following format.\n\nReview: The review text to classify.**\nClassifier Decision: The sentiment classification proposed by a model fine-tuned on sentiment.**\nClassification: One word representing the sentiment classification: 'negative', 'neutral', or 'positive' (do not repeat the field name, do not use 'mixed')\n\n—\n\nReview: Those 2 drinks are part of the HK culture and has years of history. It is so bad.**\nClassifier Decision: negative**\nClassification:"
Assistant	"negative"

E DSPy Prompt Signature Examples

Figure 5: Basic Prompt DSPy Signature

```
Classify the sentiment of a review as either 'negative', 'neutral', or 'positive'.

---

Follow the following format.

Review: The review text to classify.
Classification: One word representing the sentiment classification: 'negative', 'neutral', or 'positive'
(do not repeat the field name, do not use 'mixed').

---

Review: Those 2 drinks are part of the HK culture and has years of history. It is so bad.
Classification:
```

Figure 6: Prompt with Predicted Label DSPy Signature

```
Classify the sentiment of a review as either 'negative', 'neutral', or 'positive'.

---

Follow the following format.

Review: The review text to classify.
Classifier Decision: The sentiment classification proposed by a model fine-tuned on sentiment.
Classification: One word representing the sentiment classification: 'negative', 'neutral', or 'positive'
(do not repeat the field name, do not use 'mixed')

---

Review: I was told by the repair company that was doing the car repair that fixing the rim was
"impossible" and to replace it.
Classifier Decision: negative
Classification:
```

Figure 7: Prompt with Probabilities DSPy Signature

```
Classify the sentiment of a review as either 'negative', 'neutral', or 'positive'.

---

Follow the following format.

Review: The review text to classify.

Negative Probability: Probability the review is negative from a model fine-tuned on sentiment

Neutral Probability: Probability the review is neutral from a model fine-tuned on sentiment

Positive Probability: Probability the review is positive from a model fine-tuned on sentiment

Classification: One word representing the sentiment classification: 'negative', 'neutral', or 'positive'
(do not repeat the field name, do not use 'mixed')

---

Review: Those 2 drinks are part of the HK culture and has years of history. It is so bad.

Negative Probability: 99.85%

Neutral Probability: 0.04%

Positive Probability: 0.12%

Classification:
```

Figure 8: Prompt with Predicted Label and Probabilities DSPy Signature

```
Classify the sentiment of a review as either 'negative', 'neutral', or 'positive'.

---

Follow the following format.

Review: The review text to classify.

Classifier Decision: The sentiment classification proposed by a model fine-tuned on sentiment.

Negative Probability: Probability the review is negative

Neutral Probability: Probability the review is neutral

Positive Probability: Probability the review is positive

Classification: One word representing the sentiment classification: 'negative', 'neutral', or 'positive'
(do not repeat the field name, do not use 'mixed')

---

Review: Those 2 drinks are part of the HK culture and has years of history. It is so bad.

Classifier Decision: negative

Negative Probability: 99.85%

Neutral Probability: 0.04%

Positive Probability: 0.12%

Classification:
```

Figure 9: Top Examples DSPy Signature

```
Classify the sentiment of a review as either 'negative', 'neutral', or 'positive'.

---

Follow the following format.

Examples: A list of examples that demonstrate different sentiment classes.

Review: The review text to classify.

Classifier Decision: The sentiment classification proposed by a model fine-tuned on sentiment.

Classification: One word representing the sentiment classification: 'negative', 'neutral', or 'positive'
(do not repeat the field name, do not use 'mixed')

---

Examples:
- negative: We've been to about 5 or 6 other Verizon stores in Vegas, and they all give us a hard time
about everything and never solve any issue.
- negative: Then Raj then had the balls to send me an email after my box was closed to tell me they were
ready to receive the key for my mailbox after closing it.!
- negative: Always and issue here even with take out orders.
- negative: SHOULD YOU HAVE ANY DISPUTE, THEY IMMEDIATELY WILL THREATEN YOU WITH MECHANICS LIENS.
- negative: We were waiting for them to get our order out, but the lady came out and gave the car behind
us their order first!

Review: I went back in to ask for cilantro dressing the shift leader even smile or greet me.

Classifier Decision: negative

Classification:
```

Figure 10: Balanced Examples DSPy Signature

```
Classify the sentiment of a review as either 'negative', 'neutral', or 'positive'.

---

Follow the following format.

Examples: A list of examples that demonstrate different sentiment classes.

Review: The review text to classify.

Classifier Decision: The sentiment classification proposed by a model fine-tuned on sentiment.

Classification: One word representing the sentiment classification: 'negative', 'neutral', or 'positive'
(do not repeat the field name, do not use 'mixed')

---

Examples:
- negative: Beware of all the fake 5 star reviews of this place, just take a look at these people.
- negative: 3- girls look even cheaper than the club.
- neutral: Not to mention the esso across the street also has cheaper gas.
- neutral: I wish that they would open up by 6am so that I can pick up a coffee or tea before work, but
what boba place is opened that early?
- positive: The plumbers did not give up and continued to work on the drain for two days.
- positive: This is my 6th gun to add to my collection and if I had not wanted it so bad, I would have
walked out 2 minutes after walking in.

Review: She greeted customers by holding the scanner toward them without even looking.

Classifier Decision: negative

Classification:
```

Figure 11: All Context DSPy Signature

```
Classify the sentiment of a review as either 'negative', 'neutral', or 'positive'.

---

Follow the following format.

Examples: A list of examples that demonstrate different sentiment classes.

Review: The review text to classify.

Classifier Decision: The sentiment classification proposed by a model fine-tuned on sentiment.

Negative Probability: Probability the review is negative

Neutral Probability: Probability the review is neutral

Positive Probability: Probability the review is positive

Classification: One word representing the sentiment classification: 'negative', 'neutral', or 'positive'
(do not repeat the field name, do not use 'mixed')

---

Examples:
- negative: The only negative I can think for this place is it's price-point.
- positive: This place will be the death of my waist (but not my wallet).
- negative: Expensive, if you are looking for something more affordable, don't go here; you will miss
  the best dishes.
- positive: Thank you so much for dealing with my crabby ass
- positive: I think I scarfed it down so quickly because it was that good! It was bad.

Review: The gentleman staffing the bar seemed a bit gruff, but a good caffeine fix will help me forgive
even the orneriest grump.

Classifier Decision: negative

Negative Probability: 84.37%

Neutral Probability: 0.53%

Positive Probability: 15.10%

Classification:
```

Retrieval of Temporal Event Sequences from Textual Descriptions

Zefang Liu*
Georgia Institute of Technology
Atlanta, GA 30332, USA
liuzefang@gatech.edu

Yinzhu Quan*
Georgia Institute of Technology
Atlanta, GA 30332, USA
yquan9@gatech.edu

Abstract

Retrieving temporal event sequences from textual descriptions is crucial for applications such as analyzing e-commerce behavior, monitoring social media activities, and tracking criminal incidents. To advance this task, we introduce TESRBench, a comprehensive benchmark for temporal event sequence retrieval (TESR) from textual descriptions. TESRBench includes diverse real-world datasets with synthesized and reviewed textual descriptions, providing a strong foundation for evaluating retrieval performance and addressing challenges in this domain. Building on this benchmark, we propose TPP-Embedding, a novel model for embedding and retrieving event sequences. The model leverages the TPP-LLM framework, integrating large language models (LLMs) with temporal point processes (TPPs) to encode both event texts and times. By pooling representations and applying a contrastive loss, it unifies temporal dynamics and event semantics in a shared embedding space, aligning sequence-level embeddings of event sequences and their descriptions. TPP-Embedding demonstrates superior performance over baseline models across TESRBench datasets, establishing it as a powerful solution for the temporal event sequence retrieval task.

1 Introduction

Temporal event sequence retrieval (Gupta et al., 2022) plays a crucial role in various applications, such as e-commerce user activity analysis, social media monitoring, and crime tracking. These sequences combine temporal information with event types, making them more complex than traditional text data. Effective retrieval requires models capable of capturing both time-sensitive dynamics and structured relationships within the sequences. While traditional language models perform well for general text retrieval (Kashyap et al., 2024), they often struggle to handle the unique temporal and structural complexities of event sequences.

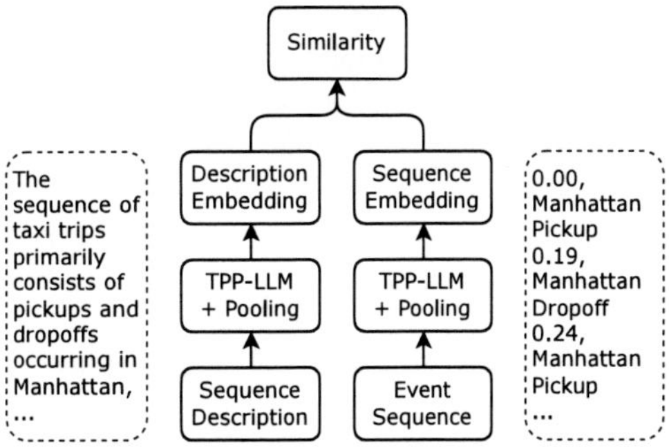

Figure 1: TPP-Embedding framework with one TESRBench example, where the model embeds both textual descriptions and temporal event sequences using a shared TPP-LLM framework, applies pooling to generate fixed-length representations, and uses contrastive learning with similarity scores to align matching pairs for effective event sequence retrieval.

To address these challenges, we introduce TESRBench[1], a comprehensive benchmark for evaluating temporal event sequence retrieval (TESR) from textual descriptions. TESRBench comprises diverse real-world event sequence datasets with synthesized and reviewed textual descriptions, offering a strong foundation for benchmarking retrieval models. It highlights the complexities of aligning event sequences with textual descriptions and provides a standardized platform for evaluating model performance, uncovering key challenges, and identifying opportunities for improvement in temporal and contextual modeling.

Building on this benchmark, we propose TPP-Embedding[2], a novel framework for temporal event sequence retrieval that extends the TPP-LLM

*These authors contributed equally to this work.

[1]Benchmark available on https://huggingface.co/tppllm.

[2]GitHub repository available on https://github.com/zefang-liu/TPP-Embedding.

Proceedings of the 4th International Workshop on Knowledge-Augmented Methods for Natural Language Processing (KnowledgeNLP'25), pages 37–49
May 3, 2025 ©2025 Association for Computational Linguistics

model (Liu and Quan, 2024). TPP-LLM integrates temporal encoding for event times and textual embeddings for event types within a large language model (LLM) backbone to model temporal point processes (TPPs). Extending this framework, TPP-Embedding aligns sequence-level representations of event sequences and their textual descriptions in a shared embedding space. By modeling the interdependencies between events and their temporal context, TPP-Embedding generates richer, contextually informed embeddings optimized for retrieval tasks. Evaluated across TESRBench datasets, TPP-Embedding demonstrates superior performance over text-based baselines and generalizes effectively across different event domains.

In this paper, our key contributions are: (1) Introducing TESRBench, a benchmark for evaluating TESR models with diverse datasets; (2) Proposing TPP-Embedding, which integrates temporal and event-type information for accurate event sequence retrieval from descriptions; and (3) Showcasing the scalability and flexibility of our approach through multi-domain experiments.

2 Related Work

Recent developments in sentence representation models, such as Sentence-BERT (Reimers and Gurevych, 2019), have significantly improved retrieval tasks by enabling efficient semantic similarity searches using transformer-based embeddings (Vaswani et al., 2017). While these models perform well in standard text retrieval tasks (Lin et al., 2022), they struggle with the temporal and event-specific complexities of event sequence data. To address these challenges, temporal point process (TPP) models (Mei and Eisner, 2017; Shchur et al., 2021; Xue et al., 2023) have been adapted for retrieval tasks. NeuroSeqRet (Gupta et al., 2022, 2023) introduces a neural framework for continuous-time event sequence retrieval by leveraging marked TPPs to model temporal dynamics and using a trainable unwarping function, neural relevance models, and hashing techniques to optimize retrieval efficiency. However, despite these advancements, existing models either treat event types as categorical inputs, limiting their ability to capture rich event semantics, or treat entire sequences as text, ignoring their temporal dependencies.

Recently, Liu and Quan (2024) proposed TPP-LLM, a framework that integrates large language models (LLMs) with TPPs to capture event semantics and temporal dynamics for event sequence modeling and prediction. While TPP-LLM focuses on predicting future event types and times using both textual and temporal information, our proposed TPP-Embedding extends this framework to the task of retrieving temporal event sequences from textual descriptions. By introducing a shared embedding space for sequences and descriptions and employing contrastive learning, our model effectively aligns sequence-level representations with natural language descriptions, enabling retrieval while maintaining temporal and semantic dependencies.

3 Benchmark

In this section, we present TESRBench, a comprehensive benchmark designed to evaluate temporal event sequence retrieval (TESR) from textual descriptions. We provide an overview of its key components, including detailed dataset summaries, the methodology for generating event sequence descriptions, and the evaluation process used to assess the quality of these descriptions.

3.1 Dataset Summaries

TESRBench is built on five real-world datasets from diverse domains: Stack Overflow, Chicago Crime, NYC Taxi Trip, U.S. Earthquake, and Amazon Review. Each dataset captures sequences of event-based information within specific time periods but lacks accompanying textual sequence descriptions. To address this, we generate textual descriptions for these event sequences using GPT-4o-mini (Achiam et al., 2023), creating objective summaries that emphasize the order and timing of events while preserving their essential structure. Details of the description generation and evaluation processes are provided in subsequent subsections. Examples of the data from TESRBench are included in Appendix A for further reference.

The datasets in TESRBench span various domains and offer rich opportunities for analysis. Table 1 presents an overview of their key statistics, using the same train/validation/test splits as Liu and Quan (2024), which are detailed in Table 2. The **Stack Overflow** (Stack Exchange, Inc., 2024) dataset tracks non-tag-related badges earned between January 2022 and December 2023, comprising 3,336 sequences across 25 event types. The **Chicago Crime** (Chicago Police Department,

Dataset	Domain	# of Types	# of Events	# of Seq.	Avg. Seq. Length	Time Unit
Stack Overflow	Social Networks	25	187,836	3,336	56.31	Month
Chicago Crime	Urban Dynamics	20	202,333	4,033	50.17	Month
NYC Taxi Trip	Transportation	8	362,374	2,957	122.55	Hour
U.S. Earthquake	Natural Disasters	3	29,521	3,009	9.81	Day
Amazon Review	E-Commerce	18	127,054	2,245	56.59	Week

Table 1: Dataset statistics overview of event sequences in TESRBench. (# = Number.)

Dataset	Seq.	Train	Val.	Test
Stack Overflow	3,336	2,668	334	334
Chicago Crime	4,033	3,226	403	404
NYC Taxi Trip	2,957	2,365	296	296
U.S. Earthquake	3,009	2,407	301	301
Amazon Review	2,245	1,796	224	225

Table 2: Numbers of sequences in train, validation, and test sets of TESRBench datasets.

2024) dataset focuses on the top 20 crime types and blocks with 30-120 incidents during the same time period, yielding 4,033 sequences across 20 crime categories. The **NYC Taxi Trip** (Monroy-Hernandez, 2014) dataset captures trips from May 1-7, 2013, excluding Staten Island, with 2,957 sequences across 8 location categories. The **U.S. Earthquake** (U.S. Geological Survey, 2024) dataset records 3,009 sequences of earthquake events from January 2020 to December 2023, categorized into 3 magnitude levels. Finally, the **Amazon Review** (Ni et al., 2019) dataset comprises 2,245 sequences of 40-200 reviews per user between January and June 2018, spanning 18 categories. Collectively, these datasets establish a robust foundation for evaluating models on diverse temporal event sequence retrieval tasks.

3.2 Description Generation

To create textual descriptions for the event sequences in TESRBench, we employ a structured process using GPT-4o-mini (Achiam et al., 2023). The process begins with crafting a system message, as illustrated in Figure 2, which guides GPT-4o-mini to produce objective summaries that focus on the order and timing of events. The instructions explicitly avoid interpreting behaviors or including specific numbers or timestamps, ensuring consistency and objectivity in the generated summaries. For each dataset, specific prompts are designed to reflect the context of the event sequences, as detailed in Table 3. These prompts present sequences of events with timestamps and event types, formatted to highlight the unique characteristics of each dataset. GPT-4o-mini processes these prompts and generates concise textual descriptions that capture key patterns and trends, providing an accurate summary of how events unfold over time. This approach ensures that the generated descriptions are well-aligned with the underlying temporal and contextual dynamics of the event sequences.

System Message:
You are an expert in summarizing event sequences. Your task is to provide a 2-5 sentence objective summary of the sequence's key patterns and trends without interpreting any behaviors or motivations. Focus on the sequence's order and timing, emphasizing how the events unfold over time. Describe general trends such as whether certain event types occur earlier or later, or if events cluster in certain periods. Avoid including exact numbers or timestamps.

Figure 2: Instructions for generating objective summaries of event sequences, focusing on the order, timing, and general trends without including specific numbers or timestamps.

3.3 Description Evaluation

To evaluate the quality of the generated descriptions for temporal event sequences, we establish a set of assessment criteria and scoring scales. Leveraging LLMs as evaluators (Zheng et al., 2023), we assess the descriptions across five key dimensions: accuracy, coverage, fidelity, clarity, and conciseness. The definitions of these criteria, along with their respective scoring scales, are outlined below:

- **Accuracy**: Does the description correctly represent the sequence of events, focusing on the event types, their order, and timing? (1 = Completely inaccurate, 5 = Completely accurate)
- **Coverage**: Does the description include all significant events and key details of the se-

Dataset	Description
Stack Overflow	Here is a sequence of badges earned by a user on Stack Overflow, with relative timestamps (in months) and badge names. Please provide a summary that describes the timing and order of events: {event_sequence}
Chicago Crime	Here is a sequence of crime incidents reported at a block in Chicago, with relative timestamps (in months) and crime types. Please provide a summary that describes the timing and order of events: {event_sequence}
NYC Taxi Trip	Here is a sequence of taxi trips taken by a driver in New York City, with relative timestamps (in hours) and trip locations. Please provide a summary that describes the timing and order of events: {event_sequence}
U.S. Earthquake	Here is a sequence of earthquake events in the U.S., with relative timestamps (in days) and magnitude categories. Please provide a summary that describes the timing and order of events: {event_sequence}
Amazon Review	Here is a sequence of product reviews submitted by a user on Amazon, with relative timestamps (in weeks) and review categories. Please provide a summary that describes the timing and order of events: {event_sequence}

Table 3: Overview of dataset-specific prompts, describing event sequences from various domains.

quence, without omitting critical information? (1 = Very incomplete, 5 = Fully comprehensive)

- **Fidelity**: To what extent does the description capture and reflect the temporal relationships and patterns (e.g., clustering, trends, or intervals) in the event sequence? (1 = No temporal fidelity, 5 = High temporal fidelity)
- **Clarity**: Is the description easy to understand, with clear language and a logical structure that aids comprehension? (1 = Very unclear, 5 = Very clear)
- **Conciseness**: Does the description provide the necessary information in a succinct manner, avoiding unnecessary verbosity or redundancy? (1 = Overly verbose or incomplete, 5 = Very concise and complete)

The averaged evaluation scores across datasets are presented in Tables 4, 5, and 6, which report the evaluation of event sequence descriptions using three evaluators: GPT-4o, GPT-4o-mini, and Claude 3.5 Haiku. GPT-4o's evaluation scores highlight strong performance, particularly in clarity and conciseness, while showing slightly lower scores in accuracy, coverage, and fidelity compared to GPT-4o-mini's evaluation. GPT-4o-mini assigns consistently high scores across all dimensions, indicating a strong alignment with the generated descriptions. Meanwhile, Claude 3.5 Haiku presents a different evaluation pattern, demonstrating relatively strong clarity and fidelity scores but notably lower coverage ratings. The varying assessments from these evaluators provide complementary perspectives on the quality of the descriptions, reinforcing their effectiveness in summarizing event sequences while preserving key temporal and contextual relationships. These results further emphasize the robustness of the generated descriptions when assessed across different evaluation frameworks.

Dataset	Acc.	Cov.	Fid.	Cla.	Con.
StackOverflow	4.10	4.05	4.25	4.94	4.56
Crime	4.01	4.00	4.18	4.98	4.67
Taxi	4.44	4.03	4.46	4.89	4.36
Earthquake	4.36	4.31	4.42	4.96	4.95
Amazon	4.66	4.33	4.74	4.99	4.82

Table 4: Evaluation scores from GPT-4o for event sequence descriptions in TESRBench. (Acc. = Accuracy, Cov. = Coverage, Fid. = Fidelity, Cla. = Clarity, Con. = Conciseness.)

4 Methodology

In this section, we introduce TPP-Embedding, an extension of TPP-LLM (Liu and Quan, 2024), de-

Dataset	Acc.	Cov.	Fid.	Cla.	Con.
StackOverflow	5.00	5.00	5.00	5.00	5.00
Crime	5.00	4.87	4.96	5.00	4.86
Taxi	5.00	4.99	4.99	5.00	4.99
Earthquake	4.99	4.99	4.85	5.00	4.93
Amazon	5.00	5.00	4.98	5.00	5.00

Table 5: Evaluation scores from GPT-4o-mini for event sequence descriptions in TESRBench. (Acc. = Accuracy, Cov. = Coverage, Fid. = Fidelity, Cla. = Clarity, Con. = Conciseness.)

Dataset	Acc.	Cov.	Fid.	Cla.	Con.
StackOverflow	4.00	3.27	4.11	4.93	4.00
Crime	4.00	3.05	3.96	4.93	4.00
Taxi	4.00	3.00	3.84	4.84	4.00
Earthquake	4.11	3.32	4.22	4.95	4.00
Amazon	4.18	3.70	4.48	4.80	3.98

Table 6: Evaluation scores from Claude 3.5 Haiku for event sequence descriptions in TESRBench. (Acc. = Accuracy, Cov. = Coverage, Fid. = Fidelity, Cla. = Clarity, Con. = Conciseness.)

signed to embed both event sequences and textual descriptions into a shared embedding space, enabling effective retrieval based on similarity.

4.1 Model Architecture

Given a set of textual descriptions $\mathcal{D} = \{d_1, d_2, \dots, d_m\}$ and a set of temporal event sequences $\mathcal{S} = \{s_1, s_2, \dots, s_n\}$, the task is to retrieve the most relevant sequence $s^* \in \mathcal{S}$ for a given description d_j. Each event sequence s_i consists of a series of events $\{e_{i,1}, e_{i,2}, \dots, e_{i,n_i}\}$, where each event $e_{i,j}$ is represented by an event time $t_{i,j}$ and an event type $k_{i,j}$. Thus, the sequence can be written as $s_i = \{(t_{i,1}, k_{i,1}), (t_{i,2}, k_{i,2}), \dots, (t_{i,n_i}, k_{i,n_i})\}$. The goal is to embed both descriptions d_j and event sequences s_i into a shared embedding space for effective retrieval.

Embedding Event Sequences. As illustrated by Figure 3, TPP-Embedding builds upon TPP-LLM (Liu and Quan, 2024) by embedding event sequences through the integration of temporal and event-type representations. For each event $e_{i,j}$, the temporal embedding is computed as $\boldsymbol{t}_{i,j} = f_t(t_{i,j})$, where f_t is a temporal encoding function (Zhang et al., 2020; Zuo et al., 2020). Each event type text $k_{i,j}$ is tokenized by the large language model (LLM) tokenizer and embedded using its embedding layer, resulting in $\boldsymbol{X}_{i,j} = [\boldsymbol{x}_{i,j,1}, \boldsymbol{x}_{i,j,2}, \dots, \boldsymbol{x}_{i,j,n_j}]$. The temporal and type

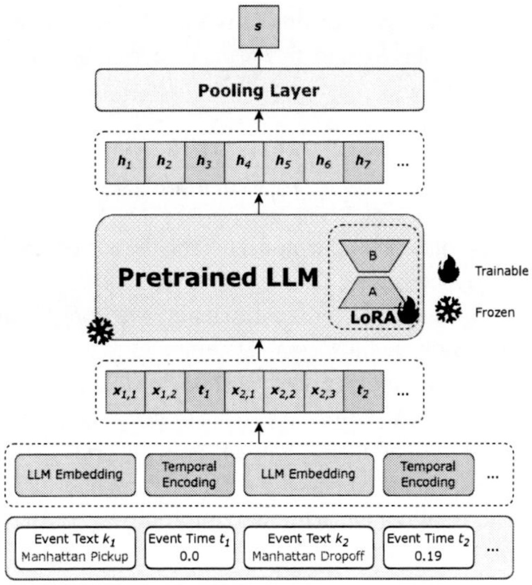

Figure 3: TPP-Embedding architecture, illustrating the embedding process for a event sequence through the integration of temporal and text representations, followed by processing with a large language model and a pooling layer to generate a fixed-length sequence representation.

embeddings are concatenated to form the final event representation $\boldsymbol{E}_{i,j}$. These event embeddings are then passed through the LLM to obtain hidden states $\boldsymbol{H}_i = [\boldsymbol{h}_{i,1}, \boldsymbol{h}_{i,2}, \dots, \boldsymbol{h}_{i,l_i}] = \text{LLM}([\boldsymbol{E}_{i,1}, \boldsymbol{E}_{i,2}, \dots, \boldsymbol{E}_{i,n_i}])$. Finally, a pooling operation (Reimers and Gurevych, 2019) is applied to produce a fixed-length representation of the sequence: $\boldsymbol{s}_i = \text{Pool}(\boldsymbol{H}_i)$.

Embedding Descriptions. Textual descriptions d_j are embedded using the same LLM and tokenizer as the event sequences. The description is tokenized and passed through the LLM, resulting in hidden states. A pooling operation is then applied to obtain the final description embedding: $\boldsymbol{d}_j = \text{Pool}(\text{LLM}(d_j))$. By embedding descriptions and sequences in the same space, TPP-Embedding enables retrieval based on their similarity.

4.2 Training Objective

To align the embeddings of descriptions and their corresponding event sequences, we employ a contrastive learning framework. Positive pairs (d_i, s_i) consist of a description and its matching event sequence, while other sequences in the batch serve as negatives. The cosine similarity between description and sequence embeddings is computed as $\text{sim}(d_i, s_j) = \frac{\boldsymbol{d}_i \cdot \boldsymbol{s}_j}{\|\boldsymbol{d}_i\| \|\boldsymbol{s}_j\|}$. The training objective uses a multiple negatives ranking loss (Henderson et al.,

2017) to maximize similarity for positive pairs and minimize it for negative pairs. The loss function is given by:

$$\mathcal{L} = -\log \frac{\exp(\text{sim}(d_i, s_i))}{\sum_j \exp(\text{sim}(d_i, s_j))}. \quad (1)$$

This encourages the model to rank the correct event sequence higher than incorrect ones for each description. To improve efficiency, we apply 4-bit precision quantization (Dettmers et al., 2024) to reduce memory usage and use low-rank adaptation (LoRA) (Hu et al., 2021) to fine-tune a small subset of parameters while keeping the rest frozen. These enhancements allow for efficient fine-tuning and deployment without compromising retrieval performance.

5 Experiments

In this section, we present a detailed overview of the baseline models used for comparison, the evaluation metrics employed, the experimental setup, the results obtained, and the ablation studies conducted.

5.1 Baselines

To enable evaluation with common embedding models, we transform temporal event sequences into a textual format by concatenating events within a sequence. Each event is represented by its relative timestamp followed by the corresponding event type text, separated by a comma. These events are concatenated with line breaks, resulting in a single textual representation for each event sequence. This approach ensures that the temporal and semantic information is preserved for text-based embeddings.

We compare TPP-Embedding against several widely used embedding models: All-MiniLM-L12-v2 (Wang et al., 2020), All-MPNet-Base-v2 (Song et al., 2020), BGE-Large-En-v1.5 (Xiao et al., 2023), MxbAI-Embed-Large-v1 (Li and Li, 2023; Lee et al., 2024), Multilingual-E5-Large-Instruct (Wang et al., 2024), and GTE-Qwen2-1.5B-instruct (Li et al., 2023). These models are designed for generating sentence embeddings and are adapted here for retrieving the most relevant event sequences based on descriptions.

To ensure a fair comparison, all baseline models are fine-tuned using a contrastive learning framework. Specifically, we employ the multiple negatives ranking loss (Henderson et al., 2017), which treats a description and its corresponding event sequence as a positive pair, while all other mismatched pairs within the batch are considered negatives. This fine-tuning process aligns the embeddings of matching descriptions and sequences while separating non-matching ones. In addition, Table 7 provides an overview of the total parameters and trainable parameters for each baseline model. While the baseline models (besides Qwen2-1.5B) require fine-tuning all parameters, TPP-Embedding models and Qwen2-1.5B leverage LoRA for efficient fine-tuning.

Model	Parameters	Trainable
MiniLM-L12	33.4M	33.4M
MPNet-Base	109M	109M
BGE-Large	335M	335M
MxbAI-Large	335M	335M
mE5-Large	560M	560M
Qwen2-1.5B	1.5B	4.4M
TPP-Llama	1.1B	4.5M
TPP-Llama-Chat	1.1B	4.5M

Table 7: Numbers of total and trainable model parameters. (M = Million, B = Billion.)

5.2 Evaluation Metrics

The temporal event sequence and description matching task is framed as a retrieval problem, where the model retrieves the correct event sequence for each description by ranking all event sequences based on their similarity to the description embeddings. We evaluate retrieval quality using two metrics: Mean Reciprocal Rank (MRR) and Recall@K. MRR measures the ranking position of the correct sequence, providing an average of reciprocal ranks across all queries, while Recall@K calculates the proportion of cases where the correct sequence is included in the top K results.

5.3 Experimental Setups

For the baseline models (besides Qwen2-1.5B), we use the AdamW optimizer (Loshchilov and Hutter, 2017), training for 15 epochs with a learning rate of 2e-5, a cosine scheduler, a warmup ratio of 0.1, and a batch size of 8. Qwen2-1.5B uses the same LoRA and training settings as the TPP-Embedding models described below.

TPP-Embedding integrates temporal positional encoding for event times (Zuo et al., 2020), with event type embeddings placed before the temporal embedding (Liu and Quan, 2024). Two foundation models are employed: TinyLlama-1.1B-

Intermediate-Step-1431k-3T (TPP-Llama) and TinyLlama-1.1B-Chat-v1.0 (Zhang et al., 2024) (TPP-Llama-Chat). We utilize all hidden states with mean pooling (Reimers and Gurevych, 2019) and apply 4-bit quantization (Dettmers et al., 2024). LoRA (Hu et al., 2021) is used with a rank of 16 and dropout of 0.05, targeting the attention projection matrices. The model is trained for 25 epochs with a learning rate of 4e-4, a cosine scheduler, a warmup ratio of 0.02, and a batch size of 8. All experiments are conducted five times, with average results reported. The experiments were run on NVIDIA A100 and H100 GPUs. Additional experimental setups are provided in Appendix B.

5.4 Experimental Results

The experimental results demonstrate the effectiveness of our proposed models compared to traditional text-based embedding models. As shown in Table 8, along with Figures 4 and 5, TPP-Llama and TPP-Llama-Chat consistently outperform the baselines across most datasets in terms of both MRR and Recall@5. TPP-Llama achieves the highest MRR and Recall@5 on Stack Overflow and remains competitive across the benchmark except for Amazon Review, while TPP-Llama-Chat attains the best Recall@5 on U.S. Earthquake and leads on Chicago Crime and NYC Taxi Trip in both metrics. While Qwen2-1.5B demonstrates strong performance on U.S. Earthquake and MPNet-Base achieves the highest MRR on Amazon Review, the TPP-based models exhibit superior generalization across the majority of datasets. These results highlight the advantage of the temporal and event-type-aware design of TPP-Embedding, which effectively captures the structure and dependencies within event sequences compared to traditional models.

5.5 Multi-Domain Results

In real-world applications, it is often necessary to retrieve event sequences that span different domains, requiring models to handle various event sequence types. Multi-domain retrieval refers to a model's ability to effectively process and retrieve information across diverse datasets or domains simultaneously, rather than being specialized for a single domain. To simulate such settings, we created a multi-domain dataset by combining 30% of the data from the five datasets. As shown in Table 9, Qwen2-1.5B achieves the highest MRR, while TPP-Llama-Chat attains the best Recall@5. Although Qwen2-1.5B performs strongly, TPP-Llama and TPP-Llama-Chat achieve competitive retrieval effectiveness, particularly excelling in Recall@5, which is crucial for practical multi-domain retrieval scenarios. These results highlight the robustness of TPP-Embedding in retrieving diverse event sequences and its ability to generalize effectively across multiple domains, making it a strong choice for real-world applications.

5.6 Ablation Studies

In this subsection, we perform ablation studies to evaluate the effects of various model configurations on event sequence retrieval performance.

5.6.1 Embedding Inclusions

We conduct an ablation study to assess the impact of using only temporal tokens or only type (textual) tokens on retrieval performance. As shown in Table 10, using only textual tokens achieves performance comparable to using all tokens on the Stack Overflow dataset. However, this approach leads to a significant performance drop on the U.S. Earthquake dataset, likely due to the nature of the datasets: Stack Overflow includes 25 event types, allowing the model to rely primarily on textual contents, whereas the U.S. Earthquake dataset contains only 3 event types, making temporal information essential for accurate retrieval.

5.6.2 Hidden State Selections

We evaluate the impact of different hidden state selections from the last hidden layer of the model for event sequences, specifically choosing only temporal tokens, a combination of temporal tokens and the last token of event type text tokens for each event, or all tokens. As shown in Table 11, using all tokens generally provides strong results, achieving the highest MRR on the StackOverflow dataset and the highest Recall@5 on the Earthquake dataset. While selecting temporal tokens and the last type tokens slightly improves MRR on the Earthquake dataset, using only temporal tokens lags behind both strategies on both datasets. Overall, choosing all tokens yields consistently good performance.

5.6.3 Pooling Modes

In experiments with different pooling modes as Table 12, we observe that the mean pooling method consistently performs well, achieving the highest MRR and Recall@5 on the StackOverflow dataset. However, for the Earthquake dataset, last token pooling (Muennighoff, 2022) slightly outperforms mean pooling. Max pooling shows competitive

Model	StackOverflow	Crime	Taxi	Earthquake	Amazon
MiniLM-L12	0.501 / 0.695	0.808 / 0.931	0.159 / 0.239	0.676 / 0.895	0.459 / 0.573
MPNet-Base	0.620 / 0.775	0.924 / 0.980	0.246 / 0.364	0.733 / 0.923	**0.665** / 0.756
BGE-Large	0.632 / 0.786	0.922 / 0.985	0.286 / 0.415	0.736 / 0.928	0.656 / 0.746
MxbAI-Large	0.627 / 0.782	0.924 / 0.982	0.271 / 0.426	0.717 / 0.914	0.650 / 0.747
mE5-Large	0.658 / 0.804	0.941 / 0.987	0.261 / 0.389	0.748 / 0.921	0.617 / 0.716
Qwen2-1.5B	0.660 / 0.804	0.921 / 0.982	0.448 / 0.662	**0.770** / 0.950	0.629 / 0.756
TPP-Llama	**0.741 / 0.880**	0.958 / 0.992	0.468 / 0.680	0.760 / 0.946	0.641 / 0.763
TPP-Llama-Chat	0.729 / 0.865	**0.961 / 0.994**	**0.475 / 0.691**	0.759 / **0.953**	0.646 / **0.767**

Table 8: Comparison of average MRR and Recall@5 across TESRBench datasets in event sequence retrieval.

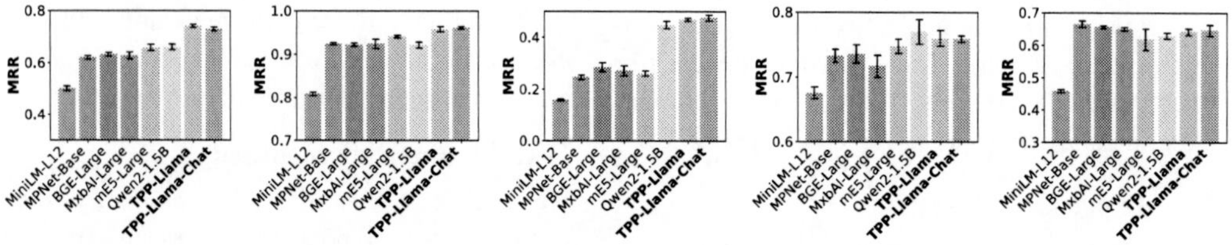

(a) Stack Overflow (b) Chicago Crime (c) NYC Taxi Trip (d) U.S. Earthquake (e) Amazon Review

Figure 4: Comparison of average MRRs with standard deviations on TESRBench in event sequence retrieval.

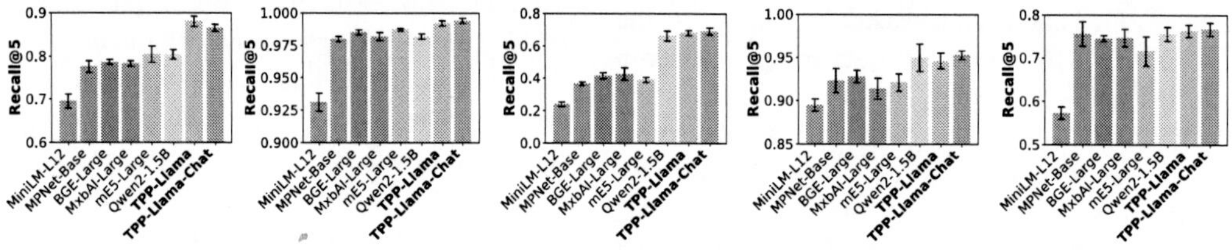

(a) Stack Overflow (b) Chicago Crime (c) NYC Taxi Trip (d) U.S. Earthquake (e) Amazon Review

Figure 5: Comparison of average Recall@5 with standard deviations on TESRBench in event sequence retrieval.

Model	MRR	Recall@5
MiniLM-L12	0.634 ± 0.007	0.795 ± 0.009
MPNet-Base	0.748 ± 0.003	0.889 ± 0.007
BGE-Large	0.744 ± 0.010	0.888 ± 0.010
MxbAI-Large	0.744 ± 0.006	0.876 ± 0.010
mE5-Large	0.749 ± 0.013	0.888 ± 0.012
Qwen2-1.5B	**0.783** ± 0.005	0.914 ± 0.013
TPP-Llama	0.772 ± 0.009	0.914 ± 0.008
TPP-Llama-Chat	0.770 ± 0.005	**0.919** ± 0.009

Table 9: Comparison of average MRRs and Recall@5 with standard deviations on the multi-domain dataset.

Embeddings	StackOverflow	Earthquake
Temporal Tokens	0.037 / 0.040	0.179 / 0.281
Textual Tokens	0.726 / **0.870**	0.675 / 0.890
All Tokens	**0.729** / 0.865	**0.759 / 0.953**

Table 10: Comparison of average MRRs and Recall@5 of TPP-Llama-Chat with different embedding inclusions.

Hidden States	StackOverflow	Earthquake
Temporal Tokens	0.718 / 0.862	0.754 / 0.939
+ Last Type Tokens	0.727 / **0.875**	**0.766 / 0.953**
All Tokens	**0.729** / 0.865	0.759 / **0.953**

Table 11: Comparison of average MRRs and Recall@5 of TPP-Llama-Chat with different hidden state selections.

performance on the StackOverflow dataset but performs considerably worse on the Earthquake dataset. Overall, mean pooling offers a balanced performance, making it a reliable choice.

Pooling	StackOverflow	Earthquake
Mean	**0.729 / 0.865**	0.759 / 0.953
Max	0.712 / 0.857	0.627 / 0.853
Last Token	0.728 / 0.848	**0.772 / 0.960**

Table 12: Comparison of average MRRs and Recall@5 of TPP-Llama-Chat with different pooling modes.

5.6.4 Loss Functions

To examine the impact of the loss function on retrieval performance, we replace the contrastive loss with a Mean Squared Error (MSE) loss, which optimizes cosine similarity to 1 for matched pairs. As shown in Table 13, this substitution leads to a pronounced decline in both metrics across all datasets, emphasizing the pivotal role of contrastive loss in capturing subtle relationships between closely related event sequences. These results highlight the effectiveness of contrastive learning in enhancing retrieval accuracy.

Loss	StackOverflow	Earthquake
MSE	0.020 / 0.016	0.020 / 0.015
Contrastive	**0.729 / 0.865**	**0.759 / 0.953**

Table 13: Comparison of average MRRs and Recall@5 of TPP-Llama-Chat with different loss functions.

6 Conclusion

In this paper, we introduce TESRBench, a comprehensive benchmark for evaluating temporal event sequence retrieval, alongside TPP-Embedding, a novel model designed to integrate temporal and event-type-aware representations. TESRBench provides a diverse set of datasets with synthesized textual descriptions, offering a robust foundation for benchmarking models in this domain. Our proposed TPP-Embedding model combines temporal encoding and event text embedding with a large language model backbone, enabling it to effectively capture the structure and dependencies of temporal event sequences. Extensive experiments conducted on TESRBench demonstrate its superior performance compared to traditional text-based baselines, particularly in handling temporally complex, multi-type event sequences. Furthermore, multi-domain experiments underscore the flexibility and adaptability of our approach across diverse event domains. Together, TESRBench and TPP-Embedding represent a significant step forward in advancing research on temporal event sequence retrieval.

Limitations

TESRBench, while providing a robust foundation for evaluating temporal event sequence retrieval, relies on synthesized textual descriptions generated by GPT-4o-mini, which may not fully capture the variability and complexity of real-world user-generated descriptions. A limitation of our TPP-Embedding model is its reliance on high-quality temporal and event-type data, which could pose challenges when dealing with noisy or incomplete event sequences encountered in real-world scenarios. Furthermore, while TPP-Embedding achieves strong retrieval performance, its dependence on large-scale language models can introduce computational latency on extremely large datasets, necessitating further optimization strategies. Finally, our current baselines are restricted to text-based methods, and future research could explore integrating recent time-context-aware sequential recommendation techniques (Li et al., 2020; Rashed et al., 2022; Tran et al., 2023; Liu et al., 2024) to further improve the retrieval of temporal event sequences from textual descriptions.

Ethical Considerations

In constructing TESRBench, we acknowledge potential ethical concerns related to the use of synthesized textual descriptions and real-world event data. While the textual descriptions are generated objectively, they may still inadvertently reflect biases or limitations inherent in the data sources. For TPP-Embedding, its ability to retrieve temporal event sequences could be misused in privacy-sensitive applications, such as personal activity tracking. It is crucial to ensure that all data used for training and retrieval is anonymized and managed responsibly. Additionally, biases in training data, such as uneven representation of event types or domains, could result in biased retrieval outcomes. Future work should emphasize dataset curation and the implementation of bias mitigation strategies to minimize potential harms.

References

Josh Achiam, Steven Adler, Sandhini Agarwal, Lama Ahmad, Ilge Akkaya, Florencia Leoni Aleman, Diogo Almeida, Janko Altenschmidt, Sam Altman, Shyamal Anadkat, et al. 2023. Gpt-4 technical report. *arXiv preprint arXiv:2303.08774*.

Chicago Police Department. 2024. Crimes - 2001 to present.

Tim Dettmers, Mike Lewis, Younes Belkada, and Luke Zettlemoyer. 2022. Llm.int8(): 8-bit matrix multiplication for transformers at scale. *arXiv preprint arXiv:2208.07339*.

Tim Dettmers, Artidoro Pagnoni, Ari Holtzman, and Luke Zettlemoyer. 2024. Qlora: Efficient finetuning of quantized llms. *Advances in Neural Information Processing Systems*, 36.

Vinayak Gupta, Srikanta Bedathur, and Abir De. 2022. Learning temporal point processes for efficient retrieval of continuous time event sequences. In *Proceedings of the AAAI Conference on Artificial Intelligence*, volume 36, pages 4005–4013.

Vinayak Gupta, Srikanta Bedathur, and Abir De. 2023. Retrieving continuous time event sequences using neural temporal point processes with learnable hashing. *ACM Transactions on Intelligent Systems and Technology*.

Matthew Henderson, Rami Al-Rfou, Brian Strope, Yun-Hsuan Sung, László Lukács, Ruiqi Guo, Sanjiv Kumar, Balint Miklos, and Ray Kurzweil. 2017. Efficient natural language response suggestion for smart reply. *arXiv preprint arXiv:1705.00652*.

Edward J Hu, Yelong Shen, Phillip Wallis, Zeyuan Allen-Zhu, Yuanzhi Li, Shean Wang, Lu Wang, and Weizhu Chen. 2021. Lora: Low-rank adaptation of large language models. *arXiv preprint arXiv:2106.09685*.

Abhinav Ramesh Kashyap, Thanh-Tung Nguyen, Viktor Schlegel, Stefan Winkler, See Kiong Ng, and Soujanya Poria. 2024. A comprehensive survey of sentence representations: From the bert epoch to the chatgpt era and beyond. In *Proceedings of the 18th Conference of the European Chapter of the Association for Computational Linguistics (Volume 1: Long Papers)*, pages 1738–1751.

Sean Lee, Aamir Shakir, Darius Koenig, and Julius Lipp. 2024. Open source strikes bread - new fluffy embeddings model.

Quentin Lhoest, Albert Villanova Del Moral, Yacine Jernite, Abhishek Thakur, Patrick Von Platen, Suraj Patil, Julien Chaumond, Mariama Drame, Julien Plu, Lewis Tunstall, et al. 2021. Datasets: A community library for natural language processing. *arXiv preprint arXiv:2109.02846*.

Jiacheng Li, Yujie Wang, and Julian McAuley. 2020. Time interval aware self-attention for sequential recommendation. In *Proceedings of the 13th international conference on web search and data mining*, pages 322–330.

Xianming Li and Jing Li. 2023. Angle-optimized text embeddings. *arXiv preprint arXiv:2309.12871*.

Zehan Li, Xin Zhang, Yanzhao Zhang, Dingkun Long, Pengjun Xie, and Meishan Zhang. 2023. Towards general text embeddings with multi-stage contrastive learning. *arXiv preprint arXiv:2308.03281*.

Jimmy Lin, Rodrigo Nogueira, and Andrew Yates. 2022. *Pretrained transformers for text ranking: Bert and beyond*. Springer Nature.

Yang Liu, Yitong Wang, and Chenyue Feng. 2024. Unirec: A dual enhancement of uniformity and frequency in sequential recommendations. In *Proceedings of the 33rd ACM International Conference on Information and Knowledge Management*, pages 1483–1492.

Zefang Liu and Yinzhu Quan. 2024. Tpp-llm: Modeling temporal point processes by efficiently fine-tuning large language models. *arXiv preprint arXiv:2410.02062*.

Ilya Loshchilov and Frank Hutter. 2017. Decoupled weight decay regularization. *arXiv preprint arXiv:1711.05101*.

Sourab Mangrulkar, Sylvain Gugger, Lysandre Debut, Younes Belkada, Sayak Paul, and B. Bossan. 2022. PEFT: State-of-the-art parameter-efficient fine-tuning methods.

Hongyuan Mei and Jason M Eisner. 2017. The neural hawkes process: A neurally self-modulating multivariate point process. *Advances in neural information processing systems*, 30.

Andres Monroy-Hernandez. 2014. NYC taxi trips.

Niklas Muennighoff. 2022. Sgpt: Gpt sentence embeddings for semantic search. *arXiv preprint arXiv:2202.08904*.

Jianmo Ni, Jiacheng Li, and Julian McAuley. 2019. Justifying recommendations using distantly-labeled reviews and fine-grained aspects. In *Proceedings of the 2019 conference on empirical methods in natural language processing and the 9th international joint conference on natural language processing (EMNLP-IJCNLP)*, pages 188–197.

Adam Paszke, Sam Gross, Francisco Massa, Adam Lerer, James Bradbury, Gregory Chanan, Trevor Killeen, Zeming Lin, Natalia Gimelshein, Luca Antiga, et al. 2019. Pytorch: An imperative style, high-performance deep learning library. *Advances in neural information processing systems*, 32.

Ahmed Rashed, Shereen Elsayed, and Lars Schmidt-Thieme. 2022. Context and attribute-aware sequential recommendation via cross-attention. In *Proceedings of the 16th ACM Conference on Recommender Systems*, pages 71–80.

Nils Reimers and Iryna Gurevych. 2019. Sentence-bert: Sentence embeddings using siamese bert-networks. In *Proceedings of the 2019 Conference on Empirical Methods in Natural Language Processing*.

Oleksandr Shchur, Ali Caner Türkmen, Tim Januschowski, and Stephan Günnemann. 2021. Neural temporal point processes: A review. *arXiv preprint arXiv:2104.03528*.

Kaitao Song, Xu Tan, Tao Qin, Jianfeng Lu, and Tie-Yan Liu. 2020. Mpnet: Masked and permuted pre-training for language understanding. *Advances in neural information processing systems*, 33:16857–16867.

Stack Exchange, Inc. 2024. Stack exchange data dump.

Viet Anh Tran, Guillaume Salha-Galvan, Bruno Sguerra, and Romain Hennequin. 2023. Attention mixtures for time-aware sequential recommendation. In *Proceedings of the 46th International ACM SIGIR Conference on Research and Development in Information Retrieval*, pages 1821–1826.

U.S. Geological Survey. 2024. USGS earthquake catalog.

Ashish Vaswani, Noam Shazeer, Niki Parmar, Jakob Uszkoreit, Llion Jones, Aidan N Gomez, Łukasz Kaiser, and Illia Polosukhin. 2017. Attention is all you need. *Advances in neural information processing systems*, 30.

Liang Wang, Nan Yang, Xiaolong Huang, Linjun Yang, Rangan Majumder, and Furu Wei. 2024. Multilingual e5 text embeddings: A technical report. *arXiv preprint arXiv:2402.05672*.

Wenhui Wang, Furu Wei, Li Dong, Hangbo Bao, Nan Yang, and Ming Zhou. 2020. Minilm: Deep self-attention distillation for task-agnostic compression of pre-trained transformers. *Advances in Neural Information Processing Systems*, 33:5776–5788.

Thomas Wolf, Lysandre Debut, Victor Sanh, Julien Chaumond, Clement Delangue, Anthony Moi, Pierric Cistac, Tim Rault, Rémi Louf, Morgan Funtowicz, et al. 2020. Transformers: State-of-the-art natural language processing. In *Proceedings of the 2020 conference on empirical methods in natural language processing: system demonstrations*, pages 38–45.

Shitao Xiao, Zheng Liu, Peitian Zhang, Niklas Muennighoff, Defu Lian, and Jian-Yun Nie. 2023. C-pack: Packaged resources to advance general chinese embedding. *arXiv preprint arXiv:2309.07597*.

Siqiao Xue, Xiaoming Shi, Zhixuan Chu, Yan Wang, Fan Zhou, Hongyan Hao, Caigao Jiang, Chen Pan, Yi Xu, James Y Zhang, et al. 2023. Easytpp: Towards open benchmarking the temporal point processes. *arXiv preprint arXiv:2307.08097*.

Peiyuan Zhang, Guangtao Zeng, Tianduo Wang, and Wei Lu. 2024. Tinyllama: An open-source small language model. *arXiv preprint arXiv:2401.02385*.

Qiang Zhang, Aldo Lipani, Omer Kirnap, and Emine Yilmaz. 2020. Self-attentive hawkes process. In *International conference on machine learning*, pages 11183–11193. PMLR.

Lianmin Zheng, Wei-Lin Chiang, Ying Sheng, Siyuan Zhuang, Zhanghao Wu, Yonghao Zhuang, Zi Lin, Zhuohan Li, Dacheng Li, Eric Xing, et al. 2023. Judging llm-as-a-judge with mt-bench and chatbot arena. *Advances in Neural Information Processing Systems*, 36:46595–46623.

Simiao Zuo, Haoming Jiang, Zichong Li, Tuo Zhao, and Hongyuan Zha. 2020. Transformer hawkes process. In *International conference on machine learning*, pages 11692–11702. PMLR.

A Data Examples

This appendix presents selected examples of event sequences from the validation sets in TESRBench, along with their corresponding descriptions, as shown in Table 14. These descriptions highlight key temporal patterns and provide context for the diversity of events and their occurrences across the benchmark's datasets.

B More Experimental Setup

Our experiments were conducted using several key Python libraries, including `pytorch` (Paszke et al., 2019) for deep learning, `transformers` (Wolf et al., 2020) for working with pre-trained language models, `sentence-transformers` (Reimers and Gurevych, 2019) for embedding and retrieval tasks, `datasets` (Lhoest et al., 2021) for data handling, `peft` (Mangrulkar et al., 2022) for parameter-efficient fine-tuning, and `bitsandbytes` (Dettmers et al., 2022) for model quantization.

C More Experimental Results

In this appendix, we provide additional experimental results to further analyze the performance of our models, both before and after fine-tuning.

C.1 Experimental Results before Fine-Tuning

The performance of all models before fine-tuning in Table 15 shows significantly lower retrieval accuracy, with the highest MRR achieved by BGE-Large across most datasets. TPP-based models perform poorly at this stage, due to unaligned temporal and textual spaces, indicating the necessity of fine-tuning to improve event sequence retrieval.

C.2 More Experimental Results after Fine-Tuning

The results after fine-tuning demonstrate a significant improvement across all models, as shown in Tables 16, 17, and 18. TPP-Llama and TPP-Llama-Chat consistently outperform baseline models in MRR, Recall@1, and Recall@5 across most datasets. These improvements highlight the importance of fine-tuning in enhancing their retrieval capabilities.

Dataset	Event Sequence	Description
Stack Overflow	0.00,Nice Question 0.57,Good Answer 0.66,Popular Question 0.83,Famous Question 0.89,Nice Question 2.25,Popular Question 2.32,Necromancer 2.43,Notable Question 3.00,Great Question 3.40,Good Question 3.64,Popular Question 3.69,Notable Question 4.00,Notable Question ... 23.41,Popular Question	The sequence of badges earned by the user on Stack Overflow shows a progression of achievements over time, with certain types of badges appearing more frequently at different intervals. Initially, badges such as "Nice Question" and "Good Answer" are earned in the first few months, followed by a cluster of "Popular Question" and "Notable Question" badges around the two to four-month mark. As time progresses, there is a notable increase in the frequency of "Famous Question" and "Popular Question" badges, particularly in the later months, indicating a trend toward these types of achievements. The sequence also includes several clusters of "Nice Question" badges, particularly around the seven-month mark and again towards the end of the timeline. Overall, the user's badge accumulation reflects a gradual increase in the variety and frequency of achievements over the course of the observed period.
Chicago Crime	0.00,Battery 0.26,Battery 0.52,Theft 0.69,Motor Vehicle Theft 0.74,Assault 0.99,Motor Vehicle Theft 0.99,Motor Vehicle Theft 1.08,Criminal Sexual Assault ... 23.72,Deceptive Practice	The sequence of crime incidents shows a notable clustering of certain crime types over time, particularly motor vehicle thefts, which appear frequently throughout the timeline, especially in the earlier months. Battery incidents are also prevalent, occurring multiple times in the first half of the sequence. Other offenses such as robbery and criminal damage emerge at various intervals, with some clustering in the middle to later months. Overall, there is a trend of increasing diversity in crime types as the timeline progresses, with a gradual rise in the frequency of theft-related incidents towards the end.
NYC Taxi Trip	0.00,Manhattan Pickup 0.19,Manhattan Dropoff 0.24,Manhattan Pickup 0.68,Manhattan Dropoff 0.73,Manhattan Pickup 0.99,Manhattan Dropoff 1.13,Manhattan Pickup 1.43,Manhattan Dropoff 1.45,Manhattan Pickup 1.54,Manhattan Dropoff ... 31.87,Brooklyn Dropoff	The sequence of taxi trips primarily consists of pickups and dropoffs occurring in Manhattan, with a notable concentration of events in the first few hours. Early in the sequence, the driver consistently alternates between pickups and dropoffs, with a high frequency of trips. As the sequence progresses, there are brief periods where trips shift to Queens and Brooklyn, particularly after a long duration of Manhattan trips. The latter part of the sequence shows a gradual transition to more pickups and dropoffs in Brooklyn, indicating a shift in location focus. Overall, the events are clustered closely together in time, with significant activity in the first half of the sequence before expanding to other boroughs.
U.S. Earthquake	0.00,Medium 0.66,Large 0.72,Large 0.99,Large 1.07,Large 1.08,Large 1.67,Large	The sequence of earthquake events begins with a medium magnitude event, followed closely by a series of large magnitude events occurring within a short time frame. The large events cluster together, with multiple occurrences happening within the first two days. This indicates a trend of increasing magnitude shortly after the initial medium event, with the majority of the large events occurring in rapid succession.
Amazon Review	0.00,Books 0.14,Sports and Outdoors 0.14,Books 0.29,Books 0.43,Books 0.57,Books 1.00,Books 1.14,Books ... 25.29,Books	The sequence of product reviews shows a predominant focus on the "Books" category, which appears consistently throughout the timeline, especially in the initial weeks. Other categories such as "Pet Supplies" and "Grocery and Gourmet Food" emerge intermittently, often clustering around specific weeks, particularly in the middle and later parts of the sequence. "Clothing Shoes and Jewelry" and "Movies and TV" also appear, but less frequently, with some clustering noted in the later weeks. Overall, there is a clear trend of sustained interest in "Books," with other categories appearing in a more sporadic manner.

Table 14: Event sequence examples with their descriptions from the validation sets of TESRBench.

Model (before FT)	StackOverflow	Crime	Taxi	Earthquake	Amazon	Multi-Domain
MiniLM-L12	0.091 / 0.123	0.071 / 0.111	0.028 / 0.024	0.037 / 0.043	0.142 / 0.200	0.154 / 0.208
MPNet-Base	0.068 / 0.087	0.027 / 0.020	0.022 / 0.017	0.031 / 0.027	0.068 / 0.071	0.102 / 0.127
BGE-Large	0.122 / 0.162	0.126 / 0.158	0.042 / 0.051	0.039 / 0.040	0.215 / 0.293	0.196 / 0.247
MxbAI-Large	0.085 / 0.102	0.091 / 0.134	0.039 / 0.037	0.038 / 0.043	0.174 / 0.227	0.170 / 0.221
mE5-Large	0.065 / 0.078	0.078 / 0.087	0.028 / 0.024	0.037 / 0.040	0.142 / 0.187	0.145 / 0.191
Qwen2-1.5B	0.047 / 0.054	0.032 / 0.032	0.025 / 0.020	0.027 / 0.027	0.109 / 0.116	0.095 / 0.114
TPP-Llama	0.022 / 0.021	0.019 / 0.020	0.020 / 0.014	0.022 / 0.020	0.033 / 0.027	0.025 / 0.030
TPP-Llama-Chat	0.020 / 0.015	0.018 / 0.012	0.019 / 0.014	0.023 / 0.020	0.033 / 0.031	0.021 / 0.017

Table 15: Comparison of MRRs and Recall@5 on TESRBench in event sequence retrieval before fine-tuning.

Model	StackOverflow	Crime	Taxi	Earthquake	Amazon
MiniLM-L12	0.501 $\pm$ 0.009	0.808 $\pm$ 0.004	0.159 $\pm$ 0.003	0.676 $\pm$ 0.009	0.459 $\pm$ 0.005
MPNet-Base	0.620 $\pm$ 0.007	0.924 $\pm$ 0.003	0.246 $\pm$ 0.009	0.733 $\pm$ 0.010	**0.665** $\pm$ 0.010
BGE-Large	0.632 $\pm$ 0.007	0.922 $\pm$ 0.004	0.286 $\pm$ 0.017	0.736 $\pm$ 0.014	0.656 $\pm$ 0.004
MxbAI-Large	0.627 $\pm$ 0.013	0.924 $\pm$ 0.011	0.271 $\pm$ 0.020	0.717 $\pm$ 0.017	0.650 $\pm$ 0.005
mE5-Large	0.658 $\pm$ 0.012	0.941 $\pm$ 0.003	0.261 $\pm$ 0.010	0.748 $\pm$ 0.011	0.617 $\pm$ 0.033
Qwen2-1.5B	0.660 $\pm$ 0.011	0.921 $\pm$ 0.007	0.448 $\pm$ 0.014	0.770 $\pm$ 0.019	0.629 $\pm$ 0.009
TPP-Llama	**0.741** $\pm$ 0.006	0.958 $\pm$ 0.006	0.468 $\pm$ 0.006	**0.760** $\pm$ 0.012	0.641 $\pm$ 0.010
TPP-Llama-Chat	0.729 $\pm$ 0.008	**0.961** $\pm$ 0.003	**0.475** $\pm$ 0.011	0.759 $\pm$ 0.005	0.646 $\pm$ 0.017

Table 16: Comparison of average MRRs with standard deviations on TESRBench in event sequence retrieval.

Model	StackOverflow	Crime	Taxi	Earthquake	Amazon
MiniLM-L12	0.353 $\pm$ 0.006	0.711 $\pm$ 0.005	0.063 $\pm$ 0.007	0.513 $\pm$ 0.013	0.348 $\pm$ 0.007
MPNet-Base	0.497 $\pm$ 0.009	0.878 $\pm$ 0.006	0.123 $\pm$ 0.013	0.598 $\pm$ 0.015	**0.579** $\pm$ 0.012
BGE-Large	0.509 $\pm$ 0.011	0.875 $\pm$ 0.006	0.155 $\pm$ 0.023	0.595 $\pm$ 0.026	0.569 $\pm$ 0.011
MxbAI-Large	0.502 $\pm$ 0.017	0.879 $\pm$ 0.019	0.130 $\pm$ 0.023	0.573 $\pm$ 0.019	0.564 $\pm$ 0.010
mE5-Large	0.540 $\pm$ 0.016	0.904 $\pm$ 0.006	0.132 $\pm$ 0.006	0.612 $\pm$ 0.013	0.520 $\pm$ 0.034
Qwen2-1.5B	0.541 $\pm$ 0.018	0.872 $\pm$ 0.012	0.284 $\pm$ 0.012	**0.638** $\pm$ 0.031	0.523 $\pm$ 0.009
TPP-Llama	**0.637** $\pm$ 0.010	0.930 $\pm$ 0.011	0.301 $\pm$ 0.010	0.622 $\pm$ 0.021	0.538 $\pm$ 0.015
TPP-Llama-Chat	0.620 $\pm$ 0.012	**0.936** $\pm$ 0.003	**0.305** $\pm$ 0.014	0.619 $\pm$ 0.013	0.546 $\pm$ 0.021

Table 17: Comparison of average Recall@1 with standard deviations on TESRBench in event sequence retrieval.

Model	StackOverflow	Crime	Taxi	Earthquake	Amazon
MiniLM-L12	0.695 $\pm$ 0.016	0.931 $\pm$ 0.007	0.239 $\pm$ 0.014	0.895 $\pm$ 0.007	0.573 $\pm$ 0.014
MPNet-Base	0.775 $\pm$ 0.014	0.980 $\pm$ 0.002	0.364 $\pm$ 0.011	0.923 $\pm$ 0.014	0.756 $\pm$ 0.028
BGE-Large	0.786 $\pm$ 0.006	0.985 $\pm$ 0.002	0.415 $\pm$ 0.019	0.928 $\pm$ 0.007	0.746 $\pm$ 0.007
MxbAI-Large	0.782 $\pm$ 0.007	0.982 $\pm$ 0.003	0.426 $\pm$ 0.037	0.914 $\pm$ 0.012	0.747 $\pm$ 0.020
mE5-Large	0.804 $\pm$ 0.019	0.987 $\pm$ 0.001	0.389 $\pm$ 0.016	0.921 $\pm$ 0.010	0.716 $\pm$ 0.034
Qwen2-1.5B	0.804 $\pm$ 0.011	0.982 $\pm$ 0.002	0.662 $\pm$ 0.030	0.950 $\pm$ 0.016	0.756 $\pm$ 0.016
TPP-Llama	**0.880** $\pm$ 0.012	0.992 $\pm$ 0.002	0.680 $\pm$ 0.016	0.946 $\pm$ 0.009	0.763 $\pm$ 0.014
TPP-Llama-Chat	0.865 $\pm$ 0.008	**0.994** $\pm$ 0.002	**0.691** $\pm$ 0.021	**0.953** $\pm$ 0.005	**0.767** $\pm$ 0.015

Table 18: Comparison of average Recall@5 with standard deviations on TESRBench in event sequence retrieval.

Generating Tables from the Parametric Knowledge of Language Models

Yevgeni Berkovitch[1] **Oren Glickman**[1] **Amit Somech**[1] **Tomer Wolfson**[2]
[1]Bar-Ilan University [2]Tel Aviv University
taoberkovitch@gmail.com {oren.glickman, somecha}@cs.biu.ac.il tomerwol@mail.tau.ac.il

Abstract

We explore generating factual tables from the parametric knowledge of large language models (LLMs). While LLMs have demonstrated impressive capabilities in recreating knowledge bases and generating free-form text, their ability to generate structured tabular data has received little attention. To address this gap, we explore the table generation abilities of eight state-of-the-art LLMs, including GPT-4o and Llama3.1-405B, using three prompting methods: full-table, row-by-row, and cell-by-cell. To facilitate evaluation we introduce WIKITABGEN, a new benchmark consisting of 119 manually curated Wikipedia tables and their description. Our findings show that table generation remains challenging, with the best performing model (LLaMA3.1-405B) reaching only 25.4% accuracy. We further analyze how properties like table size, popularity, and numerical content impact performance. This study highlights the unique challenges of LLM-based table generation and offers a foundation for future research in this area. All code, data, and prompts are publicly available.[1]

1 Introduction

Automated table generation has broad applications in fields such as healthcare, finance, scientific research and education (Chen et al., 2021; Johnson et al., 2016; Berant et al., 2018) where converting unstructured factual data into structured tables can significantly enhance decision-making, streamline workflows, and improve data accessibility enabling knowledge extraction and facilitating further analysis through statistical and visualization tools (Shen et al., 2021). Large language models (LLMs) (Brown et al., 2020; Chowdhery et al., 2022; Kadavath et al., 2022; Touvron et al., 2023a) have demonstrated remarkable performance on various natural language processing tasks, including free-form text generation, knowledge retrieval, and summarization. However, despite their success in generating free-form text, LLMs face distinct challenges when tasked with producing complex structured data, and their ability to generate long and factually accurate tables from their parametric knowledge remains largely unexplored (Akhtar et al., 2024; Zhao et al., 2024).

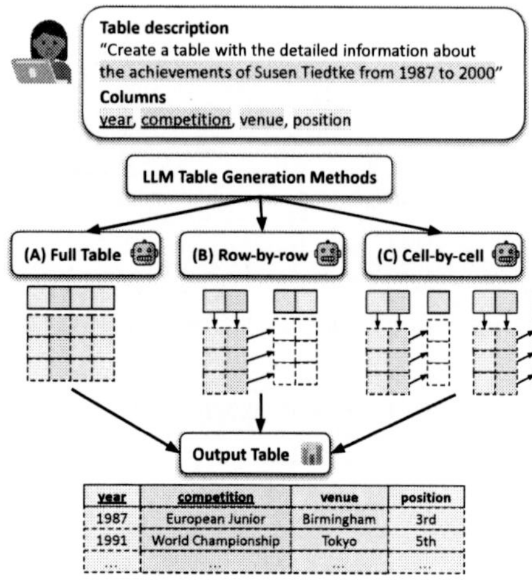

Figure 1: An example LLM-based table generation task along with three alternative prompting methods.

LLMs are pre-trained on vast amounts of text, which includes factual information presented in both plain text and structured formats, such as tables (Elazar et al., 2023; Fang et al., 2024). Through this training, LLMs encode a wealth of factual information in their parameters. While previous studies have shown that LLMs can retrieve factual information for tasks like recreating knowledge bases (KBs) (Petroni et al., 2019; AlKhamissi et al., 2022; Cohen et al., 2023) or generating Wikipedia-like articles (Shao et al., 2024), little attention has been given to their ability to generate structured tables from their parametric knowledge. Unlike question answering over tables or text-to-SQL translation (Pasupat and Liang, 2015;

[1]https://github.com/analysis-bots/WikiTabGen

Proceedings of the 4th International Workshop on Knowledge-Augmented Methods for Natural Language Processing (KnowledgeNLP'25), pages 50–65
May 3, 2025 ©2025 Association for Computational Linguistics

Chen et al., 2021), generating tables requires models to retrieve and organize specific factual data into structured formats, posing unique challenges. The lack of dedicated methods for table generation and appropriate evaluation benchmarks highlights a particular gap in current research.

To address this gap, we introduce WIKITABGEN, a benchmark designed to evaluate LLMs' ability to generate tables from their parametric knowledge. It consists of 119 manually curated Wikipedia tables, each paired with a textual description and a set of target columns. With an average of 1,457 tokens per table, WIKITABGEN features significantly larger tables compared to previous tabular generation tasks (Parikh et al., 2020; Nan et al., 2022). This benchmark facilitates a systematic evaluation of how factors such as table size, numerical content, and popularity (Mallen et al., 2022) affect table generation. We also introduce and evaluate three prompting methods: full-table generation, row-by-row generation and cell-by-cell generation.

Our key contributions are: (1) Formulating the problem of generating structured tables from LLMs' parametric knowledge. (2) Introducing WIKITABGEN, a benchmark consisting of diverse tables that vary in size, structure, and content, to evaluate table generation capabilities. (3) Implementing and evaluating three prompting methods across eight state-of-the-art LLMs, including GPT-4 and LLaMA3.1-405B. (4) Providing a comprehensive analysis of the factors that impact table generation performance.

Our experiments reveal that generating tables from LLMs remains a challenging task, with the highest F1 score reaching only 25.4%. We observe that factors such as table size and numerical content significantly affect performance. These findings highlight the need for further research to improve LLM-based table generation. We hope that our benchmark and analysis will inspire future research on generating structured data from LLMs.

2 Problem Definition

Given a short user description, our task is to generate a factually accurate table.

Following Codd (1990), a relational table $T = (R, C)$ is a set of rows $R = \{r_1, r_2, \dots\}$ and a set of columns $C = \{c_1, c_2 \dots\}$. A table cell, denoted $r[c]$, contains the value of column c in row r. Key columns are a subset $C_k \subset C$ that uniquely define each entry (row) in T and the corresponding cells do not contain null or empty values. For example, the table in Fig. 1 has the columns `year` and `competition` as its keys. Each table entry such as `venue`, corresponds to a unique `year`, `competition` pair.

Given a table description d and a list of desired table columns C, our task is to generate a corresponding table $T(\hat{R}, C)$, where the generated rows $\hat{R}$ contain factually accurate information. An example problem is shown in Fig. 1, where the table description is *"Achievements of Susen Tiedke from 1987 to 2000"* and the target columns are: *year, competition, venue*, and *position*. Each of our proposed prompting methods (§3) can then be used for the LLM to generate table $T(\hat{R}, C)$, as shown in the bottom of the figure.

3 Prompting LLMs to Generate Tables

Given a table description and list of target columns C, we evaluate LLM performance on generating the corresponding table $T(\hat{R}, C)$. Our focus is on extracting the knowledge stored in the LLM, with retrieval-augmented methods (Lewis et al., 2020; Yoran et al., 2023) being orthogonal to our study.

We implement three prompting methods to generate tables, shown in Fig. 1. First, the full table method prompts the LLM to generate the table all at once. However, the output table may be quite large, with evaluation tables have 1.5K tokens on average (§4). Therefore, we also experiment with a modular prompting approach (Khot et al., 2023, 2022), where one LLM instance generates the table *keys*, and another generates either complete rows or individual cells. We refer to these two modular prompting methods as row-by-row and cell-by-cell respectively. An in-depth example of our prompting methods is provided in Fig. 2. Note that all prompts in the figure are appended with the table description and columns (prompt 1 in Fig. 2). Next, we describe each of the prompts used in our three methods. All of our prompts are listed in §A and in our public code repository.

(a) Full-table. Given the table description and target columns the LLM is prompted to generate all table rows. Example prompts are prompts 1 and 2.A in Fig. 2 which are both concatenated and provided as the input to the LLM.

(b) Row-by-row. This is a two-stage prompting method, prompting two separate instances of the LLM. First, we prompt the LLM for key generation

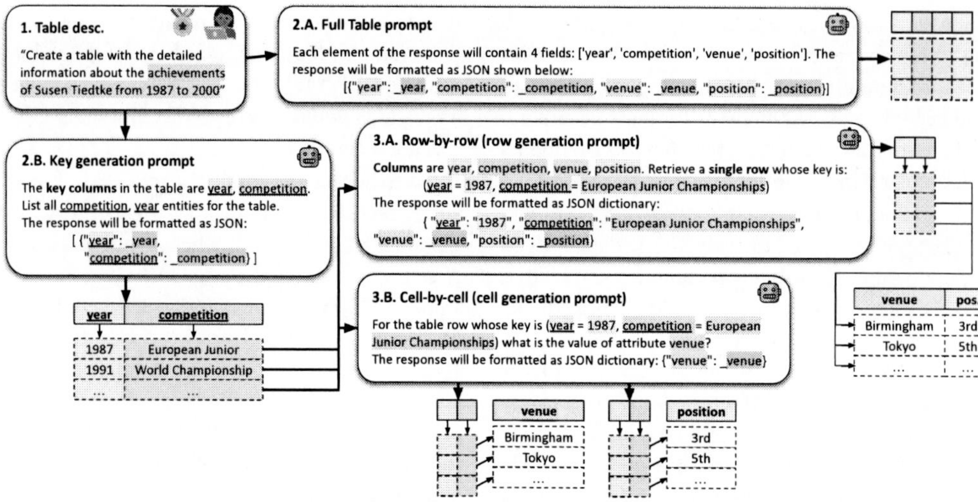

Figure 2: An overview of our three separate prompting methods for table generation, given a short user description and table metadata (Fig. 1): (2.A) Full table directly generates the table given the user desc. and its columns; (2.B) Key-generation is used in both the row-by-row and cell-by-cell methods; (3.A) Row-by-row generates a table row given a unique key value, e.g. (1987, EU Junior Championship); (3.B) Cell-by-cell generates a single table cell given a key value and specific target column e.g. *venue* → *Birmingham*.

i.e. to generate all values of the key columns C_k. As key values are a unique identifier for each table entry (§2), we then prompt a second instance of the LLM, to generate a full table row given a key value. Thus, for each key value $\hat{r}_i[C_k]$ generated by the first LLM, we generate a subsequent prompt to retrieve the remaining row entries $\hat{r}_i[C \setminus C_k]$. Overall, we are required to generate $|\hat{R}| + 1$ prompts, where $|\hat{R}|$ is the number of key values output by the key generation LLM.

In Fig. 2, box 2.B describes the key generation prompt. Given the table description, and key columns *competition* and *year*, the LLM generates a list of corresponding years and competitions which Susen Tiedtke participated in. Next, each key value returned by the first LLM, is used to generate the remaining row entries. Prompt 3.A prompts the row generation LLM to populate columns `venue`, `position` which correspond to key ⟨*"European Junior"*, *"1987"*⟩. The generated values being *"Birmingham"*, and "3rd". A new row-by-row prompt is then generated for the following keys, e.g. ⟨*"World Championship"*, *"1991"*⟩.

(c) Cell-by-cell. This two-stage approach generates each table cell individually. The first stage is identical to row-by-row, using prompt 2.B to generate all key column values. Then, we use a separate prompt for each table cell, rather than a full row. For each column $c \in C \setminus C_k$ we create a dedicated prompt to generate the cell $\hat{r}_i[c]$, based on the target column and the generated key for r_i. In total, we use $|\hat{R}| \cdot |C \setminus C_k| + 1$ prompts, one to generate the keys, and $|\hat{R}| \cdot |C \setminus C_k|$ to generate each of the non-key cells.

Prompt 3.B in Fig. 2 describes the cell-by-cell method. Given key ⟨*"European Junior"*, *"1987"*⟩, the corresponding cell in column `venue` is generated (*Birmingham*). The same prompt is then used for different keys and columns (`position`).

Generated Output Format. When prompting the LLM it is instructed to return its output in JSON format, as shown in Fig. 2. We chose JSON following past work (Singha et al., 2023) and based on our own results. Namely, we observed a better performance compared to formats such as CSV and SQL when evaluated on our held-out development set (see §4). For the row-by-row and cell-by-cell methods, we process and merge all individual JSON responses to construct the full output table.

4 WikiTabGen Benchmark

To evaluate our methods (§3), we introduce a new table generation benchmark called WikiTabGen. Each instance of WikiTabGen consists of a short manually written description d, a list of target columns C and a corresponding table $T = (R, C)$. As this benchmark targets LLM table generation based on their parametric knowledge, we followed

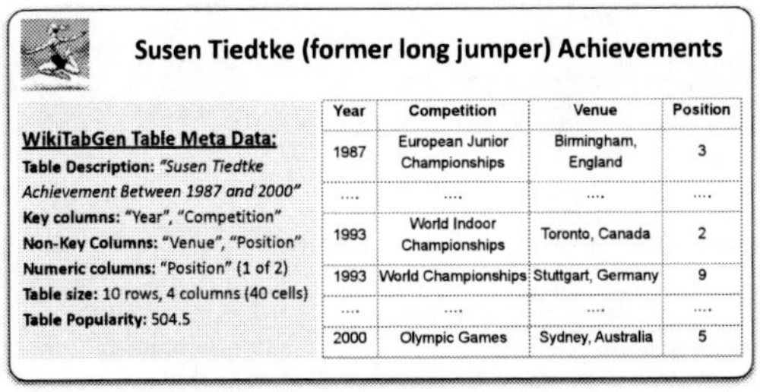

Figure 3: WIKITABGEN example table and metadata.

several key principles in its construction:

- Information Coverage: evaluation tables must contain complete information to prevent cases where the LLM generates correct entries that are not present in the ground-truth tables.
- Factual Consistency: tables should include static factual data, to ensure consistent evaluation over time as LLMs evolve (Zhang and Choi, 2021).
- Conciseness: table cells should contain concise string, categorical or numeric information, to avoid lengthy descriptive text that is harder to evaluate against the ground truth.
- Diversity: the benchmark should include a diverse range of tables with respect to structural properties such as size, data types (e.g., the ratio of numeric data), and table "popularity" which may indicate the prevalence of its content during the LLM's pre-training (Mallen et al., 2022).

Following these principles, we opted to use tables from Wikipedia, as our evaluation benchmark. Wikipedia is often used to assess LLMs' closed-book performance because it contains factual and objective information (Kwiatkowski et al., 2019). unlike certain domain-specific datasets (Yu et al., 2018). Additionally, since Wikipedia is part of LLMs' pre-training data (Brown et al., 2020; Touvron et al., 2023a), it is ideal for evaluating how well these models can generate tabular data.

To construct the benchmark, we iterate over the Wikipedia tables provided by Bhagavatula et al. (2015).[2] We first discarded all non-relational tables (those with composite headers, nested tables, or inverted tables) and excluded tables that were too small ($|R| < 10$ or $|C| < 2$).

Next, we manually selected 119 random tables with diverse number of columns, rows and portion of numeric values (numbers and dates). To ensure evaluation coverage we removed columns with partial entries. In addition, columns containing long texts were omitted to ensure a concise evaluation. Each table was manually annotated with a short, natural language description, as original captions were often ambiguous or not descriptive. Additionally, for tables that could change over time (e.g. new NBA championship teams), we ensured temporal specificity, as suggested by Zhang and Choi (2021), e.g. "*George Clooney Films released between 1983 and 2013*"

As shown in Fig. 3, each table in WIKITABGEN is provided with additional metadata, consisting of its: text description; table size (number of columns, rows and cells); key-columns; numeric columns (containing numbers or dates); and table popularity. Inspired by Mallen et al. (2022), we define table popularity as the average number of monthly views to the Wikipedia page containing the said table. To measure pages views we use the Wikipedia API.[3]

Overall, WIKITABGEN consists of 119 examples, with 100 used for evaluation (§5) and the remaining 19 serving as a held-out development set for method implementation. In Fig. 4 shows the distribution of three key properties in WIKITABGEN: size, numeric column ratio and popularity. On average, the evaluation tables have 77.5 rows, 6.9 columns and 453 cells, with an average length of 1,497 tokens. The average proportion of numeric columns per table is 62% of columns, showcasing the prevalence of numerical data in our tables. The average number of monthly views per table is 8,449. In §6 we further explore the effects of these properties on table generation performance.

5 Experimental Setting

We describe our experimental setting for evaluating the table generation capabilities of LLMs. All models were evaluated on the WIKITABGEN benchmark. Next, we list the LLMs, prompts and evaluation methods used for table generation. Last, we detail our different experimental scenarios.

5.1 Language Models and Prompts

In our experiments we evaluate 8 popular LLMs: three closed-weights models by OpenAI (Achiam et al., 2023): GPT-4o, GPT-4-Turbo, GPT3.5; four open-weights LLMs by MetaAI (Touvron et al., 2023b): Llama3.1-405B, Llama3.1-70B, Llama2-70B, and Llama2-13B; and Gemma2-27B, an open-weights LLM by Google (Riviere et al., 2024).

The same prompting methods described in §3 were used across all LLMs, whereas prompt-

[2]Creative Commons Attribution 4.0 International License.

[3]https://api.wikimedia.org

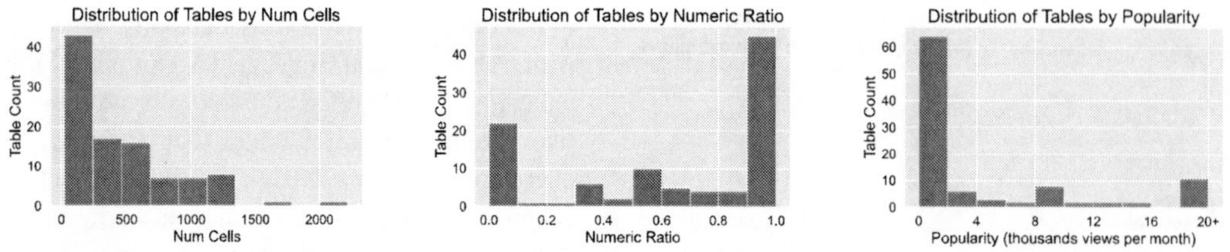

(a) Number of cells per table (b) Numeric columns ratio (c) Table popularity

Figure 4: WIKITABGEN properties distribution: number of cells, ratio of numeric columns, and table popularity.

engineering was done specifically for each model, using the held-out development set as described in §4. For all LLMs, we set the generation temperature to zero.

5.2 Evaluation Methods

Since the order of the rows and columns in the generated table may not match the ground truth, we use the following two-step process to evaluate the generation accuracy: We align rows by key attributes, then match non-key cells.

In more detail, given output table $\hat{T}(\hat{R}, C)$ and ground-truth table $T(R, C)$, we first align the rows $\hat{R}$ to their corresponding rows in R by matching their respective keys, namely $\hat{r} \rightsquigarrow r \iff \hat{r}[C_k] = r[C_k]$. For rows with multiple key columns, all values must be identical.

We then use two methods to evaluate the accuracy of cell content: *(1) exact matching*, in which we check for exact match for string content, but allow for a $\pm 0.1\%$ error for numeric content (in §B, we describe how we compare date values and handle null, missing and duplicate cells). *(2) semantic matching*, in which we first apply text-embedding on the generated and gold cell tokens, then compute the cosine similarity between them. We chose a threshold of 0.5 as our criteria for determining whether the two cells are semantically aligned.

For both matching methods we then calculate Table Precision as $\frac{\text{\# Correct Cells}}{\text{\# Generated Cells}}$, and Table Recall as $\frac{\text{\# Correct Cells}}{\text{\# Ground-Truth Cells}}$ and corresponding F1 score.

For our analysis in §6, we also consider the precision, recall, and F1 scores separately for *keys* and *non-keys*. The *keys* scores are calculated based on the number of matching keys, where for each row all the cells of C_k must match. For non-key cell scores we consider only cells in $C \backslash C_k$. We provide the full formulas in Appendix B.

5.3 Table Generation Scenarios

In addition to the table generation scenario described in §2, where the generation request contains only the table description and list of columns, we considered two alternative scenarios where additional information is provided to the LLM:

Table Row Example. In this scenario, in addition to the description and list of columns, we also provide the LLM with an example row $r[C]$ from the target table. We examine if such an example improves the LLM's performance in generating the rest of the table. We tested this scenario on all prompting methods (§3) by concatenating the first row of the target table to the table description.

Oracle Keys. This ablation provides the LLM the ground-truth set of keys cells $R[C_k]$ and measures the model's performance in generating the remaining cells. This scenario is particularly relevant for applications where the keys are known in advance, and the task involves filling in the associated data. We conducted this experiment for both the row-by-row and cell-by-cell prompting methods by skipping the keys generation prompt (prompt 2.B in Fig. 2), and providing the ground-truth keys instead.

6 Results and Analysis

Following, we summarize results obtained by the 8 LLMs, 3 prompting methods and two evaluation metrics. We then analyze the generation cost and accuracy trade-offs of the prompting methods. Next, we discuss the table generation performance in our additional scenarios: *example row* and *oracle keys*, and finally, examine the effect of table properties on the LLM generation performance.

6.1 Main Results

Tab. 1 provides a comparison of the overall F1 scores for the eight LLMs highlighting the best performing prompting method for each model (using

LLM	Method	Overall F1 (%)	
		Exact	Semantic
LLaMa3.1-405B	Full table	**23.4**	**25.4**
GPT-4o	Row-by-row	20.8	23.1
LLaMa3.1-70B	Full table	20.0	22.1
GPT4-Turbo	Row-by-row	18.9	21.6
GPT3.5-Turbo	Full table	16.1	18.0
LLaMa2-70b	Row-by-row	9.4	10.5
Gemma2-27B	Row-by-row	7.6	8.4
LLaMa2-13b	Full table	7.5	8.4

Table 1: Ranking of 8 different LLMs based on their overall F1 score (for both exact and semantic matching of tabe cells). For each LLM we only list only its best performing method.

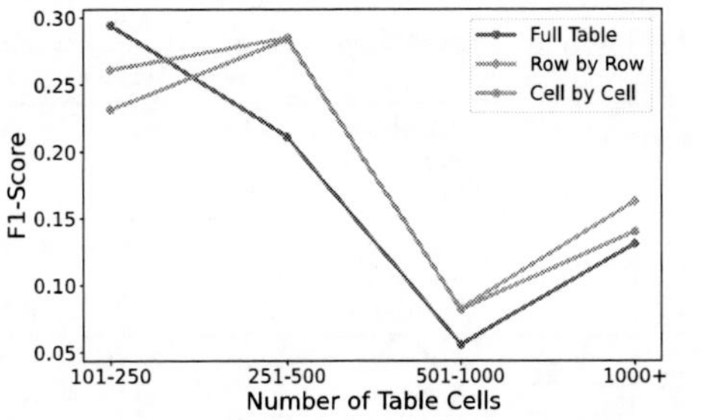

Figure 5: The performance of each prompting method for LLaMa3.1-405B with respect to the table size.

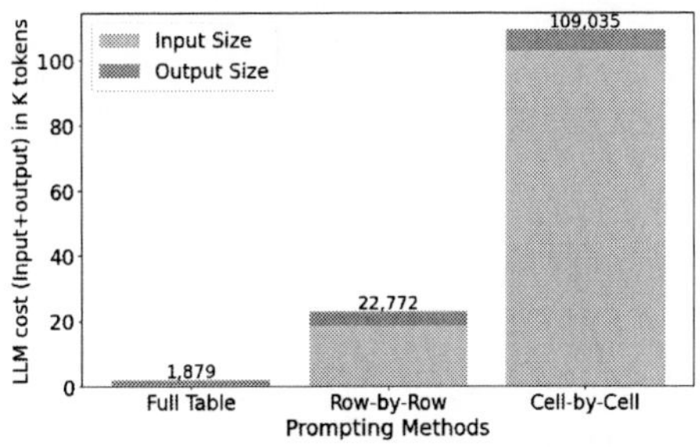

Figure 6: Cost analysis of our prompting methods.

both the exact and semantic evaluation). The top-performing model is LLaMa3.1-405B (full-table), achieving 23.4% and 25.4% F1 using the exact and semantic evaluation respectively.

We note that across all models, the semantic and exact scores are highly correlated, (semantic matching typically being approximately 10% higher than the exact score). We focus through the rest of this section on the semantic evaluation, and the top-4 performing models.

Next, Tab. 2 provides a breakdown of the performance results of the top-4 models. We list the precision, recall, and F1 scores for keys, non-keys, and the full tables (averaged across all tables), obtained for each model and prompting method.

For all LLMs, we observe that the row-by-row and cell-by-cell methods significantly improve the *keys* generation performance (see keys F1 scores in Tab. 2). Interestingly, for the two LLaMa models best performance is obtained with the full-table method, whereas for the GPT models row-by-row prompting obtained better results. Also, observe that the key generation performance is about 3X better than the non-keys, for all models. This demonstrate the inherent difficulty of current LLMs in accurately retrieving the "data" for tabular entities (as identified by the key attributes).

6.2 Prompting Cost Tradeoff

We analyze the performance of our prompting methods as a function of their accuracy and cost. As the row-by-row and cell-by-cell methods are suggested to handle larger tables. In Fig. 5 we examine their performance compared to the full-table method, focusing on tables with 100 or more cells on the best performing model, LLaMa3.1-405B. For medium-sized tables (100-250 cells), full-table still outperforms row-by-row. However, as the number of cells increases further, row-by-row outperforms full-table.

Next, to evaluate the cost of the prompting methods, we examine the average number of input and output tokens used for generating tables, as described in Fig. 6. While the output number of tokens is roughly similar for all approaches, see that the two-stage methods (row-by-row and cell-by-cell) have a significantly larger input due to the repeated use of distinct row and cell generation prompts (prompts 3.A, 3.B in Fig. 2).

6.3 Additional Generation Scenarios

We measure the effect of providing additional information during table generation: (1) an example row, (2) the ground-truth table keys.

Table Row Example. Tab. 3 lists the performance results when including an example row from the target table[4]. Cell-by-cell scores were omitted due to higher costs and inferior performance, as discussed in §6.2. We note that performance consistently improves when the models are given an example first row, except for GPT4-o (row-by-row), which performs slightly better given no example.

[4]As we omit the example row from the F1 calculations our

LLM	Method	Keys			Non-Keys			Overall		
		Recall	Precision	F1	Recall	Precision	F1	Recall	Precision	F1
GPT4-Turbo	Full table	43.4%	66.1%	46.8%	12.1%	20.6%	13.3%	18.0%	28.4%	19.4%
	Row-by-row	53.9%	57.6%	**53.2%**	14.9%	18.5%	**15.3%**	21.4%	25.0%	**21.6%**
	Cell-by-cell	53.9%	57.6%	**53.2%**	13.5%	17.0%	13.8%	20.1%	23.6%	20.2%
GPT-4o	Full table	35.8%	66.0%	40.3%	11.1%	23.6%	12.9%	15.7%	30.8%	17.9%
	Row-by-row	53.9%	60.8%	**53.5%**	16.3%	21.3%	**16.8%**	22.8%	28.0%	**23.1%**
	Cell-by-cell	53.9%	60.7%	**53.5%**	15.8%	20.6%	16.3%	22.3%	27.3%	22.5%
LLaMa3.1-70B	Full table	46.1%	63.8%	49.9%	14.3%	21.4%	**16.0%**	20.1%	28.6%	**22.1%**
	Row-by-row	50.2%	55.5%	**50.0%**	14.3%	16.6%	14.3%	20.6%	23.3%	20.5%
	Cell-by-cell	50.2%	55.3%	**50.0%**	13.0%	14.8%	13.0%	19.4%	21.8%	19.4%
LLaMa3.1-405B	Full table	44.1%	68.6%	48.8%	17.5%	29.0%	**19.8%**	22.7%	36.0%	**25.4%**
	Row-by-row	50.5%	61.5%	**51.7%**	15.1%	20.4%	15.9%	21.2%	27.4%	22.1%
	Cell-by-cell	50.4%	61.4%	51.6%	11.8%	15.5%	12.3%	18.7%	23.7%	19.3%

Table 2: Table generation performance metrics for the different models and prompting methods.

LLM	Method	Keys F1 (%)		Non-Keys F1 (%)		Overall F1 (%)	
		No-Example	Example	No-Example	Example	No-Example	Example
GPT4-Turbo	Full table	46.3	**51.9**	13.0	**17.4**	19.2	**23.8**
	Row-by-row	53.0	**54.1**	15.1	**16.4**	21.3	**22.5**
GPT-4o	Full table	39.7	**47.1**	12.6	**16.3**	17.7	**22.0**
	Row-by-row	**53.3**	53.3	**16.7**	16.5	**22.9**	22.8
LLaMa3.1-70B	Full table	49.4	**51.6**	15.5	**18.2**	21.6	**24.2**
	Row-by-row	49.6	**51.6**	14.0	**16.6**	20.2	**22.5**
LLaMa3.1-405B	Full table	47.9	**50.7**	19.2	**25.2**	24.7	**29.8**
	Row-by-row	51.0	**51.9**	15.5	**19.9**	21.6	**25.6**

Table 3: Performance comparison with and without an example row, using full table and row-by-row methods.

LLM	Non-Keys F1 (%)		Overall F1 (%)	
	Base.	Orac.	Base.	Orac.
GPT4-Turbo	11.7	22.9 (+11.2)	18.9	39.2 (+20.3)
GPT-4o	13.8	26.1 (+12.3)	20.8	41.7 (+20.9)
LLaMa3.1-70B	12.2	25.6 (+13.4)	19.0	41.4 (+22.4)
LLaMa3.1-405B	14.1	30.9 (+16.8)	20.7	45.5 (+24.8)

Table 4: Performance comparison of the row-by-row method with and without oracle keys.

Oracle Keys. Tab. 4 describes the performance of all LLMs, using the row-by-row method, when given the ground-truth key values. As expected, the overall F1 scores are significantly higher when using oracle keys, because now $\hat{R}[C_k] = R[C_k]$. We observe an additional improvement in the non-keys F1, which is expected as more table rows were aligned to the target table (given the keys), and thus more cells were successfully matched.

6.4 Table Properties Effect on Performance

As noted in §4, we systematically measure the effect of table properties such as the size, numeric data and table popularity affect the LLM generation performance.

Fig. 7 displays the table F1 scores as a function of the number of table cells, percentage of numerical data columns (number or date cells) and the table popularity score. These results are provided for all four LLMs, using the full-table generation method. As our aim is to measure the effect each property has on the LLM (not to compare different methods). A further breakdown of the properties' effect on the keys and non-keys F1 scores is provided in Appendix §C.

As shown in Fig. 7a, the larger the table, the lower the F1 scores are for all LLMs. In §6.2 we observed this trend to be less apparent for the row-by-row and cell-by-cell methods.

Fig. 7b measures the effect the percentage of columns containing numbers or dates has on performance. We observe a general decreasing trend in F1 as the portion of numerical content is higher. Fig. 7c displays the positive effect of table popularity on performance. This potentially stems from the prevalence of more popular Wikipedia pages (or related entities) in the LLMs' training data. Unsur-

results slightly differ from Tab. 2.

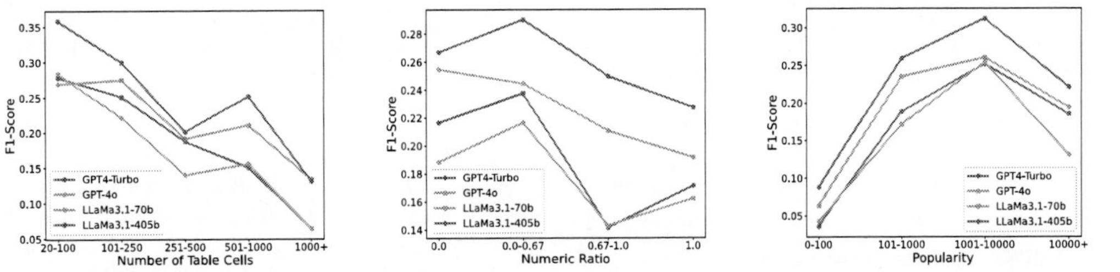

(a) Table Cells Num. (b) Numeric Cols. % (c) Table Popularity Score

Figure 7: The effect of table size, the ratio of numeric columns, and table popularity on the generation performance (F1 score). The results are of the 4 top performing LLMs and using the full-table prompting method.

prising, the less common the tabular information is, the more difficult it is for the LLM to generate. We attribute the slight decrease in F1 on the top popular tables to an artifact of the data in which these tables include census related data which the LLM have difficulty to generate.

From this analysis, we conclude that generating tables from LLMs' parametric knowledge is more challenging when the tables are larger, when they contain a higher portion of numerical data and when its content concerns less popular topics.

7 Related Work

Machine reasoning on table using pre-trained LLMs has largely been explored in the context of data augmentation (Borisov et al., 2022; Zhang et al., 2023) to improve the performance on downstream tasks. The focus has largely been on tasks where a table is provided as input to the model namely: QA over tables (Chen et al., 2020, 2022; Seedat et al., 2023), text-to-SQL translation (Deng et al., 2021; Wolfson et al., 2022), table editing (Li et al., 2023; Sui et al., 2023) and table-to-text generation (Parikh et al., 2020). Conversely, our approach receives only a user query and schema as input, and is tasked with generating an entire table.

Closest to ours are the recent table generation datasets by Pal et al. (2023); Akhtar et al. (2024); Tang et al. (2024). In these works the LLM is provided with a user query (in text or SQL) and is tasked with generating a table, as the query answer. Pal et al. (2023) evaluate on tables from the Spider dataset (Yu et al., 2018), which contains domain-specific information that is less likely to be stored in the parametric knowledge of LLMs. In Tang et al. (2024) the authors evaluate table generation from long-form text describing NBA games, taken from the RotoWire dataset (Wiseman et al., 2017). In their setting the generated table content is already present as part of the user query, where the LLM challenge is to re-structure the user input as a table. By contrast, our setting requires the LLM to generate information that does not explicitly appear in the user input query (Fig. 1). Similar to us, Akhtar et al. (2024) rely on Wikipedia however, they automatically construct new tables which are relatively small (average of 6.7 rows, 4 columns). By comparison our evaluation is on larger tables with the median number of rows being 48 (average of 77.5 rows, 6.9 columns). This emphasizes our focus on extracting long-form tabular data from LLMs, thereby extending past attempts on KBs and text (Cohen et al., 2023; Mallen et al., 2022; Carlini et al., 2022).

Our key generation phase in §3 is an instance of a list question answering problem. The challenge of list QA in LLMs has been explored in recent works (Amouyal et al., 2022; Malaviya et al., 2023). However, we further expand this challenge by focusing on generating the entire table.

8 Conclusion

This paper explores the capability of state-of-the-art LLMs to generate entire tables, by relying exclusively on their parametric knowledge. We introduced three prompt-based table generation methods and evaluated them on our newly constructed benchmark, WIKITABGEN. Our results underscore the challenge table generation poses to LLMs. We hope that WIKITABGEN and our comprehensive analysis will provide a concrete framework for future research on table generation using LLMs.

9 Limitations

We now list the limitations to our work.

Our first limitation is the size of the WIKITABGEN evaluation benchmark, which contains 119 tables. We attribute this constraint to the intensity of the manual processing required to ensure the tables' factual correctness and robustness as well as to the high generation costs of running state-of-the-art LLMs on large tables §6.2. As noted in §4, the tables in WIKITABGEN contain close to 1,500 tokens on average, evaluating them using commercial, state-of-the-art LLMs is non-trivial.

Second, all tables in WIKITABGEN are based on Wikipedia articles. This choice was made to ensure that the underlying information exists in common LLMs training data. However, we did not examine the performance on tables generated from other sources, such as news articles or tables that require multi-source integration.

Acknowledgements

This research was partially funded by a grant from the Data Science Institute at Bar-Ilan University.

References

OpenAI Josh Achiam, Steven Adler, Sandhini Agarwal, Lama Ahmad, Ilge Akkaya, Florencia Leoni Aleman, Diogo Almeida, Janko Altenschmidt, Sam Altman, Shyamal Anadkat, Red Avila, Igor Babuschkin, Suchir Balaji, Valerie Balcom, Paul Baltescu, Haiming Bao, Mo Bavarian, Jeff Belgum, Irwan Bello, Jake Berdine, Gabriel Bernadett-Shapiro, Christopher Berner, Lenny Bogdonoff, Oleg Boiko, Madelaine Boyd, Anna-Luisa Brakman, Greg Brockman, Tim Brooks, Miles Brundage, Kevin Button, Trevor Cai, Rosie Campbell, Andrew Cann, Brittany Carey, Chelsea Carlson, Rory Carmichael, Brooke Chan, Che Chang, Fotis Chantzis, Derek Chen, Sully Chen, Ruby Chen, Jason Chen, Mark Chen, Benjamin Chess, Chester Cho, Casey Chu, Hyung Won Chung, Dave Cummings, Jeremiah Currier, Yunxing Dai, Cory Decareaux, Thomas Degry, Noah Deutsch, Damien Deville, Arka Dhar, David Dohan, Steve Dowling, Sheila Dunning, Adrien Ecoffet, Atty Eleti, Tyna Eloundou, David Farhi, Liam Fedus, Niko Felix, Sim'on Posada Fishman, Juston Forte, Isabella Fulford, Leo Gao, Elie Georges, Christian Gibson, Vik Goel, Tarun Gogineni, Gabriel Goh, Raphael Gontijo-Lopes, Jonathan Gordon, Morgan Grafstein, Scott Gray, Ryan Greene, Joshua Gross, Shixiang Shane Gu, Yufei Guo, Chris Hallacy, Jesse Han, Jeff Harris, Yuchen He, Mike Heaton, Johannes Heidecke, Chris Hesse, Alan Hickey, Wade Hickey, Peter Hoeschele, Brandon Houghton, Kenny Hsu, Shengli Hu, Xin Hu, Joost Huizinga, Shantanu Jain, Shawn Jain, Joanne Jang, Angela Jiang, Roger Jiang, Haozhun Jin, Denny Jin, Shino Jomoto, Billie Jonn, Heewoo Jun, Tomer Kaftan, Lukasz Kaiser, Ali Kamali, Ingmar Kanitscheider, Nitish Shirish Keskar, Tabarak Khan, Logan Kilpatrick, Jong Wook Kim, Christina Kim, Yongjik Kim, Hendrik Kirchner, Jamie Ryan Kiros, Matthew Knight, Daniel Kokotajlo, Lukasz Kondraciuk, Andrew Kondrich, Aris Konstantinidis, Kyle Kosic, Gretchen Krueger, Vishal Kuo, Michael Lampe, Ikai Lan, Teddy Lee, Jan Leike, Jade Leung, Daniel Levy, Chak Ming Li, Rachel Lim, Molly Lin, Stephanie Lin, Mateusz Litwin, Theresa Lopez, Ryan Lowe, Patricia Lue, Anna Adeola Makanju, Kim Malfacini, Sam Manning, Todor Markov, Yaniv Markovski, Bianca Martin, Katie Mayer, Andrew Mayne, Bob McGrew, Scott Mayer McKinney, Christine McLeavey, Paul McMillan, Jake McNeil, David Medina, Aalok Mehta, Jacob Menick, Luke Metz, Andrey Mishchenko, Pamela Mishkin, Vinnie Monaco, Evan Morikawa, Daniel P. Mossing, Tong Mu, Mira Murati, Oleg Murk, David M'ely, Ashvin Nair, Reiichiro Nakano, Rajeev Nayak, Arvind Neelakantan, Richard Ngo, Hyeonwoo Noh, Ouyang Long, Cullen O'Keefe, Jakub W. Pachocki, Alex Paino, Joe Palermo, Ashley Pantuliano, Giambattista Parascandolo, Joel Parish, Emy Parparita, Alexandre Passos, Mikhail Pavlov, Andrew Peng, Adam Perelman, Filipe de Avila Belbute Peres, Michael Petrov, Henrique Pondé de Oliveira Pinto, Michael Pokorny, Michelle Pokrass, Vitchyr H. Pong, Tolly Powell, Alethea Power, Boris Power, Elizabeth Proehl, Raul Puri, Alec Radford, Jack Rae, Aditya Ramesh, Cameron Raymond, Francis Real, Kendra Rimbach, Carl Ross, Bob Rotsted, Henri Roussez, Nick Ryder, Mario D. Saltarelli, Ted Sanders, Shibani Santurkar, Girish Sastry, Heather Schmidt, David Schnurr, John Schulman, Daniel Selsam, Kyla Sheppard, Toki Sherbakov, Jessica Shieh, Sarah Shoker, Pranav Shyam, Szymon Sidor, Eric Sigler, Maddie Simens, Jordan Sitkin, Katarina Slama, Ian Sohl, Benjamin D. Sokolowsky, Yang Song, Natalie Staudacher, Felipe Petroski Such, Natalie Summers, Ilya Sutskever, Jie Tang, Nikolas A. Tezak, Madeleine Thompson, Phil Tillet, Amin Tootoonchian, Elizabeth Tseng, Preston Tuggle, Nick Turley, Jerry Tworek, Juan Felipe Cer'on Uribe, Andrea Vallone, Arun Vijayvergiya, Chelsea Voss, Carroll L. Wainwright, Justin Jay Wang, Alvin Wang, Ben Wang, Jonathan Ward, Jason Wei, CJ Weinmann, Akila Welihinda, Peter Welinder, Jiayi Weng, Lilian Weng, Matt Wiethoff, Dave Willner, Clemens Winter, Samuel Wolrich, Hannah Wong, Lauren Workman, Sherwin Wu, Jeff Wu, Michael Wu, Kai Xiao, Tao Xu, Sarah Yoo, Kevin Yu, Qiming Yuan, Wojciech Zaremba, Rowan Zellers, Chong Zhang, Marvin Zhang, Shengjia Zhao, Tianhao Zheng, Juntang Zhuang, William Zhuk, and Barret Zoph. 2023. Gpt-4 technical report.

Mubashara Akhtar, Chenxi Pang, Andreea Marzoca, Yasemin Altun, and Julian Martin Eisenschlos. 2024. Tanq: An open domain dataset of table answered questions.

Badr AlKhamissi, Millicent Li, Asli Celikyilmaz, Mona T. Diab, and Marjan Ghazvininejad. 2022. A review on language models as knowledge bases. ArXiv, abs/2204.06031.

Samuel Joseph Amouyal, Tomer Wolfson, Ohad Rubin, Ori Yoran, Jonathan Herzig, and Jonathan Berant. 2022. Qampari: : An open-domain question answering benchmark for questions with many answers from multiple paragraphs. ArXiv, abs/2205.12665.

Jonathan Berant, Daniel Deutch, Amir Globerson, Tova Milo, and Tomer Wolfson. 2018. Explaining queries over web tables to non-experts. 2019 IEEE 35th International Conference on Data Engineering (ICDE), pages 1570–1573.

Chandra Bhagavatula, Thanapon Noraset, and Doug Downey. 2015. Tabel: Entity linking in web tables. In International Workshop on the Semantic Web.

Vadim Borisov, Kathrin Seßler, Tobias Leemann, Martin Pawelczyk, and Gjergji Kasneci. 2022. Language models are realistic tabular data generators. ArXiv, abs/2210.06280.

Tom B. Brown, Benjamin Mann, Nick Ryder, Melanie Subbiah, Jared Kaplan, Prafulla Dhariwal, Arvind Neelakantan, Pranav Shyam, Girish Sastry, Amanda Askell, Sandhini Agarwal, Ariel Herbert-Voss, Gretchen Krueger, Tom Henighan, Rewon Child, Aditya Ramesh, Daniel M. Ziegler, Jeffrey Wu, Clemens Winter, Christopher Hesse, Mark Chen, Eric Sigler, Mateusz Litwin, Scott Gray, Benjamin Chess, Jack Clark, Christopher Berner, Sam McCandlish, Alec Radford, Ilya Sutskever, and Dario Amodei. 2020. Language models are few-shot learners. In Advances in Neural Information Processing Systems 33: Annual Conference on Neural Information Processing Systems 2020, NeurIPS 2020, December 6-12, 2020, virtual.

Nicholas Carlini, Daphne Ippolito, Matthew Jagielski, Katherine Lee, Florian Tramèr, and Chiyuan Zhang. 2022. Quantifying memorization across neural language models. ArXiv, abs/2202.07646.

Wenhu Chen, Hanwen Zha, Zhiyu Chen, Wenhan Xiong, Hong Wang, and William Yang Wang. 2020. Hybridqa: A dataset of multi-hop question answering over tabular and textual data. In Findings.

Zhiyu Chen, Wenhu Chen, Charese Smiley, Sameena Shah, Iana Borova, Dylan Langdon, Reema N Moussa, Matthew I. Beane, Ting-Hao 'Kenneth' Huang, Bryan R. Routledge, and William Yang Wang. 2021. Finqa: A dataset of numerical reasoning over financial data. ArXiv, abs/2109.00122.

Zhiyu Chen, Shiyang Li, Charese Smiley, Zhiqiang Ma, Sameena Shah, and William Yang Wang. 2022. ConvFinQA: Exploring the chain of numerical reasoning in conversational finance question answering. In Proceedings of the 2022 Conference on Empirical Methods in Natural Language Processing, pages 6279–6292, Abu Dhabi, United Arab Emirates. Association for Computational Linguistics.

Aakanksha Chowdhery, Sharan Narang, Jacob Devlin, Maarten Bosma, Gaurav Mishra, Adam Roberts, Paul Barham, Hyung Won Chung, Charles Sutton, Sebastian Gehrmann, Parker Schuh, Kensen Shi, Sasha Tsvyashchenko, Joshua Maynez, Abhishek Rao, Parker Barnes, Yi Tay, Noam M. Shazeer, Vinodkumar Prabhakaran, Emily Reif, Nan Du, Benton C. Hutchinson, Reiner Pope, James Bradbury, Jacob Austin, Michael Isard, Guy Gur-Ari, Pengcheng Yin, Toju Duke, Anselm Levskaya, Sanjay Ghemawat, Sunipa Dev, Henryk Michalewski, Xavier García, Vedant Misra, Kevin Robinson, Liam Fedus, Denny Zhou, Daphne Ippolito, David Luan, Hyeontaek Lim, Barret Zoph, Alexander Spiridonov, Ryan Sepassi, David Dohan, Shivani Agrawal, Mark Omernick, Andrew M. Dai, Thanumalayan Sankaranarayana Pillai, Marie Pellat, Aitor Lewkowycz, Erica Moreira, Rewon Child, Oleksandr Polozov, Katherine Lee, Zongwei Zhou, Xuezhi Wang, Brennan Saeta, Mark Díaz, Orhan Firat, Michele Catasta, Jason Wei, Kathleen S. Meier-Hellstern, Douglas Eck, Jeff Dean, Slav Petrov, and Noah Fiedel. 2022. Palm: Scaling language modeling with pathways. ArXiv, abs/2204.02311.

Edgar F Codd. 1990. The relational model for database management: version 2. Addison-Wesley Longman Publishing Co., Inc.

Roi Cohen, Mor Geva, Jonathan Berant, and Amir Globerson. 2023. Crawling the internal knowledge-base of language models. In Findings.

Xiang Deng, Ahmed Hassan Awadallah, Christopher Meek, Oleksandr Polozov, Huan Sun, and Matthew Richardson. 2021. Structure-grounded pretraining for text-to-SQL. In Proceedings of the 2021 Conference of the North American Chapter of the Association for Computational Linguistics: Human Language Technologies, pages 1337–1350, Online. Association for Computational Linguistics.

Yanai Elazar, Akshita Bhagia, Ian H. Magnusson, Abhilasha Ravichander, Dustin Schwenk, Alane Suhr, Pete Walsh, Dirk Groeneveld, Luca Soldaini, Sameer Singh, Hanna Hajishirzi, Noah A. Smith, and Jesse Dodge. 2023. What's in my big data? ArXiv, abs/2310.20707.

Xi Fang, Weijie Xu, Fiona Anting Tan, Jiani Zhang, Ziqing Hu, Yanjun Qi, Scott Nickleach, Diego Socolinsky, Srinivasan Sengamedu, and Christos Faloutsos. 2024. Large language models(llms) on tabular data: Prediction, generation, and understanding - a survey. ArXiv, abs/2402.17944.

Alistair E. W. Johnson, Tom J. Pollard, Lu Shen, Li wei H. Lehman, Mengling Feng, Mohammad Mahdi Ghassemi, Benjamin Moody, Peter Szolovits, Leo Anthony Celi, and Roger G. Mark. 2016. Mimic-iii, a freely accessible critical care database. Scientific Data, 3.

Saurav Kadavath, Tom Conerly, Amanda Askell, T. J. Henighan, Dawn Drain, Ethan Perez, Nicholas Schiefer, Zachary Dodds, Nova DasSarma, Eli Tran-Johnson, Scott Johnston, Sheer El-Showk, Andy Jones, Nelson Elhage, Tristan Hume, Anna Chen, Yuntao Bai, Sam Bowman, Stanislav Fort, Deep Ganguli, Danny Hernandez, Josh Jacobson, John Kernion, Shauna Kravec, Liane Lovitt, Kamal Ndousse, Catherine Olsson, Sam Ringer, Dario Amodei, Tom B. Brown, Jack Clark, Nicholas Joseph, Benjamin Mann, Sam McCandlish, Christopher Olah, and Jared Kaplan. 2022. Language models (mostly) know what they know. ArXiv, abs/2207.05221.

Tushar Khot, Harsh Trivedi, Matthew Finlayson, Yao Fu, Kyle Richardson, Peter Clark, and Ashish Sabharwal. 2022. Decomposed prompting: A modular approach for solving complex tasks. ArXiv preprint, abs/2210.02406.

Tushar Khot, Harsh Trivedi, Matthew Finlayson, Yao Fu, Kyle Richardson, Peter Clark, and Ashish Sabharwal. 2023. Decomposed prompting: A modular approach for solving complex tasks.

Tom Kwiatkowski, Jennimaria Palomaki, Olivia Redfield, Michael Collins, Ankur Parikh, Chris Alberti, Danielle Epstein, Illia Polosukhin, Jacob Devlin, Kenton Lee, Kristina Toutanova, Llion Jones, Matthew Kelcey, Ming-Wei Chang, Andrew M. Dai, Jakob Uszkoreit, Quoc Le, and Slav Petrov. 2019. Natural questions: A benchmark for question answering research. Transactions of the Association for Computational Linguistics, 7:452–466.

Patrick Lewis, Ethan Perez, Aleksandara Piktus, Fabio Petroni, Vladimir Karpukhin, Naman Goyal, Heinrich Kuttler, Mike Lewis, Wen tau Yih, Tim Rocktäschel, Sebastian Riedel, and Douwe Kiela. 2020. Retrieval-augmented generation for knowledge-intensive nlp tasks. ArXiv, abs/2005.11401.

Peng Li, Yeye He, Dror Yashar, Weiwei Cui, Song Ge, Haidong Zhang, Danielle Rifinski Fainman, Dongmei Zhang, and Surajit Chaudhuri. 2023. Table-gpt: Table-tuned gpt for diverse table tasks. ArXiv, abs/2310.09263.

Chaitanya Malaviya, Peter Shaw, Ming-Wei Chang, Kenton Lee, and Kristina Toutanova. 2023. Quest: A retrieval dataset of entity-seeking queries with implicit set operations. ArXiv, abs/2305.11694.

Alex Troy Mallen, Akari Asai, Victor Zhong, Rajarshi Das, Hannaneh Hajishirzi, and Daniel Khashabi. 2022. When not to trust language models: Investigating effectiveness of parametric and non-parametric memories. In Annual Meeting of the Association for Computational Linguistics.

Linyong Nan, Chiachun Hsieh, Ziming Mao, Xi Victoria Lin, Neha Verma, Rui Zhang, Wojciech Kryściński, Hailey Schoelkopf, Riley Kong, Xiangru Tang, Mutethia Mutuma, Ben Rosand, Isabel Trindade, Renusree Bandaru, Jacob Cunningham, Caiming Xiong, Dragomir Radev, and Dragomir Radev. 2022. FeTaQA: Free-form table question answering. Transactions of the Association for Computational Linguistics, 10:35–49.

Vaishali Pal, Andrew Yates, E. Kanoulas, and M. de Rijke. 2023. Multitabqa: Generating tabular answers for multi-table question answering. In Annual Meeting of the Association for Computational Linguistics.

Ankur Parikh, Xuezhi Wang, Sebastian Gehrmann, Manaal Faruqui, Bhuwan Dhingra, Diyi Yang, and Dipanjan Das. 2020. ToTTo: A controlled table-to-text generation dataset. In Proceedings of the 2020 Conference on Empirical Methods in Natural Language Processing (EMNLP), pages 1173–1186, Online. Association for Computational Linguistics.

Panupong Pasupat and Percy Liang. 2015. Compositional semantic parsing on semi-structured tables. In Annual Meeting of the Association for Computational Linguistics.

Fabio Petroni, Tim Rocktäschel, Sebastian Riedel, Patrick Lewis, Anton Bakhtin, Yuxiang Wu, and Alexander Miller. 2019. Language models as knowledge bases? In Proceedings of the 2019 Conference on Empirical Methods in Natural Language Processing and the 9th International Joint Conference on Natural Language Processing (EMNLP-IJCNLP), pages 2463–2473, Hong Kong, China. Association for Computational Linguistics.

Gemma Team Morgane Riviere, Shreya Pathak, Pier Giuseppe Sessa, Cassidy Hardin, Surya Bhupatiraju, L'eonard Hussenot, Thomas Mesnard, Bobak Shahriari, Alexandre Ram'e, Johan Ferret, Peter Liu, Pouya Dehghani Tafti, Abe Friesen, Michelle Casbon, Sabela Ramos, Ravin Kumar, Charline Le Lan, Sammy Jerome, Anton Tsitsulin, Nino Vieillard, Piotr Stańczyk, Sertan Girgin, Nikola Momchev, Matt Hoffman, Shantanu Thakoor, Jean-Bastien Grill, Behnam Neyshabur, Alanna Walton, Aliaksei Severyn, Alicia Parrish, Aliya Ahmad, Allen Hutchison, Alvin Abdagic, Amanda Carl, Amy Shen, Andy Brock, Andy Coenen, Anthony Laforge, Antonia Paterson, Ben Bastian, Bilal Piot, Boxi Wu, Brandon Royal, Charlie Chen, Chintu Kumar, Chris Perry, Christoper A. Welty, Christopher A. Choquette-Choo, Danila Sinopalnikov, David Weinberger, Dimple Vijaykumar, Dominika Rogozi'nska, D. Herbison, Elisa Bandy, Emma Wang, Eric Noland, Erica Moreira, Evan Senter, Evgenii Eltyshev, Francesco Visin, Gabriel Rasskin, Gary Wei, Glenn Cameron, Gus Martins, Hadi Hashemi, Hanna Klimczak-Pluci'nska, Harleen Batra, Harsh Dhand, Ivan Nardini, Jacinda Mein, Jack Zhou, James Svensson, Jeff Stanway, Jetha Chan, Jin Zhou, Joana Carrasqueira, Joana Iljazi, Jocelyn Becker, Joe Fernandez, Joost R. van Amersfoort, Josh Gordon, Josh Lipschultz, Joshua Newlan, Junsong Ji, Kareem Mohamed, Kartikeya Badola, Kat Black, Katie Millican, Keelin McDonell, Kelvin Nguyen, Kiranbir Sodhia, Kish Greene,

Lars Lowe Sjoesund, Lauren Usui, L. Sifre, L. Heuermann, Leticia Lago, Lilly McNealus, Livio Baldini Soares, Logan Kilpatrick, Lucas Dixon, Luciano Martins, Machel Reid, Manvinder Singh, Mark Iverson, Martin Gorner, Mat Velloso, Mateo Wirth, Matt Davidow, Matt Miller, Matthew Rahtz, Matthew Watson, Meg Risdal, Mehran Kazemi, Michael Moynihan, Ming Zhang, Minsuk Kahng, Minwoo Park, Mofi Rahman, Mohit Khatwani, Natalie Dao, Nenshad Bardoliwalla, Nesh Devanathan, Neta Dumai, Nilay Chauhan, Oscar Wahltinez, Pankil Botarda, Parker Barnes, Paul Barham, Paul Michel, Pengchong Jin, Petko Georgiev, Phil Culliton, Pradeep Kuppala, Ramona Comanescu, Ramona Merhej, Reena Jana, Reza Rokni, Rishabh Agarwal, Ryan Mullins, Samaneh Saadat, S. Mc Carthy, Sarah Perrin, S'ebastien Arnold, Sebastian Krause, Shengyang Dai, Shruti Garg, Shruti Sheth, Sue Ronstrom, Susan Chan, Timothy Jordan, Ting Yu, Tom Eccles, Tom Hennigan, Tomás Kociský, Tulsee Doshi, Vihan Jain, Vikas Yadav, Vilobh Meshram, Vishal Dharmadhikari, Warren Barkley, Wei Wei, Wenming Ye, Woohyun Han, Woosuk Kwon, Xiang Xu, Zhe Shen, Zhitao Gong, Zichuan Wei, Victor Cotruta, Phoebe Kirk, Anand Rao, Minh Giang, Ludovic Peran, Tris Brian Warkentin, Eli Collins, Joelle Barral, Zoubin Ghahramani, Raia Hadsell, D. Sculley, Jeanine Banks, Anca Dragan, Slav Petrov, Oriol Vinyals, Jeffrey Dean, Demis Hassabis, Koray Kavukcuoglu, Cl'ement Farabet, Elena Buchatskaya, Sebastian Borgeaud, Noah Fiedel, Armand Joulin, Kathleen Kenealy, Robert Dadashi, and Alek Andreev. 2024. Gemma 2: Improving open language models at a practical size. ArXiv, abs/2408.00118.

Nabeel Seedat, Nicolas Huynh, Boris van Breugel, and Mihaela van der Schaar. 2023. Curated llm: Synergy of llms and data curation for tabular augmentation in ultra low-data regimes. ArXiv, abs/2312.12112.

Yijia Shao, Yucheng Jiang, Theodore A. Kanell, Peter Xu, Omar Khattab, and Monica S. Lam. 2024. Assisting in writing wikipedia-like articles from scratch with large language models. ArXiv, abs/2402.14207.

Leixian Shen, Enya Shen, Yuyu Luo, Xiaocong Yang, Xuming Hu, Xiongshuai Zhang, Zhiwei Tai, and Jianmin Wang. 2021. Towards natural language interfaces for data visualization: A survey. IEEE Transactions on Visualization and Computer Graphics, 29:3121–3144.

Ananya Singha, José Cambronero, Sumit Gulwani, Vu Le, and Chris Parnin. 2023. Tabular representation, noisy operators, and impacts on table structure understanding tasks in llms.

Yuan Sui, Mengyu Zhou, Mingjie Zhou, Shi Han, and Dongmei Zhang. 2023. Table meets llm: Can large language models understand structured table data? a benchmark and empirical study. In Web Search and Data Mining.

Xiangru Tang, Yiming Zong, Jason Phang, Yilun Zhao, Wangchunshu Zhou, Arman Cohan, and Mark Gerstein. 2024. Struc-bench: Are large language models good at generating complex structured tabular data? In Proceedings of the 2024 Conference of the North American Chapter of the Association for Computational Linguistics: Human Language Technologies (Volume 2: Short Papers), pages 12–34, Mexico City, Mexico. Association for Computational Linguistics.

Hugo Touvron, Thibaut Lavril, Gautier Izacard, Xavier Martinet, Marie-Anne Lachaux, Timothée Lacroix, Baptiste Rozière, Naman Goyal, Eric Hambro, Faisal Azhar, Aur'elien Rodriguez, Armand Joulin, Edouard Grave, and Guillaume Lample. 2023a. Llama: Open and efficient foundation language models. ArXiv, abs/2302.13971.

Hugo Touvron, Louis Martin, Kevin R. Stone, Peter Albert, Amjad Almahairi, Yasmine Babaei, Nikolay Bashlykov, Soumya Batra, Prajjwal Bhargava, Shruti Bhosale, Daniel M. Bikel, Lukas Blecher, Cristian Cantón Ferrer, Moya Chen, Guillem Cucurull, David Esiobu, Jude Fernandes, Jeremy Fu, Wenyin Fu, Brian Fuller, Cynthia Gao, Vedanuj Goswami, Naman Goyal, Anthony S. Hartshorn, Saghar Hosseini, Rui Hou, Hakan Inan, Marcin Kardas, Viktor Kerkez, Madian Khabsa, Isabel M. Kloumann, A. V. Korenev, Punit Singh Koura, Marie-Anne Lachaux, Thibaut Lavril, Jenya Lee, Diana Liskovich, Yinghai Lu, Yuning Mao, Xavier Martinet, Todor Mihaylov, Pushkar Mishra, Igor Molybog, Yixin Nie, Andrew Poulton, Jeremy Reizenstein, Rashi Rungta, Kalyan Saladi, Alan Schelten, Ruan Silva, Eric Michael Smith, R. Subramanian, Xia Tan, Binh Tang, Ross Taylor, Adina Williams, Jian Xiang Kuan, Puxin Xu, Zhengxu Yan, Iliyan Zarov, Yuchen Zhang, Angela Fan, Melanie Kambadur, Sharan Narang, Aurelien Rodriguez, Robert Stojnic, Sergey Edunov, and Thomas Scialom. 2023b. Llama 2: Open foundation and fine-tuned chat models. ArXiv, abs/2307.09288.

Sam Wiseman, Stuart Shieber, and Alexander Rush. 2017. Challenges in data-to-document generation. In Proceedings of the 2017 Conference on Empirical Methods in Natural Language Processing, pages 2253–2263, Copenhagen, Denmark. Association for Computational Linguistics.

Tomer Wolfson, Daniel Deutch, and Jonathan Berant. 2022. Weakly supervised text-to-SQL parsing through question decomposition. In Findings of the Association for Computational Linguistics: NAACL 2022, pages 2528–2542, Seattle, United States. Association for Computational Linguistics.

Ori Yoran, Tomer Wolfson, Ori Ram, and Jonathan Berant. 2023. Making retrieval-augmented language models robust to irrelevant context.

Tao Yu, Rui Zhang, Kai Yang, Michihiro Yasunaga, Dongxu Wang, Zifan Li, James Ma, Irene Li, Qingning Yao, Shanelle Roman, Zilin Zhang, and Dragomir Radev. 2018. Spider: A large-scale human-labeled dataset for complex and cross-domain semantic parsing and text-to-SQL task. In Proceedings of the

2018 Conference on Empirical Methods in Natural Language Processing, pages 3911–3921, Brussels, Belgium. Association for Computational Linguistics.

Michael Zhang and Eunsol Choi. 2021. SituatedQA: Incorporating extra-linguistic contexts into QA. In Proceedings of the 2021 Conference on Empirical Methods in Natural Language Processing, pages 7371–7387, Online and Punta Cana, Dominican Republic. Association for Computational Linguistics.

T. Zhang, Shaowen Wang, Shuicheng Yan, Jian Li, and Qian Liu. 2023. Generative table pre-training empowers models for tabular prediction. ArXiv, abs/2305.09696.

Yilun Zhao, Lyuhao Chen, Arman Cohan, and Chen Zhao. 2024. TaPERA: Enhancing faithfulness and interpretability in long-form table QA by content planning and execution-based reasoning. In Proceedings of the 62nd Annual Meeting of the Association for Computational Linguistics (Volume 1: Long Papers), pages 12824–12840, Bangkok, Thailand. Association for Computational Linguistics.

A Table Generation Prompts

In this section we provide the prompt templates used in each of our table generation methods. Figs. 8-11 present our prompt templates used for: full table generation method, keys generation, row-by-row, and cell-by-cell method.

B Evaluation Method Details

B.1 Precision-Matching of Cell Values

We next describe our precision matching for cell values in more detail, given an output table $\hat{T}(\hat{R}, C)$ and ground-truth table $T(R, C)$.

As described in §5.2, we use *exact* value comparison of cell textual content and allow a $\pm 0.1\%$ error for numeric values. Before comparing textual cells, we first convert them to lower case, and remove non alphanumeric symbols and spaces.

As for date values, we first parse and convert cells with date values to a Python Date object, and then compare the canonical dates. This is to avoid cases where cells are deemed as a non-match due to differences in the date format. For example, in our evaluation process, two date values representing the same date, such as "2014-05-16" and "16th, May, 2014", will be considered the same.

We further treat “none”, “n/a” ,“nan” and empty cells as identical in terms of value matching.

B.2 Precision and Recall Computation for Tables

For a given output table $\hat{T}(\hat{R}, C)$ and ground-truth table $T(R, C)$, we first align the rows $\hat{R}$ to their corresponding rows in R by matching their respective keys, namely $\hat{r} \rightsquigarrow r \iff \hat{r}[C_k] = r[C_k]$. For rows with composite keys, all key values must be identical, i.e., $\forall c_k \in C_k \hat{r}[c_k] = r[c_k]$.

Recall that a *correct* cell in $T(\hat{R}, C)$ is a cell $\hat{r}[c]$ such that $\hat{r}[c] \approx r[c] \wedge \hat{r} \rightsquigarrow r$. Namely, row $\hat{r}$ is aligned with a row r in the ground-truth table, and their corresponding cell values in column c is matching (using either the precision or semantic matching definition).

We next provide the precision and recall formulas we used for keys, non-keys, and tables.

For keys, we compare $\hat{R}[C_k]$ and $R[C_k]$ as follows. Let the number of matching keys $\phi = |\{r \in \hat{R}, \forall c_k \in C_k \; \hat{r}[c_k] = r[c_k]\}|$ Then *keys precision* is calculated by $\frac{\phi}{|\hat{R}|}$ and *keys recall* is given by $\frac{\phi}{|R|}$.

For non-keys, we compare $\hat{R}[C \setminus C_k]$ and $R[C \setminus C_k]$. After aligning $\hat{R}$ and R, we compute the num-

Full-table generation template:
You are a retriever of facts. List all `{table description}`. The response will be formatted as JSON shown below. Each element of the response will contain `{num columns}` fields: `{column1, column2, ...}`
Do not output any additional text that is not in JSON format.
RESPONSE FORMAT: [{ `column1: value1, column2: value2, ... }]`

Full-table generation (populated example):
You are a retriever of facts. List all achievements of Susen Tiedtke from 1987 to 2000. The response will be formatted as JSON shown below. Each element of the response will contain 4 fields: ['year', 'competition', 'venue', 'position']. Do not output any additional text that is not in JSON format.
RESPONSE FORMAT: [{ "year": _year, "competition": _competition, "venue": _venue, "position": _position }]

Figure 8: Full-table generation prompt.

Keys generation template:
You are a retriever of facts. We want to create a table with the detailed information about `{table description}`. The key columns in the table are `{key1, (key2, ...)}`. List all `{key1, (key2, ...)}` entities for the table. The response will be formatted as JSON list shown below.
RESPONSE FORMAT: [{ `key: value1, key2: value2, ... }]`

Keys generation (populated example):
You are a retriever of facts. We want to create a table with the detailed information about achievements of Susen Tiedtke from 1987 to 2000. The key columns in the table are competition, year. List all competition, year entities for the table. The response will be formatted as JSON list shown below.
RESPONSE FORMAT: [{ "competition": _competition, "year": _year }]

Figure 9: Key columns generation prompt.

ber of *correct* keys, denoted by $\psi = |\{(r, c), r \in \hat{R} \wedge c \in C \setminus C_k \wedge r \rightsquigarrow \hat{r} \wedge \hat{r}[c] = r[c]\}|$. Then the *non-keys precision* is calculated by $\frac{\psi}{|\hat{R}[C \setminus C_k]|}$ and *non-keys recall* is calculated by $\frac{\psi}{|R[C \setminus C_k]|}$.

Last, for the table precision and recall, we perform a similar evaluation, now defining the number of correct cells, denoted by τ, as all correct cells in the table. Namely, $\tau = |\{(r, c), r \in \hat{R} \wedge c \in C \wedge r \rightsquigarrow \hat{r} \wedge \hat{r}[c] \approx r[c]\}|$, then the *table precision* is simply calculated by $\frac{\tau}{|\hat{R}[C]|}$ and *table recall* is calculated by $\frac{\tau}{|R[C]|}$.

C Table Properties Effect on Performance

In §6.4 we examine how the table properties such as the size, amount of numeric data, and table popularity affect the generation performance. In Fig. 12 we present the effect of these three properties on both the keys F1, non-keys F1, and full table F1. We can see, for instance, that the table size negatively affects both the keys F1 and the non-keys F1 scores (see Fig. 12 (a) and Fig. 12 (b)), and the ratio of numeric columns has a negative effect, as expected, only the non-keys F1 (see Fig. 12 (e)). The table popularity also have a strong effect on both the keys F1 and the non-keys F1 (Fig. 12 (g) and Fig. 12 (h)).

Row generation template:
You are a retriever of facts. We want to create a table with the detailed information about `{table description}`. Columns in the table are `{columns}`. The key columns in the table are `{key1, (key2, ...)}`. Retrieve a single row whose key is `({key = value})`. The response will be formatted as JSON dictionary shown below. Pay special attention to wrap all values in double quotes!
RESPONSE FORMAT: [{ `column1: value1, column2: value2, ...` }]

Row generation (populated example):
You are a retriever of facts. We want to create a table with the detailed information about achievements of Susen Tiedtke from 1987 to 2000. Columns in the table are year, competition, venue, position. The key columns in the table are competition, year. Retrieve a single row whose key is (year = 1987, competition = World Championships). The response will be formatted as JSON dictionary shown below. Pay special attention to wrap all values in double quotes!
RESPONSE FORMAT: { "year": 1987, "competition": World Championships, "venue": _venue, "position": _position }

Figure 10: Row-by-row (row generation) prompt.

Cell generation template:
You are a retriever of facts. We want to create a table with the detailed information about `{table description}`. Columns in the table are `{column1, column2, ...}`. The key columns in the table are `{key1, (key2, ...)}`. For the table row whose key is is `({key = value})` what is the value of attribute `{column}`. The response will be formatted as JSON dictionary shown below. Pay special attention to wrap all values in double quotes!
RESPONSE FORMAT: { `column: value` }

Cell generation (populated example):
You are a retriever of facts. We want to create a table with the detailed information about achievements of Susen Tiedtke from 1987 to 2000. Columns in the table are year, competition, venue, position. The key columns in the table are competition, year. For the table row whose key is (year = 1987, competition = World Championships) what is the value of attribute venue. The response will be formatted as JSON dictionary shown below. Pay special attention to wrap all values in double quotes!
RESPONSE FORMAT: { "venue": _venue }

Figure 11: Cell-by-cell (cell generation) prompt.

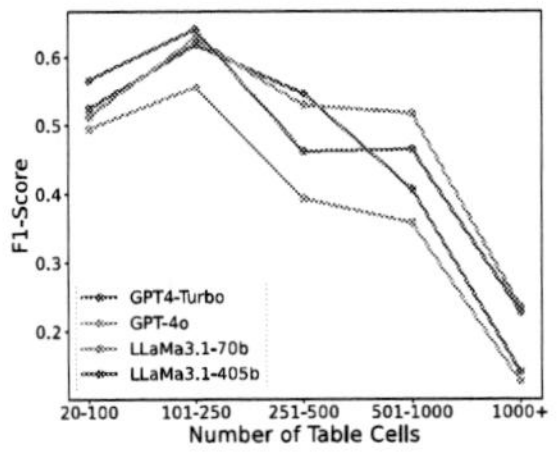

(a) Table Cells Num. - Keys F1

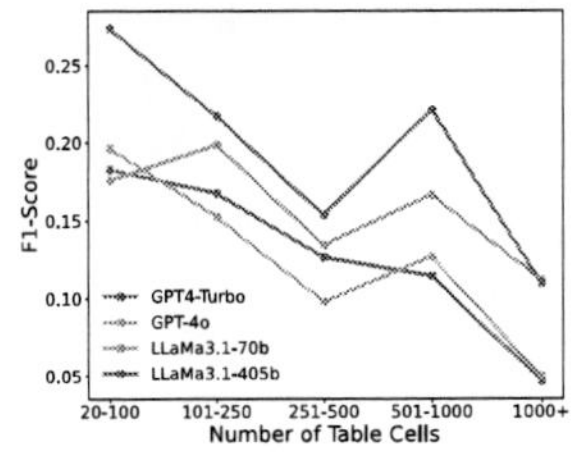

(b) Table Cells Num. - Non-Keys F1

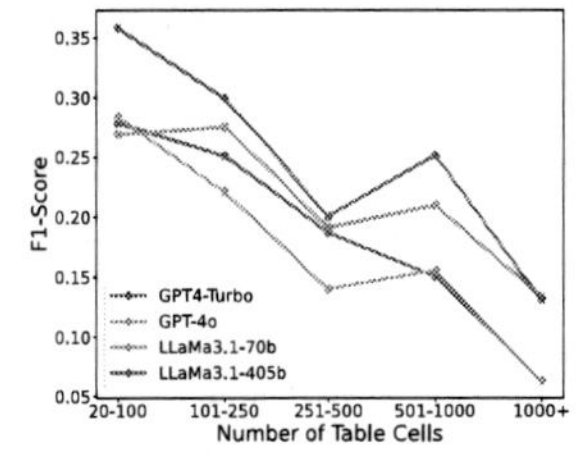

(c) Table Cells Num. - Table F1

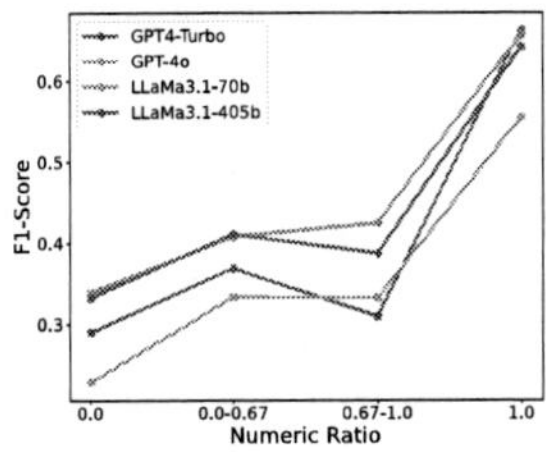

(d) Numeric Cols. % - Keys F1

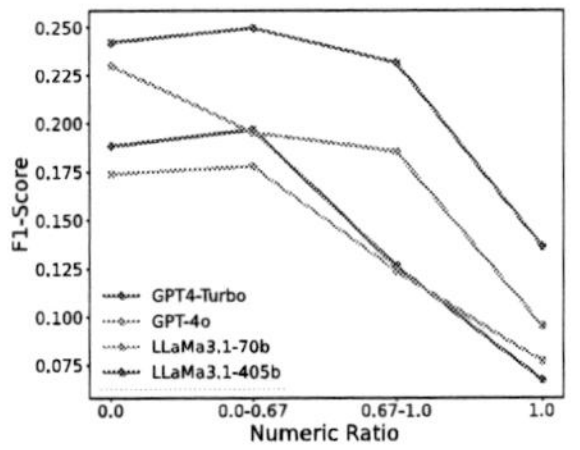

(e) Numeric Cols. % - Non-Keys F1

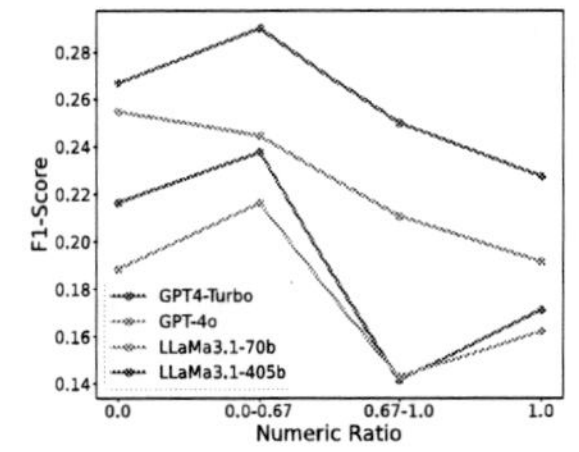

(f) Numeric Cols. % - Table F1

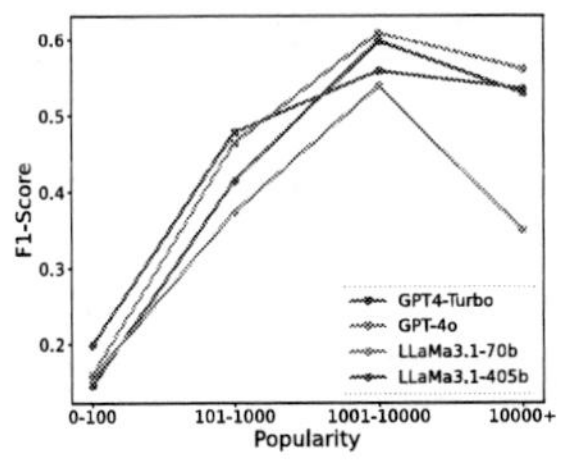

(g) Table Popularity - Keys F1

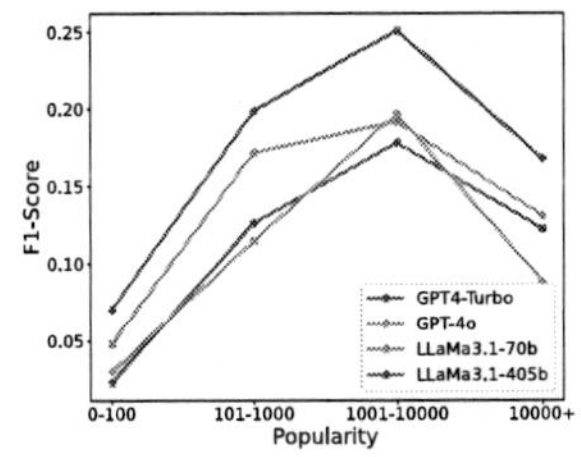

(h) Table Popularity - Non-Keys F1

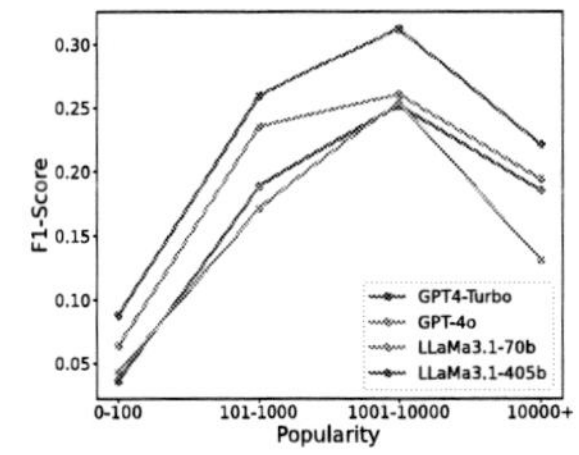

(i) Table Popularity - Table F1

Figure 12: The effect of table size, the ratio of numeric columns, and table popularity on the generation performance of the full-table method, with four different LLMs. Additional breakdown of generation performance based on cells in key columns versus non-key columns.

Investigating Large Language Models for Text-to-SPARQL Generation

Jacopo D'Abramo
Amazon Spain, Spain*
jdabramo@amazon.com

Andrea Zugarini
expert.ai, Italy
azugarini@expert.ai

Paolo Torroni
Department of Computer Science and Engineering,
University of Bologna, Italy
paolo.torroni@unibo.it

Abstract

Large Language Models (LLMs) have demonstrated strong capabilities in code generation, such as translating natural language questions into SQL queries. However, state-of-the-art solutions often involve a costly fine-tuning step. In this study, we extensively evaluate In-Context Learning (ICL) solutions for text-to-SPARQL generation with different architectures and configurations, based on methods for retrieving relevant demonstrations for few-shot prompting and working with multiple generated hypotheses. In this way, we demonstrate that LLMs can formulate SPARQL queries achieving state-of-the-art results on several Knowledge Graph Question Answering (KGQA) benchmark datasets without fine-tuning.

1 Introduction

The advent of Large Language Models (LLMs) has significantly advanced the field of Natural Language Processing (NLP), with particular success in the domain of code generation (Chen et al., 2021; Rozière et al., 2024).

At the same time, the growing complexity and scale of Knowledge Graphs (Pellissier Tanon et al., 2016; Lehmann et al., 2014; Bollacker et al., 2008) highlighted the need for robust and accurate mechanisms to query such data stores, for instance, within Knowledge Graph Question Answering (KGQA) pipelines (Li et al., 2023; Nie et al., 2024).

In this paper, we carry out an extensive evaluation of LLM-based In-Context Learning (ICL) for text-to-SPARQL generation. Text-to-SPARQL is a crucial component of many KGQA systems, that typically make use of different modules to assembly the query, such as Entity and Relation Linking. To this end, we define a simple and modular approach to address the text-to-SPARQL task without fine-tuning. The evaluation is focussed on the following key aspects: (1) the influence of various In-Context Learning strategies on the quality of the generated queries; (2) the impact of different state-of-the-art model backbones, varying in architecture, size, and training data; (3) the potential of beam search to generate multiple query candidates, thereby enhancing the results;(4) a comparison between ICL and specialized models fine-tuned for the task. The code is publicly available at `https://github.com/jacopodabramo/DFSL`.

In the interest of reproducibility, as backbones, we use three state-of-the-art open-weight LLMs: Mixtral 8x7B, Llama-3 70B, and CodeLlama 70B. We run experiments on two widely-used Knowledge Bases, DBpedia and Wikidata, using four publicly available datasets: QALD-9, based on DBpedia, and QALD-9 plus, QALD-10 and LC-QuAD 2.0, based on Wikidata.

Our experimental results demonstrate that LLMs In-Context Learning solutions achieve state-of-the-art results, without the need of any fine-tuning. The injection of demonstrations similar to the input question into the prompt combined with the generation of multiple query candidates directly from beam search hypotheses, yield the best results, exceeding in most of the benchmarks state-of-the-art models fine-tuned for the task. Finally, we also run ablation studies to gauge the effectiveness of the approach without gold information from the EL and RL modules.

2 Related work

We first provide an overview of most related In-Context-Learning approaches. Then, we discuss text-to-SPARQL methods, including KGQA systems that typically make use of text-to-SPARQL techniques to tackle the problem.

*Work done while being at expert.ai.

Proceedings of the 4th International Workshop on Knowledge-Augmented Methods for Natural Language Processing (KnowledgeNLP'25), pages 66–80
May 3, 2025 ©2025 Association for Computational Linguistics

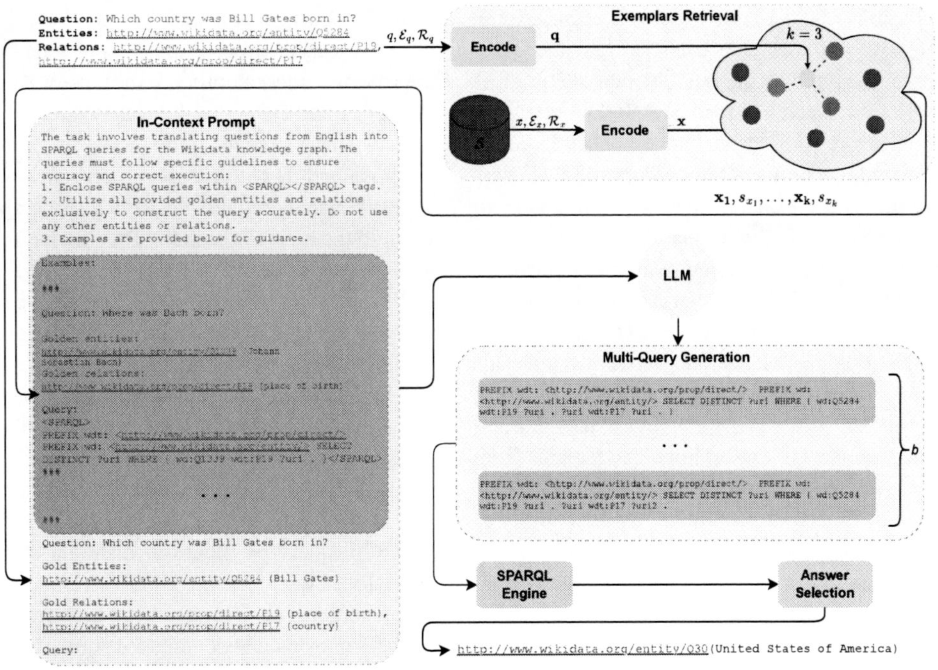

Figure 1: Sketch of the ICL approach. Given a question, its entities and its relations, k-most similar examples are retrieved from a text-to-SPARQL collection $\mathcal{S}$ and injected into the in-context prompt. Then, the LLM generates one or more queries that are all executed by a SPARQL engine. An answer selection strategy identifies which response to pick.

2.1 In-Context Learning

ICL is a paradigm that leverages reasoning through analogies. A task description, question, and demonstration context are usually concatenated to create a prompt, which is then input into an LLM for prediction. Unlike fine-tuning, ICL performs predictions without gradient updates (Dong et al., 2023). Few-Shot Learning is a type of ICL where the demonstration context includes a few examples. Owing to the effectiveness of ICL and the obvious advantage of building systems that don't need domain-specific training, a great deal of research and engineering efforts have been devoted to designing suitable prompts. ICL has been successfully applied to many NLP problems, including QA (Chada and Natarajan, 2021; Chen et al., 2023).

Some studies have also focused on the selection of in-context examples. In particular, Liu et al. (2022) developed KATE, an unsupervised retriever that utilizes k-nearest neighbors and distance metrics (e.g., L2 distance and cosine similarity) to select in-context examples for tasks such as sentiment analysis, table-to-text generation, and question answering. Levy et al. (2023) explored the incorporation of diverse demonstrations into prompts for compositional semantic parsing task, demonstrating that such diversity leads to better structural coverage in target utterances. Kim et al. (2022) leveraged the generative capabilities of pre-trained language models to generate demonstrations for each class in downstream tasks, conditioned on test inputs and class information. Gonen et al. (2022) found that selecting examples based on perplexity, in particular lower perplexity, is an effective strategy.

Similar principles have been adopted in code generation tasks (Cheng et al., 2022), including text-to-SQL (Cheng et al., 2022; Nan et al., 2023; Zhang et al., 2023; Wei et al., 2023) and KGQA (Li et al., 2023). In the same vein, our study investigates ICL strategies to address text-to-SPARQL. However, while all these approaches are based on proprietary LLMs, such as GPT-3, GPT-4 (Brown et al., 2020) and Codex (Chen et al., 2021), we focus on open-weight LLMs.

2.2 Text-to-SPARQL

With the recent wave of decoder-based LLMs such as GPT (Brown et al., 2020), Mixtral (Jiang et al., 2024), and Llama (Touvron et al., 2023), generative AI was also used to translate questions into SPARQL queries. Notably, Zou et al. (2021) introduced a text-to-SPARQL model that leverages a relation-aware attention decoder and a pointer network encoder, incorporating three separate scaled dot-product attention mechanisms to generate SPARQL queries that capture entity, relation, and keyword representations. Banerjee et al. (2022) experimented with various models, including T5 (Raffel et al., 2020), BART (Lewis et al., 2019), and Pointer Generation Networks (See et al., 2017), to explore their efficacy in KGQA tasks. Rony et al. (2022)'s SGPT employs a stack of transformer encoders to extract linguistic features from the natural question and GPT-2 as a decoder. However, this architecture is limited by its inability to capture connections among entities and relations in the underlying knowledge graph, leading to errors in generating triple sequences in the final SPARQL queries. Pliukhin et al. (2023) presented a one-shot generative approach, where the prompt is augmented with a KG fragment required to construct the query and a question-subgraph query example.

Despite promising results, these architectures are prone to systematic errors. One such error, the so-called "triple-flip", refers to the reversal of subject and object positions in the generated SPARQL triples, yielding wrong, often empty answers. Qi et al. (2024) addressed this issue by developing TSET, a fine-tuned T5 model with a pre-training stage called Triplet Structure Correction.

All these works propose dedicated architectures or training objectives designed for the task at hand. This requires fine-tuning, that may be expensive in terms of resources, thus limiting the choice of backbones to specialize. We take a different approach and investigate ICL solutions that do not require any fine-tuning.

Text-to-SPARQL methods are typically evaluated in KGQA tasks, and they all share a similar pipeline, where entities and relations are given or extracted from other modules and the goal of the model is to translate a natural language question, associated with its entities and relations, into the SPARQL query.

KGQA. Being text-to-SPARQL an important ingredient in KGQA, many KGQA approaches are inherently related with our work. Early research in KG query generation was rule-based (Guo et al., 2005; Owens et al., 2008), template-based (Zenz et al., 2009; Unger et al., 2012; Görlitz et al., 2012) or search-based. However, manual or semi-manual approaches hit scalability issues with KGs like WikiData and DBpedia. Nowadays, research follows two main streams: information-retrieval based methods and Text-to-SPARQL approaches. The former generally require identifying sub-graphs relevant to the natural question. They include divide-and-conquer (Kim et al., 2023), fact retrieval based on linked entities (Baek et al., 2023), more complex methods involving hops, relation predictions, and triple sampling (Wu et al., 2023), or Evidence Pattern Retrieval (EPR) through structural dependency modeling (Ding et al., 2024). Conversely, solutions based on text-to-SPARQL typically use ICL approaches to build a query draft in a logical form that is then refined and converted into a formal SPARQL query by means of different strategies. KB-BINDER (Li et al., 2023) leverages LLMs for generating preliminary logical forms and refines them using a lexicon-based similarity search, achieving notable performance on several KBQA datasets without customized heuristics for specific knowledge bases. In (Nie et al., 2024) authors propose converting logical form generation into Python function call sequences, reducing format errors and enhancing performance in zero-shot and few-shot settings, establishing new state-of-the-art results on multiple datasets. In the same spirit, other methods generate natural language questions starting from SPARQL queries instead (Li et al., 2024; Liang et al., 2023).

Our study departs from the KGQA works listed above in several ways. First, it focuses on the text-to-SPARQL task starting from a natural question and gold entities/relations, whereas KB-BINDER and other methods address a different task: the production of a logical form starting from a natural question, without gold entities/relations. The SPARQL query can be constructed afterward, and entities/relations can be predicted based on the logical form, which is what KB-BINDER does; nevertheless, the task is a different one. For this reason, we only consider text-to-SPARQL benchmarks with gold entities/relations, as in (Banerjee et al., 2022; Rony et al., 2022; Qi et al., 2024). Another difference is the choice of the KG: instead of freebase, a project closed in 2016, we adopt Wikidata, an ongoing project with 1.57 billion semantic triples to date.[1]

[1] https://grafana.wikimedia.org/d/000000175/

3 Method

Given a collection of natural language questions $\mathcal{Q}$ and a knowledge graph $\mathcal{G} := (\mathcal{E}, \mathcal{R}, \mathcal{F})$, where $\mathcal{E}$ are *entities*, $\mathcal{R}$ are *relations*, and $\mathcal{F} \subseteq \mathcal{E} \times \mathcal{R} \times \mathcal{E}$ are *facts*, KGQA is the problem of answering questions in $\mathcal{Q}$ based on $\mathcal{G}$. KGQA can be framed as a **text-to-SPARQL** task, where a question q must be translated into a SPARQL query s_q to be executed on $\mathcal{G}$ by a SPARQL engine, to return a (possibly empty) answer a. The entities and relations in q, denoted as $\mathcal{E}_q$ and $\mathcal{R}_q$, may be, and usually are, extracted from q before generating s_q. Hence, query generation can be tackled as a conditional text generation problem given $q, \mathcal{E}_q$ and $\mathcal{R}_q$. Within the scope of ICL, P_θ is a pre-trained LLM and the conditional input $\mathcal{E}_q, \mathcal{R}_q, q$ is combined with other contextual information C, such as additional instructions, guidelines, constraints and demonstrations, all expressed via natural language text. Accordingly, the generated query is:

$$s_q = \arg\max_s P_\theta(s|C, \mathcal{E}_q, \mathcal{R}_q, q). \quad (1)$$

3.1 Exemplary Demonstrations Retrieval

In few-shot ICL, the choice of demonstrations to inject in the prompt can significantly affect performance. Usually, few-shot examples are predetermined representative instances of the task, handpicked during prompt design. Conversely, we aim to retrieve good examples dynamically, based on their relevance to the input question. Inspired by Liu et al. (2022) and Li et al. (2023), we adopt a retrieval approach based on the similarity between a question q and a set of previously answered text-to-SPARQL examples collected in a storage $\mathcal{S}$ (see Figure 1), where each example is a tuple including a question x, its entities $\mathcal{E}_x$ and relations $\mathcal{R}_x$, and the associated SPARQL query s_x. Differently from (Li et al., 2023), we encode examples with dense representations instead of BM25. Moreover, beside the question itself, we also encode its entities and relations, i.e. $\langle q, \mathcal{E}_q, \mathcal{R}_q \rangle$ are mapped onto a vector representation $e_q \in \mathbb{R}^d$ using a sentence encoder. To properly feed such information to an encoder-only LM, we concatenate question, entities and relations in a single input sequence $\boldsymbol{q} := [q, \mathcal{E}_q, \mathcal{R}_q]$. Likewise, we encode each example $x \in \mathcal{S}$ into a vector $e_x \in \mathbb{R}^d$ and then compute the similarity between the target question and the storage:

$$score(\boldsymbol{q}, \boldsymbol{x}) = sim(e_q, e_x), \forall x \in \mathcal{S}, \quad (2)$$

where sim is a similarity function. Based on such a scoring, we retrieve the k-most similar examples $\mathcal{S}$ and include them as demonstrations in the in-context prompt. From now on, we refer to this exemplary demonstration retrieval strategy as DFSL, standing for Dynamic Few-Shot Learning.

3.2 In-Context Prompt

The in-context prompt has three parts. The first is the task description, instructing the LLM with a numbered list of guidelines on the output format and on the available information. The second, highlighted in Figure 1 with a green block, contains the k retrieved demonstrations. Each demonstration consists of a question, its entities and relations, denoted as *gold* entities/relations, all paired with their SPARQL query delimited by `<SPARQL></SPARQL>` tags. The ### symbol delimits each example. The last part is the question, associated with its gold entities and relations. The answer returned by the LLM prompted as such is then parsed to extract the generated text enclosed in `<SPARQL></SPARQL>` tags. The resulting query s_q is executed by a SPARQL engine on $\mathcal{G}$ to yield the answer to q.

3.3 Multi-Query Generation

A typical challenge faced by LLMs in SPARQL query generation is the understanding of what is the subject and what is the object of a relation, an information the model does not have. LLMs often end up in swapping the subject with the object in the query, almost choosing one way or the other randomly. This problem is called triple-flip error (Qi et al., 2024). Thanks to ICL, this issue may be alleviated whenever there are similar demonstrations in the in-context prompt that clarify the subject-object roles. To further reduce triple-flip errors, we propose the generation of multiple SPARQL queries by retaining all the final hypotheses generated during beam search. The model uncertainty in placing subject and object is likely to be reflected in the beam search exploration. Intuitively, both triple-ordering hypotheses are considered plausible by the model. Thus, instead of just returning the most probable sequence s according to Equation 1, we keep the whole b queries $\{s_{q,1}, \ldots, s_{q,b}\}$ formulated by beam search.

wikidata-datamodel-statements?orgId=1&refresh=30m

Approach	Backbone	QALD-9 Plus	QALD-10	LC-QUAD 2.0	QALD-9 DB
Zero-shot Learning		49.90	33.76	40.66	65.73
Few-shot Learning	Mixtral 7x8	54.80 (**+4.90**)	50.26 (**+16.50**)	61.04 (**+20.38**)	63.86 (**-1.87**)
DFSL		71.75 (**+21.85**)	49.90 (**+16.14**)	81.81 (**+41.15**)	72.74 (**+7.01**)
Zero-shot Learning		63.01	**58.31**	54.21	70.49
Few-shot Learning	Llama-3 70B	67.69 (**+4.68**)	51.28 (**-7.03**)	68.52 (**+14.31**)	68.84 (**-1.65**)
DFSL		73.60 (**+10.59**)	56.59 (**-1.72**)	81.93 (**+27.72**)	72.66 (**+2.17**)
Zero-shot Learning		45.94	33.36	38.40	66.43
Few-shot Learning	CodeLlama 70B	64.49 (**+18.55**)	57.38 (**+24.02**)	64.46 (**+26.06**)	72.67 (**+6.24**)
DFSL		**76.59** (**+30.65**)	57.69 (**+24.33**)	**85.45** (**+47.05**)	**75.14** (**+8.71**)

Table 1: ICL techniques comparison on different backbones. Absolute F1 gains with respect to zero-shot are reported between parenthesis.

Approach	QALD-9 Plus	QALD-10	LC-QUAD 2.0	QALD-9 DB
DFSL	76.59	57.69	85.45	75.14
DFSL-MQP$_{LS}$	73.67	58.85	85.06	73.25
DFSL + Multi-Query Prompt$_{FS}$	74.40	58.34	85.38	73.92
DFSL-MQ$_{LS}$	83.21	60.48	85.54	72.06
DFSL-MQ$_{FS}$	**84.45 (+7.86)**	**62.20 (+4.51)**	**89.10 (+3.65)**	**77.89 (+2.75)**

Table 2: Multi-query Generation: comparing DFSL-MQ with DFSL and Multi-Query Prompting baselines. Absolute F1 gains with respect to DFSL are reported for the best performing configuration.

Answer Selection. Executing multiple queries inevitably leads to multiple possible answers. Therefore, we must define an answer selection criterion. We designed two heuristics: Largest Set (LS) and First Set (FS). LS executes all the b queries, obtaining with each query $s_{q,j}$ a (possibly empty) answer set $\mathcal{A}_j$. LS then selects, among $\{\mathcal{A}_1, \ldots, \mathcal{A}_b\}$, the largest one[2], i.e:

$$\mathcal{A} = \arg\max_{\mathcal{A}_i}(|\mathcal{A}_1|, \ldots, |\mathcal{A}_b|),$$

the rationale being that incorrect candidates will likely have empty results. However, LS can be misled into selecting answers from under-constrained queries that return many irrelevant instances. FS adheres to the natural beams ordering by selecting the first query that yields a non-empty answer set.

4 Experiments

In this section, we conduct the investigation of LLMs capabilities in text-to-SPARQL query generation. KGQA serves as a benchmark task to measure the quality of the generated queries.

4.1 Datasets

To make our analysis more robust, we evaluate models and methods on four heterogeneous KGQA benchmarks based on two different Knowledge Graphs (Wikidata, DBpedia).

[2]In case of ties, we take the first largest set.

QALD-9 DB. QALD-9 (Ngomo, 2018) is a dataset from the Question Answering over Linked Data (QALD) challenge series. It comprises 408 training questions and 150 test questions. Unlike the other KGQA benchmarks, the SPARQL queries are meant for a DBpedia Knowledge Graph. We refer to it as QALD-9 DB to emphasize that.

QALD-9 plus. QALD-9 plus extends QALD-9 on new languages and transfers SPARQL queries from DBpedia to Wikidata. Although some queries were not portable to Wikidata due to the absence of corresponding information, it still comprises 371 training questions and 136 test questions. In our experiments, we only consider English questions.

QALD-10. QALD-10 (Usbeck et al., 2023) is the latest dataset in the QALD series, designed to increase the complexity of gold SPARQL queries. It consists of 412 training questions extracted from QALD-9 plus Wikidata. The test set was created from scratch, comprising 394 test questions that express real-world information needs. Test questions significantly differ from those in training.

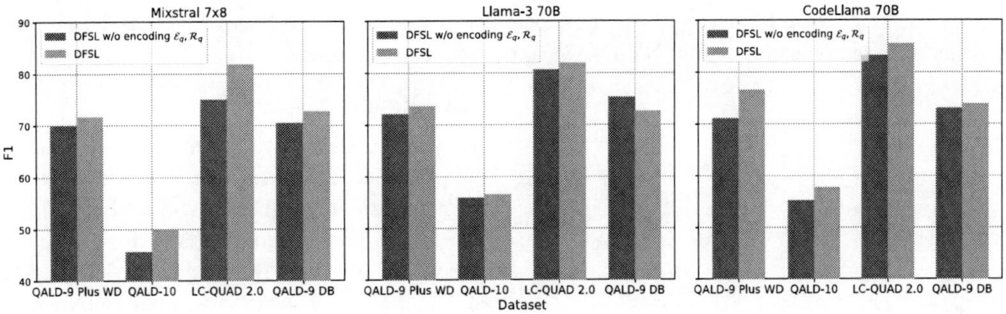

Figure 2: Comparison of Embeddings: DFSL (in orange) encoding that incorporates question, entities and relations versus an embedding solely based on the question q (in blue).

LC-QuAD 2.0. LC-QuAD 2.0 (Dubey et al., 2019) is a large-scale dataset grounded on Wikidata. It consists of 30,226 simple and complex questions: 24,180 in training, and 6,046 in test. Questions are diverse. They include single- and multi-fact, boolean, count, and other query types. With such a large and diverse text-to-SPARQL storage, LC-QuAD 2.0 allows us to gauge the benefits of retrieving similar exemplary demonstrations.

4.2 Backbones

Mixtral 8x7B. Based on the Sparse Mixture of Experts (SMoE) architecture (Fedus et al., 2022), Mixtral 8x7B (Jiang et al., 2024) is a 46.7B parameters model. Among the backbones adopted in this paper, Mixtral is the smallest. Moreover, thanks to the characteristics of its SMoE architecture, less than 13B are active at each inference step, making Mixtral particularly efficient.

Llama-3 70B. Built upon the Llama architecture (Touvron et al., 2023), Llama-3 70B has been trained on 15T tokens, a 650% increase from its predecessor, Llama 2. At the time of writing, Llama-3 70B is one of the best-performing open-weights LLMs available.

CodeLlama 70B. Initialized from Llama2 70B, CodeLlama (Rozière et al., 2024) is a specialized version fine-tuned on 1T tokens of code-heavy data. Therefore, we expect CodeLlama to be particularly suitable for SPARQL query generation.

4.3 Baselines

Plain Question. This is a naive baseline where we feed an LLM only with the task description and the question q. Without in-context examples nor any entity or relation associated with q, the LLM can only rely on its parameter memory.

Zero-Shot Learning. Here we do not provide any demonstrative example in the prompt. However, unlike the plain question baseline, we do inject golden entities and relations into the prompt. With reference to Figure 1, the In-Context prompt remains the same but without the green-like block containing the demonstrations.

Few-Shot Learning. The prompt is filled with a single set of k manually selected examples, used for all the questions in the test set. The examples were chosen to maximize diversity and cover different kinds of queries[3].

Multi Query Prompting (DFSL-MQP). As an alternative to our proposed multi-query generation (DFSL-MQ), this baseline consists in a naive multi-query prompting strategy. Essentially, we ask the model to generate more queries to answer the question. To ease the creation of inverted subject-object queries that can solve triple-flip errors, we extend the prompt to explicitly ask the model to produce this kind of SPARQL queries. Answer selection uses LS and FS heuristics, like with DFSL-MQ.

4.4 Experimental Setup

Implementation. In our experiments, the training set of each dataset serves as storage for the retrieval of the k most similar examples (see the next paragraph for details on k tuning) with DFSL. Examples are encoded with a sentence transformer[4], all-mpnet-base-v2[5], and sim is defined as the cosine similarity. Inference is performed via beam search in all ICL approaches, where b is set to 3,

[3]The chosen examples and more details are provided in Appendix B.

[4]https://www.sbert.net/index.html

[5]huggingface.co/sentence-transformers/all-mpnet-base-v2

and DFSL-MQ, where b is set to 10. All the experiments were run on a cluster of 4 NVIDIA A100 GPUs.

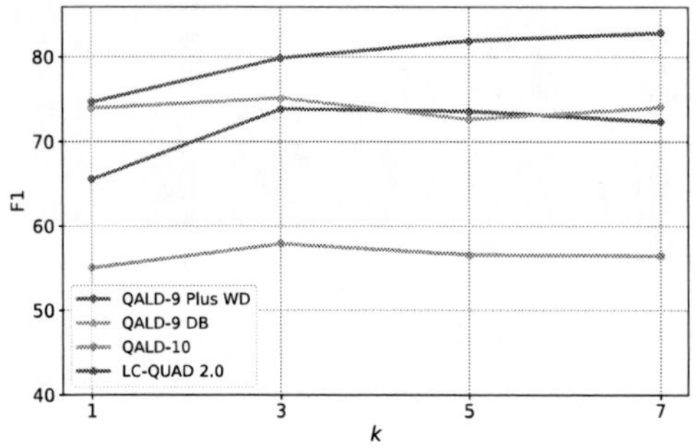

Figure 3: Impact of the number of in-context examples on the four benchmarks.

Number of Few-shot Examples. We first analyzed how the number of few-shot examples k retrieved by DFSL affects the performance. We chose among $k = \{1, 3, 5, 7\}$ and evaluated DFSL with Llama 3 70B backbone on the four datasets. The results shown in Figure 3 suggest that values of k greater than one perform comparably well on smaller benchmarks, while on LC-QUAD 2.0, where there are about 25 thousands examples as storage, increasing k seems to be beneficial. This may be due to the increased likelihood of finding similar examples in larger datasets as k grows. We set $k = 5$ for all the forthcoming experiments, which is a good trade-off across all the datasets.

Prompt. The prompt illustrated in Figure 1 constitutes the default template in our experimentations. However, slight variations are required in certain cases. For example, when running experiments on DBpedia knowledge graph, we replace the Wikidata reference with DBpedia in the first text segment. When we study the absence of gold information instead, we remove all the references to gold entities/relations (according to the ablation) from the entire prompt. There are no differences in the prompts layout when running few-shot-learning baseline experiments. In zero-shot learning, only the in-context examples any reference to them are removed, all else being equal.

Evaluation metric. We follow a standard F1 score evaluation in KGQA benchmarks. The F1 is computed between the answer set returned by the target SPARQL query and the predicted one. When both the queries return an empty set, we assign an F1 score of 1. The F1 scores of all the examples are then averaged.

4.5 Results

In-Context Learning. To measure how ICL techniques affect the generation of SPARQL queries, we compare Zero-Shot, Few-Shot Learning and DFSL on three different LLMs. Results are outlined in Table 1. Both few-shot learning and DFSL generally yield substantial gains with respect to zero-shot baseline on all the backbones and datasets. An exception occurs in QALD-10 with Llama-3. Notably, when comparing DFSL and Few-shot Learning baseline, we can see how examples selection approach improves F1 scores by a large margin in LC-QUAD 2.0, QALD-9 Plus and QALD-9 DB, with F1 increasing up to 21 absolute points[6]. In QALD-10 instead, where the test set has a different distribution from its training, there are no significant differences between DFSL and the standard few-shot learning approach. Indeed, an approach like DFSL brings little benefits when the storage only contains unrelated examples.

Backbones Comparison. In terms of backbones, Llama-3 consistently outperforms both Mixtral and CodeLlama in zero-shot learning scenario, whereas in few-shot, results are generally comparable between Llama-3 and CodeLlama. Such a strong Llama-3 zero-shot performance may be caused by some sort of data contamination, however we leave such an investigation for future works. Overall, DFSL with CodeLlama achieved the greatest performance with respect to all the other configurations. Therefore, we adopt CodeLlama as our backbone in the following experiments.

Impact of Multi-Query Generation. Here we investigate DFSL-MQ, the multi-query approach extending DFSL. We evaluate both answer selection strategies, LS and FS, and compare them against the plain DFSL and the multi-query prompting baseline described in Section 4.3. All the results are outlined in Table 2. Having multiple queries is not necessarily beneficial. Indeed, the multi-query prompting baseline under-performs in three datasets out of four with respect to (single query) DFSL, regardless of the answer selection method adopted. On the contrary, DFSL-MQ proves to positively increase results. Both Largest Set and First Set heuristics are effective when the

[6]Some qualitative examples illustrate the benefits of DFSL over few-shot learning in Appendix A (see Table 6).

Approach	QALD-9 Plus	QALD-10	LC-QUAD 2.0	QALD-9 DB
Plain Question	0.08	0.02	12.00	16.42
BART (Banerjee et al., 2022)	-	-	64.00	-
PGN-BERT-BERT (Banerjee et al., 2022)	-	-	86.00	-
SGPT (Rony et al., 2022)	-	-	89.04	67.82
TSET-small (Qi et al., 2024)	72.86	47.15	94.00	-
TSET-base (Qi et al., 2024)	75.85	51.37	**95.00**	-
Zero-shot Learning	45.94	33.36	38.40	66.43
Few-shot Learning	64.49	57.38	64.46	72.67
DFSL	76.59	57.69	85.45	75.14
DFSL-MQ beam FS	**84.45 (+8.60)**	**62.20 (+10.83)**	89.10 (**-5.90**)	**77.89 (+10.07)**

Table 3: DFSL and ICL approaches vs state-of-the-art fine-tuned models.

hypotheses come from the beams. Furthermore, FS consistently outperforms LS, even by substantial margins in QALD-9 DB. This shows that exploiting the information coming from beam search hypotheses is a promising strategy to obtain more query candidates.

In-context Learning vs Fine-tuning. Up to this point, we have assessed In-Context Learning approaches. In Table 3 instead, we compare them against state-of-the-art models trained and/or fine-tuned for specific downstream KGQA datasets. Without any training, DFSL-MQ outperforms current state-of-the-art approaches in three out of four benchmarks, namely QALD-9 Plus, QALD-10 and QALD-9 DB, even with the single query DFSL setup. DFSL-MQ does not obtain state-of-the-art results in LC-QUAD 2.0, the dataset mostly affected by triple-flip errors. This means that multi-query generation only alleviates the issue, but does not solve it entirely.

4.6 Ablation studies

Different Example Encoding. As described in Section 3.1, to compute the embeddings we concatenated the textual input made of the question and its list of entities and relations. Here, we gauge the impact of this additional information on DFSL performance. In Figure 2 we compare it, with a variant where only the natural language question q is embedded, without any additional data concatenated. The evaluation carried out in all the benchmarks and with all the backbones, demonstrates that such information improves the quality of the generated queries.

Absence of gold information. In KGQA, text-to-SPARQL generation usually relies not only on the question itself, but also on entities and relations associated to it. Here we assess DFSL when either the entities $\mathcal{E}_q$ or the relations $\mathcal{R}_q$, or both are missing. The information is removed throughout the entire process. For example, when removing entities, we discard them from both the storage and the prompt. Even the embeddings for the retrieval are computed by encoding an input without any entity concatenated in $\boldsymbol{q}$, i.e. becoming $\boldsymbol{q} = [q, \mathcal{R}_q]$. We report this on both Wikidata and DBpedia KGs. Results outlined in Table 4, clearly show how the knowledge about entities and the relations is essential for generating the query, indeed without performance drop significantly. Nonetheless, even in the case where no information is given (DFSL w/o $\mathcal{E}_q$, $\mathcal{R}_q$), the presence of dynamic demonstrations drastically help, yielding respectively a 33+ and 25+ absolute F1 increase compared to plain question baseline in Table 3.

	QALD 9 DB	QALD 9 Plus
DFSL	75.14	76.59
w/o Rq	56.62	49.47
w/o Eq	60.92	31.83
w/o Eq, Rq	49.59	26.16

Table 4: DFSL in the absence of entities and/or relations.

5 Conclusion

In this paper, we investigated the use of out-of-the-box Large Language Models for text-to-SPARQL generation. We carried out an extensive evaluation of several backbones and configurations on four KGQA benchmarks. By leveraging different In-Context Learning (ICL) approaches, we have shown that LLMs can effectively generate SPARQL queries. When demonstrations similar to the input question are injected into the prompt, LLMs achieve performance exceeding state-of-the-art models fine-tuned on the downstream task. The generation of multiple SPARQL query hypotheses from beam search candidates enhances the performance further, even with a simple query selection criterion.

Future work will focus on extending the investigation to multiple languages and (possibly private) KGs.

Limitations

We recognize some limitations in our work. Our experiments are all on English-based datasets, where notoriously LLMs are better performing. Moreover, the massive pre-training of those LLMs on a vast portion of the Web, may expose those models to unintended data contamination, a phenomenon already observed in similar domains (Ranaldi et al., 2024). Experiments only focused on LLMs with large number of parameters, without investigating the behaviour of smaller models. To encode examples, we limited the investigation to what kind of text to encode (just the question, or the question and its entities and relations), without exploring different embedding models, similarity criteria or other input concatenation strategies. We leave these investigations to future work.

Acknowledgments

This work was supported by the Cineca consortium, and it was partially funded by:

- PNRR - M4C2 - Investimento 1.3, Partenariato Esteso PE00000013 - "FAIR - Future Artificial Intelligence Research" - Spoke 8 "Pervasive AI", funded by the European Commission under the NextGeneration EU programme.

- PNRR - M4C2 - Investimento 1.3, Partenariato Esteso PE00000013 - Spoke 2 "FAIR - Future Artificial Intelligence Research" - "ReSpiRA - REplicabilità, SPlegabilità e Ragionamento", funded by the European Commission under the NextGeneration EU programme, CUP B43D22000900004 [7];

- "MAESTRO - Mitigare le Allucinazioni dei Large Language Models: ESTRazione di informazioni Ottimizzate" a project funded by Provincia Autonoma di Trento with the Lp 6/99 Art. 5: ricerca e sviluppo, PAT/RFS067-05/06/2024-0428372, CUP: C79J23001170001 [8].

References

Jinheon Baek, Alham Fikri Aji, and Amir Saffari. 2023. Knowledge-augmented language model prompting for zero-shot knowledge graph question answering. *Preprint*, arXiv:2306.04136.

Debayan Banerjee, Pranav Ajit Nair, Jivat Neet Kaur, Ricardo Usbeck, and Chris Biemann. 2022. Modern baselines for sparql semantic parsing. In *Proceedings of the 45th International ACM SIGIR Conference on Research and Development in Information Retrieval*, SIGIR '22. ACM.

Kurt Bollacker, Colin Evans, Praveen Paritosh, Tim Sturge, and Jamie Taylor. 2008. Freebase: a collaboratively created graph database for structuring human knowledge. In *Proceedings of the 2008 ACM SIGMOD International Conference on Management of Data*, SIGMOD '08, page 1247–1250, New York, NY, USA. Association for Computing Machinery.

Tom B. Brown, Benjamin Mann, Nick Ryder, Melanie Subbiah, Jared Kaplan, Prafulla Dhariwal, Arvind Neelakantan, Pranav Shyam, Girish Sastry, Amanda Askell, Sandhini Agarwal, Ariel Herbert-Voss, Gretchen Krueger, Tom Henighan, Rewon Child, Aditya Ramesh, Daniel M. Ziegler, Jeffrey Wu, Clemens Winter, Christopher Hesse, Mark Chen, Eric Sigler, Mateusz Litwin, Scott Gray, Benjamin Chess, Jack Clark, Christopher Berner, Sam McCandlish, Alec Radford, Ilya Sutskever, and Dario Amodei. 2020. Language models are few-shot learners. *CoRR*, abs/2005.14165.

Rakesh Chada and Pradeep Natarajan. 2021. Fewshotqa: A simple framework for few-shot learning of question answering tasks using pre-trained text-to-text models. In *Proceedings of the 2021 Conference on Empirical Methods in Natural Language Processing*, pages 6081–6090.

Mark Chen, Jerry Tworek, Heewoo Jun, Qiming Yuan, Henrique Ponde de Oliveira Pinto, Jared Kaplan, Harri Edwards, Yuri Burda, Nicholas Joseph, Greg Brockman, Alex Ray, Raul Puri, Gretchen Krueger, Michael Petrov, Heidy Khlaaf, Girish Sastry, Pamela Mishkin, Brooke Chan, Scott Gray, Nick Ryder, Mikhail Pavlov, Alethea Power, Lukasz Kaiser, Mohammad Bavarian, Clemens Winter, Philippe Tillet, Felipe Petroski Such, Dave Cummings, Matthias Plappert, Fotios Chantzis, Elizabeth Barnes, Ariel Herbert-Voss, William Hebgen Guss, Alex Nichol, Alex Paino, Nikolas Tezak, Jie Tang, Igor Babuschkin, Suchir Balaji, Shantanu Jain, William Saunders, Christopher Hesse, Andrew N.

[7]ReSPiRA: https://www.opencup.gov.it/portale/web/opencup/home/progetto/-/cup/B43D22000900004

[8]MAESTRO: https://www.opencup.gov.it/portale/web/opencup/home/progetto/-/cup/C79J23001170001

Carr, Jan Leike, Josh Achiam, Vedant Misra, Evan Morikawa, Alec Radford, Matthew Knight, Miles Brundage, Mira Murati, Katie Mayer, Peter Welinder, Bob McGrew, Dario Amodei, Sam McCandlish, Ilya Sutskever, and Wojciech Zaremba. 2021. Evaluating large language models trained on code. *Preprint*, arXiv:2107.03374.

Xiusi Chen, Yu Zhang, Jinliang Deng, Jyun-Yu Jiang, and Wei Wang. 2023. Gotta: generative few-shot question answering by prompt-based cloze data augmentation. In *Proceedings of the 2023 SIAM International Conference on Data Mining (SDM)*, pages 909–917. SIAM.

Zhoujun Cheng, Tianbao Xie, Peng Shi, Chengzu Li, Rahul Nadkarni, Yushi Hu, Caiming Xiong, Dragomir Radev, Mari Ostendorf, Luke Zettlemoyer, et al. 2022. Binding language models in symbolic languages. *arXiv preprint arXiv:2210.02875*.

Wentao Ding, Jinmao Li, Liangchuan Luo, and Yuzhong Qu. 2024. Enhancing complex question answering over knowledge graphs through evidence pattern retrieval. *Preprint*, arXiv:2402.02175.

Qingxiu Dong, Lei Li, Damai Dai, Ce Zheng, Zhiyong Wu, Baobao Chang, Xu Sun, Jingjing Xu, Lei Li, and Zhifang Sui. 2023. A survey on in-context learning. *Preprint*, arXiv:2301.00234.

Mohnish Dubey, Debayan Banerjee, Abdelrahman Abdelkawi, and Jens Lehmann. 2019. Lc-quad 2.0: A large dataset for complex question answering over wikidata and dbpedia. page 69–78, Berlin, Heidelberg. Springer-Verlag.

William Fedus, Jeff Dean, and Barret Zoph. 2022. A review of sparse expert models in deep learning. *Preprint*, arXiv:2209.01667.

Hila Gonen, Srini Iyer, Terra Blevins, Noah A. Smith, and Luke Zettlemoyer. 2022. Demystifying prompts in language models via perplexity estimation. *Preprint*, arXiv:2212.04037.

Olaf Görlitz, Matthias Thimm, and Steffen Staab. 2012. Splodge: Systematic generation of sparql benchmark queries for linked open data. In *The Semantic Web – ISWC 2012*, pages 116–132, Berlin, Heidelberg. Springer Berlin Heidelberg.

Yuanbo Guo, Zhengxiang Pan, and Jeff Heflin. 2005. Lubm: a benchmark for owl knowledge base systems. *Web Semantics: Science, Services and Agents on the World Wide Web*, 3:158–182.

Albert Q. Jiang, Alexandre Sablayrolles, Antoine Roux, Arthur Mensch, Blanche Savary, Chris Bamford, Devendra Singh Chaplot, Diego de las Casas, Emma Bou Hanna, Florian Bressand, Gianna Lengyel, Guillaume Bour, Guillaume Lample, Lélio Renard Lavaud, Lucile Saulnier, Marie-Anne Lachaux, Pierre Stock, Sandeep Subramanian, Sophia Yang, Szymon Antoniak, Teven Le Scao, Théophile Gervet, Thibaut Lavril, Thomas Wang, Timothée Lacroix, and William El Sayed. 2024. Mixtral of experts. *Preprint*, arXiv:2401.04088.

Hyuhng Joon Kim, Hyunsoo Cho, Junyeob Kim, Taeuk Kim, Kang Min Yoo, and Sang goo Lee. 2022. Self-generated in-context learning: Leveraging autoregressive language models as a demonstration generator. *Preprint*, arXiv:2206.08082.

Jiho Kim, Yeonsu Kwon, Yohan Jo, and Edward Choi. 2023. Kg-gpt: A general framework for reasoning on knowledge graphs using large language models. *Preprint*, arXiv:2310.11220.

Jens Lehmann, Robert Isele, Max Jakob, Anja Jentzsch, Dimitris Kontokostas, Pablo Mendes, Sebastian Hellmann, Mohamed Morsey, Patrick Van Kleef, Sören Auer, and Christian Bizer. 2014. Dbpedia - a large-scale, multilingual knowledge base extracted from wikipedia. *Semantic Web Journal*, 6.

Itay Levy, Ben Bogin, and Jonathan Berant. 2023. Diverse demonstrations improve in-context compositional generalization. *Preprint*, arXiv:2212.06800.

Mike Lewis, Yinhan Liu, Naman Goyal, Marjan Ghazvininejad, Abdelrahman Mohamed, Omer Levy, Veselin Stoyanov, and Luke Zettlemoyer. 2019. BART: denoising sequence-to-sequence pre-training for natural language generation, translation, and comprehension. *CoRR*, abs/1910.13461.

Tianle Li, Xueguang Ma, Alex Zhuang, Yu Gu, Yu Su, and Wenhu Chen. 2023. Few-shot in-context learning on knowledge base question answering. In *Proceedings of the 61st Annual Meeting of the Association for Computational Linguistics (Volume 1: Long Papers)*, pages 6966–6980.

Zhenyu Li, Sunqi Fan, Yu Gu, Xiuxing Li, Zhichao Duan, Bowen Dong, Ning Liu, and Jianyong Wang. 2024. Flexkbqa: A flexible llm-powered framework for few-shot knowledge base question answering. In *Proceedings of the AAAI Conference on Artificial Intelligence*, volume 38, pages 18608–18616.

Yuanyuan Liang, Jianing Wang, Hanlun Zhu, Lei Wang, Weining Qian, and Yunshi Lan. 2023. Prompting large language models with chain-of-thought for few-shot knowledge base question generation. *arXiv preprint arXiv:2310.08395*.

Jiachang Liu, Dinghan Shen, Yizhe Zhang, Bill Dolan, Lawrence Carin, and Weizhu Chen. 2022. What makes good in-context examples for GPT-3? In *Proceedings of Deep Learning Inside Out (DeeLIO 2022): The 3rd Workshop on Knowledge Extraction and Integration for Deep Learning Architectures*, pages 100–114, Dublin, Ireland and Online. Association for Computational Linguistics.

Linyong Nan, Yilun Zhao, Weijin Zou, Narutatsu Ri, Jaesung Tae, Ellen Zhang, Arman Cohan, and Dragomir Radev. 2023. Enhancing few-shot text-to-sql capabilities of large language models: A study on prompt design strategies. *Preprint*, arXiv:2305.12586.

Ngonga Ngomo. 2018. 9th challenge on question answering over linked data (qald-9). *language*, 7(1):58–64.

Zhijie Nie, Richong Zhang, Zhongyuan Wang, and Xudong Liu. 2024. Code-style in-context learning for knowledge-based question answering. In *Proceedings of the AAAI Conference on Artificial Intelligence*, volume 38, pages 18833–18841.

Alisdair Owens, Nick Gibbins, and m.c Schraefel. 2008. Effective benchmarking for rdf stores using synthetic data.

Thomas Pellissier Tanon, Denny Vrandečić, Sebastian Schaffert, Thomas Steiner, and Lydia Pintscher. 2016. From freebase to wikidata: The great migration. In *Proceedings of the 25th international conference on world wide web*, pages 1419–1428.

Dmitrii Pliukhin, Daniil Radyush, Liubov Kovriguina, and Dmitry Mouromtsev. 2023. Improving subgraph extraction algorithms for one-shot sparql query generation with large language models. In *Scholarly-QALD-23: Scholarly QALD Challenge at The 22nd International Semantic Web Conference (ISWC 2023)(Athens, Greece*, volume 3592, pages 1–10.

Jiexing Qi, Chang Su, Zhixin Guo, Lyuwen Wu, Zanwei Shen, Luoyi Fu, Xinbing Wang, and Chenghu Zhou. 2024. Enhancing sparql query generation for knowledge base question answering systems by learning to correct triplets. *Applied Sciences*, 14(4).

Colin Raffel, Noam Shazeer, Adam Roberts, Katherine Lee, Sharan Narang, Michael Matena, Yanqi Zhou, Wei Li, and Peter J. Liu. 2020. Exploring the limits of transfer learning with a unified text-to-text transformer. *Journal of Machine Learning Research*, 21(140):1–67.

Federico Ranaldi, Elena Sofia Ruzzetti, Dario Onorati, Leonardo Ranaldi, Cristina Giannone, Andrea Favalli, Raniero Romagnoli, and Fabio Massimo Zanzotto. 2024. Investigating the impact of data contamination of large language models in text-to-sql translation. *arXiv preprint arXiv:2402.08100*.

Md Rashad Al Hasan Rony, Uttam Kumar, Roman Teucher, Liubov Kovriguina, and Jens Lehmann. 2022. Sgpt: A generative approach for sparql query generation from natural language questions. *IEEE Access*, 10:70712–70723.

Baptiste Rozière, Jonas Gehring, Fabian Gloeckle, Sten Sootla, Itai Gat, Xiaoqing Ellen Tan, Yossi Adi, Jingyu Liu, Romain Sauvestre, Tal Remez, Jérémy Rapin, Artyom Kozhevnikov, Ivan Evtimov, Joanna Bitton, Manish Bhatt, Cristian Canton Ferrer, Aaron Grattafiori, Wenhan Xiong, Alexandre Défossez, Jade Copet, Faisal Azhar, Hugo Touvron, Louis Martin, Nicolas Usunier, Thomas Scialom, and Gabriel Synnaeve. 2024. Code llama: Open foundation models for code. *Preprint*, arXiv:2308.12950.

Abigail See, Peter J. Liu, and Christopher D. Manning. 2017. Get to the point: Summarization with pointer-generator networks. *Preprint*, arXiv:1704.04368.

Hugo Touvron, Thibaut Lavril, Gautier Izacard, Xavier Martinet, Marie-Anne Lachaux, Timothée Lacroix, Baptiste Rozière, Naman Goyal, Eric Hambro, Faisal Azhar, Aurelien Rodriguez, Armand Joulin, Edouard Grave, and Guillaume Lample. 2023. Llama: Open and efficient foundation language models. *Preprint*, arXiv:2302.13971.

Christina Unger, Lorenz Bühmann, Jens Lehmann, Axel-Cyrille Ngonga Ngomo, Daniel Gerber, and Philipp Cimiano. 2012. Template-based question answering over rdf data. *WWW'12 - Proceedings of the 21st Annual Conference on World Wide Web*.

Ricardo Usbeck, Xi Yan, Aleksandr Perevalov, Longquan Jiang, Julius Schulz, Angelie Kraft, Cedric Möller, Junbo Huang, Jan Reineke, Axel-Cyrille Ngonga Ngomo, et al. 2023. Qald-10–the 10th challenge on question answering over linked data. *Semantic Web*, (Preprint):1–15.

Jason Wei, Xuezhi Wang, Dale Schuurmans, Maarten Bosma, Brian Ichter, Fei Xia, Ed Chi, Quoc Le, and Denny Zhou. 2023. Chain-of-thought prompting elicits reasoning in large language models. *Preprint*, arXiv:2201.11903.

Yike Wu, Nan Hu, Sheng Bi, Guilin Qi, Jie Ren, Anhuan Xie, and Wei Song. 2023. Retrieve-rewrite-answer: A kg-to-text enhanced llms framework for knowledge graph question answering. *Preprint*, arXiv:2309.11206.

Gideon Zenz, Xuan Zhou, Enrico Minack, Wolf Siberski, and Wolfgang Nejdl. 2009. From keywords to semantic queries—incremental query construction on the semantic web. *Journal of Web Semantics*, 7(3):166–176. The Web of Data.

Hanchong Zhang, Ruisheng Cao, Lu Chen, Hongshen Xu, and Kai Yu. 2023. ACT-SQL: In-context learning for text-to-SQL with automatically-generated chain-of-thought. In *Findings of the Association for Computational Linguistics: EMNLP 2023*, pages 3501–3532, Singapore. Association for Computational Linguistics.

Jianyun Zou, Min Yang, Lichao Zhang, Yechen Xu, Qifan Pan, Fengqing Jiang, Ran Qin, Shushu Wang, Yifan He, Songfang Huang, and Zhou Zhao. 2021. A chinese multi-type complex questions answering dataset over wikidata. *Preprint*, arXiv:2111.06086.

A Qualitative Analysis

In this appendix we provide some qualitative analyses of DFSL and DFSL-MQ. First of all, we report some examples in Table 6 that highlight the benefits from introducing similar examples with DFSL with respect to standard few-shot learning approach.

Then, we show some examples in Table 7 where the multi-query approach solves triple-flip errors. In Table 5 instead, we showcase errors caused by employing LS answer selection heuristic. Notably, by choosing larger sets, LS sometimes selects queries that are often relegated to latter positions in the beam hypotheses, which tend to be more general, thus more prone to returning a greater number of results.

B Few-shot Learning Examples

We report in Figure 4 the examples selected for the Few-shot learning baseline prompt. The five examples were chosen to be the most representative of the training set, including queries of different kind and structure, such as ASK, COUNT and SELECT.

Question	Target Query	Answer Selection	Predicted Query	Beam
What is manufactured NEC PC-9800 series whose sector is electronics?	`SELECT ?answer WHERE { wd:Q183505 wdt:P176 ?answer . ?answer wdt:P452 wd:Q11650 }`	LS	`SELECT ?answer WHERE { wd:Q183505 wdt:P176 ?X . ?X wdt:P452 wd:Q11650 . ?X wdt:P31 ?answer}`	7
		FS	`select distinct ?obj where { wd:Q183505 wdt:P176 ?obj . ?obj wdt:P452 wd:Q11650 }`	4
What is the enthalpy of vaporization for potassium hydroxide?	`select distinct ?answer where { wd:Q132298 wdt:P2116 ?answer}`	LS	`ASK WHERE { wd:Q14982 wdt:P2116 ?obj filter(?obj = 37400) }`	3
		FS	`select distinct ?answer where { wd:Q132298 wdt:P2116 ?answer}`	1
Which is the rural city of Fukushim?	`SELECT ?answer WHERE { wd:Q161176 wdt:P131 ?answer . ?answer wdt:P150 wd:Q1347240}`	LS	`SELECT ?answer WHERE { wd:Q161176 wdt:P131 ?X . ?X wdt:P150 ?answer}`	3
		FS	`SELECT ?answer WHERE { wd:Q161176 wdt:P131 ?answer . ?answer wdt:P150 wd:Q1347240}`	1

Table 5: Qualitative comparison between different answer selection strategies in DFSL-MQ.

Question	Target Query	Approach	Predicted Query	Similar In-context Example
Who is the daughter of Robert Kennedy married to?	SELECT DISTINCT ?uri WHERE { wd:Q25310 wdt:P40 ?daughter . ?daughter wdt:P21 wd:Q6581072 . ?daughter wdt:P26 ?uri .}	Few-Shot	SELECT DISTINCT ?uri WHERE { ?uri wdt:P40 wd:Q25310 ; wdt:P21 wd:Q6581072 ; wdt:P26 ?spouse .	-
		DFSL	SELECT DISTINCT ?uri WHERE { wd:Q25310 wdt:P40 ?child . ?child wdt:P21 wd:Q6581072 . ?child wdt:P26 ?uri . }	SELECT DISTINCT ?uri WHERE { wd:Q43247 wdt:P40 ?child . ?child wdt:P26 ?uri . }
Which countries are connected by the Rhine?	SELECT DISTINCT ?uri WHERE { wd:Q584 wdt:P17 ?uri . ?uri wdt:P31 wd:Q6256 . }	Few-Shot	SELECT DISTINCT ?uri WHERE { ?uri wdt:P31 wd:Q6256 ; wdt:P17 wd:Q584 .}	-
		DFSL	SELECT DISTINCT ?uri WHERE { wd:Q584 wdt:P17 ?uri . ?uri wdt:P31 wd:Q6256 . }	SELECT DISTINCT ?res WHERE { wd:Q3392 wdt:P885/wdt:P17 ?res . }
Give me the capitals of all countries in Africa.	SELECT DISTINCT ?uri WHERE { ?country wdt:P31 wd:Q6256 . ?country wdt:P30 wd:Q15 . ?country wdt:P36 ?uri . }	Few-Shot	SELECT DISTINCT ?uri WHERE { ?uri wdt:P31 wd:Q6256 ; wdt:P30 wd:Q15 ; wdt:P36 ?capital . }	-
		DFSL	SELECT DISTINCT ?uri WHERE { ?country wdt:P31 wd:Q6256 . ?country wdt:P30 wd:Q15 . ?country wdt:P36 ?uri . }	SELECT DISTINCT ?uri WHERE { wd:Q5451 wdt:P17 ?country . ?country wdt:P36 ?uri . }

Table 6: A qualitative comparison between DFSL and Few-shot Learning. Thanks to the similar in-context examples retrieval, the LLMs generates the correct query.

Question	Target Query	Approach	Predicted Query
Who is the enclave within of Montreal?	select distinct ?sbj where { ?sbj wdt:P501 wd:Q340 . ?sbj wdt:P31 wd:Q171441 }	DFSL	select distinct ?obj where { wd:Q340 wdt:P501 ?obj . ?obj wdt:P31 wd:Q171441 }
		DFSL-MQ	select distinct ?sbj where { ?sbj wdt:P501 wd:Q340 . ?sbj wdt:P31 wd:Q171441 }
The trachea is of what anatomical branch?	select distinct ?answer where { ?answer wdt:P3261 wd:Q175449}	DFSL	select distinct ?answer where { wd:Q175449 wdt:P3261 ?answer}
		DFSL-MQ	select distinct ?answer where { ?answer wdt:P3261 wd:Q175449}
What revolution caused the destruction of the Russian Empire?	select distinct ?obj where { wd:Q34266 wdt:P770 ?obj . ?obj wdt:P31 wd:Q10931 }	DFSL	select distinct ?sbj where { ?sbj wdt:P770 wd:Q34266 . ?sbj wdt:P31 wd:Q10931 }
		DFSL-MQ	select distinct ?obj where { wd:Q34266 wdt:P770 ?obj . ?obj wdt:P31 wd:Q10931 }

Table 7: Some triple-flip errors that are solved by DFSL-MQ.

```
Examples:

Question: Give me all companies in Munich.

Entities:
http://www.wikidata.org/entity/q4830453 (business), http://www.wikidata.org/entity/q1726 (Munich)

Relations:
http://www.wikidata.org/prop/direct/p279 (subclass of), http://www.wikidata.org/prop/direct/p31 (instance of),
http://www.wikidata.org/prop/direct/p159 (headquarters location)

Query:
<SPARQL>
PREFIX wdt: <http://www.wikidata.org/prop/direct/> PREFIX wd: <http://www.wikidata.org/entity/> SELECT DISTINCT ?uri WHERE { ?type wdt:P279*
wd:Q4830453 . ?uri wdt:P31 ?type ; wdt:P159 wd:Q1726 . }
</SPARQL>
###

Question: Was Marc Chagall a jew?

Entities:
http://www.wikidata.org/entity/q93284 (Marc Chagall), http://www.wikidata.org/entity/q7325 (Jewish people)

Relations:
http://www.wikidata.org/prop/direct/p172 (ethnic group)

Query:
<SPARQL>
PREFIX wdt: <http://www.wikidata.org/prop/direct/> PREFIX wd: <http://www.wikidata.org/entity/> ASK WHERE { wd:Q93284 wdt:P172 wd:Q7325 . }
</SPARQL>
###

Question: How many films did Leonardo DiCaprio star in?

Entities:
http://www.wikidata.org/entity/q11424 (film), http://www.wikidata.org/entity/q38111 (Leonardo DiCaprio)

Relations:
http://www.wikidata.org/prop/direct/p31 (instance of), http://www.wikidata.org/prop/direct/p161 (cast member)

Query:
<SPARQL>
PREFIX wdt: <http://www.wikidata.org/prop/direct/> PREFIX wd: <http://www.wikidata.org/entity/> SELECT (COUNT(DISTINCT ?uri) AS ?c) WHERE { ?uri
wdt:P31 wd:Q11424 ; wdt:P161 wd:Q38111 . }
</SPARQL>
###

Question: Give me all libraries established earlier than 1400.

Entities:
http://www.wikidata.org/entity/q7075 (library)

Relations:
http://www.wikidata.org/prop/direct/p31 (instance of), http://www.wikidata.org/prop/direct/p571 (inception)

Query:
<SPARQL>
PREFIX wdt: <http://www.wikidata.org/prop/direct/> PREFIX wd: <http://www.wikidata.org/entity/> SELECT DISTINCT ?uri WHERE { ?uri wdt:P31 wd:Q7075
; wdt:P571 ?date . FILTER (YEAR(?date) < 1400 ) }
</SPARQL>
###

Question: Is Christian Bale starring in Batman Begins?

Entities:
http://www.wikidata.org/entity/q166262 (Batman Begins), http://www.wikidata.org/entity/q45772 (Christian Bale)

Relations:
http://www.wikidata.org/prop/direct/p161 (cast member)

Query:
<SPARQL>
PREFIX wdt: <http://www.wikidata.org/prop/direct/> PREFIX wd: <http://www.wikidata.org/entity/> ASK WHERE { wd:Q166262 wdt:P161 wd:Q45772 }
</SPARQL>
```

Figure 4: Examples injected in the Few-shot-learning prompt.

GAVEL: Generative Attribute-Value Extraction Using LLMs on LLM-Augmented Datasets

Pollawat Hongwimol, Dong Sheng, Zhang Li, Kai Liu, Xiufei Wang
Lazada, Alibaba Group
pollwat.h@alibaba-inc.com
frank.dong@lazada.com, zhangli835@gmail.com

Abstract

In the evolving e-commerce landscape, accurate product attribute-value extraction is crucial for enhancing user experience and increasing sales. This paper introduces GAVEL, a generative approach leveraging large language models (LLMs) to augment training data for attribute extraction from diverse textual sources. Our method extracts over 1,000 unique attributes across 2,000 product categories in multiple Southeast Asian languages, including Thai, Vietnamese, and Indonesian. Rigorous evaluations show significant improvements in accuracy and coverage compared to seller-provided attributes, with enhanced recall and F1 scores. Additionally, GAVEL reduces operational costs by minimizing instruction token usage and improves inference speed. The results of the A/B test indicate that our model has a positive impact on Gross Merchandise Value (GMV) per page view (PV) across all three operating countries. This research highlights the potential of generative techniques for optimizing attribute extraction in multi-language e-commerce applications.

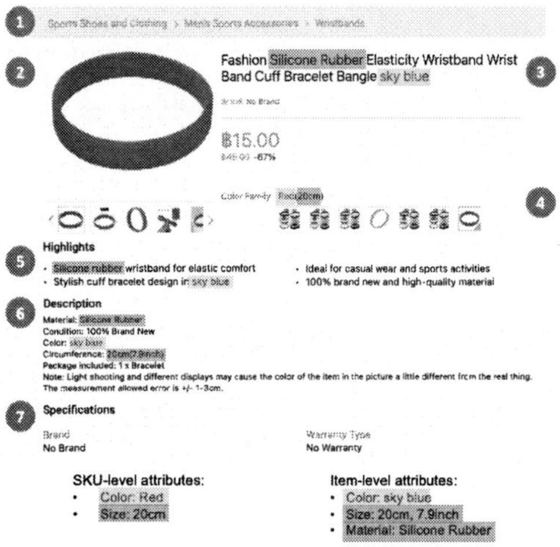

Figure 1: An example of seller-provided information, including extracted attributes. The information consists of (1) category, (2) images, (3) title, (4) SKU variants, (5) highlights, (6) description, and (7) specifications. In this case, the color 'sky blue' appears in the title, highlights, and description; however, it contradicts the SKU variant's color, which is red.

1 Introduction

Product attributes significantly influence product search (Ai et al., 2019; Luo et al., 2022), recommendation systems (Luo et al., 2022; Gao et al., 2023), and buyers' decision-making processes (Zheng et al., 2020; Hafiz and Ali, 2019; Helfi et al., 2019). Inadequate or erroneous information on product pages can lead to adverse outcomes, such as a poor shopping experience, decreased visibility, and lower sales. For instance, Figure 1 illustrates a case where the color 'sky blue' is mentioned in the title, highlights, and description; however, it contradicts the Stock Keeping Unit (SKU) variant, which is listed as red. Such discrepancies can confuse potential buyers and negatively impact their purchasing decisions.

In recent years, there has been significant research on Product Attribute-Value Extraction (PAVE) (Shinzato et al., 2023; Zou et al., 2024b; Zhu et al., 2020). Initial studies primarily employed sequence tagging methods using encoder-only models like BERT (Wang et al., 2020; Zhu et al., 2020; Chen et al., 2022; Embar et al., 2021; Xu et al., 2019; Deng et al., 2022). However, this approach has limitations in handling unseen and canonicalized values (Shinzato et al., 2023). To overcome these challenges, subsequent research has shifted from sequence tagging to sequence-to-sequence generation models, such as T5 and BART, which support more flexible output formats (Shinzato et al., 2023; Nikolakopoulos et al., 2023; Gong and Eldardiry, 2024; Wang et al., 2022; Roy et al., 2022; Sabeh et al., 2024; Roy et al., 2021). Addi-

Proceedings of the 4th International Workshop on Knowledge-Augmented Methods for Natural Language Processing (KnowledgeNLP'25), pages 81–90
May 3, 2025 ©2025 Association for Computational Linguistics

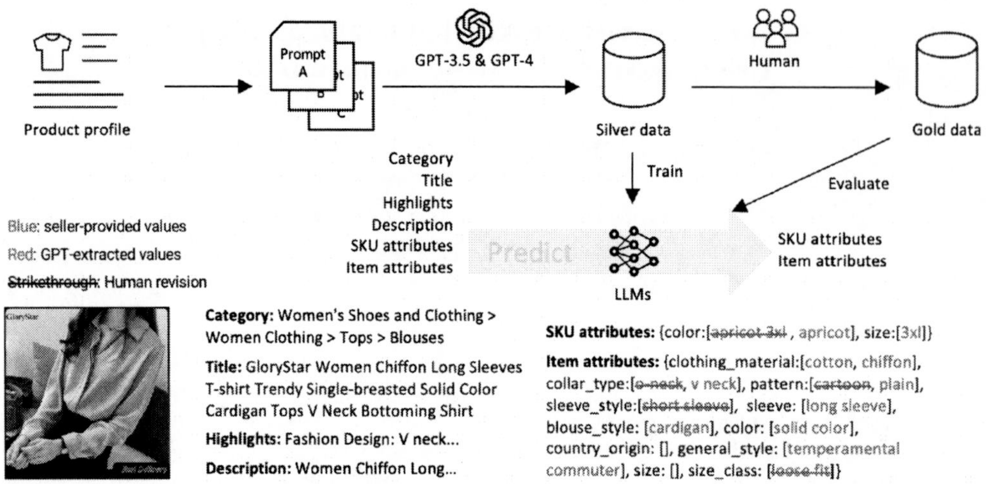

Figure 2: An overview of the GAVEL pipeline for generative attribute-value extraction using LLMs on LLM-augmented datasets. The GAVEL process begins with a product profile containing seller-provided information (indicated in blue) and employs prompts to extract and predict attributes (highlighted in red) utilizing GPT-3.5 and GPT-4. Silver data is used for training, while human evaluation is conducted to refine the final gold data for testing purposes.

tionally, current research leverages the zero-shot and few-shot capabilities of large-scale autoregressive models, such as GPT-3.5 and GPT-4, to enhance attribute extraction processes (Brinkmann et al., 2024b; Brinkmann et al., 2024a; Fang et al., 2024). This evolution has demonstrated that effective attribute value extraction significantly improves key e-commerce metrics, including Click-Through Rate (CTR) and Add-To-Cart Rate (ATC) (Fang et al., 2024).

Despite these advancements, existing publicly available datasets for PAVE face several limitations. For instance, the AE-110k dataset (Xu et al., 2019) is confined to the Sports & Entertainment category, offering data in the form of title-attribute-value triplets. While MEPAVE (Zhu et al., 2020) broadens its data sources to include images and descriptions, it still possesses a limited number of unique attributes. OA-Mine (Zhang et al., 2022) encompasses titles for 100 product types but lacks comprehensive information beyond the title itself. MAVE (Yang et al., 2021) includes 1,257 categories and various input types; however, it requires that explicit attribute values be present in the text, which complicates the extraction of unseen and canonicalized values. Although ImplicitAVE (Zou et al., 2024a) aims to address this shortcoming through a two-round human inspection process that annotates 25 attributes across five domains, it remains limited to titles and images. Furthermore, existing datasets predominantly rely on item-level information, which may lead to inaccuracies in attribute value extraction for a specific SKU variant, as demonstrated in Figure 1.

Expanding beyond these challenges, it is crucial to recognize the growing e-commerce landscape in Southeast Asia, where the need for PAVE solutions is becoming increasingly pressing. This region is home to a rich diversity of languages, including Thai, Vietnamese, Indonesian, and English. However, most PAVE research to date has primarily focused on English (Brinkmann et al., 2024b; Fang et al., 2024; Yang et al., 2023), Chinese (Zhu et al., 2020; Deng et al., 2023), and Japanese (Shinzato et al., 2023; Chen et al., 2022). To the best of our knowledge, there has been no prior study exploring the potential for enhancing PAVE in Southeast Asian languages.

To tackle these challenges, we propose an efficient pipeline for augmenting training data for generative attribute-value extraction, as depicted in Figure 2. Our key contributions are summarized as follows:

- We experiment with a comprehensive set of attributes, consisting of over 1,000 unique attributes across 2,000 categories.
- We incorporate successful methodologies

from prior research, including the utilization of generation-based models with zero-shot capabilities, the effective incorporation of textual data from product profiles, and the prediction of multiple attribute values.

- We reformulate the task to include seller-provided attribute values within input data. This enhancement improves output quality, as valuable information is sometimes misallocated under incorrect attribute values.
- We introduce GAVEL, a novel pipeline for generating high-quality training data for PAVE, enabling the training of smaller models with shorter, more concise prompts.

2 Related Work

2.1 Attribute Value Extraction

Attribute value extraction aims to derive specific values from product information. Traditionally, this has involved sequence tagging techniques employing models like Long Short-Term Memory (LSTM) or Bidirectional Encoder Representations from Transformers (BERT) (Embar et al., 2021; Xu et al., 2019; Wang et al., 2020). However, these methods often struggle with unseen values. To address these limitations, Roy et al. (2022) proposed generative frameworks that jointly extract attributes and values using the Text-to-Text Transfer Transformer (T5), demonstrating that such approaches outperform traditional tagging for single-value sentences.

Recent work has explored LLMs like GPT-3.5 and GPT-4 for attribute extraction, showing improved data efficiency and robustness to unseen values compared to traditional pretrained language models (Brinkmann et al., 2024b). Despite these advancements, many studies focus on English products, with few addressing the complexities of Southeast Asian languages (Brinkmann et al., 2024b; Yang et al., 2023), underscoring a significant gap in multilingual PAVE research.

2.2 Attribute Value Extraction Datasets

A variety of datasets have been created to support PAVE research. Table 1 offers a detailed summary of existing datasets alongside our datasets. Notably, these datasets vary significantly across several dimensions, including product categories, SKU counts, attribute counts, unique attributes, languages, and data sources.

OpenTag (Zheng et al., 2018) comprises 10k SKUs, with a total of 13k attribute instances, across three categories collected from Amazon. This dataset includes attributes extracted from product titles, descriptions, and highlights, and is exclusively presented in English. AE-110k (Xu et al., 2019) is concentrated within a single Sports & Entertainment category, featuring a considerably larger SKU count of 50k, yielding 110k attribute instances. Attributes derive solely from product titles, with data collected from AliExpress and created without human annotation. MEPAVE (Zhu et al., 2020) offers a broader variety of categories, containing seven categories with 34k SKUs and 87k attributes, with human annotations. Attributes in this dataset are predominantly extracted from images and descriptions and are published in Chinese. MAVE (Yang et al., 2021) includes an extensive catalog of 1.3k categories and a substantial total of 3 million attribute instances. The products are sourced from the Amazon Review Dataset and do not include any human annotations. OA-Mine (Zhang et al., 2022) encompasses ten distinct categories, comprising 11k attributes. This dataset focuses on attributes derived from titles, descriptions, and highlights, all collected from Amazon in English. Only the development and test sets are annotated by human. ImplicitAVE (Zou et al., 2024a) presents a dataset featuring five categories and 70k attributes, focusing on attributes sourced from title and image data. This dataset represents an enhanced version of MAVE, with the evaluation set re-annotated by a team of five Ph.D. students to improve reliability.

3 Methods

3.1 Attribute Mining

Our approach to enhancing seller-provided attributes utilizes three distinct prompts submitted to GPT-3.5 (Ouyang et al., 2024) and GPT-4 (OpenAI et al., 2024), as illustrated in Figure 3. The first prompt verifies brand names in the title and highlights. The second prompt focuses on SKU-level attributes, addressing frequent misclassifications by providing detailed instructions for the extraction of five common attributes. The third prompt targets item-level attributes from titles, highlights, and descriptions, requiring comprehensive instructions to avoid the model simply replicating examples instead of accurately extracting values. This prompt includes value examples and bullet-point instructions to regulate the expected output format.

Dataset	#Cate	#SKU	#Attr	#Unique	Lang	Source
OpenTag	3	10k	13k	4	en	title, desc, highlights
AE-110k	1	50k	110k	4	en	title
MEPAVE	7	34k	87k	26	zh	image, desc
MAVE	1.3k	2.2M	3M	2.5k	en	title, desc, highlights
OA-Mine	10	2k	11k	10	en	title, desc, highlights
ImplicitAVE	5	70k	70k	25	en	title, image
Lzd-ID-train (ours)	2k	163k	739k	1.2k	en, id	title, desc, highlights, sku attributes, specifications
Lzd-TH-train (ours)	2k	152k	648k	1.2k	en, th	
Lzd-VN-train (ours)	2k	152k	705k	1.2k	en, vi	
Lzd-ID-test (ours)	314	1k	6.3k	313	en, id	
Lzd-TH-test (ours)	352	1k	5.8k	372	en, th	
Lzd-VN-test (ours)	353	1k	6.3k	417	en, vi	
Total (ours)	**2k**	**470k**	**2.1M**	**1.2k**	**en, th, id, vi**	

Table 1: A summary of existing datasets compared to our datasets.

3.2 Dataset Construction

The attributes mined in Section 3.1, along with seller-provided attributes, are categorized as silver labels. A rule-based processing algorithm resolves conflicts by prioritizing mined attributes; if there are no contradictions, both types are retained. Experienced e-commerce annotators from Indonesia, Thailand, and Vietnam evaluate these silver-labeled attributes to generate gold labels.

To optimize token efficiency during training and inference, we compile all attribute information into a concise prompt (see Figure 3). This prompt includes seller-provided data such as titles, highlights, descriptions, SKU attributes, and item specifications, allowing models to predict multiple attributes and values simultaneously.

Table 1 summarizes our three datasets, encompassing 2,000 categories and over two million attribute instances. Each training category includes an equal number of SKUs, while the test set consists of 1,000 randomly selected and mutually exclusive SKUs, ensuring diverse representation and comprehensive evaluation of model performance.

3.3 Model Fine-tuning

In this study, we fine-tune four LLMs with comparable parameter counts, which are accessible on Hugging Face[1]. The models include *Gemma-2-9b* (Team et al., 2024), *Llama-3.1-8B* (Dubey et al., 2024), *Qwen2.5-7B* (Yang et al., 2024), and *SeaLLMs-v3-7B* (Zhang et al., 2024). Our training employs Low-Rank Adaptation (LoRA) (Hu et al., 2022) with bf16 precision, specifically setting `lora_target=all` to facilitate comprehensive adaptation across all layers of the models. We split the dataset into training and validation sets, allocating 15% for validation to ensure robust evaluation of model performance. The training process utilizes a cosine learning rate scheduler and incorporates early stopping criteria to further optimize performance. We set the training and evaluation batch sizes to 2 and employ gradient accumulation over 8 steps, leading to a total of 10 training epochs, which allows for thorough learning from the dataset. Additionally, evaluations and logging are conducted at intervals of 500 steps to monitor convergence effectively. Notably, this experiment utilizes 4 PPU 810 cards provided by Alibaba Cloud to fine-tune the models.

[1]https://huggingface.co/

4 Experimental Setup

In this section, we outline the experimental framework employed in this study, utilizing data sourced from Lazada, a prominent e-commerce platform in Southeast Asia. The information collected encompasses product profiles and various attributes relevant to our analysis, establishing a comprehensive basis for the subsequent investigations.

4.1 Data Sources

The product pages on Lazada contain extensive information furnished by sellers, which includes both textual and visual components, as illustrated in Figure 1. SKU-level attributes refer to specific variants of a product, while item-level attributes cover common characteristics shared across all variants. We extract SKU-level attributes from individual

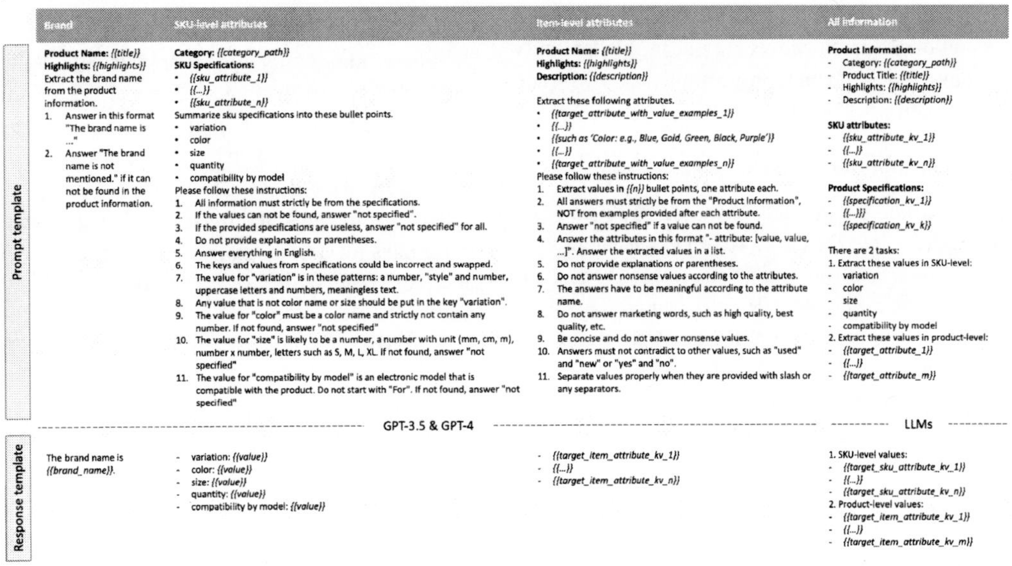

Figure 3: Structured templates for extracting product information, including brand, SKU-level attributes, item-level attributes, and all relevant details. The first three prompts are designed for dataset development using GPT models, while the last prompt is intended for training and inference with internal models.

product variants, whereas item-level attributes are derived from the product specifications. All SKUs associated with a particular item share identical title, highlights, description, and specifications.

It is imperative to recognize that the attributes supplied by sellers may be the least reliable source of information. This unreliability stems from potential inaccuracies, such as incorrect categorization of values or arbitrary selections from platform-provided dropdown menus. In instances where an attribute value contradicts information presented in the title, highlights, or description, there exists a considerable probability that the attribute value is erroneous. Consequently, this study does not treat seller-provided attributes as definitive ground truth; rather, these attributes are meticulously revised for accuracy and subsequently used as golden labels.

4.2 Large Language Models

GPT-3.5 and GPT-4, developed by OpenAI, are advanced large language models that employ deep learning to generate human-like text. They demonstrate exceptional performance in zero-shot and few-shot contexts on datasets like OA-Mine and AE-110k (Brinkmann et al., 2024b). Following previous research, we utilize these models to extract and verify product attributes, which are then combined with seller-provided data to create silver datasets for training and evaluation.

To assess the performance of various LLMs, we selected multilingual models proficient in languages including English, Thai, Indonesian, and Vietnamese. SeaLLMs 3 (Zhang et al., 2024) from Alibaba's DAMO Academy excels in Southeast Asian languages. Qwen2.5 (Yang et al., 2024), developed by Alibaba Cloud, offers decoder-only models ranging from 0.5 to 72 billion parameters with capabilities in natural language understanding, coding, and mathematics. Gemma 2 (Team et al., 2024) from Google DeepMind includes lightweight models with 2 to 27 billion parameters, utilizing architectural innovations and knowledge distillation. Llama 3.1 (Dubey et al., 2024) from Meta AI features multilingual models competitive with leading closed-source variants, excelling in coding, reasoning, and mathematics.

Licensing is pivotal for compliance and intellectual property respect. OpenAI's terms for GPT-3.5 and GPT-4 restrict modifications but allow usage for specific tasks. Our work involves generating a small-sized model that does not directly compete with OpenAI, aligning with their guidelines. Other models have varying licenses: SeaLLMs 3 permits modification under a worldwide, non-exclusive, non-transferable agreement; Gemma 2 allows reproduction and modification within certain limits; Qwen2.5 operates under the permissive Apache License 2.0; and Llama 3.1's Community License

Agreement permits modifications with specified conditions. These licenses provide us the flexibility to innovate while ensuring compliance with each organization's guidelines.

4.3 Evaluation Metrics

We evaluate our models based on Precision (*P*), Recall (*R*), and the F1 score (*F1*), consistent with prior research (Brinkmann et al., 2024b; Yang et al., 2021). In addition, we calculate accuracy (*Acc*) and coverage (*Cov*) based on the first predicted value for each attribute.

Our predictions are classified into five distinct categories: no prediction when there is no attribute (*NN*), incorrect prediction where no attribute exists (*NV*), no prediction despite the existence of an attribute (*VN*), correct prediction that matches the attribute (*VC*), and incorrect prediction that does not align with the attribute (*VW*). The subscripted numbers (e.g., VC_1, NV_1, etc.) denote the counts of correct and incorrect predictions associated with the first predicted value. The evaluation metrics are computed as follows:

$$P = VC\,/\,(NV+VC+VW)$$
$$R = VC\,/\,(VN+VC+VW)$$
$$F1 = 2PR\,/\,(P+R)$$
$$Acc = VC_1\,/\,(NV_1+VC_1+VW_1)$$
$$Cov = (NV_1+VC_1+VW_1)\,/\,All_1$$

Importantly, we follow standard practice by assessing accuracy solely on the attributes provided by sellers, which allows us to focus our evaluation on the correctness of the available information without penalizing for any missing attributes. This practice is also applied to outputs generated by LLMs. In contrast, coverage accounts for both available and missing information, providing a comprehensive view of the model's performance.

This evaluation framework enables us to assess model performance through metrics such as precision, recall, and F1 score, while also providing insights into attribute quality via accuracy and coverage.

5 Results

This section presents performance metrics and evaluations of four selected LLMs across three datasets. We benchmark the models against the seller attribute values and assess their effectiveness in predicting multiple attributes, the quality of the first predicted value, and inference speed.

5.1 Human Annotation

To assess the quality of Seller Attribute Values (SAV) and Mined Attribute Values (MAV), we conducted a human annotation evaluation focusing on SKU-level and item-level attributes across three distinct test datasets.

The results, presented in Table 2, show acceptance rates for SAV and MAV, denoted as %ASAV and %AMAV. While SAV exhibits higher acceptance rates, its volume is considerably lower than that of MAV, with accepted SAV totaling 7,710 compared to 21,742 for MAV. This gap highlights the significant potential of MAV in identifying new attribute values that sellers may overlook, as approximately 75% of accepted attribute values arise from our mining pipeline, even though they are evaluated as less accurate. These findings underscore the complementary functions of SAV and MAV; SAV provides reliable attributes, while MAV enriches the dataset by introducing three times more newly identified values.

Dataset	SAV	MAV	%ASAV	%AMAV
SKU-level attributes				
ID-test	1221	512	48.16	99.22
TH-test	885	583	58.53	25.73
VN-test	735	608	35.92	74.18
Item-level attributes				
ID-test	3170	6062	96.97	86.69
TH-test	1871	9473	81.88	77.56
VN-test	1950	12443	88.92	64.54
Total	**9832**	**29681**	**78.42**	**73.25**

Table 2: Results of human annotation for Seller Attribute Values (SAV) and Mined Attribute Values (MAV), categorized into SKU-level and item-level attributes. Acceptance rates (%ASAV and %AMAV) indicate the proportion of attribute values recognized as accurate by human annotators for both SAV and MAV.

5.2 Multiple Attribute Values Prediction

To evaluate the models' efficacy in predicting multiple attribute values, we focus on precision, recall, and F1 score as key performance metrics. These metrics serve as indicators of the models' capabilities to accurately identify and extract valid attribute values from product listings.

As illustrated in Table 3, the models exhibit varying performance across distinct datasets. For Lzd-ID, Llama 3.1 emerges as the top performer, achieving the highest F1 score of 77.36, which indicates

Dataset	Model	P	R	F1	Acc	Cov	Speed (s)
Lzd-ID	*Seller attribute values*	**84.92**	74.16	**79.18**	85.09	69.40	-
	Gemma 2	76.29	76.19	76.24	90.61	78.44	5587
	Llama 3.1	77.34	**77.38**	77.36	**91.30**	78.51	**642**
	Qwen2.5	74.33	74.49	74.41	90.34	78.88	859
	SeaLLMs 3	77.68	76.87	77.27	91.27	**78.96**	832
Lzd-TH	*Seller attribute values*	**67.26**	44.54	53.59	67.63	50.86	-
	Gemma 2	50.18	56.24	53.04	**77.42**	77.09	8287
	Llama 3.1	52.81	56.00	54.36	73.52	**81.21**	**1226**
	Qwen2.5	51.38	52.47	51.92	75.54	76.77	1914
	SeaLLMs 3	55.27	**57.20**	**56.22**	74.64	79.16	2098
Lzd-VN	*Seller attribute values*	**72.26**	45.07	55.52	72.17	44.00	-
	Gemma 2	67.77	**69.57**	**68.66**	**78.04**	72.31	6251
	Llama 3.1	64.45	67.61	66.00	75.85	**73.95**	**716**
	Qwen2.5	65.33	67.64	66.47	75.93	73.38	1017
	SeaLLMs 3	65.66	67.38	66.51	77.09	72.36	1042

Table 3: Performance of four LLMs fine-tuned and evaluated on three datasets, compared against seller-provided attribute values.

its effectiveness in this specific context. Conversely, SeaLLMs 3 demonstrates superior performance on Lzd-TH, suggesting a heightened suitability for processing Thai-language attributes. Meanwhile, Gemma 2 excels in the Lzd-VN dataset, highlighting the necessity of aligning model selection with the unique linguistic and contextual features inherent in each dataset.

The models consistently outperformed seller-provided attributes in terms of recall, highlighting the potential for generative approaches. Although these models may identify a broader range of potential attribute values, they often fall short of the precision achieved by sellers for attributes that encompass multiple values. This observation underscores the fundamental trade-offs between precision and recall in automated prediction systems.

5.3 First Predicted Attribute Value

In our evaluation, we also examine the accuracy and coverage of the first predicted attribute value for each attribute. This perspective is crucial for assessing how effectively the models retrieve the most relevant attribute value when multiple options are available.

The results shown in Table 3 reveal significant variability in the accuracy of the first predicted value across different models and datasets. Notably, Llama 3.1 achieves the highest accuracy of 91.30% alongside a commendable coverage of 78.51% on Lzd-ID. This model consistently demonstrates strong coverage across Lzd-TH and Lzd-VN. Conversely, Gemma 2 excels in terms of accuracy on Lzd-TH and Lzd-VN, underscoring its effectiveness in these contexts.

Overall, our findings indicate that all models enhance the attribute values provided by sellers, reflecting improvements in both accuracy and coverage. This highlights the potential of utilizing automated models to complement seller-supplied data, thereby enriching the attribute extraction process across various datasets.

5.4 Inference Speed Analysis

Inference speed is a crucial consideration for deploying model solutions in real-world scenarios. In this analysis, we measure the inference time for each model while processing data from 1,000 SKUs under specific testing conditions. The inference was conducted using a batch size of 2 and a single PPU 810 card on Alibaba Cloud. The evaluation was performed using the following parameters: `temperature=0.2`, `top_p=0.1`, and `top_k=100`.

The results reveal considerable variation across models, as indicated in Table 3. Gemma 2 exhibits the longest inference time, whereas Llama 3.1 demonstrates significantly faster processing capabilities. The prolonged inference time associated with Gemma 2 may be attributed to the incompatibility between Flash Attention 2 (Dao, 2024) and Gemma 2, resulting in a marked decrease in processing efficiency.

5.5 Comparative Analysis of Models

The performance of the four selected LLMs varies significantly across evaluated datasets, presenting an opportunity to analyze their strengths and weaknesses in real-world applications. Llama 3.1 stands out on Lzd-ID, achieving an F1 score of 77.36 and an impressive accuracy of 91.30% for the first predicted value. This consistent performance indicates its suitability for applications demanding precision in multi-attribute extraction. In contrast, SeaLLMs 3 excels in Lzd-TH, highlighting the importance of language and locale.

Gemma 2 displays high accuracy in specific contexts but struggles with inference speed, making it less viable for real-time applications. Conversely, Llama 3.1 maintains swift processing times without sacrificing accuracy, making it an optimal choice for environments requiring rapid decision-making. Qwen2.5 delivers moderate performance across datasets but lacks standout features, suggesting its suitability for general applications.

Considering the trade-offs in accuracy, coverage, and speed, Llama 3.1 is the most balanced model for deployment. Its combination of high accuracy, solid coverage, and efficient processing makes it ideal for commercial applications that require reliable attribute extraction and the ability to handle large data volumes swiftly.

5.6 Online Performance

An A/B experiment was conducted to evaluate the impact of Llama 3.1 on online performance. Orders per item page view, also known as conversion rates (CVR), showed a 0.70% increase for ID, a 0.68% decrease for VN, and a 1.19% increase for TH. Additionally, orders per page view improved by 0.47% in ID and 1.40% in TH, with VN experiencing a decrease of 0.79%. Gross Merchandise Value (GMV) per page view saw substantial increases, with VN leading at 6.73%, followed by ID at 1.61% and TH at 1.44%. These findings underscore the ability of LLMs to enhance user engagement and optimize business outcomes, thereby contributing to overall revenue growth.

6 Conclusion

In this study, we introduced an innovative approach for attribute-value extraction by leveraging generative LLMs on augmented datasets. Our method capitalizes on the zero-shot capabilities of advanced LLMs, facilitating the extraction of over 1,000 unique attributes across diverse categories with enhanced accuracy and speed. The empirical results demonstrate significant improvements in the quality of attributes provided by sellers, with notable increases in accuracy, coverage, and overall market performance metrics. By fine-tuning smaller models, we not only reduced operational costs but also enhanced efficiency, allowing for rapid inference while maintaining high prediction quality. The successful outcomes from our experiments underscore the viability of our GAVEL pipeline for wide-scale implementation in multilingual e-commerce platforms. This research paves the way for further exploration of generative approaches to attribute extraction, offering organizations valuable insights into optimizing their inventory and enhancing customer experiences.

7 Limitations

Despite the promising results of this study, several limitations should be noted. Firstly, while our augmented datasets cover a diverse range of attributes, performance may vary significantly across different product categories and languages, limiting the generalizability of our findings, particularly in regions underrepresented in the training data. Future research should aim to enhance model robustness across a broader spectrum of inputs. Additionally, our approach does not currently incorporate visual data, which is vital in e-commerce. The lack of image data may hinder comprehensive attribute extraction, especially in categories where visual representation is critical. Integrating multimodal data in future studies could enhance extraction accuracy. Another important limitation is the potential generation of erroneous data through LLM augmentation, which could result in misleading product attributes, damaging sellers' reputations and causing customer dissatisfaction. Implementing strategies for validation and verification of generated data is essential to mitigate these risks. Addressing these limitations will enable further refinement of attribute-value extraction models, enhancing their applicability in the e-commerce sector.

References

Qingyao Ai, Daniel N. Hill, S. V. N. Vishwanathan, and W. Bruce Croft. 2019. A zero attention model for personalized product search. *Proceedings of the 28th ACM International Conference on Information and Knowledge Management*.

Alexander Brinkmann, Nick Baumann, and Christian Bizer. 2024a. *Using LLMs for the Extraction and Normalization of Product Attribute Values*, page 217–230. Springer Nature Switzerland.

Alexander Brinkmann, Roee Shraga, and Christian Bizer. 2024b. Extractgpt: Exploring the potential of large language models for product attribute value extraction. *Preprint*, arXiv:2310.12537.

Wei-Te Chen, Yandi Xia, and Keiji Shinzato. 2022. Extreme multi-label classification with label masking for product attribute value extraction. In *Proceedings of the Fifth Workshop on e-Commerce and NLP (ECNLP 5)*, pages 134–140, Dublin, Ireland. Association for Computational Linguistics.

Tri Dao. 2024. FlashAttention-2: Faster attention with better parallelism and work partitioning. In *International Conference on Learning Representations (ICLR)*.

Zhongfen Deng, Wei-Te Chen, L. Chen, and Philip S. Yu. 2022. Ae-smnsmlc: Multi-label classification with semantic matching and negative label sampling for product attribute value extraction. *2022 IEEE International Conference on Big Data (Big Data)*, pages 1816–1821.

Zhongfen Deng, Hao Peng, Tao Zhang, Shuaiqi Liu, Wenting Zhao, Yibo Wang, and Philip S. Yu. 2023. Jpave: A generation and classification-based model for joint product attribute prediction and value extraction. *2023 IEEE International Conference on Big Data (BigData)*, pages 1087–1094.

Abhimanyu Dubey, Abhinav Jauhri, Abhinav Pandey, Abhishek Kadian, Ahmad Al-Dahle, et al. 2024. The llama 3 herd of models. *Preprint*, arXiv:2407.21783.

Varun Embar, Andrey Kan, Bunyamin Sisman, Christos Faloutsos, and Lise Getoor. 2021. Diffxtract: Joint discriminative product attribute-value extraction. In *2021 IEEE International Conference on Big Knowledge (ICBK)*, pages 271–280.

Chenhao Fang, Xiaohan Li, Zezhong Fan, Jianpeng Xu, Kaushiki Nag, Evren Korpeoglu, Sushant Kumar, and Kannan Achan. 2024. Llm-ensemble: Optimal large language model ensemble method for e-commerce product attribute value extraction. *Preprint*, arXiv:2403.00863.

Chen Gao, Yu Zheng, Nian Li, Yinfeng Li, Yingrong Qin, Jinghua Piao, Yuhan Quan, Jianxin Chang, Depeng Jin, Xiangnan He, and Yong Li. 2023. A survey of graph neural networks for recommender systems: Challenges, methods, and directions. *ACM Trans. Recomm. Syst.*, 1(1).

Jiaying Gong and Hoda Eldardiry. 2024. Multi-label zero-shot product attribute-value extraction. In *Proceedings of the ACM Web Conference 2024*, WWW '24, page 2259–2270, New York, NY, USA. Association for Computing Machinery.

Khalilah Abd Hafiz and Khairul Anuar Mohd Ali. 2019. The influence of product attributes on young consumers' purchase decision of makeups among malaysian: The mediating effects of perceived brand image, ceo's image, and quality.

Yudi Helfi, Fatihatul Akbar, Dinda Mutiara Pratiwi, and Fakhri Mujahid Maolani. 2019. How product attributes affect consumer decision to purchase a premium scooter matic? *JEMA: Jurnal Ilmiah Bidang Akuntansi dan Manajemen*.

Edward J Hu, Yelong Shen, Phillip Wallis, Zeyuan Allen-Zhu, Yuanzhi Li, Shean Wang, Lu Wang, and Weizhu Chen. 2022. LoRA: Low-rank adaptation of large language models. In *International Conference on Learning Representations*.

Chen Luo, William Headden, Neela Avudaiappan, Haoming Jiang, Tianyu Cao, Qingyu Yin, Yifan Gao, Zheng Li, Rahul Goutam, Haiyang Zhang, and Bing Yin. 2022. Query attribute recommendation at amazon search. In *RecSys 2022*.

Athanasios N. Nikolakopoulos, Swati Kaul, Siva Karthik Gade, Bella Dubrov, Umit Batur, and Suleiman Ali Khan. 2023. Sage: Structured attribute value generation for billion-scale product catalogs. *Preprint*, arXiv:2309.05920.

OpenAI, Josh Achiam, Steven Adler, Sandhini Agarwal, Lama Ahmad, et al. 2024. Gpt-4 technical report. *Preprint*, arXiv:2303.08774.

Long Ouyang, Jeff Wu, Xu Jiang, Diogo Almeida, Carroll L. Wainwright, Pamela Mishkin, Chong Zhang, Sandhini Agarwal, Katarina Slama, Alex Ray, John Schulman, Jacob Hilton, Fraser Kelton, Luke Miller, Maddie Simens, Amanda Askell, Peter Welinder, Paul Christiano, Jan Leike, and Ryan Lowe. 2024. Training language models to follow instructions with human feedback. In *Proceedings of the 36th International Conference on Neural Information Processing Systems*, NIPS '22, Red Hook, NY, USA. Curran Associates Inc.

Kalyani Roy, Pawan Goyal, and Manish Pandey. 2021. Attribute value generation from product title using language models. In *Proceedings of the 4th Workshop on e-Commerce and NLP*, pages 13–17, Online. Association for Computational Linguistics.

Kalyani Roy, Tapas Nayak, and Pawan Goyal. 2022. Exploring generative models for joint attribute value extraction from product titles. *ArXiv*, abs/2208.07130.

Kassem Sabeh, Robert Litschko, Mouna Kacimi, Barbara Plank, and Johann Gamper. 2024. An empirical comparison of generative approaches for product attribute-value identification. *Preprint*, arXiv:2407.01137.

Keiji Shinzato, Naoki Yoshinaga, Yandi Xia, and Wei-Te Chen. 2023. A unified generative approach to product attribute-value identification. In *Findings of the Association for Computational Linguistics: ACL*

2023, pages 6599–6612, Toronto, Canada. Association for Computational Linguistics.

Gemma Team, Morgane Riviere, Shreya Pathak, Pier Giuseppe Sessa, Cassidy Hardin, et al. 2024. Gemma 2: Improving open language models at a practical size. *Preprint*, arXiv:2408.00118.

Qifan Wang, Li Yang, Bhargav Kanagal, Sumit K. Sanghai, D. Sivakumar, Bin Shu, Zac Yu, and Jonathan L. Elsas. 2020. Learning to extract attribute value from product via question answering: A multi-task approach. *Proceedings of the 26th ACM SIGKDD International Conference on Knowledge Discovery & Data Mining*.

Qifan Wang, Li Yang, Jingang Wang, Jitin Krishnan, Bo Dai, Sinong Wang, Zenglin Xu, Madian Khabsa, and Hao Ma. 2022. SMARTAVE: Structured multimodal transformer for product attribute value extraction. In *Findings of the Association for Computational Linguistics: EMNLP 2022*, pages 263–276, Abu Dhabi, United Arab Emirates. Association for Computational Linguistics.

Huimin Xu, Wenting Wang, Xin Mao, Xinyu Jiang, and Man Lan. 2019. Scaling up open tagging from tens to thousands: Comprehension empowered attribute value extraction from product title. In *Proceedings of the 57th Annual Meeting of the Association for Computational Linguistics*, pages 5214–5223, Florence, Italy. Association for Computational Linguistics.

An Yang, Baosong Yang, Binyuan Hui, Bo Zheng, Bowen Yu, Chang Zhou, Chengpeng Li, Chengyuan Li, Dayiheng Liu, Fei Huang, Guanting Dong, Haoran Wei, Huan Lin, Jialong Tang, Jialin Wang, Jian Yang, Jianhong Tu, Jianwei Zhang, Jianxin Ma, Jianxin Yang, Jin Xu, Jingren Zhou, Jinze Bai, Jinzheng He, Junyang Lin, Kai Dang, Keming Lu, Keqin Chen, Kexin Yang, Mei Li, Mingfeng Xue, Na Ni, Pei Zhang, Peng Wang, Ru Peng, Rui Men, Ruize Gao, Runji Lin, Shijie Wang, Shuai Bai, Sinan Tan, Tianhang Zhu, Tianhao Li, Tianyu Liu, Wenbin Ge, Xiaodong Deng, Xiaohuan Zhou, Xingzhang Ren, Xinyu Zhang, Xipin Wei, Xuancheng Ren, Xuejing Liu, Yang Fan, Yang Yao, Yichang Zhang, Yu Wan, Yunfei Chu, Yuqiong Liu, Zeyu Cui, Zhenru Zhang, Zhifang Guo, and Zhihao Fan. 2024. Qwen2 technical report. *Preprint*, arXiv:2407.10671.

Li Yang, Qifan Wang, Jingang Wang, Xiaojun Quan, Fuli Feng, Yu Chen, Madian Khabsa, Sinong Wang, Zenglin Xu, and Dongfang Liu. 2023. MixPAVE: Mix-prompt tuning for few-shot product attribute value extraction. In *Findings of the Association for Computational Linguistics: ACL 2023*, pages 9978–9991, Toronto, Canada. Association for Computational Linguistics.

Li Yang, Qifan Wang, Zac Yu, Anand Kulkarni, Sumit K. Sanghai, Bin Shu, Jonathan L. Elsas, and Bhargav Kanagal. 2021. Mave: A product dataset for multisource attribute value extraction. *Proceedings of the Fifteenth ACM International Conference on Web Search and Data Mining*.

Wenxuan Zhang, Hou Pong Chan, Yiran Zhao, Mahani Aljunied, Jianyu Wang, Chaoqun Liu, Yue Deng, Zhiqiang Hu, Weiwen Xu, Yew Ken Chia, Xin Li, and Lidong Bing. 2024. Seallms 3: Open foundation and chat multilingual large language models for southeast asian languages. *Preprint*, arXiv:2407.19672.

Xinyang Zhang, Chenwei Zhang, Xian Li, Xin Luna Dong, Jingbo Shang, Christos Faloutsos, and Jiawei Han. 2022. Oa-mine: Open-world attribute mining for e-commerce products with weak supervision. In *Proceedings of the ACM Web Conference 2022*, WWW '22, page 3153–3161, New York, NY, USA. Association for Computing Machinery.

Guineng Zheng, Subhabrata Mukherjee, Xin Luna Dong, and Feifei Li. 2018. Opentag: Open attribute value extraction from product profiles. In *Proceedings of the 24th ACM SIGKDD International Conference on Knowledge Discovery & Data Mining*, KDD '18, page 1049–1058, New York, NY, USA. Association for Computing Machinery.

Qiujie Zheng, Junhong Chen, Robin Zhang, and H. Holly Wang. 2020. What factors affect chinese consumers' online grocery shopping? product attributes, e-vendor characteristics and consumer perceptions. *China Agricultural Economic Review*, 12:193–213.

Tiangang Zhu, Yue Wang, Haoran Li, Youzheng Wu, Xiaodong He, and Bowen Zhou. 2020. Multimodal joint attribute prediction and value extraction for E-commerce product. In *Proceedings of the 2020 Conference on Empirical Methods in Natural Language Processing (EMNLP)*, pages 2129–2139, Online. Association for Computational Linguistics.

Henry Zou, Vinay Samuel, Yue Zhou, Weizhi Zhang, Liancheng Fang, Zihe Song, Philip Yu, and Cornelia Caragea. 2024a. ImplicitAVE: An open-source dataset and multimodal LLMs benchmark for implicit attribute value extraction. In *Findings of the Association for Computational Linguistics ACL 2024*, pages 338–354, Bangkok, Thailand and virtual meeting. Association for Computational Linguistics.

Henry Zou, Gavin Yu, Ziwei Fan, Dan Bu, Han Liu, Peng Dai, Dongmei Jia, and Cornelia Caragea. 2024b. EIVEN: Efficient implicit attribute value extraction using multimodal LLM. In *Proceedings of the 2024 Conference of the North American Chapter of the Association for Computational Linguistics: Human Language Technologies (Volume 6: Industry Track)*, pages 453–463, Mexico City, Mexico. Association for Computational Linguistics.

Leveraging Domain Knowledge at Inference Time for LLM Translation: Retrieval versus Generation

Bryan Li[*]
University of Pennsylvania
bryanli@seas.upenn.edu

Jiaming Luo, Eleftheria Briakou, Colin Cherry
Google
{jmluo,ebriakou,colincherry}@google.com

Abstract

While large language models (LLMs) have been increasingly adopted for machine translation (MT), their performance for specialist domains such as medicine and law remains an open challenge. Prior work has shown that LLMs can be *domain-adapted* at test-time by *retrieving* targeted few-shot demonstrations or terminologies for inclusion in the prompt. Meanwhile, for *general-purpose* LLM MT, recent studies have found some success in *generating* similarly useful domain knowledge from an LLM itself, prior to translation. Our work studies domain-adapted MT with LLMs through a careful prompting setup, finding that demonstrations consistently outperform terminology, and retrieval consistently outperforms generation. We find that generating demonstrations with weaker models can close the gap with larger model's zero-shot performance. Given the effectiveness of demonstrations, we perform detailed analyses to understand their value. We find that domain-specificity is particularly important, and that the popular multi-domain benchmark is testing adaptation to a particular writing style more so than to a specific domain.

1 Introduction

Large language models (LLMs) have emerged as the next major paradigm for machine translation (MT), with increasing use in both industrial and academic settings. These models are exciting not only for their strong base (or *zero-shot*) translation capabilities, but also for their ability to be modified at inference time through alternate prompts (Kojima et al., 2022; Kong et al., 2024), in-context learning (Brown et al., 2020) and the use of intermediate reasoning (Wei et al., 2024).

This flexibility is particularly exciting for adapting LLMs to translate specialist domains, such as legal or medical texts. In the statistical and neural MT eras, domain adaptation would typically take the form of an expensive continued training procedure on in-domain data (Freitag and Al-Onaizan, 2016; Thompson et al., 2019). With LLMs, there is the promise of simple adaptation at inference time.

One promising technique is the retrieval of instance-specific demonstrations of translation from a bitext datastore for few-shot in-context learning, which has shown large improvements for domain-adapted MT (Agrawal et al., 2023; Tan et al., 2024), rivaling the performance of specialized nearest-neighbor MT systems (Khandelwal et al., 2021). LLMs have also been shown to make good use of bilingual terminology dictionaries for lexical translation hints (Ghazvininejad et al., 2023; Lu et al., 2023; Moslem et al., 2023).

Intriguingly, two recent approaches have forgone external resources in favor of querying an LLM to generate useful knowledge from its internal memory. First, the MAPS approach issues LLM queries for topics, terminology, and demonstrations based on the source text (He et al., 2024). Their terminology and demonstrations mirror the knowledge sourced from retrieval steps in earlier work. The idea is that the LLM has seen relevant information during pre-training, and would benefit from explicitly surfacing it before translation. Second, the step-by-step MT approach queries its LLM to translate and discuss idiomatic phrases before performing a complete translation (Briakou et al., 2024). However, both these works only consider the general domain. This inspires us to consider the applicability of internal memory approaches to domain adaptation, for which relevant external resources may be more difficult to obtain.

In this work, we study the effectiveness of different representations of domain-specific knowledge, in *strategies* – external retrieval vs. internal generation – and *sources* – translation demonstrations and bilingual terminology. We consider three domains (law, medical, and Koran) from the commonly-

[*]Work done at an internship at Google Translate Research.

Proceedings of the 4th International Workshop on Knowledge-Augmented Methods for Natural Language Processing (KnowledgeNLP'25), pages 91–106
May 3, 2025 ©2025 Association for Computational Linguistics

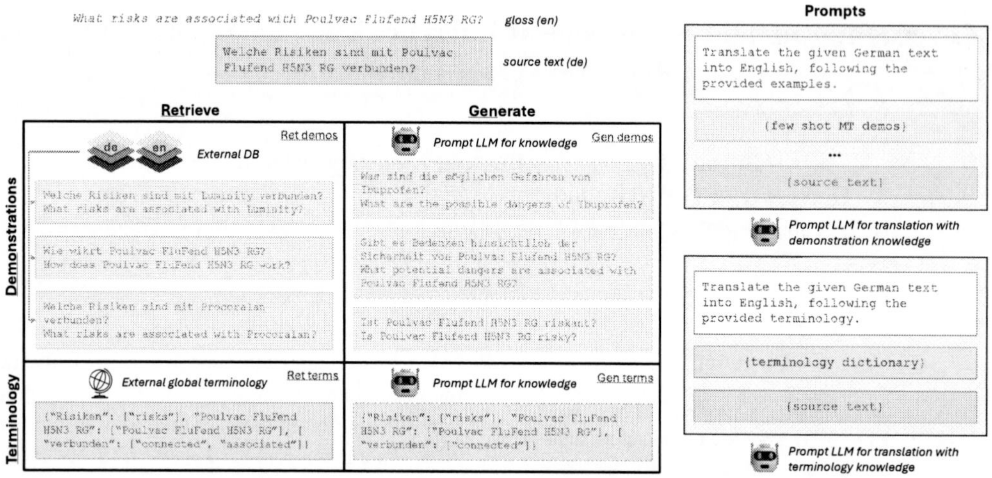

Figure 1: Illustration of the main MT settings, for an example source text in German. The two knowledge strategies are demonstrations vs. terminology; the two sources are retrieval vs. generation. This gives 4 settings for comparison. Within a strategy, we use the same prompts, varying only the provided information.

used multi-domain dataset (Aharoni and Goldberg, 2020), and experiment with two LLMs (Gemini 1.5 and Gemma-2). Our study addresses three main research questions:

RQ1. For improving domain-adapted MT, how viable is generation from an LLM's parametric memory compared to retrieval from external resources?

RQ2. Likewise, how does adapting MT with demonstrations compare with terminologies, regardless of their source?

RQ3. Given the effectiveness of demonstrations, can we attribute which of their aspects contribute the most for both retrieval and generation?

We discuss knowledge sourced from retrieval in §2.1 and from generation in §2.2. Comparisons between terminology and demonstrations are enabled by our use of a silver terminology dictionary, built by LLM analysis of the same bitext used as the datastore of demonstrations (§3.1). This allows us to study demonstrations and terminology as alternate views into the same base data in the retrieval setting. We address RQ1 and RQ2 with the results in §4. We explore RQ3 through several analyses in §5; the main takeaways are that retrieved demonstrations mainly provide hints of target style rather than terminology, and that generated ones can viably boost performance, albeit to the same level as static domain-specific demonstrations.

2 Leveraging Domain Knowledge

Comparisons between representations of domain knowledge are enabled by our careful prompting setup which decouples the *source* and *strategy*, as sketched in Figure 1. Bilingual terms, whether retrieved externally or generated by an auxiliary LLM call, feed into the same translate-with-terms prompt, and likewise for demonstrations. On *sources*, retrieval leverages resources such as datastores and dictionaries, while generation elicits information from an LLM's own parametric memory. On *strategies*, demonstrations provide source-target example pairs, whereas terminology focuses on domain-specific lexical items. This section details the integration of these strategies and knowledge sources within our experimental framework for domain adaptation of LLM MT.

2.1 Knowledge from Retrieval

We describe two successful approaches to retrieve domain knowledge from external resources: *demonstration retrieval* and *terminology lookup*. The two related approaches operate in different fashions. Demonstration retrieval has the model *implicitly* learn from the characteristics of the exemplars, both style and terminology. Terminology lookup has the model *explicitly* see which source terms are important and also how to translate them.

Resource requirements These methods, while effective, are expensive, as they require the existence of high-quality and domain-specific resources. The former requires a large pool of bitext demonstrations, and the latter requires the creation of a term-rich bilingual dictionary.

2.1.1 Demonstration Retrieval

Demonstrations are provided as exemplars in the prompt to facilitate in-context learning (ICL) (Brown et al., 2020; Patel et al., 2023). These exemplars can either be *static*, the same across all instances, or *instance-specific*, in which different exemplars are retrieved for each instance to provide specific guidance and hints.

The typical setup for demonstration retrieval for MT is as follows. Given a source text, we find k closest source-side matches in an external datastore, using some similarity metric, such as BM25 or cosine similarity of embedding vectors. Then, we include in the LLM prompt these k source texts paired with the gold target translations.

Prior work The use of demonstrations has a long history in MT, with some of the oldest data-driven approaches to MT having as their first step finding the most relevant examples from a bilingual translation memory. This idea has been used for computer-aided translation (Yamada, 2011), example-based MT (Somers, 1999; Lepage and Denoual, 2005) and statistical MT (Koehn and Senellart, 2010).

Several recent papers have studied what constitutes effective demonstration retrieval for MT with LLMs, with a particular focus on the multi-domain dataset. Agrawal et al. (2023) found a strong baseline to be example-specific BM25 retrieval of bitexts, which can be strengthened further by re-ranking for lexical diversity. Tan et al. (2024) use a much larger LLM, and show that BM25 retrieval of target sentences alone can compare favorably with both sides of bitexts. Conversely, in the general-domain, researchers have found that a demonstration's quality matters more than its proximity (Vilar et al., 2023; Zhang et al., 2023).

Our Setup For our few-shot implementation, we design a simple prompt (shown in Figure 5). We use k=3 exemplars, [1] and retrieve using the BM25 metric. Our datastore, derived from the train split of multi-domain, has 16,775 demonstrations for Koran, 234,352 for medical, and 464,295 for law.

[1]Prior work often chooses $k \geq 10$. As we find COMET for k=3 and k=10 differ by ~0.3 we thus choose k=3 to fairly compare to the 3 generated demonstrations in a later setting.

2.1.2 Terminology Lookup

Intuitively, one of the major challenges when translating in a specialist domain is the adaptation to domain-specific terminology. Especially in high-stakes legal, medical or business domains, precision of terminology can be crucial. Bilingual dictionaries of terminology are therefore likely sources of useful external knowledge to add into an MT system. These resources can be easier to construct than the large datastore of translation demonstrations needed in §2.1.1. In fact, the construction of a clear terminology may very well be a prerequisite to creating human translations.

Prior Work Improving translations with terminologies has been heavily studied. In the statistical and neural eras, solutions could take the form of incorporating dictionaries into training (Wu et al., 2008), or controllable MT systems that respect example-specific terminology constraints included in the input (Post and Vilar, 2018; Wang et al., 2022). More recently, terminology constraints have been studied at two WMT shared tasks (Alam et al., 2021; Semenov et al., 2023). These approaches illustrate two different motivations for the use of terminology dictionaries in MT: the dictionary can be viewed as a useful source of domain-specific information, or as a set of constraints that must be followed consistently. Our work aligns with the former motivation, viewing bilingual terminologies only as hints to improve overall quality.

With the advent of LLMs, terminologies can be included in the prompt, with additional instructions on their usage. Most LLMs follow these instructions easily, as shown at the WMT23 shared task on terminology (Semenov et al., 2023). For example, Moslem et al. (2023) find that for the COVID-19 domain, a prompt using retrieved terminologies significantly boosts term success rate and also improves human evaluation scores. Other works have explored how to more effectively format dictionaries (Lu et al., 2023; Ghazvininejad et al., 2023).

Our Setup Since the multi-domain dataset does not have a provided domain-specific terminology, we derive one from the multi-domain training set, as described in §3.1. Keeping with our theme of providing hints rather than constraints, the dictionary gives a list of possible translations for each source term, each licensed by at least one example in the training set.

With this dictionary in place, we look up terms

by exact lexical match to the source text currently being translated, and include any matches in our prompt for translation with terminology (shown in Figure 6). The LLM is instructed to pick the most appropriate translation among the choices, given the source. Note that the translation prompt also includes three domain-specific examples of how to translate with terminologies.

2.2 Knowledge from Generation

While external knowledge retrieval demonstrably benefits knowledge-intensive NLP tasks, whether it is truly necessary for domain-adapted MT still warrants investigation, given that LLMs are explicitly trained on massive corpora including texts from specialist domains. Therefore, we investigate whether leveraging LLMs' internal parametric memory can offer comparable benefits, and thus circumvent the costly acquisition and curation of external resources. This approach effectively simulates external retrieval by prompting the LLM to generate relevant information.

Resource requirements By design, the generation setting requires almost no external resources. The approaches discussed below only required us to manually create a handful of static exemplars for each subtask, which are used for all of its prompts.

2.2.1 Prior Work

Prior work has explored several methods to leverage an LLM's parametric knowledge to improve MT quality, either post-translation, or pre-translation. Most relevant to our work are two studies which operate at the pre-translation stage.

He et al. (2024) propose a human-like translation process, where they separately prompt LLMs for 3 aspects related to a source text (demonstrations, topics, and terms). Directly using these generated knowledge pieces in another LLM interaction is insufficient, and so they rely on an external quality estimation (QE) method to select among candidates, improving general domain MT quality. Our generation setting also use demonstrations and terms, but without any external feedback from QE.

Briakou et al. (2024) propose a method to model the LLM translation process step-by-step. Their 2-step approach has an LLM first perform research on idiomatic expressions, then perform the full translation. For document-level MT datasets, they find this consistently outperforms zero-shot MT.

2.2.2 Demonstration Generation

We author a prompt to generate demonstrations (Figure 8). For each domain, we provide 3 example demonstrations for 2 static, real source sentences. This is inspired by the demonstration aspect of He et al. (2024), but we elicit 3 demonstration pairs at a time instead of 1.

Best practices To easily parse the 3 demonstration pairs, we ask for a prescribed JSON output format. We also find that providing static few-shot exemplars of the demonstration task is key to both diversity among the 3 demonstrations, and output format adherence. We use a different set of exemplars for each domain, drawn from the train set. We perform ablations on the contributions of different aspects of generated demonstrations in §5.2.

2.2.3 Terminology Generation

We design a prompt to generate terminologies from a single source sentence (Figure 10), also using 2 static, real sentence pairs for each domain. This follows in the spirit of the research step of Briakou et al. (2024), where they explain this as having the LLM perform intermediate reasoning about hard-to-translate parts. However, there are several differences resulting from their focus on document-level MT. We ask generally for terminologies, while they ask specifically for idiomatic expressions, which are more prevalent in long documents. We also prescribe a JSON format (same as for retrieved terms), while theirs allows for free-form output.

Best practices We again found that best performance is achieved with static, domain-specific few-shot exemplars of the terminology task, and the prescribed JSON format.

3 Experimental Setup

Dataset We experiment with the multi-domain dataset (Aharoni and Goldberg, 2020), using the filtered version provided by Tan et al. (2024), with 3 domains: law, medical, and Koran. Multi-domain covers the German-English (de-en) direction, and consists of dev and test sets, with ~2000 entries per domain, as well as a train set with 1M+ entries.

LLMs We perform experiments with two LLMs, the open LLM Gemma-2 27B IT (Team, 2024b), and the proprietary Gemini 1.5 Pro (Team, 2024a). We thus can investigate which settings, if any, are more effective with the smaller model vs. a much larger model respectively.

Evaluation We perform zero-shot MT as a baseline, and employ the four settings described in §2 for comparison: retrieved demonstrations, retrieved terminologies, generated demonstrations, and generated terminologies. Appendix B lists all prompts used in this work. Following Vilar et al. (2023), we use a neural automated metric, COMET (Rei et al., 2022). While prior work also considered the lexical metric BLEU, we found that it was overly sensitive to minor rephrasing. This is in line with studies that show neural metrics correlate much better with human judgments of LLM translation quality (Freitag et al., 2021; Kocmi et al., 2021).

3.1 Terminology Dictionary Creation

Our multi-domain test scenario does not come with bilingual terminology dictionaries for its domains. However, we can create them from the provided training split, following the methodology in prior work (Moslem et al., 2023; Semenov et al., 2023).[2] We design a prompt (Figure 12) to extract terminologies from a given source-target text pair, providing 5 static exemplars to demonstrate what is meant by "terminology". We then apply this to each pair from the train split. Then, we aggregate all of the output terms, to get one large dictionary with one-to-many mappings.[3] We create a separate global terminology for each of the three domains.

Given the large size of the training split (700K entries), we make two adjustments to reduce the number of model calls. First, we batch five test pairs at a time into a single call. Second, we consider only the subset of train entries that were ever retrieved by BM25 over the test set (i.e. the entries that are actually relevant); this constitutes 70K entries, or about 10% of the total entries.

Note that the train split is also used for demonstration retrieval, therefore enabling a controlled comparison between the two external knowledge sources. Furthermore, unlike prior work using one-to-one terminology mappings, we explore a more realistic one-to-many scenario, with all possible translations in the prompt for the LLM to select.

4 Results

Table 1 presents our primary results, comparing LLM translation enhanced with domain-specific knowledge in the form of translation demonstrations or bilingual terminology, with the artifacts derived from either external retrieval (§2.1) or internal generation (§2.2). First, in line with prior work, we confirm that retrieved demonstrations improve over zero-shot across models and domains studied. We next describe the three main findings.

Demonstrations outperform terminology For all models and domains studied, knowledge provided in the form of demonstrations consistently outperforms terminology. For Gemma, we see that all settings improve performance,[4] but the improvements from demonstrations are markedly larger. The differential is more pronounced for Gemini, which starts from a much stronger baseline than Gemma. Terms, either retrieved or generated, do not provide much of a boost over zero-shot for Gemini, while demonstrations result in significant improvements. The takeaway for this finding is that for weaker models, providing domain knowledge from any source or strategy is beneficial. Conversely, stronger models do not benefit from domain-specific terminology, but only from more complete demonstrations of the task.

Retrieval outperforms generation The second notable trend across models and domains is that retrieval consistently outperforms generation. With Gemma, demonstration generation outperforms zero-shot by +2.3 (averaged across domains), while retrieval further improves to +3.4. For the more powerful Gemini, the differential is larger – demonstration generation outperforms zero-shot by +0.5, while retrieval by +1.8.

Generated domain-specific demonstrations boost weaker model's translations Taking the prior two findings together, we can bootstrap domain-adapted MT knowledge from an LLM's own parametric memory, with the two-stage approach of first generating demonstrations, then translating. This improvement especially pronounced with Gemma (+2.3 vs. +0.5 over respective zero-shot). In fact, this empowers a smaller model (Gemma) to close the gap with a larger model's (Gemini) zero-shot results, as can be seen by comparing, in Table 1, the bottom left and top right rows. The gains in medical (+2.9) and Koran domains (+1.0) result in statistically

[2] We did not perform human post-editing due to the datastore's size (700K), but we note in an experiment by Moslem et al. (2023), they found humans rated 95%+ terms as accurate.

[3] For quality controls, we kept only entries where 1) target terms have >10% usage and 2) both sides of terms match.

[4] To explain the outliers for Koran (−1.4, −0.5), our manual analysis found term inconsistency – high-frequency source terms mapped to multiple, equally-valid target terms.

Domain Knowledge?		Gemma-2 27B IT						Gemini 1.5 Pro					
		Law		**Med.**		**Koran**		**Law**		**Med.**		**Koran**	
zero-shot		84.8		85.2		75.1		86.6		88.2		76.3	
retrieved	terms	85.9*	↑1.1	87.8*	↑2.6	74.6	↓0.5	86.9*	↑0.3	88.5	↑0.3	74.9	↓1.4
	demos	88.6*	↑3.8	89.9*	↑4.7	76.7*	↑1.6	89.3*	↑2.7	89.9*	↑1.7	76.4	↑0.1
generated	terms	85.2	↑0.4	87.1*	↑1.9	75.7*	↑0.6	86.7	↑0.1	88.1	↓0.1	76.9*	↑0.6
	demos	86.0*	↑1.2	88.1*	↑2.9	76.1*	↑1.0	87.2*	↑0.6	88.8*	↑0.6	76.7*	↑0.4

Table 1: Results for MT using the COMET22 metrics, comparing the knowledge sources, retrieved and generated, and the strategies, demonstrations (demos) or terminology (terms). Significant improvements ($p < 0.05$) over the zero-shot baseline are marked with *. Demonstrations outperform terminology, and retrieval outperforms generation. Generation is especially effective for the smaller Gemma model.

equivalent scores. Law domain incurs a decent gain (+1.2), but still is below Gemini (86.0 < 86.6). It is worth emphasizing that acquiring extensive resources for novel specialist domains is expensive; but this straightforward approach can be effective.[5]

Comparisons with Prior Results We can also compare our results with demonstrations to those from the recent study by Tan et al. (2024), who use the `gpt-3.5-turbo-0301` LLM. Their zero-shot results are most comparable to Gemma's: 84.4, 86.2, 75.1. Their results for retrieved demonstrations are also comparable: 88.2, 89.6, 76.5. The other 3 settings, retrieving terms and both generation ones, are new to our work – and we re-emphasize here the value of our controlled setting in facilitating fair comparison between them all.

5 Analysis

Demonstrations (both retrieved and generated) are by far the most effective domain adaptation strategy we explored, providing a large boost to both LLMs. In the following sections, we turn to analyses to understand better where the gains are coming from. We begin by analyzing retrieved demonstrations to disentangle contributions from style vs. terminology (§5.1). Then, we investigate the importance of various in-context learning decisions for generating demonstrations (§5.2). Finally, we study how generated domain knowledge can be distilled at test-time from larger to smaller models (§5.3).

5.1 Retrieved Demonstrations: Contributions from Style vs. Terminology

What exactly is being conveyed by the retrieved demonstrations? In this section, we take advantage of our careful experimental setup, where our

[5]Note that the experiment from §5.2 shows that domain-specificity is the main contributor, rather than proximity to the current instance. These generated demos are only as effective as real static, but domain-specific demos.

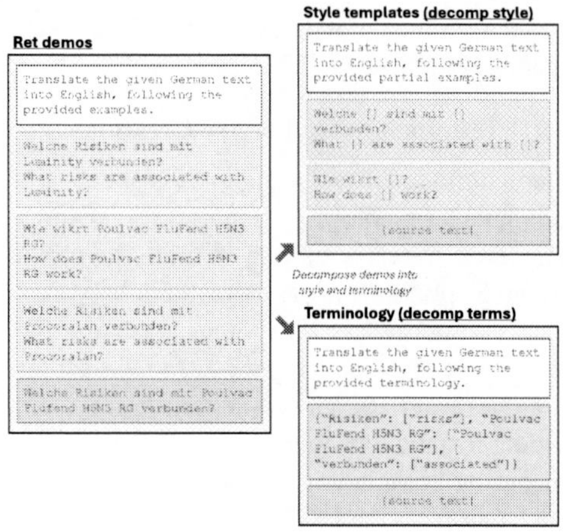

Figure 2: Illustration of our process to decompose the contributions of retrieved demonstrations into style and terminology. We first extract the source-target term pairs using a simple function, and aggregate them into a local terminology. Then, the remaining tokens are the style templates, with the terms masked. Note that in the actual data, we use <MASK> instead of [].

bilingual terminology is derived from the same parallel text used for demonstrations, to disentangle whether demonstrations are more valuable because they assist with proper *terminology* translations in context, or with matching the *style* of the corpus.

The core idea behind this experiment is that we can use the same technique to extract bilingual terminology pairs from a translation demonstration (§3.1), but instead of running it on the whole training corpus, we can run it only on the k demonstrations retrieved to match the current source sentence. This gives us a *local* terminology, as opposed to a *global* one. Crucially, where the global terminology would present the union of all possible target language translations found throughout the training set for a given source term, the local terminology only presents translations licensed by the k demonstrations. This allows it to take advantage of any

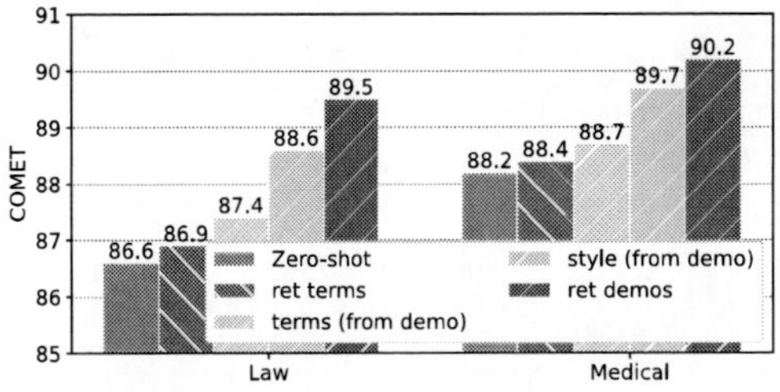

Figure 3: Results for zero-shot, external retrieval, terms from demonstrations, and style from demonstrations.

disambiguating context in the demonstrations to create more relevant term translations.

We then define style templates as the inverse – the remaining tokens, with the bilingual terms on both sides replaced with a `<MASK>` mask token. For this, we use a similar prompt as for demonstration retrieval, but also explicitly instruct the LLM to not generate mask tokens in its output (as shown in Figure 7). Upon manual inspection, these masks appear quite thorough, with most anything that could be considered terminology being masked out.

Results We carry out the decomposition experiment using Gemini 1.5 Pro. Figure 3 presents our results. We see that compared to zero-shot, using local terms (terms from demonstrations) more than doubles the gains of global terms (retrieved terms). However, style templates (style from demonstrations) further narrow the gap to retrieved demonstrations by 60% (law) and 75% (medical).

The combined results from the *terms from demonstrations* and *style from demonstrations* experiments indicate that the primary value from retrieved demonstrations is not contextually appropriate translations of domain-specific terminology. While this is a part of the story, it accounts for only 0.8 (law) and 0.5 (medical) points of the 2.9- and 2.0-point improvements from the retrieved demonstrations. Meanwhile, the *style from demonstrations* scores almost perfectly account for the remainder. This is a strong indicator that the majority of the value of retrieved demonstrations comes from matching the publication style of these corpora, rather than carrying out adaptation to a medical or legal domain. That is, we are doing domain adaptation, but it is to a much more narrow domain than is usually discussed.

These results agree with and reinforce conclusions from recent work. Tan et al. (2024) perform a targeted study into translation style, following the same settings – the multi-domain dataset and a strong proprietary LLM. Their findings between zero-shot and few-shot concur – while there is a observable COMET difference (2.7), nevertheless zero-shot translations "have already conveyed the *semantic meaning* of the source sentence, albeit with some variations in *lexical choices* and sentence structure." They therefore propose a style learning method to retrieves related target sentences from a monolingual target corpus, finding this achieves 70% of few-shot's gains. However, by only removing the source side of the demonstrations, the exemplars still implicitly provide both style and terminology hints. We add to the discussion by providing a precise, alternative definition of "style" as anything outside of terminology. This in turn allows us to cleanly decompose the tokens from each demonstration into two subsets, and assign credit accordingly.

5.2 Ablation on Generated Demonstrations

Generation of demonstrations (`generate demos`) is by far the most successful of the two approaches. As described in §2.2, we made several decisions here: 1) using domain-specific exemplars; 2) using the intermediate generation of demonstration step; 3) in that step, selection of the ICL exemplars. We explore the impact of the decisions by comparing the `zero-shot`, `retrieved demos`, and `generate demos` results to the following ablations:

Static few-shot Drop the generate demo step, and use the 2x3 domain-specific examples[6] directly as static demonstrations of translation. This investigates the impact of domain-specificity alone.

No ICL With the generated demo step, but remove all exemplars from that step's instructions. This investigates the impact of ICL at all.

General ICL With the generated demo step, but use the 5x1 general-domain examples from He et al. (2024) instead of the 2x3. This investigates the impact of the domain-specificity of ICL.

Results are shown in Table 2. First, we consider ablation results on Gemini. There is a large drop between `zero-shot` and 'no ICL' (e.g., 88.2 -> 83.8 for medicine). Our manual analysis of a few 'no ICL' outputs finds that the generated demonstrations on the target side are often quite lexically close; we hypothesize these are unhelpful and affect downstream translations. Comparing general ICL to `generated demos`, we see that roughly

[6] 2x3 means there are two example source texts, which are each followed by three example translation pairs.

Setting	Domain-specific	Generate demo step	Demo # ICL	Gemma-2 27B IT law	Gemma-2 27B IT med.	Gemma-2 27B IT Koran	Gemini 1.5 Pro law	Gemini 1.5 Pro med.	Gemini 1.5 Pro Koran
`zero-shot`	N/A	✗	N/A	84.8	85.2	75.1	86.6	88.2	76.3
static few-shot	✓	✗	N/A	86.3	88.2	76.3	87.2	89.1	76.4
`retrieved demos`	✓	✗	N/A	88.6	89.9	76.7	89.3	89.9	76.4
no ICL	N/A	✓	0	85.2	87.5	75.1	83.9	83.8	75.6
general ICL	✗	✓	5x1	85.7	87.8	75.6	86.9	88.5	76.0
`generated demos`	✓	✓	2x3	86.0	88.1	76.1	87.2	88.8	76.7

Table 2: COMET22 Results for the study on demonstration generation, using Gemma (left) and Gemini (right). The *italicized* settings are ablations, while the `monospace` settings are the same as in Table 1.

half the value of demonstration generation can be retained with general ICL. However, comparing 'static few-shot' to generate demos (rows 7 & 10), both achieve similar scores across domains. This adds a caveat to our earlier findings, suggesting the domain-specificity of the generated demos is more important to downstream MT than the demos alone.

Now, we consider ablation results on Gemma. Interestingly, unlike for Gemini, for Gemma even the 'no ICL' setting improves upon zero-shot (85.2 -> 87.5 for medicine). We observe that, compared to `generated demos`, 'General ICL' slightly underperforms it, while 'static few-shot' matches it. This again underscores the value of the demonstration stage in improving the smaller LLM's translations, as well as key role of domain-specificity.

Our results add insight into two formerly disparate findings. Prior work on older LLMs discussed two factors for ICL exemplars: lexical coverage within a domain (Agrawal et al., 2023), and their quality (Vilar et al., 2023). Our finding here provides evidence that, for current LLMs with strong zero-shot MT performance, the primary value of ICL is in the domain-specificity, especially in style. Quality examples can be equally as validly obtained from static few-shot exemplars or generated demonstrations.

5.3 Cross-LLM Knowledge Generation

For the two generation-based settings, the same LLM is used in both the generation stage and the translation stage. To further understand how generation quality affects the final performance, we conduct additional experiments to reuse the generated demonstrations or terminology from Gemini 1.5 Pro to prompt the Gemma 2 27B model for translation. As shown in Table 3, demonstration generation and terminology generation both benefit greatly from higher quality generations from Gemini, with significant gains in all three domains. This shows that higher-quality generated knowledge result in higher-quality translations. The larger Gemini model's knowledge can be effectively distilled to the smaller Gemma model, at inference-time, through its translation demonstrations.

strategy	gen. LLM	law	med.	koran
⚙ `demos`	Gemma	86.0	88.1	76.1
	Gemini	86.9*	88.6*	76.6*
⚙ `terms`	Gemma	85.2	87.1	75.7
	Gemini	85.8*	87.5*	76.4*

Table 3: Results for the ablation on generation-based strategies. Gemma-2 27B IT is always used for translation, but the generation model can be either LLM. Significant improvements when using Gemini's generated outputs instead of Gemma's are marked with *.

6 Discussion and Conclusion

We study the problem of domain adaptation for MT with LLMs, one which intuitively speaking, should be well addressed by prompting-time adaptation. Building upon prior work which injects domain-specific knowledge into prompts, we perform a thorough study into how this knowledge can best be acquired in terms of strategy, demonstrations or terminologies, and sources, retrieval or generation.

Our main study shows that demonstrations outperform terminology, and knowledge retrieval consistently outperforms generation. Furthermore, generation of domain-specific demonstrations can viably improve weaker model's performance, closing the gap with a larger model's zero-shot performance (though comparable to static exemplars). We gain additional insights with our further analyses. Notably, we explore the connection between the strategies, characterizing demonstrations as providing both terminology hints and style hints. Our decomposition of the contributions of demonstrations finds that the majority of the gains (~65%) come from style over terminology.

Taken together, our work indicates that for the law, medical and Koran domains of the commonly-used multi-domain scenario, large LLMs need very little terminology help, and the improvements from demonstrations are more so from matching corpus style than from better conveying domain-specific semantics. Our work takes a first step in surfacing the domain-specific knowledge of smaller LLMs through generation, and we look forward to more informed approaches in future work. Meanwhile for the largest LLMs, we recommend as the most promising direction to construct a new MT adaptation scenario that challenges even their broad base of parametric knowledge, perhaps with reference to pretraining cut-off dates.

Limitations

While our work aims to generally study the problem domain adaptation for MT, we considered only a single dataset, multi-domain, with 3 domains and 1 language pair. This is following prior work, and also as there no other suitable datasets for our comparative setting. This is further discussed in Appendix A. We noted the limitations of this dataset, in not posing enough of a domain-adaptation challenge for current LLMs. We call on future work to design more up-to-date, comprehensive domain-adapted MT datasets.

We acknowledge that the multi-domain dataset is fairly well-worn, and there is possible data leakage into current LLMs, given the availability of the entire dataset online. This is a general concern with research using proprietary LLMs. However, the fact that demonstration retrieval does improve COMET scores for multi-domain indicates that, at the very least, the paired translations have not exactly memorized. Also, consider the Koran domain. While an LLM have undoubtedly seen Koran text during training, because there are multiple translations of the Koran into both English and in German, there is no exact 1-1 mapping with respect to the translations used in this dataset.

For demonstration retrieval, we used only the BM25 algorithm. Prior works have explored more informed retrieval approaches; however they were starting from much weaker zero-shot baseline, meaning that demo quality should matter less in our case. We reiterate that improving retrieval-based few-shot MT is not the goal of this work; rather, we aim to understand why it works well, and whether generating from parametric memory alone is viable. Our analysis, including our decomposition of demonstrations into style and terminology, can also be applied to demonstrations from any other similarity method.

Our use of a silver terminology built by LLM may lead to an under-estimation of the value of retrieved knowledge from bilingual terminology dictionaries. Likewise, our decomposition of demonstrations into terminology entries and style templates may be affected by the LLM's terminology-extraction errors. As mentioned in the main text, prior work indicates that these techniques (with older LLMs) should be roughly 95% accurate (Moslem et al., 2023).

7 Acknowledgments

We thank the members of Google Translate Research for their guidance throughout the course of this project. We thank Weiting Tan for providing us with the filtered version of the multi-domain test set, and the anonymous reviewers and area chair for their feedback.

References

Sweta Agrawal, Chunting Zhou, Mike Lewis, Luke Zettlemoyer, and Marjan Ghazvininejad. 2023. In-context examples selection for machine translation. In *Findings of the Association for Computational Linguistics: ACL 2023*, pages 8857–8873, Toronto, Canada. Association for Computational Linguistics.

Roee Aharoni and Yoav Goldberg. 2020. Unsupervised domain clusters in pretrained language models. In *Proceedings of the 58th Annual Meeting of the Association for Computational Linguistics*, pages 7747–7763, Online. Association for Computational Linguistics.

Md Mahfuz Ibn Alam, Ivana Kvapilíková, Antonios Anastasopoulos, Laurent Besacier, Georgiana Dinu, Marcello Federico, Matthias Gallé, Kweonwoo Jung, Philipp Koehn, and Vassilina Nikoulina. 2021. Findings of the WMT shared task on machine translation using terminologies. In *Proceedings of the Sixth Conference on Machine Translation*, pages 652–663, Online. Association for Computational Linguistics.

Seth Aycock and Rachel Bawden. 2024. Topic-guided example selection for domain adaptation in LLM-based machine translation. In *Proceedings of the 18th Conference of the European Chapter of the Association for Computational Linguistics: Student*

Research Workshop, pages 175–195, St. Julian's, Malta. Association for Computational Linguistics.

Eleftheria Briakou, Jiaming Luo, Colin Cherry, and Markus Freitag. 2024. Translating step-by-step: Decomposing the translation process for improved translation quality of long-form texts. *Preprint*, arXiv:2409.06790.

Tom Brown, Benjamin Mann, Nick Ryder, Melanie Subbiah, Jared D Kaplan, Prafulla Dhariwal, Arvind Neelakantan, Pranav Shyam, Girish Sastry, Amanda Askell, Sandhini Agarwal, Ariel Herbert-Voss, Gretchen Krueger, Tom Henighan, Rewon Child, Aditya Ramesh, Daniel Ziegler, Jeffrey Wu, Clemens Winter, Chris Hesse, Mark Chen, Eric Sigler, Mateusz Litwin, Scott Gray, Benjamin Chess, Jack Clark, Christopher Berner, Sam McCandlish, Alec Radford, Ilya Sutskever, and Dario Amodei. 2020. Language models are few-shot learners. In *Advances in Neural Information Processing Systems*, volume 33, pages 1877–1901. Curran Associates, Inc.

Markus Freitag and Yaser Al-Onaizan. 2016. Fast domain adaptation for neural machine translation. *Preprint*, arXiv:1612.06897.

Markus Freitag, Ricardo Rei, Nitika Mathur, Chi-kiu Lo, Craig Stewart, George Foster, Alon Lavie, and Ondřej Bojar. 2021. Results of the WMT21 metrics shared task: Evaluating metrics with expert-based human evaluations on TED and news domain. In *Proceedings of the Sixth Conference on Machine Translation*, pages 733–774, Online. Association for Computational Linguistics.

Marjan Ghazvininejad, Hila Gonen, and Luke Zettlemoyer. 2023. Dictionary-based phrase-level prompting of large language models for machine translation. *arXiv preprint arXiv:2302.07856*.

Zhiwei He, Tian Liang, Wenxiang Jiao, Zhuosheng Zhang, Yujiu Yang, Rui Wang, Zhaopeng Tu, Shuming Shi, and Xing Wang. 2024. Exploring human-like translation strategy with large language models. *Transactions of the Association for Computational Linguistics*, 12:229–246.

Urvashi Khandelwal, Angela Fan, Dan Jurafsky, Luke Zettlemoyer, and Mike Lewis. 2021. Nearest neighbor machine translation. In *International Conference on Learning Representations*.

Tom Kocmi, Christian Federmann, Roman Grundkiewicz, Marcin Junczys-Dowmunt, Hitokazu Matsushita, and Arul Menezes. 2021. To ship or not to ship: An extensive evaluation of automatic metrics for machine translation. In *Proceedings of the Sixth Conference on Machine Translation*, pages 478–494, Online. Association for Computational Linguistics.

Philipp Koehn and Jean Senellart. 2010. Convergence of translation memory and statistical machine translation. In *Proceedings of the Second Joint EM+/CNGL Workshop: Bringing MT to the User: Research on Integrating MT in the Translation Industry*, pages 21–32, Denver, Colorado, USA. Association for Machine Translation in the Americas.

Takeshi Kojima, Shixiang (Shane) Gu, Machel Reid, Yutaka Matsuo, and Yusuke Iwasawa. 2022. Large language models are zero-shot reasoners. In *Advances in Neural Information Processing Systems*, volume 35, pages 22199–22213. Curran Associates, Inc.

Aobo Kong, Shiwan Zhao, Hao Chen, Qicheng Li, Yong Qin, Ruiqi Sun, Xin Zhou, Enzhi Wang, and Xiaohang Dong. 2024. Better zero-shot reasoning with role-play prompting. In *Proceedings of the 2024 Conference of the North American Chapter of the Association for Computational Linguistics: Human Language Technologies (Volume 1: Long Papers)*, pages 4099–4113, Mexico City, Mexico. Association for Computational Linguistics.

Yves Lepage and Etienne Denoual. 2005. Purest ever example-based machine translation: Detailed presentation and assessment. *Machine Translation*, 19(3/4):251–282.

Hongyuan Lu, Haoyang Huang, Dongdong Zhang, Haoran Yang, Wai Lam, and Furu Wei. 2023. Chain-of-dictionary prompting elicits translation in large language models. *arXiv preprint arXiv:2305.06575*.

Yasmin Moslem, Rejwanul Haque, John D. Kelleher, and Andy Way. 2023. Adaptive machine translation with large language models. In *Proceedings of the 24th Annual Conference of the European Association for Machine Translation*, pages 227–237, Tampere, Finland. European Association for Machine Translation.

Ajay Patel, Bryan Li, Mohammad Sadegh Rasooli, Noah Constant, Colin Raffel, and Chris Callison-Burch. 2023. Bidirectional language models are also few-shot learners. In *The Eleventh International Conference on Learning Representations*.

Matt Post and David Vilar. 2018. Fast lexically constrained decoding with dynamic beam allocation for neural machine translation. In *Proceedings of the 2018 Conference of the North American Chapter of the Association for Computational Linguistics: Human Language Technologies, Volume 1 (Long Papers)*, pages 1314–1324, New Orleans, Louisiana. Association for Computational Linguistics.

Ricardo Rei, José G. C. de Souza, Duarte Alves, Chrysoula Zerva, Ana C Farinha, Taisiya Glushkova, Alon Lavie, Luisa Coheur, and André F. T. Martins. 2022. COMET-22: Unbabel-IST 2022 submission for the metrics shared task. In *Proceedings of the Seventh Conference on Machine Translation (WMT)*, pages 578–585, Abu Dhabi, United Arab Emirates (Hybrid). Association for Computational Linguistics.

Kirill Semenov, Vilém Zouhar, Tom Kocmi, Dongdong Zhang, Wangchunshu Zhou, and Yuchen Eleanor

Jiang. 2023. Findings of the WMT 2023 shared task on machine translation with terminologies. In *Proceedings of the Eighth Conference on Machine Translation*, pages 663–671, Singapore. Association for Computational Linguistics.

Harold Somers. 1999. Review article: Example-based machine translation. *Machine Translation*, 14(2):113–157.

Weiting Tan, Haoran Xu, Lingfeng Shen, Shuyue Stella Li, Kenton Murray, Philipp Koehn, Benjamin Van Durme, and Yunmo Chen. 2024. Narrowing the gap between zero- and few-shot machine translation by matching styles. In *Findings of the Association for Computational Linguistics: NAACL 2024*, pages 490–502, Mexico City, Mexico. Association for Computational Linguistics.

Gemini Team. 2024a. Gemini 1.5: Unlocking multimodal understanding across millions of tokens of context. *Preprint*, arXiv:2403.05530.

Gemma Team. 2024b. Gemma: Open models based on gemini research and technology. *Preprint*, arXiv:2403.08295.

Brian Thompson, Jeremy Gwinnup, Huda Khayrallah, Kevin Duh, and Philipp Koehn. 2019. Overcoming catastrophic forgetting during domain adaptation of neural machine translation. In *Proceedings of the Second Workshop on Shortcomings in Vision and Language*, pages 2062–2068, Minneapolis, Minnesota. Association for Computational Linguistics.

David Vilar, Markus Freitag, Colin Cherry, Jiaming Luo, Viresh Ratnakar, and George Foster. 2023. Prompting PaLM for translation: Assessing strategies and performance. In *Proceedings of the 61st Annual Meeting of the Association for Computational Linguistics (Volume 1: Long Papers)*, pages 15406–15427, Toronto, Canada. Association for Computational Linguistics.

Shuo Wang, Peng Li, Zhixing Tan, Zhaopeng Tu, Maosong Sun, and Yang Liu. 2022. A template-based method for constrained neural machine translation. In *Proceedings of the 2022 Conference on Empirical Methods in Natural Language Processing*, pages 3665–3679, Abu Dhabi, United Arab Emirates. Association for Computational Linguistics.

Jason Wei, Xuezhi Wang, Dale Schuurmans, Maarten Bosma, Brian Ichter, Fei Xia, Ed H. Chi, Quoc V. Le, and Denny Zhou. 2024. Chain-of-thought prompting elicits reasoning in large language models. In *Proceedings of the 36th International Conference on Neural Information Processing Systems*, NIPS '22, Red Hook, NY, USA. Curran Associates Inc.

Hua Wu, Haifeng Wang, and Chengqing Zong. 2008. Domain adaptation for statistical machine translation with domain dictionary and monolingual corpora. In *Proceedings of the 22nd International Conference on Computational Linguistics (Coling 2008)*, pages 993–1000, Manchester, UK. Coling 2008 Organizing Committee.

Masaru Yamada. 2011. The effect of translation memory databases on productivity. *Translation research projects*, 3:63–73.

Biao Zhang, Barry Haddow, and Alexandra Birch. 2023. Prompting Large Language Model for Machine Translation: A Case Study. In *Proceedings of the 40th International Conference on Machine Learning*, pages 41092–41110. PMLR.

A Other MT with Terminology Datasets

We did not use the datasets from WMT21 and WMT23 shared tasks on MT with terminologies. They do not include datastore for retrieving demonstrations, as well as each having its own concerns. For WMT21, we found that MT performance for zero-shot and using gold terms was equivalent (87.0 vs. 86.8 COMET22). This is due to contemporary LLM pretraining data containing a lot of COVID domain text, making it no longer a specialist domain. For WMT23, terminologies are internally defined – i.e., written directly with respect to each test and dev bitext. As we argued earlier, terminologies should be considered as external, pre-defined resources. We therefore recommend that both WMT21 and WMT23 datasets are outdated with current LLMs, and their use should be avoided.

Aycock and Bawden (2024) introduce a domain-adapted MT dataset, which they curate as a subset of existing MT resources from the OPUS project. This covers 7 domains and 11 languages. However, for all domains of their dataset, there is no large-scale data-store for demonstration retrieval; they only perform retrieval – proposing a topic-model guided exemplar selection method, which they show beats BM25 – over the very small development splits. Our work therefore considers only the multi-domain dataset, as it widely used for domain-adapted MT, and also satisfies our external resource requirements.

B Prompts Used

We reproduce the exact prompts used below, where {<some_var>} are variables which are filled per prompt, and [<some_ex>] are the static exemplars which are filled per-domain.

```
Instruction: Translate the following {src_full} text into {tgt_full} and output the result
in JSON format using "translation" as the key.
{source_language_name}: {source_text}
{target_language_name}:
```

Figure 4: Prompt for zero-shot MT.

```
You are tasked with translating {source_language_name} to {target_language_name}. You are provided
several example translations, and you should follow their example to translate the given
{source_language_name} sentence.
{demo_examples}
{source_language_name}: {source_text}
{target_language_name}:
```

Figure 5: Prompt for MT with *demonstrations* (also known as few-shot MT in prior work). This prompt is used for both demonstration retrieval and demonstration generation.

```
Your task is to translate a piece of text from {source_language_name} into {target_language_name}.
You are provided a list of terminology dictionaries. Each dictionary has a single source term (key
"de"), and multiple candidate translated terms (key "en") -- pick the most appropriate translated
term for the source sentence. Note that the terminologies have lowercased terms, but you should
consider proper casing when translating into {target_language_name}. Based on these terminologies,
output your best one translation.
{examples}
Terminology: {terminology}
{source_language_name}: {source_text}
{target_language_name}:
```

Figure 6: Prompt for MT with *terminologies*. This prompt is used for both terminology retrieval and terminology generation.

```
You are tasked with translating {source_language_name} to {target_language_name}. You are provided
several example translations, and you should follow their example to translate the given
{source_language_name} sentence. Note that the examples might contain special mask tokens <MASK> but
in your output, please do not use any such tokens.

[few_shot_examples]
{source_language_name}: {source_text}
{target_language_name}:
```

Figure 7: Prompt for MT with *style from demonstrations*. Recall that in this setting, we provide the retrieved demonstrations, but with the terminologies masked out – i.e., the style contribution is the inverse of the terminology contribution.

```
You are given a {source_language_name} source text, and asked to write exactly 3 text pairs. A text
pair consists of a {source_language_name} text, which is related to but different from the source
text, and its translation into {target_language_name}. You should do your best to ensure that your
{source_language_name} texts have similar style to the source text. Following the provided examples,
output each pair as a JSON dictionary, with keys "de" and "en". Each dictionary should be on a
separate line.
[demo_examples]
{source_language_name} source: {source_text}
Pair 1:
```

Figure 8: Prompt for synthetic *demonstration generation*. `[demo_examples]` are static exemplars for this task; see below.

```
German source: Die EDGE- und EDGE-II-Studien verglichen die gastrointestinale Verträglichkeit
von Etoricoxib mit der von Diclofenac.
Pair 1: {"de": "Die kardiorenalen Ergebnisse der EDGE- und EDGE-II-Studien entsprachen den
für die MEDAL- Studie beschriebenen.", "en": "The cardiorenal results for EDGE and EDGE II
were consistent with those described for the MEDAL Study."}
Pair 2: {"de": "Eine langsame Dosissteigerung kann die gastrointestinale Verträglichkeit
ebenfalls verbessern.", "en": "A slow increase in the dose may also improve gastrointestinal
tolerability."}
Pair 3: {"de": "Die Häufigkeit von unerwünschten Ereignissen in EDGE und EDGE II sowie die
Häufigkeit von als schwerwiegend erachteten oder zum Studienabbruch führenden unerwünschten
Ereignissen in der MEDAL-Studie war unter Etoricoxib höher als unter Diclofenac.", "en": "The
incidence of adverse experiences in EDGE and EDGE II and of adverse experiences considered
serious or resulting in discontinuation in the MEDAL study was higher with etoricoxib than
diclofenac."}
---
German source: 3 ml Lösung in einer Patrone aus Glas (Glasart 1), mit einem Kolben (Brombutylgummi)
und einem Stopfen (Brombutylgummi/Polyisopren) in einem Umkarton.
Pair 1: {"de": "3 ml Lösung in einer Patrone aus Glas (Glasart 1), mit einem Kolben (Brombutylgummi)
und einem Stopfen (Brombutylgummi/Polyisopren) in einem Fertigpen (Mehrdosen-Einwegspritze aus
Polypropylen).", "en": "3 ml solution in a cartridge (type 1 glass) with a plunger (bromobutyl) and
a stopper (bromobutyl/ polyisoprene) contained in a pre-filled pen (multidose disposable pen)
(polypropylene)."}
Pair 2: {"de": "3 ml Suspension in einer Patrone (farbloses Glas, Typ 1) mit einem Kolben
(Brombutylgummi, Typ 1) und einer Bördelkappe (Aluminium) mit einem Stopfen (Brombutyl- oder
Polyisopren- Brombutylgummi, Typ 1).", "en": "3 ml suspension in a cartridge (type 1 colourless
glass) with a plunger (bromobutyl rubber (type 1)) and a flanged cap (aluminium) with a stopper
(bromobutyl or laminate of polyisoprene and bromobutyl rubber (type 1))."}
Pair 3: {"de": "5 ml Lösung in einer Durchstechflasche (farbloses Glas, Typ 1) mit einer
Bördelkappe (Aluminium), einem Stopfen (Chlorbutylgummi, Typ 1) und einem Abreißdeckel
(Polypropylen).", "en": "5 ml solution in a vial (type 1 colourless glass) with a flanged cap
(aluminium), a stopper (chlorobutyl rubber (type 1)) and a tear-off cap (polypropylene)."}
---
```

Figure 9: Static 2-shot exemplars used for the synthetic *demonstration generation* prompt (Figure 8). Each exemplar has 3 output sentences. Here we show the exemplars for the medical domain.

```
You are given a {source_language_name} source text, and asked to extract a bilingual terminology
that translates key terms from the source text into {target_language_name}. Each entry in the
terminology should have a {source_language_name} term and a list of possible {target_language_name}
translations. Following the provided examples, output each pair as a JSON dictionary, with keys "de"
and "en". Each dictionary should be on a separate line.
[term_examples]
{source_language_name} source: {source_text}
Term 1:
```

Figure 10: Prompt for synthetic *terminology generation*. `[term_examples]` are static exemplars for this task; see below.

```
German source: (6) Die Kommission unterrichtete den Antragsteller, andere Gemeinschaftshersteller,
die ausführenden Hersteller in der VR China und in den USA, bekanntermaßen betroffene Einführer
und Verwender sowie die Vertreter der Regierungen der VR China und der USA offiziell über die
Einleitung des Verfahrens.
Term 1: {"de": "einleitung des verfahrens", "en": ["initiation of the proceeding",
"opening of the proceedings"]}
Term 2: {"de": "ausführenden hersteller", "en": ["exporting producers"]}
Term 3: {"de": "gemeinschaftshersteller", "en": ["community producers"]}
Term 4: {"de": "antragsteller", "en": ["complainant"]}
Term 5: {"de": "kommission", "en": ["commission"]}
Term 6: {"de": "verfahrens", "en": ["investigation", "procedure"]}
Term 7: {"de": "einführer", "en": ["importers"]}
Term 8: {"de": "verwender", "en": ["users"]}
Term 9: {"de": "vertreter", "en": ["representatives"]}
Term 10: {"de": "vr china", "en": ["prc"]}
---
German source: ENTSCHEIDUNG DER KOMMISSION vom 25. Februar 1998 zum Fragebogen für die Berichte der
Mitgliedstaaten über die Umsetzung der Richtlinie 94/67/EG des Rates über die Verbrennung
gefährlicher Abfälle (Umsetzung der Richtlinie 91/692/EWG des Rates) (Text von Bedeutung
für den EWR) (98/184/EG)
Term 1: {"de": "verbrennung gefährlicher abfälle", "en": ["incineration of hazardous waste"]}
Term 2: {"de": "fragebogen", "en": ["questionnaire"]}
Term 3: {"de": "richtlinie", "en": ["directive", "guideline"]}
Term 4: {"de": "ewr", "en": ["eea relevance"]}
---
```

Figure 11: The static 2-shot exemplars used for the synthetic *terminology generation* prompt (Figure 10). Here we show the exemplars for the law domain.

```
Identify and annotate all terminology entities (consider only consecutive words) from the source
sentences and match them with the counterpart in the target sentences. Your response should follow
the format of the provided examples, so that each numbered source and target pair corresponds to
exactly one terminology line in your response.
[source_examples]
{source_texts}
---
[target_examples]
{target_texts}
---
[term_examples]
```

Figure 12: Prompt for *terminology extraction* from source-target text pairs. For each prompt, we batch together 5 text pairs to extract from at a time. `[source_examples]`, `[target_examples]`, `[term_examples]` are static exemplars for this task; see below.

```
source 1: Sag: "Wer hat denn die Schrift hinabgesandt, mit der Musa als Licht und als Rechtleitung
für die Menschen kam?
source 2: Sollte Seine Peinigung über euch nachts oder am Tage hereinbrechen, was wollen denn die
schwer Verfehlenden davon beschleunigen?"
source 3: Unser Herr! Du bist wahrlich Gütig, Barmherzig."
source 4: Und diejenigen, die an Allah und Seine Gesandten glauben, sind die Wahrhaftigen und die
Bezeugenden vor ihrem Herrn; sie werden ihren Lohn und ihr Licht empfangen.
source 5: "Wer sich im Irrtum befindet, dem soll Der Allgnade Erweisende noch mehr davon gewähren!"
Wenn sie dann sehen, was ihnen angedroht wurde: entweder die Peinigung oder die Stunde, dann werden
sie wissen, wer über die schlimmere Stellung und die schwächere Streitmacht verfügt.
```

```
target 1: Say: "Who sent down the Book that Moses brought as a light and a guidance to men?
target 2: If His chastisement comes upon you by night or day, what part of it will the sinners seek
to hasten?
target 3: Our Lord, surely Thou art the All-gentle, the All-compassionate."
target 4: Those who believe in God and His apostles are true of word and deed; and by their Lord are
considered testifiers of the truth. They have their guerdon and their light.
target 5: "Ar-Rahman extends the life of those who are astray until they come to realise what had
been promised them was either (physical) affliction or (the terror) of Resurrection. Then will they
know who is worse in position, and who is weak in supporters.
```

```
terminology 1: [{{"en": "Book", "de": "Schrift"}}, {{"en": "guidance", "de": "Rechtleitung"}},
{{"en": "Moses", "de": "Musa"}}]
terminology 2: [{{"en": "chastisement", "de": "Peinigung"}}, {{"en": "sinners", "de": "schwer
Verfehlenden"}}]
terminology 3: [{{"en": "Our Lord", "de": "Unser Herr"}}, {{"en": "All-gentle", "de": "Gütig"}},
{{"en": "All-compassionate", "de": "Barmherzig"}}]
terminology 4: [{{"en": "His apostles", "de": "Seine Gesandten"}} {{"en": "true of word and deed",
"de": "die Wahrhaftigen und die Bezeugenden"}}, {{"en": "by their Lord", "de": "vor ihrem Herrn"}},
{{"en": "their guerdon", "de": "ihren Lohn"}}, {{"en": "their light", "de": "ihr Licht"}}]
terminology 5: [{{"en": "Ar-Rahman", "de": "Der Allgnade Erweisende"}}, {{"en": "extends the life",
"de": "noch mehr davon gewähren"}}, {{"en": "those who are astray", "de": "Wer sich im Irrtum
befindet"}}, {{"en": "come to realise", "de": "sehen"}}, {{"en": "promised", "de": "angedroht"}},
{{"en": "(physical) affliction", "de": "Peinigung"}}, {{"en": "(the terror) of Resurrection", "de":
"Stunde"}}, {{"en": "worse in position", "de": "über die schlimmere Stellung"}}, {{"en": "weak in
supporters", "de": "die schwächere Streitmacht"}}]
```

Figure 13: Static 5-shot exemplars used for the synthetic *terminology extraction* prompt (Figure 12). We found that this format, where each of the 3 blocks (source, target, terms) are consecutive to each other, gave the most parseable output. Note that the 5 exemplars is the same size as the batches of 5 to extract terminologies from. Here we show the exemplars for the koran domain.

Enhancing Cross-Language Code Translation via Task-Specific Embedding Alignment in Retrieval-Augmented Generation

Manish Bhattarai[1], Minh Vu[1], Javier E. Santos [2], Ismael Boureima[1], Daniel O' Malley [2],

[1]Theoretical Division, Los Alamos National Laboratory, Los Alamos, NM 87544,
[2] Earth & Environmental Science Division, Los Alamos National Laboratory, Los Alamos, NM 87544
Correspondence: ceodspspectrum@lanl.gov

Abstract

We introduce a novel method to enhance cross-language code translation from Fortran to C++ by integrating task-specific embedding alignment into a Retrieval-Augmented Generation (RAG) framework. Unlike conventional retrieval approaches that utilize generic embeddings agnostic to the downstream task, our strategy aligns the retrieval model directly with the objective of maximizing translation quality, as quantified by the CodeBLEU metric. This alignment ensures that the embeddings are semantically and syntactically meaningful for the specific code translation task. Our methodology involves constructing a dataset of 25,000 Fortran code snippets sourced from Stack-V2 dataset and generating their corresponding C++ translations using the LLaMA 3.1-8B language model. We compute pairwise CodeBLEU scores between the generated translations and ground truth examples to capture fine-grained similarities. These scores serve as supervision signals in a contrastive learning framework, where we optimize the embedding model to retrieve Fortran-C++ pairs that are most beneficial for improving the language model's translation performance. By integrating these CodeBLEU-optimized embeddings into the RAG framework, our approach significantly enhances both retrieval accuracy and code generation quality over methods employing generic embeddings. On the HPC Fortran2C++ dataset, our method elevates the average CodeBLEU score from 0.64 to 0.73, achieving a 14% relative improvement. On the Numerical Recipes dataset, we observe an increase from 0.52 to 0.60, marking a 15% relative improvement. Importantly, these gains are realized without any fine-tuning of the language model, underscoring the efficiency and practicality of our approach.

1 Introduction

Cross-language code translation is a critical task in modern software development, especially as legacy programming languages, such as Fortran, continue to be prevalent in scientific computing, while more contemporary languages like C++ are favored for their performance and versatility in production environments. The goal of automatic translation from Fortran to C++ is to preserve the functionality and structure of legacy code while benefiting from the optimizations and ecosystem of C++. However, achieving high-quality translations that adhere to the syntax and semantic norms of the target language remains a challenging problem, particularly when there is a lack of large, aligned datasets or evaluation metrics that cover both source and target languages effectively.

Traditional approaches to cross-language translation, such as Retrieval-Augmented Generation (RAG) (Lewis et al., 2020) typically involve two phases: first, retrieving relevant examples from a database, followed by a language model generating code conditioned on both the query and the retrieved examples. In prior efforts, the retrieval models in RAG systems have relied on general-purpose embedding models (Bhattarai et al., 2024; Li et al.), which are not tailored to the specific nuances of code translation. These embeddings aim to retrieve relevant pairs from the source and target languages but do not directly optimize for the quality of the generated code. As a result, while the retrieved examples may be relevant in a broad sense, they often fail to guide the language model towards producing translations that maximize fidelity to the ground truth in the target language.

Given the scarcity of high-quality parallel Fortran–C++ data, we generate synthetic C++ translations from abundant Fortran code using an LLM to create a pseudo-parallel corpus. Although these synthetic translations may not be flawless, they provide a robust similarity signal that enables effective alignment of Fortran code embeddings. This "pseudo-alignment" enhances the retrieval of relevant examples in our RAG framework, lead-

Proceedings of the 4th International Workshop on Knowledge-Augmented Methods for Natural Language Processing (KnowledgeNLP'25), pages 107–117
May 3, 2025 ©2025 Association for Computational Linguistics

ing to significant improvements in downstream translation quality as demonstrated by a consistent 14–15% gain in CodeBLEU scores. We collect a dataset of 25,000 Fortran code examples from Stack V2 (Lozhkov et al., 2024) and use the LLaMA 3.1-8B (Touvron et al., 2023) model to generate corresponding C++ translations. In the absence of ground truth C++ translations, we evaluate the quality of these translations using pairwise CodeBLEU similarity scores. This metric captures both syntactic correctness and semantic fidelity, providing a robust signal for aligning the retrieval model through contrastive learning.

The proposed approach aims to addresses the shortcomings of general-purpose embedding models by integrating task-specific metrics into the retrieval optimization process. By aligning the retrieval model with the downstream task of producing high-quality C++ code, our method ensures that the examples retrieved during inference are not just broadly similar but are semantically and syntactically aligned in a way that enhances the LLM's generative performance. The result is a significant improvement in translation quality, as measured by CodeBLEU, over previous methods that lack such alignment.

Our contribution is twofold: first, we demonstrate the effectiveness of contrastive learning for fine-tuning retrieval models in the context of cross-language code translation, using a task-specific metric to guide alignment. Second, we show that optimizing retrieval for downstream generation tasks can lead to state-of-the-art results, particularly in cases where aligned datasets are not readily available for both source and target languages. This work not only advances the field of code translation but also opens up new possibilities for applying similar techniques to other language pairs and domains where task-specific evaluation metrics are available for only one side of the translation.

2 Related Work

Historically, code translation strategies before the advent of LLMs relied heavily on rule-based and statistical machine translation (SMT) systems (Koehn, 2009). These systems used predefined rules or statistical mappings between the source and target programming languages, such as tree-based translation approaches that mapped syntax trees between languages. While these methods provided structured and interpretable outputs, they were limited in their ability to handle the semantic complexities of different programming languages and struggled with code diversity, edge cases, and idiomatic translations.

With the rise of deep learning and LLMs, fine-tuning models on large datasets became the go-to method for improving code translation. Models like CodeBERT (Feng et al., 2020) and Codex (Chen et al., 2021), when fine-tuned on specific language pairs, improved translation quality by leveraging vast amounts of parallel code data. However, the main limitation of LLM fine-tuning lies in the resource-intensive process. Fine-tuning requires substantial amounts of labeled data and computational resources, making it impractical for niche or legacy languages like Fortran, where parallel data may be scarce.

As a next step, task-specific alignment of LLMs emerged to improve translation by better guiding the model's output. While alignment techniques help improve output fidelity, they still necessitate fine-tuning or explicit modification of the LLM itself, which can be resource-intensive and may still fall short of generalization when translating between languages with significant structural differences (Mishra et al., 2024).

RAG introduced a more flexible approach by allowing LLMs to retrieve and condition their outputs on example pairs from a relevant dataset. While RAG improves translation by augmenting the model's input, the effectiveness of this strategy depends on the quality and relevance of the retrieved examples. In an example case (Bhattarai et al., 2024), the retrieval step relies on general-purpose embeddings like Nomic-Embed or CodeBERT, which, although effective at retrieving semantically similar code, are not optimized for specific downstream metrics like CodeBLEU. As a result, the LLM might not always retrieve the examples that would best assist in producing translations aligned with target-specific quality metrics.

The approach we propose offers a significant advantage by focusing on semantic alignment of the retrieval mechanism without the need to fine-tune the LLM itself. Through contrastive learning, we optimize the embedding model to retrieve Fortran-C++ pairs that are more likely to maximize the downstream metric (e.g., CodeBLEU) when used by the LLM for generation. This strategy ensures that the most relevant examples are retrieved for each translation task, improving the generation quality without requiring computationally expensive fine-tuning of the LLM. This retrieval alignment makes RAG more efficient and better suited for translating between languages where high-quality paired datasets may not be available. By concentrating on improving the quality of retrieved examples, our method achieves high-quality translation with minimal additional model training, leveraging existing LLM capabilities more effectively.

3 Methods

This section provides the technical description of our proposed method.

3.1 Problem setting

We consider the standard code translation scenario leveraging a language model G, in which a target translated code c^t of a query source code c^s is generated using G:

$$c^t = G(c^s) \tag{1}$$

In practice, conditioning G on k example pairs of source and target code $D := \{(c_i^s, c_i^t)\}_{i=1}^k$, can significantly enhance translation. This few-shot learning approach can be expressed as: $c^t = G(c^s, D)$

In a RAG framework, this process is further refined by integrating a retrieval mechanism R that identifies the most pertinent k example pairs from a large corpus $\mathcal{C}$ based on the query c^s. By expressing this retrieval step as $D = R(c^s, \mathcal{C})$, we can describe the conventional translation scenario leveraging G as

$$c^t = G(c^s, R(c^s, \mathcal{C})) \tag{2}$$

In practice, the input source code for the retrieval are embedded using a neural network Ψ, which are generally agnostic to the downstream task. We denote c_Ψ^s as the embedding of the source code c^s under the embedding Ψ. Hence, Eq. 2 can be expressed as

$$c^t = G(c^s, R(c_\Psi^s, \mathcal{C}_\Psi)) \tag{3}$$

under the usage of the embedding model Ψ. Here, the notation $\mathcal{C}_\Psi$ refers to the fact that the embedding is applied onto the corpus of c^s.

Some common embedding modules for the retrieval code translation are Nomic-Embed (Nussbaum et al., 2024), StarEncoder (Li et al., 2023), and CodeBERT (Feng et al., 2020). However, as the performance of the translation task heavily depends on the relevance and the alignment of the retrieved examples with respect to the query c^s, as we will show in the following discussion, it is beneficial to optimize Ψ for better code translation performance.

3.2 Task-Specific Embedding Alignment

Our method involves aligning the Fortran embedding model Ψ using contrastive learning based on CodeBLEU similarity scores, followed by applying this aligned model within a RAG framework for improved cross-language code translation from Fortran to C++, as shown in Figure 1I.

Embedding Similarity: We directly leverage the CodeBLEU similarity computed from the language model G to train an aligned embedding module Ψ for the downstream code translation task. The following discusses how to extract the CodeBLEU similarity from G.

From a source dataset of Fortran code snippets $\mathcal{D}^F = \{c_i^s\}_{i=1}^N$, we generate the corresponding C++ translations $\mathcal{D}^C = \{c_i^t\}_{i=1}^N$ using G without RAG retrieval:

$$c_i^t = G(c_i^s), \quad \forall i = 1, \dots, N \tag{4}$$

Then, we compute the pairwise CodeBLEU similarity scores (Ren et al., 2020) between all generated translation pairs (c_i^t, c_j^t):

$$S_{ij}^t = \text{CodeBLEU}(c_i^t, c_j^t) \tag{5}$$

where the CodeBLEU score matrix $S^t \in [0,1]^{N \times N}$ is a weighted linear combination of four components: the n-gram match $S_{\text{n-gram}}$, the weighted n-gram match $S_{\text{w-n-gram}}$, the syntactic AST match S_{syntax}, and the semantic data flow match S_{semantic}. These components capture the syntactic and semantic similarities between the generated C++ translations: $S_{\text{n-gram}}$ is the traditional BLEU score up to n-grams, $S_{\text{w-n-gram}}$ assigns weights to n-grams based on their importance, S_{syntax} measures the similarity between the abstract syntax trees (AST) of the code snippets and S_{semantic} assesses the similarity in data flow between code snippets.

Intuitively, a high value of S_{ij}^t indicates that the source code snippets c_i^s and c_j^s, when translated by G, produce similar target code, suggesting that c_i^s and c_j^s are semantically similar with respect to the translation task. Therefore, our approach aims to learn a fine-tuned embedding module Ψ that

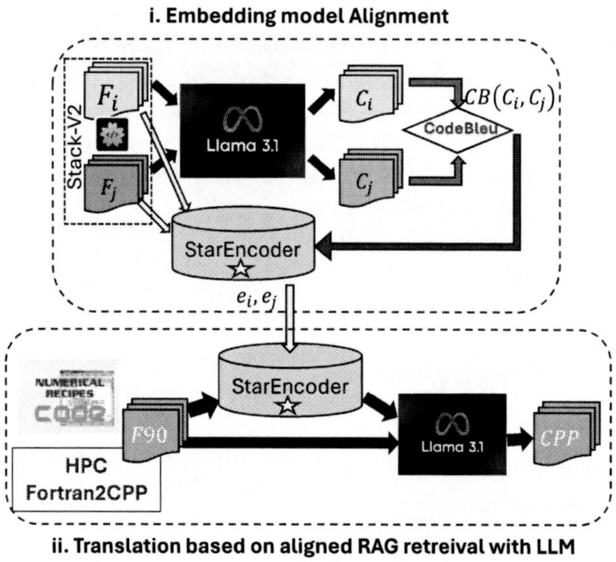

Figure 1: Overview of the proposed pipeline. i) The LLM generates pairwise code translations, which are evaluated using the CodeBLEU metric. ii) The resulting similarity scores are used to guide contrastive learning for semantic alignment of the embedding model.

utilizes S^t_{ij} to enhance code embedding alignment. The approach is expected to guide Ψ in a way that enhances the code translation task leveraging G.

Embedding Alignment: To align the embedding space of code snippets with the semantic similarities measured by CodeBLEU, we propose the Soft Information Noise-Contrastive Estimation (S-InfoNCE) loss applied to the embeddings resulting from the trainable embedding module Ψ. On a high level, our proposed S-InfoNCE can be considered a soft version of the InfoNCE loss proposed for contrastive learning (van den Oord et al., 2018). In the following, we provide the description for the S-InfoNCE loss and Lemma 1 characterizing the stationary condition resulting from the S-InfoNCE. The result helps describing the influence of the loss on the learnt representation.

Given a batch of N code snippets, we compute their embeddings $c^s_{\Psi_i} = \Psi(c^s_i)$ and then calculate the pairwise cosine similarities between those embeddings, scaled by a temperature parameter $\tau > 0$:

$$S^s_{\Psi_{ij}} = \frac{1}{\tau} \frac{c^s_{\Psi_i} \cdot c^s_{\Psi_j}}{\|c^s_{\Psi_i}\| \|c^s_{\Psi_j}\|} \tag{6}$$

Our proposed S-InfoNCE loss integrates these continuous similarity scores to weigh the contribution of each pair. Specifically, the loss component between code i with respect to code j is given as:

$$l^{\text{S-InfoNCE}}_{ij}(\Psi) = -S^t_{ij} \log \left(\frac{\exp(S^s_{\Psi_{ij}})}{\sum_{k=1}^{N} \exp(S^s_{\Psi_{ik}})} \right) \tag{7}$$

and the S-InfoNCE loss is the sum over all code pairs:

$$\mathcal{L}^{\text{S-InfoNCE}}(\Psi) = \sum_{i=1}^{N} \sum_{j=1}^{N} l^{\text{S-InfoNCE}}_{ij}(\Psi) \tag{8}$$

Finally, the embedding Ψ is optimized by minimizing $\mathcal{L}^{\text{S-InfoNCE}}(\Psi)$ using gradient descent.

Compared to the conventional InfoNCE loss for contrastive learning (van den Oord et al., 2018), our proposed loss differs in its usage of S^t_{ij} as a soft indicator for encoding a continuous similarity between the pair (i, j), rather than a binary indicator of class membership (same class or not). This gives rise to the term *soft* InfoNCE, or S-InfoNCE. In the typical InfoNCE loss, the term l_{ij} is included only if the pair (i, j) belongs to the same class, assuming discrete classes are available. However, since such discrete class labels do not exist in the code translation task, we adopt S^t_{ij} as a soft version of this indicator function, allowing for a more nuanced representation of similarity between code pairs. To further elaborate on the impact of S-InfoNCE, we provide Lemma 1 characterizing its stationary conditions:

Lemma 1. *The stationary points of the S-InfoNCE loss (Equation 8) satisfy:*

$$\frac{\exp(S^s_{\Psi^*_{ij}})}{\sum_{k=1}^{N}\exp(S^s_{\Psi^*_{ik}})} = \frac{S^t_{ij}}{\sum_{k=1}^{N} S^t_{ik}}, \tag{9}$$

for all $i, j \in \{1, \ldots, N\}$.

Furthermore, the optimal loss is the weighted sum of the entropy of the CodeBLEU similarity distribution for each input code i*:*

$$\mathcal{L}^{\text{S-InfoNCE}}(\Psi^*) = \sum_{i=1}^{N}\left(\sum_{k=1}^{N} S^t_{ik}\right) H(\boldsymbol{p}^*_i), \tag{10}$$

where H *is the entropy function and* $\boldsymbol{p}^*_i$ *is a probability vector whose* j*-th component is*

$$p^*_{ij} = \frac{S^t_{ij}}{\sum_{k=1}^{N} S^t_{ik}}. \tag{11}$$

Proof. For brevity, let us define:

- $\alpha_{ij} = S^t_{ij}$: the CodeBLEU similarity between the target code translations c^t_i and c^t_j.
- $p_{ij}(\Psi) = \exp(S^s_{\Psi_{ij}})/Z_i$, where $Z_i = \sum_{k=1}^{N}\exp(S^s_{\Psi_{ik}})$: the normalized exponential of the cosine similarity between the embeddings of source code snippets c^s_i and c^s_j.

The S-InfoNCE loss can be rewritten as:

$$\mathcal{L}^{\text{S-InfoNCE}}(\Psi) = -\sum_{i=1}^{N}\sum_{j=1}^{N}\alpha_{ij}\log p_{ij}(\Psi). \tag{12}$$

The minimization of $\mathcal{L}^{\text{S-InfoNCE}}(\Psi)$ can be viewed as a constrained optimization problem over the variables $p_{ij}(\Psi)$, subject to the normalization constraints:

$$\sum_{j=1}^{N} p_{ij}(\Psi) = 1, \quad \forall i \in \{1, \ldots, N\}. \tag{13}$$

Thus, we can formulate the Lagrangian $\mathcal{L}$:

$$\mathcal{L} = -\sum_{i=1}^{N}\sum_{j=1}^{N}\alpha_{ij}\log p_{ij}(\Psi) + \sum_{i=1}^{N}\lambda_i\left(\sum_{j=1}^{N} p_{ij}(\Psi) - 1\right). \tag{14}$$

To find the stationary points, we take the derivative of $\mathcal{L}$ with respect to $p_{ij}(\Psi)$ and set it to zero:

$$\frac{\partial \mathcal{L}}{\partial p_{ij}(\Psi)} = -\frac{\alpha_{ij}}{p_{ij}(\Psi)} + \lambda_i = 0. \tag{15}$$

Solving for $p_{ij}(\Psi)$, we get:

$$p_{ij}(\Psi) = \frac{\alpha_{ij}}{\lambda_i}. \tag{16}$$

Applying the normalization constraint gives us:

$$\sum_{j=1}^{N}\frac{\alpha_{ij}}{\lambda_i} = \sum_{j=1}^{N} p_{ij}(\Psi) = \sum_{j=1}^{N}\frac{\alpha_{ij}}{\lambda_i} = 1 \tag{17}$$

$$\Rightarrow \lambda_i = \sum_{j=1}^{N}\alpha_{ij}. \tag{18}$$

Substituting λ_i back into $p_{ij}(\Psi)$, we obtain the stationary condition:

$$p^*_{ij} = \frac{\alpha_{ij}}{\sum_{k=1}^{N}\alpha_{ik}} = \frac{S^t_{ij}}{\sum_{k=1}^{N} S^t_{ik}}. \tag{19}$$

Substituting $p_{ij}(\Psi^*)$ back into the loss function:

$$\begin{aligned}\mathcal{L}^{\text{S-InfoNCE}}(\Psi^*) &= -\sum_{i=1}^{N}\sum_{k=1}^{N}\alpha_{ik}\log\left(\frac{\alpha_{ik}}{\sum_{j=1}^{N}\alpha_{ij}}\right) \\ &= \sum_{i=1}^{N}\left(\sum_{k=1}^{N} S^t_{ik}\right) H(\boldsymbol{p}^*_i).\end{aligned} \tag{20}$$

□

From the lemma, we can see that minimizing the S-InfoNCE loss encourages embeddings of semantically similar code snippets, i.e., those with higher target CodeBLEU score S^t_{ij}, to have higher cosine similarities $S^s_{\Psi_{ij}}$, thereby aligning them closer in the embedding space. The temperature parameter τ controls the concentration of the distribution: a lower τ sharpens the softmax distribution, making the embedding model focus more on the most similar pairs.

Retrieval-Augmented Generation with Aligned Embeddings: After aligning the embedding model Ψ, we integrate it into the RAG framework to enhance the translation process (Figure 1II). In particular, given a query Fortran code snippet c^s, we compute its embedding c^s_Ψ then retrieve the top-k Fortran code snippets $\{c^s_{r_1}, c^s_{r_2}, \ldots, c^s_{r_k}\}$ from the corpus $\mathcal{C}$ by maximizing the cosine similarity between embeddings. The corresponding C++ translations $\{c^t_{r_1}, c^t_{r_2}, \ldots, c^t_{r_k}\}$ are then retrieved alongside the source code snippets. These retrieved pairs $\{(c^s_{r_j}, c^t_{r_j})\}_{j=1}^k$ are used to augment the input to the language model G, providing additional context:

$$\hat{c}^t = G\left(c^s, \{(c^s_{r_j}, c^t_{r_j})\}_{j=1}^k\right). \quad (21)$$

By incorporating the optimized embedding function Ψ into the RAG setup, we enhance the performance of the language model without the need for fine-tuning. The retrieval mechanism now provides more relevant examples that are closely aligned with the translation task, leading to more accurate and aligned translations as demonstrated in Appendix A.

4 Experiments and Results

In our study, we utilized three datasets to enhance code translation through RAG and embedding alignment. The HPC Fortran2CPP dataset (Lei et al., 2023), comprising 315 Fortran-C++ code pairs, and the Numerical Recipes dataset (Press et al., 1988), containing 298 Fortran-C++ pairs, were employed for RAG retrieval and evaluation with LLMs. Additionally, we used the Stack-V2 dataset (Lozhkov et al., 2024), which includes over 500,000 Fortran code snippets, for RAG alignment. From Stack-V2, we sampled 25,000 high-quality and diverse Fortran code snippets by selecting files larger than 500 bytes and prioritizing those with the highest combined star and fork counts, indicating relevance and popularity. Since Stack-V2 lacks Fortran-C++ pairs, we extracted files containing metadata, code, and comments, and utilized the Llama 3.1-70B Instruct model to extract executable Fortran code, discarding other metadata. We selected the StarCoder model (Li et al., 2023) with 125M parameters as the embedding backbone for our RAG pipeline and aligned it using contrastive learning on the Stack-V2 dataset. Initially, we use the LLaMA 3.1-8B model to translate the cleaned Fortran code snippets into corresponding C++ code. After code translaton, we computed pairwise CodeBLEU scores between the generated C++ code snippets to quantify the syntactic and semantic similarities of their translations. Leveraging these CodeBLEU metrics and the embeddings from the Fortran codes, we employed the proposed Soft-InfoNCE loss function with a temperature of 0.1 to align the embeddings, effectively training the embedding model to map semantically similar code snippets closer in the embedding space.

The embedding model was trained using the Adam optimizer with a learning rate of 10^{-3} and a batch size of 128 per GPU, sampling approximately 1,280,000 code pairs for alignment. This training process was distributed across 256 GH200 GPUs to accelerate the process, though it can also be performed on fewer GPUs at a significantly slower pace. Training on 256 GH200 GPUs took approximately 15 minutes per epoch, with early stopping at epoch 20. This scales to around 60 minutes per epoch with 64 GPUs and 2 hours per epoch with 32 GPUs. While training a RAG model does incur computational overhead, it remains significantly less expensive than fine-tuning a multi-billion-parameter LLM. After alignment, we integrated the embedding model into the RAG pipeline, storing Fortran-C++ pairs along with their Fortran embeddings in a vector database. We then evaluated the performance using the LLaMA 3.1-8B, LLaMA 3.1-70B, Mistral123B, and Mixtral 8x22B models—all instruct-tuned—under zero-shot, 1-shot, 2-shot, and 3-shot settings. The evaluation was conducted on the benchmark datasets HPC Fortran2C++ and Numerical Recipes, following the setup described by (Bhattarai et al., 2024). The CodeBLEU scores for both the aligned and unaligned models were obtained by comparing the RAG-augmented generated C++ translations against the ground truth C++ code.

Figure 2 shows scatter-plots of CodeBLEU scores for code samples produced using RAG retrieval with aligned versus unaligned embeddings derived from StarEncoder. Symbols crosses, pluses and triangles respectively indicate whether the sample was evaluated using a 1-shot, 2-shot, or 3-shot method. The red dashed lines delineates the boundary where the aligned samples have the same CodeBLEU score as the non-aligned ones, and across all four tested datasets, we observed a majority of samples above the red line, indicating that the aligned model produces translated codes closer to ground truth. In other words, the results in Figure 2 demonstrate that aligned embeddings significantly improve translation quality for each Fortran-to-C++ code translation task. Specifically, on the HPC Fortran2C++ dataset, averaged over all shot counts and models, the aligned embeddings achieved an average CodeBLEU score of 0.73, whereas unaligned embeddings achieve 0.64. On the Numerical Recipes dataset, aligned embeddings yielded

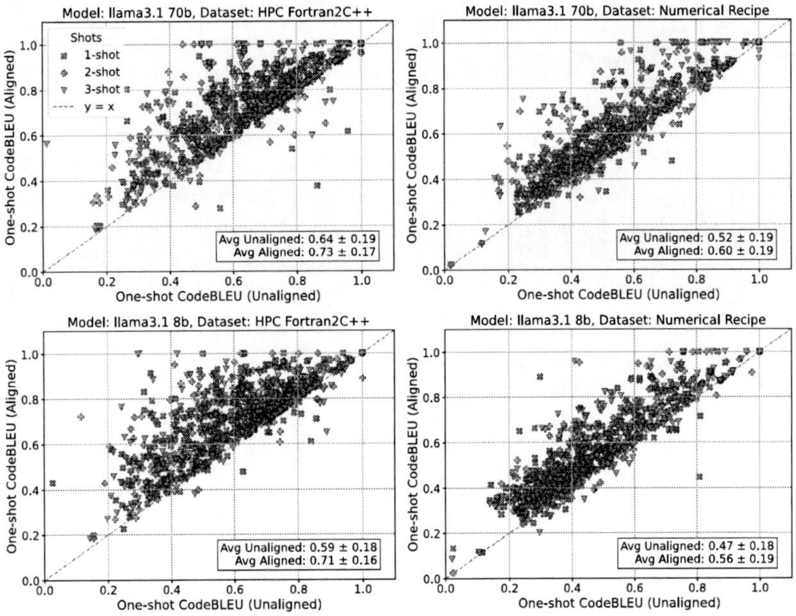

Figure 2: Scatter plots comparing the unaligned and aligned One-shot CodeBLEU scores across different shot counts (1-shot, 2-shot, 3-shot) for two models (llama3.1 70b and llama3.1 8b) and two datasets (Numerical Recipe and HPC Fortran2C++ Dataset). Each point represents a shot count, and the red dashed line represents the reference where the unaligned and aligned scores are equal. The text box in each subplot displays the average CodeBLEU performance and standard deviation for aligned vs. unaligned RAG translation across the few-shot configurations.

Table 1: Delta in Mean CodeBLEU scores between Zero- and Few-Shot prompts. The values are presented as Unaligned/Aligned scores.

		Δ in CodeBLEU scores (Unaligned / Aligned)			
Dataset	**Model**	**Zero-shot**	**1-shot**	**2-shot**	**3-shot**
HPC Fortran2++	llama3.1 70b	0.364	+0.262/+0.346	+0.275/+0.371	+0.281/+0.377
	llama3.1 8b	0.342	+0.237/+0.346	+0.261/+0.376	+0.252/+0.374
	mistral123b	0.367	+0.197/+0.241	+0.210/+0.265	+0.215/+0.271
	mixtral-8x22b	0.376	+0.237/+0.273	+0.261/+0.344	+0.233/+0.304
numerical_receipe	llama3.1 70b	0.280	+0.232/+0.313	+0.243/+0.329	+0.243/+0.317
	llama3.1 8b	0.276	+0.181/+0.268	+0.195/+0.292	+0.201/+0.289
	mistral123b	0.281	+0.138/+0.169	+0.132/+0.183	+0.135/+0.211
	mixtral-8x22b	0.280	+0.200/+0.245	+0.228/+0.296	+0.232/+0.312

an average CodeBLEU score of 0.60, outperforming the unaligned case at 0.52. These substantial improvements highlight the effectiveness of our method in enhancing translation accuracy.

Figure 3 further corroborates these findings by presenting the distribution of CodeBLEU scores across various experimental configurations. The box plots reveal that aligned embeddings not only increase the median scores but also reduce performance variability. This indicates that our approach consistently enhances translation quality and leads to more reliable code translations. The consistent improvements across different model sizes (8B and 70B parameters) and datasets demonstrate the robustness and scalability of our method.

Table 1 presents the mean CodeBLEU scores for zero-shot and few-shot prompting strategies using both unaligned and aligned embedding models across different language models and datasets. A key observation is that the aligned embedding

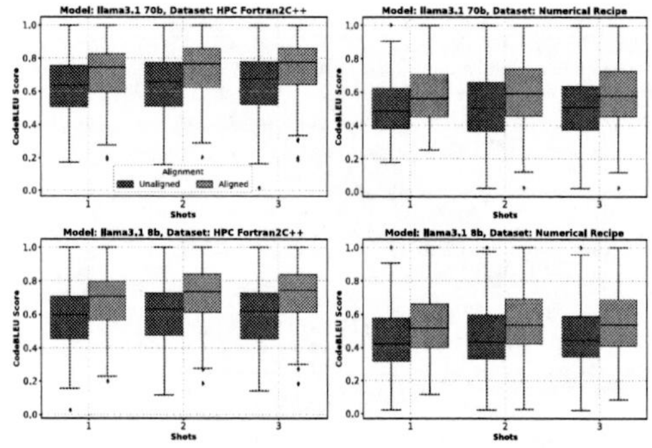

Figure 3: Box plots illustrating the distribution of CodeBLEU scores across various shot counts (1-shot, 2-shot, 3-shot) for both unaligned and aligned models. The results are presented for two models (llama3.1 70b and llama3.1 8b) across two datasets (Numerical Recipe and HPC Fortran2C++ Dataset)

models consistently achieve higher CodeBLEU scores compared to unaligned models when transitioning from zero-shot to few-shot settings. For instance, on the HPC Fortran2C++ dataset with the `LLaMA3.1 70B` model, the aligned model improves from 0.364 to 0.710 (+0.346) in the 1-shot setting, surpassing the unaligned model's improvement from 0.364 to 0.626 (+0.262). Similar trends are observed with the `LLaMA3.1 8B` model, where the aligned model increases from 0.342 to 0.688 (+0.346), compared to the unaligned model's increase from 0.342 to 0.579 (+0.237). The `Mistral 13B` and `Mixtral 8x22B` models also exhibit greater improvements with aligned embeddings in few-shot settings, confirming the benefit of embedding alignment across different architectures. On the Numerical Recipes dataset, the aligned models again demonstrate superior improvements over unaligned models. For example, the `LLaMA3.1 70B` aligned model improves from 0.280 to 0.593 (+0.313) in the 1-shot setting, exceeding the unaligned model's increase from 0.280 to 0.512 (+0.232). This consistent pattern across datasets reinforces the advantage of embedding alignment in enhancing code translation performance. We acknowledge that CodeBLEU may not capture all functional nuances. Therefore, we performed a small-scale manual check (Appendix A) on a subset of translations. While we observed that a majority compiled and produced the expected outputs, further large-scale functional evaluation remains an important future direction.

These results indicate that embedding alignment significantly enhances the models' capacity to exploit few-shot prompts, leading to superior code translation performance as measured by CodeBLEU scores. Alignment optimizes the embedding space to better capture the syntactic and semantic nuances of code translation tasks, thereby augmenting the models' few-shot learning capabilities. Additionally, larger models tend to outperform smaller ones. The `LLaMA3.1 70B` model consistently achieves higher CodeBLEU scores than the `LLaMA3.1 8B` model across both datasets and embedding types. The strong performance of the `Mixtral 8x22B` model, which combines multiple experts, highlights the benefits of increased model capacity. Furthermore, diminishing marginal gains are observed when increasing the number of shots beyond two, suggesting that the majority of performance improvements are realized with just one or two examples. This indicates that while few-shot examples are beneficial, adding more beyond a certain point yields limited additional gains.

5 Conclusion

We introduced a novel method for enhancing cross-language code translation from Fortran to C++ by aligning embeddings within a RAG framework. By leveraging contrastive learning based on CodeBLEU similarity scores, we aligned the Fortran embedding model so that code snippets yielding high-quality translations are positioned closer in the embedding space. This alignment enables the RAG system to retrieve semantically meaningful examples that effectively guide th LLM during code generation. Our experimental results demonstrate substantial improvements in translation quality without the need for fine-tuning the LLM. Specifically, using aligned embeddings increased the average CodeBLEU score from 0.64 to 0.73 on the HPC Fortran2C++ dataset and from 0.52 to 0.60 on the Numerical Recipes dataset, representing relative improvements of approximately 14% and 15%, respectively. The larger model (`llama3.1 70b`) consistently outperformed the smaller model (`llama3.1 8b`), indicating that increased model capacity enhances the effectiveness of our approach. Additionally, we observed diminishing returns beyond two-shot prompting, suggesting that most performance gains are achieved with just one or two examples. Thus, our approach significantly improves code translation performance by optimizing the retrieval mechanism through task-specific embedding alignment, rather than relying on computationally expensive fine-tuning of the LLM. This method is computationally efficient, scalable, and adaptable to other code translation tasks, particularly when aligned datasets are scarce or evaluation metrics like CodeBLEU are critical. Future work could extend this alignment strategy to additional programming languages and explore integrating other evaluation metrics to further enhance translation quality.

6 Limitations

Our approach leverages CodeBLEU as a task-specific metric for performing contrastive learning via a custom Soft-InfoNCE loss in the alignment of embedding models for code translation. While this approach introduces several improvements, it also brings specific limitations. First, using CodeBLEU as the basis for contrastive learning focuses primarily on syntactic and semantic alignment, which may not always translate into functional equivalence. CodeBLEU, while effective at evaluating linguistic features of generated code, does not fully capture the functional behavior of code, meaning that two semantically similar snippets could still behave differently at runtime (Ren et al., 2020). This limitation can lead to cases where the retrieval mechanism selects semantically similar but functionally incorrect examples, impacting the overall quality of the translation task. Second, contrastive learning, particularly with InfoNCE loss, relies heavily on the assumption that maximizing the similarity between pairs (based on CodeBLEU) leads to better downstream performance. However, InfoNCE loss is limited by its focus on pulling positive samples closer while pushing away negative ones, which in the case of code translation, does not always capture the subtle nuances of code equivalence across languages (Khosla et al., 2020). Code snippets with different syntactic structures but similar functionality may be treated as negative examples, leading to a misaligned embedding space and suboptimal retrieval. Third, the granularity of the CodeBLEU score presents an inherent challenge. Since CodeBLEU provides a continuous similarity metric (between 0 and 1), aligning embeddings through InfoNCE loss may not fully capture the wide range of functional similarities or dissimilarities between code snippets. This results in an embedding space that reflects linguistic rather than purely functional similarity, which can lead to errors in retrieval when applied to real-world translation tasks where functional correctness is paramount (Feng et al., 2020). Additionally, the use of CodeBLEU as a basis for contrastive learning is highly dependent on the quality of the generated code samples and their reference translations. Any noise or imperfections in the training data (e.g., low-quality code or inconsistent style) may degrade the alignment process. Since InfoNCE relies on subtle positive and negative distinctions, noisy CodeBLEU scores can introduce ambiguity, further distorting the learning process and leading to poorer retrievals during generation (Wang and Liu, 2021).

7 Acknowledgement

This manuscript has been approved for unlimited release and has been assigned LA-UR-24-33137. This research was funded by the LANL ASC grant AI4Coding and the LANL Institutional Computing Program, supported by the U.S. DOE NNSA under Contract No. 89233218CNA000001.

References

Manish Bhattarai, Javier E Santos, Shawn Jones, Ayan Biswas, Boian Alexandrov, and Daniel O'Malley. 2024. Enhancing code translation in language models with few-shot learning via retrieval-augmented generation. *arXiv preprint arXiv:2407.19619*.

Mark Chen, Jerry Tworek, Heewoo Jun, Qiming Yuan, Henrique Ponde De Oliveira Pinto, Jared Kaplan, Harri Edwards, Yuri Burda, Nicholas Joseph, Greg Brockman, et al. 2021. Evaluating large language models trained on code. *arXiv preprint arXiv:2107.03374*.

Zhangyin Feng, Daya Guo, Duyu Tang, Nan Duan, Xiaocheng Feng, Ming Gong, Linjun Shou, Bing Qin, Ting Liu, Daxin Jiang, and Ming Zhou. 2020. CodeBERT: A pre-trained model for programming and natural languages. In *Findings of the Association for Computational Linguistics: EMNLP 2020*, pages 1536–1547, Online. Association for Computational Linguistics.

Prannay Khosla, Piotr Teterwak, Chen Wang, Aaron Sarna, Yonglong Tian, Phillip Isola, Aaron Maschinot, Ce Liu, and Dilip Krishnan. 2020. Supervised contrastive learning. *Advances in neural information processing systems*, 33:18661–18673.

Philipp Koehn. 2009. *Statistical machine translation*. Cambridge University Press.

Bin Lei, Caiwen Ding, Le Chen, Pei-Hung Lin, and Chunhua Liao. 2023. Creating a dataset for high-performance computing code translation using llms:

A bridge between openmp fortran and c++. In *2023 IEEE High Performance Extreme Computing Conference (HPEC)*, pages 1–7. IEEE.

Patrick Lewis, Ethan Perez, Aleksandra Piktus, Fabio Petroni, Vladimir Karpukhin, Naman Goyal, Heinrich Küttler, Mike Lewis, Wen-tau Yih, Tim Rocktäschel, et al. 2020. Retrieval-augmented generation for knowledge-intensive nlp tasks. *Advances in Neural Information Processing Systems*, 33:9459–9474.

Chuangji Li, Shizhuo Li, and Alan Wang. Retrieval-augmented multi-hop code generation with codellama and unlimiformer.

Raymond Li, Loubna Ben Allal, Yangtian Zi, Niklas Muennighoff, Denis Kocetkov, Chenghao Mou, Marc Marone, Christopher Akiki, Jia Li, Jenny Chim, et al. 2023. Starcoder: may the source be with you! *arXiv preprint arXiv:2305.06161*.

Anton Lozhkov, Raymond Li, Loubna Ben Allal, Federico Cassano, Joel Lamy-Poirier, Nouamane Tazi, Ao Tang, Dmytro Pykhtar, Jiawei Liu, Yuxiang Wei, et al. 2024. Starcoder 2 and the stack v2: The next generation. *arXiv preprint arXiv:2402.19173*.

Mayank Mishra, Matt Stallone, Gaoyuan Zhang, Yikang Shen, Aditya Prasad, Adriana Meza Soria, Michele Merler, Parameswaran Selvam, Saptha Surendran, Shivdeep Singh, et al. 2024. Granite code models: A family of open foundation models for code intelligence. *arXiv preprint arXiv:2405.04324*.

Zach Nussbaum, John X Morris, Brandon Duderstadt, and Andriy Mulyar. 2024. Nomic embed: Training a reproducible long context text embedder. *arXiv preprint arXiv:2402.01613*.

William H Press, William T Vetterling, Saul A Teukolsky, and Brian P Flannery. 1988. *Numerical recipes*. Cambridge University Press, London, England.

Shuo Ren, Daya Guo, Shuai Lu, Long Zhou, Shujie Liu, Duyu Tang, Neel Sundaresan, Ming Zhou, Ambrosio Blanco, and Shuai Ma. 2020. Codebleu: a method for automatic evaluation of code synthesis. *arXiv preprint arXiv:2009.10297*.

Hugo Touvron, Thibaut Lavril, Gautier Izacard, Xavier Martinet, Marie-Anne Lachaux, Timothée Lacroix, Baptiste Rozière, Naman Goyal, Eric Hambro, Faisal Azhar, et al. 2023. Llama: Open and efficient foundation language models. *arXiv preprint arXiv:2302.13971*.

Aaron van den Oord, Yazhe Li, and Oriol Vinyals. 2018. Representation learning with contrastive predictive coding. *arXiv preprint arXiv:1807.03748*.

Feng Wang and Huaping Liu. 2021. Understanding the behaviour of contrastive loss. In *Proceedings of the IEEE/CVF conference on computer vision and pattern recognition*, pages 2495–2504.

A Demonstration: Enhancing Fortran-to-C++ Translation Using Aligned RAG on LLaMa3.1 70b Model

A.1 Fortran Code to be Translated

Below is the original Fortran code that needs to be translated into C++:

```
program DRB011_minusminus_orig_yes
    use omp_lib
    implicit none

    integer :: i, len, numNodes, numNodes2
    integer :: x(100)

    len = 100
    numNodes = len
    numNodes2 = 0

    do i = 1, len
        if (MOD(i,2) == 0) then
            x(i) = 5
        else
            x(i) = -5
        end if
    end do

    !$omp parallel do
    do i = numNodes, 1, -1
        if (x(i) <= 0) then
            numNodes2 = numNodes2 - 1
        end if
    end do
    !$omp end parallel do

    print*, "numNodes2 =", numNodes2
end program
```

Listing 1: Fortran Code

A.2 Ground Truth

Below is the human-generated ground truth Fortran-to-C++ translation, which serves as the baseline:

```
#include <stdlib.h>
#include <stdio.h>
int main(int argc, char* argv[]) {
    int i;
    int len = 100;
    int numNodes = len;
    int numNodes2 = 0;
    int x[100];

    // initialize x[]
    for (i = 0; i < len; i++) {
        if (i % 2 == 0)
            x[i] = 5;
        else
            x[i] = -5;
    }

#pragma omp parallel for
    for (i = numNodes - 1; i > -1; --i) {
        if (x[i] <= 0) {
            numNodes2--;
```

```
        }
    }

    printf("numNodes2 = %d\n", numNodes2);
    return 0;
}
```

Listing 2: Ground Truth

A.3 Zero-shot Translation

The zero-shot output from the LLM demonstrates basic translation abilities but with structural issues:

```
#include <iostream>
#include <omp.h>

int main() {
    const int len = 100;
    int numNodes = len;
    int numNodes2 = 0;
    int x[len];

    for (int i = 1; i <= len; i++) {
        if (i % 2 == 0) {
            x[i - 1] = 5;
        } else {
            x[i - 1] = -5;
        }
    }

    #pragma omp parallel for reduction(-:numNodes2)
    for (int i = numNodes; i >= 1; i--) {
        if (x[i - 1] <= 0) {
            numNodes2--;
        }
    }

    std::cout << "numNodes2 = " << numNodes2 << std::endl;

    return 0;
}
```

Listing 3: Zero-shot Translation

A.4 Unaligned RAG One-shot Translation

The one-shot output improves the translation, but some structural issues still remain. Specifically, the initialization of variables and handling of array indices are slightly different:

```
#include <stdio.h>

int main() {
    int i, len, numNodes, numNodes2;
    int x[100];

    len = 100;
    numNodes = len;
    numNodes2 = 0;

    for (i = 0; i < len; i++) {
        if ((i + 1) % 2 == 0) {
            x[i] = 5;
        } else {
            x[i] = -5;
        }
    }

#pragma omp parallel for reduction(-:numNodes2)
    for (i = numNodes - 1; i >= 0; i--) {
        if (x[i] <= 0) {
            numNodes2--;
        }
    }

    printf("numNodes2 = %d\n", numNodes2);

    return 0;
}
```

Listing 4: One-shot Translation

A.5 Aligned RAG Translation

By aligning the retrieval process to the context of the task, the translation becomes much more accurate, closely matching the ground truth:

```
#include <stdio.h>
#include <omp.h>

int main(int argc, char* argv[]) {
    int i;
    int len = 100;
    int numNodes = len;
    int numNodes2 = 0;
    int x[100];

    for (i = 0; i < len; i++) {
        if ((i % 2) == 0) {
            x[i] = 5;
        } else {
            x[i] = -5;
        }
    }

#pragma omp parallel for
    for (i = numNodes - 1; i >= 0; i--) {
        if (x[i] <= 0) {
            numNodes2--;
        }
    }

    printf("numNodes2 = %d\n", numNodes2);
    return 0;
}
```

Listing 5: Aligned RAG-based Translation

LLM Reasoning Engine: Specialized Training for Enhanced Mathematical Reasoning

Shuguang Chen
Department of Mathematics
Purdue University
chen4914@purdue.edu

Guang Lin
Department of Mathematics
Purdue University
guanglin@purdue.edu

Abstract

Large Language Models (LLMs) have shown remarkable performance in various natural language processing tasks but face challenges in mathematical reasoning, where complex problem-solving requires both linguistic understanding and mathematical reasoning skills. Existing approaches to address this challenge often rely on ensemble methods and suffer from the problem of data scarcity in target domains. In this work, we present a novel method to enhance the capabilities of LLMs in mathematical reasoning tasks. Motivated by the need to bridge this gap, our approach incorporates a question paraphrase strategy, which aims to diversify the linguistic forms of mathematical questions to improve generalization. Additionally, specialized training objectives are employed to guide the model's learning process, focusing on enhancing its understanding of mathematical concepts and reasoning processes. We conduct experiments on four datasets using different LLMs, and demonstrate the effectiveness of our approach in improving LLMs' performance on mathematical reasoning tasks. Our findings underscore the significance of our methodology in advancing LLMs and their potential implications for real-world applications that require mathematical reasoning abilities.

1 Introduction

In recent years, Large Language Models (LLMs) (Touvron et al., 2023b; Team et al., 2023) have emerged as powerful tools in the field of machine learning, demonstrating remarkable performance in a wide range of downstream benchmarks. Their ability to understand and generate natural language text has revolutionized various applications, from language translation (Costa-jussà et al., 2022; Barrault et al., 2023) to question answering systems (Chowdhery et al., 2023; Chen et al., 2023). Central to their success is their ability to perform complex reasoning, enabling them to tackle complex problems with impressive accuracy and efficiency.

However, while LLMs excel in many domains, they face challenges when it comes to solving mathematical problems. Mathematical reasoning often requires intricate logical operations and a deep understanding of mathematical concepts (Saxton et al., 2019; Lightman et al., 2023), posing significant hurdles for conventional LLM architectures. Moreover, the scarcity of data in the mathematical domain (Liu et al., 2021; Kumar et al., 2022) further compounds these challenges, limiting the performance and generalization of these LLMs.

Some existing methods (Shen et al., 2023; Jiang et al., 2024) attempt to address these challenges by employing ensemble techniques, where multiple LLMs collaboratively solve mathematical problems. However, these methods can still be further improved, particularly in enhancing the performance of individual LLMs and mitigating performance degradation over extended reasoning steps. A major challenge when applying LLMs to complex mathematical problems is error propagation, especially in tasks requiring long reasoning chains. Figure 1 illustrates this issue with an example from the GSM8K dataset (Cobbe et al., 2021), solved by the Llama2-7B model (Touvron et al., 2023b). The problem involves multiple intermediate steps to reach the correct solution. However, the model makes an error in the initial steps, which cascades through subsequent stages of reasoning. This occurs because each reasoning step depends on the accuracy of preceding steps; even a minor initial error can compound, ultimately leading to significant deviations from the correct solution. This phenomenon highlights the limitations of current LLMs in maintaining accuracy across long reasoning sequences and underscores the need for improved methodologies to mitigate error propagation and enhance performance in mathematical tasks.

In this paper, we propose novel approaches to ad-

Proceedings of the 4th International Workshop on Knowledge-Augmented Methods for Natural Language Processing (KnowledgeNLP'25), pages 118–128
May 3, 2025

Question:
Linus works for a trading company. He buys a mobile device for \$20 and sells it for twice the amount of the original price. If he bought 2 devices last Monday and 4 devices last Tuesday, how much profit was he able to earn after selling all the mobile devices he bought last Monday and Tuesday?

Answer:
Step 1: The total cost for the devices he bought on Monday is 2*20= «2*20=40»40
Step 2: The total cost for the devices he bought on Tuesday is 4*20 = «4*20=80»80
Step 3: The total cost of these devices is 80+40= «80+40=120»120
Step 4: Linus sold each mobile device he bought for \$20 x 2 = \$«20*2=40»40.
Step 5: So, he earned \$40 x 2 = \$«40*2=80»80 for the two devices he bought last Monday.
Step 6: And he earned \$40 x 4 = \$«40*4=160»160 for the 4 devices he bought last Tuesday.
Step 7: The total amount of sales he made were worth 160+80 =«160+80=240»240
Step 8: Linus earned 240-120 =\$«240-120=120»120
Step 9: The answer is 120

Model Prediction:
Step 1: Linus was able to sell each device bought on Monday for \$20 x 2 = \$40 each.
Step 2: So, his earning is \$40 - \$20 = \$20 after selling each device he bought on Monday.
Step 3: And he was able to sell each device bought on Tuesday for \$40 x 2 = \$80 each.
Step 4: So, his earning after selling each device bought on Tuesday is \$80 - \$40 = \$40.
Step 5: And the total earnings after selling 4 devices bought on Tuesday was \$40 x 4 = \$160.
Step 6: Hence, his total profit is \$40 + \$160 = \$200
Step 7: The answer is 200

Figure 1: Llama2-7B model prediction on an example from the GSM8K dataset.

dress the limitations of existing methods in solving mathematical problems with LLMs. Our contributions include the introduction of new training objectives designed to uncover underlying patterns in data, thus improving model performance. Additionally, we leverage data augmentation techniques to maximize the utility of existing datasets to fine-tune LLMs, enhancing their effectiveness in mathematical reasoning tasks. To evaluate the efficacy of our proposed methods, we conduct experiments using four open-source LLMs—Llama (Touvron et al., 2023a), Llama2 (Touvron et al., 2023b), Mistral (Jiang et al., 2023), and Mixtral (Jiang et al., 2024)—on four widely used mathematical reasoning datasets: GSM8K (Cobbe et al., 2021), MATH (Hendrycks et al., 2021), GSM8K_Hard (Gao et al., 2022), and SVAMP (Patel et al., 2021). Our results demonstrate significant performance improvements, underscoring the effectiveness of our methods in advancing the mathematical reasoning capabilities of LLMs.

In summary, this paper presents novel contributions towards improving the performance of LLMs in solving mathematical problems, addressing the challenges posed by complex reasoning and data scarcity. Our findings have implications for advancing the field of machine learning and expanding the applicability of LLMs to various problem domains.

2 Background

The intersection of machine learning and mathematical reasoning has received significant attention from researchers seeking to enhance the capabilities of LLMs in solving complex mathematical problems. In this section, we review the previous literature exploring various approaches and methodologies to address the challenges posed by mathematical reasoning tasks and highlight the advances made in this domain.

2.1 Recent Advances in LLMs

The evolution of LLMs represents a significant milestone in the field of natural language processing (NLP) and machine learning. Over the past decade, advances in neural network architectures, coupled with the availability of large amounts of text data, have driven the development of increasingly complex and capable LLMs. Beginning with seminal works such as Google's BERT (Bidirectional Encoder Representations from Transformers) (Devlin et al., 2018) and OpenAI's GPT (Generative Pre-trained Transformer) (Radford et al., 2019), researchers have made substantial progress in enhancing LLMs' language understanding and generation capabilities (Liu et al., 2019; Raffel et al., 2020). These models leverage transformer architectures and self-attention mechanisms to capture long-range dependencies and contextual information, enabling them to generate coherent and contextually relevant text.

Further refinements, such as the introduction of GPT-3 (Brown et al., 2020) with significantly larger parameter sizes and more sophisticated training regimes, have pushed the limits of LLM performance to unprecedented levels. These advancements have paved the way for LLMs to excel in a wide range of NLP tasks, including language translation (Costa-jussà et al., 2022; Kudugunta et al., 2024), text summarization (Lewis et al., 2019; Zhang et al., 2020), and question answering (Sanh et al., 2019; He et al., 2020).

2.2 LLMs for mathematics

The application of LLMs to mathematical reasoning tasks represents a recent and growing area of research within the machine learning community. Although LLMs have demonstrated remarkable proficiency in natural language understanding, their performance in mathematical reasoning tasks has historically lagged behind.

However, recent studies (Gou et al., 2023; Shao et al., 2024) have shown promising results in using LLMs to solve mathematical problems. Transfer learning techniques, particularly fine-tuning pretrained LLMs on mathematical datasets, have emerged as effective strategies for enhancing LLMs' mathematical reasoning capabilities. By leveraging the knowledge encoded in pre-trained language models and adapting it to mathematical domains, researchers have achieved remarkable results on mathematical tasks.

Moreover, novel adaptation techniques, such as question paraphrase methods (Yu et al., 2023) and tailored training objectives (Liu et al., 2023) aimed at enhancing LLMs' understanding of mathematical reasoning processes, have further advanced LLMs in mathematical applications. These techniques enable LLMs to effectively leverage existing data and develop robust reasoning abilities, thus expanding their utility in mathematical problem solving scenarios. However, these existing methods suffer from the problem of error propagation over long reasoning paths.

Overall, the application of LLMs in mathematics has immense potential to revolutionize the way mathematical problems are approached and solved. As research in this area continues to evolve, we can expect further advancements in LLMs' mathematical reasoning capabilities and their integration into diverse mathematical domains.

3 Methodology

The motivation for our methodology arises from the observation that while LLMs excel in various natural language processing tasks, their performance in mathematical reasoning remains suboptimal. This gap is primarily due to the inherent complexity of mathematical problems, which often requires intricate reasoning and logical deduction (Saxton et al., 2019; Lightman et al., 2023). Furthermore, the limited availability of annotated data in the mathematical domain (Liu et al., 2021; Kumar et al., 2022) presents a significant obstacle to effectively training LLMs for such tasks.

To overcome these challenges, we propose a novel approach that combines question paraphrasing techniques with tailored training objectives to strengthen the mathematical reasoning capabilities of LLMs. An overview of our proposed pipeline is illustrated in Figure 2.

3.1 Question Paraphrase

Question paraphrasing is a crucial technique employed to augment existing data and enhance the model's ability to generalize across different linguistic forms of mathematical problems. This process involves leveraging the powerful generative capabilities of the GPT-4 model (Brown et al., 2020) to produce diverse paraphrases for each question in the dataset. By generating multiple variations of the same question while preserving its semantic meaning, we aim to enrich the training data and expose the model to a wider range of linguistic structures and expressions commonly encountered in mathematical problem-solving scenarios.

Paraphrasing Questions The GPT-4 model is utilized to generate the paraphrases for each question in the data set. Given a mathematical question, the model generates alternative phrasings that convey the same underlying mathematical concept. This step significantly enhances the diversity of the training data by presenting questions in various linguistic forms, such as synonyms, paraphrases, and syntactic variations.

To ensure the quality and semantic coherence of the paraphrased questions, each paraphrase, along with its corresponding answer, is inputted into the GPT-4 model. The model is then tasked with determining whether the paraphrased question-answer pairs match or not. This iterative validation process helps filter out the inconsistencies or semantic distortions, ensuring that only high-quality paraphrases are retained for training.

3.2 Special Training Objectives

Effective training objectives are critical for guiding a model's learning process and fostering a deeper understanding of mathematical concepts and rea-

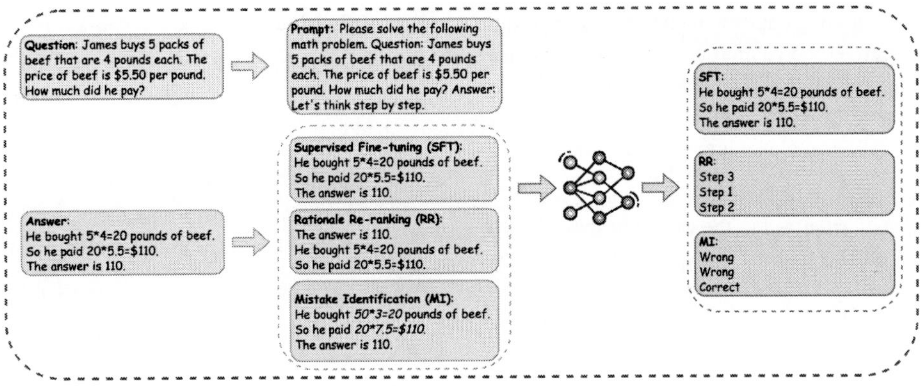

Figure 2: The overview of our proposed pipeline.

soning. Our approach incorporates specialized training objectives designed to address the unique challenges of mathematical reasoning tasks.

During training, we start with a pretrained LLM and apply a supervised fine-tuning (SFT) objective on a carefully curated dataset of mathematical problems. This data set includes a diverse range of questions and solutions to ensure a comprehensive coverage of mathematical concepts and problem types. In the SFT phase, the model is trained to minimize the loss between its predicted answers and the correct solutions provided in the dataset, effectively aligning its outputs with the desired responses.

Rationale Re-Ranking (RR) The Rationale Re-Ranking (RR) objective aims to improve the model's ability to identify and reconstruct the correct reasoning path for solving mathematical problems. This objective involves shuffling the reasoning steps associated with a given problem and reordering the models to reconstruct the proper solution sequence. By training the model to recognize and organize the logical progression of mathematical solutions, the RR objective fosters a more structured, coherent, and accurate reasoning process.

Mistake Identification (MI) The MI objective focuses on improving the robustness and error tolerance of the model by training it to differentiate between correct and erroneous reasoning steps. During training, random modifications are introduced to induce errors in the reasoning process, such as changing numerical values or altering logical operators. The model is then trained to distinguish between correct and erroneous reasoning steps, thus learning to identify and rectify potential mistakes. This objective helps mitigate the risk of erroneous predictions and enhances the model's overall performance on mathematical reasoning tasks:

Integrating these training objectives into the fine-tuning process equips LLMs with enhanced capabilities for mathematical reasoning, thereby addressing the challenges posed by complex problem-solving scenarios.

3.3 Training Process

The training process of our proposed method consists of several stages designed to enhance the mathematical reasoning capabilities of LLMs. The process begins with data augmentation through question paraphrasing, where GPT-4 generates various paraphrases for each mathematical question. To ensure data set quality and integrity, we verify the consistency of the paraphrased questions and their corresponding answers, iterating this process to achieve high accuracy.

Next, we introduce specialized training objectives to improve the model's reasoning abilities. One such objective is Rationale Re-Ranking (RR), where reasoning steps are shuffled, and the model is tasked with predicting the correct sequence. This trains the model to understand and reconstruct logical progressions. Another objective is Mistake Identification (MI), where the model learns to distinguish between correct and intentionally altered reasoning steps, enhancing its ability to detect and correct errors in complex problem-solving scenarios. These objectives are incorporated within a multitask learning framework, with weighted losses assigned to each task to ensure balanced and effective training. This approach enables the model to optimize simultaneously for various aspects of mathematical reasoning, resulting in a more robust and versatile skill set.

By combining data augmentation, targeted training objectives, and a multitask learning framework, our method equips LLMs with strong mathematical reasoning skills, significantly improving their performance on challenging mathematical tasks.

Final training objective The final training objective is formulated as the weighted sum of $\mathcal{L}_{SFT}$, $\mathcal{L}_{RR}$, and $\mathcal{L}_{MI}$:

$$\mathcal{L}_{final}(\theta) = \lambda_1 \mathcal{L}_{SFT} + \lambda_2 \mathcal{L}_{RR} + \lambda_3 \mathcal{L}_{MI}$$

where λ_1, λ_2, and λ_3 are parameters that weight the importance of each loss, and $\mathcal{L}_{SFT}$, $\mathcal{L}_{RR}$, and $\mathcal{L}_{MI}$ are cross entropy losses.

4 Experiments

Mathematical reasoning challenges LLMs, requiring both natural language understanding and mathematical problem-solving skills. Evaluating the effectiveness of LLMs in mathematical reasoning is crucial for advancing state-of-the-art NLP techniques and expanding their applicability across diverse problem domains. This study seeks to assess the performance of various LLMs on mathematical reasoning tasks through targeted experiments.

4.1 Datasets

We conducted experiments on four datasets specifically designed to assess LLMs' performance in mathematical reasoning.

- **GSM8K** (Cobbe et al., 2021): A comprehensive dataset comprising mathematical problems covering a wide range of topics and difficulty levels.
- **MATH** (Hendrycks et al., 2021): A curated collection of mathematical questions and solutions, designed to assess LLMs' ability to solve mathematical problems in various domains.
- **GSM8K-Hard** (Gao et al., 2022): A subset of the GSM8K dataset containing challenging mathematical problems aimed at evaluating the robustness of LLMs under difficult scenarios.
- **SVAMP** (Patel et al., 2021): A specialized dataset focusing on mathematical reasoning in the context of symbolic mathematics, presenting unique challenges for LLMs due to its symbolic nature.

4.2 Base Models

We employed four base models for our experiments, each representing a distinct architecture or variant of LLMs:

- **LLama** (Touvron et al., 2023a): A baseline LLM model known for its strong performance in natural language understanding tasks.
- **LLama2** (Touvron et al., 2023b): An enhanced version of LLama, incorporating improvements in model architecture and training methodology.
- **Mistral** (Jiang et al., 2023): A state-of-the-art LLM model specifically designed for mathematical reasoning tasks, leveraging advanced adaptation techniques.
- **Mixtral** (Jiang et al., 2024): A high-capacity LLM model based on the Mixtral architecture, featuring eight times the parameter size of LLama for enhanced performance.

Training Details We fine-tuned these base models on the aforementioned datasets with hyperparameters tailored to each model and dataset. The parameters are set as default to the ones used during pre-training. Note that we only experiment with the version of 7B parameters for each model. We adapt LoRA (Hu et al., 2022) to make model fine-tuning more efficient. The rank and alpha are both set as 64. Additionally, we utilized specialized training objectives, such as Rationale Re-ranking (RR) and Mistake Identification (MI), to enhance the models' understanding of mathematical reasoning. We fine-tune each model with a single Nvidia A100 GPU and the runtime of each experiment is between 2 to 6 hours.

4.3 Main Results

Our experiments resulted in notable performance improvements across all four base models. Table 1 presents a summary of the main results. Our proposed special training objectives yielded an average performance boost of 4.25% on GSM8K, 2.32% on MATH, 6.21% on GSM_HARD, and 5.15% on SVAMP datasets. Moreover, combining question paraphrase with these objectives further enhances the improvement to 7.32% on GSM8K, 3.63% on MATH, 7.72% on GSM_HARD, and 6.78% on SVAMP. Notably, our methods have a more significant impact on relatively weaker models, likely

Method	Dataset			
	GSM8K	MATH	GSM_HARD	SVAMP
Baselines (SFT Only)				
Llama-7B (Touvron et al., 2023a)	32.07	5.60	23.43	38.24
Llama2-7B (Touvron et al., 2023b)	36.92	5.68	26.72	41.07
Mistral-7B (Jiang et al., 2023)	58.68	14.08	55.42	50.25
Mixtral-8x7B (Jiang et al., 2024)	65.44	30.13	64.93	68.73
Proposed Method (SFT + MI + RR)				
Llama-7B (Touvron et al., 2023a)	37.15	6.91	29.71	44.22
Llama2-7B (Touvron et al., 2023b)	43.04	7.65	38.74	49.03
Mistral-7B (Jiang et al., 2023)	62.87	15.98	60.02	56.87
Mixtral-8x7B (Jiang et al., 2024)	67.04	34.22	66.86	68.76
Proposed Method + Question Paraphrase				
Llama-7B (Touvron et al., 2023a)	41.74	7.64	37.87	46.14
Llama2-7B (Touvron et al., 2023b)	46.86	9.05	32.96	53.04
Mistral-7B (Jiang et al., 2023)	65.82	17.27	63.25	58.03
Mixtral-8x7B (Jiang et al., 2024)	67.96	36.07	67.28	68.19

Table 1: Experimental results of base models on different datasets, respectively. Scores are calculated with the accuracy metric.

because these models benefit more from structured reasoning guidance. This aligns with findings in previous LLM fine-tuning studies, where weaker models exhibit larger relative improvements when exposed to specialized training objectives.

These findings underscore the empirical effectiveness of our methodology in improving the reasoning efficiency and accuracy of LLMs. By assessing LLMs' performance in mathematical reasoning tasks, we contribute to the ongoing efforts to advance the state-of-the-art in natural language processing and pave the way for their application in diverse problem domains requiring mathematical reasoning abilities.

5 Analysis and Discussion

In this section, we delve into a comprehensive analysis and discussion of the experimental results, focusing on the effectiveness of our proposed method in enhancing LLMs' capabilities in mathematical reasoning tasks. We begin by dissecting the model's performance over varying numbers of reasoning steps, shedding light on the impact of our approach on problem-solving efficiency. Subsequently, we present findings from an ablation study aimed at elucidating the importance of individual components within our proposed methods. Finally, through a series of case studies, we illustrate both the successes and limitations of our approach, providing valuable insights for future research directions.

5.1 Analysis on Reasoning Steps

We performed an in-depth analysis of model performance across varying reasoning steps to evaluate the effectiveness of our proposed method in solving complex mathematical problems. By examining performance at different depths of reasoning, we sought to highlight the impact of our approach on problem-solving efficiency. Figure 3 summarizes the model's performance on math questions requiring different reasoning steps. Overall, the results indicate that model performance declines as the number of reasoning steps needed to solve the problems increases. Although the improvement is minimal for questions requiring only a few reasoning steps (fewer than 4 steps), it becomes substantial for questions requiring longer reasoning chains (4–7 steps). Additionally, we note that the models struggle with questions that demand extremely long reasoning paths (more than 8 steps).

Our analysis revealed a clear trend of improved model performance as the number of reasoning steps increased. This trend indicates that our proposed method effectively enhances the model's ability to solve complex mathematical problems, leading to more accurate solutions. Specifically, we observed substantial performance improvements

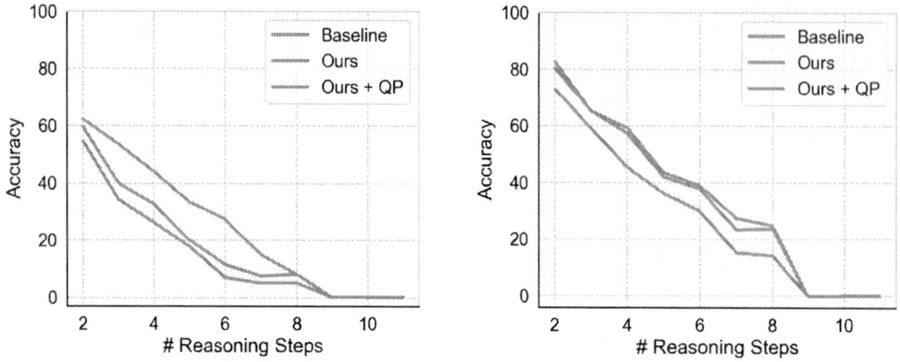

(a) Llama2-7B on different reasoning steps

(b) Mistral-7B on different reasoning steps

Figure 3: Analysis of Llama2 and Mistral on different reasoning steps, respectively. X-axis is the number of reasoning steps required to solve a math question and Y-axis the accuracy score. We use supervised fine-tuning as the baseline, and compare it with our proposed method using special training objective. QP stands for question paraphrase.

Method	GSM8K		MATH	
	Llama2-7B	Mistral-7B	Llama2-7B	Mistral-7B
Baseline (SFT)	36.92	58.68	5.68	14.08
+ RR	38.94	59.06	5.83	13.07
+ MI	40.01	61.57	7.83	15.24
+ MI + RR	43.04	62.87	7.65	15.98
+ MI + RR + QP	46.86	65.82	9.05	17.27

Table 2: Ablation Study of our proposed method on GSM8K and MATH using Llama2-7B and Mistral-7B as base models, respectively. SFT, RR, MI, and QP stand for supervised fine-tuning, rationale re-ranking, mistake identification, and question paraphrase, respectively. Scores are calculated with the accuracy metric.

on problems that involve multiple reasoning steps, which underscores the effectiveness of our approach in addressing complex problem-solving scenarios.

5.2 Ablation Study

To further evaluate the importance of each component in our proposed methods, we performed an ablation study in which we systematically removed individual components and evaluated the model performance. Table 2 presents an ablation study of our proposed method on GSM8K and MATH datasets using Llama2 and Mistral as base models, respectively. Our results demonstrated that all components of our proposed methods are integral to improve model performance in mathematical reasoning tasks.

Specifically, when components such as question paraphrase techniques and specialized training objectives were integrated, we observed a marked increase in model performance, underscoring the importance of these components in facilitating effective mathematical reasoning. These findings emphasize the holistic nature of our proposed approach, wherein each component synergistically contributes to overall model performance.

5.3 Case Study

We present a case study in Figure 4 to demonstrate the effectiveness of our method in solving complex mathematical problems. The case study includes a positive example showcasing successful problem-solving outcomes and a negative example highlighting challenges and limitations.

The positive example illustrates how our method empowers the model to navigate intricate mathematical problems and arrive at the accurate solution, even if it does not follow the exact reasoning path provided in the answer. This example validates the effectiveness of our approach in addressing real-world mathematical challenges.

In contrast, the negative example in Figure 4 reveals scenarios where our proposed method encounters limitations or fails to produce satisfactory results. Although the model follows the correct reasoning path, a common failure mode observed was arithmetic miscalculations despite correct reasoning paths. This suggests that while LLMs grasp mathematical structure, they struggle with

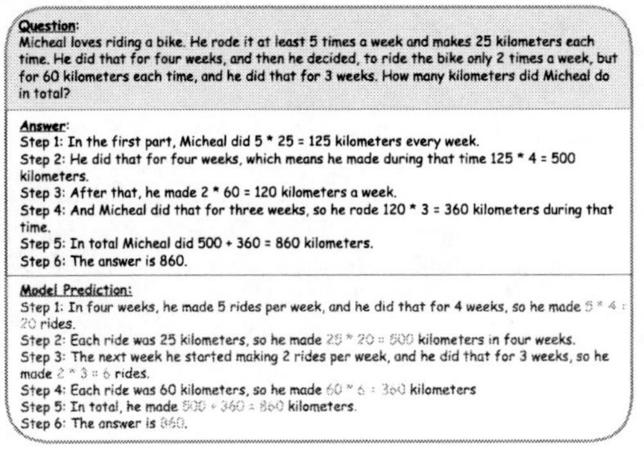

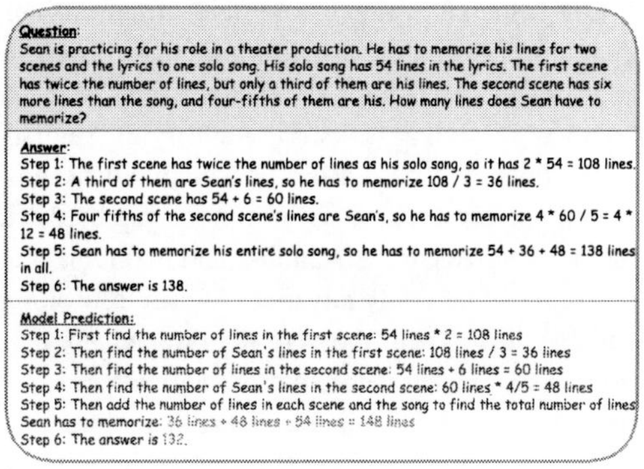

Figure 4: Case study on the GSM8K dataset using the Mistral-7B Model. The example on the left is positive while the example on the right is negative.

precise computation—an issue that could be mitigated by integrating external calculation modules. This example identifies areas for improvement and prompts discussions on potential future research directions, including refining methodologies, leveraging external calculation tools, or exploring math verification approaches to enhance model performance in challenging scenarios.

5.4 Discussion

Data Efficiency and Generalization Our question paraphrase strategy addresses a fundamental challenge in mathematical reasoning: the scarcity of diverse high-quality training data. By systematically transforming existing questions into linguistically varied forms while preserving their mathematical essence, we achieve improved generalization without requiring additional annotated examples. This approach is particularly valuable for specialized mathematical domains where expert annotation is costly and time-consuming. Our experimental results demonstrate that models trained with paraphrased questions exhibit enhanced robustness to linguistic variations, more closely mirroring the diverse ways in which mathematical problems may be encountered in real-world applications. This linguistic flexibility, combined with our specialized training objectives, enables models to focus on the underlying mathematical structures rather than become overly sensitive to specific phrasings. The data efficiency of our approach makes it particularly applicable to resource-constrained settings and suggests promising directions for self-supervised learning techniques that leverage mathematical invariance across different problem formulations.

Training-focused V.S. Test-time computational methods In recent years, the Test-Time Computation (TTC) paradigm has gained significant traction as a means to improve the reasoning skills of LLMs, particularly for complex tasks. Although training-focused and TTC methods represent different strategies, they are not mutually exclusive. In fact, their synergistic integration holds significant promise for future advancements in mathematical reasoning for LLMs. The reasoning abilities that TTC techniques leverage are fundamentally learned during the training phase, encompassing both pre-training and fine-tuning. Training on high-quality mathematical data, including examples of step-by-step reasoning, provides the essential knowledge base that enables TTC methods (e.g., CoT (Wei et al., 2022) and Self-Refine (Madaan et al., 2023)) to be effective. Furthermore, training processes can be optimized to produce models that are particularly adept at generating effective reasoning traces, which can then be further explored or verified during test time using TTC techniques. The quality of the underlying model, shaped by training, significantly influences how effectively it can utilize TTC methods.

6 Conclusion

In this study, we addressed the challenge of enhancing LLMs' capabilities in mathematical reasoning tasks. Our proposed method leverages innovative techniques to improve LLMs' understanding of mathematical concepts and reasoning processes. Through rigorous experimentation, we demonstrated the effectiveness of our approach in improving LLMs' performance on various mathematical problems.

Our research advances the field of natural language processing by providing a comprehensive approach to enhancing LLMs' capabilities in mathematical reasoning tasks. By identifying key factors influencing model performance and proposing effective solutions, we bridge the gap between natural language understanding and mathematical reasoning. Our study advances LLMs' reasoning capabilities, paving the way for broader applications in automated theorem proving, mathematical education, and AI-assisted research in scientific domains. Future work could explore integrating symbolic computation with LLMs to further enhance mathematical reliability.

Limitations

While our study demonstrates promising results in improving the reasoning efficiency and accuracy of LLMs through data enhancement and fine-tuning, several limitations should be acknowledged. First, despite efforts to create a diverse data set through enhancement, inherent biases may persist in the training data. These biases could potentially skew the model's performance towards certain types of mathematical problems or reasoning patterns. Second, although our fine-tuned model improves test performance, its generalization to out-of-distribution mathematical problems remains uncertain. Future work could explore curriculum learning strategies or hybrid neural-symbolic approaches to mitigate this limitation. Further investigation is needed to assess the model's capabilities in tackling advanced mathematical concepts or interdisciplinary problems that deviate significantly from the training examples.

References

Loïc Barrault, Yu-An Chung, Mariano Cora Meglioli, David Dale, Ning Dong, Paul-Ambroise Duquenne, Hady Elsahar, Hongyu Gong, Kevin Heffernan, John Hoffman, et al. 2023. Seamlessm4t-massively multilingual & multimodal machine translation. *arXiv preprint arXiv:2308.11596*.

Tom Brown, Benjamin Mann, Nick Ryder, Melanie Subbiah, Jared D Kaplan, Prafulla Dhariwal, Arvind Neelakantan, Pranav Shyam, Girish Sastry, Amanda Askell, et al. 2020. Language models are few-shot learners. *Advances in neural information processing systems*, 33:1877–1901.

Zeming Chen, Alejandro Hernández Cano, Angelika Romanou, Antoine Bonnet, Kyle Matoba, Francesco Salvi, Matteo Pagliardini, Simin Fan, Andreas Köpf, Amirkeivan Mohtashami, et al. 2023. Meditron-70b: Scaling medical pretraining for large language models. *arXiv preprint arXiv:2311.16079*.

Aakanksha Chowdhery, Sharan Narang, Jacob Devlin, Maarten Bosma, Gaurav Mishra, Adam Roberts, Paul Barham, Hyung Won Chung, Charles Sutton, Sebastian Gehrmann, et al. 2023. Palm: Scaling language modeling with pathways. *Journal of Machine Learning Research*, 24(240):1–113.

Karl Cobbe, Vineet Kosaraju, Mohammad Bavarian, Mark Chen, Heewoo Jun, Lukasz Kaiser, Matthias Plappert, Jerry Tworek, Jacob Hilton, Reiichiro Nakano, Christopher Hesse, and John Schulman. 2021. Training verifiers to solve math word problems. *arXiv preprint arXiv:2110.14168*.

Marta R Costa-jussà, James Cross, Onur Çelebi, Maha Elbayad, Kenneth Heafield, Kevin Heffernan, Elahe Kalbassi, Janice Lam, Daniel Licht, Jean Maillard, et al. 2022. No language left behind: Scaling human-centered machine translation. *arXiv preprint arXiv:2207.04672*.

Jacob Devlin, Ming-Wei Chang, Kenton Lee, and Kristina Toutanova. 2018. Bert: Pre-training of deep bidirectional transformers for language understanding. *arXiv preprint arXiv:1810.04805*.

Luyu Gao, Aman Madaan, Shuyan Zhou, Uri Alon, Pengfei Liu, Yiming Yang, Jamie Callan, and Graham Neubig. 2022. Pal: Program-aided language models. *arXiv preprint arXiv:2211.10435*.

Zhibin Gou, Zhihong Shao, Yeyun Gong, Yujiu Yang, Minlie Huang, Nan Duan, Weizhu Chen, et al. 2023. Tora: A tool-integrated reasoning agent for mathematical problem solving. *arXiv preprint arXiv:2309.17452*.

Pengcheng He, Xiaodong Liu, Jianfeng Gao, and Weizhu Chen. 2020. Deberta: Decoding-enhanced bert with disentangled attention. *arXiv preprint arXiv:2006.03654*.

Dan Hendrycks, Collin Burns, Saurav Kadavath, Akul Arora, Steven Basart, Eric Tang, Dawn Song, and Jacob Steinhardt. 2021. Measuring mathematical problem solving with the math dataset. *NeurIPS*.

Edward J. Hu, Yelong Shen, Phillip Wallis, Zeyuan Allen-Zhu, Yuanzhi Li, Shean Wang, Lu Wang, and Weizhu Chen. 2022. Lora: Low-rank adaptation of large language models. In *The Tenth International Conference on Learning Representations, ICLR 2022, Virtual Event, April 25-29, 2022*. OpenReview.net.

Albert Q Jiang, Alexandre Sablayrolles, Arthur Mensch, Chris Bamford, Devendra Singh Chaplot, Diego de las Casas, Florian Bressand, Gianna Lengyel, Guillaume Lample, Lucile Saulnier, et al. 2023. Mistral 7b. *arXiv preprint arXiv:2310.06825*.

Albert Q Jiang, Alexandre Sablayrolles, Antoine Roux, Arthur Mensch, Blanche Savary, Chris Bamford, Devendra Singh Chaplot, Diego de las Casas, Emma Bou Hanna, Florian Bressand, et al. 2024. Mixtral of experts. *arXiv preprint arXiv:2401.04088.*

Sneha Kudugunta, Isaac Caswell, Biao Zhang, Xavier Garcia, Derrick Xin, Aditya Kusupati, Romi Stella, Ankur Bapna, and Orhan Firat. 2024. Madlad-400: A multilingual and document-level large audited dataset. *Advances in Neural Information Processing Systems*, 36.

Vivek Kumar, Rishabh Maheshwary, and Vikram Pudi. 2022. Practice makes a solver perfect: Data augmentation for math word problem solvers. *arXiv preprint arXiv:2205.00177.*

Mike Lewis, Yinhan Liu, Naman Goyal, Marjan Ghazvininejad, Abdelrahman Mohamed, Omer Levy, Ves Stoyanov, and Luke Zettlemoyer. 2019. Bart: Denoising sequence-to-sequence pre-training for natural language generation, translation, and comprehension. *arXiv preprint arXiv:1910.13461.*

Hunter Lightman, Vineet Kosaraju, Yura Burda, Harri Edwards, Bowen Baker, Teddy Lee, Jan Leike, John Schulman, Ilya Sutskever, and Karl Cobbe. 2023. Let's verify step by step. *arXiv preprint arXiv:2305.20050.*

Qianying Liu, Wenyu Guan, Sujian Li, Fei Cheng, Daisuke Kawahara, and Sadao Kurohashi. 2021. Roda: Reverse operation based data augmentation for solving math word problems. *IEEE/ACM Transactions on Audio, Speech, and Language Processing*, 30:1–11.

Yinhan Liu, Myle Ott, Naman Goyal, Jingfei Du, Mandar Joshi, Danqi Chen, Omer Levy, Mike Lewis, Luke Zettlemoyer, and Veselin Stoyanov. 2019. Roberta: A robustly optimized bert pretraining approach. *arXiv preprint arXiv:1907.11692.*

Yixin Liu, Avi Singh, C Daniel Freeman, John D Co-Reyes, and Peter J Liu. 2023. Improving large language model fine-tuning for solving math problems. *arXiv preprint arXiv:2310.10047.*

Aman Madaan, Niket Tandon, Prakhar Gupta, Skyler Hallinan, Luyu Gao, Sarah Wiegreffe, Uri Alon, Nouha Dziri, Shrimai Prabhumoye, Yiming Yang, et al. 2023. Self-refine: Iterative refinement with self-feedback. *Advances in Neural Information Processing Systems*, 36:46534–46594.

Arkil Patel, Satwik Bhattamishra, and Navin Goyal. 2021. Are NLP models really able to solve simple math word problems? In *Proceedings of the 2021 Conference of the North American Chapter of the Association for Computational Linguistics: Human Language Technologies*, pages 2080–2094, Online. Association for Computational Linguistics.

Alec Radford, Jeffrey Wu, Rewon Child, David Luan, Dario Amodei, Ilya Sutskever, et al. 2019. Language models are unsupervised multitask learners. *OpenAI blog*, 1(8):9.

Colin Raffel, Noam Shazeer, Adam Roberts, Katherine Lee, Sharan Narang, Michael Matena, Yanqi Zhou, Wei Li, and Peter J Liu. 2020. Exploring the limits of transfer learning with a unified text-to-text transformer. *Journal of machine learning research*, 21(140):1–67.

Victor Sanh, Lysandre Debut, Julien Chaumond, and Thomas Wolf. 2019. Distilbert, a distilled version of bert: smaller, faster, cheaper and lighter. *arXiv preprint arXiv:1910.01108.*

David Saxton, Edward Grefenstette, Felix Hill, and Pushmeet Kohli. 2019. Analysing mathematical reasoning abilities of neural models. *arXiv preprint arXiv:1904.01557.*

Zhihong Shao, Peiyi Wang, Qihao Zhu, Runxin Xu, Junxiao Song, Mingchuan Zhang, YK Li, Y Wu, and Daya Guo. 2024. Deepseekmath: Pushing the limits of mathematical reasoning in open language models. *arXiv preprint arXiv:2402.03300.*

Sheng Shen, Le Hou, Yanqi Zhou, Nan Du, Shayne Longpre, Jason Wei, Hyung Won Chung, Barret Zoph, William Fedus, Xinyun Chen, et al. 2023. Mixture-of-experts meets instruction tuning: A winning combination for large language models. *arXiv preprint arXiv:2305.14705.*

Gemini Team, Rohan Anil, Sebastian Borgeaud, Yonghui Wu, Jean-Baptiste Alayrac, Jiahui Yu, Radu Soricut, Johan Schalkwyk, Andrew M Dai, Anja Hauth, et al. 2023. Gemini: a family of highly capable multimodal models. *arXiv preprint arXiv:2312.11805.*

Hugo Touvron, Thibaut Lavril, Gautier Izacard, Xavier Martinet, Marie-Anne Lachaux, Timothée Lacroix, Baptiste Rozière, Naman Goyal, Eric Hambro, Faisal Azhar, et al. 2023a. Llama: Open and efficient foundation language models. *arXiv preprint arXiv:2302.13971.*

Hugo Touvron, Louis Martin, Kevin Stone, Peter Albert, Amjad Almahairi, Yasmine Babaei, Nikolay Bashlykov, Soumya Batra, Prajjwal Bhargava, Shruti Bhosale, et al. 2023b. Llama 2: Open foundation and fine-tuned chat models. *arXiv preprint arXiv:2307.09288.*

Jason Wei, Xuezhi Wang, Dale Schuurmans, Maarten Bosma, Fei Xia, Ed Chi, Quoc V Le, Denny Zhou, et al. 2022. Chain-of-thought prompting elicits reasoning in large language models. *Advances in neural information processing systems*, 35:24824–24837.

Longhui Yu, Weisen Jiang, Han Shi, Jincheng Yu, Zhengying Liu, Yu Zhang, James T Kwok, Zhenguo Li, Adrian Weller, and Weiyang Liu. 2023. Metamath: Bootstrap your own mathematical questions for large language models. *arXiv preprint arXiv:2309.12284.*

Jingqing Zhang, Yao Zhao, Mohammad Saleh, and Peter Liu. 2020. Pegasus: Pre-training with extracted gap-sentences for abstractive summarization. In *International conference on machine learning*, pages 11328–11339. PMLR.

RouteNator: A Router-Based Multi-Modal Architecture for Generating Synthetic Training Data for Function Calling LLMs

Vibha Belavadi*, **Tushar Vatsa***, **Dewang Sultania***, **Suhas Suresha***, **Ishita Verma***,
Cheng Chen, **Tracy Holloway King**, **Michael Friedrich**
Adobe Inc.
345 Park Avenue
San Jose, CA, 95110

Abstract

This paper addresses fine-tuning Large Language Models (LLMs) for function calling tasks when real user interaction data is unavailable. In digital content creation tools, where users express their needs through natural language queries that must be mapped to API calls, the lack of real-world task-specific data and privacy constraints for training on it necessitate synthetic data generation. Existing approaches to synthetic data generation fall short in diversity and complexity, failing to replicate real-world data distributions and leading to suboptimal performance after LLM fine-tuning. We present a novel router-based architecture that leverages domain resources like content metadata and structured knowledge graphs, along with text-to-text and vision-to-text language models to generate high-quality synthetic training data. Our architecture's flexible routing mechanism enables synthetic data generation that matches observed real-world distributions, addressing a fundamental limitation of traditional approaches. Evaluation on a comprehensive set of real user queries demonstrates significant improvements in both function classification accuracy and API parameter selection. Models fine-tuned with our synthetic data consistently outperform traditional approaches, establishing new benchmarks for function calling tasks.

1 Introduction

Digital content creation platforms increasingly rely on natural language interfaces to make complex design tools accessible to non-technical users. A critical challenge lies in accurately translating user queries into appropriate function calls (Schick et al., 2023) for instance, when a user requests "Find me an image of an elephant with the background being Taj Mahal", the system must orchestrate multiple API calls for searching, background removal, and compositing.

In this paper, we specifically address the challenge of training models to classify user intent into two distinct categories: queries that can be fulfilled through search API operations versus those requiring generation through Generative-AI-powered APIs. Given a user query, our model determines: (1) whether to route the request to "Search" or "Generate" operations based on user intent, (2) the appropriate Content Type parameter selection (e.g. Photo, Template, Background, Video), and (3) prompt optimization specific to each API type—simplifying "Search" queries while preserving detailed specifications for "Generate" API requests. The examples below in Listing 1 demonstrate how our model processes and classifies different types of user queries:

Listing 1: Example function calls for user queries

```
example1 = {
'input': 'Find me an image of an
    elephant',
'output': {
    'function': 'Search',
    'content_type': 'Photo',
    'extracted_prompt': 'elephant'
    }
},
example2 = {
'input': 'Create a birthday invitation
    for my nephew whose birthday is on
    January 21',
'output': {
     'function': 'Generate',
     'content_type': 'Template',
     'extracted_prompt': 'invitation for
         nephew's birthday on January 21'
    }
}
```

While existing function calling models (Patil et al., 2023) show promise, their performance on specialized domains remains suboptimal and privacy restrictions on production data create training challenges. To address these limitations, we present two key contributions:

* These authors contributed equally to this work.

Proceedings of the 4th International Workshop on Knowledge-Augmented Methods for Natural Language Processing (KnowledgeNLP'25), pages 129–140
May 3, 2025 ©2025 Association for Computational Linguistics

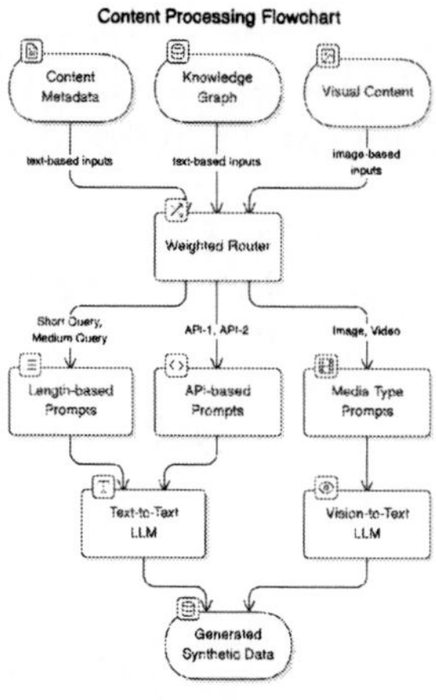

Figure 1: Data generation architecture overview integrating metadata, knowledge graph, and visual content. A "Weighted Router" directs text and image inputs to different prompt categories: length-based, API-based, and media type. They are processed by Text-to-Text and Vision-to-Text LLMs to generate synthetic data for downstream tasks.

1. A methodology for incorporating structured domain knowledge into synthetic data generation that leverages: (a) Techniques for extracting generalizable patterns from content metadata; (b) Methods for utilizing domain-specific knowledge graphs to generate contextually relevant queries.

2. A novel router-based architecture for synthetic data generation featuring: (a) Multiple specialized LLM prompt templates as distinct routes; (b) A weighted routing mechanism using population-level statistics;

(c) Integration of multi-modal language models to increase data diversity.

Our approach (Figure 1) improves downstream model performance while producing balanced training data across content types, with well-distributed keywords and diverse sentence structures that better align with real-world user interactions.

2 Related Work

The challenge of generating high-quality synthetic training data for language models has been explored through various approaches. Prior work in generating high-quality synthetic training data for language models spans three key categories: Instruction-tuning approaches have shown significant promise, starting with Self-Instruct's (Wang et al., 2023) 175-seed task framework. The field expanded through WizardLM's EvolInstruct (Xu et al., 2023), Unnatural Instructions (Honovich et al., 2022), FLAN (Wei et al., 2022), FLAN-T5 (Chung et al., 2024), Alpaca (Taori et al., 2023), Prompt-Breeder (Fernando et al., 2023), and Template-based Generation (Gholami and Omar, 2023). Multimodal synthetic data generation advanced through Visual Instruction Tuning (Liu et al., 2023), MiniGPT-4 (Zhu et al., 2023), and InternVL (Chen et al., 2024), incorporating visual and textual information for enhanced data generation. Function calling approaches, exemplified by Gorilla (Patil et al., 2023) building on Self-Instruct (Wang et al., 2023), addressed API parameter matching challenges, though lacking domain-specific knowledge integration.

Our work differs from previous approaches in several key aspects. (1) We focus specifically on generating synthetic data for function calling while maintaining real-world query distributions. Unlike general instruction tuning approaches, we target the unique challenges of function calling data generation which include precise parameter matching requirements, maintaining real-world API usage distributions and handling complex nested function calls. (2) We introduce a novel router-based architecture that combines multiple generation strategies. We extend existing router-based approaches by adding weighted probabilistic sampling and by using population-level statistics to guide routing decisions. We also combine text-to-text and vision-to-text generation paths. (3) We incorporate domain-specific knowledge while respecting privacy constraints by not directly referring to the real-world datasets. (4) We leverage multiple modalities (text and images) to increase the diversity and quality of generated data, particularly for visual content-related APIs. We introduce novel evaluation metrics measuring the qualitative alignment of the synthetic data with real-world data covering content-type alignment, diversity in data types generated, word length variability, and positional variance of key terms within sentences.

3 Methodology and Experiments

This section details how our data generation approach evolved.

3.1 Template-based Heuristic Generation

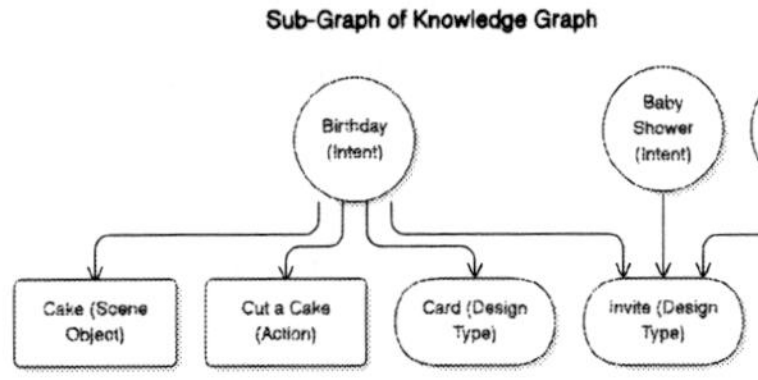

Figure 2: Knowledge Graph of concepts linked by edges

Our initial approach employed rule-based templates that combined content metadata with domain-specific Knowledge Graph (KG) relationships (Kumar et al., 2023) between different aspects of digital content creation. Consider a snapshot of the Knowledge Graph sub-graph (Figure 2). This sub-graph consists of interconnected nodes representing User Intents ("Birthday", "Diwali", "Baby shower"), Design Types ("Card", "Invite"), Scene Objects ("Cake"), and associated Actions ("Cut a cake"). Each edge between the nodes represents a relationship between them. These connections were created using the historical and semantic relationships seen between different entities like User Intents, Design Types, Scene Objects and Actions. They enable the generation of semantically coherent queries by following established relationships between concepts. We create synthetic "Search" API data by generating random prompts combining the related entities (e.g. Intent and Design Type) with search synonyms e.g. "find me", "search for", "look for", "search", "show me".

Listing 2: Examples of Image and Template metadata

```
image_asset_metadata = {
...
'title': 'Tropical frangipani flowers
    floating',
'keywords': ['flower', 'frangipani', '
    paradise', 'turquoise', 'tranquil',
    'tropical', 'summer'],
'gentech': False
...
},

template_asset_metadata = {
...
'topics': ['galactic','space','server
    banner']
'title': 'Galaxy Minecraft Server Banner
    ',
...
}
```

In addition to using the Knowledge Graph, we also use content metadata of templates and images to heuristically create data. Each image or template asset contains metadata capturing its characteristics, such as the title of the asset, keywords or tags associated with it, whether it was generated by AI, locale, aspect ratio, click through rate, etc. This metadata provides a foundation of contextually relevant information that reflects real-world content organization and classification. Listing 2 captures some of the image and template metadata tags used. For "Generate" API queries, we constructed templates that combined action verbs (e.g. "generate", "create" or "make") with content design types and titles from our metadata. For example, a template might expand to "please generate a template for" followed by the title from our content metadata. For creating "Generate" API queries for Image assets, we only use the asset if the label 'gentech' is set to True. Similarly, for "Search" API queries, we used search-related verbs (e.g. "find", "search for") with appropriate content descriptors. This approach allowed rapid generation of synthetic data with proportions matching real-world statistics, but suffered from significant limitations: The generated queries lacked diversity, often with unnatural language patterns.

3.2 Single-Prompt LLM Based Generation

To address these limitations, we experimented with a Llama-3.1-70B-Instruct model (Touvron et al., 2023) with a comprehensive set of prompts containing API specifications and few-shot examples. Different variants of the system prompt focused on different aspects of the content metadata e.g. intents, assets, actions. Examples of the Llama model prompts used used for synthesizing "Search" and "Generate" API queries are listed in appendix A.1. To mimic the characteristics of real-world data (e.g. query length for "Search" vs "Generate" queries), the system prompts used for "Search" queries specify the query to be short and crisp. Conversely the "Generate" query prompts used layout creativity and engagement as a driving factor for data generation. This approach generated more natural language queries but presented challenges in controlling output distributions and maintaining variety across generated samples. Furthermore, it was difficult to ensure appropriate coverage across different content types and query patterns.

In addition to Llama 70B model, a key innovation in our approach is the integration of multimodal capabilities for synthetic data generation on template data through the InternVL vision-to-text model (Chen et al., 2024). We prompted the 40B InternVL model to generate a few queries that would result in the creation of the input template placing emphasis on the important elements unique to the template. The prompt for InternVL model is shared in Appendix A.2. This addition of multi-modality based data generation component enables the generation of queries based on actual domain-specific corpus images and visual representations of non-image content. This provides an additional route for query generation that captures visual aspects that are not present in the metadata, leading to more natural descriptions and increased output diversity.

3.3 Router-based Multi-Modal Architecture

Our final approach introduced a novel router-based architecture that addresses the limitations of the previous two methods. The architecture consists of multiple specialized prompt templates, each designed to generate specific types of queries based on length, API type, and content requirements. These prompt templates incorporate variables from content metadata and domain-specific KG (Kumar et al., 2023) relationships, ensuring semantic relevance while maintaining natural language patterns. The architecture also employs dataset generation from the approaches discussed above: heuristic-based, Llama text-to-text model and InternVL's vision-to-text model.

The core of our architecture is a weighted router that directs query generation requests to appropriate prompt templates based on population-level statistics. This routing mechanism implements weighted sampling to maintain realistic query patterns while ensuring coverage across different query types and content categories. Table 1 gives the distribution of the synthetic dataset generated across the heuristic-, single-prompt- and router-based approaches.

Synthetic Dataset variant	Search	Generate
Heuristic Based	103,189	102,922
Single-Prompt LLM Based	100,207	100,433
Router-Based	105,100	110,000

Table 1: Number of synthetic training examples generated for Search and Generate functions for each data generation approach

3.4 Implementation Details

The router selection algorithm determines target distributions based on population statistics and selects prompt templates based on required query characteristics and content type requirements. For each synthetic data point, the router either selects a text-based route, populating templates with metadata and KG elements, or a vision-based route, processing content images through InternVL to generate contextually relevant queries.

The system includes validation checks for query realism, label accuracy, and distribution alignment. It filters out duplicate queries, unrealistic language patterns, and queries that violate length constraints. This ensures that the synthetic data is high quality and accurately reflects real-world usage patterns.

The query generation process is continuously monitored and adjusted to maintain desired distributions across query lengths, API usage patterns, and content type frequencies. This adaptive approach ensures that the generated dataset remains balanced and representative of current user behavior patterns, while the multi-modal integration provides diversity and realism in the generated queries.

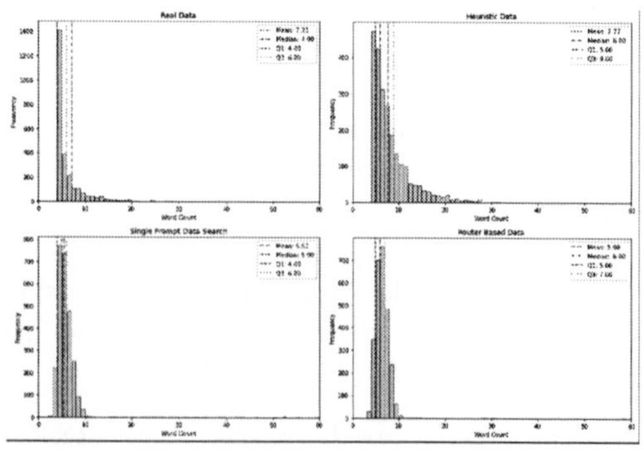

Figure 3: Comparison of word count distribution (Mean, Median and Interquartile Range) across the real and synthetically generated datasets (Heuristic, Single Prompt and Router)

3.5 Fine-tuning

To efficiently adapt the models while managing computational resources, we employ Quantized Low-Rank Adaptation (QLoRA) (Dettmers et al., 2023) across our experiments. For the Gorilla OpenFunctions v2 model (Patil et al., 2023), we utilize 4 NVIDIA A100 GPUs operating in parallel, with the base model parameters quantized to 4-bit precision while maintaining model quality through low-rank adapters. The training configuration utilizes cosine annealing for learning rate optimization (Loshchilov and Hutter, 2017) with ADAM_W (Loshchilov and Hutter, 2019) as the optimizer, and we set the LoRA rank and alpha parameters to 16 and 32 respectively to balance adaptation capability with training stability.

Additionally, we fine-tuned several small language models (SLMs) using the same QLoRA technique Phi-3.5-mini-instruct (Microsoft, 2024), Llama-3.2-1B-Instruct (LlamaTeam, 2024), Llama-3.2-3B-Instruct (LlamaTeam, 2024), Qwen2.5-1.5B-Instruct (QwenTeam, 2024), Qwen2.5-0.5B-Instruct (QwenTeam, 2024) and Gemma-2-2b-it (GemmaTeam, 2024). For these models, the training infrastructure consisted of 4 NVIDIA A10 GPUs operating in parallel. We maintained consistent quantization and adaptation strategies across all models to ensure fair comparison. The hyperparameters and prompt structure used for training, training and evaluation loss, system memory usage and GPU utilization are in Appendix B.

4 Results and Analysis

We analyze the results by first looking at the data diversity of the router based synthetic data (word count distribution, content type diversity, positional diversity of keywords and query length distribution) and comparing it with other synthetically generated datasets. We then focus on the performance metrics of different variants of Gorilla model across different synthetic datasets. We also show the performance improvement of Small Language Models (SLMs) fine-tuned on our router based synthetic dataset compared to their base model.

4.1 Word Count Distribution

Figure 3 compares the word count distribution across real-world and synthetically generated datasets, specifically analyzing the mean, median, and Interquartile Range (IQR). For this comparison, we sampled 2,500 search queries from each distribution.

The real-world dataset has a mean word length of 7 words and a median of 4 words. The distribution is right-skewed with a short IQR, suggesting that real-world queries are generally concise, typically ranging between 1 to 10 words.

In contrast, the synthetic dataset generated using Heuristic Data (KG and metadata-based) exhibits a higher median of 6 words, indicating that the generated queries tend to be more verbose. Although the Single Prompt-based data has a similar IQR, its narrower distribution suggests that the synthetic queries are, on average, shorter than real-world queries.

Finally, we observe that the Router-based synthetic data generation approach maintains a similar IQR to the real-world data, while achieving a balanced distribution between diverse and realistic queries. This means that the generated queries are neither excessively long nor too short, aligning with real-world user behavior—where users are likely to search with either "Search" (short user query) or "Generate" (long user query).

4.2 Content Type Diversity

Traditional synthetic data generation techniques often struggle to replicate a real-world data diversity, resulting in imbalanced datasets where certain content types are overrepresented. In contrast, our architecture enables a balanced and diverse distribution across content types. Figure 4 shows that our approach achieves a relatively even distribution across multiple content types (e.g. 'Templates', 'Images', 'Videos', 'Backgrounds'), allowing the model to learn from a variety of content requests without over-fitting to any single category. This balanced distribution ensures that the model is exposed to a realistic sampling of potential queries, improving its generalization ability for content-specific API calls. In contrast, traditional synthetic data generation methods (Figure 4) tend to be heavily skewed, with content types like 'Image' dominating the dataset, while others such as 'Audio' and 'Template' are underrepresented. This can limit a model's capability to handle less frequent but important content types, resulting in suboptimal performance in real-world applications.

4.3 Positional Diversity of Keywords

One of the key improvements in our synthetic data generation approach is the reduction of keyword position bias, specifically for 'Content Type' key-

User Query	Function	Content Type	Optimized Subprompt
Find me a birthday template with balloons and confetti	Search	Template	birthday balloons confetti
Create an elegant wedding invitation with gold floral borders for a December ceremony	Generate	Template	elegant wedding invitation gold floral borders December ceremony
Show me tropical beach backgrounds	Search	Background	tropical beach background
Generate a podcast cover with neon colors and retro style	Generate	Design Asset	podcast cover neon colors retro style
Find business presentation templates with data charts	Search	Template	business presentation data charts

Table 2: Representative Examples from Golden Dataset

Model and Dataset variant	Function Call F1-Score	ContentType Accuracy (CTA)	Subprompt Similarity (SS)
Pre Fine-tuned Base Gorilla	0.646	0.239	0.824
Fine-tuned Gorilla: Single Prompt dataset	0.788	0.574	0.898
Fine-tuned Gorilla: Heuristic dataset	0.801	0.676	**0.919**
Fine-tuned Gorilla: Synthetic dataset + Router	0.844	0.65	0.867
Fine-tuned Gorilla: Synthetic + Heuristic dataset + Router	0.875	0.737	0.915
Prompt Tuned Gorilla: Synthetic + Heuristic dataset + Router	**0.881**	**0.756**	0.918

Table 3: Performance summary of the fine-tuned Gorilla model trained on different datasets. The ContentType Accuracy and Subprompt Similarity are referenced as CTA and SS respectively

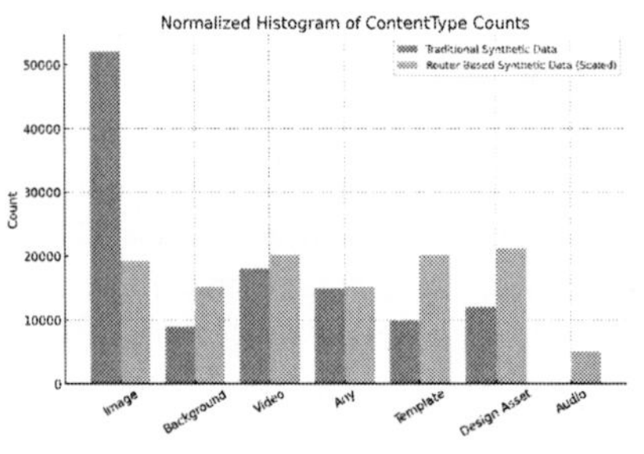

Figure 4: Comparison of Content Type distribution

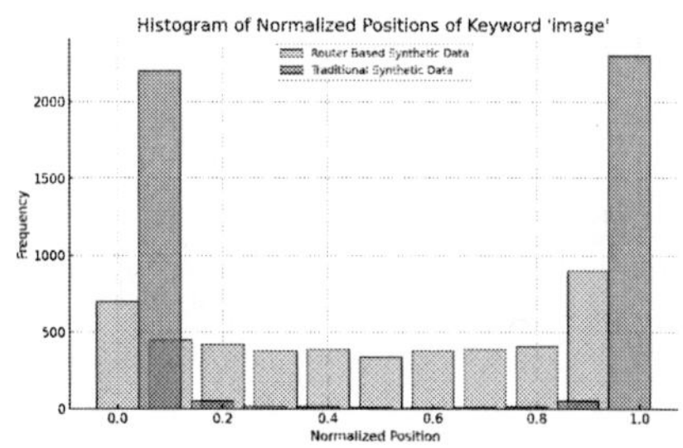

Figure 5: Comparison of normalized keyword positions

words within user queries. Traditional synthetic datasets often position these keywords (e.g. 'Image', 'Video', 'Template', 'Audio') consistently at the beginning or end of queries. This lack of positional diversity leads to models that are prone to over-fitting, as they learn to expect keywords in fixed positions, which limits their generalization capabilities in real-world scenarios.

Our router-based synthetic data generation framework creates a more even distribution of content type keywords (Figure 5) across positions in the query, which exposes the model to a wider range of query structures, helping it generalize and reducing over-fitting.

4.4 Query Length Diversity

To ensure our dataset accurately reflects real-world query variations, we designed distinct length distributions for "Search" and "Generate" queries. We observed that users tend to use the "Search" API to look for generic content and then select a result to start their design with. In contrast, they tend to use the "Generate" API to create specific content which may not exist in the content library. Consequently, "Search" queries are usually shorter than "Generate" queries. By accommodating a spectrum of query lengths, our approach improves the model's ability to handle both concise and complex user requests. For "Search" based queries, we upper-bound the length to 10 words. This allows the model to focus on short, targeted requests, enhancing retrieval performance. In contrast, "Generate" based queries allow a broader range of lengths, with an upper limit set to 40 words (Figure 6). By expanding the length allowance for "Generate" queries, the model learns to handle more descriptive inputs, improving its ability to create content that aligns with nuanced user specifications.

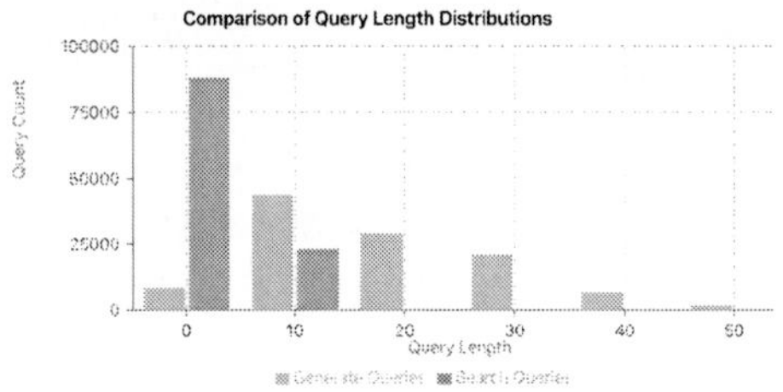

Figure 6: Comparison of search and generate query length

4.5 Performance Metrics and Evaluation

4.5.1 Golden Dataset Details

To evaluate model performance, we created a manually curated golden dataset consisting of 460 real-world user queries with high-quality labels. This dataset provides a balanced representation across query types and intents, with 237 Search queries and 223 Generate queries. The dataset exhibits natural language variation with query lengths ranging from brief phrases to detailed specifications (median length = 8 words, mean = 10.9 words, maximum = 38 words). This diverse distribution ensures comprehensive evaluation across all supported content types, with particular emphasis on commonly requested media like templates and images while maintaining representation of specialized content types.

Each query in the dataset is annotated with function classification (Search/Generate), content type label and optimized sub-prompt.The dataset includes queries ranging from simple search requests to complex generation specifications, as illustrated in Table 2. This variation in query complexity and specificity allows us to assess model performance across different difficulty levels and use cases. The content type distribution in golden dataset is in Table 5. This comprehensive labeling enables evaluation across multiple dimensions of model performance, from high-level task classification to the nuanced understanding required for subprompt optimization. The golden dataset served as our primary benchmark for comparing different model variants and synthetic data generation approaches, providing consistent and reliable metrics for Function Call F1 score, Content Type Accuracy (CTA), and Subprompt Similarity (SS) as reported in Tables 3 and 4.

4.5.2 Model Performance Metrics

We began with the baseline Gorilla openfunctions v2 model (Patil et al., 2023) fine-tuned for API calls, which yielded initial F1-Score of 0.646, Content Type Accuracy (CTA) of 0.239, and Subprompt Similarity (SS) of 0.824 (Table 3). These metrics highlighted areas for improvement to meet our query mapping requirements. Testing a single-prompt response approach resulted in F1-Score of 0.788, CTA of 0.57, and SS of 0.898, indicating modest gains but underscoring the need for additional fine-tuning strategies.

To enhance performance further, we fine-tuned the model on a heuristic dataset from our storage index, which included captions, template phrases (e.g. "birthday template" for birthday-related queries), and keywords based on query analysis. As a result, F1 rose to 0.801, CTA to 0.676, and SS to 0.919. Next, we implemented the multi-prompt router approach, generating synthetic data using domain-specific metadata from our KG. Fine-tuning on this synthetic dataset alone achieved F1 of 0.844, CTA of 0.65, and SS of 0.867, showing the effectiveness of our router-based approach in capturing nuanced query patterns and context. Combining the synthetic and heuristic datasets yielded further improvements, with F1 reaching 0.875, CTA at 0.737, and SS at 0.915, demonstrating the benefits of blending structured metadata with generated queries. Finally, we applied prompt-tuned fine-tuning to the combined dataset, achieving peak results: F1 of 0.881, CTA of 0.756, and SS of 0.918. This iterative process validated the model's capacity to handle complex queries. To assess whether the observed gains in Function Calling Accuracy between the Single Prompt Fine-Tuned Gorilla model and the Prompt Tuned Gorilla model (Synthetic + Heuristic) dataset using the router were statistically significant, we conducted McNemar's test. The p-value of 2.529 e-05 demonstrates a highly significant difference. For Subprompt Similarity (SS) metric, a paired t-test yielded a p-value of 0.064, suggesting a trend toward significance.

In addition to training on Gorilla, we compared the performance of Small Language Models (SLMs) before and after being trained

Model	Function Call F1-Score	ContentType Accuracy (CTA)	Subprompt Similarity (SS)
Vanilla Gemma2-2B-Instruction-Tuned	0.626	0.337	0.882
Fine-tuned Gemma2-2B-Instruction-Tuned	0.876	0.552	0.91
Vanilla Qwen2.5-1.5B-Instruct	0.687	0.274	0.796
Fine-tuned Qwen2.5-1.5B-Instruct	0.863	0.554	0.91
Vanilla Qwen2.5-0.5B-Instruct	0.187	0	0.02
Fine-tuned Qwen2.5-0.5B-Instruct	0.876	0.554	0.91
Vanilla Phi-3.5-mini-Instruct	0.626	0.406	0.915
Fine-tuned Phi-3.5-mini-Instruct	0.889	0.576	0.91
Vanilla Llama-3.2-1B-Instruct	0.432	0	0.182
Fine-tuned Llama-3.2-1B-Instruct	0.865	0.57	0.91

Table 4: Performance summary of the additional SLM models before/after training on the router-based synthetic dataset. The ContentType Accuracy and Sub-prompt Similarity are referenced as CTA and SS respectively

Content Type	Count	Percentage
Templates	103	22.4%
Photos/Images	97	21.1%
Audio	20	4.3%
Video	19	4.1%
Background	20	4.3%
Design Assets	17	3.7%
Text	20	4.3%
Any (type-agnostic)	164	35.7%

Table 5: Content Type Distribution in Golden Dataset

on our router-based synthetic dataset. The SLMs used for comparison were Gemma2-2B-it (Instruction-Tuned) model (GemmaTeam, 2024), Qwen2.5-1.5B-instruct and Qwen2.5-0.5B-instruct models (QwenTeam, 2024), Phi3.5-mini-instruct model (Microsoft, 2024) and Llama-3.2-1B-Instruct model (LlamaTeam, 2024). We found a significant improvement in the Function Call F1 score, CTA and SS scores across all the SLMs after fine-tuning them with the Router-based synthetic dataset. Additional details on performance improvement are provided in Table 4.

5 Conclusion

LLMs are fueling efforts to develop systems that accurately interpret user queries and map them to function calls. However, the scarcity of real-world user data and privacy constraints on training with it necessitate synthetic data generation. Existing synthetic data generation approaches lack the diversity and complexity needed to mirror real-world interactions, limiting model performance. We introduced a novel architecture for generating high-quality synthetic training data. Our approach integrates content metadata and domain-specific KGs with text-to-text and vision-to-text models, producing more varied and representative data. Through iterative development, we arrived at a router-based multi-modal architecture that enhances data diversity and improves model training outcomes. Our model demonstrates gains in function mapping accuracy, although further improvement is possible in content-type classification.

6 Future Work

This research opens several promising avenues for future investigation. One primary direction is to extend the system's linguistic capabilities to support multilingual query processing, thereby improving global accessibility. Although our architecture has proven effective in digital content creation, its underlying principles could be generalized to other domains requiring sophisticated function-calling mechanisms. Leveraging more advanced language models—such as Llama-405B (LlamaTeam, 2024) or DeepSeek (DeepSeek-AI et al., 2024)—for synthetic data generation may yield higher-quality training examples, while expanding our golden dataset could enable more rigorous model evaluation. Additionally, exploring the architecture's extensibility to support additional specialized functions and API calls would both broaden the system's applications and provide insights into the scalability of our approach across different functional domains.

References

Zhe Chen, Jiannan Wu, Wenhai Wang, Weijie Su, Guo Chen, Sen Xing, Muyan Zhong, Qinglong Zhang, Xizhou Zhu, Lewei Lu, et al. 2024. Internvl: Scaling up vision foundation models and aligning for generic visual-linguistic tasks. In *Proceedings of the IEEE/CVF Conference on Computer Vision and Pattern Recognition*, pages 24185–24198.

Hyung Won Chung, Le Hou, Shayne Longpre, Barret Zoph, Yi Tay, William Fedus, Yunxuan Li, Xuezhi Wang, Mostafa Dehghani, Siddhartha Brahma, Albert Webson, Shixiang Shane Gu, Zhuyun Dai, Mirac Suzgun, Xinyun Chen, Aakanksha Chowdhery, Alex Castro-Ros, Marie Pellat, Kevin Robinson, Dasha Valter, Sharan Narang, Gaurav Mishra, Adams Yu, Vincent Zhao, Yanping Huang, Andrew Dai, Hongkun Yu, Slav Petrov, Ed H. Chi, Jeff Dean, Jacob Devlin, Adam Roberts, Denny Zhou, Quoc V. Le, and Jason Wei. 2024. Scaling instruction-finetuned language models. *Journal of Machine Learning Research*, 25(70):1–53.

DeepSeek-AI, Aixin Liu, Bei Feng, Bing Xue, Bingxuan Wang, Bochao Wu, Chengda Lu, Chenggang Zhao, Chengqi Deng, Chenyu Zhang, Chong Ruan, Damai Dai, Daya Guo, Dejian Yang, Deli Chen, Dongjie Ji, Erhang Li, Fangyun Lin, Fucong Dai, Fuli Luo, Guangbo Hao, Guanting Chen, Guowei Li, H. Zhang, Han Bao, Hanwei Xu, Haocheng Wang, Haowei Zhang, Honghui Ding, Huajian Xin, Huazuo Gao, Hui Li, Hui Qu, J. L. Cai, Jian Liang, Jianzhong Guo, Jiaqi Ni, Jiashi Li, Jiawei Wang, Jin Chen, Jingchang Chen, Jingyang Yuan, Junjie Qiu, Junlong Li, Junxiao Song, Kai Dong, Kai Hu, Kaige Gao, Kang Guan, Kexin Huang, Kuai Yu, Lean Wang, Lecong Zhang, Lei Xu, Leyi Xia, Liang Zhao, Litong Wang, Liyue Zhang, Meng Li, Miaojun Wang, Mingchuan Zhang, Minghua Zhang, Minghui Tang, Mingming Li, Ning Tian, Panpan Huang, Peiyi Wang, Peng Zhang, Qiancheng Wang, Qihao Zhu, Qinyu Chen, Qiushi Du, R. J. Chen, R. L. Jin, Ruiqi Ge, Ruisong Zhang, Ruizhe Pan, Runji Wang, Runxin Xu, Ruoyu Zhang, Ruyi Chen, S. S. Li, Shanghao Lu, Shangyan Zhou, Shanhuang Chen, Shaoqing Wu, Shengfeng Ye, Shengfeng Ye, Shirong Ma, Shiyu Wang, Shuang Zhou, Shuiping Yu, Shunfeng Zhou, Shuting Pan, T. Wang, Tao Yun, Tian Pei, Tianyu Sun, W. L. Xiao, Wangding Zeng, Wanjia Zhao, Wei An, Wen Liu, Wenfeng Liang, Wenjun Gao, Wenqin Yu, Wentao Zhang, X. Q. Li, Xiangyue Jin, Xianzu Wang, Xiao Bi, Xiaodong Liu, Xiaohan Wang, Xiaojin Shen, Xiaokang Chen, Xiaokang Zhang, Xiaosha Chen, Xiaotao Nie, Xiaowen Sun, Xiaoxiang Wang, Xin Cheng, Xin Liu, Xin Xie, Xingchao Liu, Xingkai Yu, Xinnan Song, Xinxia Shan, Xinyi Zhou, Xinyu Yang, Xinyuan Li, Xuecheng Su, Xuheng Lin, Y. K. Li, Y. Q. Wang, Y. X. Wei, Y. X. Zhu, Yang Zhang, Yanhong Xu, Yanhong Xu, Yanping Huang, Yao Li, Yao Zhao, Yaofeng Sun, Yaohui Li, Yaohui Wang, Yi Yu, Yi Zheng, Yichao Zhang, Yifan Shi, Yiliang Xiong, Ying He, Ying Tang, Yishi Piao, Yisong Wang, Yixuan Tan, Yiyang Ma, Yiyuan Liu, Yongqiang Guo, Yu Wu, Yuan Ou, Yuchen Zhu, Yuduan Wang, Yue Gong, Yuheng Zou, Yujia He, Yukun Zha, Yunfan Xiong, Yunxian Ma, Yuting Yan, Yuxiang Luo, Yuxiang You, Yuxuan Liu, Yuyang Zhou, Z. F. Wu, Z. Z. Ren, Zehui Ren, Zhangli Sha, Zhe Fu, Zhean Xu, Zhen Huang, Zhen Zhang, Zhenda Xie, Zhengyan Zhang, Zhewen Hao, Zhibin Gou, Zhicheng Ma, Zhigang Yan, Zhihong Shao, Zhipeng Xu, Zhiyu Wu, Zhongyu Zhang, Zhuoshu Li, Zihui Gu, Zijia Zhu, Zijun Liu, Zilin Li, Ziwei Xie, Ziyang Song, Ziyi Gao, and Zizheng Pan. 2024. Deepseek-v3 technical report. *Preprint*, arXiv:2412.19437.

Tim Dettmers, Artidoro Pagnoni, Ari Holtzman, and Luke Zettlemoyer. 2023. Qlora: Efficient finetuning of quantized llms. *Preprint*, arXiv:2305.14314.

Chrisantha Fernando, Dylan Banarse, Henryk Michalewski, Simon Osindero, and Tim Rocktäschel. 2023. Promptbreeder: Self-referential self-improvement via prompt evolution. *Preprint*, arXiv:2309.16797.

GemmaTeam. 2024. Gemma.

Sia Gholami and Marwan Omar. 2023. Does synthetic data make large language models more efficient? *Preprint*, arXiv:2310.07830.

Or Honovich, Thomas Scialom, Omer Levy, and Timo Schick. 2022. Unnatural instructions: Tuning language models with (almost) no human labor. *Preprint*, arXiv:2212.09689.

Jayant Kumar, Manasi Deshmukh, Ming Liu, Ashok Gupta, Karthik Suresh, Chirag Arora, Jing Zheng, Ravindra Sadaphule, Vipul Dalal, and Andrei Stefan. 2023. Generating and utilizing a digital knowledge graph to provide contextual recommendations in digital content editing applications.

Haotian Liu, Chunyuan Li, Qingyang Wu, and Yong Jae Lee. 2023. Visual instruction tuning. *Preprint*, arXiv:2304.08485.

AI@Meta LlamaTeam. 2024. The llama 3 herd of models/. *arXiv preprint arXiv:2407.21783*.

Ilya Loshchilov and Frank Hutter. 2017. Sgdr: Stochastic gradient descent with warm restarts. *Preprint*, arXiv:1608.03983.

Ilya Loshchilov and Frank Hutter. 2019. Decoupled weight decay regularization. *Preprint*, arXiv:1711.05101.

Microsoft. 2024. Phi-3 technical report: A highly capable language model locally on your phone. *arXiv preprint arXiv:2404.14219*.

Shishir G. Patil, Tianjun Zhang, Xin Wang, and Joseph E. Gonzalez. 2023. Gorilla: Large language model connected with massive apis. *Preprint*, arXiv:2305.15334.

QwenTeam. 2024. Qwen2.5 technical report. *arXiv preprint arXiv:2412.15115*.

Timo Schick, Jane Dwivedi-Yu, Roberto Dessì, Roberta Raileanu, Maria Lomeli, Luke Zettlemoyer, Nicola Cancedda, and Thomas Scialom. 2023. Toolformer: Language models can teach themselves to use tools. *Preprint*, arXiv:2302.04761.

Rohan Taori, Ishaan Gulrajani, Tianyi Zhang, Yann Dubois, Xuechen Li, Carlos Guestrin, Percy Liang, and Tatsunori B Hashimoto. 2023. Alpaca: A strong, replicable instruction-following model. *Stanford Center for Research on Foundation Models. https://crfm. stanford. edu/2023/03/13/alpaca. html*, 3(6):7.

Hugo Touvron, Thibaut Lavril, Gautier Izacard, Xavier Martinet, Marie-Anne Lachaux, Timothée Lacroix, Baptiste Rozière, Naman Goyal, Eric Hambro, Faisal Azhar, Aurelien Rodriguez, Armand Joulin, Edouard Grave, and Guillaume Lample. 2023. Llama: Open and efficient foundation language models. *Preprint*, arXiv:2302.13971.

Yizhong Wang, Yeganeh Kordi, Swaroop Mishra, Alisa Liu, Noah A. Smith, Daniel Khashabi, and Hannaneh Hajishirzi. 2023. Self-instruct: Aligning language models with self-generated instructions. *Preprint*, arXiv:2212.10560.

Jason Wei, Maarten Bosma, Vincent Y. Zhao, Kelvin Guu, Adams Wei Yu, Brian Lester, Nan Du, Andrew M. Dai, and Quoc V. Le. 2022. Finetuned language models are zero-shot learners. *Preprint*, arXiv:2109.01652.

Can Xu, Qingfeng Sun, Kai Zheng, Xiubo Geng, Pu Zhao, Jiazhan Feng, Chongyang Tao, and Daxin Jiang. 2023. Wizardlm: Empowering large language models to follow complex instructions. *Preprint*, arXiv:2304.12244.

Deyao Zhu, Jun Chen, Xiaoqian Shen, Xiang Li, and Mohamed Elhoseiny. 2023. Minigpt-4: Enhancing vision-language understanding with advanced large language models. *Preprint*, arXiv:2304.10592.

A Model Prompts

A.1 Llama-3.1-70B-Instruct Model Prompts

Below is an example of System Prompt used for generating Search data using Llama's 70B model:

Role: System
Content: You are an AI Assistant responsible for generating a single, concise user search query based on provided metadata. The search queries are short and crisp and less than 10 words. You will be working with different assets for example (templates, images, videos, design assets, backgrounds, shapes). Help me write a search query for an Instagram story template for title:{title} focusing on intents:{intents}. The query should directly reflect the relevant title, intents, actions, or assets, without any additional explanations or unnecessary text. Do not include any introductory phrases or conclusions, just the query itself.
...
Role: System
Content: You are an AI Assistant responsible for generating a single, concise user search query based on provided metadata. The search queries are short and crisp and less than 10 words. You will be working with different assets for example (templates, images, videos, design assets, backgrounds, shapes). Help me write a search query for the vibrant background for title:{title} focusing on actions:{actions}. Please include the word background in the query.The query should directly reflect the relevant title, intents, actions, or assets, without any additional explanations or unnecessary text. Do not include any introductory phrases or conclusions, just the query itself.
....

Here are examples of some of the prompts used by Llama 70B model to synthesize Generate function data:

Role: System
Content: You are an AI that generates creative and engaging user prompts based on provided metadata. The prompt should be less than 40 words. Design a Facebook post prompt for title:{title} that encourages users to actions:{actions}. Use assets:{assets} to support intents:{intents}.The prompt should feel like something a human would write and should not include any hashtags or links or unnecessary punctuations.
....
Role: System
Content: You are an AI that generates creative and engaging user prompts based on provided metadata. The prompt should be less than 40 words. Make some prompt for title:{title} with intents:{intents}. Use assets:{assets}, or maybe not?
....

A.2 InternVL 40B Model Prompt

Role: System
Content: Based on this image, generate 2 single-sentence prompts that could have created this template. Each prompt should specify the type of material, the purpose it is for, and briefly mention key elements to include. Mention specific business name only if it is present in the image. Translate any non English sentences/words to English.

B Model fine-tuning details

For fine-tuning all models, we employed Quantized Low-Rank Adaptation (QLoRA) with consistent hyperparameters across our experiments. The training process utilized a learning rate of $1e^{-4}$ with the AdamW optimizer and cosine learning rate scheduler. We implemented gradient accumulation with 2 steps and a batch size of 4, processing sequences up to 4,096 tokens in length. The models were trained for 3 epochs with a warmup ratio of 0.03, and we applied gradient clipping with a maximum norm of 0.3 to ensure training stability.The LoRA configuration maintained consistency across all models, employing a rank of 16 with an alpha value of 32 and a dropout rate of 0.05. The adaptation targeted key transformation matrices including query, key, value, output, gate, up, and down projections. To optimize memory usage while preserving model quality, we implemented 4-bit quantization (NF4) with double quantization enabled. The training pipeline incorporated mixed precision (FP16) computation and gradient checkpointing for efficient resource utilization. Model evaluation and checkpoint saving were performed at regular intervals of 1,000 steps, with training metrics logged every 20 steps. For inference, we deployed models using vllm with carefully tuned sampling parameters. The configuration included a maximum token length of 4,096, a temperature of 0.3 for controlled randomness, and standard top-k and top-p values of 50 and 1.0 respectively. Each prompt generated a single sample to maintain consistency in our evaluation process. All experimental metrics, including training loss, validation metrics, model checkpoints, and system resource utilization, were tracked and logged using Weights & Biases (Wandb) for comprehensive experiment monitoring and reproducibility. To ensure reproducibility across all experiments, we maintained a fixed random seed of 42 throughout both training and inference phases.

The following plots capture the comparison of the training loss (Figure 7), system memory utilization (Figure 8) and GPU utilization (Figure 9) for the following models: Gorilla, Gemma2-2B-it model, Qwen2.5-1.5B-Instruct, Qwen2.5-0.5B-Instruct model and Llama3.2-1B-Instruct models.

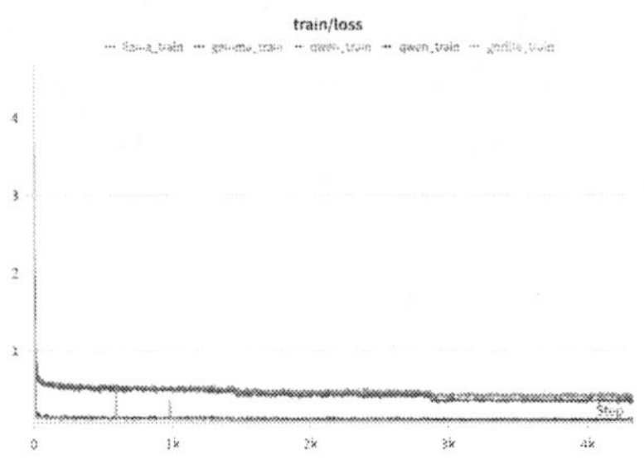

Figure 7: Training loss comparison for: Gorilla, Gemma, Qwen (both variants) and Llama models

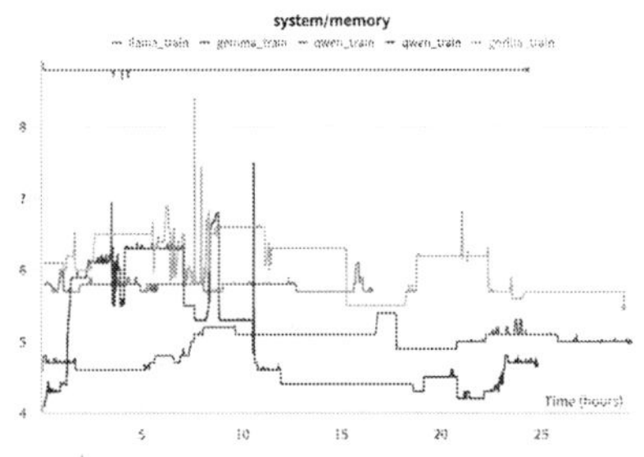

Figure 8: System memory utilization comparison for: Gorilla, Gemma, Qwen (both variants) and Llama models

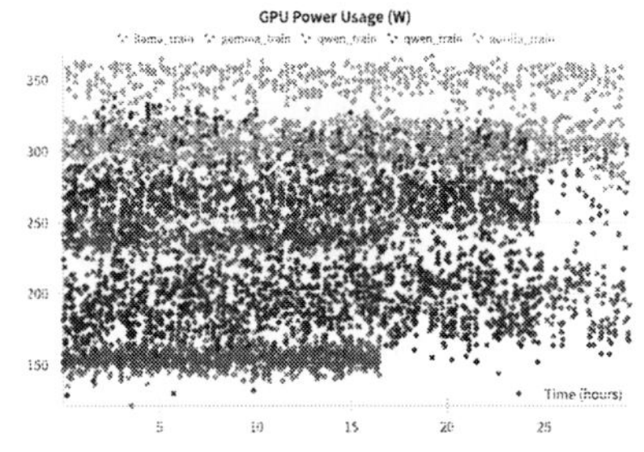

Figure 9: Process GPU utilization comparison for: Gorilla, Gemma, Qwen (both variants) and Llama models

B.1 Finetuning Data Structuring and Prompt Preparation

Before feeding data to the model, we pre-structure the input using Hugging Face's `apply_chat_template` function. This function organizes the conversation into a list of messages with defined roles (e.g. `system` and `user`), ensuring that the prompt adheres to the format expected by the model. In our implementation, the prompt is prepared in two parts: one describing the task and another providing the actual query and function descriptions.

The prompt template is defined as follows:

> **Role:** System
> **Content:** You are an expert in composing functions. You are given a set of possible functions and a question. Based on the question, you will need to make one function/tool call to achieve the purpose. You should only return the function call in your response. You MUST put it in the format of func_name(params_name1=params_value1, params_name2=params_value2...). You SHOULD NOT include any other text in the response.
> **Role:** User
> **Content:**«function»function_descriptions«question»query

The following Python code snippet demonstrates how the prompt is generated and tokenized before being passed to the model:

The `apply_chat_template` function performs several key tasks:

1. **Input Organization:** It takes a list of messages, each tagged with a role (either `system` or `user`), and concatenates them into a single input string that respects the intended conversational format.

2. **Tokenization:** The function tokenizes the structured messages, converting them into a format suitable for the model.

3. **Generation Prompt Addition:** It appends any necessary generation prompts that guide the model's response.

4. **Tensor Conversion:** Finally, the tokenized data is converted into tensors (using `return_tensors="pt"` for PyTorch), ensuring compatibility with the model's expected input format.

This preprocessing step is critical for maintaining the structure and consistency of the input data, thereby facilitating effective fine-tuning and ensuring that the model generates outputs that align with the desired format.

STOC-TOT: Stochastic Tree-of-Thought with Constrained Decoding for Complex Reasoning in Multi-Hop Question Answering

Zhenyu Bi[1], Daniel Hajialigol[1], Zhongkai Sun[2], Jie Hao[2], Xuan Wang[1]
[1]Virginia Tech [2]Amazon Alexa AI
{zhenyub, danielhajialigol, xuanw}@vt.edu, {zhongkais, jieha}@amazon.com

Abstract

Multi-hop question answering (MHQA) requires a model to retrieve and integrate information from multiple passages to answer a complex question. Recent systems leverage the power of large language models and integrate evidence retrieval with reasoning prompts (e.g., chain-of-thought reasoning) for the MHQA task. However, the complexities in the question types (bridge v.s. comparison questions) and the reasoning types (sequential v.s. parallel reasonings) require more novel and fine-grained prompting methods to enhance the performance of MHQA under the zero-shot setting. In this paper, we propose STOC-TOT, a stochastic tree-of-thought reasoning prompting method with constrained decoding for MHQA and conduct a detailed comparison with other reasoning prompts on different question types and reasoning types. Specifically, we construct a tree-like reasoning structure by prompting the model to break down the original question into smaller sub-questions to form different reasoning paths. In addition, we prompt the model to provide a probability estimation for each reasoning path at each reasoning step. At answer time, we conduct constrained decoding on the model to generate more grounded answers and reduce hallucination. Experiments comparing STOC-TOT with on two MHQA datasets and five large language models showed that STOC-TOT outperforms other reasoning prompts by a significant margin.

1 Introduction

Question answering (QA) is a fundamental task in natural language processing (NLP) that involves designing systems capable of understanding human language questions and providing accurate and relevant answers. With the recent advancement of large language models (LLMs) that demonstrated superior reasoning ability (Brown et al., 2020), researchers have been focusing more on complex QA tasks, such as multi-hop question answering (MHQA). MHQA is more challenging as it requires models to understand complicated questions, perform multiple reasoning steps, and gather evidence across documents. Figure 1 shows an example of a two-hop MHQA question. To answer that question in Figure 1, the QA model needs to first figure out who is the actor that received the 2016 Academy Honorary Award. Then based on the answer to the previous question, the QA model needs to further answer a second question about which movie the actor co-starred with Chris Tucker.

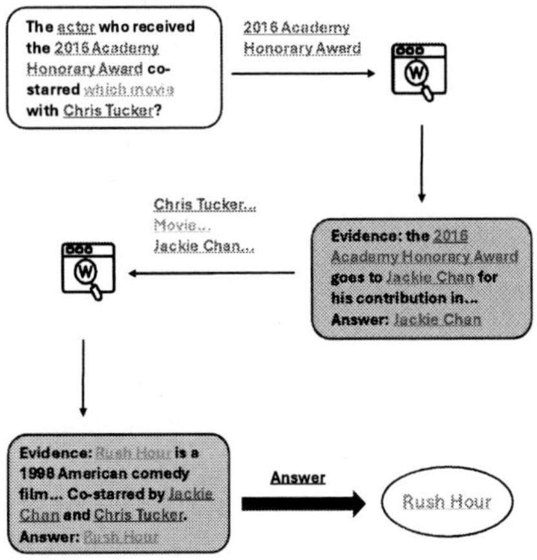

Figure 1: An example of the MHQA question. This question has two hops that require the model to reason about before answering the final question.

State-of-the-art methods for MHQA are fully-supervised methods that often follow a retrieve-and-read framework, including a passage retrieving module that gathers relative evidence from documents and a reading comprehension module to reason about the evidence (Zhu et al., 2021; Li et al., 2022). Other methods include beam-search (Zhang et al., 2023) and label-smoothing (Yin et al., 2023). However, these methods often require extensive pre-training or fine-tuning and do not generalize well to other datasets.

Proceedings of the 4th International Workshop on Knowledge-Augmented Methods for Natural Language Processing (KnowledgeNLP'25), pages 141–151
May 3, 2025 ©2025 Association for Computational Linguistics

Large language models (LLMs), on the other hand, show remarkable reasoning ability and rich knowledge of general-domain questions. Many LLMs can answer simple and straightforward questions that do not require complex reasoning without any supervision involved but often fail to deal with complex questions requiring multiple reasoning steps. To tackle the problem, researchers have developed many prompting techniques to improve LLM's reasoning ability, such as chain-of-thought (CoT) (Wei et al., 2022), self-consistency CoT (Sc-CoT) (Wang et al., 2023), and tree-of-thought (ToT) prompting (Yao et al., 2023a).

CoT has been shown effective across tasks requiring extensive, step-by-step reasoning, such as math calculation and reading comprehension. However, there could be various possible reasoning paths for many complex multi-hop questions, and CoT models cannot "turn back" when they have made a mistake along their reasoning paths. Sc-CoT further improves on CoT by proposing different chains of thought, thus expanding the reasoning space. However, there is no local reasoning expansion within each chain, and the "majority voting" strategy often fails in open-domain tasks where the output space is unlimited. ToT, designed to maintain different reasoning paths along its reasoning process, is more suitable for dealing with complex question types. However, the intermediate reasoning steps in NLP generation tasks are much less constrained and require more than a simple rule-based evaluation. The complexities in the question types (bridge v.s. comparison questions in Table 1), as well as the reasoning types (sequential v.s. parallel reasonings in Table 2), require more novel and fine-grained prompting methods to enhance the reasoning ability of LLMs.

To tackle the challenges and design a more reliable reasoning method for open-domain NLP tasks, we propose STOC-TOT, a stochastic ToT-based framework that instructs the model to generate different reasoning paths from the same question and assign probability scores to reasoning paths to effectively avoid reasoning dead-ends. To the best of our knowledge, our work is the first to adapt the tree-of-thought reasoning prompting to natural language tasks that require complex reasoning, such as MHQA. We provide an example overview of our framework in Figure 2. Specifically, we construct a tree-like reasoning structure by prompting the model to break down the original question into smaller sub-questions to form different reasoning paths. We evaluate the validity of each reasoning path on three levels of aspects and arrive at a model-given probability score. At answer time, we innovatively propose to use constrained decoding in the answering process to reduce hallucination by forcing the model to generate grounded answers from evidence and letting models give concise and exact answers. Ultimately, we arrive at the best answer by choosing the path with the highest aggregated probability score. Experiments on two benchmarking MHQA datasets demonstrate that STOC-TOT significantly improves the reasoning ability of LLMs in complex reasoning scenarios, especially with GPT-4, improving Exact Match accuracy by 7%, and F1 score by 7.8 points on the HotpotQA dataset over the original tree-of-thought prompting. Our contributions are as follows:

2 Related Work

Multi-Hop Question Answering Multi-hop Question Answering (MHQA) is a challenging task requiring models to reason over different evidence across documents to answer a complex multi-hop question. Many high-quality MHQA datasets have been developed, including HotpotQA (Yang et al., 2018), WikiHop (Welbl et al., 2018), MuSiQue (Trivedi et al., 2022), and others. Among these, HotpotQA is the task's most representative and widely used dataset. Previous state-of-the-art MHQA models often follow a two-stage pipeline: a retriever that extracts evidence from the documents, and a reader that reasons about the evidence to arrive at an answer (Zhu et al., 2021; Li et al., 2022). Other methods include beam-search (Zhang et al., 2023) and label-smoothing (Yin et al., 2023). Some LLM-based frameworks (Yao et al., 2023b; Gou et al., 2024; Cao et al., 2023) were also evaluated on the task of MHQA, but their performance fell short compared with supervised methods, and relied on retrievers instead of LLM's own reasoning ability to sort out the related evidence.

Reasoning Prompting of LLMs Various prompt engineering methods have been developed (Wei et al., 2022; Wang et al., 2023; Yao et al., 2023a; Besta et al., 2024; Sel et al., 2024; Chen et al., 2023), aiming to improve large language models' reasoning ability across various tasks and domains. Chain-of-thought (CoT) prompting (Wei et al., 2022) prompts the large language models (LLMs) to divide their reasoning process into smaller

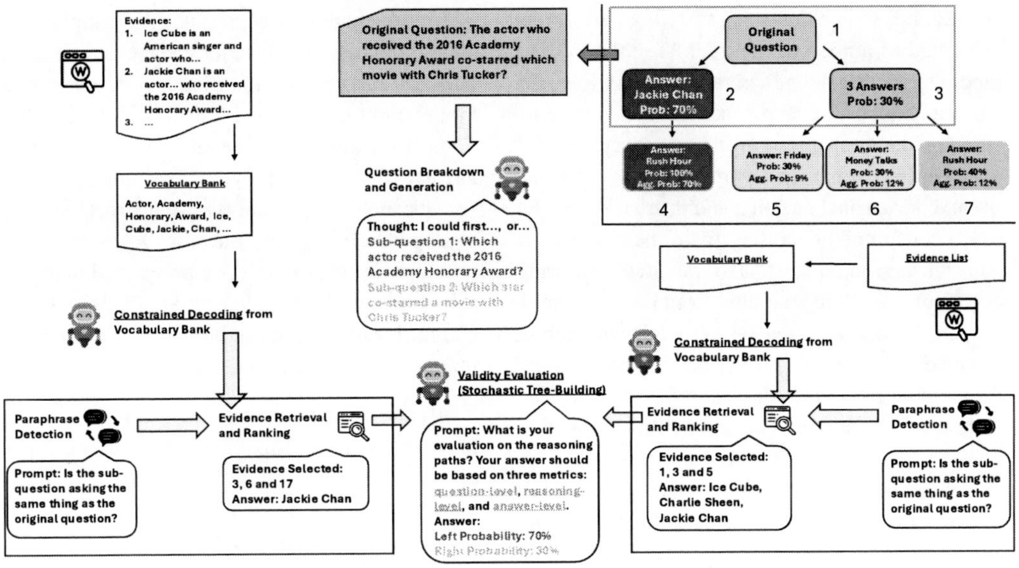

Figure 2: Overview of our framework, with the example in Figure 1. The top-right Corner shows the overall structure of the constructed tree, with each node's label on the left. **Darker green** in the nodes means a **higher evaluated probability of the reasoning path**. The original Question is colored in blue. We chose the first round of our tree-building process as an example in the purple block.

steps when solving a question, forming a chain of thoughts. Chain-of-thought self-consistency prompting (Wang et al., 2023) improves on the CoT method by proposing different reasoning chains and ensembles on the final result. Tree-of-thought (ToT) prompting method (Yao et al., 2023a) actively maintains a tree of thoughts, where each thought is a coherent language sequence that serves as an intermediate step toward problem-solving. Graph-of-thought (Besta et al., 2024) further improves ToT by constructing a Directed Graph instead of a tree. LLMs can loop over a thought to refine it and aggregate thoughts or chains.

Constrained Decoding Constrained decoding is the technique that asks the models to generate outputs following a given set of rules. The most common way of conducting constrained generation uses beam search (Och and Ney, 2004) in decoding time. Before the LLM era, works on constrained decoding focused on task-specific sequence-to-sequence models that span across many fields, such as machine translation (Hokamp and Liu, 2017; Post and Vilar, 2018), named entity recognition (Lester et al., 2020), and dialogue generation (Balakrishnan et al., 2019). Recently, Microsoft introduced Guidance [1], which allows users of various large language models to control their outputs given a human-defined vocabulary or rules.

[1]https://github.com/guidance-ai/guidance

3 Method

3.1 Task Formation

Given a multi-hop question Q and background corpus of evidence P, the goal of our framework is to output the answer A to question Q, drawing its reasoning with the support of multiple evidence passages $p_1, p_2, ...$ retrieved from corpus P.

3.2 StoC-ToT Framework

For each of the questions Q, multiple reasoning lines and, thus, multiple ways of breaking down the question could exist. However, not every reasoning line would lead us to the right answer, and they take us to dead ends. To avoid such reasoning dead-ends, we build a stochastic reasoning tree to represent the possible reasoning lines and the probability of each reasoning line taking us to the right answer. We achieve this by proposing a self-interactive framework that automatically builds the reasoning tree given a multi-hop question. Figure 2 shows our framework with an example question.

In our reasoning process, we first prompt the model to propose different possible sub-questions to solve at each reasoning step. Each sub-question corresponds to one possible reasoning path and is presented as a node in the tree. We then ask the model to answer the generated sub-questions. To prevent hallucination and make the model more focused on the given question and evidence, we build a vocabulary bank using words from the evidence list and the original question and instruct the model to do constrained decoding from the vocabulary bank when generating its answers. After answering every sub-question generated from the same question in the previous reasoning level, we prompt the model to evaluate each reasoning path and estimate how likely the reasoning path would lead us to the right answer. This probability estimation would be assigned to the corresponding node in the tree. After the reasoning process finishes, each reasoning path would have an aggregated probability calculated from nodes along the path.

Formally, given a question Q, we instruct the model to generate sub-questions $q_1, q_2, ..., q_n$, and build a tree structure with the original question Q as the root node and each question q_i as subsequent nodes. The tree would expand as each sub-question q_i has its sub-question q_j, and the reasoning paths are thus represented as branches in the tree structure. From the original question Q and the evidence list $E = e_1, e_2, ..., e_n$, we build a vocabulary bank $V = [w_1, w_2, ..., w_n], w_i \in Q, w_j \in E$. We then prompt the model to generate their answer $a_1, a_2, ..., a_n$ using only $w_i \in V$. We describe the details of our framework below.

Example-Based Sub-Question Generation Our framework starts with the sub-question generation module, which generates sub-questions $q_1, q_2, ..., q_n$ using the question Q_g from the previous reasoning level. The sub-questions are generated based on both the model's reasoning ability and the model's semantic understanding of the question Q_g. An example is given in Figure 2, where the sub-questions from nodes 2 and 3 were generated using the question from node 1. However, we cannot guarantee that each sub-question asked is a good sub-question, and sometimes, the generated sub-question merely repeats the previous question. We introduce the paraphrase detection module and pass on the generated sub-questions to reduce redundancy and improve question quality.

Paraphrase Detection Answering repetitive questions often leads to low-quality answers and time-consuming steps. Following the sub-question generation module, we introduce the paraphrase detection module to reduce redundancy and improve question quality. In this module, we prompt the model and ask it to distinguish informative questions from questions that merely repeat what is already stated at the previous reasoning level. If a sub-question is a paraphrase, we instruct the model to stop generating sub-questions from the current question. In other words, we prune the low-quality sub-branch of the tree that could otherwise be generated. By pruning these branches, we effectively improve the efficiency of our framework.

Evidence Retrieval and Answering We then move on to answering the question after our paraphrase detection module. Our evidence retrieval and answering module focuses on retrieving evidence and generating answers to the given sub-question. We also pass in the full evidence list provided and prompt the model to give out an answer to the given sub-question. The evidence retrieval and answering module selects relative evidence from an evidence pool for each sub-question and uses words only from the vocabulary bank to generate its final answer. We will discuss details of constrained decoding in Section 3.3. The generated sub-answer and the answered sub-question are then passed on to the sub-question generation module at the next level to continue the reasoning process.

Validity Estimation Not each sub-question asked is a good sub-question, and not each reasoning path is reasonable. After every sub-question q_i generated from the same question Q_g has been answered, we prompt the model to provide a probability estimation p_i for each (q_i, a_i) pair. This probability is the model's evaluation of going down the correct reasoning path. Specifically, this probability is obtained by prompting the model to consider the following three aspects:

- Question Level: Is the question semantically clear and answerable?
- Reasoning Level: Is the reasoning line coherent when considering previous levels?
- Answer Level: Does the evidence fully support the answer to the question?

As shown in Figure 2, we conduct validity estimation for sub-questions and sub-answers in nodes 2 and 3 since the sub-questions were generated from the same question in node 1.

At the leaf node of our tree, we would have a final question q_f. along with a final answer A to the original question Q, and also an aggregated probability $p_{final} = \prod_i p_i$, with each p_i being the probability of the nodes along the reasoning path. We assign p_{final} to the leaf node, representing the aggregated probability of answer A being the correct answer to Q.

3.3 Constrained Decoding

One challenge for generative LLMs in the task of question answering is hallucination. LLMs often fail to pay attention to the golden evidence and hallucinate their own reference even when large amounts of evidence exist. To alleviate the problem of LLM halluscination during evidence selection and answer generation, we innovatively propose to use constrained decoding in the answering process to reduce hallucination by forcing the model to generate grounded answers from evidence and let models give concise and exact answers. As shown in Figure 2, we conduct constrained decoding by asking the model to generate words from the vocabulary bank, consisting of words taken only from the original question and the evidence list provided. More formally, we construct a vocabulary bank $V = w_1, w_2, ..., w_i$ from all words in the provided evidence sentences. We conduct a simple filtering by removing common English stop words. We then instruct the model's evidence retrieval and answering module to construct its answers using words only from the given vocabulary V.

Code-based Constrained Decoding For open-source LLMs (e.g., Llama), we build our logit processor at the decoding time. Specifically, for every word $w_j \notin V$, we manually set the score to negative infinity to prevent the model from generating them. Thus, every answer generated will only use words from the evidence list.

Prompt-based Constrained Decoding For closed-source LLMs (e.g., GPT models), since we do not have access to their decoding function, we had to instruct the GPT models using prompts to do constrained decoding. We provide our prompt template used in Appendix A.

4 Experimental Setup

Dataset We compare STOC-TOT with baseline methods on the HotpotQA dataset (Yang et al., 2018) and the MuSiQue dataset (Trivedi et al., 2022), both of which are widely used MHQA datasets across state-of-the-art MHQA baselines. The experiments are conducted under the distractor setting, where we provide the model with an evidence pool containing both golden and irrelevant evidence. The model needs to find the golden evidence to answer the question correctly. We randomly selected 200 examples from each dataset as our evaluation set.

Baselines We included three baselines:

- Vanilla Prompting with no examples provided. We only provide the model with questions and evidence and instruct it to output the answer.
- Chain-of-Thought (CoT) prompting (Wei et al., 2022) with a standard input-output (IO) prompt. We design the prompt with one in-context example, which presents the whole reasoning chain, including all intermediate steps.
- Tree-of-Thought prompting (Yao et al., 2023a) with slight modifications to adapt to the MHQA task. None of their current decision strategies fit into the MHQA scope, where model needs to make decisions based on self-confidence, instead of pre-defined rules and metrics. Thus, we revised their decision strategy and used majority voting on the reasoning lines to decide the final answer.

We recognize that there are LLM-based retrieval augmented generation frameworks (Yao et al., 2023b; Gou et al., 2024; Cao et al., 2023) that were also evaluated on HotpotQA. However, we excluded them from our baselines as they used outside knowledge bases, which are under a different testing scenario.

4.1 Implementation

We experiment with the baselines and our model utilizing five LLMs: GPT-3.5-turbo (Brown et al., 2020) and GPT-4(OpenAI, 2023) from OpenAI, LLaMa 2-13B (Touvron et al., 2023), LLaMa 2-70B, and LLaMa 3-8B from MetaAI. Due to the lengthy running time, LLaMa 2-70B was not tested on the MusiQue dataset. For all models, We set the temperature to 0.5, top_k to 1.0, and maximum number of iterations to 5.

4.2 Evaluation Metric

Following the metrics in (Yang et al., 2018), we use Exact Match and F1 score as two evaluation metric.

Table 1: Performance comparison of STOC-TOT and baseline methods on the HotpotQA dataset.

Prompting Method	GPT3.5		GPT4		LLaMa2(13B)		LLaMa2(70B)		LLaMa3(8B)	
	EM	F1	EM	F1	EM	F1	EM	F1	EM	F1
Zero-Shot Vanilla	34.0	45.0	51.0	65.0	25.5	36.5	30.5	41.0	27.5	40.7
Chain-of-Thought	35.5	47.3	52.0	66.8	30.5	42.5	33.5	45.0	32.5	44.6
Tree-of-Thought	36.5	49.5	55.0	68.5	29.5	41.3	35.5	47.3	30.5	37.5
STOC-TOT	**45.5**	**56.2**	**62.0**	**76.3**	**31.0**	**43.0**	**43.0**	**56.3**	**33.0**	**44.5**
w/o constrained decoding	40.5	53.5	59.5	73.0	31.0	43.0	40.5	53.5	32.0	44.3

Table 2: Performance comparison of STOC-TOT and baseline methods on the MusiQue dataset.

Prompting Method	GPT3.5		GPT4		LLaMa2(13B)		LLaMa3(8B)	
	EM	F1	EM	F1	EM	F1	EM	F1
Zero-Shot Vanilla	17.0	28.8	31.5	41.2	9.5	16.0	12.0	19.2
Chain-of-Thought	18.0	29.7	32.5	44.2	11.0	17.5	12.5	21.6
Tree-of-Thought	20.5	32.0	35.0	47.3	11.0	17.2	12.0	20.6
STOC-TOT	**26.5**	**38.0**	**42.0**	**55.3**	**11.5**	**18.0**	**14.5**	**22.0**
w/o constrained decoding	24.0	35.5	38.5	51.0	11.5	18.0	14.0	22.0

For an answer a given by our framework, the Exact Match score equals 1 if the answer span matches the golden answer exactly and 0 otherwise. The F1 metric measures the average overlap between the prediction and ground truth answers.

5 Results

5.1 Overall Results

We compare STOC-TOT with LLM baselines on the HotpotQA dataset and the MusiQue dataset and present our results in Tables 1 and 2. The backbone LLMs in our experiments include GPT3.5, GPT4, Llama2-13B, Llama2-70B, and Llama3-8B. Due to time constraints, we only tested with Llama2-70B on the HotpotQA dataset. On the HotpotQA dataset, STOC-TOT attains an on-average increase in performance of over 6 % compared with vanilla prompting on GPT models, and the improvement goes up to 11% when we further implement STOC-TOT with constrained decoding. On the more challenging MusiQue dataset, we still see an increase in performance of STOC-TOT compared with the other baselines, most notably on GPT4, where we observe an 11.5% EM improvement (from 31.50 to 42.0).

Comparison with Tree-of-Thought STOC-TOT surpasses the original Tree-of-Thought prompting by 7% with the GPT4 model on both tested datasets. For LLMs with inferior reasoning ability, such as LLaMa2-8B, we still observe a performance improvement, even on the harder MusiQue dataset. These results suggest that STOC-TOT is more effective at forming and selecting reliable reasoning paths under complex reasoning scenarios.

Constrained Decoding Even though the LLM's reasoning ability can be improved by reasoning prompting, such techniques have little help in preventing hallucination. However, STOC-TOT implements constrained decoding, which makes the model much more grounded to evidence when answering the question, effectively addressing hallucination issues and improving the overall performance of our framework.

5.2 Ablation Study

Sensitivity to Demonstration Question Type We study the effect on STOC-TOT performance when different types of demonstration questions are provided in the prompt template. The HotPotQA dataset specified two types of questions. The "Bridge" question contains a "bridge entity" that connects the question and the final answer. In contrast, the "Comparison" question requires the model to compare two entities of the same type. Of the 200 questions in our evaluation set, 34 are comparison questions, and 166 are bridge questions. Examples of bridge and comparison questions are in Table 4.

We examined STOC-TOT performance under the two different question types, each with a different prompt template: one containing only a comparison question as an example and the other containing only a bridge question as an example. We

Table 3: Performance of STOC-TOT with different prompt types on the HotpotQA dataset in terms of EM score. "Com" represents comparison questions, and "Bri" represents bridge questions.

Model Variant	GPT3.5		GPT4		LLaMa2(13B)		LLaMa2(70B)		LLaMa3(8B)	
Prompt/Question Type	**Com**	**Bri**	**Com**	**Bri**	**Com**	**Bri**	**Com**	**Bri**	**Com**	**Bri**
Prompt: Comparison	58.8	41.0	76.5	57.2	38.2	31.9	58.8	41.0	44.1	33.7
Prompt: Bridge	55.9	43.4	73.5	59.0	35.3	32.5	55.9	42.2	41.2	34.9

Table 4: Question Type Examples. On the left side, the bridging entity is highlighted in red, and the final question is highlighted in orange. On the right side, entities that are being compared are highlighted in blue.

Bridge Question	Comparison Question
What distinction is held by the former NBA player who was a member of the Charlotte Hornets during their 1992-93 season and was head coach for the WNBA team Charlotte Sting?	Were Scott Derrickson and Ed Wood of the same nationality?

Table 5: Reasoning Type Examples. On the left side, the entity in red needs to be found before solving the question in orange. On the right side, questions with parallel reasoning contain parts (highlighted in blue) that can be solved in arbitrary order.

Sequential Reasoning	Parallel Reasoning
The football manager who recruited David Beckham managed Manchester United during what timeframe?	What distinction is held by the former NBA player who was a member of the Charlotte Hornets during their 1992-93 season and was head coach for the WNBA team Charlotte Sting?

provide the content of our templates in Appendix A. Results are shown in Table 3. We observe that the difference in prompt templates influences the performance of our framework under different question types by a small margin. The comparison questions are generally easier to solve, and STOC-TOT performs better on comparison questions than on bridge questions. STOC-TOT will handle comparison questions better if the prompt template contains comparison questions and vice versa.

Question and Reasoning Types We examine STOC-TOT, Tree-of-Thought prompting, and Chain-of-Thought prompting by comparing their performance under different question-type settings. Detailed results are shown in Figure 3(a). STOC-TOT performs better at both Bridge Questions and Sequential Questions, suggesting that STOC-TOT can avoid reasoning dead-ends and is better at forming intermediate reasoning lines.

We also conduct an in-depth analysis of the reasoning types in the existing MHQA datasets by randomly selecting 100 questions from our testing set. The questions are roughly divided into two categories: 1) tree-like parallel reasoning and 2) chain-like sequential reasoning. Questions with parallel reasoning contain two or more reasoning paths that can be solved arbitrarily. Questions with sequential reasoning follow a strict reasoning chain, and all the sub-questions must be solved to form the correct reasoning process. All comparison questions are parallel reasoning, but some bridge questions contain parallel reasoning. Examples of sequential and parallel reasoning questions are in Table 5. Out of the selected 100 questions, 59 questions were Sequential and 41 questions were Parallel. Results are shown in Figure 3(b). STOC-TOT performs better on both reasoning types, especially on questions containing parallel reasoning. This suggests that STOC-TOT's stochastic way of forming the tree is very effective when solving questions containing multiple reasoning paths.

Performance and Hops As the number of hops increases in a question, the reasoning line gets more complex and varied. Figure 4 shows the performances of different prompting techniques on questions in the MusiQue dataset with different numbers of hops. STOC-TOT performs best in all categories, demonstrating our framework's superior ability to deal with complex reasoning scenarios. This ablation study was conducted only on GPT4, as other models performed poorly on 3-hop and 4-hop scenarios, regardless of the reasoning prompting technique used.

Error Analysis We conduct a detailed analysis of the errors made by our framework on GPT3 and GPT4, and present our results in Figure 5. We categorize the errors into four types: (1) **No Answer**: our framework did not come up with an answer

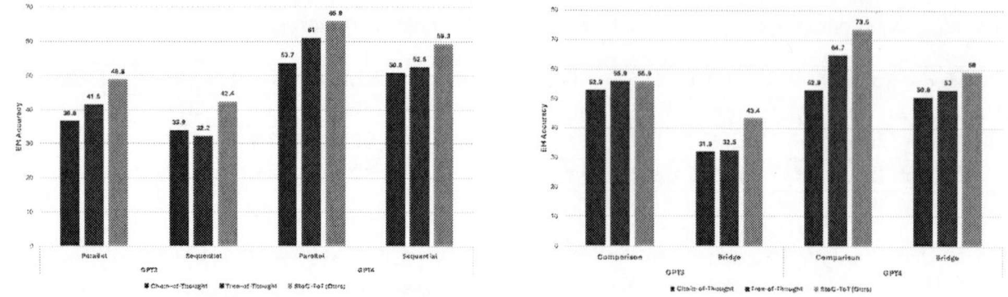

(a) Question Type (b) Reasoning Type

Figure 3: Performace comparison of Chain-of-Thought, Tree-of-Thought, and STOC-TOT on questions of different question types (Left) and reasoning types (Right). Experiments were done on the HotpotQA dataset.

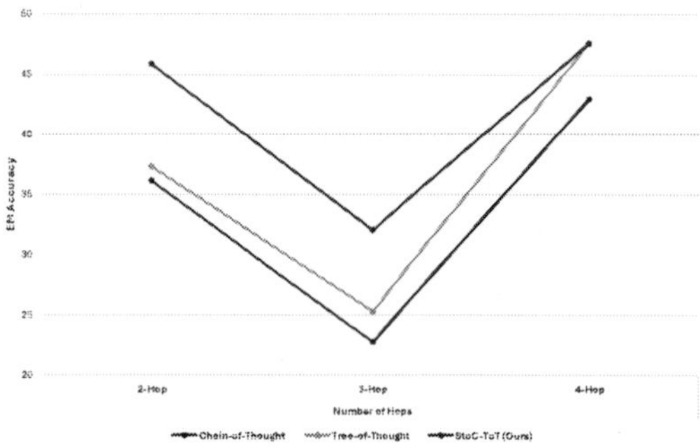

Figure 4: Performance comparison of CoT, ToT, and STOC-TOT on different number of hops in the question. Experiments done in the MusiQue dataset.

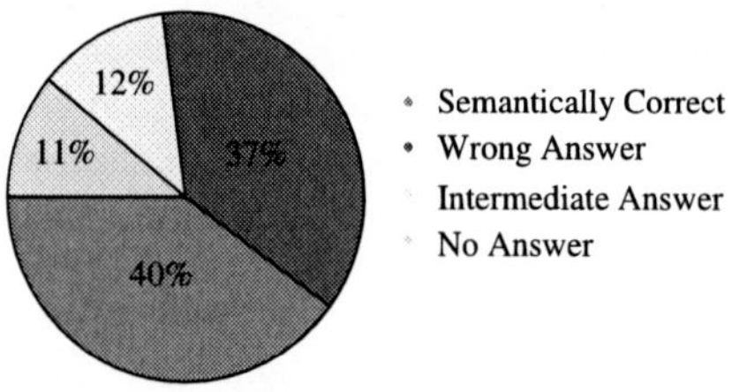

Figure 5: Ratio of different categories in error cases, on the HotpotQA dataset.

for the question due to not finishing the reasoning process; (2) **Intermediate Answer**: our framework came up with an answer for one of the intermediate hops instead of for the final question; (3) **Wrong Answer**: our framework came up with an answer that is neither the final answer nor one of the intermediate answers; (4) **Semantically Correct**: our framework came up with the right answer, but did not have an exact match with the final answer. Appendix B shows examples of each error category. Large amounts of error cases were correct answers with extra wording or hallucination errors, signaling potential improvements over our constrained decoding scheme. Reasoning process errors, including no answer and intermediate answer, make up only 25% of the total error cases. This result shows that our framework is capable of building a robust reasoning process for complex questions.

5.3 Time Analysis

We provide a brief analysis of running time for all methods reported in Table 1. The experiment was done on LLaMa2-13B model for 50 datapoints. For ToT and STOC-TOT, the running time significantly increases compared with simple prompting methods, increasing by 4.4 times and 5.2 times, respectively.

6 Conclusion

This paper proposes STOC-TOT, a stochastic tree-of-thought reasoning framework with constrained generation for multi-hop question answering. STOC-TOT is specialized in dealing with complex reasoning scenarios in natural language tasks. Experiments on two benchmark datasets show that our framework outperforms previous reasoning prompting techniques with multiple Large Language Models. Detailed analysis shows that our framework is capable of building a robust reasoning process given different types of questions. Further research can aim to enhance the reliability of our framework by proposing better validity evaluation schemes and more effective methods for improving groundedness and preventing hallucination.

Acknowledgements

Our work is sponsored by the NSF NAIRR Pilot with PSC Neocortex and NCSA Delta, Commonwealth Cyber Initiative, Children's National Hospital, Fralin Biomedical Research Institute (Virginia Tech), Sanghani Center for AI and Data Analytics (Virginia Tech), Virginia Tech Innovation Campus, and generous gifts from Cisco Research and the Amazon + Virginia Tech Center for Efficient and Robust Machine Learning.

Limitations

Our framework relies on initiating multiple model instances and requires multiple prompts per round. The repetitive callings impose heavy time costs for our framework, even after implementing our paraphrase module. Another limitation comes from how we generated sub-questions. Currently, we directly prompt the model to generate sub-questions. A more complex standard can be used to increase the quality of the sub-questions generated. Also, more extensive experiments should be provided, including experimenting on other different datasets and case studies.

Ethics Statement

This research adhered to the ethical standards and best practices outlined in the ACL Code of Ethics. Language Models can sometimes produce illogical or inaccurate reasoning paths, so their outputs should be cautiously used. The outputs are only examined to understand how a model arrives at its answers and investigate why it makes certain errors. All experiments used publicly available datasets from previously published works and did not involve ethical or privacy issues.

References

Anusha Balakrishnan, Jinfeng Rao, Kartikeya Upasani, Michael White, and Rajen Subba. 2019. Constrained decoding for neural NLG from compositional representations in task-oriented dialogue. In *Proceedings of the 57th Conference of the Association for Computational Linguistics, ACL 2019, Florence, Italy, July 28- August 2, 2019, Volume 1: Long Papers*, pages 831–844. Association for Computational Linguistics.

Maciej Besta, Nils Blach, Ales Kubicek, Robert Gerstenberger, Michal Podstawski, Lukas Gianinazzi, Joanna Gajda, Tomasz Lehmann, Hubert Niewiadomski, Piotr Nyczyk, and Torsten Hoefler. 2024. Graph of thoughts: Solving elaborate problems with large language models. In *Thirty-Eighth AAAI Conference on Artificial Intelligence, AAAI 2024, Thirty-Sixth Conference on Innovative Applications of Artificial Intelligence, IAAI 2024, Fourteenth Symposium on Educational Advances in Artificial Intelligence, EAAI 2014, February 20-27, 2024, Vancouver, Canada*, pages 17682–17690. AAAI Press.

Tom B. Brown, Benjamin Mann, Nick Ryder, Melanie Subbiah, Jared Kaplan, Prafulla Dhariwal, Arvind Neelakantan, Pranav Shyam, Girish Sastry, Amanda Askell, Sandhini Agarwal, Ariel Herbert-Voss, Gretchen Krueger, Tom Henighan, Rewon Child, Aditya Ramesh, Daniel M. Ziegler, Jeffrey Wu, Clemens Winter, Christopher Hesse, Mark Chen, Eric Sigler, Mateusz Litwin, Scott Gray, Benjamin Chess, Jack Clark, Christopher Berner, Sam McCandlish, Alec Radford, Ilya Sutskever, and Dario Amodei. 2020. Language models are few-shot learners. *CoRR*, abs/2005.14165.

Shulin Cao, Jiajie Zhang, Jiaxin Shi, Xin Lv, Zijun Yao, Qingwen Tian, Juanzi Li, and Lei Hou. 2023. Probabilistic tree-of-thought reasoning for answering knowledge-intensive complex questions. *ArXiv*, abs/2311.13982.

Wenhu Chen, Xueguang Ma, Xinyi Wang, and William W. Cohen. 2023. Program of thoughts prompting: Disentangling computation from reasoning for numerical reasoning tasks. *Transactions on Machine Learning Research*.

Zhibin Gou, Zhihong Shao, Yeyun Gong, yelong shen, Yujiu Yang, Nan Duan, and Weizhu Chen. 2024. CRITIC: Large language models can self-correct with tool-interactive critiquing. In *The Twelfth International Conference on Learning Representations*.

Chris Hokamp and Qun Liu. 2017. Lexically constrained decoding for sequence generation using grid beam search. In *Proceedings of the 55th Annual Meeting of the Association for Computational Linguistics, ACL 2017, Vancouver, Canada, July 30 - August 4, Volume 1: Long Papers*, pages 1535–1546. Association for Computational Linguistics.

Brian Lester, Daniel Pressel, Amy Hemmeter, Sagnik Ray Choudhury, and Srinivas Bangalore. 2020. Constrained decoding for computationally efficient named entity recognition taggers. In *Findings of the Association for Computational Linguistics: EMNLP 2020, Online Event, 16-20 November 2020*, volume EMNLP 2020 of *Findings of ACL*, pages 1841–1848. Association for Computational Linguistics.

Xin-Yi Li, Weixian Lei, and Yubin Yang. 2022. From easy to hard: Two-stage selector and reader for multihop question answering. *ICASSP 2023 - 2023 IEEE International Conference on Acoustics, Speech and Signal Processing (ICASSP)*, pages 1–5.

Franz Josef Och and Hermann Ney. 2004. The alignment template approach to statistical machine translation. *Comput. Linguistics*, 30(4):417–449.

OpenAI. 2023. Gpt-4 technical report.

Matt Post and David Vilar. 2018. Fast lexically constrained decoding with dynamic beam allocation for neural machine translation. In *Proceedings of the*

2018 Conference of the North American Chapter of the Association for Computational Linguistics: Human Language Technologies, NAACL-HLT 2018, New Orleans, Louisiana, USA, June 1-6, 2018, Volume 1 (Long Papers), pages 1314–1324. Association for Computational Linguistics.

Bilgehan Sel, Ahmad Tawaha, Vanshaj Khattar, Ruoxi Jia, and Ming Jin. 2024. Algorithm of thoughts: Enhancing exploration of ideas in large language models. In *Forty-first International Conference on Machine Learning*.

Hugo Touvron, Louis Martin, Kevin Stone, Peter Albert, Amjad Almahairi, Yasmine Babaei, Nikolay Bashlykov, Soumya Batra, Prajjwal Bhargava, Shruti Bhosale, Dan Bikel, Lukas Blecher, Cristian Canton Ferrer, Moya Chen, Guillem Cucurull, David Esiobu, Jude Fernandes, Jeremy Fu, Wenyin Fu, Brian Fuller, Cynthia Gao, Vedanuj Goswami, Naman Goyal, Anthony Hartshorn, Saghar Hosseini, Rui Hou, Hakan Inan, Marcin Kardas, Viktor Kerkez, Madian Khabsa, Isabel Kloumann, Artem Korenev, Punit Singh Koura, Marie-Anne Lachaux, Thibaut Lavril, Jenya Lee, Diana Liskovich, Yinghai Lu, Yuning Mao, Xavier Martinet, Todor Mihaylov, Pushkar Mishra, Igor Molybog, Yixin Nie, Andrew Poulton, Jeremy Reizenstein, Rashi Rungta, Kalyan Saladi, Alan Schelten, Ruan Silva, Eric Michael Smith, Ranjan Subramanian, Xiaoqing Ellen Tan, Binh Tang, Ross Taylor, Adina Williams, Jian Xiang Kuan, Puxin Xu, Zheng Yan, Iliyan Zarov, Yuchen Zhang, Angela Fan, Melanie Kambadur, Sharan Narang, Aurelien Rodriguez, Robert Stojnic, Sergey Edunov, and Thomas Scialom. 2023. Llama 2: Open foundation and fine-tuned chat models.

Harsh Trivedi, Niranjan Balasubramanian, Tushar Khot, and Ashish Sabharwal. 2022. Musique: Multi-hop questions via single-hop question composition. *Trans. Assoc. Comput. Linguistics*, 10:539–554.

Xuezhi Wang, Jason Wei, Dale Schuurmans, Quoc V. Le, Ed H. Chi, Sharan Narang, Aakanksha Chowdhery, and Denny Zhou. 2023. Self-consistency improves chain of thought reasoning in language models. In *The Eleventh International Conference on Learning Representations, ICLR 2023, Kigali, Rwanda, May 1-5, 2023*. OpenReview.net.

Jason Wei, Xuezhi Wang, Dale Schuurmans, Maarten Bosma, Brian Ichter, Fei Xia, Ed H. Chi, Quoc V. Le, and Denny Zhou. 2022. Chain-of-thought prompting elicits reasoning in large language models. In *Advances in Neural Information Processing Systems 35: Annual Conference on Neural Information Processing Systems 2022, NeurIPS 2022, New Orleans, LA, USA, November 28 - December 9, 2022*.

Johannes Welbl, Pontus Stenetorp, and Sebastian Riedel. 2018. Constructing datasets for multi-hop reading comprehension across documents. *Trans. Assoc. Comput. Linguistics*, 6:287–302.

Zhilin Yang, Peng Qi, Saizheng Zhang, Yoshua Bengio, William W. Cohen, Ruslan Salakhutdinov, and Christopher D. Manning. 2018. HotpotQA: A dataset for diverse, explainable multi-hop question answering. In *Conference on Empirical Methods in Natural Language Processing (EMNLP)*.

Shunyu Yao, Dian Yu, Jeffrey Zhao, Izhak Shafran, Tom Griffiths, Yuan Cao, and Karthik Narasimhan. 2023a. Tree of thoughts: Deliberate problem solving with large language models. In *Advances in Neural Information Processing Systems 36: Annual Conference on Neural Information Processing Systems 2023, NeurIPS 2023, New Orleans, LA, USA, December 10 - 16, 2023*.

Shunyu Yao, Jeffrey Zhao, Dian Yu, Nan Du, Izhak Shafran, Karthik R. Narasimhan, and Yuan Cao. 2023b. React: Synergizing reasoning and acting in language models. In *The Eleventh International Conference on Learning Representations, ICLR 2023, Kigali, Rwanda, May 1-5, 2023*. OpenReview.net.

Zhangyue Yin, Yuxin Wang, Xiannian Hu, Yiguang Wu, Hang Yan, Xinyu Zhang, Zhao Cao, Xuanjing Huang, and Xipeng Qiu. 2023. Rethinking label smoothing on multi-hop question answering. In *Chinese Computational Linguistics - 22nd China National Conference, CCL 2023, Harbin, China, August 3-5, 2023, Proceedings*, volume 14232 of *Lecture Notes in Computer Science*, pages 72–87. Springer.

Jiahao Zhang, Haiyang Zhang, Dongmei Zhang, Yong Liu, and Shen Huang. 2023. Beam retrieval: General end-to-end retrieval for multi-hop question answering. *CoRR*, abs/2308.08973.

Fengbin Zhu, Wenqiang Lei, Chao Wang, Jianming Zheng, Soujanya Poria, and Tat-Seng Chua. 2021. Retrieving and reading: A comprehensive survey on open-domain question answering. *CoRR*, abs/2101.00774.

A Prompt Templates

We provide the prompts used in the experiments below.

Sub Question Generation Template

```
Break a question into high-quality sub-
    questions that are easier to answer.
     Here are two examples as guidelines
    :
"Question: Are Tokyo and Busan in the
    same country? Thought 1: I could
    either find which country Tokyo is
    located in, or which country Busan
    is located in. Sub Question 1-1:
    Which country is Tokyo located in?
    Sub Question 1-2: Which country is
    Busan located in?"
"Question: Tokyo is located in the
    country that has what colors present
     on its national flag? Thought 1: I
    need to first find out which country
     Tokyo is located in. Sub Question
    1-1: Which country is Tokyo located
    in?"
Only give out your thought process and
    current-level sub-questions. Do not
    give out answers to your questions.
    Question: {Given Question}.
Thought 1:
```

Prompt-based Constrained Generation Template

```
Given a question and a list of evidence
    that may of help, give your answer
    directly, using words only from the
    vocabulary bank, without any
    explanations.
Question: {Given Question}. Evidence as
    reference: {Given Evidence}.
    Vocabulary Bank: {Given Vocabulary}.
     Answer:
```

B Examples of the Error Cases

We present examples of the different types of errors that our framework made. Detailed analysis is provided in the Section 5: Results.

Type-2: Intermediate Answer

```
{Question}:
Where does the hotel and casino located
    in which Bill Cosby's third album
    was recorded?
{Answer given by STOC-TOT on GPT4}:
Las Vegas.
{Golden Answer}:
Las Vegas Strip in Paradise.
```

Type-3: Wrong Answer

```
{Question}:
Aside from the Apple Remote, what other
    device can control the program Apple
     Remote was originally designed to
    interact with?
{Answer given by STOC-TOT on GPT4}:
siri remote and devices with netsupport
    manager software
{Golden Answer}:
keyboard function keys
```

Table 6: Performance comparison of STOC-TOT and baseline methods on the HotpotQA dataset.

Prompting Method	Time(mins)
Zero-Shot Vanilla	10
Chain-of-Thought	14
Tree-of-Thought	62
STOC-TOT	75

Type-4: Semantically Correct

```
{Question}:
Roger O. Egeberg was Assistant Secretary
     for Health and Scientific Affairs
    during the administration of a
    president that served during what
    years?
{Answer given by STOC-TOT on GPT4}:
1969 to 1974
{Golden Answer}:\
1969 until 1974
```

C Time Analysis

We provide a brief time analysis on LLaMa2-13B model on 50 samples and present the results in Table 6. We see that using ToT and STOC-TOT will lead to a much higher cost in terms of time efficiency compared with Zero-Shot and CoT prompting. STOC-TOT increases time complexity by a around 20 percent compared with ToT.

EKRAG: Benchmark RAG for Enterprise Knowledge Question Answering

Tan Yu*, **Wenfei Zhou***, **Lei Yang, Aaditya Shukla, Meenakshi Madugula, Pritam Gundecha**
Nick Burnett, Anbang Xu, Vishal Seth, Tamar Bar, Rama Akkiraju ,Vivienne Zhang
NVIDIA
Santa Clara, California, USA

Abstract

Retrieval-augmented generation (RAG) offers a robust solution for developing enterprise internal virtual assistants by leveraging domain-specific knowledge and utilizing information from frequently updated corporate document repositories. In this work, we introduce the Enterprise-Knowledge RAG (EKRAG) dataset to benchmark RAG for enterprise knowledge question-answering (QA) across a diverse range of corporate documents, such as product releases, technical blogs, and financial reports. Using EKRAG, we systematically evaluate various retrieval models and strategies tailored for corporate content. We propose novel embedding-model (EM)-as-judge and ranking-model (RM)-as-judge approaches to assess answer quality in the context of enterprise information. Combining these with the existing LLM-as-judge method, we then comprehensively evaluate the correctness, relevance, and faithfulness of generated answers to corporate queries. Our extensive experiments shed light on optimizing RAG pipelines for enterprise knowledge QA, providing valuable guidance for practitioners. This work contributes to enhancing information retrieval and question-answering capabilities in corporate environments that demand high degrees of factuality and context awareness.

1 Introduction

Large Language Models (LLMs) have demonstrated remarkable zero-shot reasoning capabilities (Brown et al., 2020; Achiam et al., 2023). However, their static knowledge base, acquired during pre-training, poses significant challenges in generating factual, timely, and salient responses to ambiguous and complex queries, particularly in corporate environments. This limitation is critical in enterprise settings, where accuracy and up-to-date information are paramount for a functional product. Inaccurate or outdated responses to time-sensitive queries not only erode user trust but can render AI-assisted tools impractical. For instance, using obsolete data to answer financial queries like "What was the company's last quarter revenue?" could lead to misinformed decision-making, if not panic in the stock market, even if the information was accurate once upon a time.

Retrieval-augmented generation (RAG) (Guu et al., 2020; Lewis et al., 2020) emerges as a promising solution, integrating external knowledge from domain-specific corpora to potentially generate up-to-date, factually correct answers. It is particularly suited for corporate internal chatbots, facilitating employees and external investors access to current company policies, procedures, and knowledge across public facing corporate documents.

Despite its advantages, RAG presents unique evaluation challenges compared to standalone LLMs. Their answer quality depends not only on the LLM's pre-trained knowledge and reasoning capabilities but also on the relevance of retrieved context and the model's ability to integrate and synthesize information. While recent works (Adlakha et al., 2023; Chen et al., 2024b; Gao et al., 2023; Es et al., 2023; Xiong et al., 2024) have evaluated RAG systems in general domains, assessing both answer correctness and alignment with retrieved context, the evaluation of RAG in enterprise knowledge applications remains largely unexplored.

To address this gap, we introduce the Enterprise-Knowledge RAG (EKRAG) dataset, comprising 1,347 manually curated questions, designed to systematically evaluate the influence of each RAG component on enterprise knowledge question-answering over five core question types in multi-hop settings. Using this benchmark, our extensive evaluations of various retrieval models and strategies reveal that well-known techniques like HYDE and hybrid search do not significantly improve enterprise knowledge retrieval accuracy, while

*Equal contribution.

Proceedings of the 4th International Workshop on Knowledge-Augmented Methods for Natural Language Processing (KnowledgeNLP'25), pages 152–159
May 3, 2025

some straightforward mechanisms such as multi-embedding vector achieve excellent performance.

Furthermore, we propose novel evaluation methodologies: embedding-model-as-judge and ranking-model-as-judge approaches, complementing the prevailing LLM-as-judge technique. Our comprehensive investigation provides insights into optimizing RAG pipelines for enterprise knowledge systems, offering a nuanced understanding of answer quality that could lead to more robust and reliable RAG implementations in real-world corporate applications.

2 Related Work

Adlakha, BehnamGhader, Lu, Meade, and Reddy (2023) utilizes the existing QA datasets and evaluates the answer quality of RAG along the dimensions of correctness and faithfulness. To be specific, the correctness dimension reveals the relevance between the response and the ground-truth answer. On the other hand, faithfulness measures the relevance between the answer and the retrieved context to evaluate model's capability to ground the retrieved context. RGB (Chen et al., 2024b) evaluates RAG from four aspects including noise robustness, negative rejection, information integration, and counterfactual robustness. ALCE (Gao et al., 2023) proposes evaluation metrics of RAG along three dimensions including fluency, correctness, and citation quality. RAGAS (Es et al., 2023) develops an automated evaluation pipeline by prompting LLMs and evaluate RAG from the dimensions of faithfulness, answer relevance and context relevance. MIRAGE (Xiong et al., 2024) benchmarks different RAG solutions in the field of medicine and ablates the influence of each component on the overall answer quality from a multi-dimensional perspective. CRAG (Yang et al., 2024) proposes a comprehensive RAG benchmark consisting of questions across five domains and eight categories.

3 Enterprise-Knowledge RAG Dataset

3.1 Overview

The Enterprise-Knowledge RAG (EKRAG) dataset (v.1) is an expert-curated, comprehensive evaluation resource for Retrieval-Augmented Generation (RAG) systems operating on corporate documents. Developed by Corporate's IT and data teams, EKRAG serves as a benchmark for assessing agentic RAG systems, particularly those requiring a high degree of factuality in reporting corporate financial performance and product information.

Key features of EKRAG include:

1. **Composition:** 1,348 human curated data points, each consisting of a query, relevant context chunk(s), referenced document, and ground truth answer, complemented by associated metadata. These are derived from a diverse corpus of 5,000 documents, encompassing Corporate technical blogs, news releases, SEC filings, and leadership communications.

2. **Manual Curation:** Annotations are provided by a team of 14 human experts with backgrounds in business and finance, ensuring high-quality, domain-specific data points that reflect real-world complexity and nuance.

3. **Comprehensive Task Coverage:** The dataset facilitates evaluation across five core tasks of varying complexities:

   - Extractive Question Answering
   - Abstractive Question Answering
   - Summarization
   - Financial Numerical Reasoning
   - No Answer Questions

   Each task type encompasses questions of varying complexities, characterized by 1) modality utilization (text, tables, or both), 2) intra-document reasoning (synthesizing information from non-contiguous chunks), and 3) inter-document reasoning (integrating information across multiple documents). These multi-hop tasks simulate real-world, enterprise-level scenarios, evaluating both the RAG *retriever's* ability to fetch complex information from diverse sources and the *generator's* capacity to synthesize coherent responses from retrieved chunks. This design assesses the system's end-to-end capability in handling practical information retrieval and integration problems in a corporate setting.

3.2 Annotation Methodology

3.2.1 Data Sourcing

Reference Documents: The EKRAG dataset is derived from 5,000 publicly available Corporate documents, including web pages, earnings call transcripts, and SEC reports in PDF, HTML, .docx, and .txt formats. These documents are categorized into four main groups: Corporate News and Blogs, Corporate Technical Blogs, leadership communications (including public fireside chats), and SEC

10-K and 8-K filings. The current v.1 of the dataset utilizes only the Corporate News and Blogs and Corporate Technical Blogs categories.

Queries: To ensure real-world relevance, we analyzed approximately 200 queries made by corporate finance analysts during the initial release of the chatbot. These queries were rigorously categorized to create a comprehensive taxonomy, which formed the basis for the annotation guidelines. This approach ensured alignment between annotators' efforts and real-world use cases.

3.2.2 Data Preprocessing

To facilitate human annotation, the corpus underwent a thorough cleaning process. Using the Beautiful Soup package, the team extracted crucial metadata (e.g., publication dates and titles) from HTML and PDF files while removing extraneous content such as CSS. Rigorous filtering criteria were applied, resulting in $3,620$ high-quality documents suitable for annotation.

For multi-document annotations, the team employed topic modeling and preprocessing techniques to group similar documents together, resulting in clusters of 1-4 topically related documents.

Throughout the annotation process, the annotators provided active feedback. They were given the option to skip document groupings that are 1) low-quality; 2) impossible to derive coherent queries. The annotation process is described in Appendix B.

4 RAG Pipeline

4.1 Indexing

We denote the cropped chunks by $\{c_i\}_{i=1}^N$ where N denotes the number of chunks. For each chunk, the embedding vector is extracted by

$$\mathbf{c}_i = f_{\text{emb}}(c_i), \tag{1}$$

where $f_{\text{emb}}(\cdot)$ denotes the embedding model. Since the embedding of chunks are independent to the query, a retrieval system normally precomputes chunk embedding vectors $\{\mathbf{c}_i\}_{i=1}^N$. In the retrieval phase, we just need compute the query's embedding online and compare it with the precomputed chunk embedding vectors to retrieve the most relevant chunks. When N is large, to speed up the retrieval, approximated nearest neighbor (ANN) search methods such as Hashing, Product Quatization, and HNSW are used in indexing.

4.2 Embedding Models

Dense Embedding. Trationally, the dense embedding model adapts a bi-encoder Transformer architecture (Reimers and Gurevych, 2019). To be specific, the query encoder maps the textual query into the query embedding:

$$\mathbf{q} = \text{bi-enc}_{\text{query}}(q). \tag{2}$$

In parallel, the doc encoder maps a text chunk into the chunk embedding:

$$\mathbf{c} = \text{bi-enc}_{\text{doc}}(c). \tag{3}$$

The relevance between the query and the chunk is measured by the distance/similarity between the query embedding $\mathbf{q}$ and the chunk embedding $\mathbf{c}$. Recently, with the emergence of LLM, ecoder-based embedding models (Lee et al., 2024) are obtained by fine-tuning immediate output of LLM, achieving promising performance in retrieval.

Sparse Embedding often represents the occurrence or statistics of specific features (*e.g.*, words or n-grams). It was widely used in traditional information retrieval and text classification. Traditionally, TF-IDF (Ramos et al., 2003) and BM25 (Robertson et al., 1995) are widely used term-weighting sparse embedding methods. Recently, some works such as SPLADE (Formal et al., 2021) and BGE-M3 (Chen et al., 2024a) utilize foundational BERT architecture to generate sparse embedding vectors.

4.3 Retrieval.

Hybrid search is a widely used strategy for RAG applications (Finardi et al., 2024). It conducts dense retrieval and the sparse retrieval simultaneously. To be specfic, given a query q, we retrieve t most relevant queries based on dense embedding:

$$[c_{i_1}, \cdots, c_{i_t}] = \text{dense}(q, \{c_i\}_{i=1}^t). \tag{4}$$

In parallel, another t most relevant queries are retrieved based on sparse embedding:

$$[c_{j_1}, \cdots, c_{j_t}] = \text{sparse}(q, \{c_i\}_{i=1}^t). \tag{5}$$

Then $2t$ retrieved chunks from both sparse and dense retrieval are de-duplicated and re-ranked by a ranking model, and top s ranked chunks are as the context for LLM to generate the answer:

$$[c_{k_1}, \cdots, c_{k_s}] = \text{rerank}(\{c_{i_l}\}_{l=1}^t, \{c_{j_l}\}_{l=1}^t) \tag{6}$$

Embedding Model	Recall@1	Recall@3	Recall@5	Recall@10
BM25 (Robertson et al., 1995)	0.004	0.010	0.023	0.074
NV-QA (Verma et al.)	0.277	0.540	0.651	0.752
Arctic-L (Merrick et al., 2024)	0.313	0.552	0.660	0.786
NV-EMB (Lee et al., 2024)	**0.360**	**0.618**	**0.742**	**0.839**

Table 1: The evaluation of the embedding models.

NV-QA	Arctic-L	NV-EMB	Recall@1	Recall@3	Recall@5	Recall@10
		✓	**0.360**	0.618	0.742	0.839
✓	✓		0.325	0.590	0.697	0.808
✓		✓	0.350	0.640	0.746	0.858
	✓	✓	0.358	0.639	**0.751**	**0.863**
✓	✓	✓	0.348	**0.648**	0.748	0.857

Table 2: The results from combining multiple embedding models.

4.4 Reranking

Cross-encoder. In the reranking phase, we normally takes a cross-encoder architecture. Different from bi-encoder model used in embedding model, cross-encoder takes a query-chunk pair (q, c_{k_i}) as the input and output a relevance score:

$$r_i = \text{cross-enc}(q, c_{k_i}). \quad (7)$$

Chunks $\{c_{k_i}\}_{i=1}^{s}$ are sorted by relevance scores. Detailed discussions on the cross-encoder and bi-encoder are in Appendix A.

4.5 Answer Generation

We fill the query and the chunks $\{c_{k_i}\}_{i=1}^{s}$ from reranking into the prompt template and feed the prompt into a LLM to generate answer.

5 Benchmark on Retrieval

Metrics. There are multiple metrics to evaluate the retrieval such as mAP, Precision@K, Recall@K, NDCG. In RAG scenarios, Recall@K is the most cruial metric, which reveals the coverage of relevant information in the retrieved chunks. Thus, by default, we use Recall@K as the evaluation metric.

5.1 Ablation on Embedding Models

Ablation on embedding models. We compare 4 models, including BM25 (Robertson et al., 1995), NV-QA (Verma et al.), Arctic-L (Merrick et al., 2024) and NV-EMB (Lee et al., 2024). NV-EMB is a decoder-only large language model (LLM)-based embedding model. Compared with BERT-based models, it achieves significantly higher accuracy on public benchmarks but takes much high computational cost. As shown in Table 1, NV-EMB significantly outperforms other embedding models.

Multi-embedding vector. To make use of multiple embedding model simultaneously, a straightforward method is to concatenate the embedding vectors from multiple models into a long vector, which we term as multi-embedding vector. For example, we denote the query/chunk embedding from the first embedding model by $\mathbf{q}_1/\mathbf{c}_1$ and that from the second embedding model by $\mathbf{q}_2/\mathbf{c}_2$. We normalize and concatenate the query/chunk embedding vectors into a multi-embedding vector:

$$\begin{aligned} \bar{\mathbf{q}} &= \left[\alpha_1 \frac{\mathbf{q}_1}{\|\mathbf{q}_1\|_2}, \alpha_2 \frac{\mathbf{q}_2}{\|\mathbf{q}_2\|_2}\right], \\ \bar{\mathbf{c}} &= \left[\alpha_1 \frac{\mathbf{c}_1}{\|\mathbf{c}_1\|_2}, \alpha_2 \frac{\mathbf{c}_2}{\|\mathbf{c}_2\|_2}\right], \end{aligned} \quad (8)$$

where α_1 and α_2 are pre-defined constants to weight the contributions of each embedding vector. By default, we set $\alpha_1 = \alpha_2 = 1$. Empercially, we could assign a higher weight to a better embedding. The relevance between the query and the chunk is computed by the dot product between $\bar{q}$ and $\bar{c}$:

$$\mathrm{r}(q, c) = \langle \bar{\mathbf{q}}, \bar{\mathbf{c}} \rangle = \alpha_1^2 \cos(\mathbf{q}_1, \mathbf{c}_1) + \alpha_2^2 \cos(\mathbf{q}_2, \mathbf{c}_2). \quad (9)$$

We evaluate multi-embedding vectors in Table 2. As shown, multi-embedding vector using Arctic-L and NV-EMB achieves the highest recall@5. By default, we use this setting for embedding.

Hybrid Search. In Table 4, we compare the hybrid search with methods using solely dense-embedding. To be specific, dense-based method adopts a multi-embedding settings using both NV-EMB and Archtic-L. As shown, hybrid search does not bring considerable improvement for recall. Thus, by default, we exclude hybrid search.

5.2 Retrieval boosting strategies

Average query expansion (AQE) (Carpineto and Romano, 2012) refines the query embedding by

LLM for HYDE	Recall@1	Recall@3	Recall@5	Recall@10
w/o	0.360	0.618	**0.742**	0.839
Mistal-7B (Jiang et al., 2023)	0.358	**0.625**	0.736	0.836
Llama3-8B (AI@Meta, 2024)	0.358	0.621	0.737	0.830
Gemma2-7B (Team, 2024)	0.351	0.621	0.737	0.838
Llama3-70B (AI@Meta, 2024)	**0.361**	0.624	0.740	**0.842**
Mixtral-8x7B (Jiang et al., 2024)	0.351	0.621	**0.742**	0.836
Mixtral-8x22B (Mistral AI team, 2024)	0.358	0.629	0.740	0.838

Table 3: The evaluation of the HYDE.

	Recall@1	Recall@3	Recall@5
Dense	0.403	0.688	0.707
Hybrid	0.404	0.687	0.707

Table 4: Evaluation on hybrid search.

n	0	1	2	3	4
NV-QA	0.651	0.660	0.647	0.652	0.662
Arctic-L	0.660	0.689	0.667	0.663	0.652
NV-EMB	0.742	0.725	0.716	0.721	0.731

Table 5: The influence of average query expansion.

the embeddings from the top-retrieved chunks. To be speicifc, we denote the original query embedding by $\mathbf{q}$ and the embeddings for the retrieved top n chunks as $\{\mathbf{c}_i\}_{i=1}^{n}$. AQE generates the revised query embedding by suming up the original query embedding with each chunk embedding $\mathbf{c}_i$:

$$\hat{\mathbf{q}} = \frac{\mathbf{q} + \sum_{i=1}^{n}(\mathbf{c}_i)}{n+1} \tag{10}$$

We evaluate the influence of AQE on the retrieval Recall@5. As shown in Table 5, when we set $n = 1$, AQE consistently improves Recall@5 for NV-QA and Arctic-L embedding models, but it drops Recall@5 for the NV-EMB. Considering the computation cost, we do not use AQE, by default.

HYDE (Gao et al., 2022) utilizes the LLM's knolwedge to generate a hypothetical document $d = \mathrm{LLM}(q)$ for the query q. Then the embedding model encodes document d into the embedding vector $\mathbf{d} = f_{\text{emb}}(d)$. The refined query embedding $\hat{\mathbf{q}}$ is obtained by summing up $\mathbf{q}$ and $\mathbf{d}$:

$$\hat{\mathbf{q}} = \alpha\mathbf{q} + (1-\alpha)\mathbf{d}, \tag{11}$$

where α is a pre-defined positive constant ($\alpha \in [0, 1]$) controlling the contribution from each component. We explore multiple open-source LLMs including Mistal-7B (Jiang et al., 2023), Llama3-8B (AI@Meta, 2024), Gemma2-7B (Team, 2024), Llama3-70B (AI@Meta, 2024), Mixtral-8x7B (Jiang et al., 2024) and Mixtral-8x22B (Mistral AI team, 2024) to generate the hypothetical document. As shown in Table 3, HYDE could not consistently improve the recall. Thus, we exclude HYDE in retrieval pipeline.

5.3 Reranking

By default, we use QA-Mistral-4B(NVIDIA AI, 2024) for reranking. As shown in Table 6, the reranking model consistently and significantly improves the recall of all embedding models. Therefore, we use rerakning model in default settings.

6 Benchmark on Answer Generation

6.1 Metrics

Correctness measures the alignment between the generated answer and the ground-truth answer.
Relevance quantizes the relevance between the generated answer and the ground-truth context.
Faithfulness measures the relevance between the retrieved context and generated answer.
We design three types of judge mechanisms including embedding-model-as-judge, ranking-model-as-judge and LLM-as-judge.

6.2 Embedding-model-as-judge

We denote the embedding of the ground-truth answer by $\mathbf{a}_g$, that of answer generated from RAG by $\mathbf{a}_r$, the embedding of the ground-truth context by $\mathbf{c}_g$ and that of the retrieved context by $\mathbf{c}_r$. When using embedding model as judge, correctness/relevance/faithfulness is measured by the cosine similarity between embeddings:

$$\begin{aligned} \mathrm{C_{emb}} &= \frac{\langle \mathbf{a}_r, \mathbf{a}_g \rangle}{\|\mathbf{a}_r\|_2 \|\mathbf{a}_g\|_2}, \\ \mathrm{R_{emb}} &= \frac{\langle \mathbf{a}_r, \mathbf{c}_g \rangle}{\|\mathbf{a}_r\|_2 \|\mathbf{c}_g\|_2}, \\ \mathrm{R_{emb}} &= \frac{\langle \mathbf{a}_r, \mathbf{c}_r \rangle}{\|\mathbf{a}_r\|_2 \|\mathbf{c}_r\|_2}. \end{aligned} \tag{12}$$

6.3 Ranking-model-as-judge

We denote the labeled groundtruth answer by a_g, the answer generated from RAG by a_r, the groundtruth context by c_g and the embedding of the retrieved context by c_r. We denote the $\mathrm{cross}(x, y)$ as the cross-encoder model maps a pair of texts (x, y) into a relevance score $s \in [-\infty, +\infty]$. The higher score means that x is more relevant with

Rerank	NV-QA		Arctic-L		NV-EMB		Arctic-L + NV-EMB	
	Recall@1	Recall@5	Recall@1	Recall@5	Recall@1	Recall@5	Recall@1	Recall@5
w/o	0.277	0.651	0.313	0.552	0.360	0.742	0.358	0.751
QA-Mistral-4B	0.389	0.757	0.391	0.767	0.401	0.782	0.403	0.787

Table 6: The influence of ranking model.

Models	Embedding-model-as-judge			Ranking-model-as-judge			LLM-as-judge		
	Corre.	Relev.	Faith.	Corre.	Relev.	Faith.	Corre.	Relev.	Faith.
Mistral-7B	0.789	**0.747**	0.707	0.891	0.693	0.668	0.925	0.894	0.977
Llama3-8B	0.779	0.744	0.724	0.880	0.691	**0.692**	**0.945**	**0.915**	0.976
Mixtral-8x7B	0.792	0.738	0.691	0.891	0.684	0.651	0.913	0.875	0.963
Mixtral-8x22B	0.769	0.760	**0.742**	0.885	**0.698**	0.674	0.939	0.912	0.977
Llama3-70B	**0.793**	0.739	0.694	**0.894**	0.693	0.695	0.944	**0.915**	**0.978**

Table 7: The evaluation results on the generated answers from multiple open-source LLMs.

y. To normalize the score to the range $[0, 1]$, we process the relevance score by a sigmoid function: $\hat{s} = \text{sigmoid}(s)$. We define the correctness/relevance/faithfullness as below:

$$\begin{aligned} C_{\text{rank}} &= \text{sigmoid}(\text{cross}(a_r, a_g)), \\ R_{\text{rank}} &= \text{sigmoid}(\text{cross}(a_r, c_g)), \\ F_{\text{rank}} &= \text{sigmoid}(\text{cross}(a_r, c_r)). \end{aligned} \tag{13}$$

6.4 LLM-as-judge

We design the prompt templates for correctness, relevance and faithfulness, respectively. Given the query q, ground-truth answer a_g, answer generated from RAG a_r, ground-truth context by c_g, retrieved context by c_r, we fill them into the pre-defined templates, which is further feed into an LLM:

$$\begin{aligned} C_{\text{LLM}} =& \text{LLM}(\text{Template}_\text{C}(q, a_r, a_g)) \\ R_{\text{LLM}} =& \text{LLM}(\text{Template}_\text{R}(q, a_r, c_g)) \\ F_{\text{LLM}} =& \text{LLM}(\text{Template}_\text{F}(q, a_r, c_r)). \end{aligned} \tag{14}$$

Since LLM is not good at evaluating outputs in continuous range, we prompt the LLM to output a integer score within $[1, L]$ and divide the integer score by L to normalize it. By default, we use Mistral-Large as the judge.

6.5 Experimental results

Ablation on LLMs for answer generation. We evaluate the generation capabilities across a spectrum of Large Language Models (LLMs). The assessment includes smaller-scale models such as Mistral-7B and Llama3-8B, as well as larger-scale models including Mixtral-8x7B, Mixtral-8x22B, and Llama3-70B. The comparative results, presented in Table 7, reveal that the larger-scale models do not demonstrate a substantial performance advantage over their smaller counterparts in this specific task. Given these findings, and taking into account computational efficiency, we have opted to utilize Llama3-8B as our default model for answer generation. This choice represents an optimal balance between performance and resource utilization in our experimental framework.

# chunks	0	1	3	5	10
EM-as-J	0.717	0.764	0.777	0.779	0.775
RM-as-J	0.772	0.861	0.879	0.880	0.876
LLM-as-J	0.630	0.902	0.940	0.945	0.945

Table 8: Impact of the count of chunks on correctness.

Influence of the retrieved chunks. Table 8 illustrates the impact of the number of retrieved documents on answer correctness. The results demonstrate that the absence of retrieved chunks significantly diminishes answer correctness compared to scenarios where chunks are utilized, thus validating the efficacy of RAG over standalone LLMs. As the number of retrieved chunks increases from 1 to 5, we observe a consistent improvement in answer accuracy. However, this trend plateaus and potentially reverses when the number of chunks increases from 5 to 10. This phenomenon can be attributed to the introduction of extraneous information as the chunk count rises, which may impede the generation of accurate responses. These findings suggest an optimal retrieval window that balances comprehensive context with focused relevance, highlighting the importance of judicious document retrieval in RAG systems.

7 Conclusion

Our comprehensive study on Retrieval-Augmented Generation (RAG) for enterprise knowledge question-answering has yielded several significant insights. Through the creation and utilization of the EKRAG dataset, comprising 3200 manually curated questions, we have conducted an extensive evaluation of various components within the RAG pipeline. The insights gained from this study have broad implications for the optimization of RAG pipelines in enterprise knowledge management systems. By shedding light on the effectiveness of various retrieval strategies and introducing new evaluation paradigms, our work contributes to the ongoing refinement of question-answering systems tailored to enterprise needs.

References

Josh Achiam, Steven Adler, Sandhini Agarwal, Lama Ahmad, Ilge Akkaya, Florencia Leoni Aleman, Diogo Almeida, Janko Altenschmidt, Sam Altman, Shyamal Anadkat, et al. 2023. Gpt-4 technical report. *arXiv preprint arXiv:2303.08774*.

Vaibhav Adlakha, Parishad BehnamGhader, Xing Han Lu, Nicholas Meade, and Siva Reddy. 2023. Evaluating correctness and faithfulness of instruction-following models for question answering. *arXiv preprint arXiv:2307.16877*.

AI@Meta. 2024. Llama 3 model card.

Tom Brown, Benjamin Mann, Nick Ryder, Melanie Subbiah, Jared D Kaplan, Prafulla Dhariwal, Arvind Neelakantan, Pranav Shyam, Girish Sastry, Amanda Askell, et al. 2020. Language models are few-shot learners. *Advances in neural information processing systems*, 33:1877–1901.

Claudio Carpineto and Giovanni Romano. 2012. A survey of automatic query expansion in information retrieval. *Acm Computing Surveys (CSUR)*, 44(1):1–50.

Jianlv Chen, Shitao Xiao, Peitian Zhang, Kun Luo, Defu Lian, and Zheng Liu. 2024a. Bge m3-embedding: Multi-lingual, multi-functionality, multi-granularity text embeddings through self-knowledge distillation. *arXiv preprint arXiv:2402.03216*.

Jiawei Chen, Hongyu Lin, Xianpei Han, and Le Sun. 2024b. Benchmarking large language models in retrieval-augmented generation. In *Proceedings of the AAAI Conference on Artificial Intelligence*, volume 38, pages 17754–17762.

Shahul Es, Jithin James, Luis Espinosa-Anke, and Steven Schockaert. 2023. Ragas: Automated evaluation of retrieval augmented generation. *arXiv preprint arXiv:2309.15217*.

Paulo Finardi, Leonardo Avila, Rodrigo Castaldoni, Pedro Gengo, Celio Larcher, Marcos Piau, Pablo Costa, and Vinicius Caridá. 2024. The chronicles of rag: The retriever, the chunk and the generator. *arXiv preprint arXiv:2401.07883*.

Thibault Formal, Benjamin Piwowarski, and Stéphane Clinchant. 2021. Splade: Sparse lexical and expansion model for first stage ranking. In *Proceedings of the 44th International ACM SIGIR Conference on Research and Development in Information Retrieval*, pages 2288–2292.

Luyu Gao, Xueguang Ma, Jimmy Lin, and Jamie Callan. 2022. Precise zero-shot dense retrieval without relevance labels. *arXiv preprint arXiv:2212.10496*.

Tianyu Gao, Howard Yen, Jiatong Yu, and Danqi Chen. 2023. Enabling large language models to generate text with citations. In *Empirical Methods in Natural Language Processing (EMNLP)*.

Kelvin Guu, Kenton Lee, Zora Tung, Panupong Pasupat, and Mingwei Chang. 2020. Retrieval augmented language model pre-training. In *International conference on machine learning*, pages 3929–3938. PMLR.

Albert Q Jiang, Alexandre Sablayrolles, Arthur Mensch, Chris Bamford, Devendra Singh Chaplot, Diego de las Casas, Florian Bressand, Gianna Lengyel, Guillaume Lample, Lucile Saulnier, et al. 2023. Mistral 7b. *arXiv preprint arXiv:2310.06825*.

Albert Q Jiang, Alexandre Sablayrolles, Antoine Roux, Arthur Mensch, Blanche Savary, Chris Bamford, Devendra Singh Chaplot, Diego de las Casas, Emma Bou Hanna, Florian Bressand, et al. 2024. Mixtral of experts. *arXiv preprint arXiv:2401.04088*.

Chankyu Lee, Rajarshi Roy, Mengyao Xu, Jonathan Raiman, Mohammad Shoeybi, Bryan Catanzaro, and Wei Ping. 2024. Nv-embed: Improved techniques for training llms as generalist embedding models. *arXiv preprint arXiv:2405.17428*.

Patrick Lewis, Ethan Perez, Aleksandra Piktus, Fabio Petroni, Vladimir Karpukhin, Naman Goyal, Heinrich Küttler, Mike Lewis, Wen-tau Yih, Tim Rocktäschel, et al. 2020. Retrieval-augmented generation for knowledge-intensive nlp tasks. *Advances in Neural Information Processing Systems*, 33:9459–9474.

Luke Merrick, Danmei Xu, Gaurav Nuti, and Daniel Campos. 2024. Arctic-embed: Scalable, efficient, and accurate text embedding models. *arXiv preprint arXiv:2405.05374*.

Mistral AI team. 2024. Mixtral8x22b.

NVIDIA AI. 2024. Rerank-QA-Mistral-4B.

Juan Ramos et al. 2003. Using tf-idf to determine word relevance in document queries. In *Proceedings of the first instructional conference on machine learning*, volume 242, pages 29–48. Citeseer.

Nils Reimers and Iryna Gurevych. 2019. Sentence-bert: Sentence embeddings using siamese bert-networks. *arXiv preprint arXiv:1908.10084*.

Stephen E Robertson, Steve Walker, Susan Jones, Micheline M Hancock-Beaulieu, Mike Gatford, et al. 1995. Okapi at trec-3. *Nist Special Publication Sp*, 109:109.

Gemma Team. 2024. Gemma.

Shashank Verma, Vinh Nguyen, Nguyen Lee, Nave Algarici, Gabriel Moreira, Ronay AK, Caroline Gottlieb, Benedikt Schifferer, and Wei Ping. Build Enterprise Retrieval-Augmented Generation Apps with NVIDIA Retrieval QA Embedding Model.

Guangzhi Xiong, Qiao Jin, Zhiyong Lu, and Aidong Zhang. 2024. Benchmarking retrieval-augmented generation for medicine. *arXiv preprint arXiv:2402.13178*.

Xiao Yang, Kai Sun, Hao Xin, Yushi Sun, Nikita Bhalla, Xiangsen Chen, Sajal Choudhary, Rongze Daniel Gui, Ziran Will Jiang, Ziyu Jiang, et al. 2024. Crag–comprehensive rag benchmark. *arXiv preprint arXiv:2406.04744*.

A Bi-encoder versus Cross-encoder

Bi-encoders individually encodes each input (*e.g.*, a query or a document) into dense embeddings. Bi-encoders are scalable because the embeddings for inputs can be pre-computed and stored. This allows for efficient retrieval from large datasets using approximate nearest neighbor (ANN) search techniques. Cross-encoder jointly encodes a query and a document by concatenating them and feeding the concatenated sequence through a single model. It allows the model to directly capture the interactions between the inputs. Cross-encoder normally achieves higher retrieval accuracy. Nevertheless, cross-encoder is computationally expensive since it could not pre-compute embeddings like bi-encoder. This limitation forbids its application in large-scale retrieval scenarios. Therefore, cross-encoder is only applied in re-ranking tens of candidates retrieved based on embedding models.

B Annotation Process

The annotation was conducted using the LabelStudio platform by a team of 14 experienced annotators with professional backgrounds in business and finance. The process occurred in two phases:

- **Retrieval Annotation:** Annotators were presented with individual or grouped documents and tasked with formulating queries and selecting relevant context(s) that answered these queries.
- **Generator Evaluation:** A different set of annotators reviewed the query-context pairs along with multiple LLM-generated answers (using GPT-4, Claude 3.5, and Mixtral 7x22B). These LLM outputs served as guidelines for the annotators in creating the final ground truth answers.

Each annotation underwent rigorous vetting by a lead annotator and a data team lead to ensure adherence to guidelines and maintain quality.

Towards Effectively Leveraging Execution Traces for Program Repair with Code LLMs

Mirazul Haque[1]*, Petr Babkin[2]*, Farima Farmahinifarahani[2], Manuela Veloso[1]
J. P. Morgan AI Research, {[1]New York, [2]Palo Alto}
{first.last}@jpmchase.com

Abstract

Large Language Models (LLMs) show promising performance on various programming tasks, including Automatic Program Repair (APR). However, most approaches to LLM-based APR are limited to the static analysis of the programs, while disregarding their runtime behavior. Inspired by knowledge-augmented NLP, in this work, we aim to remedy this potential blind spot by augmenting standard APR prompts with program execution traces. We evaluate our approach using the GPT family of models on three popular APR datasets. Our findings suggest that simply incorporating execution traces into the prompt provides a limited performance improvement over trace-free baselines, in only 2 out of 6 tested dataset / model configurations. We further find that the effectiveness of execution traces for APR diminishes as their complexity increases. We explore several strategies for leveraging traces in prompts and demonstrate that LLM-optimized prompts help outperform trace-free prompts more consistently. Additionally, we show trace-based prompting to be superior to finetuning a smaller LLM on a small-scale dataset; and conduct probing studies reinforcing the notion that execution traces can complement the reasoning abilities of the LLMs.

```
### Buggy Program:
def search(x, seq):
    index = 0
    def helper(index):
        if not seq:
            return 0
        elif x <= seq[index]:
            return index
        else:
            if index + 1 >= len(seq):
                return index + 1
            else:
                return helper(index+1)

### Failing test case:
result = search(42, (-5, 1, 3, 5, 7, 10))
assert result == 6,
  ↪  'Expected 6 but got %s' % result
AssertionError: Expected 6 but got None

### Execution trace:
Starting var:.. x = 42
Starting var:.. seq = (-5, 1, 3, 5, 7, 10)
call        10 def search(x, seq):
line        11     index = 0
New var:....... index = 0
line        12     def helper(index):
New var:....... helper = <function search.<locals>
  ↪  .helper at 0x7fd455b89040>
return      12     def helper(index):
Return value:.. None
```

Figure 1: Example buggy program, a failing test case and its execution trace. While the failure message simply indicates the output is wrong, the execution trace provides a detailed explanation how it was produced.

1 Introduction

Automatic Program Repair (APR) is a critical challenge in software engineering, aiming to reduce human effort in debugging and fixing software defects. Software bugs can lead to significant security vulnerabilities, financial losses, and system failures, necessitating efficient repair mechanisms. While large language models (LLMs) have demonstrated remarkable capabilities in generating and modifying code, their effectiveness in APR remains constrained by their reliance on static code analysis.

Debugging complex software issues often necessitates a deeper understanding of the program's execution behavior, including variable modifications and control flow changes, which conventional Deep Learning-based and LLM-based APR approaches fail to capture effectively (Xia and Zhang, 2022; Jiang et al., 2023; Tian et al., 2023; Sutton et al., 2023).

Recent advancements in knowledge-augmented NLP have emphasized integrating external information into language models to enhance reasoning and

*equal contribution.

Proceedings of the 4th International Workshop on Knowledge-Augmented Methods for Natural Language Processing (KnowledgeNLP'25), pages 160–179
May 3, 2025

accuracy. Inspired by this, our research explores augmenting LLM-based automated program repair (APR) with program execution traces—structured runtime data that reveal a program's actual behavior. These traces provide diagnostic insights beyond static code analysis. By embedding them into repair prompts, we aim to bridge the gap between static and dynamic program understanding, aligning with trends in knowledge-augmented NLP that leverage external sources to enhance language model capabilities.

We frame our work in terms of three research questions (RQs). In RQ1 (Section 3.2), our objective is to quantify the gains from incorporating execution traces into the APR prompt over the prompts only containing the failing test case as well as the trace-free chain-of-thought prompting baseline (Chen et al., 2023). We find that simply adding the execution trace does not consistently outperform trace-free prompts.

To inform a more finegrained approach, in RQ2 (Section 3.3), we analyze the relationship between trace complexity and the likelihood of the LLM producing a working fix. To measure this complexity, we consider two parameters: trace length and the number of variable modifications. We find that the effectiveness of trace-based prompts decreases with the growing length and number of variable assignments.

Motivated by this finding, in RQ3 (Section 4), we aim at improving the consistency of trace-based APR by experimenting with three different representations of execution traces: traces in a collated format, LLM-optimized traces, and a trace representation conditionally selected based on querying the LLM's confidence. We find that LLM-optimized trace-based prompts provide the most consistent results with respect to program repair.

We additionally perform two follow-up studies: in the first, we compare our trace-based prompting approach with a fine-tuned baseline inspired by TraceFixer (Bouzenia et al., 2023); and in the second one, we directly probe the LLM on two trace understanding tasks.

The rest of the paper is organized as follows. In Section 2, we discuss the related work and how it differs from our approach. Section 3 details our methodological setup and covers RQ1 and RQ2. Section 4 covers RQ2 and in Section 5, we discuss the additional studies.

2 Related Work

Recent work looked into augmenting code LLMs with execution information to improve performance on downstream tasks, including APR.

SelfAPR (Ye et al., 2022) proposed to use compiler and test diagnostics during self-supervised training of the language model for improving APR. Additionally, several works have proposed the use of execution traces for pretraining code LLMs. In TRACED (Ding et al., 2023), authors finetuned a BERT-like model to predict execution paths and quantized values, which allowed it to outperform an AST-based UniXcoder (Guo et al., 2022) on clone detection and vulnerability detection. Whereas, Liu et al.'s program state prediction pre-training improved code search and generation (Liu et al., 2023). Finally, TraceFixer, based on CodeT5 and finetuned with execution traces, showed a 13% improvement in APR on synthetic bugs over the code-only baseline but struggled with real bugs, hinting at potential generalization limitations (Bouzenia et al., 2023).

Among training-free approaches, Self-Debug (Chen et al., 2023) improved program generation by generating code explanations directly from the LLM, in a chain-of-thought fashion, as part of solving the APR task.

To the best of our knowledge, all of these works do not consider the effect of putting execution traces in the prompt of a pretrained LLM.

3 Analyzing the Impact of Execution Traces on Program Repair

In this section, we analyze the effects of adding traces in the LLM prompt on APR performance, compared to two trace-free baselines (Ye et al., 2022), (Chen et al., 2023). Additionally, we perform a differentiated analysis of APR performance based on trace complexity. We formulate the corresponding two research questions as follows.

RQ1. Are prompts with execution traces more effective at program repair than prompts without traces?

RQ2. How does trace complexity affect the effectiveness of trace-based prompts?

3.1 Set Up

Datasets. We surveyed 15 popular datasets across Python, Java, C++, and other major languages, focusing on dataset size, program diversity, unit test availability, and dataset origin (e.g., self-contained algorithmic problems like CodeNet (Puri et al., 2021) or full open-source projects like PyTraceBugs (Akimova et al., 2021)). While realistic datasets are ideal, evaluating them requires significant manual effort due to complex dependencies. Algorithmic datasets offer advantages like manageable length and easily testable, self-contained functions, enabling trace generation through execution.

We selected three APR datasets: Refactory (Hu et al., 2019), RunBugRun (Prenner and Robbes, 2023), and HumanEval-Java (Jiang et al., 2023). Refactory includes nearly 2000 faulty Python programs submitted by students, enabling coverage of diverse mistakes. RunBugRun, derived from CodeNet, contains a quarter million submissions for 4000 distinct problems; we sampled 1000 Python bugs for evaluation. HumanEval, originally for Python, was adapted into HumanEval-Java, injecting synthetic bugs for APR testing.

Each dataset includes at least 5 test cases per problem. For RunBugRun, we implemented a wrapper to handle input/output via standard input and print statements for accurate result comparison.

Models. With the landscape of state-of-the-art code LLMs rapidly changing, we chose use two most widely studied commercial models from OpenAI for ease of comparison with other work: GPT-3.5 Turbo (Ouyang et al., 2022) and GPT-4 (OpenAI, 2023). These two models represent two different performance tiers both in terms of the number of parameters and different release timelines, hence, studying these models could shine the light on the LLMs' evolving ability to reason about program execution across product generations. While there is undoubtedly scope for including more proprietary as well as open source models, given our narrow focus on traces, we leave this to be explored in future work.

Execution Traces Generation. As the program is being executed, it is possible to step through it programmatically, while also capturing every change to the function's variables, akin to interactive debugging. PySnooper(pys) library for Python provides this functionality via a decorator that can be added to a function of interest to automatically log state changes, such as variable initialization and modification, subroutine calls, returned values, and runtime exceptions. Crucially, each state change reference a specific line of code on which it occurred. Examples of execution traces are given in the Appendix A.2. Before appending traces to the prompt we perform basic postprocessing, including the removal of timestamps and stripping of terminal formatting command sequences.

Prompt Types. We follow the instruction template for complete function generation used by Xia et al. (2023), expanding it with two additional types of information, namely, a failing test case (henceforth, referred to as *Error Prompts*) and a program execution trace (referred as *Trace Prompts*). We offer our rationale for these choices, along with other prompt types considered, in Appendix B.

To ensure the prompt and response fit within the GPT model context size, we truncate the content of the prompt if the number of lines exceeds 200. We have added an example of all the prompts in Section A in the Appendix.

Baseline. We consider the Prompt-based baseline Self-Debug. With this baseline, we explore prompting LLMs using execution traces generated by LLMs themselves (instead of actual program execution traces). This baseline inspired by Self-Debugging (Chen et al., 2023) where LLMs are prompted to debug their own generated code. In particular, we draw inspirations from the *Explanation* step of this work where the model is asked to generate execution traces for a predicted code. We tailored Self-Debugging's prompts to fit our usecase: in our prompts, we provide LLMs with a program and a test case feedback, and ask them to trace through the execution of the program and determine the needed fix, and correct the function accordingly. We perform these experiments with both GPT-3.5 and GPT-4.

Metrics. In previous work on APR, models are evaluated either at the granularity of distinct bugs solved (Xia et al., 2023; Jiang et al., 2023) or individual test cases passed (Tian et al., 2023). In contrast, we generate multiple prompts for each program tailored to a specific failing test case and its corresponding execution trace (e.g., A.1, A.2). Rather than aggregating predictions from multiple samples, we generate a single prediction per test case-specific prompt and aggregate across prompts when computing metrics. The key metrics are ***Correct Fix Accuracy (CFA)***, the percentage of fixes passing all test cases, and ***Correct Program Accuracy (CPA)***, the percentage of programs with at least one correct fix. We do not report test case-level accuracy, as it can be too lenient and doesn't account for variations in the number of test cases per program.

Model	Dataset	Method	# FPs	# Fixes	# CF	# CP	CFA	CPA
		Self-Debug			244	73	0.421	0.529
	Refactory	**Error Prompt**	138	579	**304**	**91**	**0.525**	**0.659**
		Trace Prompt			295	87	0.509	0.630
		Self-Debug			210	75	0.331	0.477
GPT-3.5	**HumanEval-Java**	**Error Prompt**	157	634	**241**	85	**0.380**	0.541
		Trace Prompt			212	**86**	0.334	**0.547**
		Self-Debug			151	132	0.270	0.289
	RunBugRun	**Error Prompt**	456	559	**260**	**221**	**0.465**	**0.484**
		Trace Prompt			249	216	0.445	0.473
		Self-Debug			414	117	0.715	0.847
	Refactory	**Error Prompt**	138	579	**458**	**122**	**0.791**	**0.884**
		Trace Prompt			427	113	0.737	0.818
		Self-Debug			312	105	0.492	0.668
GPT-4	**HumanEval-Java**	**Error Prompt**	157	634	313	104	0.493	0.662
		Trace Prompt			**324**	**112**	**0.511**	**0.713**
		Self-Debug			**337**	**287**	**0.602**	**0.629**
	RunBugRun	**Error Prompt**	456	559	296	264	0.529	0.578
		Trace Prompt			*312*	*266*	*0.558*	*0.583*

Table 1: **RQ1 Quantitative Results.** FP = Faulty Programs, CF = Correct Fixes, CP = Correct Programs, CFA = Correct Fix Accuracy, CPA = Correct Program Accuracy.

3.2 RQ1. Are prompts with execution traces more effective at program repair than prompts without traces?

In this research question, our objective is to evaluate the effectiveness of including program execution traces into LLM prompts, for solving APR tasks, compared to the baselines. The effectiveness is measured through reporting CPA and CFA. The evaluation results can be found in Table 1. The number of faulty programs, number of fixes, and total test cases are the same for all types of prompts per each dataset.

Across the board, the Self-Debug baseline performs the worst except in one configuration using GPT-4 on the RunBugRun dataset. This general outcome is unsurprising as having the LLM generate an execution trace could introduce hallucination and thus undermine the resulting fixes. For both GPT-3.5 and GPT-4 on the Refactory dataset, prompts including just a failing test case decisively outperform ones with execution traces by multiple percentage points on both fix accuracy and program accuracy.

On the HumanEval-Java dataset with GPT-3.5, error-only prompts are only ahead of trace-based prompts in terms of fix accuracy but are slightly behind in program accuracy. Meanwhile, with GPT-4, trace-based prompts consistently outperform error-only prompts on both metrics. Results on RunBugRun paint a similar picture, where GPT-3.5 doesn't seem to benefit from including traces, while GPT-4 gets a tangible lift over the error-only prompts. Overall, on two out of three datasets, trace-based prompts significantly improve the ability of GPT-4 to generate working bug fixes.

While GPT-3.5 lagging behind in terms of absolute scores irrespective of prompt type is expected, more broadly, its inability to benefit from execution traces (even degraded performance) could highlight a qualitative generational gap when it comes to emergent abilities of LLMs. Notwithstanding, there remain a few unexplained results, such as the lack of performance gain from using traces on the Refactory dataset and the unusually strong performance of the Self-Debug baseline in one particular configuration. To gain a fine-grained understanding, in the next research question, we focus on studying the varying complexity of execution traces and how they affect downstream APR performance.

> **RQ1 Summary.** Trace prompts do not consistently outperform Error Prompts on program repair.

3.3 RQ2. How does trace complexity affect the effectiveness of trace-based prompts?

Unlike other elements of the prompt, execution traces are dynamic in nature and are highly dependent on a particular input as much as the program itself. Additionally, execution traces can be dramat-

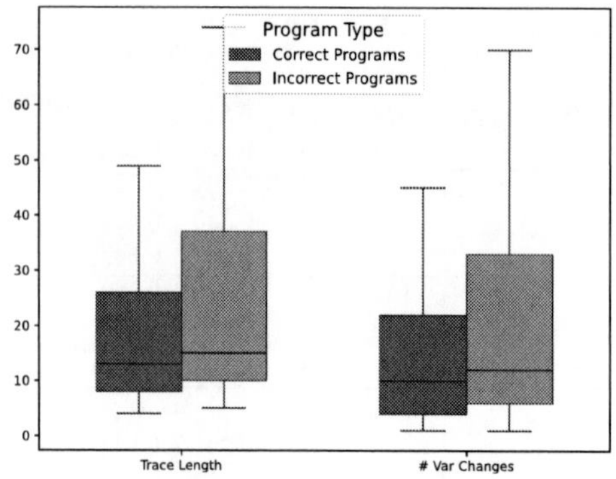

(a) HumanEval-Java Dataset with GPT-4

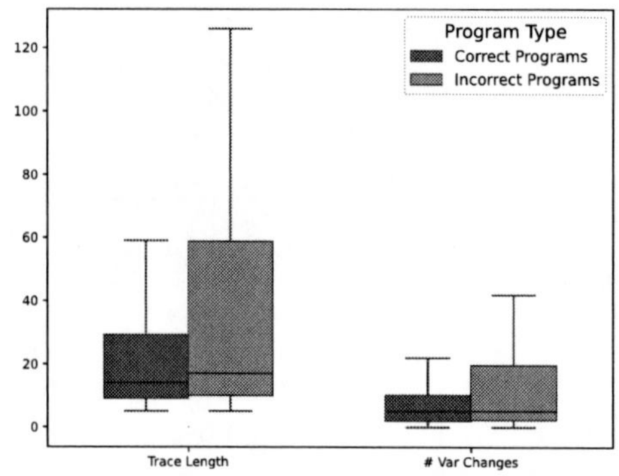

(b) RunBugRun Dataset with GPT-4

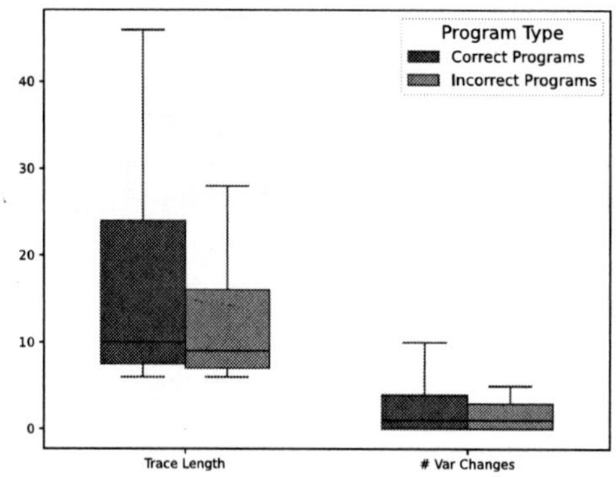

(c) Refactory Dataset with GPT-4

Figure 2: Distributions of trace lengths and variable changes across correct vs incorrect program fixes generated by GPT-4. Analysis for GPT-3.5, showing a similar trend, is given in the appendix.

ically different in the presence of a runtime error, compared to when the function finishes executing correctly (even if the returned value itself is wrong). Thus, variations in trace complexity could be a crucial factor in how beneficial their inclusion is in the prompt. On the one hand, traces that are too short may not provide much information beyond what is already conveyed by the program itself and the failing test case. On the other hand, overly long and complex traces may overwhelm LLMs' long context and ultimately confuse it. We believe there is a sweet spot at which the inclusion of traces is most beneficial. As such, we observed great variability with respect to the overall trace length, as well as in the number and type of individual state changes.

To gain insights into nuanced differences among our evaluated datasets, we compute the statistics of overall trace length and the number of variable modifications in all prompts, while differentiating by whether the resulting fix was correct (Figure 2). For both the HumanEval-Java and RunBugRun datasets, median[1] trace length and number of variable modifications were significantly higher for failing fixes than for the correct ones. This corroborates our presupposition that longer traces could undermine rather than help APR. Conversely, in the Refactory dataset, somewhat contrary to our intuitions, for failing fixes median trace length were actually lower than for successful fixes. Regarding the number of variable modifications, the median was just one, compared to 5 in RunBugRun. This disparity implies variable modifications could play a key role in the effectiveness of a trace for APR.

> **RQ2 Summary.** The prompts having longer execution traces have a lower chance of generating a correct fix.

4 Impact of Modified Traces

As we find that longer trace length could have a negative impact in the effectiveness of GPT models, we focus on modified trace strategies and their impact on the effectiveness of the model. In this section, we discuss one research question.

RQ3. Can the format of traces be optimized to guarantee gains for APR?

4.1 Modified Traces

Collated Execution Traces. Even though execution traces for both languages reference code lines from the original program, they are placed in the standalone section of the prompt, separate from the program itself. In order to thoroughly ablate

[1]In all datasets and for both correct and failing fixes we observed the presence of extremely long traces in excess of 10,000 entries. Additionally, a significant number of trace prompts got truncated (5% for Refactory and almost 10% for RunBugRun).

trace format, we experimented with combining the two by placing each trace entry directly to its corresponding line of code as an inline comment [2]. The rationale behind this design choice is to consolidate the two types of information in the common location, potentially freeing the LLM from having to constantly cross-reference between them.

LLM-Optimized Execution Traces (OPT). While in a general case deterministic traces provide valuable information regarding variable changes, logging every single event is not always ideal. In scenarios such as infinite loops, traces end up repeating the same information, while also unboundedly growing in length. It can thus be desirable to optimize potentially lengthy traces by condensing superfluous information. To optimize execution traces, we prompt a long context GPT4-32k model with the deterministic execution trace and an instruction to generate a shorter version of it, optimized for downstream APR.

Confidence Based Prompt Selection (Conf OPT). In addition to modifying the format or content of the prompt itself, we experimented with a simple prompt routing mechanism based on pre-querying LLM's confidence about correctly solving a program repair task using the deterministic trace. If the confidence level is low, we fallback onto using an LLM-optimized trace instead.

We have considered multiple ways to find the confidence value of the model. One possible way is to prompt the model to find whether it's confident or not (boolean) to use a specific prompt to repair a program. But on a small prompt set, we find that the model outputs that it is always confident for all inputs. Additionally, another way is to feed both prompts and ask the model for which prompt it is more confident to repair the program. However, based on the findings of recent work (Huang et al., 2023), LLM might be biased for a specific position (prompt one or prompt two). Hence, based on the findings of Huang et al. (Huang et al., 2023), we use a Likert-scale based confidence score. Given a score range of 1-5, if the confidence score provided by the model is less than 3, we consider that the model has low-confidence. The approach is shown in Figure 3.

Trace-length Based Prompt Selection (TRL OPT). As we have found through investigating

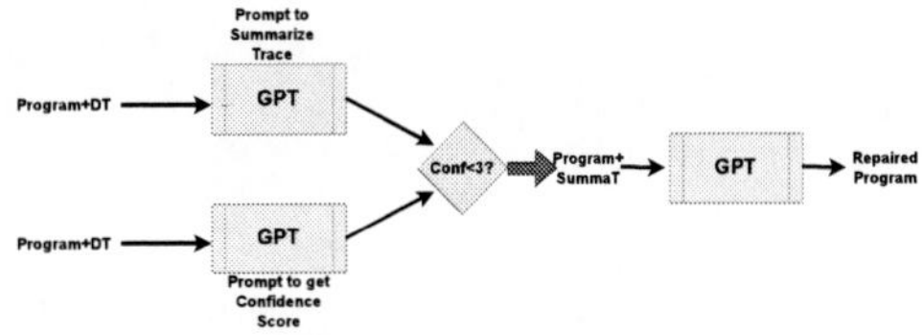

Figure 3: The Flow of Conditional Selection of Traces

RQ2 that trace prompts work well if the trace length is within a specific range; hence, switching to a different prompt given a longer trace might be beneficial. In this technique, instead of using a confidence score like Conf OPT, we use trace length for routing between prompts. The routing is investigated in two settings: trace prompt and OPT prompt, and trace prompt and error prompt. If the trace length is less than N, we use trace prompt, or we use OPT prompt or error prompt based on the setting. We use the following N values for the experiment: 25,30,35,40,45,50.

4.2 RQ3 Results.

The results could be found in Table 2. For ease of comparison, for each dataset and model we include the best performing strategy from RQ1, which could be either error prompt, trace prompt or the Self-Debug baseline. Of the three trace modification strategies, LLM-Optimized prompts (OPT) provide the most consistent performance gains on both CFA and CPA metrics. With respect to CPA, for all dataset and model pairs, OPT is among the top three performing prompting techniques. The CFA values for OPT are even more commendable, whereas, for three out of six model-dataset pairs, OPT has the best CFA (second best in the other three). Furthermore, this confirms our implication from RQ2 that less complicated traces are better for prompting for program repair tasks.

For confidence-based prompt selection, while we find the CFA and CPA values are comparatively better for GPT4, the performance in GPT3.5 is worse. This would imply that GPT-4 is significantly better in providing confidence scores for prompts than GPT-3.5. But, as the performance is significantly worse than OPT on average, the application of the method for GPT-4 is still not reliable.

For trace length-based prompt selection, we only report the best results in the table. We have two findings here; first, although routing could improve the CFA and CPA values more than individual

[2]In case of multiple passes through the same line e.g., variable changes within a loop, we concatenate each of the traced events by a new line, providing a full history of state changes at that line.

Metric	Method	GPT-3.5			GPT-4		
		Refactory	HumanEval-Java	RunBugRun	Refactory	HumanEval-Java	RunBugRun
CFA	**Collated Trace**	0.452	0.391	0.381	0.656	0.531	0.483
	OPT Trace	0.502	**0.430**	**0.472**	0.753	**0.572**	0.570
	Conf OPT Trace	0.368	0.380	0.429	0.735	0.549	0.527
	TRL OPT Trace (EP)	0.490	0.312	0.457	0.742	0.492	0.549
	TRL OPT Trace (OPT)	0.493	0.353	0.466	0.737	0.473	0.574
	RQ1 Best	**0.525**	0.380	0.465	**0.791**	0.511	**0.602**
CPA	**Collated Trace**	0.587	0.497	0.407	0.818	0.681	0.508
	OPT Trace	0.601	0.535	**0.497**	0.862	0.713	0.589
	Conf OPT Trace	0.384	0.522	0.453	0.847	**0.732**	0.550
	TRL OPT Trace (EP)	0.623	0.528	0.484	0.826	0.694	0.589
	TRL OPT Trace (OPT)	0.623	**0.573**	0.491	0.826	0.675	0.603
	RQ1 Best	**0.659**	0.547	0.484	**0.884**	0.713	**0.629**

Table 2: **RQ3 Quantitative Results.** CFA = Correct Fix Accuracy, and CPA = Correct Program Accuracy.

prompts, we find that only for the GPT-3.5 model and HumanEvalJava dataset could routing get the best CPA score among all considered techniques. Second, changing the value of N would have a limited impact on CFA and CPA values. Overall, we could not find any strong result suggesting that routing between techniques based on trace length might be significantly beneficial. Detailed results could be found in Figures 6 and 7 (in Appendix).

Lastly, collated trace prompts disappointingly do not provide an improvement over trace prompts. One possible explanation is a lack of exposure to this format during LLM training as code doesn't normally include inline comments about state changes. Second, inline traces within loops can "stretch" the length of the program quite a bit, possibly diluting LLMs attention to the continuation of the program after the loop. In our probing studies of LLM trace understanding, we find that, indeed, LLMs struggle to keep up with variable changes across multiple iterations. Finally, the problem of truncation becomes more severe with collated traces, as not just the trace but also part of the original problem could be excluded from the prompt.

RQ3 Summary. Optimized trace prompt is the most consistent type of prompting technique, specifically for CFA metric.

5 Additional Studies

5.1 Trace-based prompting compared to finetuning a smaller model.

In this RQ, we focus on evaluating if fine-tuning a small-sized LLM would generate better results w.r.t program repair rather than prompting GPT models with different prompts. For that purpose, we fine-tune the deepseek-coder-1.3b-instruct [3] model with training data extracted from HumanEval-Java and RunBugRun datasets. Finally, we compare the program repair performance of fine-tuning and prompting-based techniques on test data.

Finetuning Setup. Our finetuning approach is inspired by TraceFixer (Bouzenia et al., 2023), which finetunes a CodeT5 model using the buggy program's code, its execution trace, and the desired state of the program. As we didn't have access to TraceFixer's code, we implemented our own finetuning pipeline. In our case, the input to the model consists of a buggy program, the failing test case results, and corresponding execution traces. During training, the correct version of the program is included in the prompt, while during inference it is omitted, to be filled in by the model. For each dataset, 80% of the problems are randomly selected for training, and the rest are reserved for testing. This accounts for 459 samples for RunBugRun and 517 samples for HumanEval-Java datasets. We use the training settings and parameters suggested by deepseek-coder developers to finetune this model. Details of these parameters can be found in the model's repo.

Result. Figure 4 shows the results. For comparison purposes, we calculate CPA and CFA for prompting-based techniques on the same test programs. It can be noted that all the prompting techniques outperform fine-tuned model's CPA and CFA. It is observed that models fine-tuned with and without trace show lower CPA and CFA than prompting-based techniques. One of the reasons behind the results might be the limited training data for each task. Also, the TraceFixer technique showed better results in the original work, but the number of training examples for TraceFixer was

[3]https://github.com/deepseek-ai/DeepSeek-Coder

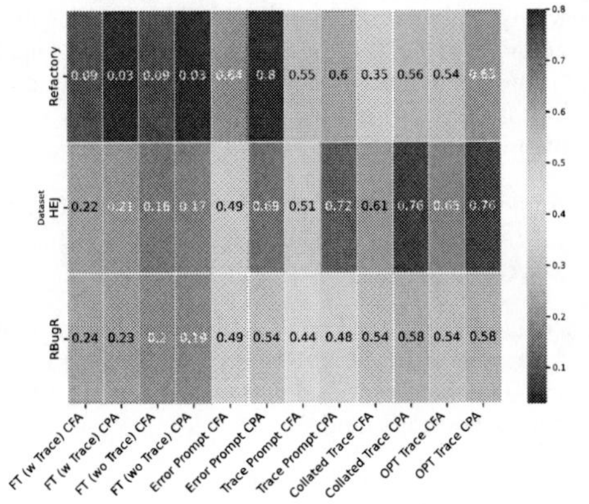

Figure 4: CPA and CFA of Prompting-Based Techniques vs. Model Fine-Tuned for APR Tasks.

significantly higher, too. In our future work, we plan to use a larger training dataset and larger models for finetuning.

5.2 Probing Studies of Trace Understanding

To gain insights into the observed lack of improvement in APR performance using collated traces and results from using traces for APR in general, we investigate two additional questions via small-scale probing experiments.

Can the LLM align the program with its execution trace? We directly measure the LLM's ability to perform trace collating given a standalone program and its execution trace. The rationale behind this experiment is that if an LLM can do this task with high accuracy, then there is no added benefit of adding collating traces into prompts.

Can the LLM infer the execution trace from the program alone? Although the Self-Debug approach implicitly traces through the program's execution, it is never formally evaluated. If an LLM can accurately generate a program's execution trace, then adding such a trace into the prompt would understandably not provide additional value for APR. Prompts used for each task can be found in Appendix C.2.

For both of these experiments we used GPT-4 on a subset of programs from the Refactory dataset. Since trace prediction behavior can be different depending on whether a function executes successfully or raises an error, for each experiment we differentiate between traces produced for working and failing programs. In addition, due to a limited number of distinct problems in Refactory, we additionally evaluate on the Geeks-for-geeks dataset[4]. To evaluate the LLM's output, we compute a diff against the ground truth trace or collated trace/program and report the exact match rate, after light post-processing, in Table 3 of Appendix C.1.

Based on these results, trace collating accuracy reaches 88% on reference Refactory programs, however it degrades by nearly ten percent on programs containing failures. Furthermore, on the more diverse Geeks for geeks dataset, which also eliminates the possibility of prompt leakage, collating performance sharply decreases to just 45%.

Prediction of a program's execution trace by an LLM from scratch is a significantly more challenging task compared to merely modifying the format of the trace. As a result, the rate of zero-diff trace predictions does not exceed 50% in the case of reference Refactory programs and is further halved for programs containing failures. Across the Geeks for geeks dataset, only 15% of generated traces perfectly match the ground truth. We provide qualitative analysis of a manually reviewed sample of diffs in the appendix.

Despite the impressive ability of GPT-4 at manipulating execution traces neither of the two tasks appear to be trivially solvable. Hence, we conclude real execution traces can contribute information for downstream tasks not yet easily inferrable by strong LLMs such as GPT-4.

6 Conclusion

In this study, we examined the impact of incorporating program execution traces into prompts on the program repair capabilities of the GPT model family. Our findings indicate that trace-based prompts do not consistently outperform error-based prompts; their effectiveness varies with the dataset and LLM used. Analysis reveals that longer traces and more variable assignments reduce prompt effectiveness. Using this insight, we developed variations of trace-based prompts, finding that LLM-optimized traces offer more consistent improvements without limiting trace complexity heuristically. We validated our results against a fine-tuned baseline and found that LLMs have limited capacity for trace generation, explaining the weaker performance of the Self-Debug baseline and highlighting the potential utility of traces in code tasks.

[4]`https://github.com/facebookresearch/TransCoder`

7 Disclaimer

Disclaimer: This paper was prepared for informational purposes by the Artificial Intelligence Research group of JPMorgan Chase & Co. and its affiliates ("JP Morgan") and is not a product of the Research Department of JP Morgan. JP Morgan makes no representation and warranty whatsoever and disclaims all liability, for the completeness, accuracy or reliability of the information contained herein. This document is not intended as investment research or investment advice, or a recommendation, offer or solicitation for the purchase or sale of any security, financial instrument, financial product or service, or to be used in any way for evaluating the merits of participating in any transaction, and shall not constitute a solicitation under any jurisdiction or to any person, if such solicitation under such jurisdiction or to such person would be unlawful.

References

Pysnooper. https://pypi.org/project/PySnooper/. (Accessed on 10/14/2023).

Elena N Akimova, Alexander Yu Bersenev, Artem A Deikov, Konstantin S Kobylkin, Anton V Konygin, Ilya P Mezentsev, and Vladimir E Misilov. 2021. Pytracebugs: A large python code dataset for supervised machine learning in software defect prediction. In 2021 28th Asia-Pacific Software Engineering Conference (APSEC), pages 141–151. IEEE.

Islem Bouzenia, Yangruibo Ding, Kexin Pei, Baishakhi Ray, and Michael Pradel. 2023. Tracefixer: Execution trace-driven program repair.

Xinyun Chen, Maxwell Lin, Nathanael Schärli, and Denny Zhou. 2023. Teaching large language models to self-debug. arXiv preprint arXiv:2304.05128.

Yangruibo Ding, Ben Steenhoek, Kexin Pei, Gail Kaiser, Wei Le, and Baishakhi Ray. 2023. Traced: Execution-aware pre-training for source code.

Daya Guo, Shuai Lu, Nan Duan, Yanlin Wang, Ming Zhou, and Jian Yin. 2022. Unixcoder: Unified cross-modal pre-training for code representation.

Yang Hu, Umair Z Ahmed, Sergey Mechtaev, Ben Leong, and Abhik Roychoudhury. 2019. Refactoring based program repair applied to programming assignments. In 2019 34th IEEE/ACM International Conference on Automated Software Engineering (ASE), pages 388–398. IEEE.

Kung-Hsiang Huang, Philippe Laban, Alexander R Fabbri, Prafulla Kumar Choubey, Shafiq Joty, Caiming Xiong, and Chien-Sheng Wu. 2023. Embrace divergence for richer insights: A multi-document summarization benchmark and a case study on summarizing diverse information from news articles. arXiv preprint arXiv:2309.09369.

Nan Jiang, Kevin Liu, Thibaud Lutellier, and Lin Tan. 2023. Impact of code language models on automated program repair.

Chenxiao Liu, Shuai Lu, Weizhu Chen, Daxin Jiang, Alexey Svyatkovskiy, Shengyu Fu, Neel Sundaresan, and Nan Duan. 2023. Code execution with pre-trained language models.

OpenAI. 2023. Gpt-4 technical report. ArXiv, abs/2303.08774.

Long Ouyang, Jeffrey Wu, Xu Jiang, Diogo Almeida, Carroll Wainwright, Pamela Mishkin, Chong Zhang, Sandhini Agarwal, Katarina Slama, Alex Ray, et al. 2022. Training language models to follow instructions with human feedback. Advances in Neural Information Processing Systems, 35:27730–27744.

Julian Aron Prenner and Romain Robbes. 2023. Runbugrun – an executable dataset for automated program repair.

Ruchir Puri, David S Kung, Geert Janssen, Wei Zhang, Giacomo Domeniconi, Vladimir Zolotov, Julian Dolby, Jie Chen, Mihir Choudhury, Lindsey Decker, et al. 2021. Codenet: A large-scale ai for code dataset for learning a diversity of coding tasks. arXiv preprint arXiv:2105.12655.

Charles Sutton, David Bieber, Kensen Shi, Kexin Pei, and Pengcheng Yin. 2023. Can large language models reason about program invariants?

Haoye Tian, Weiqi Lu, Tsz On Li, Xunzhu Tang, Shing-Chi Cheung, Jacques Klein, and Tegawendé F. Bissyandé. 2023. Is chatgpt the ultimate programming assistant – how far is it?

Chunqiu Steven Xia, Yuxiang Wei, and Lingming Zhang. 2023. Automated program repair in the era of large pre-trained language models. In 2023 IEEE/ACM 45th International Conference on Software Engineering (ICSE), pages 1482–1494.

Chunqiu Steven Xia and Lingming Zhang. 2022. Less training, more repairing please: revisiting automated program repair via zero-shot learning. In Proceedings of the 30th ACM Joint European Software Engineering Conference and Symposium on the Foundations of Software Engineering, pages 959–971.

He Ye, Matias Martinez, Xiapu Luo, Tao Zhang, and Martin Monperrus. 2022. Selfapr: Self-supervised program repair with test execution diagnostics. In Proceedings of the 37th IEEE/ACM International Conference on Automated Software Engineering, pages 1–13.

A Different Prompt Types

A.1 Error Prompt

```
### Provide a fix for the buggy function.
### Buggy Function:
def sort_age(lst):
    return lst.sort(key = lambda x: x[1])

### Failing Test Case:
 Traceback (most recent call last):
  File "temp.py", line 13, in <module>
    result = sort_age([('F', 18), ('M', 23), ('F', 19), ('M', 30)]); assert result == [('M', 30), ('M', 23), ('F', 19), ('F', 18)], 'Expected [(\'M\', 30), (\'M\', 23), (\'F\', 19), (\'F\', 18)] but got %s' % result
AssertionError: Expected [('M', 30), ('M', 23), ('F', 19), ('F', 18)] but got None

```

A.2 Trace Prompt

```
### Provide a fix for the buggy function.
### Buggy Function:
def sort_age(lst):
    return lst.sort(key = lambda x: x[1])

### Failing Test Case:
 Traceback (most recent call last):
  File "temp.py", line 13, in <module>
    result = sort_age([('F', 18), ('M', 23), ('F', 19), ('M', 30)]); assert result == [('M', 30), ('M', 23), ('F', 19), ('F', 18)], 'Expected [(\'M\', 30), (\'M\', 23), (\'F\', 19), (\'F\', 18)] but got %s' % result
AssertionError: Expected [('M', 30), ('M', 23), ('F', 19), ('F', 18)] but got None

### Function Execution Trace:
Source path:... temp.py
Starting var:.. lst = [('F', 18), ('M', 23), ('F', 19), ('M', 30)]
call        10 def sort_age(lst):
line        11     return lst.sort(key = lambda x: x[1])
Modified var:.. lst = [('F', 18), ('F', 19), ('M', 23), ('M', 30)]
return      11     return lst.sort(key = lambda x: x[1])
Return value:.. None
```

A.3 Collated Prompt

```
### Provide a fix for the buggy function, annotated with its execution trace of the below failing test case.
### Buggy Function (execution states indicated via inline comments):
# Starting var:.. lst = [('F', 18), ('M', 23), ('F', 19), ('M', 30)]
def sort_age(lst): # Call def sort_age(lst):
  lst.sort(key=lambda x: x[1],reverse=True) # Modified var:.. lst = [('M', 30), ('M', 23), ('F', 19), ('F', 18)]
  print(lst) # Return   print(lst)
  # Return value:.. None

### Failing Test Case:
[('M', 30), ('M', 23), ('F', 19), ('F', 18)]
Traceback (most recent call last):
  File "temp.py", line 14, in <module>
    result = sort_age([('F', 18), ('M', 23), ('F', 19), ('M', 30)]); assert result == [('M', 30), ('M', 23), ('F', 19), ('F', 18)], 'Expected [(\'M\', 30), (\'M\', 23), (\'F\', 19), (\'F\', 18)] but got %s' % result
AssertionError: Expected [('M', 30), ('M', 23), ('F', 19), ('F', 18)] but got None
```

A.4 OPT Prompt

```

### Provide a fix for the buggy function.
### Buggy Function:
def sort_age(lst):
  lst.sort(key=lambda x: x[1],reverse=True)
  print(lst)

```

```
### Failing Test Case:
 [('M', 30), ('M', 23), ('F', 19), ('F', 18)]
Traceback (most recent call last):
  File "temp.py", line 15, in <module>
    result = sort_age([('F', 18), ('M', 23), ('F', 19), ('M', 30)]); assert result == [('M', 30),
    ↪ ('M', 23), ('F', 19), ('F', 18)], 'Expected [(\'M\', 30), (\'M\', 23), (\'F\', 19), (\'F\',
    ↪ 18)] but got %s' % result
AssertionError: Expected [('M', 30), ('M', 23), ('F', 19), ('F', 18)] but got None
### Function Execution Trace:Source path: temp.py
Function: sort_age(lst)
Input: lst = [('F', 18), ('M', 23), ('F', 19), ('M', 30)]
Line 12: Sorted list based on age in descending order
Updated lst: [('M', 30), ('M', 23), ('F', 19), ('F', 18)]
Line 13: Printed sorted list
Return: None
```

B Rationale behind prompt choice and other prompts considered.

In our preliminary experiment error-based prompts always performed better than program-only prompts. Hence, we use Error Prompts as a point of comparison for Trace Prompts, foregoing prompts only containing the buggy program. Furthermore, we explored the option of including all failing test cases in the same prompt, however that did not provide a lift compared to a single test case, and overall performed slightly worse. We hypothesize multiple test cases could be more helpful for program generation to help define the space of valid solutions, whereas in APR the buggy function itself provides a bulk of information for fixing a bug, and a single failing test case, while inexhaustive, is generally sufficient for setting the LLM on the right path to finding a fix. The use of few-shot prompts, while feasible for improving the accuracy of error-based prompts, is problematic for traces as it can greatly increase the overall length of the prompt, potentially exceeding the 8k context window.

C Comparison of Refactory Fixes Generated by GPT 3.5 for Error and Trace Prompts

```
### Provide a fix for the buggy function.
### Buggy Function:
def sort_age(lst):
    return lst.sort(key = lambda x: x[1])

### Failing Test Case:
 Traceback (most recent call last):
  File "temp.py", line 13, in <module>
    result = sort_age([('F', 18), ('M', 23), ('F', 19), ('M', 30)]); assert result == [('M', 30),
    ↪ ('M', 23), ('F', 19), ('F', 18)], 'Expected [(\'M\', 30), (\'M\', 23), (\'F\', 19), (\'F\',
    ↪ 18)] but got %s' % result
AssertionError: Expected [('M', 30), ('M', 23), ('F', 19), ('F', 18)] but got None

### Function Execution Trace:
Source path:... temp.py
Starting var:.. lst = [('F', 18), ('M', 23), ('F', 19), ('M', 30)]
call        10 def sort_age(lst):
line        11     return lst.sort(key = lambda x: x[1])
Modified var:.. lst = [('F', 18), ('F', 19), ('M', 23), ('M', 30)]
return      11     return lst.sort(key = lambda x: x[1])
Return value:.. None
```

```
# GPT 3.5 EP Response:
'''The issue with the buggy function is that
the `lst.sort()` method modifies the list
in-place and does not return a sorted list.
To fix this, we can modify the function to
first sort the list using `lst.sort()` and
then return the sorted list by simply
returning the original list `lst`. Here's
the fixed function:'''

def sort_age(lst):
    lst.sort(key=lambda x: x[1])
    return lst

'''Now, running the failing test case
should give us the expected output:'''
```

```
# GPT 3.5 TP Response:
'''To fix the buggy function, we need to make
two changes: 1. Instead of returning the
result of the `lst.sort()` method, we need
to return the sorted list itself. 2. We need
to sort the list in descending order by
modifying the sorting key lambda function to
`lambda x: -x[1]`. Here is the fixed version
of the function:'''

def sort_age(lst):
    lst.sort(key=lambda x: -x[1])
    return lst

'''This will return the correct sorted
↪ list.'''
```

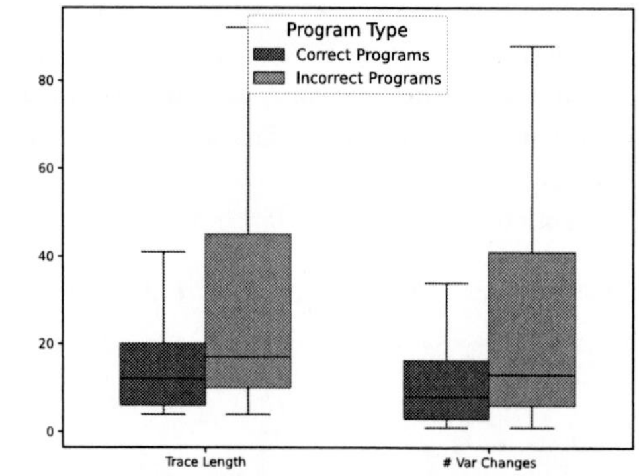

(a) HumanEval-Java Dataset with GPT-3.5

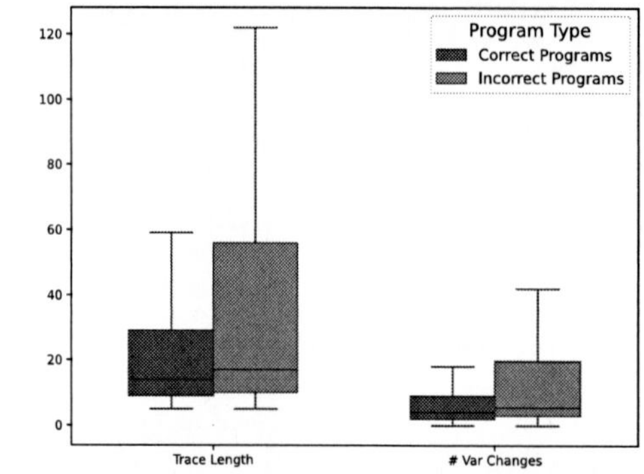

(b) RunBugRun Dataset with GPT-3.5

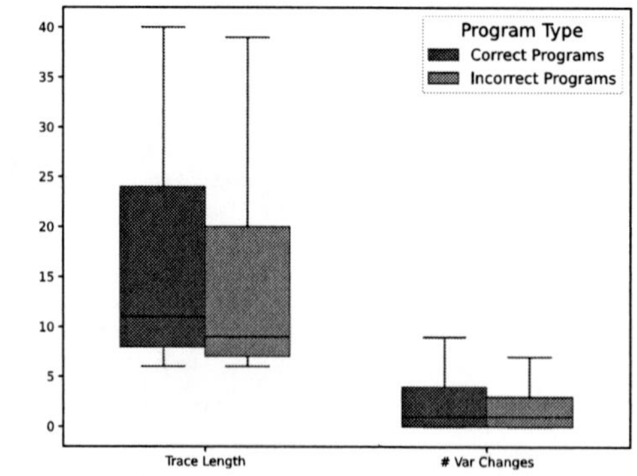

(c) Refactory Dataset with GPT-3.5

Figure 5: Distributions of trace lengths and variable changes across correct vs incorrect program fixes generated by GPT-3.5

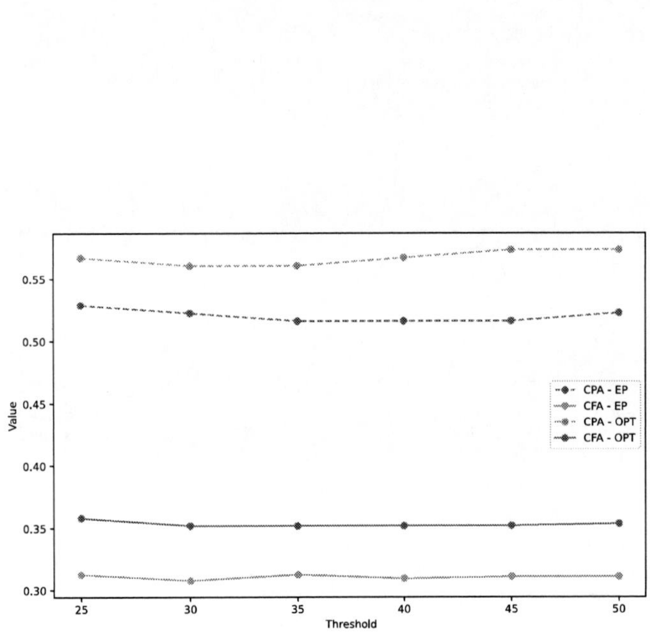

(a) HumanEval-Java Dataset with GPT-3.5

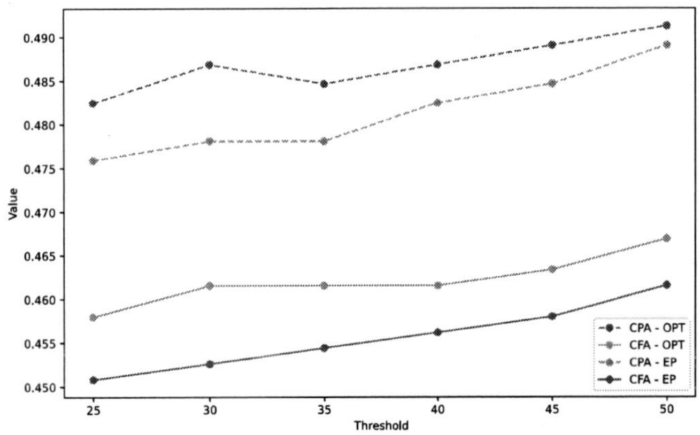

(b) RunBugRun Dataset with GPT-3.5

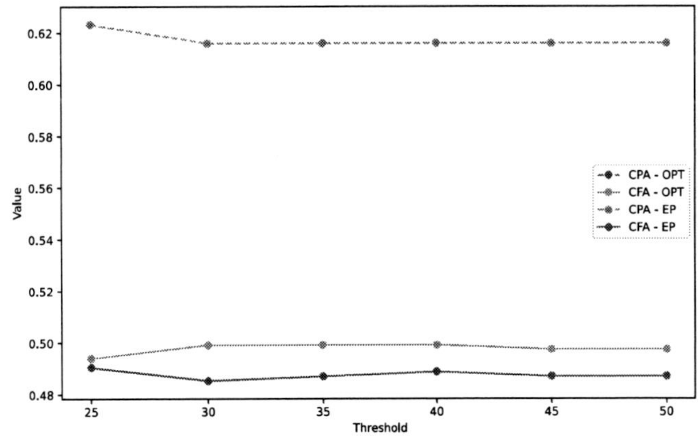

(c) Refactory Dataset with GPT-3.5

Figure 6: Ablations of trace length threshold values used with the routing strategy for GPT3.5

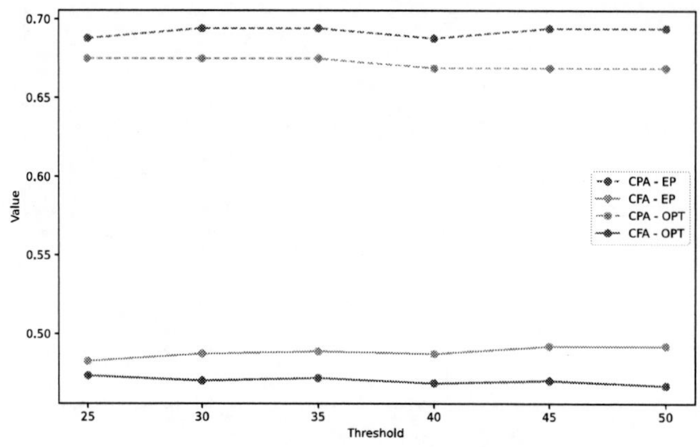

(a) HumanEval-Java Dataset with GPT-4

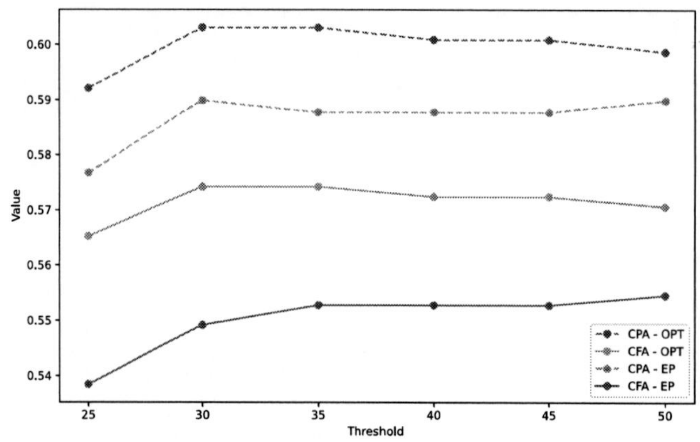

(b) RunBugRun Dataset with GPT-4

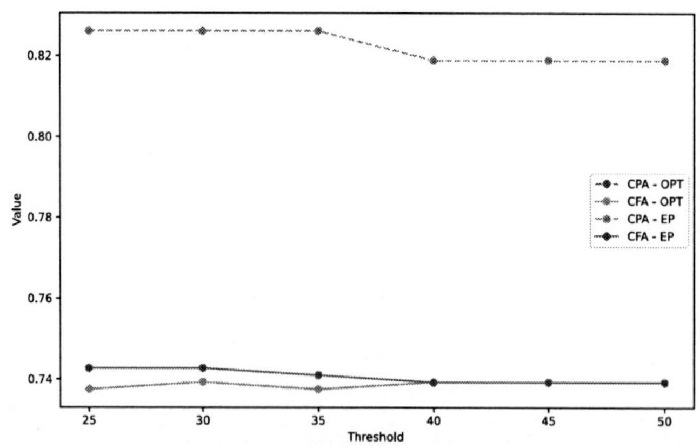

(c) Refactory Dataset with GPT-4

Figure 7: Ablations of trace length threshold values used with the routing strategy for GPT-4.

C.1 Trace Understanding Probing Studies Full Results and Qualitative Findings

Table 3: Trace Understanding Probing Results

Dataset partition (#prompts)	Trace Collating	Trace Prediction
Refactory reference (34)	88%	50%
Refactory fail (38)	79%	26%
Geeks for geeks (300)	45%	15%

We manually reviewed a sample of diffs to gain qualitative insights of LLM trace manipulation behavior. Most discrepancies between ground truth and either LLM-collated or predicted traces are due to additions or deletions of variable modifications from the trace. In particular, within loops, the LLM tends to either miss or add extra variable modifications., which could hit at a potential limitation in the depth of reasoning and memory. In the task of trace prediction from scratch, the second most erratic behavior is around predicting function returns, which can amount to both wrong value and wrong placement within the execution flow. Interestingly, in addition to generating traces, the LLM consistently attempts to fix code formatting, and in many cases optimizes away code branches not taken. Similarly, in the presence of execution failures, the LLM is unreliable at correctly predicting exceptions – either predicting exception types not commonly raised by a given operation, missing the exception altogether or, in some cases, patching the code to prevent an exception. Miscellaneous observed other discrepancies are due to the LLM adding superfluous commentary, trace formatting mistakes and hallucination of object hashes and other literals.

C.2 Prompts for Predicting and Collating Traces

```
### Given a function and its invocation, trace the function's execution, using inline comments in the format shown in the below examples:
### Example program:
def unique_day(day, possible_birthdays):
    count = 0
    for birthday in possible_birthdays:
        if birthday[1] == day:
            count += 1
    return count == 1

### Example invocation:
unique_day(day = '1', possible_birthdays = (('January', '1'), ('February', '1')))

### Example traced program:
# Starting var:.. day = '1'
# Starting var:.. possible_birthdays = (('January', '1'), ('February', '1'))
def unique_day(day, possible_birthdays):
    count = 0 # New var:....... count = 0
    for birthday in possible_birthdays: # New var:....... birthday = ('January', '1')
    # Modified var:.. birthday = ('February', '1')
        if birthday[1] == day:
            count += 1 # Modified var:.. count = 1
            # Modified var:.. count = 2
    return count == 1
    # Return value:.. False

### Example program with exception:
def remove_extras(lst):
    result = []
    for i in lst and not result:
        result += result + i
    return result

### Example invocation with exception:
remove_extras(lst = [3, 4, 5, 1, 3])

### Example traced program with exception:
# Starting var:.. lst = [3, 4, 5, 1, 3]
def remove_extras(lst):
    result = [] # New var:....... result = []
    for i in lst and not result: # Exception:..... TypeError: 'bool' object is not iterable
        result += result + i
    return result

### Valid traces types the following: 'Starting var', 'Modified var', 'New var', 'Return value', 'Exception'. Do not insert any other comments.

### Program:
def search(x, seq):
    for i in range(len(seq)):
        if x <= seq[i]:
            return i
    return len(seq)
### Invocation:
search(-100, ())

```

```
### Given a function and its execution trace, can you align each element in the trace with the corresponding line in the program, using the format
↪ shown in the below examples:
### Example program:
def unique_day(day, possible_birthdays):
    count = 0
    for birthday in possible_birthdays:
        if birthday[1] == day:
            count += 1
    return count == 1

### Example trace:
Source path:... temp.py
Starting var:.. day = '1'
Starting var:.. possible_birthdays = (('January', '1'), ('February', '1'))
call         10 def unique_day(day, possible_birthdays):
line         11     count = 0
New var:....... count = 0
line         12     for birthday in possible_birthdays:
New var:....... birthday = ('January', '1')
line         13         if birthday[1] == day:
line         14             count += 1
Modified var:.. count = 1
line         12     for birthday in possible_birthdays:
Modified var:.. birthday = ('February', '1')
line         13         if birthday[1] == day:
line         14             count += 1
Modified var:.. count = 2
line         12     for birthday in possible_birthdays:
line         15     return count == 1
return       15     return count == 1
Return value:.. False

### Example aligned:
# Starting var:.. day = '1'
# Starting var:.. possible_birthdays = (('January', '1'), ('February', '1'))
def unique_day(day, possible_birthdays):
    count = 0 # New var:....... count = 0
    for birthday in possible_birthdays: # New var:....... birthday = ('January', '1')
    # Modified var:.. birthday = ('February', '1')
        if birthday[1] == day:
            count += 1 # Modified var:.. count = 1
            # Modified var:.. count = 2
    return count == 1
    # Return value:.. False

### Example program with exception:
def remove_extras(lst):
    result = []
    for i in lst and not result:
        result += result + i
    return result

### Example trace with exception:
Source path:... temp.py
Starting var:.. lst = [3, 4, 5, 1, 3]
call         10 def remove_extras(lst):
line         11     result = []
New var:....... result = []
line         12     for i in lst and not result:
exception    12     for i in lst and not result:
Exception:..... TypeError: 'bool' object is not iterable
Call ended by exception

### Example aligned with exception:
# Starting var:.. lst = [3, 4, 5, 1, 3]
def remove_extras(lst):
    result = [] # New var:....... result = []
    for i in lst and not result: # Exception:..... TypeError: 'bool' object is not iterable
        result += result + i
    return result

### Note aligned versions only include capitalized entries from the trace. Do not insert any other comments.

### Program:
def search(x, seq):
    for i in range(len(seq)):
        if x <= seq[i]:
            return i
    return len(seq)
### Trace:
Source path:... temp.py
Starting var:.. x = 42
Starting var:.. seq = (-5, 1, 3, 5, 7, 10)
call         10 def search(x, seq):
line         11     for i in range(len(seq)):
New var:....... i = 0
line         12         if x <= seq[i]:
line         11     for i in range(len(seq)):
Modified var:.. i = 1
line         12         if x <= seq[i]:
line         11     for i in range(len(seq)):
Modified var:.. i = 2
line         12         if x <= seq[i]:
line         11     for i in range(len(seq)):
Modified var:.. i = 3
line         12         if x <= seq[i]:
line         11     for i in range(len(seq)):
Modified var:.. i = 4
line         12         if x <= seq[i]:
line         11     for i in range(len(seq)):
Modified var:.. i = 5
line         12         if x <= seq[i]:
line         11     for i in range(len(seq)):
line         14     return len(seq)
return       14     return len(seq)
Return value:.. 6
```

C.3 Qualitative Examples of Trace Prediction Errors

```
# Starting var:.. lst = [3, 4, 5, 1, 3]
def remove_extras(lst):
    i = 0 # New var:....... i = 0
    while i < len(lst):
        j = i + 1 # New var:....... j = 1
        # Modified var:.. j = 2
        # Modified var:.. j = 3
        while j < len(lst):
            if lst[i] == lst[j]:
                lst = lst[:j] + lst[j+1:] # Modified var:.. lst = [3, 4, 5, 1]
            j += 1 # Modified var:.. j = 2
            # Modified var:.. j = 3
            # Modified var:.. j = 4
            # Modified var:.. j = 5
            # Modified var:.. j = 3
            # Modified var:.. j = 4
            # Modified var:.. j = 4
        i += 1 # Modified var:.. i = 1
        # Modified var:.. i = 2
        # Modified var:.. i = 3
        # Modified var:.. i = 4
    return lst # Return value:.. [3, 4, 5, 1]
```

```
# Starting var:.. lst = [3, 4, 5, 1, 3]
def remove_extras(lst):
    i = 0 # New var:....... i = 0
    while i < len(lst):
        j = i + 1 # New var:....... j = 1
# Modified var:.. j = 2
# Modified var:.. j = 3
# Modified var:.. j = 4
# Modified var:.. j = 5
        while j < len(lst):
            if lst[i] == lst[j]:
                lst = lst[:j] + lst[j+1:] # Modified var:.. lst = [3, 4, 5, 1]
            j += 1
        i += 1 # Modified var:.. i = 1
# Modified var:.. i = 2
# Modified var:.. i = 3
# Modified var:.. i = 4
    return lst # Return value:.. [3, 4, 5, 1]


```

Figure 8: Example of erroneous variable modifications within a nested loop (Ground truth – left, prediction – right)

```
# Starting var:.. date = '3'
# Starting var:.. possible_birthdays = (('January', '1'), ('January', '2'))
def unique_day(date, possible_birthdays):
    if date in possible_birthdays[1]:
        return False
    else:
        return True # Return value:.. True
```

```
# Starting var:.. date = '3'
# Starting var:.. possible_birthdays = (('January', '1'), ('January', '2'))
def unique_day(date, possible_birthdays):
    if date in possible_birthdays[1]:
        return True # Return value:.. True
    else:
        return False
```

Figure 9: Example of wrong return value placement and code modification. (Ground truth – left, prediction – right)

```
# Starting var:.. lst = [('M', 23), ('F', 19), ('M', 30)]
def sort_age(lst):
    return lst.sort(key = lambda x: x[1], reverse = True) # Modified var:.. lst = [('M', 30), ('M', 23), ('F', 19)]
    # Return value:.. None
```

```
# Starting var:.. lst = [('M', 23), ('F', 19), ('M', 30)]
def sort_age(lst):
    return lst.sort(key = lambda x: x[1], reverse = True) # Return value:.. None
# Exception:..... AttributeError: 'NoneType' object has no attribute 'sort'
```

Figure 10: Example of a falsely predicted exception. (Ground truth – left, prediction – right)

```
# Starting var:.. lst = [('F', 19)]
def sort_age(lst):
    sort1 = [] # New var:....... sort1 = []
    while lst:
        largest = lst[0][1] # New var:.......
        ↪ largest = 19
        if i[1] > largest: # Exception:.....
        ↪ NameError: name 'i' is not defined
            largest = i[1]
        lst.remove(i)
        sort1.append(i)
    return sort1
```

```
# Starting var:.. lst = [('F', 19)]
def sort_age(lst):
    sort1 = [] # New var:....... sort1 = []
    while lst:
        largest = lst[0][1] # New var:.......
        ↪ largest = 19
        for i in lst: # New var:....... i =
        ↪ ('F', 19)
            if i[1] > largest:
                largest = i[1]
        lst.remove(i) # Modified var:.. lst =
        ↪ []
        sort1.append(i) # Modified var:..
        ↪ sort1 = [('F', 19)]
    return sort1 # Return value:.. [('F', 19)]
```

Figure 11: Example of a code modification to fix an exception. (Ground truth – left, prediction – right)

A Novel Multi-Document Retrieval Benchmark: Journalist Source-Selection in Newswriting

Alexander Spangher*[1], Tenghao Huang*[1], Yiqin Huang*[2], Lucas Spangher[3], Sewon Min[2], Mark Dredze[4]

[1]University of Southern California, [2]University of California, Berkeley, [3]Google Research, [4]Johns Hopkins University

{spangher, tenghaoh}@usc.edu, {yiqinhuang, sewonm}@berkeley.edu, spangher@google.com mdredze@cs.jhu.edu

Abstract

Multi-document retrieval approaches often overlook the ways different retrievals complement each other when addressing complex queries. In this work, we study journalist source selection in news article writing and examine the *discourse roles* that different sources serve when paired together, finding that discourse function (not simply informational content) is an important component of source usage. We introduce a novel IR task to benchmark how well language models can reason about this narrative process. We extract a journalist's initial query and the sources they used from news articles and aim to recover the sources that support this query. Then, we demonstrate that large language models (LLMs) can be employed in multi-step query planning, identifying informational gaps and enhancing retrieval performance, but current approaches to interleave queries fall short. By training auxiliary discourse planners and incorporating this information into LLMs, we enhance query planning, achieving a *significant* 5% improvement in precision and a 2% increase in F1 score over the previous SOTA, all while maintaining recall.

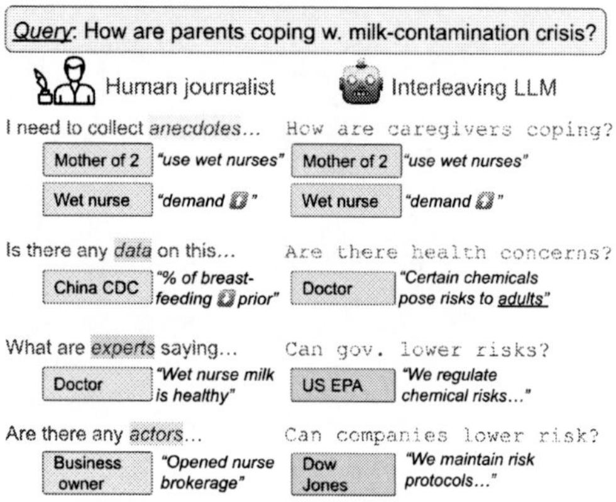

Figure 1: We present a new multi-document retrieval task: source-finding for journalism. Shown above is a complex query, extracted from news articles. On the left are the sources the journalist used to support the query, each annotated with their discourse role. Shown on the right are the queries issued by an LLM to our sandbox retrieval environment, and the sources retrieved. Although initially retrieving the same sources that the journalist used (green) the LLM soon meanders and departs from the original query, retrieving irrelevant sources (red).

1 Introduction

Tasks in information retrieval (IR) traditionally focus on retrieving documents based on factual relevance to queries (Manning, 2008), even in approaches that incorporate multi-document retrieval objectives (Zhai et al., 2015; Yu et al., 2023). This overlooks the *discourse* function that different sources of information play in addressing complex queries (Hearst, 2009). Across a variety of communicative domains – e.g. storytelling (Bruner, 1991), education (Egan, 1989) and journalism (Tuchman, 1978) – *humans* synthesize information from multiple sources to fulfill different narrative roles. For example, in news articles, it is not enough to cover different subtopics (Zhai et al., 2015): journalists bring together experts, witnesses, and authorities (Spangher et al., 2024a). Together, these sources tell a more complete story (Van Dijk, 1998).

Building off this insight, we introduce a novel IR task that requires us to retrieve multiple documents to support complex queries the way a *human* would retrieve them. Specifically, given (1) a dataset of news articles, (2) the initial queries guiding each news article, and (3) sources extracted from all articles, *our task is to retrieve the ground-truth set of sources a journalist chose for the article*. Successfully addressing this requires reasoning about the roles and contributions of each source within a narrative context (Schank and Abelson, 1977).

We start by testing an *interleaving retrieval approach* to (Trivedi et al., 2023) address this task, as shown in Figure 1. In this approach, an LLM

Proceedings of the 4th International Workshop on Knowledge-Augmented Methods for Natural Language Processing (KnowledgeNLP'25), pages 180–204
May 3, 2025

is used to iteratively: (1) issue queries to a retriever (2) reason about the sources returned (3) issue follow-up queries. *However, human validation shows that these interleaved queries frequently repeat, meander, or degenerate, ultimately failing to capture the diversity of sources present in human writing (Section 5).*

We hypothesize that a higher-level planner can guide the interleaving process towards diversity while staying focused on the query. For example, based off the example in Figure 1, we would like a higher-level planner to predict: *"this query is likely to answered by anecdotes, data, experts and actors"* – we can then use this plan to guide interleaving steps. To make training such a planner tractable, we first constrain the space of possible plans: we do this by developing a novel discourse schema (described in Section 2.2). With this lower-dimensional planning space in hand, we train a high accuracy autoregressive planner.

Finally, we introduce a novel retrieval method called *Planned Interleaved Retrieval (PIR)* to utilize retrieval plans in an interleaving fashion. PIR uses discourse labels in three ways: (1) *querier:* The LLM is given the discourse label for each interleaved query in the prompt. (2) *retriever:* The retrieval database is segmented based on discourse roles. (3) *re-ranker:* The results are reranked within each discourse segment. Taken together, we find that PIR increases retrieval precision by 5% and improves F1 score by 2%.

In summary, our contributions are threefold:

- We present a novel IR task grounded in observed sources curated by journalists. This task benchmarks our ability to reason about the different information types that contribute to comprehensive narratives.
- Through extensive analysis, we demonstrate how various sources contribute different elements to a narrative, offering unique viewpoints and fulfilling specific roles within the story's discourse structure. This understanding gives us insights into why certain sources are used together and how they collectively enhance the narrative.
- We introduce a novel method, *Planned Interleaved Retrieval*, and demonstrate that planning can be used to guide a multi-step, interleaved querying process. Incorporating discourse into the retrieval process, we show, significantly improves performance on the task.

Although we focus on news, our focus discourse in retrieval is flexible, and we have *offered a vision of how retrieval might incorporate higher-level planning structures.* We seek not only to enhance IR systems' ability to meet complex user needs, but also contribute to a deeper understanding of how source-inclusion occurs in narrative structures.

2 Task and Dataset Creation

To set up our multi-document retrieval task, we wish to create *a large retrieval database where multiple "documents" are labeled as ground-truth for answering each query.* Obtaining gold labels in journalism, though, is challenging: news is experts' domain that is difficult to crowdsource. So, to construct our task, we *reverse-engineer* the *text* of finished news articles, as described below.

2.1 Dataset Creation

For each news article, we extract two items: (1) a query describing the initial question answered by the journalist and (2) the set of informational sources used by the journalist. The queries serve as the input to our retrieval problem, while the text of each source serves as the ground truth matching "document" for each query. Following the definitions in Spangher et al. (2023), sources can be people (e.g., individuals interviewed or issuing statements), documents (e.g., studies, legal documents), or datasets. We use a dataset of articles released by Spangher et al. (2024b), which includes 380,000 news articles covering business press releases. From this dataset, we sample 50,000 articles and their corresponding press releases. *Press release coverage is a practically useful domain, because press-releases coverage is a necessary and time-sensitive part of business coverage (Petridis et al., 2023).*

Query Generation We provide an LLM with both the press release and the corresponding news article, asking it to generate a query that might describe an initial question the journalist had upon reading the press release, which led them to write the article.

Source Extraction First, we identify all informational sources in each news article using models trained by Spangher et al. (2023). Then, we use Llama-3.1-70B[1] to extract, for each source, a stand-alone packet of information provided by that source[2] "Standalone" means that we can accurately identify the source later in the retrieval database. In total, we extract 400,000 sources, averaging approximately 8.3 sources per document.

2.2 Schema Generation

As described in Section 1, we seek to create a low-dimensional schema to describe our sources (in order to ground our planner). We describe that process now. Inspired by Pham et al. (2024), we first ask an LLM to generate descriptive labels for the discourse role of each source, based on its source extraction. This allows for a broad superset of labels (examples are shown in the Appendix, Table 10.). Then, we cluster these labels by (1) annotating pairs of labels with similarity judgments using an LLM[3], (2) using these annotations to train an SBERT embedding model (Reimers and Gurevych, 2019a), and (3) clustering these embeddings using k-means. We identify eight distinct clusters that represent different narrative roles (e.g., "Main Actor," "Expert" "Background Info"). Definitions for each discourse role are shown in the Appendix, Table 5. Additionally, we ask the LLM to label the centrality of the source: "High" (the source is crucial to the narrative), "Medium" (the source plays a significant role but is not necessary) and "Low" (the source could be easily replaced with another source). We show the breakdown of Discourse Roles by Centrality in Figure 2, and give additional analysis in the Appendix.

2.3 Data Validation

Query and Source Extraction Validation First, we present two professional journalists a sample of 150 queries and ask them if these queries (1) contain the appropriate level of background information that an experienced journalist would have, and (2) reflect reasonable starting-points for stories. The journalists confirm 95% of our queries meet these criteria. Next, the journalists manually annotate a set of 396 sources using pyramid summarization evaluation (Nenkova et al., 2007): they count the informational units present in each of extracted source and then examine the news article to count the units of information attributable to that source. Overall, we find that 87% of units in source summaries correspond to units expressed in the original news article. We also manually validate whether the information in each source stands on its own or if there are unclear coreferences. In 80% of our sources, we are satisfied with the level of detail.

Discourse Label	%	Discourse Label	%
Main Actor	19.0%	Data	10.2%
Background Info.	18.9%	Confirmation	9.2%
Counterpoint	11.3%	Analysis	7.8%
Anecdotes	10.8%	Broadening	1.6%
Expert	10.5%	Subject	0.7%

Table 1: Distribution of Discourse Types in News Articles. 'Main Actor' and 'Background Info.' are the most common, and 'Subject' the least common.

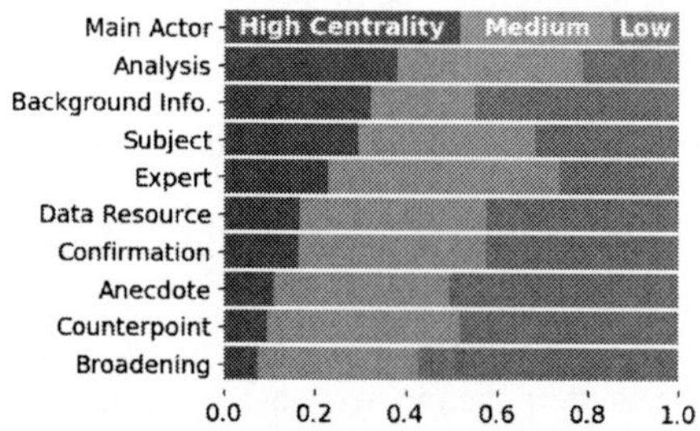

Figure 2: Proportion of sources within each discourse role that occupy High, Medium or Low Centrality in their stories.

Discourse Schema Validation To validate the reliability of these labels, we ask the same two expert journalists to manually annotate the 396 sources with labels from our schema. The journalists achieve a high inter-annotator agreement rate (Cohen's $\kappa = 0.75$) as well as a high agreement rate with our applied labels ($\kappa = 0.64$), indicating substantial agreement (Cohen, 1960).

3 Analysis

In order to better understand our dataset, we conduct a series of analyses to show how sources are used in news writing by journalists. We express our findings as three primary insights.

Insight #1: Diversity and perspective alone do not characterize source inclusion Diversity is a common threads in multi-document retrieval: the underlying assumption is that combin-

[1] https://huggingface.co/meta-llama/Meta-Llama-3.1-70B-Instruct/

[2] This includes: describing resolving all coreferences and stating the full names of places, people, and events.

[3] Specifically, whether two different narrative roles generations are substantially the same or not.

ing diverse sources leads to a more comprehensive retrieval (Carbonell and Goldstein, 1998; Allan, 2003; Clarke et al., 2008). However, we observe that, in news writing, while many sources are chosen for diverse information, others are chosen specifically to confirm facts. For example, ∼10% of sources play a Confirmation role, as in Table 1. We show more analysis in Appendix B.

What other theories exist to explain source-selection criteria in journalism? Gans (1979) suggests that supporting and opposing viewpoints are selected to give a balanced narrative, suggesting that *stance* is a primary driver for source selection. We conduct an analysis of sources' stances in the narrative, using Ma et al. (2024)'s stance-detection method[4]. We find that while some sources do fit into the "for" and "against" categories, this is not universally the case. Over 30% of sources take an informational perspective *without explicitly supporting or opposing any viewpoint*[5]. This suggests that source selection is more nuanced than the binary "for and against" model implies. Journalists often include sources to provide context, background information, or expert analysis, which may not directly relate to a polarized viewpoint (Tuchman, 1978).

Insight #2: Certain Kinds of Stories Use Different Kinds of Sources Finally, we examine whether different types of news stories use sources differently. We manually identify different kinds of coverage: investigative reports, breaking news, etc. (see Appendix E.3 for a full list). We find that different kinds coverage tend to be dominated by different source discourse roles. For instance, investigative reports tend to include more "Expert Analysis" and "Background Information" sources, while event coverage focuses on "Main Actors" and "Eyewitnesses." Detailed analysis of these is provided in Appendix E.3, along with examples of stories. This analysis highlights that source selection is context-dependent and varies across different types of journalism. Understanding these patterns can inform the development of more sophisticated information retrieval systems that tailor source recommendations based on the story type.

Insight #3: Sources used in multiple documents tend to have the same discourse roles. We expected that sources would often be used in different roles in differet articles: for instance, in Story #1, a police officer might be a "Main Actor", in Story #2 the same police officer might used for "Background info." and in Story #3, for an "Anecdote".

We conduct an analysis on all named sources that we name-match across two or more articles and find that, on average, sources tend to be classified in the same role (sources have .43 gini impurity[6], .33 label inconsistency[7], .95 entropy and .55 diversity[8] across discourse roles). One possible explanation is that journalists observe how other journalists use sources, and use them similarly. This is a crucial insight: for simplicity, in the rest of the paper, we assume that sources' discourse role is only based on their original source-text.[9]

4 Discourse in Multi-Document Information Retrieval

Given our source and query dataset, described in Section 2, we now present our methodology for discourse-aware multi-document retrieval. Motivated by our findings in Section 3, we posit that incorporating discourse structures can significantly enhance the retrieval process. In Section 4.1, we discuss how discourse information can inform the retrieval process and in Section 4.2 we discuss ways to infer a story's discourse requirements.

4.1 Overview of *Planned Interleaved Retrieval*

Our retrieval framework consists of three main stages, illustrated in Figure 3: (1) Query Planning, (2) Discourse-Specific Indexing and Retrieval, and (3) Re-ranking. We describe each of these steps, focusing on how discourse roles can be involved.

Stage 1: Interleaved Querying In the first stage, we employ an LLM to generate queries $q_1, ...q_n$ sequentially in order to retrieve sources, as in Trivedi et al. (2023). Discourse-awareness in this stage means the LLM can reference the discourse role

[4]Ma et al. (2024) used Llama 3.1 with chain-of-thought prompts to detect stance; this scored highly on popular stance benchmarks. Specifically, we prompt the model to classify the stance of each source as "supporting," "opposing," or "neutral" with respect to the main event or topic of the article (see Appendix E.4 for the full prompt).

[5]Shown in Figure 9 in the Appendix

[6]Gini impurity is measured as $1 - \sum_i \left(\frac{l_i}{l_{total}}\right)^2$, where l_i is the count of label i and l_{total} is the sum of all label counts

[7]Inconsistency is defined as $1 - l_{max}/l_{total}$ where l_{max} is the label with the maximum count.

[8]Where diversity is defined as $l_{numunique}/l_{total}$

[9]We hold this constant to simplify computation. We acknowledge this is a limiting assumption, and in follow-up work we will remove that assumption. Allowing sources to adapt their discourse roles dynamically in response to novel, unseen queries is a crucial area for future research.

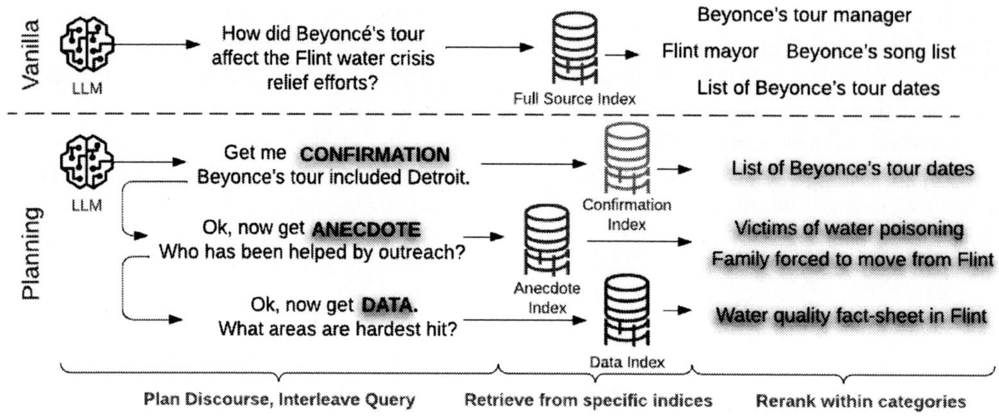

Figure 3: The three-stage discourse-aware retrieval process: (1) Discourse-aware query planning using an LLM with interleaving and discourse role planning, (2) querying discourse-specific indices, and (3) re-ranking retrieved documents within discourse categories.

of the source it desires to obtain in query round q_t while generating it's query (we will discuss in Section 4.2 how we infer these discourse roles).

Stage 2: Indexing and Retrieval Given a query, q_t, we then retrieve sources $s_1, ...s_k$ relevant to this query. Discourse-awareness in this stage means that the retrieval indices themselves are filtered to discourse roles of sources in our corpus. Traditional multi-document retrieval systems treat all documents equally (Voorhees and Tice, 1999), but our approach organizes the index into hierarchical, discourse-driven sub-indices. This stratification allows for more targeted retrieval. When the LLM generates a query for a particular discourse role, it is directed to the corresponding sub-index.

Stage 3: Re-ranking Finally, given a large set of sources $s_1, ...s_m$ retrieved in the prior steps, we re-rank them to surface the sources that are most relevant together. In this stage, discourse awareness means that we take the most relevant documents *within* each discourse category. This additional layer of categorization prioritizes documents that best fulfill the intended narrative role. We use a re-ranking model that incorporates both relevance and discourse compatibility, similar to the approach in Nogueira and Cho (2019).

4.2 Two Different Planning Approaches

As outlined in the previous section, we can incorporate discourse information at each stage in our retrieval process. However, left unexplained was how *we would infer* these discourse roles. Now we discuss the two approaches we take.

Approach #1: Sequential Planning Here, the query-generator is informed of the possible discourse categories, and is asked to pick the next discourse role that a story requires. In other words, at turn *t*, the LLM views prior $q_{1,...t-1}$ and discourse roles $d_{1,...t-1}$ of retrievals, and is asked to generate the next discourse role, d_t that the story requires.

By allowing an LLM to sequentially generate roles, we hypothesize that we can introduce a human-like planning ability – i.e. often humans do not know the exact discourse roles a story needs until they get deeper in (Sedorkin, 2015). However, this approach relies the LLM's inherent ability to reason independently about discourse roles without explicit guidance. Prior studies have shown that LLMs struggle with structural reasoning in complex tasks (Spangher et al., 2022), suggesting that this method may be less effective.

Approach #2: A-priori Planning In this approach, we train an auxiliary planner to predict the entire distribution of discourse roles the document will take, a-priori, based on the initial query. To do this, we cluster articles based on the distribution of source narrative roles, using K-means clustering with $k = 8$ clusters and train a `DistilBERT-base` classifier (Sanh et al., 2019) to *infer* which story cluster a query belongs to.

In other words, the a-prior planner predicts the proportion of each discourse role expected in the final document, based on the initial query. The predicted distribution is then provided to the LLM

Retriever	Discourse Strategy		Overall Results			Results by Centrality		
	Sequential	A-priori	Recall	Prec.	F1	High (F1)	Med. (F1)	Low (F1)
BM25 (Robertson and Walker, 1994)			0.00	0.00	0.00	0.00	0.00	0.00
DPR (Karpukhin et al., 2020)			13.98	9.12	11.04	14.42	6.82	5.68
Interleaving (Trivedi et al., 2023)			**25.81**	27.04	26.34	37.66	22.60	14.37
PIR	✓	–	24.07	25.27	24.60	33.88	21.28	14.05
	–	✓	25.49	31.61	28.04	**40.43**	22.17	14.32
	✓	✓	24.84	**33.15****	**28.12****	40.16	22.55	**14.77**
Oracle PIR	–	–	42.77	42.98	42.86	54.02	37.73	26.78

Table 2: We show retrieval strategies and methods in terms of Recall, Precision, F1 score. Each strategy uses multiple retrievers. with the Oracle strategy demonstrating the highest performance metrics. ** indicates significant increases at $p < .01$, obtained via bootstrap resampling ($b = 1,000$).

during the query planning phase[10] We train the auxiliary model on our dataset, achieving a macro F1 score of 0.72 in classifying queries into the correct discourse clusters. The average KL divergence between the predicted and true discourse distributions is 0.7, indicating a close approximation.

4.3 Experiment Setup

Retriever We use SFR[11]: a 7B text-embedding model developed by Salesforce AI Research that has demonstrated superior performance across multiple benchmarks. We choose SFR as a powerful, large instruction-tuned model in order to understand richer and more nuanced queries that we anticipate our task will require.

LLM As in Trivedi et al. (2023), an LLM is used to plan and reason about the next query to issue. As in the rest of the paper, we use Llama-3.1-70B.

Dataset We perform an 80/20 split for training and test sets. To construct the retrieval index, we aggregate all sources from both sets and organize them according to discourse role, such that each role is indexed separately. That is, for every query, a distinct retrieval index is created for each type.

Baselines (1) *BM25:* a widely-used probabilistic retrieval framework, calculating the relevance of documents to a query based on the frequency of query terms in each document. (2) *Dense Passage Retrieval (DPR)* (Karpukhin et al., 2020): *we fine-tune* a transformer-based model[12] to to effectively capture semantic similarities beyond keyword matching. Fine-tuned DPR allows us to test whether learned knowledge is more important than planning or reasoning. To finetune DPR, we build a training dataset that including negative samples for in-batch training (Karpukhin et al., 2020). For each positive pair of query q_j and its relevant sources s_j^+, we include n negative tools as negative samples. (3) *Interleaving:* we employ SFR with an identical setup to Trivedi et al. (2023) in order to test the ability of LLMs to reason about the needs of the query in the absence of discourse labels.

Oracle Finally, to differentiate the role of discourse from these two noisy discourse inference techniques, we test an oracle approach. In this approach, we provide the LLM with ground-truth discourse labels extracted during our analysis. By supplying the actual distribution of discourse roles present in the target documents, we assess how well the system can perform when it has perfect knowledge of the sources' discourse structure. Also, this highlights potential improvements in retrieval planning and reasoning mechanisms.

4.4 Results

Our main finding is that incorporating discourse labels helps us retrieve sources with significantly higher accuracy than baseline approaches (we find that these improvements are significant at $p < .01$ by running bootstrapped resamples with $b = 1,000$). As evidenced in Table 2, including discourse labels (with both **a-priori** and **sequential** strategies) elevates the F1 score from 26.34% to 28.12% compared with the baseline *Interleave*. Further, when incorporating oracle discourse information, the F1 score boosts up to 42.86%. This indicates that discourse awareness and planning can provide insights into query needs.

[10]Prompt example: "`We expect this document will contain 50% Background, 30% Expert Analysis, and 20% Main Actor information. Please choose the next discourse role you want to use.`"

[11]`https://huggingface.co/Salesforce/SFR-Embedding-2_R`

[12]`https://huggingface.co/sentence-transformers/all-MiniLM-L6-v2`

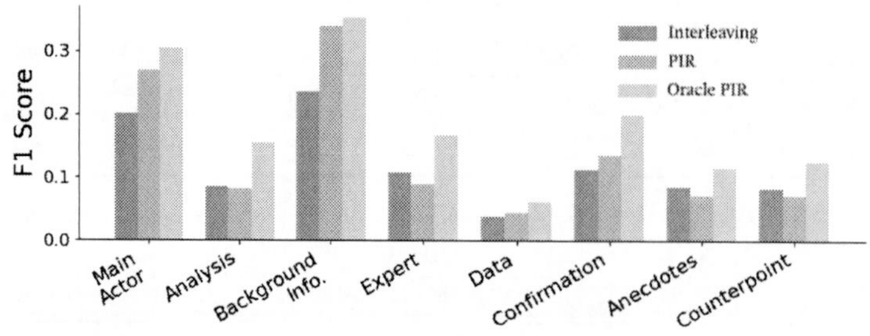

Figure 4: Retrieval accuracy scores, broken down by different discourse types. As can be seen, introducing my discourse planning has a greater impact on certain kinds of discourse categories (e.g. Main Actor and Background Info.) compared with other discourse types (e.g. "Experts", "Anecdotes" and "Counterpoint").

Secondly, and intriguingly, our results suggest that an a-prior planning-based approach has a more pronounced impact than sequential planning. According to the results in Table 2, employing a-priori planning *without* sequential planning[13] yields an F1 score of 28.04%. In contrast, combining both sequential *and* a-prior planning results in a slightly higher F1 score of 28.12%. The small difference between these two trials suggests that a-priori planning alone can substantially enhance retrieval effectiveness, potentially diminishing the incremental benefits introduced by sequential planning. This contrasts with recent results on more conventional QA-based IR tasks, where prompt-based planning strategies were shown to significantly enhance retrieval performances (Trivedi et al., 2023; Huang et al., 2024). These results suggest that our task possesses inherent differences. We do caveat our results with awareness that our a-priori planner was trained while our sequential planner relied on LLM pretraining (as did (Trivedi et al., 2023)). This suggests both that (1) a narrative-focused query objective is distinct from purely informational query tasks like those studied previously, and (2) an a-prior plan is useful in this task, indicating that templates exists that journalists follow.

5 Discussion

We investigate why incorporating the discourse aspects into the systems enhances machine's source retrieval ability above the *Interleaving* approach.

Vanilla Interleaving Tends to Meander To explain the subpar performance of *Interleaving*, which has shown state-of-the-art results on QA benchmarks, we examine multiple query threads, shown in Appendix A.1. Vanilla interleaving exhibits three notable failure modes. (1) Many queries generated by the planner tend to restate the same objectives or focus on overly narrow aspects of the broader topic without expanding into complementary dimensions (see Appendix A.1, Table 6). This restricts the planner's ability to explore the full range of sources that a humans typically consider (e.g. expert opinions, counterpoints, or data analysis), thus producing a less well-rounded article. (2) Paradoxically, while interleaving often remains closely aligned with the initial query's intent, it also suffers from a tendency to drift when progressing through subsequent queries. For instance, an initial focus on the societal consequences of an issue may eventually lead to highly specific and less generalizable topics that deviate from the core inquiry (e.g. in Figure 1 and Appendix A.1, Table 7). (3) Finally, even when the planner maintains alignment with the initial query, it often fails to explicitly request critical discourse roles, such as expert analyses or contrasting viewpoints (Appendix A.1, Table 8). Consequently, the output of vanilla interleaving lacks the depth and balance.

Varied Centrality Improvements As shown in Table 2, the retrieval system shows marked improvement in handling sources of varying centrality when informed by discourse roles, particularly with the oracle setup. For high centrality sources, the Micro-F1 score leaps from 37.66 to 54.02, indicating enhanced effectiveness in identifying and retrieving crucial sources. Similarly, for low centrality sources, the Micro-F1 score rises from 14.37 to 26.78, demonstrating the system's expanded capability to incorporate less central, yet informative perspectives into the narrative, thereby enriching the overall information retrieval process. The improvement from our planning strategies, we ob-

[13]In other words, we simply retrieve $k \times n$-rounds of candidates in the first round, without interleaving, and then re-rank according to the a-priori predicted discourse distribution

serve, originates from the enhanced retrieval of more central sources; this indicates that our planning strategies effectively identifies and prioritizes sources crucial for constructing detailed narratives. However, while the system excels at retrieving high centrality sources, there is room for improvement in capturing more medium and low centrality sources. Enhancing our planning to better include these sources could further enrich the comprehensiveness of the IR process.

Discourse Role F1 Analysis As shown in Figure 4, incorporating discourse role information significantly enhances retrieval performance across discourse roles. By accounting for the specific functions that sources play in constructing a narrative, the retrieval system is more adept at identifying and selecting *comprehensive* information. The consistent enhancements across diverse categories highlight the effectiveness of a discourse-aware approach, suggesting that a nuanced understanding of narrative structures is essential for optimizing retrieval outcomes in complex tasks such as multi-document source retrieval.

However, the selective improvements observed with our planning strategies indicate that while these strategies are beneficial, their effectiveness varies across different source categories. Significant gains are achieved in categories central to the narrative—such as Main Actor and Background Information—where the discourse roles are closely aligned with the main query and can be explicitly planned for. This suggests that planning strategies are most effective when the narrative role is straightforward and directly related to the primary focus of the query. In contrast, categories requiring nuanced understanding—such as Analysis, Expert, Anecdotes, and Counterpoint—exhibit less improvement, implying that current planning strategies may not fully capture the complexities inherent in these discourse roles. Consequently, further refinement of these strategies is necessary to enhance retrieval performance in categories that demand deeper contextual and interpretive analysis.

Retrieval Hyperparameters Our preliminary experiments reveal that the effectiveness of discourse-aware retrieval is sensitive to the choice of k, the number of documents retrieved per query. As shown in Figure 5 in the Appendix, the benefits of incorporating discourse information become more pronounced with larger k values. This is consistent with findings from Craswell et al. (2020), who note that re-ranking models have more impact when the initial retrieval set is large. We attempt different methods for learning the ideal k per query: we train a Poisson regression model using a simple Multilayer Perceptron (MLP) on SBERT embeddings (Reimers and Gurevych, 2019b). However, the model achieves a low Pearson correlation of $r = 0.35$ between the predicted and actual optimal k values. Overall, this additional planning step fails to measurably impact performance. We leave further steps to future work.

Future Work and Extensions While our current approach is specialized for journalistic source selection, we see the potential applicability to other domains like scientific literature and legal document retrieval. Adapting our method to these areas would involve redefining discourse categories relevant to the target domain, retraining discourse-role classifiers on domain-specific corpora, and validating with subject matter experts. Journalists often face time-constraints on the number of sources they can talk to, making news article analysis a particularly tractable domain to start in, but we anticipate that structured discursive frameworks common in these domains would particularly benefit from our planned retrieval methodology.

Additionally, we recognize the computational overhead introduced by large models such as Llama-3.1-70B and SFR-7B. In the future, we plan to explore smaller, distilled models and computationally efficient techniques, including knowledge distillation and quantization. Additionally, we look forward to testing additional baselines to validate our approach, such as token-level dense retrievers (Khattab and Zaharia, 2020; Santhanam et al., 2022) or in-context learning approaches (Zhao et al., 2021; Rubin et al., 2022).

6 Related Work

Traditional information retrieval (IR) frameworks primarily focus on finding individual documents that match factual relevance to a query (Manning, 2008). Extensions of these models for multi-document retrieval often target coverage or subtopic diversity, aiming to capture distinct angles of a topic to improve completeness (Carbonell and Goldstein, 1998; Allan, 2003; Clarke et al., 2008; Zhai et al., 2015). However, such methods typically overlook why sources are combined. In particular, they neglect how different documents fulfill complementary discourse functions—for example, how "expert opinions" versus "first-person accounts" each play unique roles in constructing a cohesive narrative (Hearst, 2009; Bruner, 1991; Egan, 1989).

Classical work suggests that human sense-making processes often organize multiple sources based on how those sources fit into a broader communicative structure (Tuchman, 1978; Schank and Abelson, 1977; Van Dijk, 1998). These insights pave the way for discourse-aware retrieval systems, which factor in narrative roles such as *main actors*, *background info*, or *expert analysis* when seeking relevant material. Early steps toward iterative or interleaving retrieval show promise for complex queries by harnessing large language models (LLMs) to generate sequential queries and refine results on-the-fly (Trivedi et al., 2023). Yet, these methods often lack explicit discourse planning, leading to overlapping or irrelevant retrievals.

Recent work in *LLM-based reasoning* have introduced methods such as *chain-of-thought* (Wei et al., 2022; Trivedi et al., 2023), which encourage models to articulate intermediate inferences improve multi-hop or compositional queries. While *interleaving IR* iteratively refines queries, they largely neglect explicit discourse roles. Our work addresses this gap by designing a discourse-driven selection paradigm, where roles like "expert opinion" or "background info" are explicitly modeled. We show how this lens significantly enriches the set of retrieved documents — an essential step toward tasks that value not just *what* sources provide, but *why* they are chosen.

7 Conclusion

In this work, we have introduced the concept of discourse in multi-document retrieval tasks, and have framed and introduced a novel task aimed at retrieving sources to assist journalists. We have shown that discourse planning can impact scores, and have introduced two different planners; one based on an LLM and the other based on a learned algorithm. We noted throughout the paper the numerous simplifying assumptions we made in order to implement our task, including: the lack of a trained sequential model, the reliance on ground-truth k and the assumption that sources would retain their initial discourse. We look in future work to more fully return and address these.

8 Limitations

8.1 Ethical Considerations

Our methodology relies on large-scale language models, which have known issues related to bias and fairness (Sheng et al., 2019; Bender et al., 2021). We take steps to mitigate these concerns by filtering training data for harmful content and evaluating the outputs for biased representations.

8.2 Reproducibility

We provide all code and data necessary to reproduce our experiments at [*GitHub repository link*], following the guidelines set by Pineau et al. (2021) for reproducible research in machine learning. While we provide our code and data in a public repository to promote reproducibility, the computational demands may prevent full replication by those with limited resources. Furthermore, some aspects of our work, particularly the a-priori planning strategy and the LLM's discourse role labeling, involve stochastic elements, which may lead to variations in the results when the models are retrained or fine-tuned on different hardware or datasets.

8.3 Implementation Details

The discourse role classifier and auxiliary planning model are trained with a learning rate of $2e^{-5}$ and batch size of 32.

8.4 Model Limitations

Our study, relying heavily on large language models (LLMs), presents inherent limitations in understanding complex narrative structures. While LLMs such as Llama-3.1-70B are effective at extracting and labeling discourse roles, their performance can be inconsistent when handling nuanced roles like "Anecdote" or "Expert." These roles often require deeper contextual knowledge and interpretative capabilities, which current models struggle to grasp fully. The sequential and a-priori planning strategies we employ only partially mitigate these limitations, leaving room for improvements, particularly in capturing low centrality sources.

8.5 Computational Budget

We conducted our experiments on a combination of BM25, Dense Passage Retrieval (DPR), and SFR-7B embedding models. The SFR model required significant computational resources due to its size (7B parameters). We employed a distributed cluster of 8 NVIDIA A100 GPUs for model training and testing. Fine-tuning the discourse role classifier and auxiliary planner models took approximately 72 hours on this hardware setup. Additionally, large-scale inference, especially with SFR and Llama-3.1-70B, added another 50 hours across multiple processes. This heavy reliance on high-computation hardware restricts the reproducibility of our results for researchers without access to similar resources.

8.6 Data and Annotator Limitations

Our dataset consists of 50,000 news articles sampled from a larger corpus of 380,000, but this sample size may not fully represent the diversity of journalism across various media outlets. Moreover, the annotations for discourse roles were generated using LLMs, and while we manually validated a subset of 50 documents, this represents only a small fraction of the dataset. We involved two professional journalists to assess the validity of our extracted queries and source roles, but this limited human annotation introduces the possibility of bias and errors not being sufficiently captured across the entire dataset.

8.7 Risks and Ethical Considerations

There are several risks associated with the use of LLMs in journalism-related tasks. Firstly, LLMs have known biases, which may inadvertently influence source retrieval, particularly when retrieving contentious or polarized information. Although we filtered the training data to remove harmful content, biases in the models remain a potential issue, especially in politically charged narratives or sensitive topics. Additionally, relying on automated systems for source selection in journalism introduces ethical concerns regarding the transparency of source curation, as these systems may favor certain sources or viewpoints without clear justification.

References

James Allan. 2003. Topic detection and tracking: event-based information organization. In *Topic Detection and Tracking*, pages 1–16. Springer.

Anonymous. 2023. Palm + rlhf: Training language models to follow instructions. arXiv:2308.xxxxx [cs.CL].

Emily M Bender, Timnit Gebru, Angelina McMillan-Major, and Shmargaret Shmitchell. 2021. On the dangers of stochastic parrots: Can language models be too big? *Proceedings of the 2021 ACM Conference on Fairness, Accountability, and Transparency*, pages 610–623.

Jerome Bruner. 1991. The narrative construction of reality. *Critical inquiry*, 18(1):1–21.

Sébastien Bubeck, Varun Chandrasekaran, Ronen Eldan, and et al. 2023. Sparks of artificial general intelligence: Early experiments with gpt-4. *arXiv preprint arXiv:2303.12712*.

Jaime Carbonell and Jade Goldstein. 1998. The use of mmr, diversity-based reranking for reordering documents and producing summaries. In *Proceedings of the 21st annual international ACM SIGIR conference on Research and development in information retrieval*, pages 335–336. ACM.

Charles LA Clarke, Mallik Kolla, Gordon V Cormack, Olga Vechtomova, Azin Ashkan, Stefan Büttcher, and Ian MacKinnon. 2008. Novelty and diversity in information retrieval evaluation. In *Proceedings of the 31st annual international ACM SIGIR conference on Research and development in information retrieval*, pages 659–666. ACM.

Jacob Cohen. 1960. A coefficient of agreement for nominal scales. *Educational and Psychological Measurement*, 20(1):37–46.

Nick Craswell, Bhaskar Mitra, Emine Yilmaz, Daniel Campos, and Ellen Voorhees. 2020. Overview of the trec 2019 deep learning track. In *Proceedings of the Twenty-Eighth Text REtrieval Conference (TREC 2019)*. NIST.

Antonia Creswell, Murray Shanahan, and et al. 2022. Selection-inference: Exploiting large language models for interpretable logical reasoning. *arXiv preprint arXiv:2205.09712*.

Kieran Egan. 1989. *Teaching as story telling: An alternative approach to teaching and curriculum in the elementary school*. University of Chicago Press.

Herbert J Gans. 1979. *Deciding What's News: A Study of CBS Evening News, NBC Nightly News, Newsweek, and Time*. Northwestern University Press.

Marti A Hearst. 2009. *Search user interfaces*. Cambridge university press.

Tenghao Huang, Dongwon Jung, and Muhao Chen. 2024. Planning and editing what you retrieve for enhanced tool learning. *ArXiv*, abs/2404.00450.

Gautier Izacard, Edouard Grave, and Armand Joulin. 2022. Few-shot learning with retrieval augmented language models. In *Proceedings of the 39th International Conference on Machine Learning (ICML)*.

Vladimir Karpukhin, Barlas Oguz, Sewon Min, Patrick Lewis, Ledell Wu, Sergey Edunov, Danqi Chen, and Wen-tau Yih. 2020. Dense passage retrieval for open-domain question answering. In *Proceedings of the*

2020 Conference on Empirical Methods in Natural Language Processing (EMNLP), pages 6769–6781, Online. Association for Computational Linguistics.

Omar Khattab and Matei Zaharia. 2020. Colbert: Efficient and effective passage search via contextualized late interaction over bert. In *Proceedings of the 43rd International ACM SIGIR conference on research and development in Information Retrieval*, pages 39–48.

Tushar Khot, Ashish Sabharwal, and et al. 2023. Decomposition-driven reasoning in language models. *arXiv preprint arXiv:2304.xxxxx.*

Takeshi Kojima, Shixiang Gu, Machel Reid, Yutaka Matsuo, and Yusuke Iwasaki. 2022. Large language models are zero-shot reasoners. In *Advances in Neural Information Processing Systems (NeurIPS).*

Bill Kovach and Tom Rosenstiel. 2014. *The Elements of Journalism: What Newspeople Should Know and the Public Should Expect*, 3rd edition. Three Rivers Press.

Chenfei Liang, Can Wu, et al. 2023. Taskmatrix.ai: Completing tasks by connecting foundation models with millions of apis. arXiv:2303.xxxxx [cs.CL].

Junxia Ma, Changjiang Wang, Hanwen Xing, Dongming Zhao, and Yazhou Zhang. 2024. Chain of stance: Stance detection with large language models. In *CCF International Conference on Natural Language Processing and Chinese Computing*, pages 82–94. Springer.

Christopher D Manning. 2008. Introduction to information retrieval.

Reiichiro Nakano, Jacob Hilton, Suchir Balaji, et al. 2021. Webgpt: Browser-assisted question-answering with human feedback. OpenAI Blog.

Ani Nenkova, Rebecca Passonneau, and Kathleen McKeown. 2007. The pyramid method: Incorporating human content selection variation in summarization evaluation. *ACM Transactions on Speech and Language Processing (TSLP)*, 4(2):4–es.

Rodrigo Nogueira and Kyunghyun Cho. 2019. Passage re-ranking with bert. In *arXiv preprint arXiv:1901.04085.*

Laura Parisi, Avinash Athreya, et al. 2022. Talm: Tool-augmented language models. arXiv:2210.xxxxx [cs.CL].

Savvas Petridis, Nicholas Diakopoulos, Kevin Crowston, Mark Hansen, Keren Henderson, Stan Jastrzebski, Jeffrey V Nickerson, and Lydia B Chilton. 2023. Anglekindling: Supporting journalistic angle ideation with large language models. In *Proceedings of the 2023 CHI conference on human factors in computing systems*, pages 1–16.

Chau Pham, Alexander Hoyle, Simeng Sun, Philip Resnik, and Mohit Iyyer. 2024. Topicgpt: A prompt-based topic modeling framework. In *Proceedings of the 2024 Conference of the North American Chapter of the Association for Computational Linguistics: Human Language Technologies (Volume 1: Long Papers)*, pages 2956–2984.

Joelle Pineau, Kyle Vincent, Zaid Barret, and et al. 2021. Improving reproducibility in machine learning research (a report from the NeurIPS 2019 reproducibility program). *Journal of Machine Learning Research*, 22(164):1–20.

Ofir Press, Libby Barak, and et al. 2022. Measuring and narrowing the compositionality gap in language models. *arXiv preprint arXiv:2210.03350.*

Nils Reimers and Iryna Gurevych. 2019a. Sentence-bert: Sentence embeddings using siamese bert-networks. In *Proceedings of the 2019 Conference on Empirical Methods in Natural Language Processing*. Association for Computational Linguistics.

Nils Reimers and Iryna Gurevych. 2019b. Sentence-bert: Sentence embeddings using siamese bert-networks. In *Proceedings of the 2019 Conference on Empirical Methods in Natural Language Processing*, pages 3982–3992. Association for Computational Linguistics.

Stephen E. Robertson and Steve Walker. 1994. Some simple effective approximations to the 2–poisson model for probabilistic weighted retrieval. In *Proceedings of the 17th Annual International ACM SIGIR Conference on Research and Development in Information Retrieval*, pages 232–241. Springer-Verlag.

Ohad Rubin, Jonathan Herzig, and Jonathan Berant. 2022. Learning to retrieve prompts for in-context learning. In *Proceedings of the 2022 Conference of the North American Chapter of the Association for Computational Linguistics: Human Language Technologies*, pages 2655–2671.

Gerard Salton and Michael J. McGill. 1983. *Introduction to Modern Information Retrieval*. McGraw-Hill, New York.

Victor Sanh, Lysandre Debut, Julien Chaumond, and Thomas Wolf. 2019. Distilbert, a distilled version of BERT: smaller, faster, cheaper and lighter. *arXiv preprint arXiv:1910.01108.*

Kartik A Santhanam, Omar Khattab, Theodoros Rekatsinas, and Matei Zaharia. 2022. Colbertv2: Effective and efficient retrieval via lightweight late interaction. In *Proceedings of the 45th International ACM SIGIR Conference on Research and Development in Information Retrieval*, pages 337–347. ACM.

Roger C Schank and Robert P Abelson. 1977. Scripts, plans, goals and understanding: An inquiry into human knowledge structures.

Timo Schick, Jay Dwivedi-Yu, et al. 2022. Modular reasoning, knowledge and language (mrkl) systems. arXiv:2203.xxxxx [cs.CL].

Gail Sedorkin. 2015. *Interviewing: A Guide for Journalists and Writers*, 4th edition. Allen & Unwin.

Emily Sheng, Kai-Wei Chang, Premkumar Natarajan, and Nanyun Peng. 2019. The woman worked as a babysitter: On biases in language generation. In *Proceedings of the 2019 Conference on Empirical Methods in Natural Language Processing*, pages 3407–3412. Association for Computational Linguistics.

Adam Passman Shinn, Rami Labash, Daniel Hesslow, and et al. 2023. Reflexion: Language agents with verbal reinforcement learning. arXiv:2303.xxxxx [cs.CL].

Alexander Spangher, Matthew DeButts, Nanyun Peng, and Jonathan May. 2024a. Explaining mixtures of sources in news articles. In *Conference on Empirical Methods in Natural Language Processing*.

Alexander Spangher, Yao Ming, Xinyu Hua, and Nanyun Peng. 2022. Sequentially controlled text generation. In *Findings of the Association for Computational Linguistics: EMNLP 2022*, pages 6848–6866.

Alexander Spangher, Nanyun Peng, Emilio Ferrara, and Jonathan May. 2023. Identifying informational sources in news articles. In *Proceedings of the 2023 Conference on Empirical Methods in Natural Language Processing*, pages 3626–3639.

Alexander Spangher, Nanyun Peng, Sebastian Gehrmann, and Mark Dredze. 2024b. Do llms plan like human writers? comparing journalist coverage of press releases with llms. In *Conference on Empirical Methods in Natural Language Processing*.

Harsh Trivedi, Niranjan Balasubramanian, Tushar Khot, and Ashish Sabharwal. 2023. Interleaving retrieval with chain-of-thought reasoning for knowledge-intensive multi-step questions. In *Proceedings of the 61st Annual Meeting of the Association for Computational Linguistics (Volume 1: Long Papers)*, pages 10014–10037.

Gaye Tuchman. 1972. Objectivity as strategic ritual: An examination of newsmen's notions of objectivity. *American Journal of Sociology*, 77(4):660–679.

Gaye Tuchman. 1978. Making news: A study in the construction of reality. *Free Pres.*

Teun A Van Dijk. 1998. *News as discourse*. Routledge.

Ellen M Voorhees and Dawn M Tice. 1999. The trec-8 question answering track report. In *Proceedings of the Eighth Text REtrieval Conference (TREC-8)*, pages 77–82. NIST.

Jason Wei, Xuezhi Wang, Dale Schuurmans, Maarten Bosma, Sydney Ichien, and et al. 2022. Chain-of-thought prompting elicits reasoning in large language models. *arXiv preprint arXiv:2201.11903*.

Jason Weston, Sumit Chopra, and Antoine Bordes. 2015. Memory networks. In *International Conference on Learning Representations (ICLR)*.

Puxuan Yu, Razieh Rahimi, Zhiqi Huang, and James Allan. 2023. Search result diversification using query aspects as bottlenecks. In *Proceedings of the 32nd ACM International Conference on Information and Knowledge Management*, pages 3040–3051.

ChengXiang Zhai, William W Cohen, and John Lafferty. 2015. Beyond independent relevance: methods and evaluation metrics for subtopic retrieval. In *Acm sigir forum*, volume 49, pages 2–9. ACM New York, NY, USA.

Ruiqi Zhang, Linda Li, Xiaodong Liu, Bill Dolan, and et al. 2022. Automatic chain of thought prompting in large language models. In *Proceedings of the AAAI Conference on Artificial Intelligence*.

Zihao Zhao, Eric Wallace, Shi Feng, Dan Klein, and Sameer Singh. 2021. Calibrate before use: Improving few-shot performance of language models. In *International conference on machine learning*, pages 12697–12706. PMLR.

A Appendix

A.1 Examples of Query Threads

B Further Characterization of Discourse Roles

As shown in Table 3, several sources provide overlapping or identical information (e.g. Jeff Horwitz and Newley Purnell). To investigate further, we compute the pairwise cosine similarity between the SBERT embeddings (Reimers and Gurevych, 2019b) of all sources within each article. While the average cosine similarity between source pairs is 0.45 (indicating diversity), a significant minority (7%) of source pairs have a cosine similarity above 0.70, suggesting they provide similar information. This highlights a practice of verification, where multiple sources are used to corroborate facts and enhance credibility (Tuchman, 1972; Kovach and Rosenstiel, 2014).

C Expanded Related Works

D Related Works

In this section, we situate our work at the intersection of *information retrieval (IR)*, *discourse-driven narrative construction*, and *reasoning-based NLP frameworks* (e.g., *chain-of-thought*, *interleaving retrieval*, and *agentic NLP*). We highlight how methods in each of these areas contribute to our proposed task of *multi-document source retrieval for journalism* and illustrate how discourse modeling adds a crucial layer of planning beyond conventional IR objectives.

D.1 Information Retrieval

Information retrieval has a rich history, beginning with classical keyword-based approaches (e.g., TF-IDF, BM25) that treat queries and documents as bags of words (Manning, 2008; Salton and McGill, 1983). These methods remain foundational to modern IR pipelines. Over time, specialized paradigms like *diversified retrieval* (Carbonell and Goldstein, 1998; Clarke et al., 2008) and *subtopic retrieval* (Allan, 2003) have evolved to handle broad, multi-faceted queries by reducing redundancy and maximizing coverage. Our work follows the spirit of *multi-document retrieval* (Zhai et al., 2015), emphasizing that single-document relevance alone is inadequate for tasks requiring multiple complementary sources.

Building upon these foundations, *dense vector retrieval* has emerged, leveraging neural embeddings to map queries and documents into a shared semantic space (Karpukhin et al., 2020; Reimers and Gurevych, 2019a). These approaches excel at capturing deeper lexical and semantic relationships, outperforming bag-of-words techniques in various domains. "Retrieval-augmented" language models further enhance this by prompting LLMs to iteratively refine queries and re-rank candidate documents (Izacard et al., 2022). Our framework extends this line of work by explicitly modeling *discourse roles* rather than purely semantic or topical overlaps, aiming to retrieve sources that complement each other *functionally* in narrative building.

D.2 Planning and Chain-of-Thought Reasoning

Concurrently, large language models (LLMs) have catalyzed progress in *few-shot learning*, *text generation*, and *reasoning*. *Chain-of-Thought (CoT)* prompting (Wei et al., 2022) encourages models to articulate intermediate reasoning steps, improving factual accuracy and multi-hop inference in question-answering (Zhang et al., 2022) and math tasks (Kojima et al., 2022). Our work adapts these insights to *iterative query planning*, where sub-queries are tied to distinct *discourse functions*.

Recent research has explored enhanced *planning* frameworks in LLM-driven pipelines. For instance, "self-ask" prompts (Press et al., 2022) or symbolic reasoning modules (Anonymous, 2023) help break down complex tasks. We incorporate and extend these ideas by linking intermediate reasoning steps to specific *discourse roles*—such as "expert perspective" or "main actor"—thereby imposing additional structure on the retrieval process.

D.3 Interleaving Retrieval and Follow-Ups

Interleaving retrieval (Trivedi et al., 2023) describes a process where an LLM iteratively queries a retrieval system, inspects the results, and refines queries for subsequent rounds. Follow-up works build on this paradigm with more advanced *planning modules* (Huang et al., 2024) or specialized *retrieval agents* (Nakano et al., 2021). These techniques aim to systematically explore or fill information gaps across multiple query iterations.

However, existing interleaving methods commonly focus on retrieving the *most relevant* documents. Our work posits that "relevance" alone is insufficient for tasks like *journalistic source selection*, where each source must also fulfill a particular *narrative function*. Accordingly, we propose

Query: Is Facebook's (FB) leadership inadequately addressing concerns that moderation policies are applied inconsistently in India, with regards to hate speech from Hindu nationalist politicians?		
Name	Information	Discourse
Ankhi Das (FB Public Policy team)	Opposed internal moves to apply hate-speech rules to a BJP politician and at least three other Hindu nationalist individuals and groups for violating FB's standards.	Main Actor
Former FB employees	A pattern of favoritism exists in India toward the country's ruling party and Hindu hardliners.	Confirmation
FB's Muslim affinity group	Said that Facebook needed to make its policy-enforcement process for high-profile users more transparent and less susceptible to political influence.	Counterpoint
Jeff Horwitz	Wrote an article about FB employees pressing leadership to review its handling of hate speech in India	Background Info.
Newley Purnell	Wrote an article about FB employees pressing leadership to review its handling of hate speech in India.	Confirmation

Table 3: A sample article from our corpus, with query and sources extracted. Labels from our discourse schema (induced from an LLM) is shown in the right column. As can be seen, some sources do not differ greatly from the query (e.g. Former FB employees) while others offer novel dimensions (e.g. Muslim affinity group). Some sources have nearly identical informational content to each other (e.g. Newley Purnell and Jeff Horwitz), and serve to confirm their information.

Centrality	High	Medium	Low
Percentage	21.8%	37.8%	40.0%

Table 4: Percentage of sources by centrality label, queried via LLM.

Planned Interleaved Retrieval, which explicitly encodes discourse roles in a *plan* or distribution of roles needed for a coherent story. This approach reduces the tendency for queries to meander or become repetitive, facilitating *diversity* and *functional complementarity* in the retrieved documents.

D.4 Reasoning in NLP

While NLP systems have historically tackled classification and generation tasks, *multi-step reasoning* is increasingly central to modern challenges (Creswell et al., 2022; Bubeck et al., 2023). Prior work explored neural *memory networks* for logical inference (Weston et al., 2015); LLMs, however, can now articulate more explicit, *symbolic* reasoning steps in few-shot or chain-of-thought paradigms. Yet, even advanced models struggle with tasks requiring strict logical consistency or complex entity tracking across documents (Khot et al., 2023).

Our framework adds a *discourse reasoning* lens to multi-step retrieval. Instead of merely stringing together sub-questions for coverage, we examine *why* different sources are chosen together. We label sources by *narrative role* (e.g., confirming facts, providing an anecdote, serving as an expert) and reason about how each source contributes to the story's completeness. By encoding these discourse intentions, we achieve richer retrieval outcomes aligned with real-world journalistic practices (Tuchman, 1978).

D.5 Agentic NLP

A growing interest in *agentic NLP* frames LLMs as *autonomous agents* that plan, retrieve, and act upon external tools, such as search engines or databases (Shinn et al., 2023; Liang et al., 2023). Architectures like *MRKL* (Schick et al., 2022) and *tool-augmented LLMs* (Parisi et al., 2022) treat the language model as a decision-making orchestrator that delegates subtasks to specialized APIs. Such systems can handle multi-hop QA or web browsing by adaptively issuing queries and integrating results.

Our method can be viewed as a specialized agentic approach, where an LLM "agent" controls a multi-document retrieval pipeline using *discourse-level guidance*. Instead of purely seeking factual coverage, the LLM is tasked with *ensuring* that each source fulfills a *unique narrative function*. By incorporating higher-level organizational structures (i.e., discourse roles) into the agent's plan, we steer retrieval towards more *comprehensive* and *multi-faceted* sets of sources. This approach fits into the broader shift toward agentic NLP, where language models do more than "respond"—they *coordinate* the entire solution process.

Overall, our work is informed by **classical IR** insights on coverage, strengthened by **neural retrieval** methods, and guided by **chain-of-thought**

Label	Definition
Main Actor	Individuals or entities involved in decision-making that effects events in the story.
Subject	Individuals or entities being affected/targeted by events in the story (*i.e.* The converse of "Main Actor").
Anecdote	Real-world stories of people, groups or organizations being affected by events in the story.
Background Info.	Provides broader context to events, helping readers understand the main topic in the context of what is going on and grasp peripheral details.
Broadening	Sources that induce the reader to think about the events of the news article in new or bigger picture.
Analysis	These sources offer insights and forecasts, often explaining what things mean going forward.
Counterpoint	These sources offer diverse perspectives or examples of differences, opposing opinions to provide a more balanced understanding.
Expert	These sources provide essential facts, rules or interpretations to help us understanding the events.
Confirmation	A source whose role is primarily to confirm events that occurred in the news article.
Data Resource	These sources provide statistics and other survey or scientific resources.

Table 5: Definitions for our discourse labeling scheme, generated via LLM-labeling and clustering.

style planning. We build on the **interleaving retrieval** paradigm but innovate by imposing explicit *discourse structure*, effectively bridging the gap between *unstructured multi-document IR* and *agentic NLP* approaches. By elevating *why* sources are chosen (discourse intentions) alongside *what* they contain (semantic relevance), we deliver more *journalistically valid* and *functionally diverse* retrieval outcomes. The subsequent sections introduce our dataset, experimental setup, and evaluation, illustrating how discourse reasoning substantially improves multi-document retrieval for journalism.

E Analysis of Source Centrality and Perspective in Newswriting

In this section, we explore the role that sources play in newswriting by analyzing two key attributes: *centrality* and *perspective*. Using the Llama-3.1-70B language model, we conducted experiments to label sources based on these attributes and examined how they correlate with the sources' placement and prominence within news articles.

E.1 Centrality of Sources

We employed Llama-3.1-70B to label the centrality of sources in news stories. Centrality refers to how integral a source is to the main narrative of the article. Our hypothesis was that more central sources would not only appear earlier in the articles but also be attributed more sentences.

Figure 6 illustrates the relationship between a source's centrality and its position in the story. The plot indicates that sources labeled as more central tend to appear earlier in the narrative. This suggests that journalists prioritize central sources to establish the main storyline promptly.

Figure 7 shows the number of sentences attributed to sources based on their centrality. The data reveal that more central sources are associated with a higher number of sentences, highlighting their prominence in the discourse of the article.

E.2 Perspective of Sources

In a separate experiment, Llama-3.1-70B was used to label the perspective of sources, categorizing them as either *Informational* or *Authoritative*. We investigated how these perspectives influence the placement of sources in articles and the extent of coverage they receive.

Figure 7 and 7 presents the positions of sources based on their labeled perspective. Both Informational and Authoritative sources tend to appear earlier in the articles. This pattern suggests that sources providing essential information or authoritative insights are introduced promptly to establish

Queries
1. What economic and social impacts can the local communities surrounding Mount Everest expect in the aftermath of the earthquake, and how are international aid organizations contributing to the relief and recovery efforts?"
2. What measures is the Nepalese government taking to support the recovery of the climbing industry and affected communities after the earthquake, and how will these efforts impact the long-term sustainability of climbing on Mount Everest?"
3. What specific measures did the Nepalese government take to respond to the earthquake and its impact on Mount Everest, and what lessons have been learned from the disaster to improve future disaster response and preparedness?",
4. What are the long-term plans and strategies being implemented by the Nepalese government and international aid organizations to support the recovery of local communities and the climbing industry affected by the April 2015 Nepal earthquake?"
5. What were the personal experiences and challenges faced by climbers and guides who were on Mount Everest during the April 2015 Nepal earthquake, and how did they respond to the disaster?"
6. What was the impact of the April 2015 Nepal earthquake on Mount Everest climbers, and how would it affect the climbing season?
Retrieved Sources
"A professional mountaineer who was on Makalu, a mountain in the Himalayas southeast of Everest, near the Nepal-China border: Arjun Vajpai said in a video he posted to Facebook from his campsite that there have been a lot of disturbances due to the earthquake, and that there have been a few avalanches in the area, as well as rockfalls, and that most climbers on his team were fine, but he had not yet heard from climbers who moved to other camps."
"The director general of the Nepal Tourism Department: Tulasi Prasad Gautam said that climbing Mount Everest may be canceled this year due to the avalanche, and that the cancellation of the climbing season last year was a key part of Nepal's tourism industry."
"Government officials of Nepal: Nepalese officials said that at least 17 climbers were killed and at least 37 others were injured in the avalanche on Mount Everest."
"A guide at the base camp of Mount Everest and the base camp manager for Asian Trekking: Nima Namgyal Sherpa said the avalanche caused many injuries at the base camp of Mount Everest, and that many camps have been destroyed by the shake and wind from the avalanche, and that all the doctors at the base camp are doing their best to treat and save lives."
"A hiker at the base camp of Mount Everest: Alex Gavan described on Twitter a huge earthquake then huge avalanche that sent him running for life from his tent at the base camp of Mount Everest, and warned that many of the wounded would die if they were not evacuated soon."
"An experienced guide: Ang Sherpa said that about 800 people were already staying at the Everest base camp, which is always a somewhat chaotic collection of tents, equipment and exhausted climbers and their attendants, and that a helicopter rescue operation to the base camp was planned for Sunday morning, when a full tally of the dead and injured should become available."

Table 6: Sample interleaving query for the article `www.nytimes.com/2015/04/26/world/asia/everest-climbers-killed-as-nepal-quake-sets-off-avalanche.html`, paired with the sources retrieved by this sequence. Many of the sources repeat information, and the queries appear to restate the same objective. Beyond the initial query, subsequent queries primarily pertain to government policies or personal accounts from individuals affected by the disaster. The scope of these queries remains significantly narrower than the range of sources utilized by the human journalist.

Queries
1. What strategies are technology companies, such as Facebook and Twitter, implementing to help users manage their screen time and reduce mindless social media checking, and are these efforts effective? 2. What are the potential long-term health consequences of mindless social media checking, and how have some individuals successfully broken the cycle of excessive social media use? 3. What insights do sociologists or cultural critics offer on the ways in which societal and cultural factors, such as the pressure to present a curated online persona or the fear of missing out, contribute to mindless social media checking, and how can individuals resist these influences to develop healthier social media habits? 4. What strategies or techniques do mental health professionals or behavioral psychologists recommend for individuals to break the cycle of mindless social media checking, and how can these strategies be combined with the features implemented by tech companies to achieve lasting change? 5. What strategies have individuals who have successfully reduced their social media use employed to maintain their new habits over time, and what role do they believe societal and cultural factors play in perpetuating mindless social media checking? 6. How can I, and others, break the cycle of mindless social media checking, which seems to be exacerbated by the constant stream of news and updates from sources like President Trump's Twitter feed?
Retrieved Sources
Experts in the field of neuroscience: Neuroscientists recommend techniques for coping with social media's grip on our brains. Experts in the field of psychology: Psychologists recommend techniques for coping with social media's grip on our brains. The President of the United States: Donald Trump's tweets can be annoying and disrupt your workflow, and it's not necessary to see his tweets first thing in the morning. A technology news website: TechCrunch obtained a Facebook slide deck that shows people check their phones about 100 times a day and Facebook 10-15 times a day. Surveys and polls conducted by various media outlets: According to a media poll, people don't find news anymore, the news finds them, on Facebook, Twitter, Instagram, and Snapchat. A newspaper: The New York Post found that the average American checked their phone 80 times per day, or once every 12 minutes, in 2017. One in 10 people surveyed checked it once every four minutes, or about 240 times per day. People who observe the effects of social media on others: The evidence that we aren't coping well with social media is on display at dinner tables where everyone is staring at screens–and even at crosswalks, where distracted pedestrians walk into traffic. Social media platforms: Facebook and Instagram will roll out features that show people how much time they've spent on the apps. These features include an activity dashboard that shows how long you're spending on Facebook or Instagram, a daily reminder for when you're hitting your total time for the day, and a way to tune out notifications. These tools can be accessed via the settings page on either app.

Table 7: Sample interleaving query for the article `www.wsj.com/articles/take-back-your-brain-from-social-media-1485968678`, paired with the sources retrieved by this sequence. This example highlights another failure mode of vanilla interleaving planning: its tendency to drift away from the main query. While Queries 1-5 primarily focus on the consequences of mindless social media usage, Query 6 deviates significantly, introducing highly specific and less generalizable information. This divergence results in poorer retrieval performance.

Queries
1. What role could renewable energy sources, such as solar or wind power, play in replacing the capacity lost due to nuclear power plant closures, and how might policymakers or industry leaders support the development of these alternatives?
2. What are the potential environmental and social consequences of the recent wave of nuclear power plant closures in the US, and how might policy changes or regulatory reforms help mitigate these effects?
3. What are the potential economic and social impacts of the recent wave of nuclear power plant closures on local communities, and how can policymakers or industry leaders mitigate these effects to support workers and local economies?
4. What are the potential national security implications of the recent wave of nuclear power plant closures in the US, and how might the shift towards natural gas and renewables impact the country's energy independence and security?
5. What are the potential health and safety implications of the recent wave of nuclear power plant closures in the US, and how might these closures impact local communities and the long-term stability of the US energy grid?
6. What's behind the recent wave of nuclear power plant closures in the US, and what does this trend mean for the future of nuclear energy in America?
Retrieved Sources
Official documents from the government: The government documents stated that multiple nuclear plants are at risk for early closure and several others have already closed prematurely due to economic circumstances.
A nuclear power plant located in Massachusetts: Pilgrim Nuclear Power Station is closing, with a capacity of 685 megawatts.
A US energy company: FirstEnergy Corp. has said it might decide next year to sell or close its three nuclear plants – Davis-Besse and Perry in Ohio and Beaver Valley in Pennsylvania.
One of the largest providers of nuclear power in the United States: Exelon Corp. announced that it would close two of its nuclear plants in northern Illinois, called Byron and Dresden, in roughly one year's time, even though the plants are licensed to operate for decades more. The plants face revenue shortfalls in the hundreds of millions of dollars. Exelon also said it may need to bring forward the closure dates of two other northern Illinois plants, LaSalle and Braidwood.
A nuclear power plant near Los Angeles: The second and third units of the San Onofre nuclear generating plant near Los Angeles ceased operation in 2013.
A utility company that operates nuclear power plants: Exelon recently announced that it would close the last remaining reactor at the Three Mile Island nuclear plant by 2019 unless policy makers stepped in to support it, due to cheap natural gas cutting regional electricity prices in half and pushing Pennsylvania's nine reactors toward unprofitability.
The industry that generates electricity through nuclear power in the United States: The U.S. nuclear power industry is quietly suffering, with the decline of coal power in the United States making the headlines every week, but the nuclear power industry, which accounts for about 20 percent of U.S. electricity production, is also struggling.

Table 8: Sample interleaving query for the article `slate.com/business/2015/10/nuclear-power-is-losing-its-appeal-thanks-fossil-fuels.html`, paired with the sources retrieved by this sequence. Vanilla interleaving planning often remains closely aligned with the initial query. In this instance, the queries thoroughly explore the environmental, social, security, and safety implications of nuclear power plant closures. However, they fail to explicitly request expert opinions, data, or counterpoints, critical source types essential for constructing a comprehensive news article.

Queries
1. What are the marketing and business strategies behind EVA Air's decision to introduce the Hello Kitty jet on the San Francisco-Taipei route, and how does this fit into the airline's overall brand and growth plans? 2. What do passengers who have flown on EVA Air's Hello Kitty jets think of the experience, and how does it compare to other themed flights or regular flights? 3. What are the key demographic groups that EVA Air is targeting with its Hello Kitty jet on the San Francisco-Taipei route, and how does the airline plan to tailor its marketing efforts to effectively reach and engage with these groups? 4. What demographic groups are EVA Air targeting with its Hello Kitty jet on the San Francisco-Taipei route, and how does the airline expect this unique offering to differentiate itself from competitors and attract new passengers? 5. What specific marketing and promotional efforts is EVA Air planning to undertake to attract its target demographic groups to the Hello Kitty jet on the San Francisco-Taipei route, and how does the airline expect this unique offering to impact its brand awareness and passenger loyalty in the North American market? 6. What's behind EVA Air's decision to bring its popular Hello Kitty jet to the San Francisco-Taipei route, and what can passengers expect from this unique flying experience?
Retrieved Sources
The founder of TravelSkills.com: The author stated that EVA Air made a media splash several years ago when it decided to cover its jets with cute animated characters created by Japan's Sanrio Company, the most popular of which is Hello Kitty, and that the Hello Kitty planes bring the theme to more than just their paint jobs, with passengers getting specially designed boarding passes and baggage stickers at check-in, and seeing Hello Kitty figures on the flight attendants' aprons, the headrest covers, pillows, tissues, hand cream, napkins, paper cups, and even utensils and snack packaging. A major Taiwanese airline: For the rest of April, Taiwan's EVA Air will operate three weekly Taipei-SFO flights, three to Seattle and three or four a week to LAX, all with 777-300ERs. Taiwan's flag carrier: China Airlines plans to increase capacity between San Francisco International and Taipei on May 2, boosting its schedule from seven flights a week to nine, using 777-300ERs. A Taiwanese airline: EVA Air provided delightful flights and service to the author, unlike their experience on Asiana Airlines. A Singaporean airline: Singapore Airlines plans to pull its extra-long-range A350-900ULRs off the San Francisco route next fall. The ULR version – which has only business class and premium economy seating – currently operates three of the airline's 10 weekly SFO-Singapore non-stop flights; the others use a standard three-class A350-900, and that model will be used for all 10 of the airline's weekly SFO non-stop flights beginning in October of next year. A Chinese airline: Air China is planning to boost frequencies on its San Francisco-Beijing route effective March 31 from seven flights a week to 10. The three extra flights will be operated with a 787-9 Dreamliner, while the regular daily service will use a 747-8.

Table 9: Sample interleaving query for the article `www.sfgate.com/travel/article/Hello-Kitty-jet-san-francisco-13788445.php`, paired with the sources retrieved by this sequence. All of the queries primarily focus on the effects of the new marketing campaign on the airline's passengers, neglecting other important information needs such as data, analysis, or background context. This highlights the vanilla planner's lack of creativity and strategic planning capabilities.

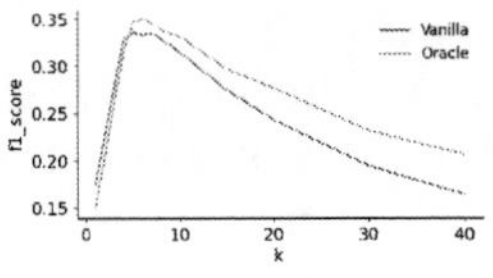

Figure 5: Retrievals benefits of discourse planning grow as k increases relative to baseline.

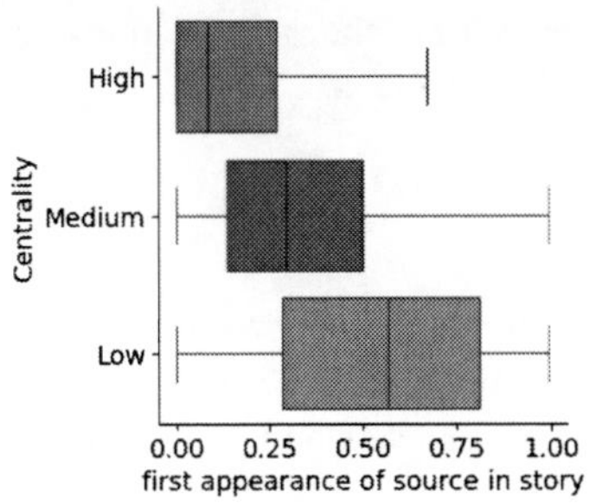

Figure 6: Correlation between centrality assigned to sources by `Llama-3.1-70B` and the first time that source is introduced in the story.

context and credibility.

As depicted in Figure 10, Authoritative sources occupy more sentences compared to Informational sources. This indicates that while both types are introduced early, Authoritative sources receive more extensive coverage, possibly due to their perceived expertise and influence on the topic.

E.3 A-prior Plans: Clustering

As described in the main body, the approach to a-priori planning involved first clustering our label distributions and then training a SequenceClassifier model to predict the cluster, based on the query. We now share more details about the clustering. We clustered KMeans with 8 clusters, cluster centers are shown in Figure 11. Example queries and documents are shown in Tables 11, 12, 13.

E.4 Prompts

Prompt to Score Centrality You will receive a news article and a set of sources to examine in that article.

For each source, provide the following information: (1) Name: who the source is. (2) Perspective: What is their perspective on the main events of the article? Choose as many labels as fit from: ("Authoritative", "Informative", "Supportive", "Skeptical", "Against", "Neutral"). (3) Centrality: How central is this source to the main events of the article? Choose from "High", "Medium", "Low". (4)

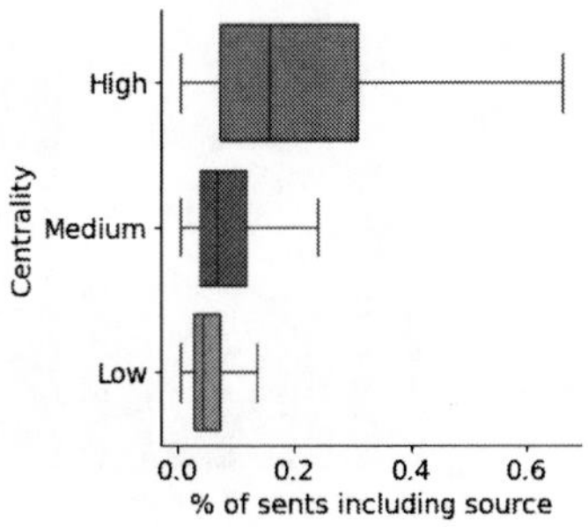

Figure 7: Correlation between centrality assigned to sources by `Llama-3.1-70B` and the percentage of sentences attributed to that source by (Spangher et al., 2023)'s methods.

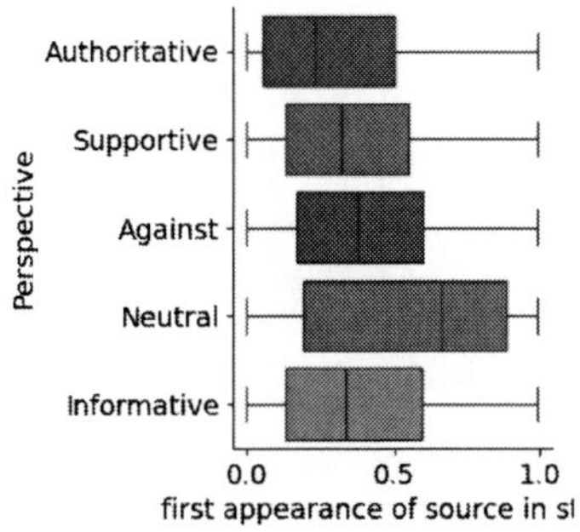

Figure 8: Correlation between perspective assigned to sources by `Llama-3.1-70B` and the first time that source is introduced in the story. Prompts for perspective are shown in Appendix E.4

Is_Error: Did we annotate this source in error? This can happen for many reasons, including if a sentence from the webpage was included in the story unintentionally. Answer with "Yes" or "No".

Here is a news article:

‘‘‘{news_article}‘‘‘

Please examine the role of each of the following sources:

‘‘‘

$$\{target\_sources\}$$

‘‘‘

For each source, answer the questions above. Output the summary in a list of python dictionaries as in the examples. Don't say anything else.

Prompt to Label Discourse Function You will receive a news article and a set of sources to examine in that article.

For each source in the list, provide the following information, once per source: (1) Name: Exactly

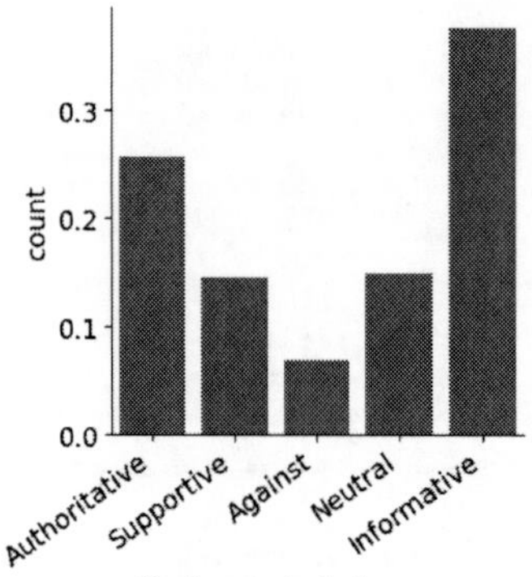

Figure 9: Percentage of sources holding each perspective role, as identified by `Llama-3.1-70B`.

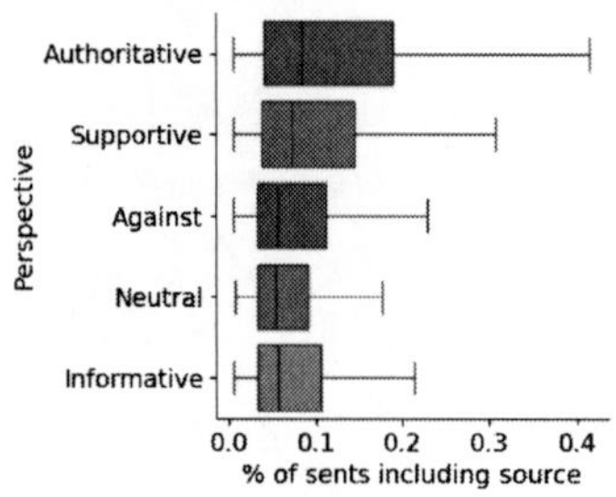

Figure 10: Correlation between perspective assigned to sources by `Llama-3.1-70B` and the percentage of sentences attributed to that source by (Spangher et al., 2023)'s methods.

copy the name of the source. (2) Narrative Function: Give a generic keyword label to categorize the narrative role the source playes in the article. Infer why the author used the source, and a generalizable statement about the role they play in the article. Don't just summarize their identity. Return in the format: "LABEL": DESCRIPTION.

Here are example outputs. Again, your main task here is to identify a generalizable label that can characterize the narrative role of each source and why the author used them.

[Examples] Example 1:

{{ "Name": "Match Group", "Narrative Function": "Counterpoint: This source is used to compare to the main actor in the news article and provide grounding." }}

Example 2:

{{ "Name": "Dubai Airshow", "Narrative Function": "More Context: This source is used to further expand the context offered and offer a visual setting." }}

Example 3: {{

"Name": "Ann Gough", "Narrative Function": "Victim": This source provides the voice of a user for the product, giving us a personal view of the harm caused by the event. }}

[Instructions]

Now it's your turn. Here is a news article:

“‘{news_article}“‘

Please examine the narrative role of each of the following sources:

“‘

$$\{target\_sources\}$$

“‘

For each source, answer the questions above. Output the summary in a list of python dictionaries as in the examples. Don't say anything else.

Prompt to extract source descriptions from news articles You are a helpful news assistant. Here is a news article:
{news_article}

Please summarize each informational source providing information in the article.
Include unnamed or passively expressed sources (e.g. "witnesses", "price signals") if there is information attributable to them.
Include any facts that might have come from the source.
Make sure each source you return refers to just one source. For example: if "John and Jane" both contribute the same information, generate two separate summaries, one for "John" and one for "Jane".
Generate only ONE summary per source.

For each source, provide the following information:
(1) Name: just the name of the source.
(2) Biography: A brief biography of the source mentioned in the article.
(3) Information: Restate the facts provided by the source. Be as SPECIFIC and as VERBOSE as possible.
Contextualize ALL the information the source describes. State the full names of all people, places, events, and ideas mentioned and everything the source says with AS MUCH BACKGROUND INFORMATION from the article so I can fully understand the information the source is giving.
I will look at each source independently without looking at any others, so help me understand the

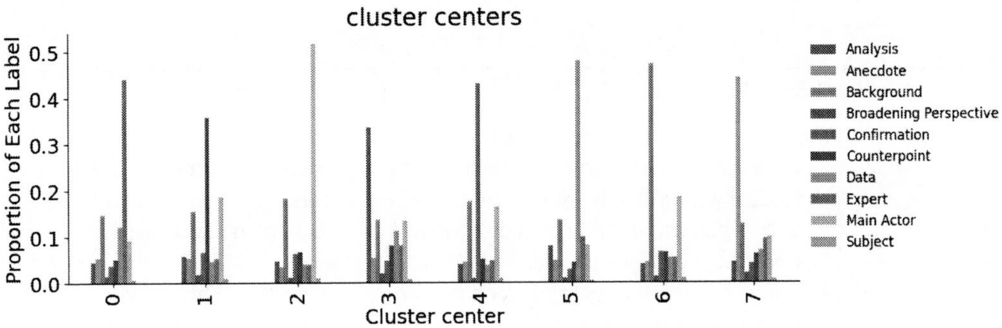

Figure 11: The cluster centers for our KMeans algorithm are distinctive and high-entropy clusters.

context.

Here are some examples:
example 1:
{ "Name": "Supermarkets around the country",
"Biography": "Retail stores that sell food and other household items",
"Information": "Supermarkets around the country alerted shoppers that prices are likely to continue going up due to the avian flu outbreak, with eggs now average $2.88 per dozen, up 52% since the first confirmed case of avian influenza in February." }

example 2:
{ "Name": "The article's author (unnamed)",
"Biography": "The author of the article",
"Information": "The author stated that Wing, which is collaborating with FedEx and Walgreens on drone delivery, was the first to receive a limited Part 135 certificate. Wing is launching operations in Virginia this month, and the Standard certification allows UPS to send an unlimited number of drones to the skies, for their cargo load to exceed 55 pounds and for them to fly at night." }

example 3:
{ "Name": "Delta's customers",
"Biography": "People who travel with Delta Air Lines",
"Information": "Delta's customers suggested that they preferred more space on flights amid the COVID-19 pandemic, and they continue to tell Delta that more space provides more peace of mind." }

example 4:
{ "Name": "European Union countries",
"Biography": "Countries that are part of the European Union",
"Information": "European Union countries are working on adopting copyright rules that allow news companies and publishers to negotiate payments with large tech companies like Facebook, Microsoft, and Google that use their content on their platforms." }

Output the summary in a list of python dictionaries as in the examples. Don't say anything else.

	Source Text (to embed)	Narrative Function	Discourse
The FBI	The Federal Bureau of Investigation: The FBI shows that 82 percent of white homicide victims were killed by other white people and 15 percent of white homicide victims were killed by black people	"Fact Checker": This source can provide accurate information and debunk the false statistics.	Data Resource
The U.S. Securities and Exchange Commission	A regulatory agency responsible for enforcing federal securities laws and regulating the securities industry: The U.S. Securities and Exchange Commission has postponed a decision on whether to allow the listing of an exchange-traded fund backed by Bitcoin...	"Authority": This source can be used to establish the regulatory framework and provide the official decision."	Main Actor
The Privacy Rights Clearinghouse	An organization that provides information on how to deal with security breaches: If you learn of a breach involving your driver's license information, contact the agency (in this case the state Department of Driver's Services)	"Authority": This source can be used to provide expert advice and recommendations on how to deal with the data breach.	Expert
CNN	A news organization: Both the Pfizer/BioNTech and Moderna vaccines use an mRNA platform and are well tolerated and safe. Moderna was estimated to be 36.8% effective against symptomatic disease for kids 2-to-5 years of age...	"Providing Data": This source can be used to provide data and statistics to support the claims made in the article.	Data Resource
Tech Crunch	A technology news website: According to a report by Tech Crunch, Detroit Mayor Mike Duggan said on Wolf Blitzer's show on CNN that the city of Detroit received the test kits manufactured by Abbott on April 1.	"Secondary Source": This source can be used to provide additional information and context to the main story.	Background Information
Anil Agarwal	The chairman of the Vedanta group: Anil Agarwal recently said that the group is scouting for more energy and metal assets across India, which includes coal, oil and iron ore.	"Company Strategy": This source can be used to provide insight into the strategy and interests of the Vedanta group.	Analysis
Experts	Unspecified experts in the field of economics or education: Some experts have raised concerns that forgiving student loans may effectively penalize people who already paid off their debt, often while making considerable financial sacrifices.	"Counterpoint": This source can be used to raise concerns and questions about the fairness and effectiveness of the policy."	Counterpoint

Table 10: An example of sources randomly selected from our retrieval database. We show the narrative function originally labeled by Llama-3.1 along with the discourse label applied after clustering. Note how initial narrative function label applied by the LLM narrative function doesn't always align with the final label: for example, row #2 and #3 are both labeled "Authority", however #2 is a more active participant while #3 is more an expert.

Query: How did news websites handle the expected surge in traffic and demand for video streams during President Barack Obama's inauguration, and what were the consequences for users trying to watch the event online?		
Name	Biography	Discourse Label
Daniel Wild	A Web site editor at the New York University School of Medicine	Anecdotes, Examples and Illustration
Akamai	A company that helps many media companies keep up with visitor demand on their Web sites	Data Resource
A Facebook representative	A spokesperson for Facebook	Data Resource
The article's author (unnamed)	The author of the article	Background Information

Table 11: Example of query and ground-truth sources in Cluster #5, the "Data and Resources" cluster.

Query: What are the unintended consequences of receiving a Michelin star, and why would a chef choose to give one up?		
Name	Biography	Discourse Label
Julio Biosca	A chef and owner of Casa Julio, a restaurant in Fontanars dels Alforins, outside of Valencia, Spain, that was awarded a Michelin star in 2009	Main Actor
Julia Perez Lozano	A Spanish food critic	Expert
Frederick Dhooge	A chef and owner of 't Huis van Lede in Belgium	Counterpoint
Skye Gyngell	An Australian chef and owner of Petersham Nurseries Cafe in London	Anecdotes, Examples and Illustration
Gary Pisano	A professor of business administration at Harvard Business School	Analysis
David Munoz	A chef and owner of DiverXo	Anecdotes, Examples and Illustration
Authors of 'Behind the stars...'	Researchers who published a study in the Cornell Hotel & Restaurant Administration Quarterly	Data Resource

Table 12: Example of query and ground-truth sources in Cluster #7, the "Data and Resources" cluster.

Query: What has been the public reaction to Target's decision to allow transgender customers and employees to use the bathroom and fitting rooms that correspond with their gender identity?		
Name	Biography	Discourse Label
Tim Wildmon	President of the American Family Association, a Christian nonprofit organization based in Mississippi	Counterpoint
Kris Hayashi	Executive director at the Transgender Legal Center	Expert
Williams Institute	An organization that conducted a study on transgender people's experiences with bathrooms	Data Resource
Article's author	The author of the article	Background Information
American Family Association	A Christian nonprofit organization based in Mississippi	Counterpoint
Southern Poverty Law Center	An organization that has deemed the American Family Association an extremist group	Counterpoint
Bill Partridge	Oxford Police Chief	Counterpoint
Human Rights Campaign	An organization that publishes the Corporate Equality Index report	Background Information
Target	The second-largest discount retailer in the nation	Main Actor
City of Oxford	A city in Alabama	Counterpoint
Supporters of the boycott	People who have taken to social media to show their support for the boycott called for in the petition	Counterpoint
Opponents of the petition	People who have shown opposition to the petition	Counterpoint

Table 13: Example of query and ground-truth sources in Cluster #1, the "Counterpoint" cluster.

HEAL: Hierarchical Embedding Alignment Loss for Improved Retrieval and Representation Learning

Manish Bhattarai[1], Ryan Barron[1,4], Maksim Eren[2], Minh Vu[1], Vesselin Grantcharov[1], Ismael Boureima[1], Valentin Stanev[3], Cynthia Matuszek[4], Vladimir Valtchinov[5], Kim Rasmussen[1], Boian Alexandrov[1]

[1]Theoretical Division, Los Alamos National Laboratory, Los Alamos, NM, USA
[2]Analytics Division, Los Alamos National Laboratory, Los Alamos, NM, USA
[3]Department of Material Science & Engineering, University of Maryland, College Park, MD, USA
[4]Department of Computer Science, University of Maryland, Baltimore County, MD, USA
[5]Department of Radiology, Brigham and Women's Hospital, Harvard Medical School, Boston MA

Correspondence: ceodspspectrum@lanl.gov

Abstract

Retrieval-Augmented Generation (RAG) enhances Large Language Models (LLMs) by integrating external document retrieval to provide domain-specific or up-to-date knowledge. The effectiveness of RAG depends on the relevance of retrieved documents, which is influenced by the semantic alignment of embeddings with the domain's specialized content. Although full fine-tuning can align language models to specific domains, it is computationally intensive and demands substantial data. This paper introduces **H**ierarchical **E**mbedding **A**lignment **L**oss (HEAL), a novel method that leverages hierarchical fuzzy clustering with matrix factorization within contrastive learning to efficiently align LLM embeddings with domain-specific content. HEAL computes level/depth-wise contrastive losses and incorporates hierarchical penalties to align embeddings with the underlying relationships in label hierarchies. This approach enhances retrieval relevance and document classification, effectively reducing hallucinations in LLM outputs. In our experiments, we benchmark and evaluate HEAL across diverse domains, including Healthcare, Material Science, Cyber-security, and Applied Maths.

1 Introduction

Large Language Models (LLMs), such as GPT-4 (OpenAI, 2023), have demonstrated exceptional capabilities in natural language understanding and generation. However, LLMs are prone to *hallucinations*, generating plausible but incorrect or nonsensical content (Ji et al., 2023). Retrieval-Augmented Generation (RAG) frameworks (Lewis et al., 2020) mitigate this issue by integrating external knowledge through document retrieval, enhancing the factual accuracy of LLM outputs. A critical component of RAG systems is the embedding model used for document retrieval. Standard embedding models, however, often fail to capture the hierarchical and semantic relationships within domain-specific corpora, leading to suboptimal retrieval and, consequently, increased hallucinations. This issue is particularly pronounced in domains with increased specificity such as Healthcare, Legal sytem, and Scientific research.

Corpus of documents for a specialized domain inherently exhibit a high degree of semantic coherence, presenting an opportunity to align embedding models for retrieving the most contextually relevant information. Hierarchical Non-negative Matrix Factorization (HNMF) (Eren et al., 2023) is a powerful technique for semantically categorizing documents into clusters that exhibit thematic coherence. By grouping documents into hierarchical clusters of supertopics and subtopics, HNMF provides a rich semantic categorization of the corpus, enabling a deeper understanding of document relationships. Leveraging this semantic knowledge in the form of hierarchical cluster labels, we can align embedding models to preserve hierarchical information within the embedding space. This alignment enhances the embeddings to capture both coarse-grained and fine-grained document similarities, improving contextual relevance in retrieval tasks and enabling better downstream capabilities.

To tackle the challenges of hallucination and suboptimal retrieval in RAG systems, we introduce the **Hierarchical Embedding Alignment Loss (HEAL)**, a refined extension of the Hierarchical Multi-label Contrastive Loss (Zhang et al., 2022). HEAL leverages an improved hierarchical weighting scheme to align embeddings more effectively with the underlying hierarchical structure. By incorporating hierarchical label structures, HEAL

Proceedings of the 4th International Workshop on Knowledge-Augmented Methods for Natural Language Processing (KnowledgeNLP'25), pages 205–214
May 3, 2025 ©2025 Association for Computational Linguistics

fine-tunes embedding models to align with document clusters derived from HNMF. The method computes contrastive losses at each hierarchical level, combining them with depth-specific penalties to emphasize distinctions at higher levels of the hierarchy.

2 Related Work

Contrastive learning has become a cornerstone of representation learning, particularly in computer vision and natural language processing. Methods like SimCLR (Chen et al., 2020) and MoCo (He et al., 2020) have achieved state-of-the-art performance in unsupervised settings by learning representations that are invariant to data augmentations. In supervised contrastive learning, Khosla et al. (2020) extended the contrastive loss to utilize label information, improving performance on classification tasks. Similarly, the SciNCL framework employs neighborhood contrastive learning to capture continuous similarity among scientific documents, leveraging citation graph embeddings to sample both positive and negative examples (Ostendorff et al., 2022). However, these methods generally assume flat label structures and do not exploit hierarchical relationships.

Hierarchical classification has been studied extensively, with approaches such as hierarchical softmax (Goodman, 2001) and hierarchical cross-entropy loss (Deng et al., 2014). These methods aim to leverage hierarchical label structures to improve classification efficiency and accuracy. In the context of representation learning, Deng et al. (2011) introduced hierarchical semantic embedding, aligning image embeddings with WordNet hierarchies. More recent works, such as Bertinetto et al. (2020), have explored hierarchical prototypes to capture hierarchical relationships. Zhang et al. (2022) propose a hierarchical multi-label contrastive learning framework that preserves hierarchical label relationships through hierarchy-preserving losses. Their method excels in scenarios with hierarchical multi-label annotations, such as biological or product classifications. In contrast, our approach focuses on enhancing information retrieval to mitigate hallucinations.

RAG frameworks combine retrieval models with generative models to enhance the factual accuracy of language generation (Lewis et al., 2020). These systems rely heavily on the quality of the embeddings used for retrieval. Prior work has focused on improving retrieval through better indexing and retrieval algorithms (Karpukhin et al., 2020), but less attention has been given to aligning embeddings with hierarchical document structures.

3 Method

In this section, we propose an embedding alignment framework comprising hierarchical label extraction with HNMF, embedding alignment using HEAL, and retrieval with aligned embeddings as outlined in Figure 1.

3.1 Hierarchical Document Clustering with HNMFk.

Hierarchical Non-negative Matrix Factorization with automatic latent feature estimation (HNMFk) Eren et al. (2023) is an advanced technique for uncovering hierarchical patterns within document collections. It builds on traditional Non-negative Matrix Factorization (NMF) Vangara et al. (2021) by dynamically and automatically determining the optimal number of latent features at each level. Effective contrastive learning relies on well-separated document cluster labels to align embeddings effectively. HNMFk's ability to automatically balance stability and accuracy using a bootstrap approach enhances the quality of clustering results. In this work, we utilize the publicly available HNMFk implementation from the TELF library [1].

Given a Term Frequency-Inverse Document Frequency (TF-IDF) matrix $\mathbf{X} \in R^{n \times m}$, where n represents the vocabulary size and m denotes the number of documents, HNMFk performs a sequence of matrix factorizations across hierarchical levels to capture the nested structure of topics. At each level l, the factorization is expressed as $\mathbf{X} \approx \mathbf{W}^{(l)}\mathbf{H}^{(l)}$, where $\mathbf{W}^{(l)} \in R^{n \times k_l}$ is the basis matrix representing latent topics, and $\mathbf{H}^{(l)} \in R^{k_l \times m}$ is the coefficient matrix quantifying the contribution of each topic to the composition of documents. Here, k_l is the number of topics at level l, which is determined automatically through stability analysis (Vangara et al., 2021). This analysis involves bootstrapping the data to create resampled versions of the TF-IDF matrix, applying NMF across a range of k values, and evaluating the stability of clusters across the resampled datasets. The optimal k_l is selected as the value that produces the most consistent clustering results, indicating a robust underlying structure

[1]TELF is available at `https://github.com/lanl/T-ELF`

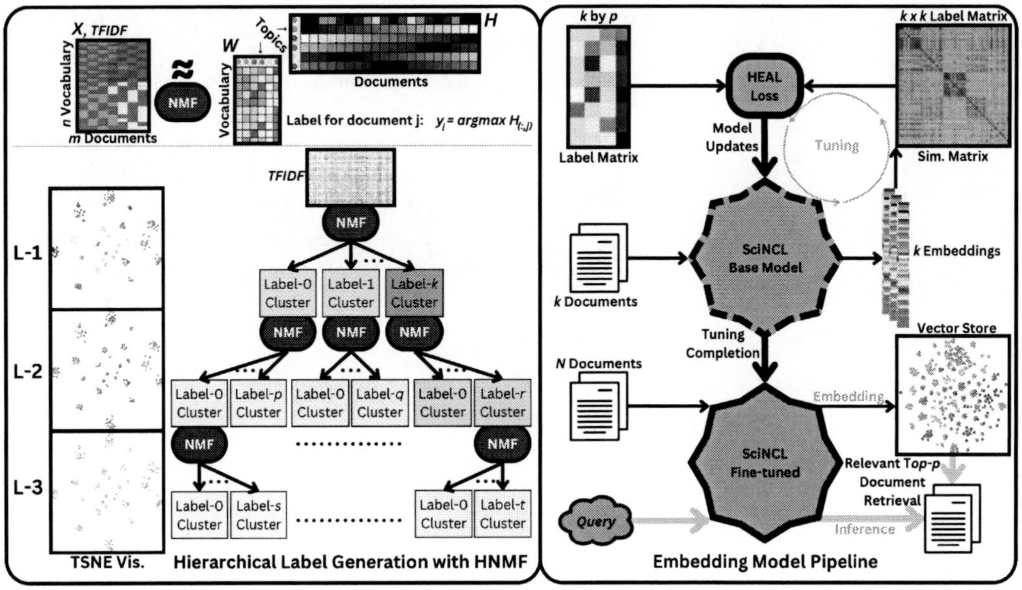

Figure 1: Overview of the HEAL-Based Embedding Model Alignment and Retrieval. *The left side* illustrates hierarchical label generation using HNMF, where documents corresponding to a cluster from each preceding depth are converted into TFIDF matrices and further decomposed to extract sub-clusters. The TSNE visualizations highlighting cluster memberships in document embeddings. *The right side* depicts fine-tuning of the SciNCL model using HEAL loss on generated embeddings and HNMF derived labels. Once trained, the aligned model computes a vector store from the corpus, enabling retrieval of the nearest p documents for a given query embedding.

in the data.

To construct hierarchical labels for each document, the coefficient matrix $\mathbf{H}^{(l)}$ is used to determine topic assignments. For each level l, the topic for document i is identified by selecting the index of the maximum value in the corresponding column of $\mathbf{H}^{(l)}$, expressed as $y_i^{(l)} = \arg\max_k \mathbf{H}_{k,i}^{(l)}$. The hierarchical label for document i is then formed by aggregating the topic assignments across all levels, resulting in $\mathbf{y}_i = (y_i^{(0)}, y_i^{(2)}, \ldots, y_i^{(L-1)})$. Here, L is the total number of hierarchical levels, or hierarchical depth that is the number of NMFk operations from the first one to the leaf. y_i^l is the label of sample i at level l, with $l = 0$ corresponding to the *shallowest*(most general or root node) level and $l = L - 1$ to the *deepest* (most fine-grained, or leaf node) level.

3.2 Hierarchical Multilevel Contrastive Loss (HEAL)

Upon the unsupervised data decomposition with HNMFk, the datasets have clusters with hierarchical structures. To incorporate such structures, we propose the HEAL, which extends supervised contrastive loss (Khosla et al., 2020) by introducing level-wise contrastive losses and aggregating them with level-specific penalties.

3.2.1 Level-wise Contrastive Loss

For a batch of N samples $\{(\mathbf{x}_i, \mathbf{y}_i)\}_{i=1}^N$, where $\mathbf{x}_i \in R^d$ is the input and $\mathbf{y}_i \in R^L$ is the hierarchical cluster label, we obtain normalized embeddings $\{\mathbf{h}_i\}_{i=1}^N$ using an encoder network $f_\theta(\cdot)$:

$$\mathbf{h}_i = \frac{f_\theta(\mathbf{x}_i)}{\|f_\theta(\mathbf{x}_i)\|_2}, \quad \mathbf{h}_i \in R^d. \tag{1}$$

For a given level l, the set of positive samples for sample i is:

$$P(i,l) = \{p \mid \mathbf{y}_p^l = \mathbf{y}_i^l, p \neq i\}. \tag{2}$$

The contrastive loss at level l for sample i is:

$$\mathcal{L}_{i,l} = \frac{-1}{|P(i,l)|} \sum_{p \in P(i,l)} \log \frac{\exp\left(\mathbf{h}_i^\top \mathbf{h}_p / \tau\right)}{\sum_{a=1}^N \exp\left(\mathbf{h}_i^\top \mathbf{h}_a / \tau\right)}. \tag{3}$$

If $P(i,l)$ is empty (i.e., no positive samples at level l for i), $\mathcal{L}_{i,l}$ is excluded from the total loss.

3.2.2 Aggregating Level-wise Losses with Penalties

To prioritize discrepancies at shallower levels, we assign penalties λ_l to each level l, where shallower levels have higher penalties. The penalties are defined as:

$$\lambda_l = \frac{2^{L-l-1}}{\sum_{k=0}^{L-1} 2^k} = \frac{2^{L-l-1}}{2^L - 1}. \tag{4}$$

The penalties λ_l satisfy:

1. $\lambda_l > \lambda_{l+1}$ for $l = 0, 1, ..., L-2$, i.e., penalties decrease for deeper levels.

2. $\sum_{l=0}^{L-1} \lambda_l = 1$, i.e., the penalties are normalized.

The total HEAL loss is then:

$$\mathcal{L}_{\text{HEAL}} = \frac{1}{N} \sum_{l=0}^{L-1} \lambda_l \sum_{i=1}^{N} \mathcal{L}_{i,l}. \tag{5}$$

Algorithm 1 Computation of HEAL Loss

Require: Mini-batch $\{(\mathbf{x}_i, \mathbf{y}_i)\}_{i=1}^N$, temperature τ, number of levels L

Compute embeddings: $\mathbf{h}_i = f_\theta(\mathbf{x}_i)/\|f_\theta(\mathbf{x}_i)\|_2$
Initialize total loss: $\mathcal{L}_{\text{HEAL}} \leftarrow 0$
for $l = 0$ to $L-1$ **do**
  Compute penalty λ_l using Eq. (4)
  for $i = 1$ to N **do**
    Determine positive set $P(i, l)$ using Eq. (2)
    if $|P(i, l)| > 0$ **then**
      Compute $\mathcal{L}_{i,l}$ using Eq. (3)
      Update total loss: $\mathcal{L}_{\text{HEAL}} \leftarrow \mathcal{L}_{\text{HEAL}} + \lambda_l \mathcal{L}_{i,l}$
    end if
  end for
end for
return $\mathcal{L}_{\text{HEAL}}$

Algorithm 1 outlines the computation of $\mathcal{L}_{\text{HEAL}}$ for a mini-batch.

3.3 Fine-tuning Embedding Models with HEAL for RAG

To enhance retrieval performance in RAG systems, we fine-tune the embedding model to align with the hierarchical structure of the document corpus. Given a specialized document corpus, we first apply HNMFk (as described in Section 3.1) to the corresponding TF-IDF matrix $\mathbf{X}$ producing hierarchical cluster labels $\mathbf{y}_i = (y_i^{(0)}, y_i^{(2)}, \ldots, y_i^{(L-1)})$ for each document i. Next, we generate embeddings from each document x_i using a pretrained embedding model $f_\theta(.)$. The embedding model is initialized with pre-trained weights and produces normalized embeddings $\mathbf{h}_i \in R^d$ for document i. To align embeddings with the hierarchical structure, we optimize the HEAL presented in 3.3.

The embedding model is trained by minimizing $\mathcal{L}_{\text{HEAL}}$ using gradient-based optimization:

$$\theta^* = \arg\min_\theta \mathcal{L}_{\text{HEAL}},$$

where θ are the parameters of the embedding model $f_\theta(\cdot)$.

After fine-tuning, the updated embeddings $\mathbf{h}_i = f_{\theta^*}(\mathbf{x}_i)$ are used to replace the initial embeddings in the vector store. During inference, a query $\mathbf{q}$ is embedded using $f_{\theta^*}(\cdot)$ as $\mathbf{h}_q = f_{\theta^*}(\mathbf{q})$, and retrieves top p documents based on cosine similarity:

$$\text{Similarity}(\mathbf{q}, \mathbf{x}_i) = \frac{\mathbf{h}_q^\top \mathbf{h}_i}{\|\mathbf{h}_q\| \|\mathbf{h}_i\|}.$$

To maximize retrieval performance in RAG systems, it is essential to align the query embeddings with the hierarchically aligned document embeddings. Since queries are typically shorter and may not capture the full semantic richness of the documents, we need to semantically align queries and documents in the embedding space. To achieve this, we generate question-answer (Q&A) pairs using a language model (e.g., LLaMA-3.1 70B) for each document and leverage HEAL to jointly align both query and document embeddings during training. For each document $\mathbf{x}_i$, we generate a set of queries $\{\mathbf{q}_{i,k}\}_{k=1}^{K_i}$, where K_i is the number of queries generated for document i. Each query $\mathbf{q}_{i,k}$ is associated with the same hierarchical labels $\mathbf{y}_i$ as its source document $\mathbf{x}_i$, since it is derived from the content of $\mathbf{x}_i$.We extend the HEAL framework to include both documents and queries by defining a unified set of samples:

$$\mathcal{S} = \{\mathbf{x}_1, \ldots, \mathbf{x}_N\} \cup \{\mathbf{q}_{i,k} \mid i = 1, \ldots, N;\ k = 1, \ldots, K_i\}.$$

Each sample $\mathbf{s}_j \in \mathcal{S}$ has an associated hierarchical label $\mathbf{y}_j$, where:

$$\mathbf{y}_j = \begin{cases} \mathbf{y}_i, & \text{if } \mathbf{s}_j = \mathbf{x}_i \text{ (document)} \\ \mathbf{y}_i, & \text{if } \mathbf{s}_j = \mathbf{q}_{i,k} \text{ (query generated from document } \mathbf{x}_i\text{)}. \end{cases} \tag{6}$$

Based on this dataset, the HEAL is leveraged to finetune the embedding model .

4 Experiments

4.1 Datasets

We evaluate our method on datasets specifically constructed from scientific publications in the domains of Material Science, Medicine, Tensor Decomposition, and Cybersecurity. To construct our datasets, we leveraged the Bibliographic Utility Network Information Expansion (BUNIE) method, a machine learning-based approach that integrates subject-matter expertise in a human-in-the-loop framework (Solovyev et al., 2023). For completeness, we briefly summarize the BUNIE approach in this paper. BUNIE begins with a small core corpus of documents selected by subject-matter experts (SMEs). From this starting point, it constructs a citation network to identify additional relevant documents, leveraging BERT based text embeddings to assess semantic similarity. Through iterative cycles of dataset expansion and pruning—guided by embedding visualization, topic modeling, and expert feedback—the method ensures the corpus is both comprehensive and domain-specific. We apply this procedure to each scientific domain with guidance from SMEs, who provide target keywords/phrases and/or a core set of papers relevant to the sub-topic of interest within the domain. Using this knowledge base, we employ BUNIE to expand the dataset from the initial core papers to a larger collection of domain-specific documents.

1. **Material Science**: A collection of 46,862 scientific articles, which explore 73 Transition Metal Dichalcogenides (TMD) compounds, combining transition-metal and chalcogen atoms (S, Se, or Te). With a layered structure similar to graphite, TMDs excel as solid lubricants and exhibit unique quantum phases like superconductivity and charge density waves. Their atomically thin layers offer tunable properties, with applications in spintronics, optoelectronics, energy harvesting, batteries, and flexible electronics.

2. **Healthcare**: A collection of 9,639 scientific articles, which examine Pulmonary Hypertension (PH) disease - a rare condition causing elevated pulmonary arterial pressure, right heart strain, and reduced oxygen delivery. The WHO classifies PH into five groups based on causes, including pulmonary arterial hypertension (PAH), which has a prevalence of 15-25 cases per million in the U.S. Treatments such as endothelin receptor antagonists and prostacyclin analogs aim to improve symptoms, but prognosis varies, with untreated PAH having a median survival of less than three years.

3. **Applied Mathematics:** A collection of 4,624 scientific articles, which explore tensor network techniques, such as Tensor-Train (TT) decomposition, which recently emerged as a powerful mathematical tool for solving large-scale Partial Differential Equations (PDEs). Tensor network PDE solvers efficiently manage high-dimensional data by mitigating the curse of dimensionality, drastically reducing computational costs and memory usage while maintaining high solution accuracy. These advancements hold significant promise for breakthroughs in scientific computing, including material science, climate modeling, and engineering design optimization.

4. **Cyber-security**: We created a dataset of 8,790 scientific publications focusing on the application of tensor decomposition methods in cybersecurity and ML techniques for malware analysis. This dataset serves as a knowledge base covering topics for cybersecurity such as ML-based anomaly detection, malware classification, novel malware detection, uncertainty quantification, real-world malware analysis challenges, tensor-based anomaly detection, malware characterization, and user behavior analysis.

4.2 Experimental Setup

For training, we used the Adam optimizer with a learning rate of 10^{-5}, a batch size of 128, and early stopping based on validation performance with a patience of 5 epochs. The experiments were conducted on a high-performance computing cluster, with each node equipped with 4 NVIDIA GH200 GPUs. Document metadata, comprising the title and abstract combined, were used as input. Hierarchical labels were generated using HNMF with dataset-specific factorization depths: Material Science (depth 3), Healthcare (depth 4), Applied Mathematics (depth 3), and Cybersecurity (depth 3). HEAL loss was applied with a temperature parameter of 0.07. The embedding base model, SciNCL (Ostendorff et al., 2022), was chosen for its robust contrastive pretraining on scientific documents, serving as a strong baseline for fine-tuning.

The data was split into 60% training, 20% validation, and 20% test sets, with early stopping monitored on the validation set. Evaluation metrics were reported on the test set, while Q&A retrieval analysis used the entire dataset (train + validation + test) for constructing the vector store.

The efficacy of the RAG system was evaluated at two levels. *First*, we characterized the embeddings on document-level tasks, including hierarchical classification, retrieval, and hallucination measurement. For hierarchical classification, we used a hierarchical classifier applying random forests to each node (Miranda et al., 2023). The classifier is trained on embeddings corresponding to train dataset and evaluated against the test set. We perform this for embeddings derived from aligned and unaligned embedding model. Retrieval performance was assessed by measuring whether retrieved documents belonged to the same hierarchical class as the query document. Hallucination likelihood was evaluated based on the retrieval of incorrect documents for a given query. *Second*, we evaluated the performance of the embedding model within a RAG framework. To support retrieval and hallucination analysis, we used the LLaMA-3.1 70B model to generate 10 Q&A pairs per document using abstracts as input, providing a robust test for embedding alignment and retrieval capabilities. Next, we leveraged the questions as queries to the embedding model to retrieve the best metadata and assessed whether the model retrieved the exact document that generated the query during Q&A analysis, as well as the rank of the returned document within the top 10 results. Furthermore, the retrieved documents were augmented with LLaMA-3.1 70B LLM to generate responses, with hallucinations evaluated based on response accuracy and relevance.

Given the specialized nature of our dataset and the requirement for hierarchical labels, fine-tuning is essential. Comparing our method to approaches that do not leverage hierarchical labels is inequitable, as they are inherently less effective for this task. Our approach simplifies training by eliminating HEAL loss hyperparameter tuning, unlike HiMulCon (Zhang et al., 2022), which requires extensive tuning of penalty parameters for optimal results. While HiMulCon focuses on root-level classification in vision datasets, our method aligns embeddings across all hierarchical depths. We optimize hierarchical metrics such as classification, retrieval, and hallucination indirectly through the HEAL loss, ensuring a robust alignment with the hierarchical structure.

For these reasons, we evaluate the performance of HEAL using the baseline model SciNCL, both without and with hierarchical alignment on our diverse specialized datasets. We evaluate performance using hierarchical metrics to capture nuances of hierarchical label structures in retrieval, classification, and hallucination assessments as presented in Appendix Table 2 .

4.3 Results

Table 1 summarizes the performance metrics for three datasets (Healthcare, Materials, Applied Mathematics, and Cybersecurity) across three tasks: classification, retrieval, and hallucination evaluation. The aligned model corresponds to the embedding model trained using the HEAL loss, whereas the non-aligned model corresponds to the original embedding model without HEAL-based training. The metrics are reported for both non-aligned and aligned SciNCL embeddings, demonstrating the significant impact of HEAL on improving performance. Figure 2 illustrates hierarchical embedding alignment achieved through HEAL training, resulting in well-separated super and sub-clusters for the Materials and Healthcare datasets which enhances the performance of downstream tasks. The density contours, computed via Kernel Density Estimation (KDE), highlight the underlying clustering structure by depicting regions of high and low embedding concentration. In subplots (a) and (c), the embeddings before model alignment appear more dispersed, indicating weaker intra-cluster cohesion and greater overlap between different data regions. However, in subplots (b) and (d), after model alignment, the contours become more compact and well-separated, signifying improved structural coherence and enhanced discriminability of the learned representations. This transformation suggests that alignment enhances the model's ability to encode meaningful relationships, ultimately improving feature organization and representation learning within the embedding space. The increased cluster compactness and separation indicate a more refined, task-specific feature space, which is crucial for downstream applications such as classification and retrieval.

First, we evaluate the performance on document-level tasks using hierarchical labels. Specifically, we assess the ability of the hierarchical classifier to predict hierarchical labels in the classification task.

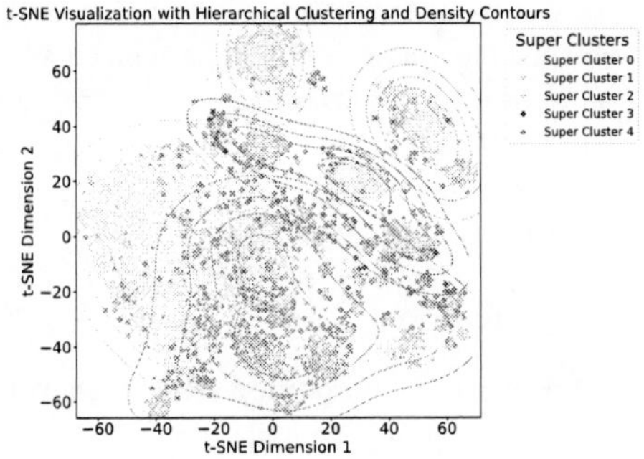

(a) Material dataset before model alignment

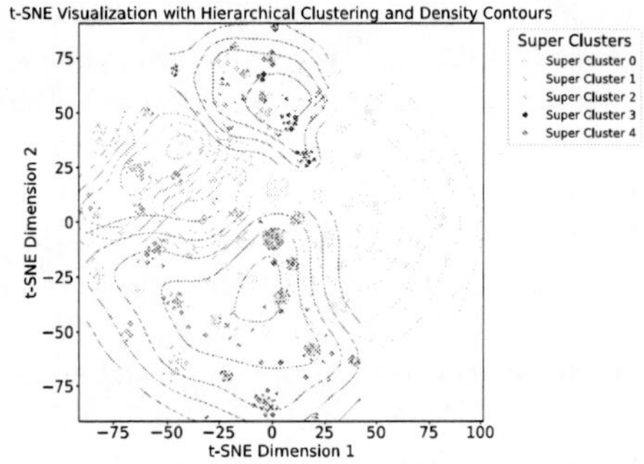

(b) Material dataset after model alignment

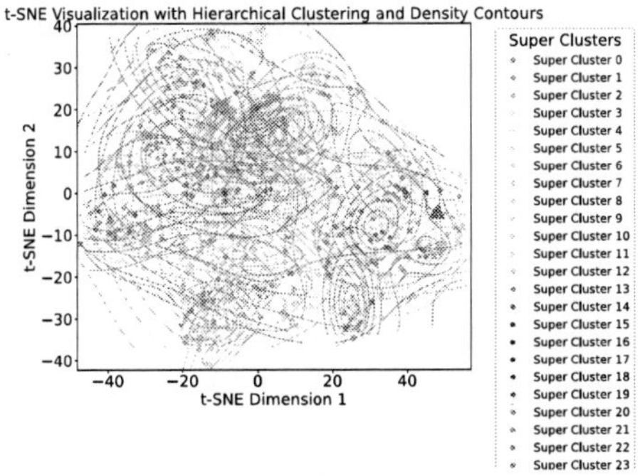

(c) Healthcare dataset before model alignment

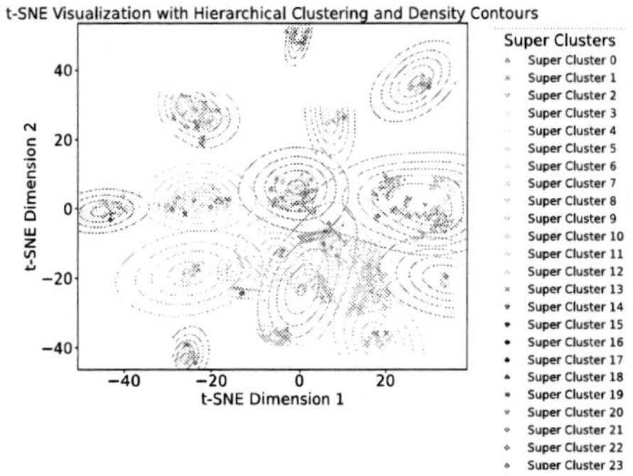

(d) Healthcare dataset after model alignment

Figure 2: Embedding visualizations for the Material and Healthcare datasets, projected using t-SNE for dimensionality reduction. The density contours represent the kernel density estimation (KDE) of the embeddings in the 2D space, highlighting the clustering structure. Subplots show the Material dataset, (a) before and (b) after model alignment, and the Healthcare dataset, (c) before and (d) after model alignment. The contours reveal changes in the density distribution of embeddings, emphasizing the effect of alignment on cluster organization and separability.

Table 1: Performance Metrics Across Datasets (Healthcare, Materials, Cyber, Applied Mathematics) for Aligned and Non-aligned Embeddings for $k = 10$

Task	*Metric	Healthcare	Materials	Cyber	Applied Mathematics				
		Non-aligned	Aligned	Non-aligned	Aligned	Non-aligned	Aligned	Non-aligned	Aligned
Classification	F1 Score	0.5164	0.6588	0.6469	0.990	0.7130	0.8151	0.7541	0.8048
	Precision	0.5134	0.6590	0.6453	0.990	0.6975	0.8121	0.7415	0.8112
	Recall	0.5194	0.6586	0.6485	0.990	0.7293	0.8180	0.7672	0.7985
Retrieval	Precision@k	0.3103	0.4983	0.4787	0.9707	0.6397	0.7518	0.6576	0.7636
	Recall@k	0.0164	0.0290	0.0058	0.0116	0.0112	0.0133	0.0182	0.0212
	MRR	1.6259	2.2525	1.6541	2.9972	2.7538	3.1482	2.9065	3.2245
	nDCG@k	0.3752	0.5908	0.4982	0.990	0.6781	0.7908	0.7187	0.8280
Hallucination	FPR@k	0.9386	0.8771	0.8534	0.0878	0.7968	0.6236	0.8191	0.6529
	Severity	0.7306	0.5533	0.6041	0.0644	0.4402	0.3654	0.4119	0.3353

Additionally, we quantify the retrieval of documents from the same hierarchical category based on a query document to characterize retrieval accuracy and evaluate hallucinations. The results presented in table 1 demonstrate that HEAL significantly improves hierarchical classification metrics across all datasets. For the Healthcare dataset, the Hierarchical F1 Score improves from 0.5164 to 0.6588, reflecting a more accurate representation of hierarchical labels. Similarly, the Materials dataset achieves near perfect classification metrics (F1 Score, Precision, Recall = 0.99) with aligned embeddings, while the most challenging Healthcare dataset (4 depth cluster label) sees improvements in F1 Score from 0.5164 to 0.6588. In retrieval tasks, HEAL aligned embeddings consistently outperform non-aligned embeddings across all metrics. For the Healthcare dataset, Hierarchical MRR improves from 1.6259 to 2.2525, and nDCG@k increases from 0.3752 to 0.5908 where $k = 10$, indicating better ranking and retrieval relevance. The Materials dataset achieves a dramatic increase in retrieval precision, with Precision@k rising from 0.4787 to 0.9707, while nDCG@k reaches 0.99, showcasing near-perfect retrieval performance. For the Cyber dataset, aligned embeddings yield an MRR improvement from 2.7538 to 3.1482 and a corresponding nDCG@k increase from 0.6781 to 0.7908. Hallucination metrics further underscore the superiority of HEAL. Aligned embeddings reduce hallucination rates significantly across all datasets. For the Healthcare dataset, FPR@k drops from 0.9386 to 0.8771, and severity decreases from 0.7306 to 0.5533, indicating fewer irrelevant or misleading retrievals. The Materials dataset shows the most striking improvement, with FPR@k reduced from 0.8534 to 0.0878 and severity declining from 0.6041 to 0.0644, nearly eliminating hallucination tendencies. For the Cyber dataset, aligned embeddings lower FPR@k from 0.7968 to 0.6236 and severity from 0.4402 to 0.3654.

Next, we evaluate the performance of aligned RAG in retrieving the correct documents for generated queries to augment the LLM and minimize hallucinations. From each test dataset, we randomly sampled 100 documents and generated 10 Q&A pairs per document using the LLAMA-3.1 70B model, resulting in a total of 1,000 Q&A pairs for each dataset. Each Q&A pair was tagged with the corresponding document from which it was generated. The prompt used for Q&A generation was as follows: *"First, provide a concise summary of the following abstract that emphasizes its key concepts and hierarchical relationships. Then, based on this summary, generate 10 unique, nuanced Q&A pairs. Focus on creating questions that delve into specialized details of the hierarchical concepts discussed."* The generated queries were used to fetch documents via both aligned and unaligned models. We assessed the ability of each model to correctly retrieve the original document and evaluated the rank/order of retrieval. On average, the unaligned model achieved an MRR of 0.273 and a Recall@10 of 0.415. These metrics represent regular retrieval scores, not hierarchical scores. In contrast, the aligned model significantly improved performance, achieving an MRR of 0.514 and a Recall@10 of 0.731, demonstrating its superior ability to retrieve the correct set of documents. Furthermore, when integrating RAG with LLAMA-3.1 70B for generating answers from the queries and retrieved documents, the unaligned model produced a ROUGE score of 0.42, while the aligned model achieved a ROUGE score of 0.68. This highlights the impact of alignment on improving the quality and relevance of generated responses.

5 Conclusion

In this work, we introduced HEAL, a novel framework for aligning embeddings in RAG systems through hierarchical fuzzy clustering and matrix factorization, integrated within a contrastive learning paradigm. HEAL effectively computes level-specific contrastive losses and applies hierarchical penalties to align embeddings with domain-specific structures, enhancing both retrieval relevance and classification performance. Experimental results across diverse domains — Healthcare, Materials Science, Cybersecurity, and Applied Mathematics — demonstrate HEAL's capability to significantly improve retrieval accuracy and mitigate hallucinations in LLM-based systems. By bridging hierarchical semantics with contrastive alignment, HEAL establishes itself as a versatile and robust tool for advancing RAG methodologies, enabling more precise, reliable, and domain-adaptive applications of large language models.

6 Acknowledgement

This manuscript has been approved for unlimited release and has been assigned LA-UR-24-32672. This research was funded by the Los Alamos National Laboratory (LANL) Laboratory Directed Research and Development (LDRD) program under grants 20230067DR & 20230287ER and supported by LANL's Institutional Computing Program, and by the U.S. Department of Energy National Nuclear Security Administration under Contract No. 89233218CNA000001.

References

Luca Bertinetto, Joao F Henriques, and Philip HS Torr. 2020. Making better mistakes: Leveraging class hierarchies with deep networks. *Proceedings of the IEEE/CVF Conference on Computer Vision and Pattern Recognition*, pages 1251–1259.

Ting Chen, Simon Kornblith, Mohammad Norouzi, and Geoffrey Hinton. 2020. A simple framework for contrastive learning of visual representations. In *International Conference on Machine Learning*, pages 1597–1607. PMLR.

Jia Deng, Alexander C Berg, and Li Fei-Fei. 2014. Large-scale object classification using label relation graphs. In *European Conference on Computer Vision*, pages 48–64. Springer.

Jia Deng, Sanjeev Satheesh, Alexander C Berg, and Fei-Fei Li. 2011. Hierarchical semantic indexing for large scale image retrieval. In *IEEE Conference on Computer Vision and Pattern Recognition*, pages 785–792. IEEE.

Maksim E Eren, Manish Bhattarai, Robert J Joyce, Edward Raff, Charles Nicholas, and Boian S Alexandrov. 2023. Semi-supervised classification of malware families under extreme class imbalance via hierarchical non-negative matrix factorization with automatic model selection. *ACM Transactions on Privacy and Security*, 26(4):1–27.

Joshua Goodman. 2001. Classes for fast maximum entropy training. In *IEEE International Conference on Acoustics, Speech, and Signal Processing*, volume 1, pages 561–564. IEEE.

Kaiming He, Haoqi Fan, Yuxin Wu, Saining Xie, and Ross Girshick. 2020. Momentum contrast for unsupervised visual representation learning. In *Proceedings of the IEEE/CVF Conference on Computer Vision and Pattern Recognition*, pages 9729–9738.

Zi Ji, Nayeon Lee, Rita Frieske, Tiezheng Yu, Dan Su, Yanlin Xu, Etsuko Ishii, Yeonseung Bang, Andrea Madotto, and Pascale Fung. 2023. A survey of hallucination in natural language generation. *arXiv preprint arXiv:2301.07128*.

Vladimir Karpukhin, Barlas Oguz, Sewon Min, Patrick Lewis, Ledell Wu, Sergey Edunov, Danqi Chen, and Wen-tau Yih. 2020. Dense passage retrieval for open-domain question answering. In *Proceedings of the 2020 Conference on Empirical Methods in Natural Language Processing (EMNLP)*, pages 6769–6781.

Prannay Khosla, Piotr Teterwak, Chen Wang, Aaron Sarna, Yonglong Tian, Phillip Isola, Aaron Maschinot, Ce Liu, and Dilip Krishnan. 2020. Supervised contrastive learning. *Advances in Neural Information Processing Systems*, 33:18661–18673.

Patrick Lewis, Ethan Perez, Aleksandra Piktus, Fabio Petroni, Vladimir Karpukhin, Naman Goyal, Urvashi Khandelwal, Mikel Artetxe, Hailey Schoelkopf, Moin Nadeem Sung, et al. 2020. Retrieval-augmented generation for knowledge-intensive nlp tasks. In *Advances in Neural Information Processing Systems*, volume 33, pages 9459–9474.

Fábio M Miranda, Niklas Köhnecke, and Bernhard Y Renard. 2023. Hiclass: a python library for local hierarchical classification compatible with scikit-learn. *Journal of Machine Learning Research*, 24(29):1–17.

OpenAI. 2023. Gpt-4 technical report. *arXiv preprint arXiv:2303.08774*.

Malte Ostendorff, Nils Rethmeier, Isabelle Augenstein, Bela Gipp, and Georg Rehm. 2022. Neighborhood Contrastive Learning for Scientific Document Representations with Citation Embeddings. In *The 2022 Conference on Empirical Methods in Natural Language Processing (EMNLP 2022)*, Abu Dhabi. Association for Computational Linguistics. 7-11 December 2022. Accepted for publication.

Nicholas Solovyev, Ryan Barron, Manish Bhattarai, Maksim E. Eren, Kim Ø. Rasmussen, and Boian S. Alexandrov. 2023. Interactive distillation of large single-topic corpora of scientific papers. In *2023 International Conference on Machine Learning and Applications (ICMLA)*, pages 1000–1005.

Raviteja Vangara, Manish Bhattarai, Erik Skau, Gopinath Chennupati, Hristo Djidjev, Tom Tierney, James P Smith, Valentin G Stanev, and Boian S Alexandrov. 2021. Finding the number of latent topics with semantic non-negative matrix factorization. *IEEE access*, 9:117217–117231.

Shu Zhang, Ran Xu, Caiming Xiong, and Chetan Ramaiah. 2022. Use all the labels: A hierarchical multi-label contrastive learning framework.

A Appendix

A.1 Evaluation Metrics

Table 2 provides a comprehensive overview of the metrics utilized to quantify different downstream tasks such as hierarchical classification and hierarchical retrieval.

Metric	Formula	Description
Hierarchical Relevance	$\text{Relevance}(q, r) = \frac{1}{L}\sum_{l=0}^{L-1} \delta(y_q^l, y_r^l)$	Average label match across hierarchy levels
Hierarchical Precision@k	$\frac{1}{k}\sum_{i=1}^{k} \text{Relevance}(q, r_i)$	Fraction of hierarchically relevant documents among top k.
Hierarchical Recall@k	$\frac{\sum_{i=1}^{k} \text{Relevance}(q,r_i)}{\sum_{r \in \text{Relevant}(q)} \text{Relevance}(q,r)}$	Fraction of hierarchically relevant documents retrieved.
Hierarchical nDCG@k	$\frac{\sum_{i=1}^{k} \frac{2^{\text{Relevance}(q,r_i)}-1}{\log_2(i+1)}}{\sum_{i=1}^{k} \frac{2^{\text{IdealRelevance}(q,r_i)}-1}{\log_2(i+1)}}$	Discounted gain based on hierarchical relevance.
Hierarchical F1 Score	$\frac{2 \cdot \text{Precision} \cdot \text{Recall}}{\text{Precision}+\text{Recall}}$	Balance between hierarchical precision and recall.
Hierarchical Severity	$1 - \frac{\sum_{i=1}^{k} \text{Relevance}(q,r_i)}{k}$	Measures retrieval of irrelevant documents in hierarchical setting.
Hierarchical False Positive Rate@k	$\frac{\text{Irrelevant hierarchical documents in top } k}{k}$	Fraction of irrelevant hierarchical documents among top k.

Table 2: Hierarchical Metrics for classification, retrieval and hallucination

Hybrid AI for Responsive Multi-Turn Online Conversations with Novel Dynamic Routing and Feedback Adaptation

Priyaranjan Pattnayak[1], **Amit Agarwal**[1], **Hansa Meghwani**[2],
Hitesh Laxmichand Patel[1], **Srikant Panda**[2]

[1]OCI, Oracle America Inc., [2]OCI, Oracle India
Correspondence: priyaranjan.pattnayak@oracle.com

Abstract

Retrieval-Augmented Generation (RAG) systems and large language model (LLM)-powered chatbots have significantly advanced conversational AI by combining generative capabilities with external knowledge retrieval. Despite their success, enterprise-scale deployments face critical challenges, including diverse user queries, high latency, hallucinations, and difficulty integrating frequently updated domain-specific knowledge. This paper introduces a novel hybrid framework that integrates RAG with intent-based canned responses, leveraging predefined high-confidence responses for efficiency while dynamically routing complex or ambiguous queries to the RAG pipeline. Our framework employs a dialogue context manager to ensure coherence in multi-turn interactions and incorporates a feedback loop to refine intents, dynamically adjust confidence thresholds, and expand response coverage over time. Experimental results demonstrate that the proposed framework achieves a balance of high accuracy (95%) and low latency (180ms), outperforming RAG and intent-based systems across diverse query types, positioning it as a scalable and adaptive solution for enterprise conversational AI applications.

1 Introduction

Recent progress in NLP has drastically changed the landscape of conversational AI, and among such new state-of-the-art solutions, a class of Retrieval-Augmented Generation (RAG) systems has emerged. By combining large language models (LLMs) with separate information retrieval pipelines, RAG systems can generate contextually rich and factually grounded responses, which are necessary for knowledge-intensive applications (Lewis et al., 2020). However, enterprise-scale conversational AI systems often face real-world challenges such as diverse user query patterns, varying levels of query complexity, and stringent latency requirements for seamless user experiences. High computational costs, susceptibility to hallucinations when retrieval is misaligned, and inefficiencies in managing frequently updated domain-specific knowledge further compound these challenges, particularly in dynamic environments like customer support (Sanh et al., 2020b; Rocktäschel et al., 2020). In practice, ensuring that such systems can scale while maintaining accuracy and low latency remains an industry pain point.

In contrast, classical intent-based chatbots are efficient in processing frequently asked questions (FAQ) and other predictable queries, thanks to using pre-defined responses. Their lightweight computational footprint and scalability also make them well-suited for high-confidence, domain-specific scenarios (Serban et al., 2017; Shah et al., 2018). However, these systems are inherently rigid and often struggle with query diversity, especially when faced with ambiguous or context-dependent user interactions. In high-demand enterprise settings, the inability of intent-based systems to adapt quickly to evolving user needs or handle complex multi-turn dialogues (Shah et al., 2018; Zhao, 2020) results in inconsistent user experiences and increased operational overhead for manual updates. The inability to balance adaptability with efficiency underscores the need for hybrid systems that synergize the strengths of RAG and intent-based approaches.

In order to solve these challenges, we propose a novel hybrid framework that combines RAG systems with intent-based canned responses for dynamic, multi-turn customer service interactions. While prior works have explored combining RAG and intent-based systems independently, our contribution lies in a cohesive framework that not only integrates these elements but also introduces a dynamic confidence-based routing mechanism refined through user feedback. This mechanism ensures that query routing decisions are continuously op-

Proceedings of the 4th International Workshop on Knowledge-Augmented Methods for Natural Language Processing (KnowledgeNLP'25), pages 215–229
May 3, 2025 ©2025 Association for Computational Linguistics

timized based on real-time user interactions, enabling a system that evolves and adapts without manual intervention. Additionally, our framework addresses scalability challenges by efficiently balancing computational resources, making it particularly suited for enterprise-scale applications where latency and accuracy are paramount. Our approach utilizes a dynamic query routing mechanism that evaluates the intent confidence level of user queries:

- *High-confidence queries* are resolved using predefined canned responses to ensure low latency and computational efficiency.
- *Low-confidence or ambiguous queries* are routed to the RAG pipeline, enabling contextually enriched responses generated from external knowledge.

The framework is further enhanced with a dialogue context manager, keeping track and managing evolving intents across multiple turns, ensuring consistent and coherent interactions. Additionally, a feedback loop continuously refines the intent repository, adapting to emerging user needs and expanding response coverage over time. Our system is designed to meet enterprise latency standards, delivering responses within an acceptable threshold (sub-200ms latency and high turn efficiency), thereby ensuring user engagement and satisfaction in real-time applications(Pattnayak et al., 2024).

Our Contributions This work makes the following key contributions:

1. **Hybrid Conversational Framework:** We propose a novel architecture which combines RAG systems with intent-based canned responses; the queries are routed dynamically for optimizing response latency and computational cost without compromising accuracy.
2. **Multi-Turn Dialogue Management:** We introduce a dialogue context manager which can track the evolving user intents and guarantee coherence in responses over multiple turns, thus addressing a key gap in the current systems.
3. **Feedback-Driven Adaptability:** Our framework incorporates a feedback loop to enable continuous refinement of intents, canned responses and confidence thresholds, thereby improving system adaptability and coverage for real-world applications.
4. **Comprehensive Evaluation:** Extensive experiments on synthetic and real-world datasets demonstrate significant improvements in accuracy, latency, and cost efficiency compared to state-of-the-art baselines.
5. **Real-World Applicability:** Our framework is designed for enterprise-scale deployment, handling diverse user queries efficiently, from repetitive FAQs to complex knowledge-based questions, while adhering to industry latency standards critical for user retention.

By addressing key challenges faced by enterprise conversational AI systems, such as query diversity, dynamic knowledge updates, and real-time latency requirements, our proposed framework offers a scalable, adaptive, and efficient solution. This work advances task-oriented dialogue systems, particularly in domains where multi-turn interactions and dynamic knowledge management are essential for operational success.

2 Related Work

2.1 Retrieval-Augmented Generation (RAG)

Recent advancements in RAG have enhanced contextual retrieval and generative capabilities, improving incident resolution in IT support (Isaza et al., 2024), question-answering systems, and domain-specific chatbots (Veturi et al., 2024). Research on noise handling (Cuconasu et al., 2024) and reinforcement learning (Kulkarni et al., 2024) further optimizes RAG for precision and adaptability in complex applications. By retrieving relevant documents during inference, RAG systems mitigate common LLM challenges such as hallucinations and outdated knowledge (Lewis et al., 2020; Sanh et al., 2020b). These systems are particularly effective for knowledge-intensive tasks where accuracy and factual grounding are critical.

Despite their effectiveness, RAG systems face significant challenges, including high computational costs and latency due to the dual retrieval and generation processes. Enterprise settings also pose unique challenges, such as diverse user queries, latency constraints, and evolving domain knowledge needs (Lewis et al., 2020; Pattnayak et al., 2025). Moreover, most existing RAG systems are optimized for single-turn interactions and struggle with maintaining coherence in multi-turn di-

Approach	Strengths	Weaknesses	Multi-Turn Support	Feedback Adaptation
RAG Systems	Accurate, dynamic responses	High latency, computationally expensive	Limited	No
Intent-Based Chatbots	Efficient, low latency	Rigid, poor adaptability	No	No
Hybrid RAG-Intent Systems	Balance between efficiency and flexibility	Limited multi-turn and feedback mechanisms	Partial	No
Proposed Framework	Low latency, multi-turn adaptable	Scalability challenges	Yes	Yes

Table 1: Comparison of Existing Approaches and the Proposed Framework.

alogues, where evolving user intents require dynamic retrieval and contextual adaptation (Rocktäschel et al., 2020). Recent efforts to optimize RAG pipelines, such as multi-stage retrieval systems (Lee et al., 2020) and model distillation (Sanh et al., 2020b), have reduced latency but do not address the complexities of multi-turn interactions (Sanh et al., 2020a).

2.2 Intent-Based Chatbots

Intent-based chatbots work well for predictable, high-confidence queries by mapping user inputs to predefined intents. These systems are widely used in domains like customer support, where they efficiently handle FAQs and repetitive queries with minimal computational overhead (Serban et al., 2017; Shah et al., 2018). However, their reliance on predefined intents limits their adaptability to ambiguous or evolving queries, particularly in multi-turn conversations (Michelson et al., 2020; Friedrich et al., 2020).

Recent developments have involved the inclusion of transformer-based models to enhance intent recognition and increase coverage (Michelson et al., 2020). However, these methods are resource-heavy, as they require a lot of labeled data and computational resources, which makes scalability quite limited for dynamic domains.

2.3 Hybrid Approaches

Hybrid retrieval systems integrating lexical search (e.g., BM25 (Robertson and Walker, 1994)) and semantic search (e.g., dense embeddings via FAISS (Douze et al., 2024)) effectively balance speed and semantic depth (Agarwal et al., 2025), improving retrieval accuracy (Mitra et al., 2021; Hernandez et al., 2020).

In conversational AI, hybrid approaches integrating RAG with intent-based responses have emerged to address limitations in single-mode systems by enhancing flexibility and efficiency (Bordes et al., 2020). Prior works, such as (Gao et al., 2020b; Zhao, 2020; Patel et al., 2024), have explored blending retrieval-augmented pipelines with canned responses to improve response efficiency and contextual depth. However, these systems are primarily designed for single-turn interactions and do not address the complexities of multi-turn dialogues, where query context evolves dynamically (Agarwal et al., 2024a). While existing research relies on static threshold-based routing, the integration of adaptive threshold driven routing and response generation for real-time, multi-turn applications remains an under explored area with significant potential for optimization.

2.4 Positioning of This Work

While prior research has advanced RAG systems, intent-based chatbots, and hybrid architectures, key limitations remain. RAG systems excel in generating contextually rich responses but struggle with coherence in multi-turn conversations, high latency, and computational costs (Lewis et al., 2020; Rocktäschel et al., 2020). Intent-based chatbots are efficient but lack flexibility for ambiguous or evolving queries in dynamic settings (Serban et al., 2017; Agarwal et al., 2024b). Hybrid systems balance efficiency and adaptability but often fail to track dialogue context or refine responses dynamically based on user feedback (Gao et al., 2020a). Table 1 summarizes the key differences between the existing work and our proposed framework.

This work addresses real-world challenges by proposing a hybrid framework that integrates RAG systems with intent-based canned responses. It uses dynamic query routing to handle high-confidence queries efficiently with canned responses while relying on RAG pipelines for complex cases. A dialogue context manager ensures coherence in multi-turn interactions, and a real-time feedback loop

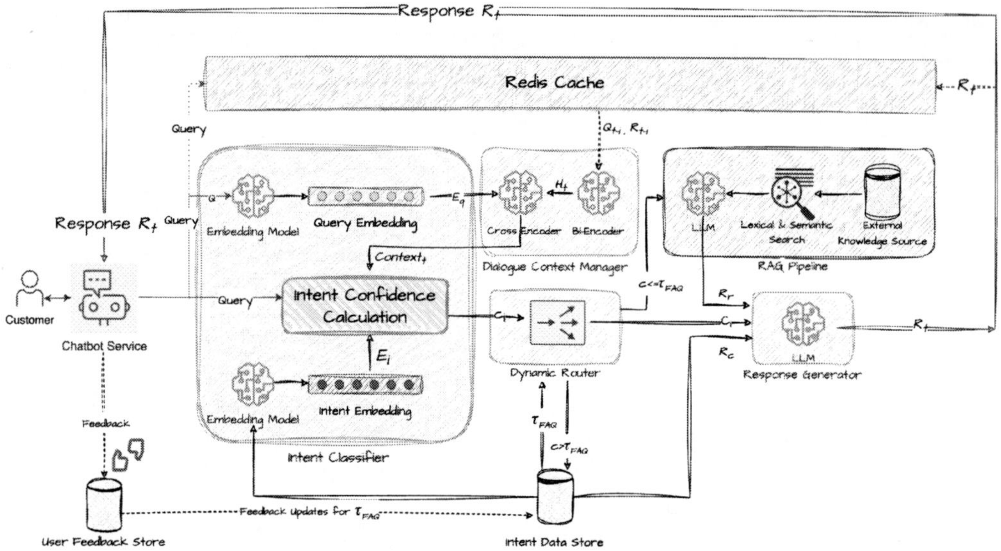

Figure 1: High-level Architecture of the Hybrid Framework.

enables continuous refinement of intents, thresholds and canned responses. For instance, in an enterprise customer support setting, our system efficiently handles high-frequency queries such as, *"How do I reset my password?"* using canned responses with minimal latency (under 200ms), ensuring quick resolution for routine tasks. In contrast, more complex queries such as, *"Can you help me troubleshoot a payment gateway integration issue with API X?"* are dynamically routed to the RAG pipeline, leveraging external documentation and past incident reports to generate accurate responses. This adaptability is further evident when users provide feedback on response quality, prompting the system to refine its intent classification and adjust confidence thresholds for future queries. Unlike existing systems that either focus on single-turn interactions or static routing and struggle with multi-turn dialogue management, our framework continuously adapts to diverse queries and user needs, optimizing latency and scalability.

By focusing on these critical aspects, this framework advances the state-of-the-art in task-oriented dialogue systems, particularly for enterprise-scale applications where efficiency, scalability, and adaptability are paramount.

3 Proposed Framework

The proposed framework integrates the efficiency of intent-based canned responses with the contextual richness and adaptability of Retrieval-Augmented Generation (RAG) systems (Lewis et al., 2020; Gao et al., 2020c). By dynamically routing queries based on intent confidence and leveraging user feedback for adaptive refinement, the framework addresses latency, accuracy, and scalability challenges while maintaining coherence across multi-turn interactions. Figure 1 illustrates the architecture with key modules, data flow and a Redis Cache which stores frequently accessed intents and responses for faster retrievals.

3.1 Key Modules

The framework comprises the following key components, each designed to address specific challenges in multi-turn dialogue systems:

Intent Classifier. The Intent Classifier utilizes a fine-tuned BERT model (Devlin et al., 2019) to encode user queries into semantic embeddings extracted from last layer of the model. See Appendix A.3 for datatset detail. Confidence scores (c) are calculated by comparing the query embedding with predefined intent embeddings: Based on c, the query is classified as:

- $c > 0.85$: **FAQ (Canned Response)**.
- $0.5 < c \leq 0.85$: **Contextual**.
- $c \leq 0.5$: **Out-of-Domain**.

The above thresholds are default for the system which are updated based on the user-feedback on

Algorithm 1 Context-Aware Intent Confidence Calculation

Require: Query Q, Set of Intent Embeddings $\{E_1, E_2, \ldots, E_n\}$, Historical Context Embeddings H_t
Ensure: Highest Confidence Score c, Corresponding Intent: $\text{Intent}_{\text{max}}$

Step 1: Calculate Query Embedding
$\mathrm{E}_q \leftarrow \mathrm{BERT}(Q)$
Step 2: Contextual Query Embedding
$\text{Context}_t \leftarrow \phi(E_q, \mathrm{H}_t)$ ▷ Augment query embedding with historical context
Step 3: Confidence Calculation
for each intent embedding E_i in $\{E_1, E_2, \ldots, E_n\}$ **do**
    $c_i \leftarrow \text{CosineSimilarity}(\text{Context}_t, E_i)$ ▷ Compute similarity for intent i
end for
Step 4: Find Best Match
$c \leftarrow \max(c_i)$ ▷ Highest confidence score
$\text{Intent}_{\text{max}} \leftarrow \text{argmax}_i(c_i)$ ▷ Intent corresponding to c
Output: c, $\text{Intent}_{\text{max}}$

the fly. Algorithm 1 provides the pseudo-code for the classification process, which incorporates historical context from the Dialogue Context Manager.

Dialogue Context Manager. The module tracks dialogue history using embeddings of prior queries and responses, stored in a sliding window. For multi-turn interactions, historical context embeddings are computed dynamically:

$$\mathrm{H}_t = \psi(\{(Q_{t-i}, R_{t-i}) \mid i = 1, ..n\})$$

where ψ represents a bi-encoder (in-house architecture) that computes the embeddings by appending prior context, queries, and responses into a string. Q_{t-i} and R_{t-i} represents previous query and corresponding responses within a chat session. The aggregated historical context H_t is then used to compute the current contextual query embedding:

$$\text{Context}_t = \phi(E_q, \mathrm{H}_t)$$

Here, ϕ represents a lightweight transformer block (in house cross-encoder) to compute attention, E_q is the current query embedding. Relevant historical context embedding is appended to the current query embedding for downstream processing.

Dynamic Routing. The module checks the confidence (c) of the classified intent: $\text{Intent}_{\text{max}}$, against the threshold (τ_{FAQ}) of the particular intent in the Intent Data Store. τ_{FAQ} for each intent is dynamically updated with user-feedback.

Response Generator. The module refines the final response to user by either blending the static canned responses (R_c) with dynamic RAG outputs (R_r) using a language module or directly passing the R_c or R_r to the user based on the Dynamic Router.

Feedback Mechanism. Explicit (ratings) and implicit (e.g., query refinements) feedback is logged and used to refine thresholds, intents, and response mappings. New intents are created for recurring unhandled queries. Specifically, recurring unhandled queries are logged and grouped based on semantic similarity. When a threshold number of similar unresolved queries is reached in a group, the system automatically flags for creation of a new intent and response. Explicit user feedback is collected via a post-response prompt in the chat interface, allowing users to rate responses positive or negative (thumbs up or thumbs down), which dynamically updates the system's confidence thresholds every 100 interactions.

3.2 Workflow

The framework integrates query classification, response routing, multi-turn handling, and feedback adaptation into a cohesive workflow:

Query Classification. Queries are classified into types (FAQ, Contextual, or Out-of-Domain) based on the confidence score c from the Intent Classifier and the threshold τ_{FAQ} & $\tau_{\text{Out-of-Domain}}$ for each intent, stored in the Intent Data Store, which is dynamically updated with the user feedback. The classification logic is as follows:

- *FAQ:* If $c > \tau_{\text{FAQ}}$, the query is resolved using a predefined canned response for the intent.
- *Out-of-Domain:* If $c \leq \tau_{\text{Out-of-Domain}}$, the

query is routed exclusively to the RAG pipeline for domain-specific response generation.

- *Contextual:* If $\tau_{\text{Out-of-Domain}} < c \leq \tau_{\text{FAQ}}$, the query is processed by both canned responses for the intent and the RAG pipeline. The Response Generator then combines the outputs.

Response Routing. The final response for the user is based on the query classification. The response generation varies by query type:

1. *Canned Response (FAQ):* The predefined the canned response for the intent is passed directly to the user for rapid resolution.
2. *RAG Response (Out-of-Domain):* The RAG output is passed as is, ensuring the most contextually rich response for undefined intents.
3. *Hybrid Response (Contextual):* Both the canned response and the RAG output are retrieved and combined into a unified response using a language model (LLM):

   $$R_f = \text{LLM}(c \cdot R_c, (1 - c) \cdot R_r),$$

   where c is the confidence of the $\text{Intent}_{\text{max}}$, passed to the LLM in to the prompt to ensures coherence and contextual alignment in the final response.

Multi-Turn Handling. Context tracking ensures coherence in multi-turn interactions by retrieving and appending the most relevant embeddings from dialogue history.

Feedback-Driven Adaptability. User feedback dynamically influences system thresholds and intent mappings. The threshold for FAQs (τ_{FAQ}) is adjusted based on feedback trends, ensuring that frequently misclassified queries are handled appropriately. The update mechanism follows::

$$\tau_{\text{FAQ}} = \tau_{\text{FAQ}} + \lambda \cdot (\text{NFR} - \text{PFR}),$$

where:

- **NFR**: Negative Feedback Rate.
- **PFR**: Positive Feedback Rate.
- λ: Scaling factor controlling the sensitivity of the adjustment.
- τ_{FAQ}: By default is set to 0.85 whenever the intents (and dependent intents) are updated in intent data store.

High negative feedback increases the threshold, reducing the likelihood of misclassification as FAQs, while positive feedback reduces the threshold to favor FAQ classification. Threshold for Out-of-Domain queries ($\tau_{\text{Out-of-Domain}}$) is kept constant at 0.5 to prevent over-restricting or over-generalizing OOD classification. This adaptive threshold mechanism ensures that the system remains responsive to user feedback while maintaining stability in query classification. Further details are provided in Appendix A.1

3.3 Prototype Implementation

The framework is implemented as a modular system using microservices:

- **Frontend:** Built with React.js for user interaction and feedback collection (Contributors, 2023).
- **Backend:** Flask microservices handle query classification, retrieval, and feedback processing (Grinberg, 2018).
- **Storage:** OCI (Oracle Cloud Infrastructure) Opensearch stores canned responses & external knowledge base, while FAISS and dense embeddings support retrieval (Karpukhin et al., 2020).
- **Memory Cache:** A memory-augmented module maintains embeddings of prior interactions in OCI Cache (Managed Redis), allowing the system to retain relevant historical context across multiple dialogue turns.
- **Model Deployment:** Models (e.g., BERT, Encoder, Cross-Encoder, GPT-3 & other proprietary LLMs) are deployed using in-house architecture and OCI Gen AI Service for scalability.

4 Experiment and Results

The hybrid framework was evaluated on four metrics: accuracy, response latency, cost efficiency, and turn efficiency. These evaluations spanned inhouse datasets of live customer queries, and scalability tests. Table 2 summarizes overall results, while Table 5 in the appendix provides category-wise performance.

4.1 Experimental Setup

The evaluation dataset comprised 10,000 queries, categorized as :- a) *Predefined FAQ Queries (40%)*:

High-confidence queries resolved via canned responses, b) *Contextual Queries (30%)*: Queries requiring both canned & RAG responses, and c) *Out-of-Domain Queries (30%)*: Undefined intents handled exclusively by RAG pipeline.

For multi-turn interactions, 20% of queries included follow-ups designed to assess context retention. Scalability tests evaluated performance with dataset sizes up to 50,000 queries, preserving category proportions. Results are shown in Table 3.

Evaluation Metrics The system was assessed using the following metrics:

- **Accuracy**: Percentage of correctly resolved queries across predefined FAQs, contextual queries, and out-of-domain scenarios. Accuracy is a fundamental evaluation metric in retrieval-based and generative NLP models (Karpukhin et al., 2020; Lewis et al., 2020), ensuring that responses align with the intended knowledge base. We determine accuracy using a cosine similarity metric, as used in prior works on retrieval-based QA systems (Reimers and Gurevych, 2019). For *Predefined FAQ*, the framework has to fetch the correct FAQ, leading to a 100% cosine similarity. For *Contextual* and *Out-of-Domain Queries*, the generated resposne needs to be similar (90%) to annotated ground truth answer.

- **Response Latency**: Average response time in milliseconds taken to generate responses. Response latency is crucial in real-time conversational AI applications, as delays directly impact user experience (Shuster et al., 2021). Faster response times enhance engagement, making this metric essential for evaluating system efficiency.

- **Cost Efficiency (CE)**: A normalized measure of cost efficiency, defined as:

$$\text{CE} = \min\left(1, \frac{\text{Latency}_{\text{baseline}}}{\text{Latency}_{\text{proposed}}} \times \frac{\text{Accuracy}_{\text{proposed}}}{\text{Accuracy}_{\text{baseline}}}\right)$$

  Inspired by cost-aware NLP evaluations (Tay et al., 2023), this metric balances accuracy and latency trade-offs. It ensures that the proposed framework maintains or improves accuracy while reducing computational costs, a key factor in large-scale AI deployment.

- **Turn Efficiency**: Average number of turns required to resolve a query in a conversation:

$$\text{Turn Efficiency} = \frac{\text{Total Turns}}{\text{Resolved Queries}}$$

  Turn efficiency measures conversational conciseness, ensuring that the system minimizes unnecessary back-and-forth interactions (Serban et al., 2017). A lower number of turns per resolved query indicates a more efficient dialogue system, reducing user dissatisfaction and operational overhead.

4.2 Results and Analysis

Overall Performance. Table 2 compares the proposed framework with baseline systems. Our proposed framework achieves a balance of high accuracy (95%) and low latency (180ms), outperforming the canned-response system and the RAG pipeline's accuracy. The proposed system reduces the chances of hallucination for the most common user queries by leveraging canned responses hence outperforming accuracy of just RAG pipeline's.

Category-Specific Insights. Table 5 (Appendix A.2) highlights performance variations across query types:

- **FAQs**: Similar accuracy compared to the canned-response system, with a 82% reduction in latency compared to RAG Pipeline.

- **Contextual Queries**: Accuracy improved over 47% compared to canned-response system, with over 50% reduction in latency compared to RAG Pipeline with similar accuracy.

- **Out-of-Domain Queries**: The RAG pipeline and our proposed framework exceed the baseline intent-based system's accuracy by over 85%, as intent systems default to fallback responses for out-of-domain queries.

Scalability. The hybrid framework's scalability was evaluated under query loads ranging from 1,000 to 50,000. We observed graceful performance degradation under increasing query loads. Accuracy remains within enterprise-grade thresholds (92% at 50,000 queries), while latency increases proportionally due to retrieval bottlenecks. Table 3 summarizes the results, demonstrating the

Framework	Accuracy (%) (↑)	Response Latency (ms) (↓)	Cost Efficiency (↑)	Turn Efficiency (↓)
Canned-Response (Baseline)	53	**68**	**1.0**	**NA**
RAG Pipeline	91	380	0.3	2.3
Proposed Framework	**95**	180	0.7	1.7

Table 2: Evaluation Results for Canned-Response (Intent) Systems, RAG, and Proposed Frameworks. Metrics represent averages across the evaluation dataset. The desired direction for improvement: (↑) higher is better, (↓) lower is better. Turn Efficiency is not available for Canned-Response as it lacks multi-turn capabilities.

frameworks ability to maintain balanced performance in terms of accuracy, latency, and cost efficiency under increasing concurrent loads.

Cost Efficiency. Proposed framework demonstrates effective trade-offs, achieving a CE score of 0.7 compared to 0.3 for RAG. The introduction of dynamic query routing minimizes computational overhead for high-confidence queries.

Turn Efficiency. Turn efficiency (1.7) highlight the framework's ability to maintain coherence and minimize dialogue complexity while trying to resolve queries, relatively outperforming both baselines when compared in conjunction with accuracy and response latency.

Multi-Turn Interaction Analysis With 20% (2,000) queries including follow-up interactions, the dialogue context manager maintained high coherence in these multi-turn interactions, effectively tracking evolving user intents and ensuring context continuity. Minor context drift was observed in sessions exceeding 10 turns, indicating that optimizing context management for prolonged dialogues remains an area for future improvement. See Appendix A.5 for common failure scenarios and error analysis.

Query Load	Accuracy (%)	Latency (ms)	Cost Efficiency
1,000	96	174	0.77
5,000	96	177	0.74
10,000	95	180	0.71
20,000	94	186	0.70
50,000	92	193	0.69

Table 3: Scalability Results for the proposed Framework. Query Load indicates the number of queries processed in the evaluation.

4.3 Error Analysis:

We conducted a manual error analysis on 500 dialogue samples covering diverse user intents. Only 32 (6%) samples were found erroneous. Three independent annotators with subject matter expertise in Oracle cloud customer support evaluated these dialogue samples with an inter-annotator agreement of 0.91. Errors were categorized into four main types: 1) Edge Cases in Intent Classification (21%) due to subtle semantic differences, 2) Long Multi-Turn Dialogues (35%) where latency and context tracking issues arose, 3) Retrieval Inaccuracy (25%) from incomplete or outdated document retrieval, and 4) Feedback Misalignment (19%) due to misinterpretation of user feedback. Future work to remediate these could include refining fallback strategies, optimizing context management, regular index updates, and context-aware feedback processing. Further details are provided in Appendix A.5.

4.4 Final Insights and Implications

The evaluation metrics, error analysis and scalability underscore the proposed framework's effectiveness:

- **Efficiency-Accuracy Trade-offs**: Dynamic query routing achieves optimal balance between computational cost and response quality.
- **Multi-Turn Adaptability**: Superior context retention validates its applicability in complex dialogue scenarios.
- **Scalability and Robustness**: Modular design ensures operational resilience under high query loads.

5 Conclusion

We proposed a hybrid conversational framework that integrates intent-based canned responses with Retrieval-Augmented Generation (RAG) systems, explicitly designed to handle multi-turn interactions. The framework dynamically routes queries based on intent confidence, ensuring low latency for predefined intents while leveraging RAG for complex or ambiguous queries. The inclusion of a dialogue context manager guarantees coherence across multi-turn interactions, and a feedback-driven mechanism continuously refines intents and confidence thresholds over time.

Experimental results demonstrated the proposed framework's ability to balance accuracy (95%), response latency (180ms), and cost efficiency (0.7), while achieving superior context retention and turn efficiency in multi-turn scenarios. The system effectively handles multi-turn dialogues with minor limitations in long conversations exceeding 10 turns. Our contributions include a scalable, adaptive solution for dynamic conversational AI, addressing key industry challenges such as query diversity, evolving knowledge bases, and real-time performance requirements. Future research will focus on enhancing multi-turn context management, conducting ablation studies to isolate module contributions, and exploring real-time learning mechanisms for continuous adaptation. This work advances the state-of-the-art in enterprise conversational AI, providing a robust framework for handling complex, multi-turn interactions efficiently.

6 Limitations and Future Work

While our system demonstrates strong performance in enterprise customer support scenarios, it is optimized for English language applications and may require adaptation for multilingual deployments. Expanding to other languages introduces challenges such as acquiring labeled training data and handling linguistic variations, which may increase operational costs and training time. Additionally, our intent classifier is trained on domain-specific datasets, and extending to new domains or industries will necessitate retraining with relevant data, impacting both cost and deployment timelines.

Lastly, integrating real-time learning mechanisms that adapt continuously without periodic retraining is an avenue for future exploration, providing a more seamless and cost-effective method for maintaining system relevance over time. Future work will also include studies to isolate the impact of the dialogue context manager and quantify its contribution to system performance, as well as extending our framework to support multilingual conversations by improving intent recognition and retrieval efficiency across diverse languages.

References

Amit Agarwal, Srikant Panda, and Kulbhushan Pachauri. 2024a. Synthetic document generation pipeline for training artificial intelligence models. US Patent App. 17/994,712.

Amit Agarwal, Srikant Panda, and Kulbhushan Pachauri. 2025. Fs-dag: Few shot domain adapting graph networks for visually rich document understanding. In Proceedings of the 31st International Conference on Computational Linguistics: Industry Track, pages 100–114, Abu Dhabi, UAE. Association for Computational Linguistics.

Amit Agarwal, Hitesh Patel, Priyaranjan Pattnayak, Srikant Panda, Bhargava Kumar, and Tejaswini Kumar. 2024b. Enhancing document ai data generation through graph-based synthetic layouts. arXiv preprint arXiv:2412.03590.

Jason Bordes et al. 2020. Contextualized end-to-end learning for conversational ai. In Proceedings of the 2020 Conference on Neural Information Processing Systems (NeurIPS).

React.js Contributors. 2023. React: A javascript library for building user interfaces. Available at https://react.dev/.

Florin Cuconasu, Giovanni Trappolini, Federico Siciliano, Simone Filice, Cesare Campagnano, Yoelle Maarek, Nicola Tonellotto, and Fabrizio Silvestri. 2024. The power of noise: Redefining retrieval for rag systems. In Proceedings of the 47th International ACM SIGIR Conference on Research and Development in Information Retrieval, SIGIR 2024, page 719–729. ACM.

Jacob Devlin, Ming-Wei Chang, Kenton Lee, et al. 2019. Bert: Pre-training of deep bidirectional transformers for language understanding. Association for Computational Linguistics (ACL), pages 4171–4186.

Matthijs Douze, Alexandr Guzhva, Chengqi Deng, Jeff Johnson, Gergely Szilvasy, Pierre-Emmanuel Mazaré, Maria Lomeli, Lucas Hosseini, and Hervé Jégou. 2024. The faiss library.

A. Friedrich et al. 2020. Context-aware robust fine-tuning for chatbots. In Proceedings of the 2020 International Conference on AI and Machine Learning.

Hao Gao, Dongxu Li, Shuohang Wang, and Wenjie Li. 2020a. Hybrid conversational frameworks for multi-domain dialogue systems. In ACL, pages 298–305.

Hao Gao, Dongxu Li, Liheng Xu, Shuohang Wang, and Wenjie Li. 2020b. Search-augmented generation for dialogue systems. In Proceedings of the 58th Annual Meeting of the Association for Computational Linguistics (ACL).

Pengfei Gao, Jianfei Gao, and et al. 2020c. Modular graph networks for reasoning over text. ACL.

Miguel Grinberg. 2018. Flask web development:

Developing web applications with Python. O'Reilly Media.

Ricardo Hernandez, Rahul Gupta, and Shubham Patel. 2020. Efficient and scalable hybrid retrieval for search engines. In Proceedings of the 43rd International ACM SIGIR Conference on Research and Development in Information Retrieval.

Paulina Toro Isaza, Michael Nidd, Noah Zheutlin, Jae wook Ahn, Chidansh Amitkumar Bhatt, Yu Deng, Ruchi Mahindru, Martin Franz, Hans Florian, and Salim Roukos. 2024. Retrieval augmented generation-based incident resolution recommendation system for it support.

Vladimir Karpukhin, Barlas Oguz, Sewon Min, et al. 2020. Dense passage retrieval for open-domain question answering. Empirical Methods in Natural Language Processing (EMNLP), pages 6769–6781.

Mandar Kulkarni, Praveen Tangarajan, Kyung Kim, and Anusua Trivedi. 2024. Reinforcement learning for optimizing rag for domain chatbots.

Jinhyuk Lee et al. 2020. Speculative rag: Enhancing retrieval augmented generation through drafting. In Proceedings of the 2020 Conference on Neural Information Processing Systems (NeurIPS).

Patrick Lewis, Ethan Perez, Aleksandra Piktus, Fabio Petroni, Vassilios Stamatescu, Tim Rocktäschel, Sebastian Ruder, Pontus Stenetorp, and LUKAS RICHTER. 2020. Retrieval-augmented generation for knowledge-intensive nlp tasks. In Proceedings of the 38th International Conference on Machine Learning (ICML).

J. Michelson et al. 2020. Expanding chatbot knowledge in customer service: Context-aware similar question generation using large language models. In Proceedings of the 2020 Conference on Natural Language Processing.

Bingqing Mitra, Karan Goel, and Nikita Soni. 2021. Hybrid retrieval and ranking methods for information retrieval. In Proceedings of the 43rd International ACM SIGIR Conference on Research and Development in Information Retrieval.

Hitesh Laxmichand Patel, Amit Agarwal, Bhargava Kumar, Karan Gupta, and Priyaranjan Pattnayak. 2024. Llm for barcodes: Generating diverse synthetic data for identity documents. arXiv preprint arXiv:2411.14962.

Priyaranjan Pattnayak, Hitesh Laxmichand Patel, Amit Agarwal, Bhargava Kumar, Srikant Panda, and Tejaswini Kumar. 2025. Improving clinical question answering with multi-task learning: A joint approach for answer extraction and medical categorization.

Priyaranjan Pattnayak, Hitesh Laxmichand Patel, Bhargava Kumar, Amit Agarwal, Ishan Banerjee, Srikant Panda, and Tejaswini Kumar. 2024. Survey of large multimodal model datasets, application categories and taxonomy. arXiv preprint arXiv:2412.17759.

Nils Reimers and Iryna Gurevych. 2019. Sentence-bert: Sentence embeddings using siamese bert-networks. arXiv preprint arXiv:1908.10084.

S. E. Robertson and S. Walker. 1994. Some Simple Effective Approximations to the 2-Poisson Model for Probabilistic Weighted Retrieval, pages 232–241. Springer London.

Tim Rocktäschel, Sebastian Ruder, Shinnosuke Takamatsu, and Pontus Stenetorp. 2020. Rethinking the role of knowledge in dialogue systems. In Proceedings of the 58th Annual Meeting of the Association for Computational Linguistics (ACL).

Victor Sanh, Thomas Wolf, Julien Chaumond, and Clément Delangue. 2020a. Multitask mixture of sequence generation tasks for diverse natural language generation. In Proceedings of the 58th Annual Meeting of the Association for Computational Linguistics, pages 1962–1971.

Victor Sanh, Thomas Wolf, Julien Chaumond, Clement Delangue, Pierrick Sprechmann, Alex Wang, Shinnosuke Takamatsu, and Tim Rocktäschel. 2020b. Realm: Retrieval-augmented language model pre-training. In Proceedings of the 37th International Conference on Machine Learning (ICML).

Iulian V. Serban, Alessandro Sordoni, Yoshua Bengio, and Jian-Yun Nie. 2017. A survey of available corpora for building data-driven dialogue systems. In Proceedings of the 2nd Workshop on Dialogue Systems Technology Evaluation (DST'17).

Vishal Shah, Pushpak Bhattacharyya, and Khurshid Ahmad. 2018. Building end-to-end dialogue systems with transformer models. In Proceedings of the 22nd Conference on Computational Natural Language Learning (CoNLL).

Kurt Shuster, Eric Smith, Stephen Roller, Y-Lan Boureau, and Jason Weston. 2021. Retrieval-augmented generation for knowledge-intensive nlp tasks. arXiv preprint arXiv:2102.09527.

Yi Tay, Mostafa Dehghani, Samira Abnar, Dara Bahri, Yikang Shen, Xingdi Zhou, and Donald Metzler. 2023. Efficient and scalable nlp with small and large pretrained language models. arXiv preprint arXiv:2305.13249.

Sriram Veturi, Saurabh Vaichal, Reshma Lal Jagadheesh, Nafis Irtiza Tripto, and Nian Yan. 2024. Rag based question-answering for contextual response prediction system.

et al. Zhao, W. 2020. A retrieval-augmented encoder-decoder for knowledge-intensive nlp tasks. In Proceedings of the 58th Annual Meeting of the Association for Computational Linguistics (ACL).

A Appendix

A.1 Extended Workflow

Feedback-Driven Adaptability. The feedback rates are used to dynamically change the thresholds

Scenario	Query Type	Response Type	Impact
Predefined FAQ	High-confidence intent	Canned Response	Reduced Latency, Cost Savings
Contextual Query	Low-confidence intent	Hybrid (RAG + canned)	Increased Coherence, Cost Saving
Out-of-Domain Query	Undefined intent	Full RAG pipeline	Increased Accuracy

Table 4: Query Handling Scenarios in the Hybrid Framework.

Framework	Category	Accuracy (%)	Response Latency (ms)	Cost Efficiency
Canned Response	Predefined FAQ	93	65	1.00
	Contextual	49	65	1.00
	Out-of-Domain	5	75	0.08
RAG	Predefined FAQ	91	376	0.31
	Contextual	92	381	0.31
	Out-of-Domain	90	379	0.31
Proposed Framework	Predefined FAQ	96	65	1.00
	Contextual	96	182	0.67
	Out-of-Domain	93	379	0.32

Table 5: Performance comparison of different frameworks across various categories. Baseline cost efficiency is established using average latency and accuracy for canned responses across the entire evaluation dataset as mentioned in Table 2.

defined as follows:

$$\text{NFR} = \frac{\text{NegativeFeedback}}{\text{TotalQueries}}$$

$$\text{PFR} = \frac{\text{PositiveFeedback}}{\text{TotalQueries}}$$

New intents are generated from user feedback and query patterns, which are processed offline to update the Intent Data Store. Intent classification is refined continuously by an adaptive system feedback loop. Unresolved queries are logged, clustered on the basis of semantic similarity, and flagged for review. When a cluster reaches a certain size, a new intent is created offline and integrated into the classifier. Additionally, confidence thresholds are periodically adjusted based on user feedback to improve the routing of ambiguous queries.

A.1.1 Intent Evolution through Feedback

In addition to threshold tuning, the system expands its intent data store based on observed usage patterns and unresolved queries. The intent creation process operates in the following stages:

1. **Logging and Clustering**: All unhandled queries are logged and grouped using semantic similarity clustering.

2. **Pattern Detection**: If a cluster of unresolved queries exceeds a predefined frequency threshold, it is flagged for intent creation.

3. **New Intent Generation**: A new intent is proposed & validated by SMEs, and added to the Intent Data Store.

This process ensures that frequently occurring unresolved queries are automatically handled by the intent classifier going forward, thereby improving future query routing.

Improving FAQ Classification via Threshold Adjustment

Query: *"Why am I seeing high costs for my Oracle Autonomous Database instance?"*

The system classifies this as an FAQ and responds: **Response:** *"Oracle Autonomous Database costs depend on the compute shape, storage capacity, and workload type. You can adjust your settings to optimize cost."*

However, users frequently provide negative feedback, indicating that the response lacks details on Auto Scaling, Always Free tier limits, and OCI pricing policies. This causes NFR to increase, leading to an increase in τ_{FAQ}. The system becomes more selective in assigning queries to FAQs. More complex cost-related queries are routed to context-aware retrieval mechanisms rather than FAQs.

Intent Creation for Repeated OOD Queries
Query: *"How do I configure OCI Object Storage to replicate data to another region?"*

Initially, the system classifies this as Out-of-Domain (OOD), as no existing intent covers cross-region object storage replication. However, after multiple users ask similar questions, the system clusters these unresolved queries. Once the cluster surpasses the predefined frequency threshold, it is flagged for new intent creation by SMEs:

New Intent: *"OCI Object Storage Cross-Region Replication"*
Associated Response: *"Detailed steps to enabled and configure cross-region replication as determined by SME"*

The system proactively resolves similar future queries by classifying them under the newly created intent. Users receive accurate responses immediately instead of being redirected to general support.

Proposed Framework. The workflow of the proposed system is summarized in Table 4

A.2 Detailed Performance Comparison

This section provides a detailed breakdown of the performance of the proposed hybrid framework compared to baseline systems (Canned Response System) and RAG Pipeline across different query categories: Predefined FAQs, Contextual Queries, and Out-of-Domain Queries. The metrics include accuracy, response latency, and cost efficiency, highlighting the strengths and trade-offs of each approach.

Analysis The results in Table 5 demonstrate the trade-offs between accuracy, latency, and cost efficiency:

- **Predefined FAQs:** The proposed framework achieves a balance, with similar accuracy with the canned-response system while reducing latency by 82% compared to the RAG pipeline.
- **Contextual Queries:** The proposed framework strikes a balance between RAG's accuracy (92%) and the canned-response system's latency (65ms), achieving 96% accuracy with an acceptable latency of 182ms.
- **Out-of-Domain Queries:** The RAG Pipeline and the proposed framework have a very similar latency and performance with our proposed framework have slight better accuracy (3%) owing to the better handling of context and queries.

A.3 In-House Dataset Overview

The evaluation leveraged a in-house dataset on customer support for OCI Cloud based Services of 10,000 queries across three categories: predefined FAQs, contextual queries, and out-of-domain queries. Table 6 provides a sample of the queries used in the evaluation.

For BERT fine-tuning, we used in-house conversational dataset which is domain specific, with 35,000 human-customer conversations curated over a period of 6 months.

A.4 Multi-Turn Interaction Examples

To demonstrate the framework's adaptability, Table 7 outlines examples of evolving user queries and how the system dynamically adapts to maintain coherence.

A.5 Failure Cases and Error Analysis

We conducted a manual error analysis on 500 dialogue samples spanning diverse user intents. Three independent annotators with experience in enterprise conversational AI systems evaluated these dialogues, with an inter-annotator agreement of 0.91 (Cohen's Kappa). Inter-annotator agreement was calculated by comparing the categorical labels assigned (out of 4 shown below) by each annotator across all 500 dialogue samples. Annotators independently labeled each dialogue, and disagreements were resolved through discussion to refine the labeling criteria. The high agreement score (0.91) reflects consistency in identifying and categorizing errors across evaluators.

Errors were categorized as follows:

Query	Category	Confidence Level
How do I reset my password?	Predefined FAQ	0.95
What are the steps to integrate autoscaling?	Contextual	0.70
What are compliance requirements for data?	Out-of-Domain	0.40
Can you elaborate on scaling options?	Multi-Turn Follow-Up	0.75

Table 6: Sample Queries from the in-house Dataset.

Turn	User Query	Framework	System Response
1	What are the steps to enable advanced analytics?	Canned Response	Analytics can be enabled in the dashboard settings.
2	Can you explain what metrics are available?	Hybrid Response	Available metrics include user engagement, retention, and revenue.
3	How can I visualize these metrics effectively?	RAG Response	Visualization tools like Tableau and Power BI integrate seamlessly with our platform.
4	What steps are required to connect Tableau?	Hybrid Response	Refer to the integration settings under "Analytics" and provide your Tableau API key.
5	Are there any tutorials for advanced analytics setup?	RAG Response	Yes, detailed tutorials can be found in the documentation section under "Advanced Analytics."

Table 7: Multi-Turn Example Showcasing Evolving Intents and Follow-Ups.

- **Edge Cases in Intent Classification (21% of errors):** Queries were misclassified due to subtle semantic differences. For example, the query *"Can you assist with integrating API X for multi-platform deployment?"* was routed to a general FAQ response about API usage due to high lexical similarity.
- **Long Multi-Turn Dialogues (35% of errors):** In conversations exceeding 10 turns, latency increased, and context tracking sometimes failed. For instance, after handling a billing query, the system mistakenly retained billing context when the user shifted to technical support.
- **Retrieval Inaccuracy (25% of errors):** Some queries led to incomplete or off-topic document retrieval. For example, a query like *"Provide the latest number of regions your cloud service is available in"* retrieved outdated documents due to incomplete index updates.
- **Feedback Misalignment (19% of errors):** User feedback was sometimes misinterpreted. For instance, a user rated a correct response poorly due to slow response time rather than content accuracy, leading to unnecessary adjustments in the intent classifier.

Table 8 summarizes these failure cases and suggested remedies. This detailed error analysis highlights both the strengths of our system and areas for future improvement.

A.6 Prototype Implementation

The framework is implemented as a modular system using microservices:

- **Frontend:** Built with React.js for user interaction and feedback collection (Contributors, 2023).
- **Backend:** Flask microservices handle query classification, retrieval, and feedback processing (Grinberg, 2018).
- **Storage:** Elasticsearch stores canned responses & external knowledge base, while FAISS and dense embeddings support retrieval (Karpukhin et al., 2020).
- **Memory Cache:** A memory-augmented module maintains embeddings of prior inter-

Scenario	Issue	Remedy	Error Distribution (%)
Edge Cases in Intent Classification	Query incorrectly routed to canned responses	A stronger fallback strategy could improve reliability	21% (7/32)
Long Multi-Turn Dialogues	Latency for very long conversations	Optimize dialog context manager to reduce latency.	35% (11/32)
Retrieval Inaccuracy	Incomplete or outdated documents retrieved	Regular index updates and improved retrieval ranking	25% (8/32)
Feedback Misalignment	User feedback misinterpreted during adjustments	Implement context-aware feedback processing	19% (6/32)

Table 8: Failure Cases and Suggested Remedies. A total of 32 erroneous dialogues were identified out of 500 tested samples.

actions in OCI Cache (Managed Redis), allowing the system to retain relevant historical context across multiple dialogue turns.

- **Model Deployment:** Models (e.g., BERT, Encoder, Cross-Encoder, GPT-3 & other proprietary LLMs) are deployed using in-house architecture and OCI Gen AI Service for scalability.

B Technical Implementation of Multi-Turn Adaptation

The **Dialogue Context Manager** is implemented using a transformer-based architecture with the following components:

- **Context Embeddings:** Queries are encoded using fine-tuned BERT embeddings capturing semantic information and historical contexts are encoded using an in-house Bi-Encoder.
- **Memory Module:** A memory-augmented module maintains embeddings of prior interactions in cache (Redis), allowing the system to retain relevant historical context across multiple dialogue turns.
- **Context Attention Mechanism:** An attention layer prioritizes recent or semantically relevant interactions, dynamically retrieving context embeddings as input to the intent classifier and response generator.
- **Sliding Context Window:** Implements a fixed-length sliding window to limit the memory footprint and computational complexity by retaining only the most relevant context from prior turns.

The context manager utilizes the embeddings and attention scores to generate a composite representation of the current dialogue state, which is passed to downstream components, such as the hybrid response generator. The dynamic adaptation ensures responses remain coherent and contextually grounded in multi-turn settings.

C Technical Implementation of Hybrid Routing

Hybrid routing combines canned responses and RAG outputs using a confidence-based decision-making pipeline:

- **Confidence Scoring:** The intent classifier assigns a confidence score to each query based on the similarity between the query embedding and predefined intent embeddings.
- **Thresholding Mechanism:** Queries with a confidence score above a pre-defined threshold (e.g., 85%) are routed to the canned response repository for rapid resolution.
- **Response Generation:** For low-confidence queries or multi-turn scenarios, responses are generated by blending canned responses with retrieved content from the RAG pipeline. Sample prompt used for blending the responses using confidence scores is shown in Figure 2

This mechanism optimizes query handling for diverse scenarios while ensuring minimal latency and maximal accuracy.

Prompt Template
You are an AI assistant tasked with synthesizing responses to a given query. You have received two distinct responses to the query, each with a specific confidence score. Your goal is to produce a refined and cohesive final response that:

1. Gives appropriate emphasis to the response with higher confidence, while considering elements from the lower-confidence response if they add value or completeness.
2. Avoids contradictions and ensures clarity, consistency, and factual correctness in the final output.
3. Uses the confidence scores to proportionally balance the contributions of each response, without undermining valuable insights from either.
Instructions:

- *Consider the following inputs:*
- *Query: [Insert query here]*
- *Response 1: [Insert response 1 here]*
- *Confidence 1: [Insert weightage for response 1]*
- *Response 2: [Insert response 2 here]*
- *Confidence 2: [Insert weightage for response 2]*
- *Combine the two responses into a single, well-structured response by prioritizing the higher-confidence response while integrating any complementary information from the other response.*

***Output:** Provide a single, refined response to the query. Ensure the response is logically structured, concise, and addresses the query comprehensively.*

Figure 2: Prompt for Blending Responses

D Feature Limitations & Related Future Work

D.1 Limitations

Despite the strong performance of the proposed framework on a variety of metrics, certain feature-specific limitations remain:

- *Edge Cases in Intent Classification*: Ambiguous queries near confidence thresholds may cause inconsistencies, as seen in our error analysis, where subtle semantic differences led to misclassification. A stronger fallback strategy could improve reliability.
- *Latency in Long Multi-Turn Dialogues*: Latency issues for very long conversations (over 10 turns) were identified in 30% of errors, highlighting the need to optimize the dialogue context manager for faster context updates.
- *Retrieval Inaccuracy*: Incomplete or outdated document retrieval (20% of errors) due to index inconsistencies highlights the need for regular index updates and improved retrieval ranking.
- *Feedback Misalignment*: User feedback misinterpretation (10% of errors) occasionally led to suboptimal adjustments, suggesting the need for context-aware feedback processing.

D.2 Future Work

Future research could address these limitations by:

- Developing advanced intent detection techniques and fallback mechanisms to handle ambiguous and low-confidence queries more effectively.
- Enhancing multi-turn context tracking with memory-augmented models to improve coherence across long dialogues.
- Implementing regular index updates and fine-tuned retrieval processes to ensure accurate document retrieval.
- Integrating context-aware feedback processing to ensure accurate adaptation of system responses based on user ratings.
- Exploring distributed architectures and load-balancing techniques for scalability under peak query loads.

Chain of Evidences and Evidence to Generate: Prompting for Context Grounded and Retrieval Augmented Reasoning

Md Rizwan Parvez
Qatar Computing Research Institute (QCRI)
mparvez@hbku.edu.qa

Abstract

While chain-of-thoughts (CoT) prompting has revolutionized how LLMs perform reasoning tasks, its current methods and variations (e.g, Self-consistency, ReACT, Reflexion, Tree-of-Thoughts (ToT), Cumulative Reasoning (CR) etc.,) suffer from limitations like limited context grounding, hallucination/inconsistent output generation, and iterative sluggishness. To overcome these challenges, we introduce a novel mono/dual-step zero-shot prompting framework built upon two unique strategies **Chain of Evidences (CoE)** and **Evidence to Generate (E2G)**. Instead of unverified reasoning claims, our innovative approaches leverage the power of "evidence for decision making" by first focusing exclusively on the thought sequences explicitly mentioned in the context which then serve as extracted evidence, guiding the LLM's output generation process with greater precision and efficiency. This simple yet potent approach unlocks the full potential of chain-of-thoughts prompting, facilitating faster, more reliable, and contextually aware reasoning in LLMs. Our framework consistently achieves remarkable results across various knowledge-intensive reasoning and generation tasks, surpassing baseline approaches with state-of-the-art LLMs. For instance, (i) on the LogiQA benchmark using GPT-4, CoE achieves a new state-of-the-art accuracy of 53.8%, surpassing CoT by 18%, ToT by 11%, and CR by 9%; (ii) CoE with PaLM-2 outperforms the variable-shot performance of Gemini Ultra by 0.9 F1 points, achieving an F1 score of 83.3 on DROP. We release our prompts and outputs on these benchmarks as a new instruction tuning dataset for future research at *Hugging Face*[1].

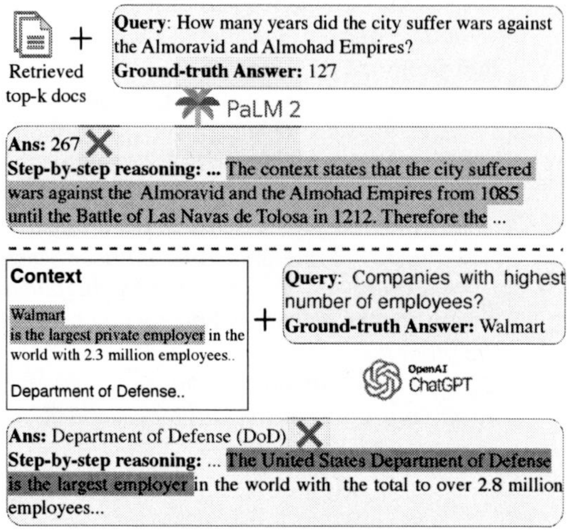

Figure 1: CoT & variants falter in context-aware reasoning. Top: Overwhelming long-text complexity leads models' failure even when it generates partially/fully correct reasoning (in green). Bottom: Ungrounded internal reasoning fails to grasp context, confusing "DoD" (ungroundeded private org in red) vs Walmart (in green).

1 Introduction

Retrieval-augmented or context-based generation serves as a mean for leveraging relevant information, empowering large language models (LLMs) to reduce the factual errors in their generation (Islam et al., 2024b; Asai et al., 2023a,b). However, despite the expansion in model and data size, LLMs struggle in contextual reasoning. This challenge is further amplified when dealing with retrieved information that are often long and imperfect text with distractive contents.

To bolster LLM's reasoning capabilities, the Chain-of-Thought (CoT) prompting paradigm has emerged as a potent tool (Wei et al., 2022). Subsequent methods, including Self-consistency (SC; (Wang et al., 2022)), ReACT (Yao et al., 2022), Reflexion (Shinn et al., 2023), Tree of Thoughts (ToT; (Yao et al., 2023)), and Cumulative Reasoning (CR; (Zhang et al., 2023b)), generalize CoT with various multi-objective, ensemble-based, or tool-augmented, and trial & error approaches but do not address the complexities of context-grounded or retrieval augmented generations (RAG). We highlight two of their pivotal bottlenecks: (i) CoT focuses solely on expanding steps without verifying hypotheses; (ii) excessively long retrieved text can lead to incorrect conclusions even with valid CoT reasonings (example in Figure 1).

Multi-step reasoning prompting has emerged as a promising alternative to traditional chain-of-thought (CoT) approaches by decomposing complex problems

[1]https://huggingface.co/datasets/kagnlp/Chain-of-Evidences/

Proceedings of the 4th International Workshop on Knowledge-Augmented Methods for Natural Language Processing (KnowledgeNLP'25), pages 230–245
May 3, 2025 ©2025 Association for Computational Linguistics

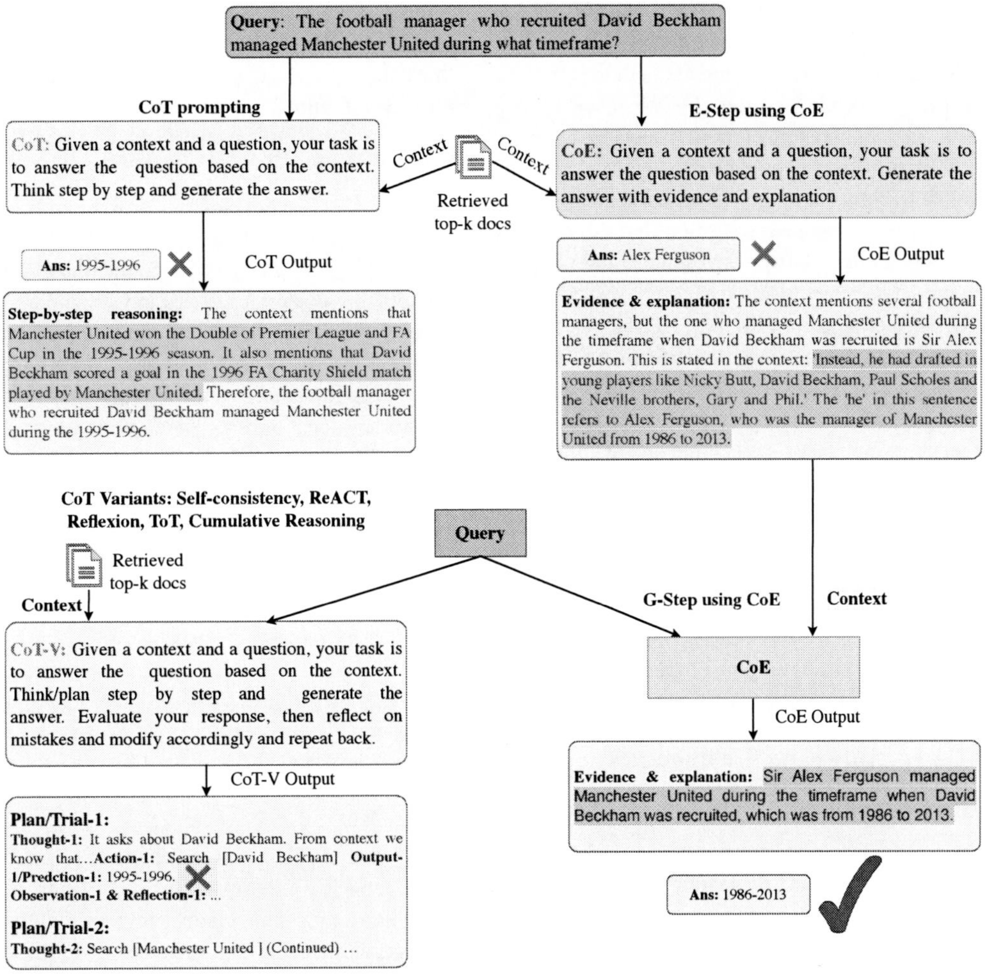

Figure 2: (left) CoT and generic view of its (iterative) variants, (right) The E2G pipeline: In E-step our "generate ans with evidence and explanation" instruction extracts the rationales, coupled with the ans, grounded in the original context, then in G step we use the same instruction to derive the final answer solely from the "evidence and explanation" or along with the original context.

into sequential reasoning substeps (Dhuliawala et al., 2023; Wang et al., 2023a; Zhao et al., 2023; Trivedi et al., 2023; Fu et al., 2022; Creswell et al., 2022; Li et al., 2023). However, these techniques typically require rigorous verification of each intermediate step. Although simpler iterative verification strategies—such as self-check (Miao et al., 2023) and self-refine (Madaan et al., 2024)—have been proposed, they do not fully address the challenges inherent in long-context processing or retrieval-augmented generation. Moreover, they often rely on disparate intermediate prompts—such as rationale selection and inference/premise derivation—that necessitate k-shot annotated in-context exemplars, which are often difficult to construct (Islam et al., 2025, 2024a; Yasunaga et al., 2024). Therefore, unlocking CoT's true potential for RAG & context driven reasoning remains unanswered. To address, in this paper, we propose a simple verification-free zero-shot prompting framework for context-grounded and retrieval augmented reasoning.

Our framework consists of two unique and real-time prompting strategies particularly tailored for long context reasoning. First, single-step **Chain-of-Evidences (CoE):** to address the problem of ungrounded reasoning hypotheses, our designed prompt asks for specific thought sequences that are explicitly mentioned in the context. We call this series of intermediate reasoning steps, with directly extracted rationales from the given context, '*Evidence*' (as in human decision making). Our key distinction from existing CoT approaches is that instead of mere "thinking step-by-step" (Kojima et al., 2022) our prompt instruction asks for "step-by-step reasoning with explicit evidence and explanation".

Second, dual-step **Evidence to Generate (E2G):** to facilitate LLMs' answering the query properly even with retrieval augmented long-text contexts, we split the task into steps. In the first step (E), we adopt prompts similar to CoE and generate both the *Answer* & *Evidence* . Then in next step (G), we pass only the *Evidence* as context for a second round of CoE to LLM. G Step *Answer* is predicted as the final answer. In contrast to complex long original context in E step, the *Evidence* is a concise short text that directly answer the input query, G step is very fast, and simpler for the model to generate answer.

In experiments with different LLMs, we show that our prompts consistently outperform existing approaches in a diverse set of eight context-driven tasks, including natural QA, complex multi-hop, long-form QA, fact checking, dialog generation, and reading comprehension tasks. Since, even with such techniques, it is non-trivial to comprehend why and how this works and how to setup the prompt to function correctly, cost-effectively, and robustly. To this end, we perform case studies, analyze different alternatives and reveal the strengths and weaknesses of our approach. We open-source our prompts and outputs on these benchmarks as a new instruction tuning dataset for future research.

2 Related Works and Preliminaries

2.1 Prompting LLMs

Various prompting paradigms have been studied in literature toward enhancing reasoning in LLMs. In Section 1, we provide a (non-exhaustive) list of CoT approaches. Among others, search-based (Pryzant et al., 2023; Lu et al., 2021), Program-aided LLM generation (Liu et al., 2023a; Gao et al., 2023; Jung et al., 2022; Zhu et al., 2022), self generation of prompts (He et al., 2023; Yasunaga et al., 2023; Sun et al., 2022; Kim et al., 2022; Li et al., 2022), self evaluation based approaches (Madaan et al., 2023; Xie et al., 2023; Kim et al., 2023; Paul et al., 2023) have been studied. Other works have also been extended with more complex multi-step reasoning procedure (e.g., using a different fine-tuned model (Yu et al., 2023; Nye et al., 2021; Lester et al., 2021)) or for domain specific applications (Parvez et al., 2023, 2021; Ouyang et al., 2022; Sanh et al., 2021; Wei et al., 2021).

2.2 Chain-of-Thoughts (CoT) Prompting

Chain-of-thoughts (CoT; (Wei et al., 2022)) is a prompting framework that guides LLMs to produce intermediate reasoning steps towards the final answer, enhancing its reasoning. Original version of CoT employs a few-shot version by providing multiple exemplars of the reasoning process (question–reasoning–answer), leveraging LLMs' in-context learning abilities. However, due to the requirement of labeled exemplars, it quickly evolved with a 0-shot instance (Kojima et al., 2022). 0-shot CoT prompts LLMs with a general instruction like "think step by step" to produce intermediate reasoning steps (See Figure 2).

3 Our Prompting Framework

In this section, we develop our prompting framework for context-grounding and retrieval augmented long-text reasoning. We design two unique (mono/dual-step) prompts that does not require any exemplars and removes the hurdles of choosing multi-objective instructions. Below we first present the prompt instruction for defining the objective for the target task (a.k.a system prompt), next the single-step prompting technique **Chain of Evidences (CoE)** and finally dual-step **Evidence to Generate (E2G)** that uses CoE twice.

3.1 System/Objective Instruction

Our proposed framework is a single-intent system, having only one target task to solve at a time. Given a target task T, our objective/system prompt is:

```
# You are a/an [T] agent. Given a context and a [T[x]] as input, please give a [T[y]] output based on the context.
```

`T[x]` and `T[y]` depends on the task `T`. Examples of `T`, `T[x]` and `T[y]` are (QA, fact verification, dialogue generation), (question, claim, previous dialogue), and (answer, judgement, next turn dialogue) respectively. An example for fact checking:

```
# You are a text classification agent. Given a context and a claim, please give a judgement to the claim ('SUPPORTS' or 'REFUTES') based on the context.
```

3.2 Chain of Evidences (CoE)

While the 0-shot CoT instruction (i.e., Answer the question. Think step-by-step.) expands the query answer generation into small reasoning steps, it does not focus on context-grounding and generate imaginary hypotheses. To address, our prompt asks for answering the query specifically with evidence and explanation from context. We design two alternatives CoE-SHORT & CoE-LONG.

CoE-Short

```
# Objective Instruction from Section 3.1
# Generate the answer with evidence and explanation.
```

|Context| >200	Multi-Query	Context-Aware	Cost-Minimize	E-step		G-step	
				Prompt	Context	Prompt	Context
✗	✗	✗	✗	CoE-Long	-	-	-
✗	✗	✗	✓	CoE-Short	-	-	-
✗	✗	✓	✗	CoE-Long	OC	-	-
✗	✗	✓	✓	CoE-Short	OC	-	-
✗	✓	✗	✗	CoE-Long	-	-	-
✗	✓	✗	✓	CoE-Short	-	-	-
✗	✓	✓	✗	CoE-Long	OC	CoE-Long	E + OC
✗	✓	✓	✓	CoE-Short	OC	CoE-Short	E + OC
✓	✗	✓	✗	CoE-Long	OC	CoE-Long	E
✓	✗	✓	✓	CoE-Short	OC	CoE-Short	E
✓	✓	✓	✗	CoE-Long	OC	CoE-Long	E + OC
✓	✓	✓	✓	CoE-Short	OC	CoE-Short	E + OC

Table 1: Recommended alternative mono/2-step prompts, & contexts in each step. OC, E refer to original context, *Evidence*.

CoE-Long

```
# Objective Instruction from Section
3.1
# Think step-by-step and generate the
answer with evidence and explanation.
```

An overview is in Figure 2. However, depending on the task T, we add one or two additional instructions to clarify how the answer should be generated, and what should be the output format:

```
# Your answer must be the either of
('SUPPORTS' or 'REFUTES') based on the
claim and the context.
# Generate your response in a json
output format with an 'answer' tag and
an 'evidence and explanation' tag
```

While both CoE prompts generates more context-driven reasonings which are often very concise w.r.t the original context, CoE-LONG prompt, which includes "step-by-step" command, instructs the model to generate more verbose and expanded reasoning paths in compare to CoE-SHORT. Hence, typically CoE-LONG tends to be more accurate (e.g., for commonsense, multi-step reasoning, or arithmetic cases) while CoE-SHORT is more cost-effective.

3.3 Adaptation

In this section, we outline how our framework adapts to various tasks and objectives. Our framework offers choices between mono/dual step prompting, CoE alternatives, and context inputs. Considering task complexity, we examine the nature of the task (context-aware or context-free), context length, and query complexity (single or multi-question). Regarding objectives, we prioritize cost optimization or performance triggering. Our design principles are mainly three-folds:

1. Single-step CoE is generally sufficient, except for longer contexts where E2Gis employed.
2. Cost-effectiveness is tied to the number of steps or LLM API calls. Thus, for E2G, CoE-SHORT is more cost-effective in each step, while CoE-LONG offers granular reasoning steps, enhancing performance, particularly in context-less reasoning tasks like arithmetic and commonsense.
3. The G-step context is typically derived from *Evidence* from the E-step. However, for queries involving multiple sub-queries or answers, a brief *Evidence* may provide only partial answers. In such cases, the G-step context should include *Evidence* concatenated with the original context. Table 1 summarizes these principles.

Another objective, we consider is inference time. While the worst-case runtime of our approach is approximately double that of CoT, shorter *Evidence* reduces runtime (e.g., 1.5s vs CoT's 1s on average), making it suitable for practical use cases. However, more constrained inference time can be achieved via single-step CoE.

4 Experimental Setup

We evaluate our prompting framework across eight context-intensive language tasks, requiring reasoning over given contexts, including those with distracting documents and retrieval augmentation for generation. Using three LLMs (ChatGPT, GPT-4, PaLM-2 (540B)) via APIs, we conduct comprehensive experiments. Due

Dataset	Size	Reasoning	|Context|	Task	Metric
LogiQA	651	MRC	77	Logical Reasoning	Acc
DROP	500		196	Arithmetic Reasoning	F1
HotpotQA	$7.41K^{CG}/1.5K^{P}$	Distarctor	1106	Multi-hop QA	EM, F1
NQ	500	RAG	650-675	Open-domain QA	
TQA	1.5K				
WOW	500			Know. Grounded Dialouge Gen.	F1
ELI5	300			Long Form QA	
FEVER	$10.1K^{CG}/.1K^{P}$			Fact Verification	Acc

Table 2: Evaluation Datasets. MRC, and distractor denote machine reading comprehension, and context with distracting documents. |Context| denotes avg token length. $^{CG/P}$ denotes with ChatGPT and PALM-2 respectively.

to the size of the datasets, we use sampling and dev splits for evaluation, following established practices. We compare our results with CoT baselines and other frameworks from the literature, reproducing 0-shot CoT where necessary. For retrieval tasks, we utilize datasets from Wang et al. (2023b), comprising DPR (Karpukhin et al., 2020) retrieved top-5 context documents from Wikipedia. Benchmark summaries are in Table 2. By default, we use the single-step CoE-LONG for LogiQA & DROP, and two-step E2G (with CoE-SHORT) for other tasks where G-step contexts are sourced from *Evidence*, unless otherwise specified. We use Dalvi et al. (2024) in implementation.

5 Main Results

Arithmetic/Logical Context Reasoning We evaluate our approach on the MRC tasks LogiQA and DROP, known for heavy arithmetic and logical reasoning complexities. LogiQA tasks involve choosing among four options inferred from a small context, while DROP tasks require answering questions with complex arithmetic computations from the context.[2] Although reasoning in both tasks is largely independent, LLMs still need to align their reasoning with the context. Our method, presented in Table 3 for LogiQA and Table 5 for DROP, robustly enhances real-time contextual reasoning in both benchmarks, achieving new state-of-the-art 0-shot results. In both benchmarks, CoE-LONG significantly outperformed existing approaches.

For instance, in Table 3 using GPT-4 as backbone CoE-LONG achieves 9% and 11% higher Acc than CR and ToT respectively on LogiQA while their iterations are much higher in number. This reveals that variants built on CoT also suffer from generating outputs inconsistent to context, and guiding their reasoning paths with grounding precision can enhance CoT approaches broadly. We find that while CoT prompts give

Backbone	Method	Acc	Steps
GPT-4	CoT^{a}	38.6	1
	$CoT\text{-}SC^{a}$	40.4	16
	ToT^{a}	43.0	19.87
	CR^{a}	45.3	17
	CoE-LONG	**53.8%**	1
PaLM-2	CoT	35.0	1
	CoT-SC	36.3	3
	CoE-LONG	36.4	1
PREVIOUS SOTA[b]	-	45.8	-

Table 3: Performance on LogiQA. $^{a-b}$ refer to Zhang et al. (2023b) and Ouyang et al. (2021) respectively.

decisions for MCQ options directly in every step, CoE-LONG explains how the option can/not be inferred from the context (example: Appendix Fig 5). Similarly, Table 4 shows an example how CoE provides superior reasoning w.r.t CoT (more in Appendix). On DROP, PaLM-2 achieves higher performances than GPT-4 in general, and with CoE-LONG it outperforms the few-shot F1 scores of recent performer LLM Gemini Ultra.

Besides, in compare to the best performances of CoE-LONG in these two tasks, F1 performances of CoE-SHORT are (LogiQA 53.8 vs 51.8) and (83.3 vs 82.7) which validates our intuition that CoE-LONG excels more when the task is based on arithmetic and logical reasoning. In addition, replacing the CoE-LONG with CoE-SHORT, we observe a performance drop of around 2% & 0.6% in LogiQA amd DROP respectively– which validates our intuition that CoE-LONG reasoning is both more context-driven and modular combining both the CoE-SHORT and CoT. In simple math tasks (e.g., GSM8K), our method performs as good as CoT as they are often context-free.

Multi-hop QA with Distracting Contexts We tackle more complex QA challenges, evaluating on the dis-

[2]We compare with baseline performances (i.e., CoT, CoT-SC) reported in previous works if they are higher than our reproduced ones.

Q:	How many field goals of at least 40 yards did Neil Rackers make
Ans:	['2', '2']
Context:	.. In the fourth quarter, the Seahawks took the lead with Brown kicking another 28-yard field goal. However, Arizona rallied to tie the game on a Rackers 52-yard .. Arizona quickly moved into field goal range after the Seahawk TD, but Rackers hit the upright from 53 yards as time expired. .. Arizona then drove to the Seahawks' 25-yard line, where Rackers kicked a game-winning 42-yard field goal with 11 seconds left.
CoT Reasonings:	The question is asking for the number of field goals of at least 40 yards that Neil Rackers made. The context states that Rackers made a 52 yard field goal , a 42-yard field goal , and a 53-yard field goal . Therefore, the answer is 3.
CoE-Short Reasonings:	The question is asking for the number of field goals of at least 40 yards that Neil Rackers made. The context states that Rackers made a 52 yard field goal and a 42-yard field goal . Hence, the answer is 2.

Table 4: CoT distracted by focusing on numerical precision only. CoE-LONG provides superior reasoning by considering both arithmetic and validity of rationales.

Backbone	Method	EM	F1
GPT-4	CoT	56.2	71.3
	CoE-LONG	56.4	73.7
PaLM-2	CoT	-	82.0[a]
	CoE-LONG	**79.6**	**83.3**
FEW-SHOT SOTA		-	82.4[a]/83.0[b]

Table 5: Results on DROP. [a–b] refer to Gemini Technical Report (Team et al., 2023) and Huang et al. (2022).

Backbone	Method	HotpotQA EM	HotpotQA F1	FEVER Acc
ChatGPT	CoT	43.4	55.3	76.7
	Rct+Rfl[3] (t=2)	42	-	-
	E2G	**47.1**	**59.6**	80.7
PaLM-2	CoT	44.49	55.76	78.0
	E2G	46.76	57.90	**82.0**
SOTA	-	72.7[1]	85.0[1]	94.2[2]

Table 6: Performance on HotpotQA. [1–3] refers to Zhang et al. (2023a), Wang et al. (2023b), Shinn et al. (2023) respectively. t=2 refers to our equivalent 2 trials. Rct, Rfl denote ReACT, and Reflexion respectively.

tractor split of HotpotQA (Yang et al., 2018), where each query faces a large context with two relevant and eight irrelevant documents, with only 2-5 far-apart sentences serving as rationales. Results in Table 6 show that E2G , using both ChatGPT and PaLM-2, outperforms CoT and other variants by a large margin. With ChatGPT, E2G achieves a 4% gain in both EM and F1 scores over CoT, while with PaLM-2, the gains are 2%. Other iterative baselines like ReACT and Reflexion find the relevant texts one by one, leading to longer trials or failure to utilize all relevant hops effectively. Note that with PaLM-2, their literature reported performances are found with PaLM-1 and we do not reproduce them as they use few-shot examples, leverage external tools, and involve iterative generations. In contrast, both E and G steps of E2G address the entire problem in each step, demonstrating greater efficiency. As connecting the relevant texts distant apart is one of the key challenges in multi-hop QA, to understand the advantages of extracting `Evidence` along with the answer (i.e., single objective in both steps), we perform an additional experiment towards a multi-agent or multi-objective approach. We employ ChatGPT to establish one agent tasked with co-reference resolution, another as a retriever model for sentence ranking, and a third as a QA agent for generating the final answer. However, this approach lags behind by 10EM points compared to ours. We identify multiple issues, including each agent contributing to propagating its own errors such as imperfect co-reference resolution and ranking. We also find that the agents are overly sensitive to input objective instructions.

In addition, a key bottleneck arises from the retriever agent as it is unaware of how its outputs will be combined by the later QA agent, leading to sub-optimal ranking. For instance, when queried about two persons, all top-k sentences pertaining to one same person may be ranked higher than those about the other, adding complexity to the task. In addition, we observe some interesting hallucination trends with CoT when the context contains distractions: LLMs' hallucination even

Q:	Are both Dafeng District and Dazhou located in the same province?
Ans:	No
CoT Reasonings:	Dafeng District and Dazhou are both located in the same province, which is Sichuan province. False information is given in the context that Dafeng and Dazhou are located in different provinces.
Ans:	Yes
CoE-SHORT Reasonings:	Dafeng District and Dazhou are not located in the same province. Dafeng District is in Jiangsu province while Dazhou is in Sichuan province.
Ans:	No

Table 7: CoT reasoning does not account for grounding–even overrides the contextual fact with its pre-trained knowledge (or hallucinates). Finding Evidence, E2G enables more factually verified reasoning.

Backbone	Method	NQ EM	NQ F1	TQA EM	TQA F1	WOW F1	ELI5 F1
ChatGPT	CoT	41.6	51.9	68.3	75.4	13.4	**27.0**
	E2G	**42.8**	**53.0**	**69.5**	**76.9**	**15.0**	25.1
PaLM-2	CoT	28.4	36.6.	46.9	51.9	12.2	15.3
	E2G	31.2	39.5	46.7	52.1	12.4	17.4
SUP. SOTA[1]			61.8	-	71.1	68.3	73.9

Table 8: Results on NQ, TQA, WOW, and ELI5. [1] & Red refer to Wang et al. (2023b) & an inferior performance.

override the factual information in the context. Table 7 illustrates this with an example where E2G constructively emphasizes on evidences and tackles this. In a further experiment, we find an increase of 5 points both EM and F1 score when using CoE-LONG instead of CoE-SHORT –validating its higher effectiveness.

Retrieval Augmented Generation In addition to the MRC and Distractor, we evaluate our framework on the following five RAG tasks in the KILT benchmark (Petroni et al., 2021).

Fact Verification: We adopt the Fact Extraction and VERification (FEVER) dataset (Thorne et al., 2018). The task involves determining whether a claim aligns with facts in a Wikipedia reference ("SUPPORTS") or contradicts them ("REFUTES"). As shown in Table 6, E2G outperforms strong baselines by more than 4% across both LLMs. Further comparisons with CoT-SC (Self-consistency; (Wang et al., 2022)) validate that performance gaps of over 2% persist. Our Evidence captures essential rationales for claim evaluation, and akin to HotpotQA, our global problem-solving approach provides advantages over iterative CoT variants (FEVER reasoning examples are in Appendix).

Open-Domain Question Answering: We adopt the Natural Questions (NQ) (Kwiatkowski et al., 2019) and TriviaQA (TQA) (Joshi et al., 2017) benchmark to analyze our prompting framework. For each example, there is a short associated answers (less than five tokens) to generate. We present model performances w/ E2G in Table 8. We note that questions in NQ are often joint or has multiple named entity answers, and hence we choose to the analyze the affect of different alternatives for the G-Step context. As shown in Table 9, LLMs outputs can answer partially in E-step and using `Evidence + Original Context` as G-step context provides additional chances to the model for answering the query fully - consequently enhances model enhances. To grasp more on improving E2G, investi-

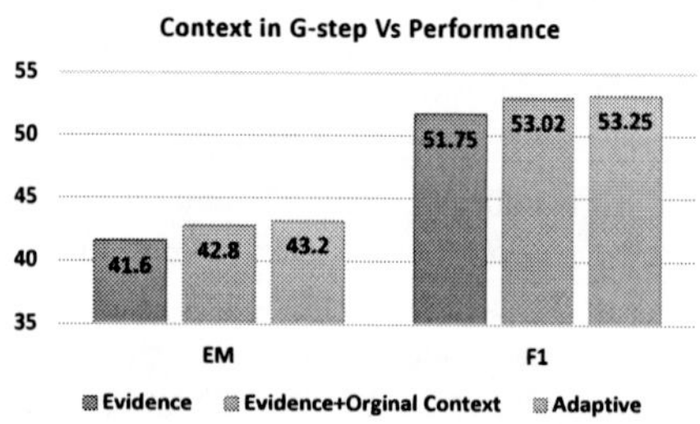

Figure 3: Reasoning with different "Context" in G-step. Adaptive means selecting them dynamically on the fly.

gating the dataset more, we further develop an adaptive G-step context with a heuristic that the well formed questions (starts with *wh* words or "be/do/have/modal" words) are often from this multi-query type. Hence using `Evidence + Original Context` for them and using only `Evidence`) for ill-formed others (e.g., my age is what?)–leading to even better performances. Figure 3 compares them.

Open-ended Long Form Generation: Though, our

Q:	Who was in dont worry be happy video?
Ans:	['Bill Irwin', 'Robin Williams', 'McFerrin']
E-Step (CoE-Short) Reasonings:	The comedic original video for 'Don't Worry Be Happy' stars Bobby McFerrin, Robin Williams, and Bill Irwin.
Ans:	Robin Williams
G-Step (CoE-Short) Reasonings	The video for 'Don't Worry Be Happy' stars Robin Williams and Bill Irwin along with McFerrin.
Ans:	Robin Williams and Bill Irwin

Table 9: E-step may focus on answering partially when asked joint questions or multiple named entity answers. Hence, to increase our chances, in second step (G) Context, we use the `Evidence + Original Context`.

Q:	Sounds complicated. How long did it take you to learn to do that?
Ans:	It depends on how fast you can learn the languages such as COBOL, C, C++, C#, Java, Lisp, Python, etc
CoT Reasonings:	The context provided discusses various topics such as game programming..The user's claim does not relate to any of these topics.
Ans:	I am sorry, but your claim does not relate to the context provided.
Our final G-Step Reasonings:	Based on the context, it is mentioned that software development takes weeks or months to complete, but it depends on the complexity of the software. Some complex software may require more than a year of work, while others are..
Ans:	Learning to create software can take varying amounts of time depending on the complexity of the software and the individual's learning ability.

Table 10: Dialogue by ChatGPT using CoT and E2G.

focus is toward the reasoning tasks, we also explore its potential in open-ended generation tasks. We examine two verbose QA tasks: (i) Knowledge-Grounded Dialog Generation using the WoW dataset (Dinan et al., 2019), where short dialog histories are provided as context for generating next-turn responses; (ii) Long Form QA on the ELI5 dataset (Fan et al., 2019), requiring detailed answers to open-ended questions. Table 8 compares E2G with CoT baseline. Although the performance difference is marginal due to verbosity, E2G shows a slight gain over CoT in WoW. A small-scale human evaluation also favored E2G responses by 71% for factual correctness, similarity to gold responses, and naturalness. Table 10 illustrates a dialogue example, where the overall responses are similar despite verbosity. However, our results in both benchmarks lag behind recent Supervised SOTA models. In Appendix A.1, we perform additional experiments and further discuss the generalizability.

6 Qualitative Case Study: Why and How Our Methods Work?

To understand more on why and how CoE and E2G enhance CoT like reasoning in RAG or with long context, we conduct a case study on CoT reasoning on complex multihop HotpotQA with a set of 50 examples. We observe 4 types of errors: (a) when the question is very hard in reasoning (even for human) (b) when relevant text lies in the middle or at bottom of retrieved context, as noted in (Liu et al., 2023b). (c) linguistically or logically challenging questions with long contexts (d) reasoning is not mentioned in the context. We focus on c, and d. For problem c, among the erroneous *wh* questions, in 23% of them, the gold answer span is actually present in the reasoning, and for the erroneous *yes/no* questions, 75% of their reasoning actually hypotheses opposite of the predicted answer (e.g., "yes" should be derived from reasoning but the predicted answer is "no"). This indicates that just using the reasoning to answer the question can achieve quite some improvements–justifying our intuition for two-step E2G prompt. For problem d, in our analyses, 23% of erroneous *wh* and 25% of *yes/no* questions are of this category. This suggests a root change in the prompting strategy to focus on verification of the reasoning rationales and to verify, CoE shows an 8% lower error rate. In addition to qualitative analysis, we employ the self-reflection approach (Shinn et al., 2023) by deliberately querying two state-of-the-art LLMs (ChatGPT and Gemini Pro) about the internal advantages of our designed instruction over CoT. Details are provided in Appendix A.2.

Q:	Who has the most trophies in the premier league?
Ans:	Manchester United
CoT Reasonings:	Manchester United has won more trophies than any other club in English football, with a record 20 League titles, 12 FA Cups, 5 League Cups and a ...
Ans:	Manchester United
Our final G-Step Reasonings:	Former Blackburn Rovers and Newcastle United striker Alan Shearer holds the record for most Premier League goals with 260...
Ans:	Alan Sheare

Table 11: Overemphasizing on grounding can hinder model from leveraging world knowledge, common sense, etc., (e.g., Manchester United is a team in premier league).

7 Error Analysis and Challenges

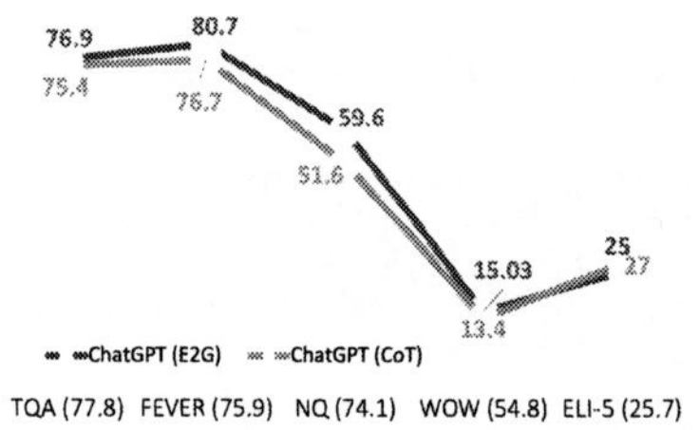

Figure 4: F1 scores w/ E2G & CoT vs (sorted) recall.

Apart from persisted hallucination to some extent, our experiments and ablations reveal two main limitations of our framework. **Overemphasis in context-grounding** Some overemphasis on grounding leading to the model's failure to infer simple common sense, leverage generic world knowledge, arithmetic, logic, and principles (See Table 11), and in many cases, it causing the model to generate responses such as "unknown," or "cannot be determined". Specific examples of categorical mistakes are provided in the Appendix. **Low performance in long form generation** We find that the retrieval recalls in WoW and ELI5 are lower than our other RAG tasks (See Figure 4) which may cause this. Upon investigating more on a performance drop in ELI5: while the task is to generate verbose answers, ours are still short (Word length 130 vs <100) and may actually not fulfilling the target requirements–suggesting a future work of model fine-tuning/domain adaptation.

8 Conclusion

In this paper, we address the limitations of existing prompting frameworks for context-aware and retrieval augmented reasoning. We highlight the challenge of ungrounded reasoning rationales leading to potential hallucinations in LLMs. Our novel framework introduces two new prompting methods to identify evidences in the context and generate answers based on that evidence. Across various tasks, our approach empowers LLMs to deliver robust, and accurate. Future work involves LLM instruction fine-tuning using our prompted outputs.

9 Limitations

Our proposed inference framework has achieved significant gains over baseline approaches across various tasks, and in English. However, in certain data domains (e.g., bio-medical domain (Nentidis et al., 2023)), or language (e.g., low-resource languages (Parvez and Chang, 2021)), under automatic evaluation metrics, and with sufficient computational resources or LLMs, it may not exhibit such trends. Another aspect is that the performance scale in RAG tasks may also vary if the retrieval accuracy is quite different than ours. Our evaluation considers the EM, F1, Accuracy, and such matrices for method comparisons, and a different comparison outcomes may be found while using different sets of matrices. For RAG tasks, we use top-5 retrieved documents with any context filtering (e.g., (Parvez et al., 2023)) and for all tasks, we did not adopt any model fine-tuning. Under these change in settings, a different kind of results may be obtained regarding which we do not conduct any experiments on. We also note an additional risk of getting different performances on a different number of test instances in the benchmark datasets we reported.

Ethics

In this paper, we conduct a small scale human evaluation. All our participants were pre-informed about the voluntary nature of our survey, approximated required time, criteria of the feedback. An example human evaluation screen-shot can be found: https://forms.gle/h6WJtC7TrDj9LUNc6. The participants span different continents, and asked through author's research channels.

References

Akari Asai, Sewon Min, Zexuan Zhong, and Danqi Chen. 2023a. Retrieval-based language models and applications. In *Proceedings of the 61st Annual Meeting of the Association for Computational Linguistics (Volume 6: Tutorial Abstracts)*, pages 41–46.

Akari Asai, Zeqiu Wu, Yizhong Wang, Avirup Sil, and Hannaneh Hajishirzi. 2023b. Self-rag: Learning to retrieve, generate, and critique through self-reflection. *arXiv preprint arXiv:2310.11511*.

Antonia Creswell, Murray Shanahan, and Irina Higgins. 2022. Selection-inference: Exploiting large language models for interpretable logical reasoning. *arXiv preprint arXiv:2205.09712*.

Fahim Dalvi, Maram Hasanain, Sabri Boughorbel, Basel Mousi, Samir Abdaljalil, Nizi Nazar, Ahmed Abdelali, Shammur Absar Chowdhury, Hamdy Mubarak, Ahmed Ali, Majd Hawasly, Nadir Durrani, and Firoj Alam. 2024. LLMeBench: A flexible framework for accelerating llms benchmarking.

Shehzaad Dhuliawala, Mojtaba Komeili, Jing Xu, Roberta Raileanu, Xian Li, Asli Celikyilmaz, and Jason Weston. 2023. Chain-of-verification reduces hallucination in large language models. *arXiv preprint arXiv:2309.11495*.

Emily Dinan, Stephen Roller, Kurt Shuster, Angela Fan, Michael Auli, and Jason Weston. 2019. Wizard of Wikipedia: Knowledge-powered conversational agents. In *International Conference on Learning Representations*.

Angela Fan, Yacine Jernite, Ethan Perez, David Grangier, Jason Weston, and Michael Auli. 2019. ELI5: Long form question answering. In *Proceedings of the 57th Annual Meeting of the Association for Computational Linguistics*, pages 3558–3567, Florence, Italy. Association for Computational Linguistics.

Yao Fu, Hao Peng, Ashish Sabharwal, Peter Clark, and Tushar Khot. 2022. Complexity-based prompting for multi-step reasoning. In *The Eleventh International Conference on Learning Representations*.

Luyu Gao, Aman Madaan, Shuyan Zhou, Uri Alon, Pengfei Liu, Yiming Yang, Jamie Callan, and Graham Neubig. 2023. Pal: Program-aided language models. In *International Conference on Machine Learning*, pages 10764–10799. PMLR.

Zhiwei He, Tian Liang, Wenxiang Jiao, Zhuosheng Zhang, Yujiu Yang, Rui Wang, Zhaopeng Tu, Shuming Shi, and Xing Wang. 2023. Exploring human-like translation strategy with large language models. *arXiv preprint arXiv:2305.04118*.

Jiaxin Huang, Shixiang Shane Gu, Le Hou, Yuexin Wu, Xuezhi Wang, Hongkun Yu, and Jiawei Han. 2022. Large language models can self-improve. *arXiv preprint arXiv:2210.11610*.

Md. Ashraful Islam, Mohammed Eunus Ali, and Md Rizwan Parvez. 2024a. MapCoder: Multi-agent code generation for competitive problem solving. In *Proceedings of the 62nd Annual Meeting of the Association for Computational Linguistics (Volume 1: Long Papers)*, pages 4912–4944, Bangkok, Thailand. Association for Computational Linguistics.

Md Ashraful Islam, Mohammed Eunus Ali, and Md Rizwan Parvez. 2025. Codesim: Multi-agent code generation and problem solving through simulation-driven planning and debugging. *arXiv preprint arXiv:2502.05664*.

Shayekh Bin Islam, Md Asib Rahman, K S M Tozammel Hossain, Enamul Hoque, Shafiq Joty, and Md Rizwan Parvez. 2024b. Open-RAG: Enhanced retrieval augmented reasoning with open-source large language models. In *Findings of the Association for Computational Linguistics: EMNLP 2024*, pages 14231–14244, Miami, Florida, USA. Association for Computational Linguistics.

Mandar Joshi, Eunsol Choi, Daniel Weld, and Luke Zettlemoyer. 2017. TriviaQA: A large scale distantly supervised challenge dataset for reading comprehension. In *Proceedings of the 55th Annual Meeting of the Association for Computational Linguistics (Volume 1: Long Papers)*, pages 1601–1611, Vancouver, Canada. Association for Computational Linguistics.

Jaehun Jung, Lianhui Qin, Sean Welleck, Faeze Brahman, Chandra Bhagavatula, Ronan Le Bras, and Yejin Choi. 2022. Maieutic prompting: Logically consistent reasoning with recursive explanations. *arXiv preprint arXiv:2205.11822*.

Vladimir Karpukhin, Barlas Oguz, Sewon Min, Patrick Lewis, Ledell Wu, Sergey Edunov, Danqi Chen, and Wen-tau Yih. 2020. Dense passage retrieval for open-domain question answering. In *Proceedings of the 2020 Conference on Empirical Methods in Natural Language Processing (EMNLP)*, pages 6769–6781, Online. Association for Computational Linguistics.

Geunwoo Kim, Pierre Baldi, and Stephen McAleer. 2023. Language models can solve computer tasks. *arXiv preprint arXiv:2303.17491*.

Hyuhng Joon Kim, Hyunsoo Cho, Junyeob Kim, Taeuk Kim, Kang Min Yoo, and Sang-goo Lee. 2022. Self-generated in-context learning: Leveraging auto-regressive language models as a demonstration generator. *arXiv preprint arXiv:2206.08082*.

Takeshi Kojima, Shixiang Shane Gu, Machel Reid, Yutaka Matsuo, and Yusuke Iwasawa. 2022. Large language models are zero-shot reasoners. *Advances in neural information processing systems*, 35:22199–22213.

Tom Kwiatkowski, Jennimaria Palomaki, Olivia Redfield, Michael Collins, Ankur Parikh, Chris Alberti, Danielle Epstein, Illia Polosukhin, Jacob Devlin, Kenton Lee, Kristina Toutanova, Llion Jones, Matthew Kelcey, Ming-Wei Chang, Andrew M. Dai, Jakob Uszkoreit, Quoc Le, and Slav Petrov. 2019. Natural questions: A benchmark for question answering research. *Transactions of the Association for Computational Linguistics*, 7:452–466.

Brian Lester, Rami Al-Rfou, and Noah Constant. 2021. The power of scale for parameter-efficient prompt tuning. In *Proceedings of the 2021 Conference on Empirical Methods in Natural Language Processing*, pages 3045–3059,

Online and Punta Cana, Dominican Republic. Association for Computational Linguistics.

Junlong Li, Zhuosheng Zhang, and Hai Zhao. 2022. Self-prompting large language models for open-domain qa. *arXiv preprint arXiv:2212.08635*.

Xingxuan Li, Ruochen Zhao, Yew Ken Chia, Bosheng Ding, Lidong Bing, Shafiq Joty, and Soujanya Poria. 2023. Chain of knowledge: A framework for grounding large language models with structured knowledge bases. *arXiv preprint arXiv:2305.13269*.

Bo Liu, Yuqian Jiang, Xiaohan Zhang, Qiang Liu, Shiqi Zhang, Joydeep Biswas, and Peter Stone. 2023a. Llm+p: Empowering large language models with optimal planning proficiency. *arXiv preprint arXiv:2304.11477*.

Nelson F Liu, Kevin Lin, John Hewitt, Ashwin Paranjape, Michele Bevilacqua, Fabio Petroni, and Percy Liang. 2023b. Lost in the middle: How language models use long contexts. *arXiv preprint arXiv:2307.03172*.

Ximing Lu, Sean Welleck, Peter West, Liwei Jiang, Jungo Kasai, Daniel Khashabi, Ronan Le Bras, Lianhui Qin, Youngjae Yu, Rowan Zellers, et al. 2021. Neurologic a* esque decoding: Constrained text generation with lookahead heuristics. *arXiv preprint arXiv:2112.08726*.

Aman Madaan, Niket Tandon, Prakhar Gupta, Skyler Hallinan, Luyu Gao, Sarah Wiegreffe, Uri Alon, Nouha Dziri, Shrimai Prabhumoye, Yiming Yang, et al. 2023. Self-refine: Iterative refinement with self-feedback. *arXiv preprint arXiv:2303.17651*.

Aman Madaan, Niket Tandon, Prakhar Gupta, Skyler Hallinan, Luyu Gao, Sarah Wiegreffe, Uri Alon, Nouha Dziri, Shrimai Prabhumoye, Yiming Yang, et al. 2024. Self-refine: Iterative refinement with self-feedback. *Advances in Neural Information Processing Systems*, 36.

Ning Miao, Yee Whye Teh, and Tom Rainforth. 2023. Self-check: Using llms to zero-shot check their own step-by-step reasoning. *arXiv preprint arXiv:2308.00436*.

Anastasios Nentidis, Anastasia Krithara, Georgios Paliouras, Eulàlia Farré-Maduell, Salvador Lima-López, and Martin Krallinger. 2023. Bioasq at clef2023: The eleventh edition of the large-scale biomedical semantic indexing and question answering challenge. In *Advances in Information Retrieval*.

Maxwell Nye, Anders Johan Andreassen, Guy Gur-Ari, Henryk Michalewski, Jacob Austin, David Bieber, David Dohan, Aitor Lewkowycz, Maarten Bosma, David Luan, et al. 2021. Show your work: Scratchpads for intermediate computation with language models. *arXiv preprint arXiv:2112.00114*.

Long Ouyang, Jeffrey Wu, Xu Jiang, Diogo Almeida, Carroll Wainwright, Pamela Mishkin, Chong Zhang, Sandhini Agarwal, Katarina Slama, Alex Ray, et al. 2022. Training language models to follow instructions with human feedback. *Advances in Neural Information Processing Systems*, 35:27730–27744.

Siru Ouyang, Zhuosheng Zhang, and Hai Zhao. 2021. Fact-driven logical reasoning. *CoRR*, abs/2105.10334.

Md Rizwan Parvez, Wasi Ahmad, Saikat Chakraborty, Baishakhi Ray, and Kai-Wei Chang. 2021. Retrieval augmented code generation and summarization. In *Findings of the Association for Computational Linguistics: EMNLP 2021*, pages 2719–2734, Punta Cana, Dominican Republic. Association for Computational Linguistics.

Md Rizwan Parvez and Kai-Wei Chang. 2021. Evaluating the values of sources in transfer learning. In *Proceedings of the 2021 Conference of the North American Chapter of the Association for Computational Linguistics: Human Language Technologies*, pages 5084–5116.

Md Rizwan Parvez, Jianfeng Chi, Wasi Uddin Ahmad, Yuan Tian, and Kai-Wei Chang. 2023. Retrieval enhanced data augmentation for question answering on privacy policies. In *Proceedings of the 17th Conference of the European Chapter of the Association for Computational Linguistics*, pages 201–210, Dubrovnik, Croatia. Association for Computational Linguistics.

Debjit Paul, Mete Ismayilzada, Maxime Peyrard, Beatriz Borges, Antoine Bosselut, Robert West, and Boi Faltings. 2023. Refiner: Reasoning feedback on intermediate representations. *arXiv preprint arXiv:2304.01904*.

Fabio Petroni, Aleksandra Piktus, Angela Fan, Patrick Lewis, Majid Yazdani, Nicola De Cao, James Thorne, Yacine Jernite, Vladimir Karpukhin, Jean Maillard, Vassilis Plachouras, Tim Rocktäschel, and Sebastian Riedel. 2021. KILT: a benchmark for knowledge intensive language tasks. In *Proceedings of the 2021 Conference of the North American Chapter of the Association for Computational Linguistics: Human Language Technologies*, pages 2523–2544, Online. Association for Computational Linguistics.

Reid Pryzant, Dan Iter, Jerry Li, Yin Tat Lee, Chenguang Zhu, and Michael Zeng. 2023. Automatic prompt optimization with" gradient descent" and beam search. *arXiv preprint arXiv:2305.03495*.

Victor Sanh, Albert Webson, Colin Raffel, Stephen H Bach, Lintang Sutawika, Zaid Alyafeai, Antoine Chaffin, Arnaud Stiegler, Teven Le Scao, Arun Raja, et al. 2021. Multitask prompted training enables zero-shot task generalization. *arXiv preprint arXiv:2110.08207*.

Noah Shinn, Beck Labash, and Ashwin Gopinath. 2023. Reflexion: an autonomous agent with dynamic memory and self-reflection. *arXiv preprint arXiv:2303.11366*.

Zhiqing Sun, Xuezhi Wang, Yi Tay, Yiming Yang, and Denny Zhou. 2022. Recitation-augmented language models. *arXiv preprint arXiv:2210.01296*.

Gemini Team, Rohan Anil, Sebastian Borgeaud, Jean-Baptiste Alayrac, Jiahui Yu, Radu Soricut, Johan Schalkwyk, Andrew M Dai, Anja Hauth, Katie Millican, et al. 2023. Gemini: a family of highly capable multimodal models. *arXiv preprint arXiv:2312.11805*.

James Thorne, Andreas Vlachos, Christos Christodoulopoulos, and Arpit Mittal. 2018. FEVER: a large-scale dataset for fact extraction and VERification. In *Proceedings of the 2018 Conference of the North American Chapter of the Association for Computational Linguistics: Human Language Technologies, Volume 1 (Long Papers)*, pages

809–819, New Orleans, Louisiana. Association for Computational Linguistics.

Harsh Trivedi, Niranjan Balasubramanian, Tushar Khot, and Ashish Sabharwal. 2023. Interleaving retrieval with chain-of-thought reasoning for knowledge-intensive multi-step questions. In *Proceedings of the 61st Annual Meeting of the Association for Computational Linguistics (Volume 1: Long Papers)*, pages 10014–10037, Toronto, Canada. Association for Computational Linguistics.

Jianing Wang, Qiushi Sun, Nuo Chen, Xiang Li, and Ming Gao. 2023a. Boosting language models reasoning with chain-of-knowledge prompting. *arXiv preprint arXiv:2306.06427*.

Xuezhi Wang, Jason Wei, Dale Schuurmans, Quoc Le, Ed Chi, Sharan Narang, Aakanksha Chowdhery, and Denny Zhou. 2022. Self-consistency improves chain of thought reasoning in language models. *arXiv preprint arXiv:2203.11171*.

Zhiruo Wang, Jun Araki, Zhengbao Jiang, Md Rizwan Parvez, and Graham Neubig. 2023b. Learning to filter context for retrieval-augmented generation. *arXiv preprint arXiv:2311.08377*.

Jason Wei, Maarten Bosma, Vincent Y Zhao, Kelvin Guu, Adams Wei Yu, Brian Lester, Nan Du, Andrew M Dai, and Quoc V Le. 2021. Finetuned language models are zero-shot learners. *arXiv preprint arXiv:2109.01652*.

Jason Wei, Xuezhi Wang, Dale Schuurmans, Maarten Bosma, Fei Xia, Ed Chi, Quoc V Le, Denny Zhou, et al. 2022. Chain-of-thought prompting elicits reasoning in large language models. *Advances in Neural Information Processing Systems*, 35:24824–24837.

Yuxi Xie, Kenji Kawaguchi, Yiran Zhao, Xu Zhao, Min-Yen Kan, Junxian He, and Qizhe Xie. 2023. Decomposition enhances reasoning via self-evaluation guided decoding. *arXiv preprint arXiv:2305.00633*.

Zhilin Yang, Peng Qi, Saizheng Zhang, Yoshua Bengio, William Cohen, Ruslan Salakhutdinov, and Christopher D. Manning. 2018. HotpotQA: A dataset for diverse, explainable multi-hop question answering. In *Proceedings of the 2018 Conference on Empirical Methods in Natural Language Processing*, pages 2369–2380, Brussels, Belgium. Association for Computational Linguistics.

Shunyu Yao, Dian Yu, Jeffrey Zhao, Izhak Shafran, Thomas L Griffiths, Yuan Cao, and Karthik Narasimhan. 2023. Tree of thoughts: Deliberate problem solving with large language models. *arXiv preprint arXiv:2305.10601*.

Shunyu Yao, Jeffrey Zhao, Dian Yu, Nan Du, Izhak Shafran, Karthik Narasimhan, and Yuan Cao. 2022. React: Synergizing reasoning and acting in language models. *arXiv preprint arXiv:2210.03629*.

Michihiro Yasunaga, Xinyun Chen, Yujia Li, Panupong Pasupat, Jure Leskovec, Percy Liang, Ed H Chi, and Denny Zhou. 2023. Large language models as analogical reasoners. *arXiv preprint arXiv:2310.01714*.

Michihiro Yasunaga, Xinyun Chen, Yujia Li, Panupong Pasupat, Jure Leskovec, Percy Liang, Ed H. Chi, and Denny Zhou. 2024. Large language models as analogical reasoners. In *The Twelfth International Conference on Learning Representations*.

Weihao Yu, Zihang Jiang, Yanfei Dong, and Jiashi Feng. 2020. Reclor: A reading comprehension dataset requiring logical reasoning. *arXiv preprint arXiv:2002.04326*.

Wenhao Yu, Hongming Zhang, Xiaoman Pan, Kaixin Ma, Hongwei Wang, and Dong Yu. 2023. Chain-of-note: Enhancing robustness in retrieval-augmented language models. *arXiv preprint arXiv:2311.09210*.

Jiahao Zhang, Haiyang Zhang, Dongmei Zhang, Yong Liu, and Shen Huang. 2023a. Beam retrieval: General end-to-end retrieval for multi-hop question answering. *arXiv preprint arXiv:2308.08973*.

Yifan Zhang, Jingqin Yang, Yang Yuan, and Andrew Chi-Chih Yao. 2023b. Cumulative reasoning with large language models. *arXiv preprint arXiv:2308.04371*.

Ruochen Zhao, Xingxuan Li, Shafiq Joty, Chengwei Qin, and Lidong Bing. 2023. Verify-and-edit: A knowledge-enhanced chain-of-thought framework. *arXiv preprint arXiv:2305.03268*.

Xinyu Zhu, Junjie Wang, Lin Zhang, Yuxiang Zhang, Ruyi Gan, Jiaxing Zhang, and Yujiu Yang. 2022. Solving math word problem via cooperative reasoning induced language models. *arXiv preprint arXiv:2210.16257*.

Method	LogiQA	DROP	
	Acc	EM	F1
CoT	35.0	51.0	62.06
CoE-LONG	**41.0**	**52.0**	**63.77**

Table 12: Results on LogiQA and DROP using Gemini-Pro.

Method	ReCLOR (Acc)
CoT	46
CoT-SC	49
CoE-LONG	**53.0**

Table 13: Results on ReCLOR using ChatGPT.

A Appendix

A.1 Additional Experiments on Generalizability

To further discuss the generalizability of our approach with new LLM models and on new benchmark datasets, we consider two additional experiments on logical/-factual reasoning tasks on a randomly sampled 100 examples from (i) LogiQA and DROP dataset using Gemini-Pro as backbone foundation model in Table 12 (ii) ReCLOR dataset (Yu et al., 2020) using ChatGPT as backbone LLM in Table 13.

Question: Which of the following can be the order of recording these 7 records from 1 to 7?

context: A producer is recording 7 albums one after another? F, G, H, J, K, L and M, but it is not necessary to record in this order. When arranging the sequence of recording these 7 albums, the following conditions must be met? (l) F must be ranked second. (2) J cannot be ranked seventh. (3) G can neither be directly in front of H nor immediately after H. (4) H must be somewhere in front of L. (5) L must be somewhere before M

options': ['F, K, G, L, H, J, M.', 'G, F, H, K, L, J, M.', 'G, F, H, K, L, M, J.', 'K, F, G, H, J, L, M.']
Answer: 1

```
cot ans: {
 "answer": 0,
 "step_by_step_reasoning": [
  "Step 1: F must be ranked second. This eliminates option 2 and 3 as they have F in the wrong position.",
  "Step 2: J cannot be ranked seventh. This eliminates option 3.",
  "Step 3: G can neither be directly in front of H nor immediately after H. This eliminates option 4 as G is immediately after H.",
  "Step 4: H must be somewhere in front of L. Option 1 satisfies this condition.",
  "Step 5: L must be somewhere before M. Option 1 satisfies this condition.",
  "Conclusion: Option 0 (F, K, G, L, H, J, M) is the correct order of recording the albums."
 ]
}
e2g: {
 "answer": 1,
 "step_by_step_reasoning_with_evidence_and_explanation": [
  "Step 1: F must be ranked second. We can eliminate option 3 because F is not in the second position.",
  "Step 2: J cannot be ranked seventh. We can eliminate option 2 because J is in the seventh position.",
  "Step 3: G can neither be directly in front of H nor immediately after H. We can eliminate option 4 because G is immediately after H.",
  "Step 4: H must be somewhere in front of L. Option 1 meets this condition.",
  "Step 5: L must be somewhere before M. Option 1 meets this condition.",
  "Based on the given conditions, option 1 ('G, F, H, K, L, J, M.') is the correct order of recording the 7 albums."
 ]
}
```

Figure 5: Example-1 w/ different prompting for LogiQA benchmarks

A.2 Self-Reflection: Why CoE Works?

Along with statistical motivation, to further understand why it works, we consider the self-reflection (Shinn et al., 2023) approach–deliberately asking two different SoTA LLMs (ChaTGPT and Gemini Pro) the internal advantages of our designed instruction over CoT. Below we summarize them.

1. **Logical Reasoning:** promotes more structured and logical thought process, reducing unsupported statements.
2. **Factual Basis:** Explicitly asking to focus on justifying its answer by providing evidence & explanation encourages the LLM to ground its reasoning in the context and relevant facts, making it less likely to resort to imaginary or unsupported claims.
3. **Reduced Speculation:** Prompting for evidence encourages to rely on what is known or can be reasonably inferred from existing information.
4. **Accountability:** When prompted to provide evidence, models are held accountable for the accuracy and reliability of their responses.

A.3 Qualitative Examples

context: July 16, 2013, Snowden, the whistleblower of the US "Prism Gate" incident, formally submitted an application for asylum to Russia. The United States has been hunting for Snowden. If Russia accepts Snowden\'s application, it will surely lead to the deterioration of Russia-US relations. However, there are high voices in Russia and other countries in the world that Snowden is a defender of the rights of the people of the world. If he refuses his application, Russia will suffer moral and national dignity.

Q: If the above statement is true, which of the following statements must be true?

Gold answer: 3

Options : ['Russia does not want the Snowden incident to harm Russia-US relations.', 'Russia will not give Snowden to the United States, but may send him to a third country.', "If Snowden's asylum application is accepted, Russia will not be compromised morally or nationally.", 'If Russia does not want to worsen relations between Russia and the United States, it will suffer morally and national dignity.'],

cot ans: {
 "answer": 0,
 "step_by_step_reasoning": [
  "The context states that if Russia accepts Snowden's application, it will lead to the deterioration of Russia-US relations.",
  "The context also mentions that if Russia refuses his application, it will suffer moral and national dignity.",
  "Option 0 states that Russia does not want the Snowden incident to harm Russia-US relations, which aligns with the context.",
  "Option 1 is not supported by the context.",
  "Option 2 is not supported by the context.",
  "Option 3 is partially true but does not fully capture the situation described in the context.",
  "Therefore, the best answer is option 0."
 ]
}

E2G: {
 "answer": 3,
 "step_by_step_reasoning_with_evidence_and_explanation": [
  "Step 1: Identify the key points in the context. The context states that if Russia accepts Snowden's application, it will lead to the deterioration of Russia-US relations
. If Russia refuses his application, it will suffer moral and national dignity.",
  "Step 2: Evaluate each option based on the context.",
  "Option 0: 'Russia does not want the Snowden incident to harm Russia-US relations.' - This statement is true, but it does not necessarily follow from the context that it
must be true.",
  "Option 1: 'Russia will not give Snowden to the United States, but may send him to a third country.' - This statement is a possible outcome, but it is not mentioned in th
e context and therefore cannot be considered as a must-be-true statement.",
  "Option 2: \"If Snowden's asylum application is accepted, Russia will not be compromised morally or nationally.\" - This statement is not true, as the context states that
 if Russia accepts Snowden's application, it will lead to the deterioration of Russia-US relations.",
  "Option 3: 'If Russia does not want to worsen relations between Russia and the United States, it will suffer morally and national dignity.' - This statement is true and f
ollows directly from the context, as it states that if Russia refuses Snowden's application, it will suffer moral and national dignity.",
  "Step 3: Select the index of the option that must be true based on the context. In this case, the correct answer is option 3."
 ]
}

Figure 6: Example-2 w/ different prompting for LogiQA benchmarks

HotpotQA

Q1: Are both Dafeng District and Dazhou located in the same province? **A:** No

(CoT) Step by step reasoning: Dafeng District and Dazhou are both located in the same province, which is Sichuan province. False information is given in the context that Dafeng and Dazhou are located in different provinces. **(CoT) Output:** Yes.

(E2G) Evidence & explanation: Dafeng District and Dazhou are not located in the same province. Dafeng District is in Jiangsu province while Dazhou is in Sichuan province. (E2G) Output: No.

Q2: This Celtic ruler who was born in AD 43 ruled southeastern Britain prior to conquest by which empire? **A:** Roman

(CoT) Step by step reasoning: The Celtic ruler who was born in AD 43 ruled southeastern Britain prior to conquest by the Catuvellauni tribe, as mentioned in the context.

(CoT) Output: Catuvellauni

(E2G) Evidence & explanation: The context mentions that the Celtic ruler ruled southeastern Britain prior to conquest by the Roman Empire, so the answer is Roman.

(E2G) Output: Roman

DROP

Q1: What ancestries were self-identified by fewer than 7% of the population?

A: ["English", "Polish", "French", "English", "Polish", "French"]

(CoT) Step by step reasoning: The context states that the top ancestries self-identified by people on the census are talian (13.6%), Guyanese (12.3%), Irish (12.1%), Puerto Rican (10.1%), German (8.7%), English (6.0%), Polish (5.4%), French (4.4%). Therefore, the ancestries that were self-identified by fewer than 7% of the population are Race (United States Census), two or more races, Asian (U.S. Census), Native American (U.S.Census), and Pacific Islander (U.S. Census).

(CoT) Output: Asian (U.S. Census), Native American (U.S.Census), and Pacific Islander (U.S. Census).

E2G) Evidence & explanation: The context states that the top ancestries self-identified by people on the census are Italian (13.6%), Guyanese (12.3%), Irish (12.1%), Puerto Rican (10.1%), German (8.7%), English (6.0%), Polish (5.4%), French (4.4%). (E2G) Output: English, Polish, French

Q2: How many years was it in between when Ava ceded to Mohny in all northern Avan territory down to present-day Shwebo and the confederation wiping out Ava's defences in Shwebo? **A:** [17, 20]

(CoT) Step by step reasoning: n 1507, Ava ceded to Mohnyin all northern Avan territory down to present-day Shwebo. he confederation wiped out Ava's defences in Shwebo in 1524. 1524-1507=7 **(CoT) Output:** 7

(E2G) Evidence & explanation: In 1507, Ava ceded to Mohnyin all northern Avan territory down to present-day Shwebo in the vain hope that the raids would stop. It did not. The confederation wiped out Ava's defences in Shwebo in 1524. (E2G) Output: **17**

WoW

Q: I am a retired computer programmer. I enjoyed my life as a person who creates computer software.\nThat sounds interesting, what kind of software did you create?\nI create all sort of software as long as long it is an executable code consisting of machine language instructions\nThat sounds complicated. How long did it take you to learn to do that?

A: It depends on how fast you can learn the languages such as COBOL, C, C++, C#, Java, Lisp, Python, etc

(CoT) Step by step reasoning: The context provided discusses various topics such as game programming, software maintenance, and computer-aided maintenance. The user's claim does not relate to any of these topics. However, it is interesting to know that the user enjoyed creating all sorts of software as a retired computer programmer.

(CoT) Output: I am sorry, but your claim does not relate to the context provided. However, it is interesting to know that you enjoyed creating all sorts of software as a retired computer programmer.

(E2G) Evidence & explanation: Based on the context, it is mentioned that software development takes weeks or months to complete, but it depends on the complexity of the software. Some complex software may require more than a year of work, while others are never considered 'complete' but rather are continuously improved as long as they stay in use. Therefore, the time it takes to learn to create software may vary depending on the complexity of the software and the individual's learning ability.

(E2G) Output: Learning to create software can take varying amounts of time depending on the complexity of the software and the individual's learning ability.

WoW

Q: Target always felt like the slightly classier walmart.

A: They have certainly always seemed to have a better reputation, considering all the protest from small-town advocates, labor unions, and the like.

(CoT) Step by step reasoning: Based on the context, Target is known for offering more upscale, trend-forward merchandise at lower costs, which differentiates it from its competitors like Walmart. This concept attracts younger customers than Walmart, and the median Target shopper is 40, the youngest of all major discount retailers that Target competes directly against. Additionally, the median household income of Target's customer base is roughly $64,000. It is also worth noting that roughly 76% of Target customers are female. Lastly, Target has acquired the San Francisco-based jeweler Shreve & Co., which it merged with previously acquired J.B. Hudson & Son to become Dayton Jewelers.

(CoT) Output: Target is known for offering more upscale, trend-forward merchandise at lower costs, which attracts younger customers than Walmart. The median Target shopper is 40, the youngest of all major discount retailers that Target competes directly against. The median household income of Target's customer base is roughly $64,000. Roughly 76% of Target customers are female, and more than 43% have acquired the San Francisco-based jeweler Shreve & Co., which it merged with previously acquired J.B. Hudson & Son to become Dayton Jewelers.

(E2G) Evidence & explanation: As mentioned in the context, Target has intended to differentiate its stores from its competitors by offering what it believes is more upscale, trend-forward merchandise at lower costs, rather than the traditional concept of focusing on low-priced goods. This has resulted in Target stores attracting younger customers than Walmart, among other competitors. Additionally, the median household income of Target's customer base is roughly $64,000, which is higher than Walmart's customer base. While Walmart is a discount department store that carries general merchandise and limited groceries, Target is often considered a slightly classier version of Walmart due to its focus on more upscale merchandise and attracting a slightly more affluent customer base.

(E2G) Output: Yes, Target is often considered a slightly classier version of Walmart.

FEVER

Q: There is not a computer game that goes by the name of Firefox. A: SUPPORTS

(CoT) Step by step reasoning: The context states that Firefox is a web browser. The context does not mention anything about a computer game that goes by the name of Firefox. **(CoT) output:** REFUTES. (E2G) Evidence & explanation: The context states that Firefox is a web browser, not a computer game. (E2G) Output: SUPPORTS

Q: There exists a punk band called The Times.

True answer and e2g answer: REFUTES

(CoT) Step by step reasoning: The first context states that The Times are a British indie band. Therefore, the claim is supported. **(CoT) output:** SUPPORTS

(E2G) Evidence & explanation: The first context states that The Times are a British indie band. (E2G) Output: REFUTES

Q: The English Wikipedia is definitely not an edition of a free online almanac.

True answer and e2g answer: SUPPORTS

(CoT) Step by step reasoning: English Wikipedia is not an edition of a free online almanac. The English Wikipedia is a free encyclopedia. An almanac is a reference book that contains information about the year, such as weather forecasts, astronomical events, and sports schedules. The English Wikipedia does not contain information about the year, such as weather forecasts, astronomical events, and sports schedules. **(CoT) output:** REFUTES

(E2G) Evidence & explanation: The context states that the English Wikipedia is not an edition of a free online almanac. This supports the claim that the English Wikipedia is definitely not an edition of a free online almanac. (E2G) Output: SUPPORTS

Figure 7: Example Model I/O (E2G vs CoT)

NQ

Q: when does not going out series 9 start? **A:** ['8 March 2018']
(CoT) Step by step reasoning: The eighth series of 'Not Going Out' began airing on 13 January 2017 and ended on 3 March 2017. Therefore, the ninth series did not start before 8 January 2017 **(CoT) output:** 8 January 2017 (E2G) Evidence & explanation: Series 9 of 'Not Going Out' began on 8 March 2018. (E2G) Output: 8 March 2018

Q: when did honolulu become the capital of Hawaii? **A:** ['1845']
(CoT) Step by step reasoning: In 1850, Kamehameha III declared Honolulu to be the official capital of the Kingdom of Hawai'i. **(CoT) output:** 1850 (E2G) Evidence & explanation: In 1845, Kamehameha III moved the permanent capital of the Hawaiian Kingdom from Lahaina on Maui to Honolulu. (E2G) Output: 1845

TQA

Q: In which Formula One team did Damon Hill replace Nigel Mansell? A: ['Williams (disambiguation)', 'Williams (company)', 'Williams']
(CoT) Step by step reasoning: "Damon Hill replaced Alain Prost in Williams team in 1994. In the previous season, Nigel Mansell was the driver for Williams. So, Damon Hill replaced Nigel Mansell in Williams team."
(CoT) output: "Nigel Mansell
(E2G) Evidence & explanation: Damon Hill replaced Nigel Mansell in the Williams team." ", (E2G) output: Williams",

Q: Before breaking up, how was the Union of Soviet Socialist Rebublics abbreviated in Russian, using the Russian Cyrillic alphabet? **A:** ['C C C P', 'The C. C. C. P.', 'The C–C–C–P', 'U.-S.-S.-R.', 'CCCP', 'The U.–S.–S.–R.', 'Советской Социалистической Республикаослэн Союззы', 'Совет, Ушем', 'The Soviet–Union', 'The Soviet-Union',]
(CoT) Step by step reasoning: The abbreviation for the Russian Soviet Federative Socialist Republic (Russian SFSR) was commonly used as RSFSR. This abbreviation was used until the Soviet Union officially ceased to exist on December 26, 1991. During 1992, it was allowed to use the old name of the RSFSR for official business (forms, seals and stamps).
(CoT) output: RSFSR (E2G) Evidence & explanation: The abbreviation for the Union of Soviet Socialist Republics (USSR) in Russian Cyrillic alphabet was 'CCCP'.
(E2G) output: CCCP

Negative Results NQ (Gen knowledge)

Q: who has the most trophies in the premier league?
A: ['Manchester United]
(CoT) Step by step reasoning: Manchester United has won more trophies than any other club in English football, with a record 20 League titles, 12 FA Cups, 5 League Cups and a
(CoT) output: 'Manchester United (E2G) Evidence & explanation: Former Blackburn Rovers and Newcastle United striker Alan Shearer holds the record for most Premier League goals with 260.. (E2G) Output: Alan Shearer

Negative Results HotpotQA (Low conf. and hallucinate)

Q: who is younger Keith Bostic or Jerry Glanville ?
A: [Keith Bostic]
(CoT) Step by step reasoning: We do not have any information about the age of Jerry Glanville or Keith Bostic in the given context except for their birth years. Therefore, we cannot determine who is younger based on the given context.
(CoT) output: Keith Bostic (E2G) Evidence & explanation: The context does not provide information about who is younger between Keith Bostic and Jerry Glanville. (E2G) Output: Unknown
Q: Which Australian city founded in 1838 contains a boarding school opened by a Prime Minister of Australia and named after a school in London of the same name.
A: [Marion, South Australia]
(CoT) Step by step reasoning: The only city mentioned in the context that can fit the query is Marion.
(CoT) output: Marion (E2G) Evidence & explanation: The Australian city founded in 1838 that contains a boarding school opened by a Prime Minister of Australia and named after a school in London of the same name is Melbourne. The boarding school is called Melbourne Grammar School and was opened by Prime Minister James H. Scullin in 1930. It was named after the prestigious school in London, Westminster School. E2G) Output: Melbourne

Negative Results FEVER (Commonsense)

Q: Brian De Palma is a writer.
A: ['SUPPORTS']
(CoT) Step by step reasoning: The context states that Brian De Palma is a director. The context also states that Brian De Palma is a graduate student in their theater department. The context also states that Brian De Palma is a composer. Therefore, the claim that Brian De Palma is a writer is supported by the context.'**(CoT) output:** SUPPORTS (E2G) Evidence & explanation: The context does not mention that Brian De Palma is a writer. (E2G) Output: REFUTES

Negative Results DROP (Arithmetic)

Q: How many percent combined did the smallest three racial groups have?
A: 3.45
(CoT) Step by step reasoning: the smallest three racial groups are Asian, Native American, and Pacific Islander.', 'The percentage of Asian people in the city is 2.62%.', 'The percentage of Native American people in the city is 0.69%.', 'The percentage of Pacific Islander people in the city is 0.14%.', 'Adding these three percentages together, we get 3.45%. CoT) **output:** 3.45 (E2G) Evidence & explanation: The smallest three racial groups are Asian, Native American, and Pacific Islander. The percentage of people in these groups combined is 3.55%. (E2G) Output: 3.55%

Q: How many points did the Ravens have at the half? **A:** 17
(CoT) Step by step reasoning: The game was tied 3-3 with 4:32 remaining in the first half. Quarterback Joe Flacco struck quickly, however, completing touchdown passes of 65 yards and 10 yards, to Todd Heap and Derrick Mason respectively, just before half time.', 'So the Ravens had 3 + 7 + 7 = 17 points at the half.
CoT) output: 3.17 (E2G) Evidence & explanation: The Ravens scored two touchdowns just before half time, giving them 10 points. (E2G) Output: 10

Figure 8: Example Model I/O (correct and incorrect outcome)

Expertly Informed, Generatively Summarized: A Hybrid RAG Approach to Informed Consent Summarization with Auxiliary Expert Knowledge

Autumn Toney-Wails
SciTech Strategies, Inc.
Georgetown University
autumn@mapofscience.com

Ryan Wails
Georgetown University
rsw66@georgetown.edu

Caleb Smith
University of Michigan
Syntheos, Corp.
calebs@med.umich.edu

Abstract

The utility of retrieval augmented generation (RAG) systems is actively being explored across a wide range of domains. Reliable generative output is increasingly useful in fields where routine tasks can be streamlined and potentially improved by integrating domain-specific data in addition to individual expert knowledge, such as medical care. To that end, we present a hybrid RAG and GraphRAG user interface system to summarize the key information (KI) section in IRB informed consent documents. KI summaries are a unique task, as generative summarization helps the end user (clinical trial expert) but can pose a risk to the affected user (potential study participants) if inaccurately constructed. Thus, the KI summarization task requires reliable, structured output with input from an expert knowledge source outside of the informed consent document. Reviewed by IRB domain experts and clinical trial PIs, our summarization application produces accurate (70% to 100% varied by accuracy type) and useful summaries (63% of PIs stating summaries were as good as or better than their accepted summaries).

1 Introduction

Applied in the medical field, retrieval augmented generation (RAG) systems have shown promise in streamlining routine tasks, providing structure for standard medical procedures, and ensuring current information is integrated into decision making (Hammane et al., 2024; Unlu et al., 2024; Zhang, 2024; Jeong et al., 2024). However, there is concern surrounding the reliability and trustworthiness of generative output in high-risk, real-world implementations in which incorrect information can lead to severe personal harm. Researchers and practitioners have focused on studying and identifying reliable generative artificial intelligence (GenAI) use cases to optimize a routine procedure for the end user (e.g., medical professional) and minimize potential harm for the affected individual (e.g., patient receiving care).

As technical advances in GenAI, natural language generation, and information retrieval continue, applications of these systems and models become viable tools for real-world implementation. Building on the RAG pipeline (a user query coupled with an LLM and knowledge base), the development of GraphRAG created a retriever system that uses a knowledge graph to provide context and entity relationships derived from the selected knowledge base (Edge et al., 2024). Thus, GraphRAG systems can be used to extract key information with known feature relationships, providing more transparent outputs linked directly to data sources in the knowledge base.

In this study, we design a hybrid RAG and GraphRAG system to optimize summaries of key information in IRB informed consent documents. Informed consent documents (ICDs) are provided to individuals who are considering participating in a medical study for new treatment that may affect their health and path to recovery. Thus, ICDs are required and reviewed to ensure that participants are well-informed about their rights as well as the nature, risks, and benefits of the study. The key information portion of the ICD serves as a concise summary highlighting the most critical aspects of the study. Specifically, it helps potential participants understand the key information to make a well-informed decision about agreeing to participate. It is important that these summaries balance providing comprehensive details with clarity and minimizing technical jargon.

We designed and evaluated a pilot key information summary application on four key measurements: (1) factual accuracy, (2) standard of care vs. research differentiation, (3) information weighting, and (4) style and structure. Evaluations were performed by three IRB subject matter experts to iteratively improve our model design and output

Proceedings of the 4th International Workshop on Knowledge-Augmented Methods for Natural Language Processing (KnowledgeNLP'25), pages 246–258

over 11 cycles. Additionally, eight senior principal investigators assessed the machine-generated summaries for further improvement input. We found that the key challenge in our pilot summarizer was differentiating between standard of care risks versus research risks (i.e., what risks were associated explicitly with participating in the study outside of standard treatment?).

To address the risk differentiation challenge we implement **T**emporary **A**uxiliary **G**raph**RAG** (**TAGRAG**) for expert question and answering. Using search terms associated with the proposed study's disease focus and standard of care medical treatment, we query open-source articles via PubMed Central's API and select relevant research publications as input to a GraphRAG system. The GraphRAG is instantiated for each summary instance and removed after each summary is generated. Our TAGRAG component enables expert information to support current and relevant standard of care risks associated with the corresponding study's disease focus without maintaining a large knowledge graph of medical research.

2 GenAI in Medical Research

Prior research has investigated the utility of GenAI in the medical field for a wide range of tasks using text and image data. Sai et al. (2024) provide a survey on how models like ChatGPT and DALL-E can be implemented in medical tasks such personalized patient treatment, healthcare operations and research, and clinical trial optimization. The authors highlight four directions for future research: (1) customized/personalized suggestions and a platform for information exchange, (2) enhanced patient and worker interactions, (3) streamlining administrative operations, and (4) enhancing decision making and bridging the knowledge gap. Researchers have studied the utility of chatbots as tools to reduce time on routine tasks and assist non-experts with understanding technical medical language (Barak-Corren et al., 2024; Shyr et al., 2024; Zaretsky et al., 2024). Specifically, using retrieval augmented generation (RAG) systems in the medical field has been recently explored (Alkhalaf et al., 2024; Hammane et al., 2024; Jeong et al., 2024; Unlu et al., 2024; Zhang, 2024). We summarize the work that follows similar processes to our KI summary application.

Alkhalaf et al. (2024) use zero-shot prompting with Llama 2 (13B model) to generate structured summaries for clients describing their nutritional status and extracting key information about malnutrition risk factors. Implementing RAG improved their accuracy results from 93% to 99%; however, the authors note that RAG did not improve extracting risk factors (accuracy maintained at 90%). Unlu et al. (2024) implement a RAG system, RAG-Enabled Clinical Trial Infrastructure for Inclusion Exclusion Review (RECTIFIER), to evaluate if GenAI could "improve the accuracy, efficiency, and reliability of screening for a trial involving patients with symptomatic heart failure." The authors find that RECTIFIER (achieving 97.9% accuracy) outperforms medical professionals (achieving 91.7% accuracy) at determining symptomatic heart failure.

Jeong et al. (2024) present Self-BioRAG, a RAG system trained on 84k filtered biomedical instruction sets that provides customized explanations; the authors highlight the benefit of domain-specific components (e.g., a retriever, related document corpus, and instruction sets) for high performance. Self-BioRAG achieves an average of 7.2% improvement over the state-of-the-art open-foundation models and outperforms traditional RAG by 8% Rouge-1 score. Hammane et al. (2024) design SelfRewardRAG, a RAG system that references PubMed for evidence-based responses to user queries and includes a self evaluation layer to thoroughly evaluate and update its output. The authors evaluate the model on three benchmarks: (1) PubMedQA (achieving 81.1% accuracy), (2) MedQA-USMLE (achieving 50% accuracy), and (3) BioASQ (achieving 95% accuracy).

Our work covers each of the four areas highlighted by Sai et al. (2024), as we designed, developed, and deployed a generative summarization tool that incorporates expert knowledge (enhancing decision making and bridging the knowledge gap), decreases administrative work for clinical experts (streamlining administrative operations), supports effective communication between clinical experts and non-expert study participants (enhanced patient and worker interactions), and provides a user interface for summarizing a document based on the domain-specific implementation (customized/personalized suggestions and a platform for information exchange).

3 Informed Consent Key Information Summary Structure

An Institutional Review Board (IRB) works to regulate human-subject research, ensuring ethical procedures and minimal risk to participants. Research institutions are required to receive IRB approval prior to engaging with any potential participants or beginning any human-subject experiments. Producing an informed consent document is a requirement of the IRB approval process and these documents follow a regulated structure and format to maintain consistency across research studies—they are designed to consistently protect participants.

A critical component (and requirement) of an informed consent document is the key information section, which explains the details of the study in clear language (with minimal technical jargon) and identifies the potential risks involved as a participant that are distinct from the risks involved from standard of care treatment. Specifically, key information summaries are designed to support potential participants in deciding whether or not they would like to be a part of the research study. According to U.S. federal regulations, key information summaries should include the following five elements: (1) a statement acknowledging that the project is research and participation is completely voluntary; (2) a summary of the proposed research (purpose, duration, and list of procedures); (3) potential risks (distinct from standard of care treatment); (4) expected benefits; and (5) alternative treatment options or procedures (if applicable).

With their structured output and routine requirement for researchers, writing key information summaries is a suitable task for experimentation using generative AI. Additionally, key information summaries require knowledge of the informed consent document and context-relevant medical expertise for the proposed study.

4 Pilot RAG KI Summary Application

Given the application setting, our experimental design involved iterating through results with evaluations from three subject matter experts (SMEs). Our pilot RAG system (shown in Figure 1) takes two inputs: (1) one informed consent document used as the knowledge base in the RAG system, and (2) a prompt dictionary for structured question-and-answering for reliable KI summary output.

In Sections 4.1 and 4.2 we describe the details of the pilot KI summary application after 11 iterations[1]. Section 4.4 provides the details on the SME evaluations for each evaluation, and Section 4.5 provides the details on the PI evaluations. Table 1 contains brief summaries of the main changes made in each iteration.

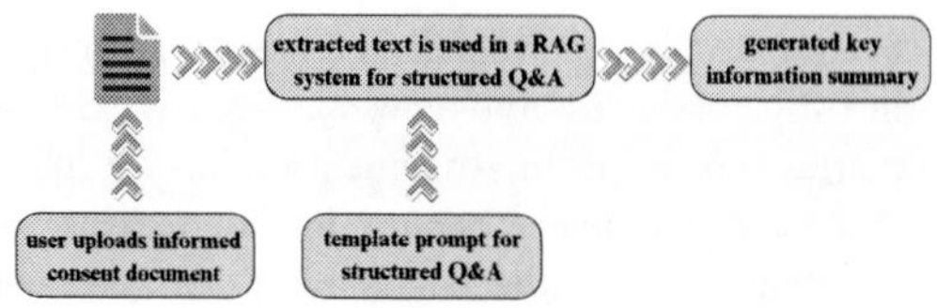

Figure 1: Pilot RAG system diagram for key information summaries.

4.1 Informed Consent Documents as Knowledge bases

We used 18 human-authored informed consent documents approved by an institution's medical school IRB. This set of ICDs covered studies on clinical trials for drugs and medical devices, data registries, cancer and other health studies, and pediatric populations. Table 2 displays the descriptive statistics on the ICDs page length and token count.

Each user-uploaded ICD is used as the knowledge base in the RAG system for summarization, thus the document text extraction, chunking, and vectorization is computed in real time. Our system processes .pdf and .docx files; we used `pypdf` to extract text from .pdf files and `docx2txt` to extract text from .docx files. We built the RAG framework with `llama-index`[2], and selected the `HierarchicalNodeParser` to chunk the parsed document text (with `chunk_sizes` $\in [128, 256, 512]$). Node parsing enables efficient and scalable text processing with the hierarchical structure maintaining the relationship between sections. The chunked documents are stored using the `VectorStorageIndex` using the default parameters for the `StorageContext`.

4.2 Agentic Summarization

Using OpenAI's GPT-4 (`gpt-4-0125-preview`), we instantiate a chatbot with the following persona assigned in the system prompt:

```
## YOUR ROLE
You are a bioethicist specializing in
patient advocacy and human subjects
research. Your focus is on interpreting
and explaining Informed Consent
```

[1] https://github.com/autumntoney/TAGRAG

[2] https://pypi.org/project/llama-index/

Version	Design Details/Changes
v1	Naive, general instructions with reference to template content.
v2	Single prompt with each paragraph of the Key Information template was included. Similar to how a human would generate a summary (e.g., "Fill in the blanks on the provided template.").
v3	**<major change>** Single prompt is still used, but instructions are more detailed and we begin using meta-language to exert more fine-grained control on the model's choices.
v4	**<major change>** Each paragraph of the KI section is given it's own custom prompt. We load the complete ICD as context for each paragraph. *We no longer use a single prompt.*
v5	**<major change>** Use simple sub-questions to distill information from the ICD in a decision tree format. The answers from the sub-questions are used to inform the KI sections. *Example: "Will the study enroll children?" If yes, use paragraph option 1; if no, use paragraph option 2*
v6	Same approach as v5 but question decomposition is more elaborate, with more sub-questions used to distill knowledge.
v7	Same approach as v6 but we create a draft KI, then the model evaluates this draft KI before generating its final response. V7 has the following system components: (1) decompose the content needed to generate a paragraph into sub-questions, (2) answer the sub-questions, (3) use those answers to complete the paragraph, (4) join all paragraphs together into a "draft" KI, and (5) edit the draft into a final version.
v8	**<major change>** Test the newly introduced "Assistant" functionality where all questions and answers are fed into a continuing conversation that the chatbot can draw on (i.e., when the chatbot is given a task such as answering a question or completing a paragraph, it is able to draw on all previous questions and tasks it has completed for the provided ICD).
v9	Continue with v8 but continue prompt engineering for improved question/instruction phrasing
v10	**<major change>** Stop using the Assistant thread approach due to: (1) cost (it is significantly more expensive), (2) availability (it is available on OpenAI but not Azure), and (3) control (we do not have as much control over structured and reliable responses). New prompt engineering designs with tehcnical experts to provide similar performance using the original `chatCompletion` framework.
v11	Finalized prompt instruction design to optimally manage section-level changes and provide generalizability for other implementations.

Table 1: RAG system pipeline design details and changes throughout each of the 11 iterations.

	Mean	Min	Max	Std. Dev
Page Count	17	7	41	10
Token Count	8,081	3,939	16,718	4,547

Table 2: Descriptive statistics on the 18 ICDs page length and token count.

```
documents to potential human subjects
research participants.

## RULES
- Ensure all responses are directly
grounded in the context you are provided
- Responses should be clear and
authoritative, delivered in a more
formal tone.
- Avoid conjunctive adverbs, discourse
markers, and both introductory and
conclusive statements.
- Do not include disclaimers or refer to
 yourself as an AI.
- Provide information in a way that is
clear and understandable to potential
research participants.
- Prioritize accuracy and relevance in
your responses. Do not include
unnecessary information.
```

The assigned role is written to encourage a focus on the affected user (potential participant) and the rules are written to provide explicit instruction to the chatbot that will produce reliable and consistently formatted results for the summarization task.

We formulate a structured open-ended prompt dictionary, containing nine sections, for an automated question and answering pipeline that generates the components for the key information summary. These prompts were designed by technical experts and SMEs to ensure relevant information is extracted and to further instruct the chatbot on how to formulate responses for the corresponding section. For example, the section 6 prompt reads:

```
"section6": [
        (
            "Imagine that I am the study
 participant and you are explaining the
most important risks that are introduced
 or enhanced because of participation in
 this research study to me.\n"
            "Rather than trying to
explain every risk, focus on the risks
that will cause me pain or emotional
distrees. What are the most important
risks that you would explain to me?\n"
            "Do not include risks
associated with standard of care
treatments. Only include risks that
could reasonably be introduced or
enhanced due to participation in this
research study.\n"
            "Use plain language to
describe the risks with few words. Your
response should be no more than 3
sentences in length."
            ),
        (
            "You have been provided with
 template text after the triple dashes
below. Adhere to this text in your
response. When you encounter a phrase in
 this text that is enclosed by double
brackets ([[example instructions]]),
replace it with relevant details based
on what you have learned about this
research study. \n\n"
            "---\n\n"
            "There can be risks
associated with joining any research
study. The type of risk may impact
whether you decide to join the study.
For this study, some of these risks may
include [[Briefly describe the risks
while maintaining a formal tone]]. More
detailed information will be provided
later in this document."
        )
    ],
```

There are portions of the summaries that maintain standardized phrasing (e.g., "There can be risks associated with joining any research study. The type of risk may impact whether you decide to join the study. For this study, some of these risks may include [*identified risks*]"); all templates are included in the Appendix.

4.3 Generated Text Post-Processing

The output text of each relevant section is cleaned and joined together to form the final key information summary text returned to the end-user. We implement basic text cleaning functions and remove unwanted characters (e.g., extra quotation marks, brackets, or special characters), correct text spacing (e.g., remove extra spaces or line breaks), and standardize the formatting to ensure consistency across each section. With the cleaned text, we assemble the responses to form one summary. We remove any sections that are empty, as not all sections are relevant to each ICD and proposed study, and we set predefined text for two sections if the chatbot did not generate a response. The predefined text provides general information about research using standard language. For example, section 2 reads:

```
predefined_entries = {
        "section2": "A research study is
 different from the regular medical care
 you receive from your doctor. Research
studies hope to make discoveries and
learn new information about diseases and
 how to treat them. You should consider
the reasons why you might want to join a
 research study or why it is not the
best decision for you at this time."}
```

4.4 SME Evaluation Criteria

With the support of three IRB subject matter experts, we evaluated our key information summary system continuously over the course of 11 iterations, with two distinct cohorts. In the first cohort, IRB SME evaluators compared the same AI-generated summaries against existing human-authored key information summary sections. In the second cohort, IRB SME evaluators examined a new series of informed consents to assess the AI tool's adaptability to content it had not previously encountered. SMEs were asked to evaluate the model's response on four key components: (1) factual accuracy, (2) standard of care vs. research differentiation, (3) information weighting, and (4) style and structure.

The three IRB SMEs provided scores between 0 and 1 and we present the average scores in Table 3. The result of these evaluations prompted our final model design (presented in Section 6), as a key challenge for RAG system was presenting information surrounding the risks associated with the proposed study that were *distinct* from risks associated with standard of care. Our prompt engineering experiments resulted in the highest performing feature, style and structure, achieving 0.72 accuracy (cf. the accuracy score is 0.4 in version 1). The RAG system demonstrated improved factual accuracy with each version, improving from 0.3 to 0.7 with the final model. The two lowest performing features are information weighting and standard of care versus research differentiation, with both achieving 0.63.

	v1	v2	v3	v4	v5	v6	v7	v8	v9	v10	v11
Factual Accuracy	0.3	0.35	0.43	0.42	0.5	0.55	0.53	0.62	0.6	0.65	0.7
Risk Differentiation	0.33	0.38	0.43	0.4	0.45	0.5	0.47	0.55	0.53	0.58	0.63
Information Weighting	0.22	0.28	0.37	0.35	0.43	0.48	0.47	0.55	0.53	0.58	0.63
Style and Structure	0.4	0.45	0.5	0.47	0.52	0.57	0.55	0.63	0.62	0.67	0.72

Table 3: Average SME ratings on the four evaluation metrics for RAG output. (Risk differentiation references the standard of care versus research risk differentiation.)

4.5 Clinical Trial PI Evaluations

After iterating through system versions with IRB SMEs, eight PIs evaluated their accepted KI summaries (from previous studies with accepted ICDs) against the draft generative summaries. Answering six survey questions the PIs provided their assessments of the generative summaries; the percentages of their agreement is presented in Figure 2.

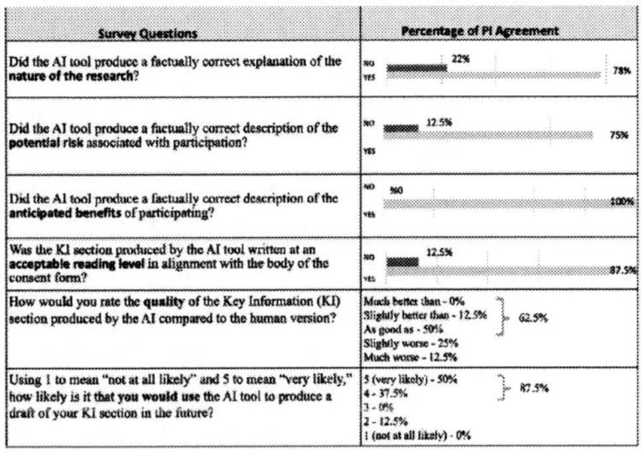

Figure 2: Percentage of PI agreement for six evaluation questions.

We found that 78% of PIs assessed the generated summary drafts to contain factually accurate explanations of the nature of the research proposed in the study. Notably, 100% of PIs found that the generated summaries described the anticipated benefits accurately, with 75% stating that the generated summaries produced accurate descriptions of potential risks. Finally, 87.5% of the PIs gave a score of 3 or higher (on a five point scale) that they were likely to use our tool to draft KI summaries.

5 Hybrid RAG Application Design

Improving on our pilot key information summary application described in Section 4, we introduce a GraphRAG component (TAGRAG) to our RAG summary pipeline to address the challenge of risk differentiation between the current standard of care and the proposed study. We maintain the same inputs from our pilot application (a user-uploaded informed consent document and a prompt message dictionary), and implement the GraphRAG using information extracted from the RAG component and an expert document database. The full end-to-end pipeline is shown in Figure 3.

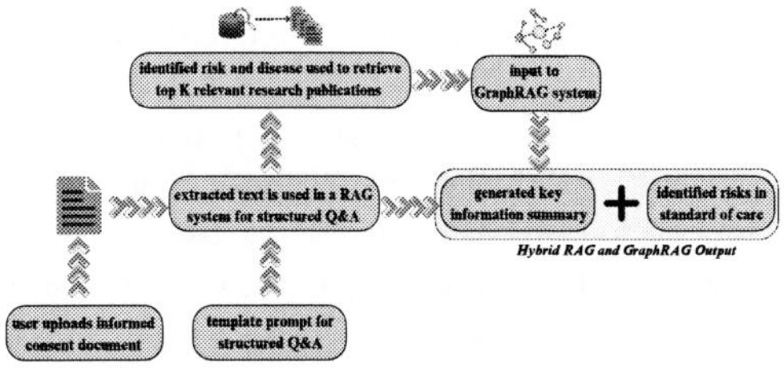

Figure 3: End-to-end hybrid RAG and graph RAG pipeline diagram for key information summaries.

5.1 Expert Document Database

We use the PubMed Central (PMC) dataset as our expert document database to select current medical research on the standard of care for a given disease (National Center for Biotechnology Information, 2000). PMC is the largest subset of PubMed[3], with over 10 million open-source, full-text biomedical and life science research publications. We query PMC via the API tool available through the `pymed`[4] Python package.

Following the PMC query format, we search the database for the top 10 most relevant articles. Our query is formatted to always contain "Standard of Care" and "Practice Guidelines as Topic" in addition to disease-relevant terms identified in the RAG component of our pipeline. For example, if the ICD was for a proposed study for diabetic treatment a PMC query would be composed as:

```
("diabete"[All Fields] OR "diabetes
mellitus"[MeSH Terms] OR ("diabetes"[All
Fields] AND "mellitus"[All Fields]) OR
```

[3]PubMed contains over 37 million research publications that are both open-source and pay-walled.

[4]https://pypi.org/project/pymed/

```
"diabetes mellitus"[All Fields] OR "
diabetes"[All Fields] OR "diabetes
insipidus"[MeSH Terms] OR ("diabetes"[
All Fields] AND "insipidus"[All Fields])
 OR "diabetes insipidus"[All Fields] OR
"diabetic"[All Fields] OR "diabetics"[
All Fields] OR "diabets"[All Fields])
AND "standard of care"[MeSH Terms] AND "
practice guidelines as topic"[MeSH Terms
]
```

This query then returns the research publications' sections (e.g., title, abstract, methods, results, and conclusion) and corresponding metadata (e.g., keywords, doi, pubmed id, authors, and journal).

5.2 Temporary Auxiliary GraphRAG

The expert TAGRAG component is instantiated in real time with each summary, similar to the RAG component. In addition to the document extraction, text chunking, and vectorization required in a RAG system, a GraphRAG requires a schema for entity extraction to build its knowledge graph. We define the entities and relationships for optimal retrieval on research publications for our risk differentiation task; Table 4 lists the terms selected for our schema builder. We select more general entities for generalizability to other areas of research.

Using `neo4j` and `neo4j_graphrag`, we design our knowledge graph pipeline with the `SimpleKGPipeline` and OpenAI models (`text-embedding-3-large` for embeddings and `gpt-4o-mini` for the chatbot). The subset of expert documents for the given instance are input to the knowledge graph pipeline; no additional data is used. The GraphRAG system is then finalized by setting the `retriever` with the expert document vectors and the `llm` to `gpt-4o-mini`.

To generate the output for standard of care and research risk differentiation, we set the following prompts for TAGRAG Q&A:

```
``You are a medical researcher
tasked with extracting information from
papers surrounding the potential risks
during medical treatment and care.
Please answer the following two
questions:
    1) What is the standard of care for
{disease} based on the PubMed articles?
    2) What are the main differences
between the risks associated with
standard of care and the following risks
 associated with a proposed study for
new medical treatment:
    {RAG_extracted_risks}''
```

The TAGRAG prompt takes `disease` and `RAG_extracted_risks` as arguments that are extracted from the RAG component (described in Section 4). We consider the output from the TAGRAG to be expert input to the ICD key information summary, as the knowledge graph is derived from peer-reviewed, relevant research publications from global research institutions and researchers.

6 KI Summary Application UI

Our finalized informed consent document key information summary application is deployed on Vercel[5] with a private server connection for the Python backend. The webpage displays a file upload box via drag-and-drop or directory search. Once uploaded, users can generate the KI summary which references the hybrid RAG and TAGRAG described in Sections 4 and 5. The section summaries are computed concurrently for efficient processing and then used to compose the final summary. Each section summary is displayed to the user in order, with the final summary including the standard of care and proposed study risk differentiation highlighted. Figure 4 displays the various components of the deployed application (file upload, subset of the drafted KI summary, and Section 6 summary) and Figure 5 displays the corresponding risk differentiation output resulting from TAGRAG.

The KI summary application includes how-to guidance, to emphasize that the summary output is a draft that requires review. We also state the limitations in using GenAI tools, reminding users not to upload sensitive or prohibited materials into the system. Lastly, we clarify that the users must ensure the accuracy and appropriateness of the final document. To encourage author review and summary refinement, our application provides the end-user with the summaries of each section as well as the final summary with academic references for the stated risks associated with the proposed study. We additionally do not include a download format that would enable immediate download and submission—a user can download the final summary in a `.txt` file. There is a "view pdf" button that allows the user to view their uploaded pdf next to the summaries for additional review and validation of the drafted summary.

7 Ethical Considerations and Discussion

There are ethical considerations when using closed source, privately owned large language models for medical-care related tasks. While chatbots are highly functional, it is necessary to understand the

[5]https://vercel.com/

Type	Terms
Entities	
General	"Object", "Entity", "Group", "Person", "Organization", "Place"
Research	"Intervention", "AdverseEvent", "Outcome", "StandardOfCare", "Condition", "Disease", "Population" "RiskMitigation", "RiskFactor", "Complication", "LevelOfEvidence", "Citation", "StudyType"
Relationships	"HAS_RISK", "HAS_OUTCOME", "SUPPORTED_BY", "REFUTED_BY", "INCREASES_RISK", "REDUCES_RISK"

Table 4: Terms used for entity and relationship schema builder.

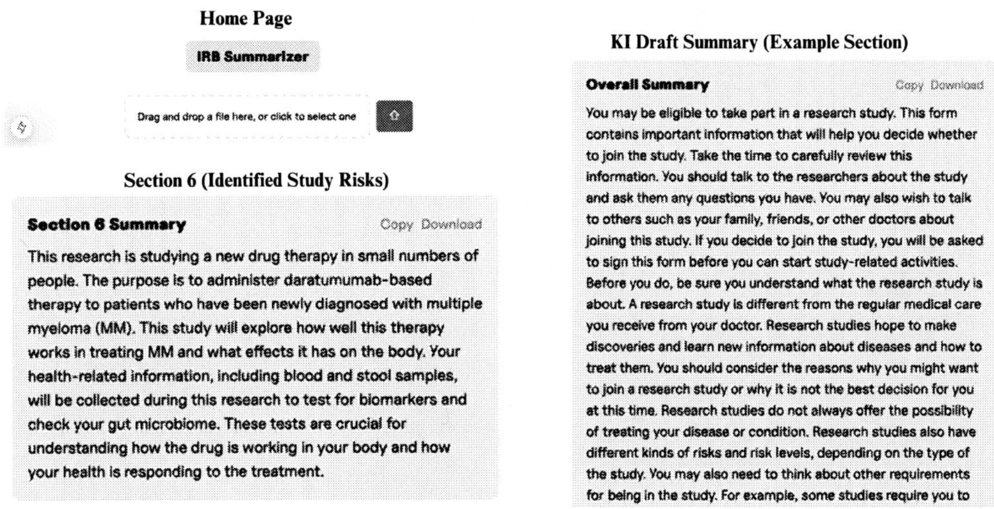

Figure 4: TAGRAG system UI and output example.

implications of using personally identifiable information (PII) data as input. Medical professionals using chatbots should evaluate the appropriate use-cases and data for a given task.

In our experimental design process, we identified three main challenges in using a RAG system for KI summary generation of ICDs: (1) preserving medical accuracy, (2) differentiating ambiguous topics, and (3) using simple language where appropriate. Balancing simple language for non-experts while maintaining necessary medical terms is difficult for a chabot, thus we assigned a persona that that explicitly stated the task of focusing and interpreting ICDs to potential non-expert study participants. Additionally, the RAG system struggled to different more ambiguous topics such as distinct risks associated with the proposed study, which we addressed by including the TAGRAG component in our final version of the KI summary application.

The challenges we identified aligned with prior work in related application areas (Alkhalaf et al., 2024; Shyr et al., 2024) and we focused on addressing these challenges via our hybrid RAG and GraphRAG system. We believe that other RAG systems can also benefit from including external expert knowledge base that can provide auxiliary information for the domain-specific task. While our study focused on IRB informed consent documents and medical research, the general pipeline of our hybrid system can be adapted to other domains.

8 Conclusion

Our hybrid RAG and TAGRAG system improves the routine procedure of generating key information sections of IRB informed consent documents. The KI summary application leverages GenAI to assist clinical trial experts in the preparation of informed consent documents and improves the communication between experts and non-expert potential participants. By including the expert TAGRAG

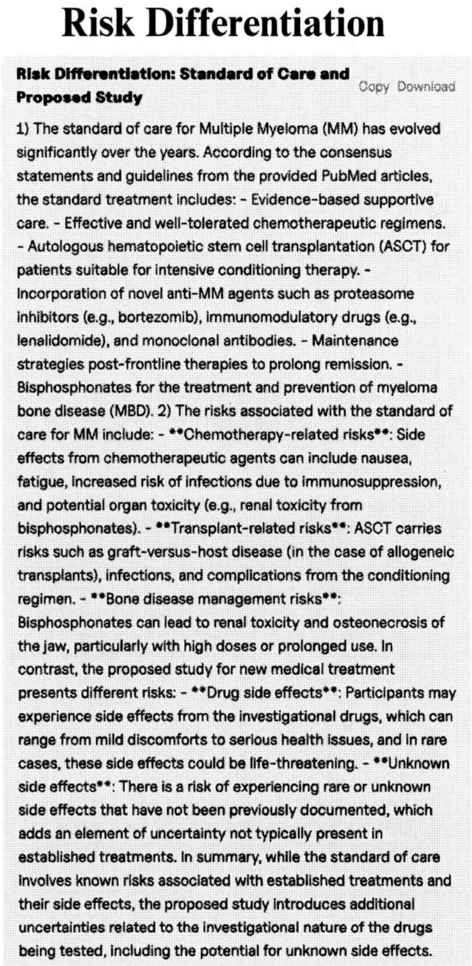

Risk Differentiation

Risk Differentiation: Standard of Care and Proposed Study Copy Download

1) The standard of care for Multiple Myeloma (MM) has evolved significantly over the years. According to the consensus statements and guidelines from the provided PubMed articles, the standard treatment includes: - Evidence-based supportive care. - Effective and well-tolerated chemotherapeutic regimens. - Autologous hematopoietic stem cell transplantation (ASCT) for patients suitable for intensive conditioning therapy. - Incorporation of novel anti-MM agents such as proteasome inhibitors (e.g., bortezomib), immunomodulatory drugs (e.g., lenalidomide), and monoclonal antibodies. - Maintenance strategies post-frontline therapies to prolong remission. - Bisphosphonates for the treatment and prevention of myeloma bone disease (MBD). 2) The risks associated with the standard of care for MM include: - **Chemotherapy-related risks**: Side effects from chemotherapeutic agents can include nausea, fatigue, increased risk of infections due to immunosuppression, and potential organ toxicity (e.g., renal toxicity from bisphosphonates). - **Transplant-related risks**: ASCT carries risks such as graft-versus-host disease (in the case of allogeneic transplants), infections, and complications from the conditioning regimen. - **Bone disease management risks**: Bisphosphonates can lead to renal toxicity and osteonecrosis of the jaw, particularly with high doses or prolonged use. In contrast, the proposed study for new medical treatment presents different risks: - **Drug side effects**: Participants may experience side effects from the investigational drugs, which can range from mild discomforts to serious health issues, and in rare cases, these side effects could be life-threatening. - **Unknown side effects**: There is a risk of experiencing rare or unknown side effects that have not been previously documented, which adds an element of uncertainty not typically present in established treatments. In summary, while the standard of care involves known risks associated with established treatments and their side effects, the proposed study introduces additional uncertainties related to the investigational nature of the drugs being tested, including the potential for unknown side effects.

Figure 5: Risk differentiation sample output.

in our system we address the current challenge of risk extraction in RAG systems, and ensure that the end-user (clinical trial expert) is well-informed with relevant research evidence to support their summaries to the affected users (potential study participants).

Acknowledgments

We would like to thank the subject matter experts and principal investigators affiliated with the University of Michigan's Michigan Institute for Clinical and Health Research. This work was conducted under the MICHR Clinical and Translational Science Pilot Award (Grant UM1TR004404).

References

Mohammad Alkhalaf, Ping Yu, Mengyang Yin, and Chao Deng. 2024. Applying generative ai with retrieval augmented generation to summarize and extract key clinical information from electronic health records. *Journal of Biomedical Informatics*, page 104662.

Yuval Barak-Corren, Rebecca Wolf, Ronen Rozenblum, Jessica K Creedon, Susan C Lipsett, Todd W Lyons, Kenneth A Michelson, Kelsey A Miller, Daniel J Shapiro, Ben Y Reis, et al. 2024. Harnessing the power of generative ai for clinical summaries: Perspectives from emergency physicians. *Annals of Emergency Medicine*.

Darren Edge, Ha Trinh, Newman Cheng, Joshua Bradley, Alex Chao, Apurva Mody, Steven Truitt, and Jonathan Larson. 2024. From local to global: A graph rag approach to query-focused summarization. *arXiv preprint arXiv:2404.16130*.

Zakaria Hammane, Fatima-Ezzahraa Ben-Bouazza, and Abdelhadi Fennan. 2024. Selfrewardrag: enhancing medical reasoning with retrieval-augmented generation and self-evaluation in large language models. In *2024 International Conference on Intelligent Systems and Computer Vision (ISCV)*, pages 1–8. IEEE.

Minbyul Jeong, Jiwoong Sohn, Mujeen Sung, and Jaewoo Kang. 2024. Improving medical reasoning through retrieval and self-reflection with retrieval-augmented large language models. *Bioinformatics*, 40(Supplement_1):i119–i129.

National Center for Biotechnology Information. 2000. Pubmed database. Accessed: 2025-01-01.

Siva Sai, Aanchal Gaur, Revant Sai, Vinay Chamola, Mohsen Guizani, and Joel JPC Rodrigues. 2024. Generative ai for transformative healthcare: A comprehensive study of emerging models, applications, case studies and limitations. *IEEE Access*.

Cathy Shyr, Randall W Grout, Nan Kennedy, Yasemin Akdas, Maeve Tischbein, Joshua Milford, Jason Tan, Kaysi Quarles, Terri L Edwards, Laurie L Novak, et al. 2024. Leveraging artificial intelligence to summarize abstracts in lay language for increasing research accessibility and transparency. *Journal of the American Medical Informatics Association*, 31(10):2294–2303.

Ozan Unlu, Jiyeon Shin, Charlotte J Mailly, Michael F Oates, Michela R Tucci, Matthew Varugheese, Kavishwar Wagholikar, Fei Wang, Benjamin M Scirica, Alexander J Blood, et al. 2024. Retrieval-augmented generation–enabled gpt-4 for clinical trial screening. *NEJM AI*, page AIoa2400181.

Jonah Zaretsky, Jeong Min Kim, Samuel Baskharoun, Yunan Zhao, Jonathan Austrian, Yindalon Aphinyanaphongs, Ravi Gupta, Saul B Blecker, and Jonah Feldman. 2024. Generative artificial intelligence to transform inpatient discharge summaries to patient-friendly language and format. *JAMA network open*, 7(3):e240357–e240357.

Zhaoyan Zhang. 2024. Rag for personalized medicine: A framework for integrating patient data and pharmaceutical knowledge for treatment recommendations. *Optimizations in Applied Machine Learning*, 1(1).

A Structured Prompts for KI Summarization

Here we provide each section prompt used to generate the full KI summary:

Section 1

```
    "section1": [
        "Who can take part in this study?",
        "What are the eligibility criteria for this study?",
        "Are children eligible to participate in this study, either as primary participants or in any other capacity?",
        (
            "Choose the text below that is most appropriate.\n"
            "---\n\n"
            "If children are eligible to participate in the study, write the following text verbatim:\n"
            "You, or your child, may be eligible to take part in a research study. Parents or legal guardians who are giving permission for a child's participation in the research, note that in the sections that follow the word 'you' refers to 'your child'. This form contains information that will help you decide whether to join the study. All of the information in this form is important. Take time to carefully review this information. After you finish, you should talk to the researchers about the study and ask them any questions you have. You may also wish to talk to others such as your friends, family, or other doctors about your possible participation in this study. If you decide to take part in the study, you will be asked to sign this form. Before you do, be sure you understand what the study is about.\n\n"
            "Otherwise, if children are not eligible to participate in the study, or it is not possible to determine whether they are, then write the following text verbatim:\n"
            "You may be eligible to take part in a research study. This form contains important information that will help you decide whether to join the study. Take the time to carefully review this information. You should talk to the researchers about the study and ask them any questions you have. You may also wish to talk to others such as your family, friends, or other doctors about joining this study. If you decide to join the study, you will be asked to sign this form before you can start study-related activities. Before you do, be sure you understand what the research study is about."
        )
    ],
```

Section 2 (used if relevant and no generative text required)

```
            "section2": "A research study is different from the regular medical care you receive from your doctor. Research studies hope to make discoveries and learn new information about diseases and how to treat them. You should consider the reasons why you might want to join a research study or why it is not the best decision for you at this time.",
```

Section 3 (used if relevant and no generative text required)

```
            "section3": "Research studies do not always offer the possibility of treating your disease or condition. Research studies also have different kinds of risks and risk levels, depending on the type of the study. You may also need to think about other requirements for being in the study. For example, some studies require you to travel to scheduled visits at the study site in Ann Arbor or elsewhere. This may require you to arrange travel, change work schedules, find child care, or make other plans. In your decision to participate in this study, consider all of these matters carefully."
```

Section 4

```
    "section4": [
        "What is the disease or condition targeted by the research study?",
        "What is the purpose or objective of the research study?",
        "How many people are expected to take part in the research study?",
        "Will the research study involve the collection of biological specimens such as blood, urine, tissue, cells, DNA, etc.?",
        "What types of specimens will be collected and for what purposes?",
        (
            "You have been provided with template text and instructions below. To customize the text:\n"
            "1. Make a decision at each choice point indicated by angle brackets (<< >>) with options separated by slashes (//). Select the option that best matches the study particulars. If the existing options are not appropriate, you may choose to omit them or to create a more appropriate alternative.\n"
```

```
            "2. Replace placeholders
enclosed in double brackets ([[ ]]) with
 pertinent details based on your
understanding of the research study.\n"
            "3. Use lay-friendly
language to describe the study. Do not
use technical or scientific jargon
unless there is no plain language
alternative or converting to plain
language would change the meaning of the
 text, such as in the case of disease or
 procedure names.\n"
            "5. When technical terms,
scientific jargon, or acronyms must be
used, attempt to define them using plain
 language the first time they are used.
For example, 'This research is studying
DIPG (diffuse intrinsic pontine glioma),
 a type of brain tumor that occurs in
children.'\n"
            "---\n\n"
            "This research is <<
studying // collecting >> << a // a new
//  >> [[state the general category of
the object of the study, for example: '
drug', 'device', 'procedure', '
information', 'biospecimens', '
behavioral change', 'diagnostic tool',
etc. If applicable, also indicate
whether or not the object of the study
has already been approved by the Food
and Drug Administration (FDA) and for
what]] in << people // large numbers of
people // small numbers of people //
children // large numbers of children //
 small numbers of children >>. The
purpose is to [[briefly describe the
purpose of the study]]. This study will
[[briefly describe goals or objectives
]]. Your health-related information will
 be collected during this research. [[If
 any biospecimen collection will be
performed, indicate it here; otherwise,
do not mention biospecimen collection
]]."
        )
    ],
```

Section 5

```
    "section5": [
        "Does the study involve
randomization? Answer this question by
checking the Informed Consent document
for any of the following words: '
randomize', 'randomization', 'randomized
'? If any of these EXACT terms are
present, then the study involves
randomization and you should respond, '
Yes, this study involves randomization.'
 Otherwise you should respond, 'No, the
study does not involve randomization.'",
        "Review the Informed Consent
document with the aim of identifying if
it is a 'washout' study. A 'washout'
study is characterized by requiring
participants to discontinue certain
prescribed medications for a period
BEFORE or DURING the study. This
discontinuation is typically to ensure
that the effects of the study treatments
 can be observed without interference
from other medications. Analyze the
document for any instructions or
requirements that align with this
definition of a washout study. Based on
your analysis, determine if the provided
 example text indicates that the study
is a washout study. Respond with a clear
 'Yes' or 'No'.",
        (
            "You have been provided with
 template text and instructions after
the triple dashes below.\n"
            "Choose the text that is
most appropriate based on what you have
learned about this research study.\n"
            "When you encounter a choice
 enclosed in double angle brackets and
delimited by double forward slashes (<<
choice one // choice two>>), replace it
with the choice that best fits the study
's specifics. If you do not see an
appropriate choice, then you may choose
not to include any of the choices in
your response or you may choose to
generate an additional choice that is
more appropriate. \n"
            "When you encounter a phrase
 in this text that is enclosed by double
 brackets ([[example instructions]]),
replace it with relevant details derived
 from the STUDY INFORMATION provided
above. \n\n"
            "---\n\n"
            "Step 1: If the study
involves randomization, write the
following text, otherwise skip this step
:\n"
            "\n\nThis study involves a
process called randomization. This means
 that the << drug // device // procedure
 >> you receive in the study is not
chosen by you or the researcher. The
study design divides study participants
into separate groups, based on chance (
like the flip of a coin), to compare
different treatments or procedures. If
you decide to be in the study, you need
to be comfortable not knowing which
study group you will be in.\n\n"
            "Step 2: If the study
requires me to stop taking any
medications before I can participate,
write the following text, otherwise skip
 this step:\n"
            "\n\nThis study may require
you to stop taking certain medications
before and possibly during the research
study. If you decide to be in the study,
 you should understand that some
symptoms that were controlled by that
medication may worsen.\n\n"
            "If both Step 1 and Step 2
are skipped, meaning the study neither
involves randomization nor requires me
to stop taking a particular medication
before I can participate, then simply
write an empty space: "
        )
    ],
```

Section 6

```
    "section6": [
        (
            "Imagine that I am the study
 participant and you are explaining the
most important risks that are introduced
 or enhanced because of participation in
 this research study to me.\n"
            "Rather than trying to
explain every risk, focus on the risks
that will cause me pain or emotional
distrees. What are the most important
risks that you would explain to me?\n"
            "Do not include risks
associated with standard of care
treatments. Only include risks that
could reasonably be introduced or
enhanced due to participation in this
research study.\n"
            "Use plain language to
describe the risks with few words. Your
response should be no more than 3
sentences in length."
        ),
        (
            "You have been provided with
 template text after the triple dashes
below. Adhere to this text in your
response. When you encounter a phrase in
 this text that is enclosed by double
brackets ([[example instructions]]),
replace it with relevant details based
on what you have learned about this
research study. \n\n"
            "---\n\n"
            "There can be risks
associated with joining any research
study. The type of risk may impact
whether you decide to join the study.
For this study, some of these risks may
include [[Briefly describe the risks
while maintaining a formal tone]]. More
detailed information will be provided
later in this document."
        )
    ],
```

Section 7

```
    "section7": [
        (
            "Imagine that I am the study
 participant and you are explaining the
benefits of participating in this study.
 \n"
            "Create a list of the
benefits and categorize them based on
whether they will directly benefit me. \
n"
            "Do not mention financial
compensation.\n"
            "---\n\n"
            "[Direct personal benefits
to me]\n"
            "<List direct personal
benefits to me. If there are no direct
personal benefits me, then skip this
section>\n\n"
            "[Other potential benefits]\
n"
            "<List other significant
potential benefits>"
        ),
        (
            "You have been provided with
 template text after the triple dashes
below. Adhere to this text in your
response. "
            "When you encounter a choice
 enclosed in double angle brackets and
delimited by double forward slashes (<<
choice one // choice two>>), "
            "replace it with the choice
that best fits the study's specifics. If
 you do not see an appropriate choice,
then you may choose not to include "
            "any of the choices in your
response or you may choose to generate
an additional choice that is more
appropriate."
            "\n\n"
            "When you encounter a phrase
 in this text that is enclosed by double
 brackets ([[example instructions]]),
replace it with relevant details based "
            "on what you have learned
about this research study.\n"
            "If there are no meaningful
direct personal benefits to me, then
select the second choice in the template
 text below. Otherwise, select the first
 choice.\n"
            "---\n\n"
            "<<This study may offer some
 benefit to you now or others in the
future by "
            "[[Briefly summarize
benefits based on what you have learned
about this research study. Make sure the
 summarized text fits with the rest of
this sentence and doesn't repeat or
restate information that has already
been provided.]]>> "
            "// "
            "This study may not offer
any benefit to you now but may benefit
others in the future by "
            "[[Briefly summarize
potential benefits based on what you
have learned about this research study.
Make sure the summarized text fits with
the rest of this sentence and doesn't
repeat or restate information that has
already been provided.]]>>. More
information will be provided later in
this document."
        )
    ],
```

Section 8

```
    "section8": [
        "How much of my time, in total,
will be needed to take part in this
study? How long will I be in the study?
What is the total duration of the study?
 In other words, how much of my time
will be taken up by the study and how
long will the overall study last?",
        (
            "After the triple dashes
```

```
below, you have been provided with
template text. Adhere to this text in
your response, replacing any double
bracketed instructions ([[example
instructions]]), with relevant
information about the research study.\n"
            "---\n\n"
            "The study will take [[
Indicate how long the subject will be in
 the study based on what you have
learned about this research study]]."
        )
    ],
```

Section 9

```
     "section9": [
        "If I decide not to take part in
 this study, what other options do I
have?",
        (
            "If participating in the
study will not affect my current or
future treatment/care options, or if
this question is not applicable to this
study, respond with the following text:
\n"
            "'Even if you decide to join
 the study now, you are free to leave at
 any time if you change your mind.'\n\n"
            "Otherwise, respond with the
 following text:\n"
            "'You can decide not to be
in this study. Alternatives to joining
this study include [[Based on what you
have learned about this research study,
briefly specify potential treatment/care
 alternatives for this disease or
condition such as the current standard
of care]].\n\n"
            "Even if you decide to join
the study now, you are free to leave at
any time if you change your mind.'"
        )
    ]
```

MSR^2: A Benchmark for Multi-Source Retrieval and Reasoning in Visual Question Answering

Kuo-Han Hung* **Hung-Chieh Fang*** **Chao-Wei Huang** **Yun-Nung Chen**
National Taiwan University, Taipei, Taiwan
{b0990120, b09902106, f07922069}@csie.ntu.edu.tw y.v.chen@ieee.org

Abstract

This paper introduces MSR^2, a benchmark for multi-source retrieval and reasoning in visual question answering. Unlike previous knowledge-based visual question answering datasets, MSR^2 focuses on questions involving multiple fine-grained entities, providing a unique opportunity to assess a model's spatial reasoning ability and its capacity to retrieve and aggregate information from various sources for different entities. Through comprehensive evaluation using MSR^2, we gain valuable insights into the capabilities and limitations of state-of-the-art large vision-language models (LVLMs). Our findings reveal that even state-of-the-art LVLMs struggle with questions requiring multi-entities and knowledge-intensive reasoning, highlighting important new directions for future research. Additionally, we demonstrate that enhanced visual entity recognition and knowledge retrieval can significantly improve performance on MSR^2, pinpointing key areas for advancement.[1]

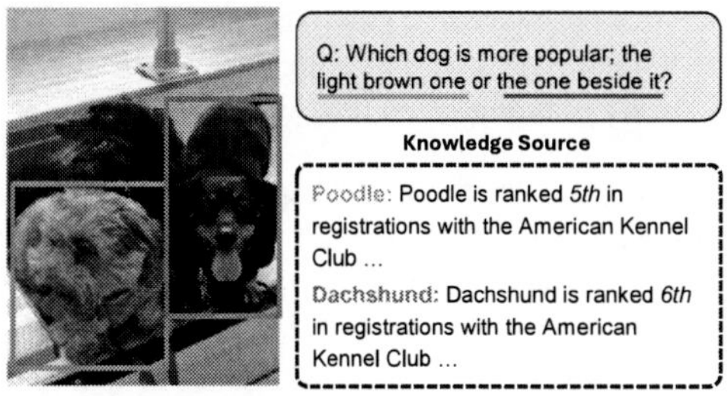

Figure 1: MSR^2 requires an understanding of spatial relationships and the ability to retrieve information from various sources for different entities.

1 Introduction

Knowledge-based visual question answering (KB-VQA) is a challenging visual question answering task that requires integration of external knowledge. It assesses a model's ability to recognize entities within images, interpret spatial relationships between them, and retrieve relevant information from a knowledge corpus to answer questions accurately.

There are several existing KBVQA datasets. Early datasets (Wang et al., 2017; Marino et al., 2019; Jain et al., 2021; Schwenk et al., 2022) typically involves questions requiring commonsense knowledge. This requirement made retrieval necessary for models at that time to answer the questions. However, due to the emergence of large vision language models (LVLMs) (Chen et al., 2023a; Li et al., 2023a; Dai et al., 2023; Achiam et al., 2023), the knowledge required by earlier datasets has become too simple for LVLMs. Recent KBVQA datasets (Mensink et al., 2023; Lin et al., 2023; Chen et al., 2023b) have increased the complexity of questions, making them challenging for LVLMs to answer directly. Nevertheless, due to the difficulty of annotating these datasets, these datasets still focus on single entity, limiting their applicability to more complex, real-world scenarios.

In this work, we explore the question: *Can current LVLMs handle questions involving multiple entities that require information retrieval?* To answer this, we propose a dataset with the following characteristics, as illustrated in Figure 1:

- Questions should reference *multiple* entities within the image, requiring the model to integrate information from diverse sources. For example, identifying the light brown dog requires knowledge about Poodles, while the dog beside it corresponds to a Dachshund.

- Questions should emphasize *spatial* relationships. For example, "the light brown dog and the one next to it" requires the model to understand the arrangement of the dogs.

- Questions should involve *knowledge* that is not based on commonsense, so the model

[1] https://github.com/MiuLab/MSR-VQA

Proceedings of the 4th International Workshop on Knowledge-Augmented Methods for Natural Language Processing (KnowledgeNLP'25), pages 259–271
May 3, 2025 ©2025 Association for Computational Linguistics

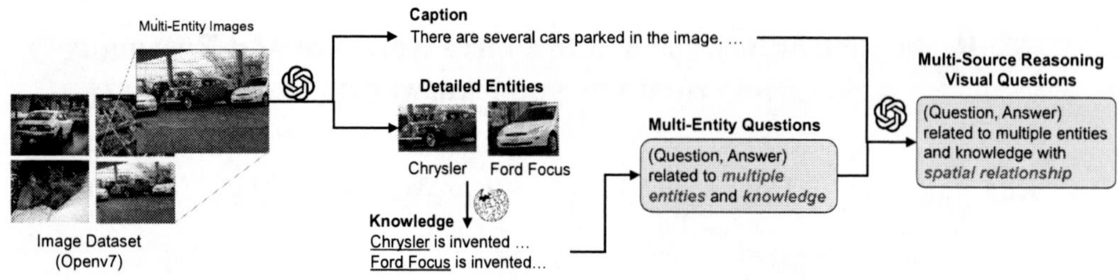

Figure 2: Data generation pipeline for MSR^2.

needs to retrieve external information beyond the image content. For example, the popularity of a dog breed may vary over time.

We evaluate several state-of-the-art LVLMs and pipeline baselines, including an entity tagging model followed by an LLM. Our results reveal that current models struggle in recognizing fine-grained entities and exhibit poor performance in spatial reasoning involving multiple entities. Additionally, we demonstrate that performance significantly improves when entity recognition is more accurate and supported by external knowledge sources. The dataset will be released publicly upon acceptance.

2 Dataset Construction

We present our data generation pipeline in Figure 2. Below are the detailed steps for constructing the MSR^2 dataset.

Image Source We utilize the Openv7 dataset (Kuznetsova et al., 2020) as our source of images. This dataset originally includes images accompanied by bounding boxes with coarse labels. To align with our objective of analyzing multi-entity images, we apply the following filtering criteria: (1) Each selected image must contain multiple objects with the same coarse, broad label; (2) We focus on a limited set of categories–AIRCRAFT, AIRPLANE, ANIMAL, CAR, CAT, DOG, DOLPHIN, INSECT, MOTORCYCLE, VEGETABLE, MUSICAL INSTRUMENT, SHARK, HORSE, FRUIT, WEAPON, TRUCK, TOOL, and FISH, since most other labels lack the fine-grained categorization necessary for our subsequent analysis.

Entity Finding After filtering the images, our next step is to identify these entities and filter those relevant for VQA generation. For each image retained from the previous step, we employ GPT-4V (Achiam et al., 2023) to generate fine-grained object labels by querying the model with object images cropped from the bounding boxes. Once all entities within an image are tagged, we retain only those images that contain distinct fine-grained labels. In addition, we also apply filtering to check whether the labeled fine-grained object labels match the original coarse label type.

Knowledge Retrieval Next, we perform knowledge retrieval for each entity by querying relevant wiki titles and their corresponding contents. We use BM25 (Robertson and Zaragoza, 2009), a traditional sparse retrieval method, to select the top-k passages. These passages are then filtered using GPT-4 (Achiam et al., 2023), which evaluates their relevance to the entity. As a result, for each entity, we retain the top-k' passages. In our implementation, k and k' is set to 50 and 1, respectively.

Question Generation With the entity names and their corresponding knowledge, we proceed to generate the corresponding questions. We utilize GPT-4 (Achiam et al., 2023) to generate these questions by providing the model with the entity labels and their associated knowledge.

Visual Question Generation In order to incorporate the visual information into the questions, we first generate image captions using GPT-4V (Achiam et al., 2023). Next, we query GPT-4 (Achiam et al., 2023) to replace the entities mentioned in the question-answer pair with the corresponding objects identified in the image captions.

LLM/VLM Filtering To ensure dataset quality, we utilize various GPT-based filtering mechanisms for entity extraction, question generation, and visual question generation.

Human Filtering To ensure the quality of our dataset, we have human evaluators on Amazon MTurk filter out any data that is incorrect or insufficiently natural after generation. Given the complexity of our data, we divide the human evalua-

Dataset	Fine-grained Entity	Knowledge Retrieval	Multiple Entities
FVQA (Wang et al., 2017)	✗	✗	✓
OKVQA (Marino et al., 2019)	✗	✗	✓
S3VQA (Jain et al., 2021)	✗	✓	✗
A-OKVQA (Schwenk et al., 2022)	✗	✗	✓
Encyclopedic VQA (Mensink et al., 2023)	✓	✓	✗
InfoSeek (Chen et al., 2023b)	✓	✓	✗
Ours: MSR^2	✓	✓	✓

Table 1: In comparison to existing knowledge-based VQA datasets, we focus on three primary aspects. (1) Fine-grained Entities: whether the model recognizes specific entities or relies on broad categories; (2) Knowledge Retrieval: whether external knowledge is needed or only image-based information suffices; and (3) Multiple Entities: whether questions involve multiple entities in the image.

tion into two steps: (1) Image Labels Reference: This step checks the correctness of entity labeling and the associated references. (2) Knowledge-Based QA Validation: This step verifies whether the provided knowledge source correctly answers the question and whether the answer itself is accurate. The evaluation user interfaces for the Mechanical Turk workers are shown in Figures 3. Only data that passes both evaluations is included in our final dataset. Originally, our dataset contained 2.8k entries; after human filtering, we retained 1.3k entries.

For further details on the data generation and filtering, please refer to Appendix A.1.

3 MSR^2: Benchmarking Multi-Source Retrieval and Reasoning in Visual Question Answering

3.1 Dataset Statistics

We compare the statistics of our dataset with those of recently proposed datasets that share some similar characteristics with MSR^2, as shown in Table 2. Note that we focus exclusively on the test set, as we aim to evaluate LVLM's zero-shot capabilities. K-VQA (Shah et al., 2019) is a multi-entity dataset that requires understanding relationships between entities to provide answers. However, its entity types are limited to humans, restricting its applicability across different domains. Encyclopedic VQA (Mensink et al., 2023) and InfoSeek (Chen et al., 2023b) are both datasets that require fine-grained entity and knowledge retrieval. However, their questions and images primarily focus on single entities, limiting their effectiveness on testing spatial reasoning.

3.2 Evaluation Metrics

Previous work primarily relied on VQA accuracy (Goyal et al., 2017) as the evaluation metric. However, Mañas et al. (2024) highlighted that VQA accuracy can be overly rigid, often marking correct answers as incorrect due to formatting discrepancies. To address this, they proposed using LLM-based evaluation for reliable accuracy. Building on this approach, we utilize GPT-4 as the evaluator to assess VQA performance. Details of the evaluation prompts are provided in Appendix A.2.

3.3 Qualitative Analysis

We show several random examples and quality assessment of our dataset in Figure 4 and Appendix A.3. This dataset offers a broad range of object categories (e.g., cars, airplanes, animals) and scenes (e.g., outdoor shows, hangars, parks), fostering comparative visual reasoning through questions about foreground vs. background objects and attributes like historical significance or function. Its strength lies in filtering overly specialized subcategories while retaining sufficient detail for tasks such as distinguishing car models or dog breeds. However, due to the nature of the dataset, some images show partially occluded or out-of-frame entities, leading to ambiguous tagging and inaccurate identification—especially when key distinguishing features fall outside the frame or are blocked by other objects. This limitation can hinder tasks requiring fine-grained classification or detailed object-specific reasoning. Despite these challenges, the dataset remains a rich multimodal resource for VQA, reference resolution, and spatial reasoning, provided that annotations and bounding

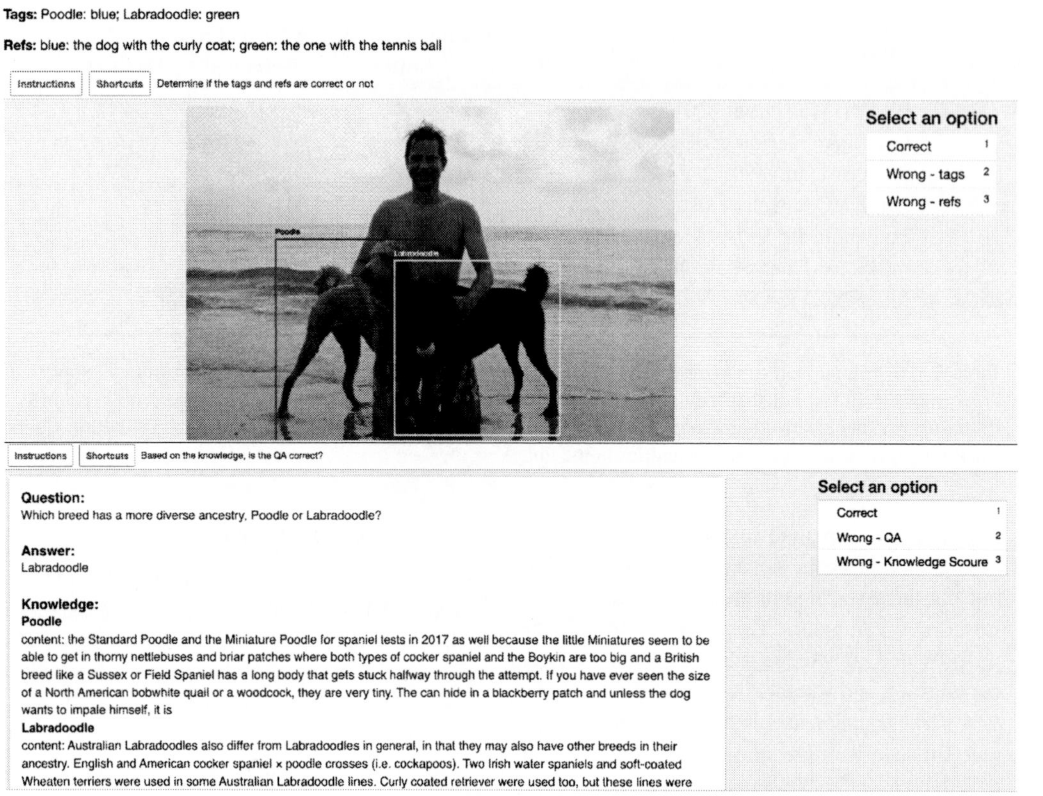

Figure 3: UI of human filtering for Mturk human evaluation. *Top:* Filtering of tags. *Bottom:* Filtering of generated questions and answers based on the provided knowledge.

boxes are carefully maintained and extended metadata is considered to address issues of ambiguity and partial visibility.

4 Experiments

4.1 Tested Models and Settings

We adopt the evaluation method from InfoSeek (Chen et al., 2023b), which includes an end-to-end approach without knowledge retrieval and a pipeline approach with knowledge retrieval.

Large Models without Retrieval We assessed existing LVLMs—BLIP2 (Li et al., 2023a), LLaVA (Liu et al., 2024), and GPT-4V (Achiam et al., 2023)—to evaluate their ability to answer VQA questions without external knowledge sources.

Large Models with Retrieval Following Chen et al. (2023b), we first use CLIP (Radford et al., 2021) to tag the visual entities. Then, an LLM/LVLM (GPT4-V in our case) is employed to answer the question, leveraging knowledge either within its parameters or from an external source.

We also include oracle toplines in our ablation studies to evaluate the model's performance in identifying fine-grained entities, spatial reasoning, and knowledge coverage. Two methods are used to incorporate entities: (1) entities are provided without being mapped to the question, and (2) entities are provided and mapped to the question. This setup allows us to evaluate the model's spatial reasoning, specifically whether it can accurately map entities to their corresponding references in the question.

4.2 Evaluation Results

As shown in Table 3, existing LVLMs perform poorly on MSR^2, achieving only a 10% improvement over the random baseline. Furthermore, pipeline methods, which first identify entities and then use an LVLM to answer, demonstrate even worse performance. We further discuss the results from the following aspects:

Existing models fail to identify fine-grained entities. The oracle baselines demonstrate an improvement of 15.9% when entity recognition is

Dataset	# {Q, I}	Avg # Ent. per I	# Ent. Type	Rationale
K-VQA (Shah et al., 2019)	183k	> 1	1	✗
Encyclopedic VQA (Mensink et al., 2023)	5.7k	1	2.1k	✗
InfoSeek$_{Human}$ (Chen et al., 2023b)	8.9k	1	527	✗
Ours: MSR^2	1.3k	2.25	53	✓

Table 2: Dataset Statistics. Q: Questions; I: Images; Ent.: Entities. The test set is used for comparison.

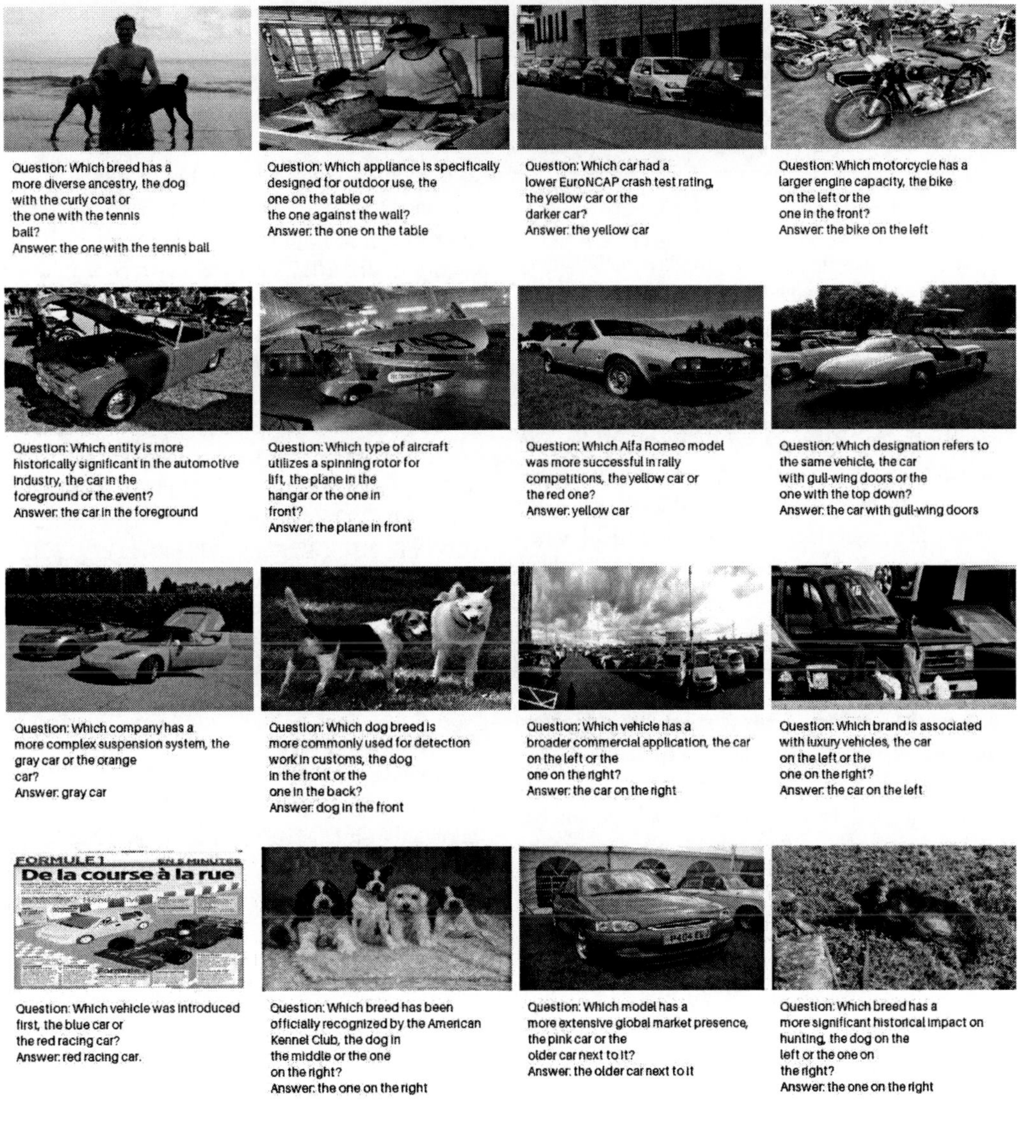

Figure 4: Random examples VQA question of MSR^2.

accurate. This highlights the limitations of LVLMs in identifying fine-grained entities.

Since the image contains multiple entities, pipeline methods using CLIP to compute embeddings for the image and match them to the closest entity embedding may be too coarse, potentially missing the details of individual entities.

Model	Accuracy
Without KB	
Random	50.00
BLIP2 (Li et al., 2023a)	54.45
LLaVA (Liu et al., 2024)	53.05
GPT4-V (Achiam et al., 2023)	62.47
With KB	
CLIP → GPT4-V (parameter)	51.73
CLIP → GPT4-V (wiki)	57.86
Oracle ent. → GPT4-V (parameter)	63.96
Oracle ent. → GPT4-V (wiki)	69.35
Oracle → GPT4-V (parameter)	76.97
Oracle → GPT4-V (wiki)	81.44

Table 3: Main results on MSR^2 (%). The "Oracle ent." toplines provide the entity without mapping it to the question, whereas the "Oracle" toplines include both the entity and its mapping to the question.

LVLMs are poor at spatial reasoning. We compare the performance of 'Oracle ent.' to 'Oracle' to evaluate the spatial reasoning ability of LVLM. The results show that providing entities improves performance by 6.9% compared to GPT4-V, where no entities are given. However, there is an 12.1% performance gap between the 'Oracle' toplines (where entities are mapped to the question) and 'Oracle ent.', indicating that LVLM struggles with correctly mapping entities back to the questions.

External knowledge can further boost performance. The 'Oracle → GPT-4 (parameter)' approach shows a significant improvement over existing baselines, demonstrating that a large number of questions can be effectively answered using the knowledge encoded within the model's parameters. Additionally, integrating external knowledge from Wikipedia further boosts performance by 4.47%, highlighting the importance of the external knowledge.

4.3 Qualitative Study

In Figure 5, we study two different types of errors. The top image illustrates that answering more precise questions (e.g., identifying a specific span) requires verifying information across multiple sources. The bottom image reveals a failure in entity mapping, where the model struggles to link the correct entity to the question despite possessing accurate knowledge.

5 Related Work

Visual Question Answering. Visual Question Answering (VQA) is a long-standing problem where models must answer questions based on a given image. There have been numerous benchmark datasets proposed for the VQA task, including VQAv1 (Antol et al., 2015), VQAv2 (Goyal et al., 2017), DAQUAR (Malinowski and Fritz, 2014), FMIQA (Gao et al., 2015) and Visual Madlibs (Yu et al., 2015).

Knowledge-based VQA. Knowledge-based VQA is a type of VQA where the questions require external knowledge beyond the image content. Some of the well-known benchmarks include OKVQA (Marino et al., 2019), which focuses on open-ended questions that require world knowledge, FVQA (Wang et al., 2017), where answers are derived from facts stored in a structured knowledge base, S3VQA (Jain et al., 2021), which involves selective question answering using different knowledge sources, and A-OKVQA (Schwenk et al., 2022), which emphasizes the reasoning ability of models. Several solutions have been proposed to solve these problems (Salemi et al., 2023; Lin and Byrne, 2022; Lin et al., 2022; Ma et al., 2024; Si et al., 2023; Hu et al., 2023; Lin et al., 2024; Hu et al., 2024). Most models use a two-stage approach: retrieving relevant knowledge then answering the question. However, much of the knowledge required by these benchmarks is commonsense, which recent (LVLMs) can handle directly through their embedded knowledge.

Knowledge-based VQA with LVLMs. Prior research has demonstrated LVLMs' capabilities for knowledge-intensive VQA. Li et al. (2023b) provides a comprehensive evaluation of GPT-4V on its knowledge-based VQA capabilities. PROOFREAD (Zhou et al., 2023) and Prophet (Shao et al., 2023) leverage LLMs as implicit knowledge engines, paired with visual-language models to filter irrelevant or noisy information and improve accuracy. Uehara et al. (2024) introduces a chain-of-thought framework with question-asking capabilities, leveraging LLM-generated datasets for knowledge-based VQA. Xu et al. (2024) proposes a novel reverse image retrieval approach for improving multimodal LLM performance on knowledge-intensive VQA tasks. Cao and Jiang (2024) uses LLMs as a knowledge source which generates relevant knowledge snippets for the downstream VQA task. To evaluate LVLMs on knowledge-intensive

Q: Which vehicle had a longer production span, the blue car on the right or the white cars to its left?

Oracle ent. -> GPT-4V (parameter)

- **Answer:** The blue car on the right (Borgward Isabella).
- **Reasoning:** The Borgward Isabella (blue car) was produced from 1954 to 1962, while the Ford Consul Cortina I (white car) was produced from 1962 to 1966

Oracle ent. -> GPT-4V (wiki)

- **Answer:** The white cars on the left.
- **Reasoning:** The Ford Consul Cortina (white car) had a longer production span, from 1962 to 1970, compared to the Borgward Isabella (blue car), which

---

Q: Which compact car was introduced later, the car in red or the car in black?

Oracle ent. -> GPT-4V (wiki)

- **Answer:** The car in red.
- **Reasoning:** The Chevrolet Cobalt was introduced later, in 2004 for the 2005 model year. The Honda Civic was introduced earlier, with its second generation debuting in June 1979 for the 1980 model year.

Oracle -> GPT-4V (wiki)

- **Answer:** The car in black was introduced later.
- **Reasoning:** The Chevrolet Cobalt was introduced in 2004 as a 2005 model, while the Honda Civic was first introduced in 1972, making the Cobalt the later introduction among

Figure 5: Qualitative analysis of two different error types: (1) **Insufficient Multi-Source Knowledge**: The top image illustrates that answering more precise questions requires integrating knowledge from multiple sources. **Entity Mapping Failure**: The bottom image demonstrates the model's inability to correctly map the relevant entity to the question, despite having accurate knowledge.

and information-seeking questions that go beyond visual content, we need more rigorous benchmarks with detailed knowledge. Recent benchmarks like Infoseek (Chen et al., 2023b) and Encyclopedic VQA (Mensink et al., 2023) assess models' capabilities in fine-grained object recognition and answering rare questions about those objects. Building on these efforts, we introduce a new benchmark with multi-entity, knowledge-intensive, and spatial reasoning questions.

6 Conclusion

We introduce MSR^2, a VQA dataset focused on KBVQA questions involving multiple entities, requiring both multi-retrieval and spatial reasoning. Our experiments demonstrate that MSR^2 presents a substantial challenge for standard LVLMs. However, incorporating an oracle retrieval component significantly enhances performance. We anticipate that MSR^2 will inspire future research into more generalized retrieval-augmented LVLMs.

Limitations

MSR^2 is limited to English; future research could extend it to a multilingual setting. Additionally, the image sources employed in our study lack sufficient diversity—particularly regarding images containing multiple objects within the same broad category.

This limitation may affect the quality and diversity of the generated dataset. Future work should explore more varied and representative image datasets that include multiple instances of different objects within the same category to improve the robustness and generalizability of the approach.

Acknowledgements

We thank the reviewers for their insightful comments. This work was financially supported by the National Science and Technology Council (NSTC) in Taiwan, under Grants 111-2222-E-002-013-MY3 and 112-2223-E002-012-MY5. We thank the National Center for High-performance Computing (NCHC) of National Applied Research Laboratories (NARLabs) in Taiwan for providing computational and storage resources.

References

Josh Achiam, Steven Adler, Sandhini Agarwal, Lama Ahmad, Ilge Akkaya, Florencia Leoni Aleman, Diogo Almeida, Janko Altenschmidt, Sam Altman, Shyamal Anadkat, et al. 2023. Gpt-4 technical report. *arXiv preprint arXiv:2303.08774*.

Stanislaw Antol, Aishwarya Agrawal, Jiasen Lu, Margaret Mitchell, Dhruv Batra, C Lawrence Zitnick, and Devi Parikh. 2015. Vqa: Visual question answering. In *Proceedings of the IEEE international conference on computer vision*, pages 2425–2433.

Rui Cao and Jing Jiang. 2024. Knowledge generation for zero-shot knowledge-based VQA. In *Findings of the Association for Computational Linguistics: EACL 2024*, pages 533–549, St. Julian's, Malta. Association for Computational Linguistics.

Xi Chen, Xiao Wang, Soravit Changpinyo, AJ Piergiovanni, Piotr Padlewski, Daniel Salz, Sebastian Goodman, Adam Grycner, Basil Mustafa, Lucas Beyer, Alexander Kolesnikov, Joan Puigcerver, Nan Ding, Keran Rong, Hassan Akbari, Gaurav Mishra, Linting Xue, Ashish V Thapliyal, James Bradbury, Weicheng Kuo, Mojtaba Seyedhosseini, Chao Jia, Burcu Karagol Ayan, Carlos Riquelme Ruiz, Andreas Peter Steiner, Anelia Angelova, Xiaohua Zhai, Neil Houlsby, and Radu Soricut. 2023a. PaLI: A jointly-scaled multilingual language-image model. In *The Eleventh International Conference on Learning Representations*.

Yang Chen, Hexiang Hu, Yi Luan, Haitian Sun, Soravit Changpinyo, Alan Ritter, and Ming-Wei Chang. 2023b. Can pre-trained vision and language models answer visual information-seeking questions? In *Proceedings of the 2023 Conference on Empirical Methods in Natural Language Processing*, pages 14948–14968, Singapore. Association for Computational Linguistics.

Wenliang Dai, Junnan Li, Dongxu Li, Anthony Tiong, Junqi Zhao, Weisheng Wang, Boyang Li, Pascale Fung, and Steven Hoi. 2023. InstructBLIP: Towards general-purpose vision-language models with instruction tuning. In *Thirty-seventh Conference on Neural Information Processing Systems*.

Haoyuan Gao, Junhua Mao, Jie Zhou, Zhiheng Huang, Lei Wang, and Wei Xu. 2015. Are you talking to a machine? dataset and methods for multilingual image question. *Advances in neural information processing systems*, 28.

Yash Goyal, Tejas Khot, Douglas Summers-Stay, Dhruv Batra, and Devi Parikh. 2017. Making the v in vqa matter: Elevating the role of image understanding in visual question answering. In *Proceedings of the IEEE conference on computer vision and pattern recognition*, pages 6904–6913.

Yushi Hu, Hang Hua, Zhengyuan Yang, Weijia Shi, Noah A Smith, and Jiebo Luo. 2023. Promptcap: Prompt-guided image captioning for vqa with gpt-3. In *Proceedings of the IEEE/CVF International Conference on Computer Vision*, pages 2963–2975.

Yushi Hu, Otilia Stretcu, Chun-Ta Lu, Krishnamurthy Viswanathan, Kenji Hata, Enming Luo, Ranjay Krishna, and Ariel Fuxman. 2024. Visual program distillation: Distilling tools and programmatic reasoning into vision-language models. In *Proceedings of the IEEE/CVF Conference on Computer Vision and Pattern Recognition*, pages 9590–9601.

Aman Jain, Mayank Kothyari, Vishwajeet Kumar, Preethi Jyothi, Ganesh Ramakrishnan, and Soumen Chakrabarti. 2021. Select, substitute, search: A new benchmark for knowledge-augmented visual question answering. In *Proceedings of the 44th International ACM SIGIR Conference on Research and Development in Information Retrieval*, pages 2491–2498.

Alina Kuznetsova, Hassan Rom, Neil Alldrin, Jasper Uijlings, Ivan Krasin, Jordi Pont-Tuset, Shahab Kamali, Stefan Popov, Matteo Malloci, Alexander Kolesnikov, Tom Duerig, and Vittorio Ferrari. 2020. The open images dataset v4: Unified image classification, object detection, and visual relationship detection at scale. *IJCV*.

Junnan Li, Dongxu Li, Silvio Savarese, and Steven Hoi. 2023a. Blip-2: Bootstrapping language-image pre-training with frozen image encoders and large language models. In *International conference on machine learning*, pages 19730–19742. PMLR.

Yunxin Li, Longyue Wang, Baotian Hu, Xinyu Chen, Wanqi Zhong, Chenyang Lyu, Wei Wang, and Min Zhang. 2023b. A comprehensive evaluation of gpt-4v on knowledge-intensive visual question answering. *arXiv preprint arXiv:2311.07536*.

Weizhe Lin and Bill Byrne. 2022. Retrieval augmented visual question answering with outside knowledge. *arXiv preprint arXiv:2210.03809*.

Weizhe Lin, Jingbiao Mei, Jinghong Chen, and Bill Byrne. 2024. Preflmr: Scaling up fine-grained late-interaction multi-modal retrievers. *arXiv preprint arXiv:2402.08327*.

Weizhe Lin, Zhilin Wang, and Bill Byrne. 2023. FVQA 2.0: Introducing adversarial samples into fact-based visual question answering. In *Findings of the Association for Computational Linguistics: EACL 2023*, pages 149–157, Dubrovnik, Croatia. Association for Computational Linguistics.

Yuanze Lin, Yujia Xie, Dongdong Chen, Yichong Xu, Chenguang Zhu, and Lu Yuan. 2022. Revive: Regional visual representation matters in knowledge-based visual question answering. *Advances in Neural Information Processing Systems*, 35:10560–10571.

Haotian Liu, Chunyuan Li, Qingyang Wu, and Yong Jae Lee. 2024. Visual instruction tuning. *Advances in neural information processing systems*, 36.

Ziyu Ma, Shutao Li, Bin Sun, Jianfei Cai, Zuxiang Long, and Fuyan Ma. 2024. Gerea: Question-aware prompt captions for knowledge-based visual question answering. *arXiv preprint arXiv:2402.02503*.

Mateusz Malinowski and Mario Fritz. 2014. A multi-world approach to question answering about real-world scenes based on uncertain input. *Advances in neural information processing systems*, 27.

Oscar Mañas, Benno Krojer, and Aishwarya Agrawal. 2024. Improving automatic vqa evaluation using large language models. In *Proceedings of the AAAI Conference on Artificial Intelligence*, volume 38, pages 4171–4179.

Kenneth Marino, Mohammad Rastegari, Ali Farhadi, and Roozbeh Mottaghi. 2019. Ok-vqa: A visual question answering benchmark requiring external knowledge. In *Proceedings of the IEEE/cvf conference on computer vision and pattern recognition*, pages 3195–3204.

Thomas Mensink, Jasper Uijlings, Lluis Castrejon, Arushi Goel, Felipe Cadar, Howard Zhou, Fei Sha, André Araujo, and Vittorio Ferrari. 2023. Encyclopedic vqa: Visual questions about detailed properties of fine-grained categories. In *Proceedings of the IEEE/CVF International Conference on Computer Vision*, pages 3113–3124.

Alec Radford, Jong Wook Kim, Chris Hallacy, Aditya Ramesh, Gabriel Goh, Sandhini Agarwal, Girish Sastry, Amanda Askell, Pamela Mishkin, Jack Clark, et al. 2021. Learning transferable visual models from natural language supervision. In *International conference on machine learning*, pages 8748–8763. PMLR.

Stephen Robertson and Hugo Zaragoza. 2009. The probabilistic relevance framework: Bm25 and beyond. *Found. Trends Inf. Retr.*, 3(4):333–389.

Alireza Salemi, Juan Altmayer Pizzorno, and Hamed Zamani. 2023. A symmetric dual encoding dense retrieval framework for knowledge-intensive visual question answering. In *Proceedings of the 46th International ACM SIGIR Conference on Research and Development in Information Retrieval*, SIGIR '23, page 110–120, New York, NY, USA. Association for Computing Machinery.

Dustin Schwenk, Apoorv Khandelwal, Christopher Clark, Kenneth Marino, and Roozbeh Mottaghi. 2022. A-okvqa: A benchmark for visual question answering using world knowledge. In *European conference on computer vision*, pages 146–162. Springer.

Sanket Shah, Anand Mishra, Naganand Yadati, and Partha Pratim Talukdar. 2019. Kvqa: Knowledge-aware visual question answering. *Proceedings of the AAAI Conference on Artificial Intelligence*, 33(01):8876–8884.

Zhenwei Shao, Zhou Yu, Meng Wang, and Jun Yu. 2023. Prompting large language models with answer heuristics for knowledge-based visual question answering. In *Proceedings of the IEEE/CVF Conference on computer vision and pattern recognition*, pages 14974–14983.

Qingyi Si, Yuchen Mo, Zheng Lin, Huishan Ji, and Weiping Wang. 2023. Combo of thinking and observing for outside-knowledge vqa. *arXiv preprint arXiv:2305.06407*.

Kohei Uehara, Nabarun Goswami, Hanqin Wang, Toshiaki Baba, Kohtaro Tanaka, Tomohiro Hashimoto, Kai Wang, Rei Ito, Takagi Naoya, Ryo Umagami, et al. 2024. Advancing large multi-modal models with explicit chain-of-reasoning and visual question generation. *arXiv preprint arXiv:2401.10005*.

Peng Wang, Qi Wu, Chunhua Shen, Anthony Dick, and Anton Van Den Hengel. 2017. Fvqa: Fact-based visual question answering. *IEEE transactions on pattern analysis and machine intelligence*, 40(10):2413–2427.

Jialiang Xu, Michael Moor, and Jure Leskovec. 2024. Reverse image retrieval cues parametric memory in multimodal llms. *arXiv preprint arXiv:2405.18740*.

Licheng Yu, Eunbyung Park, Alexander C Berg, and Tamara L Berg. 2015. Visual madlibs: Fill in the blank image generation and question answering. *arXiv preprint arXiv:1506.00278*.

Yang Zhou, Pengfei Cao, Yubo Chen, Kang Liu, and Jun Zhao. 2023. Prompting vision language model with knowledge from large language model for knowledge-based vqa. *arXiv preprint arXiv:2308.15851*.

A Appendix

A.1 Details for data generation

The following section are the prompts for different stage of our generation pipeline.

Entity Finding The following are the prompts for entity finding.

```
Given the object, you have to generate
    ↪ one question to gain a more
    ↪ detailed class of the object.
    ↪ The answer of the question
    ↪ should be the detailed class of
    ↪ the object.

Examples:
{examples}
Object: {label}
Question:
```

Listing 1: Prompt for entity finding query generation

```
{generated_query} Answer with a  noun.
```

Listing 2: Prompt for entity finding

```
Decide whether the statement is true.
Examples:
Question: Panther is a type/class of
    ↪ Giraffe,
Answer: False
{more examples}
Question: {tag} is a type/class of {
    ↪ label}
Answer:
```

Listing 3: Prompt for entity filtering - subclass

```
Given a tag list, decide whether the
    ↪ tag list contains multiple
    ↪ different entities.
Examples:
Entities:['volkswagen t1', 'audi a4']
Answer: True
{more examples}
Entities:{tags}
Answer:
```

Listing 4: Prompt for entity filtering - different tags

Question Generation The following are the prompts for question generation.

```
You are a knowledge-based question
    ↪ answer generator. Given the
    ↪ objects and knowledge of each
    ↪ objects, generate a question and
    ↪  answer with rationale and a
    ↪ short answer.
Rules:
1. Answer should be a word, not a
    ↪ sentence.
2. Only ask one short question.
3. Question should be generated based
    ↪ on the object and knowledge.
4. Question should be related to at
    ↪ least two objects and the object
    ↪  must be in the Object List.
5. Question should be hard, do not ask
    ↪ common question that can be
    ↪ easily answered without
    ↪ knowledge source.
6. **All the options in the question
    ↪ and answer should be in the
    ↪ Objects List, question should
    ↪ contain the choices. i.e. _____,
    ↪  A or B?. Both A and B should in
    ↪  the Object List**
7. Do not output Objects List and
    ↪ Knowledge, only output Question,
    ↪  Rationale and Answer.
Format: {...}
Examples: {examples}
Objects List: {objects_list}
Knowledge: {knowledge}
```

Listing 5: Prompt for QA generation

```
Decide whether the QA question follow
    ↪ this criteria.
1. All the entities in the question are
    ↪  in the object list, it can be a
    ↪  slightly calling difference
2. The question contains more than one
    ↪ entities. If the provided
    ↪ question and object list satisfy
    ↪  the criteria above, output True
    ↪  Otherwise output False. Do not
    ↪ output any other information
    ↪ other than True or False.
Question: {question}
Object List: {objects_list}
```

Listing 6: Prompt for QA filtering

Visual Question Generation The following are the prompts for visual question generation.

```
There are {tags} in the image.
Describe their (1) appearance (2) place
    ↪  it located (3) other objects/
    ↪ people that are related to this
    ↪ object in the image.
Do not describe objects that are not
    ↪ related to the provided object
    ↪ list.
Write the response in a short passsage.
```

Listing 7: Prompt for image captioning

```
You are a VQA rewriter. Given a QA
    ↪ question and an image caption,
    ↪ rewrite the part after the comma
    ↪  in the question to create a
    ↪ more natural and human-like
    ↪ visual question answering format
    ↪ .

Rules:
1. Rewrite the entities in both the
    ↪ answer and the part of the
    ↪ question after the comma, using
    ↪ the visual information provided
    ↪ in the image.
```

```
2. The part of the question before the
    ↪ comma should remain unchanged.
3. Rewrite with simpler words and fewer
    ↪  object details.

Format: {...}
Examples: {examples}
Caption: {caption}
Question: {question}
Answer: {answer}
```

Listing 8: Prompt for VQA generation

A.2 Details for evaluation

The following are the prompts for model evaluation.

```
Given a question, a prediction, and an
    ↪ answer, evaluate whether the
    ↪ prediction aligned with the
    ↪ answer based on the question.
    ↪ Answer with Yes or No.

Question: {question}
Prediction: {prediction}
Answer: {answer}
```

Listing 9: Prompt for model answer evaluation

A.3 Example data of MSR^2

Figure 4, 6 and 7 contain some random example data of MSR^2.

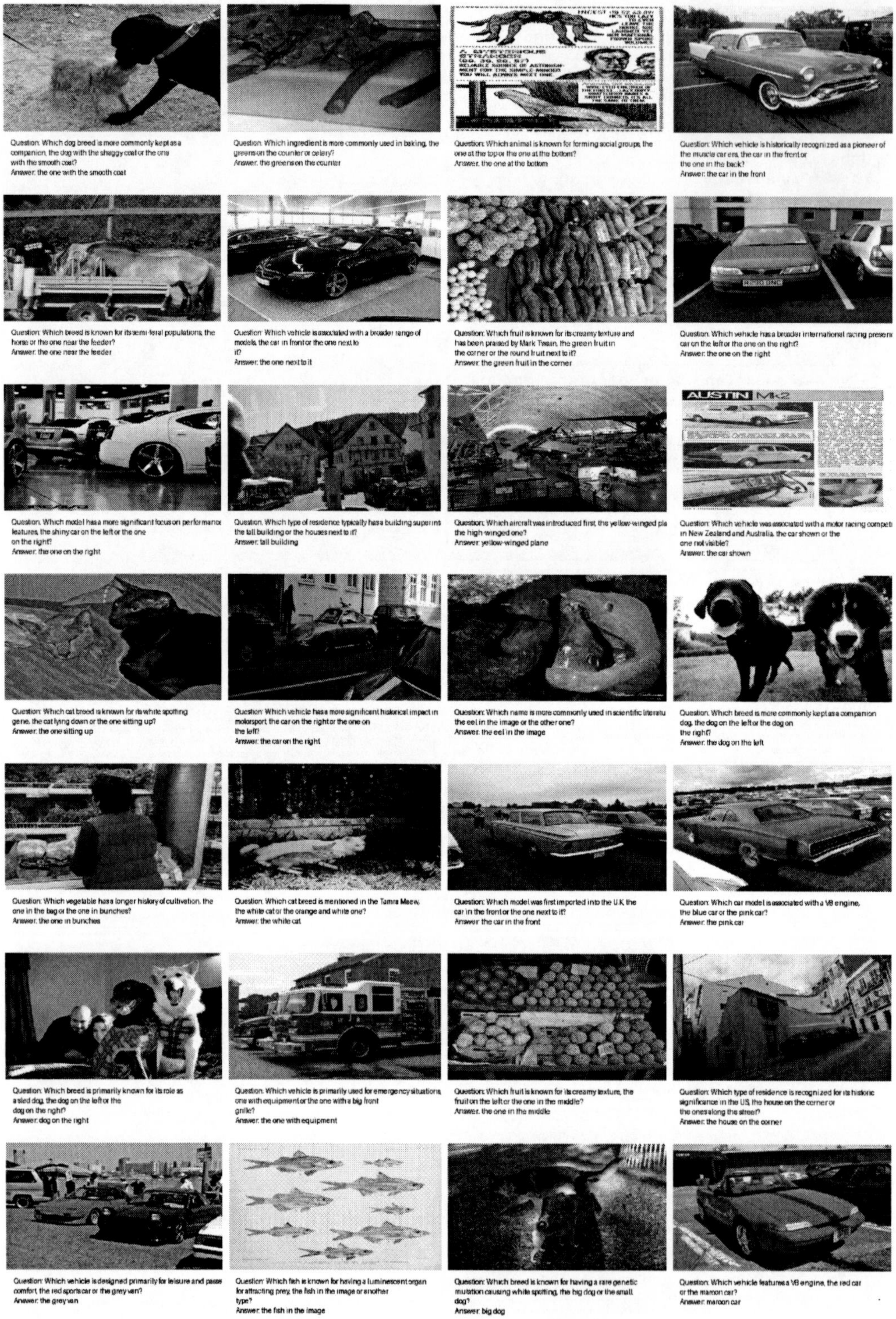

Figure 6: Random examples VQA question of MSR^2 - group2

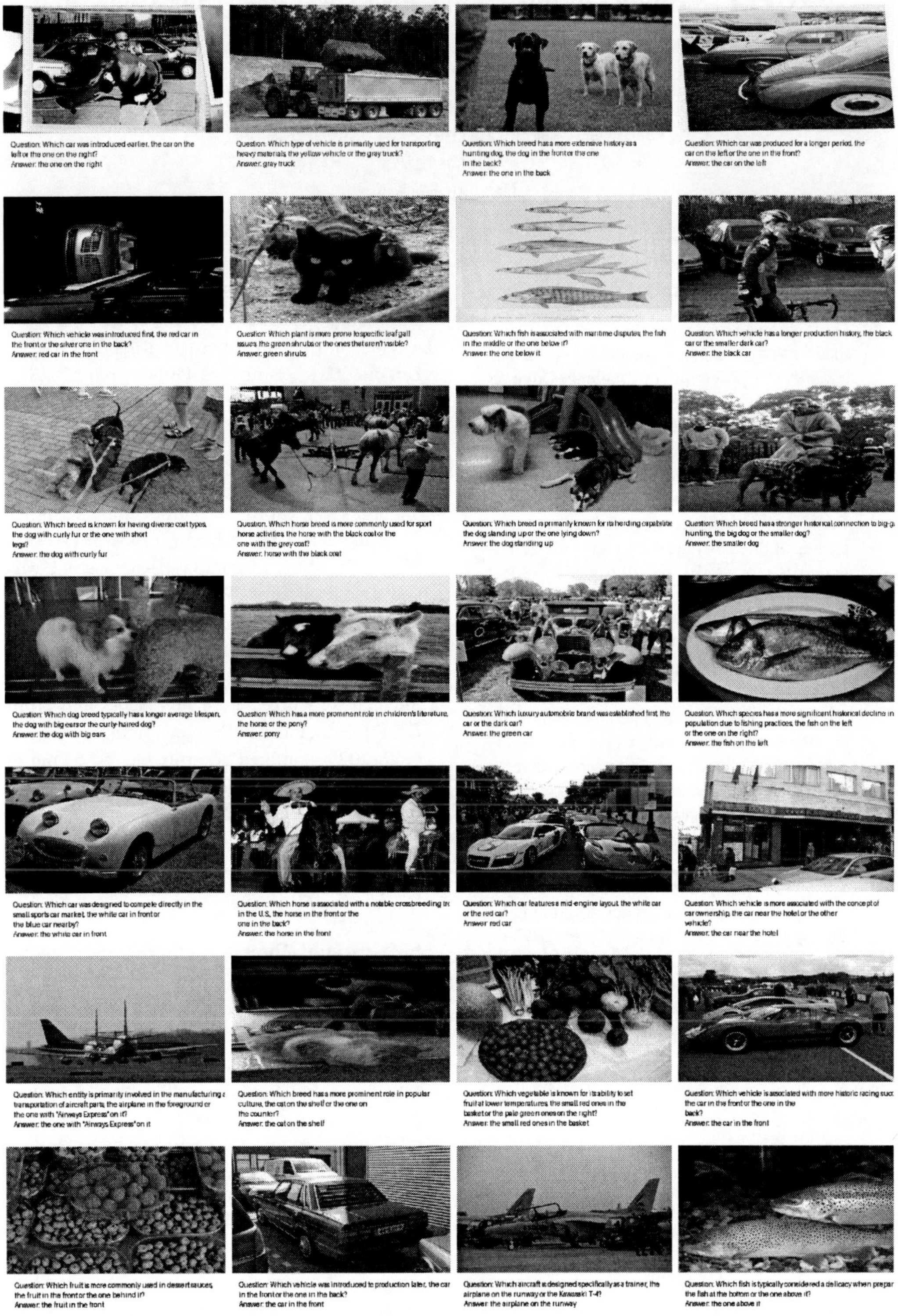

Figure 7: Random examples VQA question of MSR^2 - group3

PROPEL: Prompt Optimization with Expert Priors for Small and Medium-sized LLMs

Kawin Mayilvaghanan, Varun Nathan and **Ayush Kumar**
{kawin.m, varun.nathan, ayush}@observe.ai
Observe.AI
Bangalore, India

Abstract

Optimizing discrete prompts for small and medium-sized language models (1–8 billion parameters) poses unique challenges due to their relatively weaker instruction-following capabilities compared to larger counterparts. We present **PRompt OPtimization with Expert priors for LLMs (PROPEL)**, a novel knowledge-augmented iterative optimization framework leveraging the collaborative capabilities of three distinct roles assigned to large language models (LLMs): Responder, Judge, and Optimizer. Unlike prior works that focus on larger LLMs for prompt optimization with natural language feedback, our approach emphasizes improving prompt effectiveness for resource-efficient smaller and medium-sized models through structured iteration and the integration of prompt design principles as expert priors. Our experiments across diverse tasks such as long-text summarization and entity extraction demonstrate significant improvements. **PROPEL** improves response quality by **10–24%** for **Query-Based Summarization** and **5–16%** for **Query-Based Entity Extraction** over initial prompts, outperforming baseline approaches by at least **12%** and **9%**, respectively. Ablation studies further show that incorporating **prompt design principles as priors** enhances response quality by **21%** for Llama-3.2 1B and **9%** for Llama-3.2 3B.

1 Introduction and Related Works

Large Language Models (LLMs) have excelled in various NLP tasks, including summarization, question answering, and classification (OpenAI et al., 2024b; Grattafiori et al., 2024; Abdin et al., 2024). This success stems from extensive pretraining on diverse datasets and advancements in prompting techniques (Brown et al., 2020). Prompt engineering-designing task-specific instructions or queries to elicit optimal responses—has proven critical for achieving high performance across tasks and domains (Reynolds and McDonell, 2021).

However, creating effective prompts requires substantial manual effort (Jiang et al., 2022), often relying on domain expertise (Reynolds and McDonell, 2021; Zamfirescu-Pereira et al., 2023), intuition, and trial-and-error. This resource-intensive process poses challenges for non-expert users. Moreover, LLM performance is highly sensitive to prompt quality (Gao et al., 2021), emphasizing the importance of robust prompt engineering.

Techniques such as Chain-of-Thought (Wei et al., 2023), Few-Shot Prompting (Brown et al., 2020), and Role Prompting (Wang et al., 2024) introduce prompting strategies to improve response quality. Survey Works (Schulhoff et al., 2024; Sahoo et al., 2024; Chen et al., 2024) have systematically compiled and organized these approaches into Prompt Design Principles or Prompt Principles. Bsharat et al. 2024 identified 26 principles, showing that their effectiveness varies across LLMs, indicating model-specific applicability.

To mitigate the challenges of manual prompt engineering, various automated methods have been proposed, categorized by their underlying techniques:

Soft Prompt-Tuning Methods: Soft prompt-tuning represents prompts as continuous task-specific vectors optimized using gradient-based techniques (Lester et al., 2021; Li and Liang, 2021; Liu et al., 2023; Qin and Eisner, 2021). This method fine-tunes a small subset of trainable parameters while keeping the LLM frozen, achieving strong task performance. However, it requires access to the LLM's internal state variables, making it unsuitable for black-box APIs or closed-source models (Shin et al., 2020; Lester et al., 2021).

Iterative Scoring-Based Optimization: These approaches iteratively refine a discrete base prompt. GrIPS (Prasad et al., 2023) uses phrasal edits, while APE (Zhou et al., 2023) and OPRO (Yang et al., 2024) generate semantically similar prompts

Proceedings of the 4th International Workshop on Knowledge-Augmented Methods for Natural Language Processing (KnowledgeNLP'25), pages 272–302
May 3, 2025

via LLMs, scoring responses with an evaluation function—often another LLM—to select the next best prompt. OPRO (Yang et al., 2024) also incorporates the history of previous best prompts but doesn't explicitly generate natural language feedback. Numerical scores offer limited insights, failing to pinpoint specific response strengths or weaknesses. Our ablation study on PROPEL (Table 5) highlights the value of descriptive feedback. Moreover, these methods narrowly explore the initial prompt space, neglecting diverse strategies that could yield more robust solutions.

Iterative Feedback-Driven Optimization: These techniques use iterative feedback loops for prompt refinement. Methods like SelfRefine (Madaan et al., 2023), APO (Pryzant et al., 2023), and Self-Debugging (Chen et al., 2023) leverage LLM feedback to enhance prompts, with APO (Pryzant et al., 2023) introducing textual gradients to target weaknesses. However, APO (Pryzant et al., 2023) does not utilize the history of prompts, scores, and feedback, which we demonstrate as crucial in PROPEL (Table 4). SelfRefine (Madaan et al., 2023) and Self-Debugging (Chen et al., 2023) rely on the Responder LLM for both response and feedback. However, these methods are demonstrated on larger models, which we hypothesize are better equipped to process detailed feedback. In contrast, small- and medium-scale LLMs struggle with capability to fully utilize such feedback for self-improvement (Saunders et al., 2022; Huang et al., 2023), rendering this approach for prompt optimization ineffective when applied to these smaller models.

LLM-Based Evolutionary Techniques: Evolutionary algorithms, like the Genetic Algorithm (Holland, 1992) and Differential Algorithm (Storn and Price, 1997), have been adapted for discrete prompt optimization. Methods such as PromptBreeder (Fernando et al., 2023), PromptWizard (Agarwal et al., 2024), and EvoPrompt (Guo et al., 2024) refine prompts through iterative techniques, applying thinking styles, and leveraging LLM-driven operations like crossover and mutation. While promising, these approaches are predominantly evaluated on larger LLMs. However, as noted by (Bsharat et al., 2024), effectiveness of mutation can vary for small and medium-scale models, raising concerns about generalizability to smaller LLMs.

In this work, we tackle the critical yet underexplored challenge of optimizing discrete prompts for small and medium-sized LLMs (1–8 billion parameters), which exhibit weaker instruction-following capabilities compared to larger models (Qin et al., 2024). To address this, we propose PROPEL (PRompt OPtimization with Expert Priors for LLMs), a novel knowledge-augmented framework that leverages expert-informed prompt principles as priors and orchestrates a structured iteration among three distinct LLM roles: **Responder LLM**, responsible for response generation; **Judge LLM**, tasked with response evaluation; and **Optimizer LLM**, which refines prompts using expert priors and historical state information comprising prompts, feedback, and scores. This approach strategically incorporates structured knowledge into the prompt optimization process, enabling more effective knowledge utilization and enhancing the performance of small and medium-sized LLMs.

Unlike existing approaches that overlook the integration of prompt design principles into the optimization process, PROPEL systematically identifies task- and model-specific easy or hard to follow prompt principles. These principles are incorporated as priors over the optimal prompt space, enabling the discovery of prompts that are both effective and tailored to the specific LLM and task. Extensive experiments on summarization, entity extraction, and multi-turn QnA show improvements of at least 12%, 9% and 3% over state-of-the-art baselines, respectively, highlighting the effectiveness of the PROPEL framework.

2 Methodology

2.1 Problem Formulation

Given an initial prompt p_0 for a Responder LLM $\mathcal{M}$, our goal is to iteratively transform p_0 into $\hat{p}$, an approximation of the optimized prompt p^* which maximizes the quality of the generated responses. We assume access to an i.i.d training dataset consisting of pairs of input context and reference output: $D_{train} = \{(x_1, y_1), \ldots, (x_n, y_n)\}$ where $x_1, \ldots, x_n$ represents the input context and $y_1, \ldots, y_n$ represents the reference outputs. Note that all prompts p are drawn from the space of coherent natural language L. The quality of the generated responses $\hat{y} = \mathcal{M}(y|p, x)$ is evaluated using a metric function $m(y, \hat{y})$.

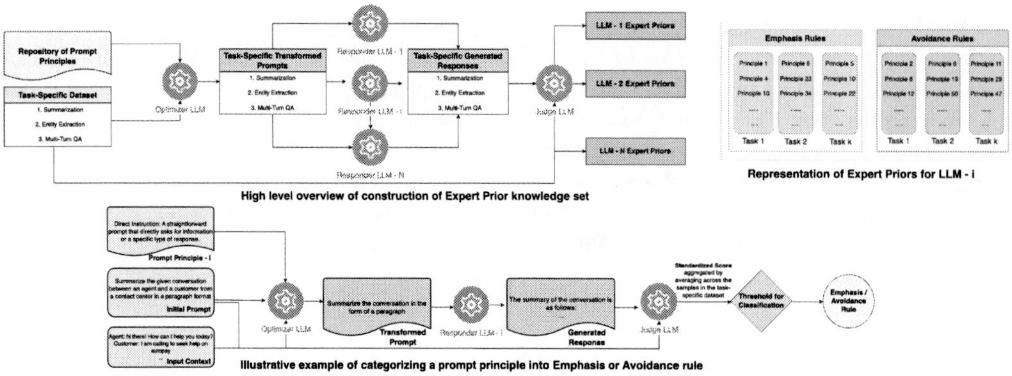

Figure 1: Visual representation of construction of Expert Prior knowledge store, which guides the prompt optimization workflow described in the next subsection.

The optimization task can be expressed as:

$$\hat{p} = \arg\max_{p \in L} \mathbb{E}[m(y, \mathcal{M}(y|p,x))] \quad \forall x, y \in D_{train}$$

The optimization process proceeds iteratively:

$$p_{k+1} = A(p_k, \text{State}, \text{Priors}),$$

where A is the algorithm explained in A.1, *State* stores the history of prompts, scores, and feedback from previous iterations, and *Priors* encode the principles to design prompts which is provided to the Optimizer LLM to guide prompt optimization.

2.2 Expert Priors

Inspired by the work of Bsharat et al. (2024), which examines the influence of LLM size on prompt design, we hypothesize that explicitly encoding the structured knowledge of the strengths and weaknesses of the Responder LLM's ability to follow specific prompt styles into the prompt optimization process will significantly enhance the quality of the prompts, as measured by the response quality. To achieve this, we define *Expert Priors*, a knowledge-augmented approach that systematically encodes the capabilities and challenges of the Responder LLM in adhering to various prompt principles. These priors guide optimization by defining *emphasis rules*, which correspond to design principles classified as *Easy* for the Responder LLM to follow, and *avoidance rules*, which correspond to design principles classified as *Hard* for the Responder LLM to follow.

As depicted in Figure 1, the *Expert Priors* are constructed as knowledge corpora[1] that capture the Responder LLM's proficiency in following different prompt styles. This is achieved by systematically transforming task-specific initial prompts with GPT-4 (OpenAI et al., 2024b) for each of the 50 prompt principles (see Tables 6 & 7) and then evaluating the Responder LLM's performance on the transformed prompts. These principles are informed by previous work, including Bsharat et al. 2024 and Chen et al. 2024, and are evaluated on a minimal dataset of 10 task-specific samples to identify *Easy* or *Hard* principles. Easy principles represent design strategies of the prompts that the Responder LLM can reliably respond with minimal errors, and these are encoded into the optimization process as *emphasis rules*, directing the optimizer to create the prompt by reinforcing these principles. Conversely, Hard principles represent design strategies of prompts where the Responder LLM is more likely to struggle, and these are encoded as *avoidance rules*, signaling the optimizer to create prompt that does not adhere to the characteristics defined by these principles to minimize errors and maintain high-quality responses.

Our approach leverages Expert Priors as structured knowledge in a plug-and-play manner, enhancing prompt optimization without requiring fine-tuning of the Responder LLM. By strategically utilizing knowledge, the Optimizer LLM generates high-quality prompts tailored to the Responder LLM's strengths and weaknesses. The 50 principles are automatically classified as Easy or Hard once per Responder LLM per task, enabling scalable and efficient knowledge elicitation. The detailed implementation of this automated classification process is described in Section 7i.

[1]Expert priors are available in Section A.11.

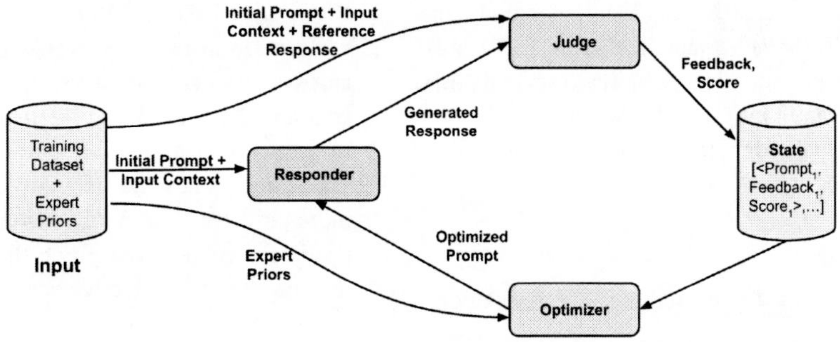

Figure 2: Proposed workflow: The Responder generates responses, the Judge evaluates them with feedback and score, and the Optimizer optimizes prompt using expert priors and state. This process is repeated iteratively.

2.3 Framework Design and Workflow

As shown in Figure 2, PROPEL operates as an iterative framework involving the coordinated interaction of three key components: the Responder LLM, Judge LLM, and Optimizer LLM. Each component is driven by role-specific meta-prompts, ensuring alignment with their designated functions:

1. **Response Generation by Responder LLM**: The Responder LLM generates a response ($\hat{y}$) based on the *input*, which consists of the current prompt p_k and the training dataset D_{train}. At the beginning of the process, the current prompt p_k is initialized to the initial prompt p_0.

2. **Evaluation by Judge LLM**: The Judge LLM evaluates the generated response ($\hat{y}$) using the current prompt p_k, the input context x, and the reference response y. This evaluation follows predefined criteria outlined in Section A.6. The Judge provides detailed feedback and assigns a score between 1 and 5 for each training data point (x, y). The feedback and scores are then summarized using the *Feedback Summary* meta-prompt (refer to Section A.8). The summarized insights, representing knowledge extracted from the evaluation process, are stored in the **State** as a triplet $\langle p_k, \text{Feedback}_k, \text{Score}_k \rangle$. This approach effectively curates and utilizes evaluation knowledge, aligning with knowledge-augmented methodologies.

3. **Prompt Optimization by Optimizer LLM**: The Optimizer LLM generates a refined prompt p_{k+1} based on the analysis of the **State** and adherence to *Expert Priors*. The metaprompt (Refer "Optimizer LLM" in section A.8) ensures that the optimizations preserve the intent of the original task while enhancing the response quality.

4. **Repeat**: Steps 1–3 are repeated iteratively for a specified number of iterations or until a stopping criteria defined by a threshold on the score of quality of responses.

For further implementation details, refer to *Key Implementation Details for PROPEL* in Section A.7.

3 Experimentation Details

3.1 Dataset and Tasks

This work utilizes the public **QMSum** (Zhong et al., 2021) dataset for the task of query-based summarization and the public benchmark **MT Bench** (Zheng et al., 2023) for evaluating QnA performance in multi-turn chat scenarios. Additionally, an **in-house** dataset[2] is employed for tasks including query-based summarization and entity extraction. Comprehensive details about these datasets, associated tasks, and rationale for their selection are provided in Section A.2.

3.2 Models used as Responder LLM

We select a diverse range of open-source models, including small models (1–3 billion parameters) and medium-sized models (7-8 billion parameters). Further details on the specific characteristics and rationale for choosing these models can be found in Section A.4.

3.3 Baselines

The study uses Self-Refine (Madaan et al., 2023), GrIPS (Prasad et al., 2023), Prompt Wizard (Agarwal et al., 2024), APO (Pryzant et al., 2023), and

[2]Due to proprietary restrictions, this dataset cannot be released.

OPRO (Yang et al., 2024) as baseline methods. In the *PROPEL (Self)* variant, the same LLM employed as the Responder LLM also serves as the Judge LLM and Optimizer LLM. Further details and the rationale for selecting these baselines are provided in Section A.5.

3.4 Metrics

Response quality for evaluating summarization, QnA in multi-turn chat and entity extraction tasks is obtained using *LLM Score*, a rating on a scale of 1–5 provided by GPT-4o (OpenAI et al., 2024a); Rouge-1 (Lin, 2004) is applied to entity extraction tasks. Table 1 presents the standardized metric differences between responses generated using optimized prompts and initial prompts. Details of the metrics, their computation, and standardization procedures are provided in Section A.6.

3.5 Implementation Details

Evaluation was conducted on the final optimized prompt, defined as either the last iteration's prompt or an intermediate one when early stopping occurred. Further details on the implementation can be found in Section A.7.

4 Experimental Results

4.1 Overall Results

We evaluate PROPEL against several baselines across two categories of Responder LLMs: Small Models (1–3 Billion parameters) and Medium-Sized Models (7–8 Billion parameters). The results are summarized in Tables 1 and key observations are detailed below:

Small Models (1–3 Billion Parameters)

1. **Superior Performance of PROPEL:** PROPEL outperforms all baselines across datasets and tasks, highlighting the crucial role of knowledge-informed Expert Priors in boosting performance for smaller models. Specifically, PROPEL achieves substantial margins over baselines, with improvements of 20%, 6% and 4% for Llama 3.2 1B, Llama 3.2 3B and Flan-T5 3B in summarization, and 14%, 10% and 13.7% for entity extraction. The more pronounced improvements in the smaller 1B model underscore the value of knowledge-augmented priors in guiding prompt optimization and maximizing the potential of resource-efficient LLMs.
2. **PROPEL (Self) vs. PROPEL**: PROPEL (Self) performs substantially worse than PROPEL across datasets and tasks, highlighting that smaller LLMs are less effective at evaluating responses and generating optimized prompts. This emphasizes the necessity of leveraging more powerful external LLMs (e.g., GPT-4) to provide feedback and guide the prompt optimization process effectively.

Medium-Sized Models (7–8 Billion Parameters)

1. **Superior Performance of PROPEL:** Similar to the small models, **PROPEL** consistently outperforms the baselines across datasets and tasks. This highlights the effectiveness of integrating knowledge-informed Expert Priors in optimizing prompt design, thereby enhancing the capabilities of medium-sized models.
2. **PROPEL (Self) vs. PROPEL:** Unlike smaller models, **PROPEL (Self)** demonstrates significantly improved performance relative to the baselines when using medium-sized models, although it still lags behind **PROPEL**. This indicates that medium-sized models are better equipped to serve as both evaluators and optimizers. However, achieving enhanced response quality still requires the coordination of a more powerful LLM for Judge and Optimizer LLM roles.

The key takeaways are as follows:

1. **Significance of Knowledge-Informed Expert Priors: Expert Priors** are particularly critical for smaller and medium-sized models (1–8 Billion parameters), significantly boosting performance across all of the tasks and datasets by leveraging knowledge-informed guidance in prompt optimization.
2. **Role of powerful LLM in Evaluation and Optimization:** Using a powerful external LLM like GPT-4 for evaluation and optimization is more effective than relying on the smaller Responder LLM. A more capable LLM offers detailed, accurate assessments by better understanding the prompt-response-reference response alignment. During optimization, it identifies prompt issues and generates improved versions that better align with task objectives and the characteristics of smaller Responder LLMs.

Responder LLM	Methods	Summarization		Entity Extraction		Chat
		Inhouse	QMSum	Inhouse		MT-Bench
		ΔLLM Score	ΔLLM Score	ΔLLM Score	ΔROUGE-1	ΔLLM Score
Llama 3.2 1B	Self-Refine	-29.00	-12.74	-46.82	-33.64	-10.04
	GrIPS	3.28	4.53	2.94	2.19	1.25
	Prompt-Wizard	-5.20	-2.64	-2.95	-3.70	-1.52
	APO	-3.20	-3.96	-9.20	-11.50	2.86
	OPRO	-2.00	-1.28	-1.75	-3.27	1.67
	PROPEL (Self)	-14.00	-10.27	-48.00	-25.04	-9.82
	PROPEL	**22.67**	**7.91**	**11.00**	**16.43**	**8.46**
Llama 3.2 3B	Self-Refine	-13.54	-8.37	-30.16	-18.48	-5.39
	GrIPS	2.79	2.92	3.16	2.65	1.69
	Prompt-Wizard	-7.44	-6.34	-1.65	-1.80	1.18
	APO	2.67	3.42	-6.40	-8.89	3.27
	OPRO	8.00	4.58	1.50	1.68	2.50
	PROPEL (Self)	-12.34	-5.90	-29.00	-13.57	-2.26
	PROPEL	**14.17**	**6.29**	**8.00**	**12.58**	**6.79**
Flan-T5 3B	Self-Refine	-3.80	-9.75	-6.30	-1.57	-1.13
	GrIPS	5.60	4.51	1.90	4.00	2.60
	Prompt-Wizard	-1.27	-4.98	-2.60	-2.38	-1.20
	APO	1.58	3.91	-7.56	-6.73	-1.48
	OPRO	6.56	-7.42	-6.02	-6.25	-7.83
	PROPEL (Self)	-8.38	-4.38	-2.02	-1.86	-2.16
	PROPEL	**10.29**	**7.03**	**15.61**	**13.7**	**6.63**
Mistral 7B	Self-Refine	3.71	2.85	1.48	0.95	-0.74
	GrIPS	5.96	3.13	-1.64	0.73	-0.58
	Prompt-Wizard	3.02	3.58	-0.84	-1.18	-1.92
	APO	-13.00	-2.68	-9.63	-8.79	-0.84
	OPRO	10.05	3.76	-0.80	-3.14	0.37
	PROPEL (Self)	17.39	3.62	2.40	1.83	1.09
	PROPEL	**21.50**	**8.73**	**3.90**	**8.96**	**3.73**
Llama 3 8B	Self-Refine	-2.00	-1.08	-3.00	-1.54	2.17
	GrIPS	-2.32	1.40	-3.80	-0.20	1.84
	Prompt-Wizard	-1.96	2.73	-1.20	-1.83	1.37
	APO	-7.46	-3.40	-3.20	-2.84	1.25
	OPRO	5.00	-1.26	-3.59	-3.42	1.89
	PROPEL (Self)	21.35	5.70	6.40	2.67	2.04
	PROPEL	**23.68**	**12.20**	**8.20**	**4.64**	**2.45**

Table 1: The table compares PROPEL with baselines across tasks and models, using *GPT-4* as Judge and Optimizer. It shows the difference in standardized LLM scores ('Δ') between responses generated with optimized prompts and initial prompts for Summarization and Chat tasks. Raw LLM scores are standardized from the GPT-4o ratings (1–5 scale) to percentages. ΔROUGE-1 is used for Entity Extraction task. Higher scores indicate better performance, with the best results for each model in bold and color. Negative scores indicate worse performance with optimized prompts.

3. **Consistent Task Performance: PROPEL** consistently delivers strong performance across tasks, demonstrating exceptional effectiveness in knowledge-intensive scenarios, including query-based summarization, entity extraction, and QnA over multi-turn chat, underscoring its versatility and robust design.

4.2 Ablation Studies

We focus on the Query-Based Summarization task in the in-house dataset containing five prompts and the Llama-3.2 1B and 3B models as the basis for all the ablation studies.

Impact of Initial Prompt: Certain prompts pose varying levels of difficulty for different models, making harder prompts more challenging to optimize. These harder prompts often require additional training data or more iterations in the optimization algorithm to converge effectively. The objective of this study is to check if PROPEL can work as effectively with "hard" prompts as they do with "easy" prompts.

For each of the considered prompts, the Optimizer LLM generates an "easy" and a "hard" version by following specific rules derived from a one-time evaluation of the Responder LLM on 50 prompt principles (Refer table 6). The "easy" prompts emphasize aspects the Responder LLM excels at, while the "hard" prompts intentionally include elements the Responder LLM struggles with. This process is conducted for two models: Llama-3.2-1B and Llama-3.2-3B.

We measure the effect of prompt difficulty on the effectiveness of PROPEL by calculating the average LLM Scores for responses generated with initial prompts (LLM $\text{Score}_{\text{init}}$) and the average improvement in scores after optimization (ΔLLM Score). The sum of these metrics gives the final LLM Scores for the optimized prompts.

The results in Table 2 show that while the LLM Scores for the final optimized prompts are higher for "easy" prompts compared to "hard" prompts, the improvements in ΔLLM Scores are significantly greater for "hard" prompts. In other words, the gap in LLM Scores between the initial "easy" and "hard" prompts is much larger than the gap between the optimized "easy" and "hard" prompts. This indicates that PROPEL is highly effective even for "hard" prompts, despite their greater optimization challenge.

Initial Prompt	Llama-3.2 1B		Llama-3.2 3B	
	LLM $\text{Score}_{\text{init}}$	ΔLLM Score	LLM $\text{Score}_{\text{init}}$	ΔLLM Score
Easy	67.60	13.47	70.04	7.83
Hard	40.06	33.47	43.86	25.47

Table 2: Impact of initial prompt on ΔLLM Score for Llama-3.2 1B and 3B models.

Impact of Expert Priors on Knowledge-Guided Prompt Optimization: The goal of this study is to evaluate how the quality of expert priors influences the effectiveness of the knowledge-augmented prompt optimization algorithm. We test the following scenarios:

1. **Good Priors:** Rules derived directly from the one-time evaluation of the Responder LLM using 50 prompt principles (Refer table 6). These "emphasis" and "avoidance" rules, which serve as structured knowledge priors, are incorporated into the Optimizer LLM's prompts during optimization.

2. **No Priors:** The Optimizer LLM operates without any knowledge-augmented rules, relying solely on iterative feedback for prompt optimization.

3. **Random Priors:** Seven prompt principles are randomly selected from the curated list for each rule type ("emphasis" and "avoidance"), and the resulting rules are included in the Optimizer LLM's prompts. This tests the impact of unstructured knowledge injection on optimization performance.

4. **Bad Priors:** The "emphasis" and "avoidance" rules are reversed, such that principles the Responder LLM excels at are treated as "avoidance" rules and vice versa. This setup evaluates the negative influence of inaccurately encoded knowledge on prompt optimization.

The effectiveness of each scenario is measured by the average change in LLM scores after optimization (ΔLLM Score). Results in Table 3 show that "Good Priors" lead to the highest improvement of 10-15%, followed by "Random Priors," "No Priors", and "Bad Priors." The decline in performance with "Bad Priors" stems from the propagation of incorrect information into the optimization process.

Priors Applied	ΔLLM Score	
	Llama 3.2 1B	Llama 3.2 3B
Bad Priors	-6.74	-7.84
Random Priors	7.62	4.86
No Priors	1.67	5.14
Good Priors	22.67	14.17

Table 3: Impact of priors on ΔLLM Score for Llama-3.2 1B and 3B models.

Effect of State History as Knowledge Context: This study investigates the role of state history (prompts, feedback, and scores) as Knowledge Context in guiding the prompt optimization process. Two settings are compared: (1) Without History — Only the latest state (prompt, feedback, and score) is provided to the Optimizer LLM for refining prompts, without any historical context.; and (2) With History — The Optimizer LLM is supplied with a sequence of the last 10 states (Refer Section A.7), effectively leveraging historical knowledge comprising prompts, feedback, and scores. Results in Table 4 show that using state history improves ΔLLM Score by 8.9% for Llama-3.2 1B and 4% for Llama-3.2 3B. This highlights the importance of historical knowledge patterns in improving prompt optimization, demonstrating the value of knowledge persistence and contextual learning in iterative LLM interactions.

History Applied	ΔLLM Score	
	Llama-3.2 1B	Llama-3.2 3B
Without History	13.80	10.13
With History	22.67	14.17

Table 4: Impact of State History on ΔLLM Score for Llama-3.2 1B and 3B models.

Impact of Using Feedback and Scores as Knowledge Signals in State: This study examines the impact of incorporating feedback and scores as knowledge signals in the State on prompt optimization effectiveness. Three settings are evaluated: (1) Feedback Only: State includes a history of size 10 with prompts and their corresponding feedback from the Judge LLM. (2) Scores Only: State includes a history of size 10 with prompts and their corresponding scores. (3) Feedback & Scores: State includes prompts, feedback, and scores (default setting).

The effectiveness is measured by the average change in LLM scores after optimization (ΔLLM Score). Results in Table 5 show that using only scores slightly outperforms using only feedback, while combining feedback and scores significantly improves performance, with gains of 14.5% and 8% for Llama-3.2 1B and 3B models, respectively. This suggests that feedback and scores provide complementary insights—feedback highlights areas for improvement, while scores offer a performance baseline. Together, they give the Optimizer LLM a richer context, enabling more effective prompt refinements.

Evaluator Output	ΔLLM Score	
	Llama-3.2 1B	Llama-3.2 3B
With Feedback Only	7.30	5.83
With Scores Only	8.20	6.21
With Feedback & Scores	22.67	14.17

Table 5: Impact of Evaluator and State on ΔLLM Score for Llama-3.2 1B and 3B models.

5 Conclusion

We introduce **PROPEL**, a novel prompt optimization framework that leverages expert priors and iterative feedback from a Judge LLM to improve LLM performance across various tasks. By integrating knowledge-informed priors, **PROPEL** effectively guides the optimization process, particularly benefiting small and medium-sized models. Experimental results demonstrate that **PROPEL** outperforms existing baselines, showing substantial gains in query-based summarization, entity extraction, and QnA over multi-turn interactions. Ablation studies reveal that the inclusion of expert priors enhances LLM scores by 10–15%, highlighting their pivotal role in aligning prompt design with model-specific strengths and limitations.

6 Limitations

We recognize certain limitations in the scope of the presented work. First, while the reliance on expert priors requires a one-time evaluation, this process may not be readily applicable to all scenarios, particularly those with highly dynamic requirements. Second, **PROPEL** relies on reference responses for evaluation, which, while effective, may pose challenges for fully automated scalability in tasks without readily available references. Third, the current evaluation focuses on tasks such as query-based summarization, entity extraction, and multi-turn QnA. While these tasks demonstrate the versatility of **PROPEL**, additional testing on more complex and diverse modeling challenges would further validate its generalizability. Additionally, the present study is confined to small and medium-sized models up to 8B parameters. Extending the analysis to larger models would better demonstrate **PROPEL**'s adaptability and effectiveness across a broader range of model architectures. Finally, the testing was conducted exclusively on English-language tasks, leaving multilingual capabilities an area for future exploration to ensure broader applicability across diverse linguistic settings.

References

Marah Abdin, Sam Ade Jacobs, Ammar Ahmad Awan, Jyoti Aneja, Ahmed Awadallah, Hany Hassan Awadalla, Nguyen Bach, Amit Bahree, Arash Bakhtiari, Harkirat Singh Behl, Alon Benhaim, Misha Bilenko, Johan Bjorck, Sébastien Bubeck, Martin Cai, Caio C'esar Teodoro Mendes, Weizhu Chen, Vishrav Chaudhary, Parul Chopra, Allison Del Giorno, Gustavo de Rosa, Matthew Dixon, Ronen Eldan, Dan Iter, Abhishek Goswami, Suriya Gunasekar, Emman Haider, Junheng Hao, Russell J. Hewett, Jamie Huynh, Mojan Javaheripi, Xin Jin, Piero Kauffmann, Nikos Karampatziakis, Dongwoo Kim, Young Jin Kim, Mahoud Khademi, Lev Kurilenko, James R. Lee, Yin Tat Lee, Yuanzhi Li, Chen Liang, Weishung Liu, Eric Lin, Zeqi Lin, Piyush Madan, Arindam Mitra, Hardik Modi, Anh Nguyen, Brandon Norick, Barun Patra, Daniel Perez-Becker, Thomas Portet, Reid Pryzant, Heyang Qin, Marko Radmilac, Corby Rosset, Sambudha Roy, Olli Saarikivi, Amin Saied, Adil Salim, Michael Santacroce, Shital Shah, Ning Shang, Hiteshi Sharma, Xianmin Song, Olatunji Ruwase, Praneetha Vaddamanu, Xin Wang, Rachel Ward, Guanhua Wang, Philipp Witte, Michael Wyatt, Can Xu, Jiahang Xu, Sonali Yadav, Fan Yang, Ziyi Yang, Donghan Yu, Cheng-Yuan Zhang, Cyril Zhang, Jianwen Zhang, Li Lyna Zhang, Yi Zhang, Yunan Zhang, and Xiren Zhou. 2024. Phi-3 technical report: A highly capable language model locally on your phone. *ArXiv*, abs/2404.14219.

Eshaan Agarwal, Vivek Dani, Tanuja Ganu, and Akshay Nambi. 2024. Promptwizard: Task-aware agent-driven prompt optimization framework. *Preprint*, arXiv:2405.18369.

Ahmed Ali and Steve Renals. 2018. Word error rate estimation for speech recognition: e-WER. In *Proceedings of the 56th Annual Meeting of the Association for Computational Linguistics (Volume 2: Short Papers)*, pages 20–24, Melbourne, Australia. Association for Computational Linguistics.

Tom B. Brown, Benjamin Mann, Nick Ryder, Melanie Subbiah, Jared Kaplan, Prafulla Dhariwal, Arvind Neelakantan, Pranav Shyam, Girish Sastry, Amanda Askell, Sandhini Agarwal, Ariel Herbert-Voss, Gretchen Krueger, Tom Henighan, Rewon Child, Aditya Ramesh, Daniel M. Ziegler, Jeffrey Wu, Clemens Winter, Christopher Hesse, Mark Chen, Eric Sigler, Mateusz Litwin, Scott Gray, Benjamin Chess, Jack Clark, Christopher Berner, Sam McCandlish, Alec Radford, Ilya Sutskever, and Dario Amodei. 2020. Language models are few-shot learners. *Preprint*, arXiv:2005.14165.

Sondos Mahmoud Bsharat, Aidar Myrzakhan, and Zhiqiang Shen. 2024. Principled instructions are all you need for questioning llama-1/2, gpt-3.5/4. *Preprint*, arXiv:2312.16171.

Daniel Cer, Mona Diab, Eneko Agirre, Inigo Lopez-Gazpio, and Lucia Specia. 2017. Semeval-2017 task 1: Semantic textual similarity multilingual and crosslingual focused evaluation. In *Proceedings of the 11th International Workshop on Semantic Evaluation (SemEval-2017)*. Association for Computational Linguistics.

Banghao Chen, Zhaofeng Zhang, Nicolas Langrené, and Shengxin Zhu. 2024. Unleashing the potential of prompt engineering in large language models: a comprehensive review. *Preprint*, arXiv:2310.14735.

Xinyun Chen, Maxwell Lin, Nathanael Schärli, and Denny Zhou. 2023. Teaching large language models to self-debug. *Preprint*, arXiv:2304.05128.

Hyunlee Chung, Mitesh Tapaswi, Denny Chen, Yiming Zhao, Mehran Sadeghi, , et al. 2022. Scaling instruction-finetuned language models. *arXiv preprint arXiv:2201.11903*.

Chrisantha Fernando, Dylan Banarse, Henryk Michalewski, Simon Osindero, and Tim Rocktäschel. 2023. Promptbreeder: Self-referential self-improvement via prompt evolution. *Preprint*, arXiv:2309.16797.

J.L. Fleiss et al. 1971. Measuring nominal scale agreement among many raters. *Psychological Bulletin*, 76(5):378–382.

Tianyu Gao, Adam Fisch, and Danqi Chen. 2021. Making pre-trained language models better few-shot learners. In *Proceedings of the 59th Annual Meeting of the Association for Computational Linguistics and the 11th International Joint Conference on Natural Language Processing (Volume 1: Long Papers)*, pages 3816–3830, Online. Association for Computational Linguistics.

Aaron Grattafiori, Abhimanyu Dubey, Abhinav Jauhri, Abhinav Pandey, Abhishek Kadian, Ahmad Al-Dahle, Aiesha Letman, Akhil Mathur, Alan Schelten, Alex Vaughan, Amy Yang, Angela Fan, Anirudh Goyal, Anthony Hartshorn, Aobo Yang, Archi Mitra, Archie Sravankumar, Artem Korenev, Arthur Hinsvark, Arun Rao, Aston Zhang, Aurelien Rodriguez, Austen Gregerson, Ava Spataru, Baptiste Roziere, Bethany Biron, Binh Tang, Bobbie Chern, Charlotte Caucheteux, Chaya Nayak, Chloe Bi, Chris Marra, Chris McConnell, Christian Keller, Christophe Touret, Chunyang Wu, Corinne Wong, Cristian Canton Ferrer, Cyrus Nikolaidis, Damien Allonsius, Daniel Song, Danielle Pintz, Danny Livshits, Danny Wyatt, David Esiobu, Dhruv Choudhary, Dhruv Mahajan, Diego Garcia-Olano, Diego Perino, Dieuwke Hupkes, Egor Lakomkin, Ehab AlBadawy, Elina Lobanova, Emily Dinan, Eric Michael Smith, Filip Radenovic, Francisco Guzmán, Frank Zhang, Gabriel Synnaeve, Gabrielle Lee, Georgia Lewis Anderson, Govind Thattai, Graeme Nail, Gregoire Mialon, Guan Pang, Guillem Cucurell, Hailey Nguyen, Hannah Korevaar, Hu Xu, Hugo Touvron, Iliyan Zarov, Imanol Arrieta Ibarra, Isabel Kloumann, Ishan Misra, Ivan Evtimov, Jack Zhang, Jade Copet, Jaewon Lee, Jan Geffert, Jana Vranes, Jason Park, Jay Mahadeokar, Jeet Shah, Jelmer van der Linde,

Jennifer Billock, Jenny Hong, Jenya Lee, Jeremy Fu, Jianfeng Chi, Jianyu Huang, Jiawen Liu, Jie Wang, Jiecao Yu, Joanna Bitton, Joe Spisak, Jongsoo Park, Joseph Rocca, Joshua Johnstun, Joshua Saxe, Junteng Jia, Kalyan Vasuden Alwala, Karthik Prasad, Kartikeya Upasani, Kate Plawiak, Ke Li, Kenneth Heafield, Kevin Stone, Khalid El-Arini, Krithika Iyer, Kshitiz Malik, Kuenley Chiu, Kunal Bhalla, Kushal Lakhotia, Lauren Rantala-Yeary, Laurens van der Maaten, Lawrence Chen, Liang Tan, Liz Jenkins, Louis Martin, Lovish Madaan, Lubo Malo, Lukas Blecher, Lukas Landzaat, Luke de Oliveira, Madeline Muzzi, Mahesh Pasupuleti, Mannat Singh, Manohar Paluri, Marcin Kardas, Maria Tsimpoukelli, Mathew Oldham, Mathieu Rita, Maya Pavlova, Melanie Kambadur, Mike Lewis, Min Si, Mitesh Kumar Singh, Mona Hassan, Naman Goyal, Narjes Torabi, Nikolay Bashlykov, Nikolay Bogoychev, Niladri Chatterji, Ning Zhang, Olivier Duchenne, Onur Çelebi, Patrick Alrassy, Pengchuan Zhang, Pengwei Li, Petar Vasic, Peter Weng, Prajjwal Bhargava, Pratik Dubal, Praveen Krishnan, Punit Singh Koura, Puxin Xu, Qing He, Qingxiao Dong, Ragavan Srinivasan, Raj Ganapathy, Ramon Calderer, Ricardo Silveira Cabral, Robert Stojnic, Roberta Raileanu, Rohan Maheswari, Rohit Girdhar, Rohit Patel, Romain Sauvestre, Ronnie Polidoro, Roshan Sumbaly, Ross Taylor, Ruan Silva, Rui Hou, Rui Wang, Saghar Hosseini, Sahana Chennabasappa, Sanjay Singh, Sean Bell, Seohyun Sonia Kim, Sergey Edunov, Shaoliang Nie, Sharan Narang, Sharath Raparthy, Sheng Shen, Shengye Wan, Shruti Bhosale, Shun Zhang, Simon Vandenhende, Soumya Batra, Spencer Whitman, Sten Sootla, Stephane Collot, Suchin Gururangan, Sydney Borodinsky, Tamar Herman, Tara Fowler, Tarek Sheasha, Thomas Georgiou, Thomas Scialom, Tobias Speckbacher, Todor Mihaylov, Tong Xiao, Ujjwal Karn, Vedanuj Goswami, Vibhor Gupta, Vignesh Ramanathan, Viktor Kerkez, Vincent Gonguet, Virginie Do, Vish Vogeti, Vítor Albiero, Vladan Petrovic, Weiwei Chu, Wenhan Xiong, Wenyin Fu, Whitney Meers, Xavier Martinet, Xiaodong Wang, Xiaofang Wang, Xiaoqing Ellen Tan, Xide Xia, Xinfeng Xie, Xuchao Jia, Xuewei Wang, Yaelle Goldschlag, Yashesh Gaur, Yasmine Babaei, Yi Wen, Yiwen Song, Yuchen Zhang, Yue Li, Yuning Mao, Zacharie Delpierre Coudert, Zheng Yan, Zhengxing Chen, Zoe Papakipos, Aaditya Singh, Aayushi Srivastava, Abha Jain, Adam Kelsey, Adam Shajnfeld, Adithya Gangidi, Adolfo Victoria, Ahuva Goldstand, Ajay Menon, Ajay Sharma, Alex Boesenberg, Alexei Baevski, Allie Feinstein, Amanda Kallet, Amit Sangani, Amos Teo, Anam Yunus, Andrei Lupu, Andres Alvarado, Andrew Caples, Andrew Gu, Andrew Ho, Andrew Poulton, Andrew Ryan, Ankit Ramchandani, Annie Dong, Annie Franco, Anuj Goyal, Aparajita Saraf, Arkabandhu Chowdhury, Ashley Gabriel, Ashwin Bharambe, Assaf Eisenman, Azadeh Yazdan, Beau James, Ben Maurer, Benjamin Leonhardi, Bernie Huang, Beth Loyd, Beto De Paola, Bhargavi Paranjape, Bing Liu, Bo Wu, Boyu Ni, Braden Hancock, Bram Wasti, Brandon Spence, Brani Stojkovic, Brian Gamido, Britt Montalvo, Carl Parker, Carly Burton, Catalina Mejia, Ce Liu, Changhan Wang, Changkyu Kim, Chao Zhou, Chester Hu, Ching-Hsiang Chu, Chris Cai, Chris Tindal, Christoph Feichtenhofer, Cynthia Gao, Damon Civin, Dana Beaty, Daniel Kreymer, Daniel Li, David Adkins, David Xu, Davide Testuggine, Delia David, Devi Parikh, Diana Liskovich, Didem Foss, Dingkang Wang, Duc Le, Dustin Holland, Edward Dowling, Eissa Jamil, Elaine Montgomery, Eleonora Presani, Emily Hahn, Emily Wood, Eric-Tuan Le, Erik Brinkman, Esteban Arcaute, Evan Dunbar, Evan Smothers, Fei Sun, Felix Kreuk, Feng Tian, Filippos Kokkinos, Firat Ozgenel, Francesco Caggioni, Frank Kanayet, Frank Seide, Gabriela Medina Florez, Gabriella Schwarz, Gada Badeer, Georgia Swee, Gil Halpern, Grant Herman, Grigory Sizov, Guangyi, Zhang, Guna Lakshminarayanan, Hakan Inan, Hamid Shojanazeri, Han Zou, Hannah Wang, Hanwen Zha, Haroun Habeeb, Harrison Rudolph, Helen Suk, Henry Aspegren, Hunter Goldman, Hongyuan Zhan, Ibrahim Damlaj, Igor Molybog, Igor Tufanov, Ilias Leontiadis, Irina-Elena Veliche, Itai Gat, Jake Weissman, James Geboski, James Kohli, Janice Lam, Japhet Asher, Jean-Baptiste Gaya, Jeff Marcus, Jeff Tang, Jennifer Chan, Jenny Zhen, Jeremy Reizenstein, Jeremy Teboul, Jessica Zhong, Jian Jin, Jingyi Yang, Joe Cummings, Jon Carvill, Jon Shepard, Jonathan McPhie, Jonathan Torres, Josh Ginsburg, Junjie Wang, Kai Wu, Kam Hou U, Karan Saxena, Kartikay Khandelwal, Katayoun Zand, Kathy Matosich, Kaushik Veeraraghavan, Kelly Michelena, Keqian Li, Kiran Jagadeesh, Kun Huang, Kunal Chawla, Kyle Huang, Lailin Chen, Lakshya Garg, Lavender A, Leandro Silva, Lee Bell, Lei Zhang, Liangpeng Guo, Licheng Yu, Liron Moshkovich, Luca Wehrstedt, Madian Khabsa, Manav Avalani, Manish Bhatt, Martynas Mankus, Matan Hasson, Matthew Lennie, Matthias Reso, Maxim Groshev, Maxim Naumov, Maya Lathi, Meghan Keneally, Miao Liu, Michael L. Seltzer, Michal Valko, Michelle Restrepo, Mihir Patel, Mik Vyatskov, Mikayel Samvelyan, Mike Clark, Mike Macey, Mike Wang, Miquel Jubert Hermoso, Mo Metanat, Mohammad Rastegari, Munish Bansal, Nandhini Santhanam, Natascha Parks, Natasha White, Navyata Bawa, Nayan Singhal, Nick Egebo, Nicolas Usunier, Nikhil Mehta, Nikolay Pavlovich Laptev, Ning Dong, Norman Cheng, Oleg Chernoguz, Olivia Hart, Omkar Salpekar, Ozlem Kalinli, Parkin Kent, Parth Parekh, Paul Saab, Pavan Balaji, Pedro Rittner, Philip Bontrager, Pierre Roux, Piotr Dollar, Polina Zvyagina, Prashant Ratanchandani, Pritish Yuvraj, Qian Liang, Rachad Alao, Rachel Rodriguez, Rafi Ayub, Raghotham Murthy, Raghu Nayani, Rahul Mitra, Rangaprabhu Parthasarathy, Raymond Li, Rebekkah Hogan, Robin Battey, Rocky Wang, Russ Howes, Ruty Rinott, Sachin Mehta, Sachin Siby, Sai Jayesh Bondu, Samyak Datta, Sara Chugh, Sara Hunt, Sargun Dhillon, Sasha Sidorov, Satadru Pan, Saurabh Mahajan, Saurabh Verma, Seiji Yamamoto, Sharadh Ramaswamy, Shaun Lindsay, Shaun Lindsay, Sheng Feng, Shenghao Lin, Shengxin Cindy Zha, Shishir Patil, Shiva Shankar, Shuqiang Zhang, Shuqiang Zhang, Sinong Wang, Sneha Agarwal, Soji Sajuyigbe, Soumith Chintala, Stephanie Max, Stephen Chen, Steve Kehoe, Steve

Satterfield, Sudarshan Govindaprasad, Sumit Gupta, Summer Deng, Sungmin Cho, Sunny Virk, Suraj Subramanian, Sy Choudhury, Sydney Goldman, Tal Remez, Tamar Glaser, Tamara Best, Thilo Koehler, Thomas Robinson, Tianhe Li, Tianjun Zhang, Tim Matthews, Timothy Chou, Tzook Shaked, Varun Vontimitta, Victoria Ajayi, Victoria Montanez, Vijai Mohan, Vinay Satish Kumar, Vishal Mangla, Vlad Ionescu, Vlad Poenaru, Vlad Tiberiu Mihailescu, Vladimir Ivanov, Wei Li, Wenchen Wang, Wenwen Jiang, Wes Bouaziz, Will Constable, Xiaocheng Tang, Xiaojian Wu, Xiaolan Wang, Xilun Wu, Xinbo Gao, Yaniv Kleinman, Yanjun Chen, Ye Hu, Ye Jia, Ye Qi, Yenda Li, Yilin Zhang, Ying Zhang, Yossi Adi, Youngjin Nam, Yu, Wang, Yu Zhao, Yuchen Hao, Yundi Qian, Yunlu Li, Yuzi He, Zach Rait, Zachary DeVito, Zef Rosnbrick, Zhaoduo Wen, Zhenyu Yang, Zhiwei Zhao, and Zhiyu Ma. 2024. The llama 3 herd of models. *Preprint*, arXiv:2407.21783.

Qingyan Guo, Rui Wang, Junliang Guo, Bei Li, Kaitao Song, Xu Tan, Guoqing Liu, Jiang Bian, and Yujiu Yang. 2024. Connecting large language models with evolutionary algorithms yields powerful prompt optimizers. *Preprint*, arXiv:2309.08532.

John H. Holland. 1992. *Adaptation in Natural and Artificial Systems: An Introductory Analysis with Applications to Biology, Control and Artificial Intelligence*. MIT Press, Cambridge, MA, USA.

Jiaxin Huang, Shixiang Gu, Le Hou, Yuexin Wu, Xuezhi Wang, Hongkun Yu, and Jiawei Han. 2023. Large language models can self-improve. In *Proceedings of the 2023 Conference on Empirical Methods in Natural Language Processing*, pages 1051–1068, Singapore. Association for Computational Linguistics.

Albert Q. Jiang, Alexandre Sablayrolles, Arthur Mensch, Chris Bamford, Devendra Singh Chaplot, Diego de las Casas, Florian Bressand, Gianna Lengyel, Guillaume Lample, Lucile Saulnier, Lélio Renard Lavaud, Marie-Anne Lachaux, Pierre Stock, Teven Le Scao, Thibaut Lavril, Thomas Wang, Timothée Lacroix, and William El Sayed. 2023. Mistral 7b. *Preprint*, arXiv:2310.06825.

Ellen Jiang, Kristen Olson, Edwin Toh, Alejandra Molina, Aaron Michael Donsbach, Michael Terry, and Carrie Jun Cai. 2022. Prompt-based prototyping with large language models.

Brian Lester, Rami Al-Rfou, and Noah Constant. 2021. The power of scale for parameter-efficient prompt tuning. *Preprint*, arXiv:2104.08691.

Xiang Lisa Li and Percy Liang. 2021. Prefix-tuning: Optimizing continuous prompts for generation. *Preprint*, arXiv:2101.00190.

Chin-Yew Lin. 2004. ROUGE: A package for automatic evaluation of summaries. In *Text Summarization Branches Out*, pages 74–81, Barcelona, Spain. Association for Computational Linguistics.

Xiao Liu, Yanan Zheng, Zhengxiao Du, Ming Ding, Yujie Qian, Zhilin Yang, and Jie Tang. 2023. Gpt understands, too. *Preprint*, arXiv:2103.10385.

Aman Madaan, Niket Tandon, Prakhar Gupta, Skyler Hallinan, Luyu Gao, Sarah Wiegreffe, Uri Alon, Nouha Dziri, Shrimai Prabhumoye, Yiming Yang, Shashank Gupta, Bodhisattwa Prasad Majumder, Katherine Hermann, Sean Welleck, Amir Yazdanbakhsh, and Peter Clark. 2023. Self-refine: Iterative refinement with self-feedback. *Preprint*, arXiv:2303.17651.

OpenAI, :, Aaron Hurst, Adam Lerer, Adam P. Goucher, Adam Perelman, Aditya Ramesh, Aidan Clark, AJ Ostrow, Akila Welihinda, Alan Hayes, Alec Radford, Aleksander Mądry, Alex Baker-Whitcomb, Alex Beutel, Alex Borzunov, Alex Carney, Alex Chow, Alex Kirillov, Alex Nichol, Alex Paino, Alex Renzin, Alex Tachard Passos, Alexander Kirillov, Alexi Christakis, Alexis Conneau, Ali Kamali, Allan Jabri, Allison Moyer, Allison Tam, Amadou Crookes, Amin Tootoochian, Amin Tootoonchian, Ananya Kumar, Andrea Vallone, Andrej Karpathy, Andrew Braunstein, Andrew Cann, Andrew Codispoti, Andrew Galu, Andrew Kondrich, Andrew Tulloch, Andrey Mishchenko, Angela Baek, Angela Jiang, Antoine Pelisse, Antonia Woodford, Anuj Gosalia, Arka Dhar, Ashley Pantuliano, Avi Nayak, Avital Oliver, Barret Zoph, Behrooz Ghorbani, Ben Leimberger, Ben Rossen, Ben Sokolowsky, Ben Wang, Benjamin Zweig, Beth Hoover, Blake Samic, Bob McGrew, Bobby Spero, Bogo Giertler, Bowen Cheng, Brad Lightcap, Brandon Walkin, Brendan Quinn, Brian Guarraci, Brian Hsu, Bright Kellogg, Brydon Eastman, Camillo Lugaresi, Carroll Wainwright, Cary Bassin, Cary Hudson, Casey Chu, Chad Nelson, Chak Li, Chan Jun Shern, Channing Conger, Charlotte Barette, Chelsea Voss, Chen Ding, Cheng Lu, Chong Zhang, Chris Beaumont, Chris Hallacy, Chris Koch, Christian Gibson, Christina Kim, Christine Choi, Christine McLeavey, Christopher Hesse, Claudia Fischer, Clemens Winter, Coley Czarnecki, Colin Jarvis, Colin Wei, Constantin Koumouzelis, Dane Sherburn, Daniel Kappler, Daniel Levin, Daniel Levy, David Carr, David Farhi, David Mely, David Robinson, David Sasaki, Denny Jin, Dev Valladares, Dimitris Tsipras, Doug Li, Duc Phong Nguyen, Duncan Findlay, Edede Oiwoh, Edmund Wong, Ehsan Asdar, Elizabeth Proehl, Elizabeth Yang, Eric Antonow, Eric Kramer, Eric Peterson, Eric Sigler, Eric Wallace, Eugene Brevdo, Evan Mays, Farzad Khorasani, Felipe Petroski Such, Filippo Raso, Francis Zhang, Fred von Lohmann, Freddie Sulit, Gabriel Goh, Gene Oden, Geoff Salmon, Giulio Starace, Greg Brockman, Hadi Salman, Haiming Bao, Haitang Hu, Hannah Wong, Haoyu Wang, Heather Schmidt, Heather Whitney, Heewoo Jun, Hendrik Kirchner, Henrique Ponde de Oliveira Pinto, Hongyu Ren, Huiwen Chang, Hyung Won Chung, Ian Kivlichan, Ian O'Connell, Ian O'Connell, Ian Osband, Ian Silber, Ian Sohl, Ibrahim Okuyucu, Ikai Lan, Ilya Kostrikov, Ilya Sutskever, Ingmar Kanitscheider, Ishaan Gulrajani, Jacob Coxon, Jacob Menick, Jakub

Pachocki, James Aung, James Betker, James Crooks, James Lennon, Jamie Kiros, Jan Leike, Jane Park, Jason Kwon, Jason Phang, Jason Teplitz, Jason Wei, Jason Wolfe, Jay Chen, Jeff Harris, Jenia Varavva, Jessica Gan Lee, Jessica Shieh, Ji Lin, Jiahui Yu, Jiayi Weng, Jie Tang, Jieqi Yu, Joanne Jang, Joaquin Quinonero Candela, Joe Beutler, Joe Landers, Joel Parish, Johannes Heidecke, John Schulman, Jonathan Lachman, Jonathan McKay, Jonathan Uesato, Jonathan Ward, Jong Wook Kim, Joost Huizinga, Jordan Sitkin, Jos Kraaijeveld, Josh Gross, Josh Kaplan, Josh Snyder, Joshua Achiam, Joy Jiao, Joyce Lee, Juntang Zhuang, Justyn Harriman, Kai Fricke, Kai Hayashi, Karan Singhal, Katy Shi, Kavin Karthik, Kayla Wood, Kendra Rimbach, Kenny Hsu, Kenny Nguyen, Keren Gu-Lemberg, Kevin Button, Kevin Liu, Kiel Howe, Krithika Muthukumar, Kyle Luther, Lama Ahmad, Larry Kai, Lauren Itow, Lauren Workman, Leher Pathak, Leo Chen, Li Jing, Lia Guy, Liam Fedus, Liang Zhou, Lien Mamitsuka, Lilian Weng, Lindsay McCallum, Lindsey Held, Long Ouyang, Louis Feuvrier, Lu Zhang, Lukas Kondraciuk, Lukasz Kaiser, Luke Hewitt, Luke Metz, Lyric Doshi, Mada Aflak, Maddie Simens, Madelaine Boyd, Madeleine Thompson, Marat Dukhan, Mark Chen, Mark Gray, Mark Hudnall, Marvin Zhang, Marwan Aljubeh, Mateusz Litwin, Matthew Zeng, Max Johnson, Maya Shetty, Mayank Gupta, Meghan Shah, Mehmet Yatbaz, Meng Jia Yang, Mengchao Zhong, Mia Glaese, Mianna Chen, Michael Janner, Michael Lampe, Michael Petrov, Michael Wu, Michele Wang, Michelle Fradin, Michelle Pokrass, Miguel Castro, Miguel Oom Temudo de Castro, Mikhail Pavlov, Miles Brundage, Miles Wang, Minal Khan, Mira Murati, Mo Bavarian, Molly Lin, Murat Yesildal, Nacho Soto, Natalia Gimelshein, Natalie Cone, Natalie Staudacher, Natalie Summers, Natan LaFontaine, Neil Chowdhury, Nick Ryder, Nick Stathas, Nick Turley, Nik Tezak, Niko Felix, Nithanth Kudige, Nitish Keskar, Noah Deutsch, Noel Bundick, Nora Puckett, Ofir Nachum, Ola Okelola, Oleg Boiko, Oleg Murk, Oliver Jaffe, Olivia Watkins, Olivier Godement, Owen Campbell-Moore, Patrick Chao, Paul McMillan, Pavel Belov, Peng Su, Peter Bak, Peter Bakkum, Peter Deng, Peter Dolan, Peter Hoeschele, Peter Welinder, Phil Tillet, Philip Pronin, Philippe Tillet, Prafulla Dhariwal, Qiming Yuan, Rachel Dias, Rachel Lim, Rahul Arora, Rajan Troll, Randall Lin, Rapha Gontijo Lopes, Raul Puri, Reah Miyara, Reimar Leike, Renaud Gaubert, Reza Zamani, Ricky Wang, Rob Donnelly, Rob Honsby, Rocky Smith, Rohan Sahai, Rohit Ramchandani, Romain Huet, Rory Carmichael, Rowan Zellers, Roy Chen, Ruby Chen, Ruslan Nigmatullin, Ryan Cheu, Saachi Jain, Sam Altman, Sam Schoenholz, Sam Toizer, Samuel Miserendino, Sandhini Agarwal, Sara Culver, Scott Ethersmith, Scott Gray, Sean Grove, Sean Metzger, Shamez Hermani, Shantanu Jain, Shengjia Zhao, Sherwin Wu, Shino Jomoto, Shirong Wu, Shuaiqi, Xia, Sonia Phene, Spencer Papay, Srinivas Narayanan, Steve Coffey, Steve Lee, Stewart Hall, Suchir Balaji, Tal Broda, Tal Stramer, Tao Xu, Tarun Gogineni, Taya Christianson, Ted Sanders, Tejal Patwardhan, Thomas Cunninghman, Thomas Degry, Thomas Dimson, Thomas Raoux, Thomas Shadwell, Tianhao Zheng, Todd Underwood, Todor Markov, Toki Sherbakov, Tom Rubin, Tom Stasi, Tomer Kaftan, Tristan Heywood, Troy Peterson, Tyce Walters, Tyna Eloundou, Valerie Qi, Veit Moeller, Vinnie Monaco, Vishal Kuo, Vlad Fomenko, Wayne Chang, Weiyi Zheng, Wenda Zhou, Wesam Manassra, Will Sheu, Wojciech Zaremba, Yash Patil, Yilei Qian, Yongjik Kim, Youlong Cheng, Yu Zhang, Yuchen He, Yuchen Zhang, Yujia Jin, Yunxing Dai, and Yury Malkov. 2024a. Gpt-4o system card. *Preprint*, arXiv:2410.21276.

OpenAI, Josh Achiam, Steven Adler, Sandhini Agarwal, Lama Ahmad, Ilge Akkaya, Florencia Leoni Aleman, Diogo Almeida, Janko Altenschmidt, Sam Altman, Shyamal Anadkat, Red Avila, Igor Babuschkin, Suchir Balaji, Valerie Balcom, Paul Baltescu, Haiming Bao, Mohammad Bavarian, Jeff Belgum, Irwan Bello, Jake Berdine, Gabriel Bernadett-Shapiro, Christopher Berner, Lenny Bogdonoff, Oleg Boiko, Madelaine Boyd, Anna-Luisa Brakman, Greg Brockman, Tim Brooks, Miles Brundage, Kevin Button, Trevor Cai, Rosie Campbell, Andrew Cann, Brittany Carey, Chelsea Carlson, Rory Carmichael, Brooke Chan, Che Chang, Fotis Chantzis, Derek Chen, Sully Chen, Ruby Chen, Jason Chen, Mark Chen, Ben Chess, Chester Cho, Casey Chu, Hyung Won Chung, Dave Cummings, Jeremiah Currier, Yunxing Dai, Cory Decareaux, Thomas Degry, Noah Deutsch, Damien Deville, Arka Dhar, David Dohan, Steve Dowling, Sheila Dunning, Adrien Ecoffet, Atty Eleti, Tyna Eloundou, David Farhi, Liam Fedus, Niko Felix, Simón Posada Fishman, Juston Forte, Isabella Fulford, Leo Gao, Elie Georges, Christian Gibson, Vik Goel, Tarun Gogineni, Gabriel Goh, Rapha Gontijo-Lopes, Jonathan Gordon, Morgan Grafstein, Scott Gray, Ryan Greene, Joshua Gross, Shixiang Shane Gu, Yufei Guo, Chris Hallacy, Jesse Han, Jeff Harris, Yuchen He, Mike Heaton, Johannes Heidecke, Chris Hesse, Alan Hickey, Wade Hickey, Peter Hoeschele, Brandon Houghton, Kenny Hsu, Shengli Hu, Xin Hu, Joost Huizinga, Shantanu Jain, Shawn Jain, Joanne Jang, Angela Jiang, Roger Jiang, Haozhun Jin, Denny Jin, Shino Jomoto, Billie Jonn, Heewoo Jun, Tomer Kaftan, Łukasz Kaiser, Ali Kamali, Ingmar Kanitscheider, Nitish Shirish Keskar, Tabarak Khan, Logan Kilpatrick, Jong Wook Kim, Christina Kim, Yongjik Kim, Jan Hendrik Kirchner, Jamie Kiros, Matt Knight, Daniel Kokotajlo, Łukasz Kondraciuk, Andrew Kondrich, Aris Konstantinidis, Kyle Kosic, Gretchen Krueger, Vishal Kuo, Michael Lampe, Ikai Lan, Teddy Lee, Jan Leike, Jade Leung, Daniel Levy, Chak Ming Li, Rachel Lim, Molly Lin, Stephanie Lin, Mateusz Litwin, Theresa Lopez, Ryan Lowe, Patricia Lue, Anna Makanju, Kim Malfacini, Sam Manning, Todor Markov, Yaniv Markovski, Bianca Martin, Katie Mayer, Andrew Mayne, Bob McGrew, Scott Mayer McKinney, Christine McLeavey, Paul McMillan, Jake McNeil, David Medina, Aalok Mehta, Jacob Menick, Luke Metz, Andrey Mishchenko, Pamela Mishkin, Vinnie Monaco, Evan Morikawa, Daniel Mossing, Tong Mu, Mira Murati, Oleg Murk, David

Mély, Ashvin Nair, Reiichiro Nakano, Rajeev Nayak, Arvind Neelakantan, Richard Ngo, Hyeonwoo Noh, Long Ouyang, Cullen O'Keefe, Jakub Pachocki, Alex Paino, Joe Palermo, Ashley Pantuliano, Giambattista Parascandolo, Joel Parish, Emy Parparita, Alex Passos, Mikhail Pavlov, Andrew Peng, Adam Perelman, Filipe de Avila Belbute Peres, Michael Petrov, Henrique Ponde de Oliveira Pinto, Michael, Pokorny, Michelle Pokrass, Vitchyr H. Pong, Tolly Powell, Alethea Power, Boris Power, Elizabeth Proehl, Raul Puri, Alec Radford, Jack Rae, Aditya Ramesh, Cameron Raymond, Francis Real, Kendra Rimbach, Carl Ross, Bob Rotsted, Henri Roussez, Nick Ryder, Mario Saltarelli, Ted Sanders, Shibani Santurkar, Girish Sastry, Heather Schmidt, David Schnurr, John Schulman, Daniel Selsam, Kyla Sheppard, Toki Sherbakov, Jessica Shieh, Sarah Shoker, Pranav Shyam, Szymon Sidor, Eric Sigler, Maddie Simens, Jordan Sitkin, Katarina Slama, Ian Sohl, Benjamin Sokolowsky, Yang Song, Natalie Staudacher, Felipe Petroski Such, Natalie Summers, Ilya Sutskever, Jie Tang, Nikolas Tezak, Madeleine B. Thompson, Phil Tillet, Amin Tootoonchian, Elizabeth Tseng, Preston Tuggle, Nick Turley, Jerry Tworek, Juan Felipe Cerón Uribe, Andrea Vallone, Arun Vijayvergiya, Chelsea Voss, Carroll Wainwright, Justin Jay Wang, Alvin Wang, Ben Wang, Jonathan Ward, Jason Wei, CJ Weinmann, Akila Welihinda, Peter Welinder, Jiayi Weng, Lilian Weng, Matt Wiethoff, Dave Willner, Clemens Winter, Samuel Wolrich, Hannah Wong, Lauren Workman, Sherwin Wu, Jeff Wu, Michael Wu, Kai Xiao, Tao Xu, Sarah Yoo, Kevin Yu, Qiming Yuan, Wojciech Zaremba, Rowan Zellers, Chong Zhang, Marvin Zhang, Shengjia Zhao, Tianhao Zheng, Juntang Zhuang, William Zhuk, and Barret Zoph. 2024b. Gpt-4 technical report. *Preprint*, arXiv:2303.08774.

Archiki Prasad, Peter Hase, Xiang Zhou, and Mohit Bansal. 2023. Grips: Gradient-free, edit-based instruction search for prompting large language models. *Preprint*, arXiv:2203.07281.

Reid Pryzant, Dan Iter, Jerry Li, Yin Tat Lee, Chenguang Zhu, and Michael Zeng. 2023. Automatic prompt optimization with "gradient descent" and beam search. *Preprint*, arXiv:2305.03495.

Guanghui Qin and Jason Eisner. 2021. Learning how to ask: Querying LMs with mixtures of soft prompts. In *Proceedings of the 2021 Conference of the North American Chapter of the Association for Computational Linguistics: Human Language Technologies*, pages 5203–5212, Online. Association for Computational Linguistics.

Yiwei Qin, Kaiqiang Song, Yebowen Hu, Wenlin Yao, Sangwoo Cho, Xiaoyang Wang, Xuansheng Wu, Fei Liu, Pengfei Liu, and Dong Yu. 2024. Infobench: Evaluating instruction following ability in large language models. *Preprint*, arXiv:2401.03601.

Rafael Rafailov, Archit Sharma, Eric Mitchell, Christopher D. Manning, Stefano Ermon, and Chelsea Finn. 2023. Direct preference optimization: Your language model is secretly a reward model. In *Advances in Neural Information Processing Systems 36: Annual Conference on Neural Information Processing Systems 2023, NeurIPS 2023, New Orleans, LA, USA, December 10 - 16, 2023*.

Nils Reimers and Iryna Gurevych. 2019. Sentence-bert: Sentence embeddings using siamese bert-networks. *Preprint*, arXiv:1908.10084.

Laria Reynolds and Kyle McDonell. 2021. Prompt programming for large language models: Beyond the few-shot paradigm. *Preprint*, arXiv:2102.07350.

Pranab Sahoo, Ayush Kumar Singh, Sriparna Saha, Vinija Jain, Samrat Mondal, and Aman Chadha. 2024. A systematic survey of prompt engineering in large language models: Techniques and applications. *Preprint*, arXiv:2402.07927.

William Saunders, Catherine Yeh, Jeff Wu, Steven Bills, Long Ouyang, Jonathan Ward, and Jan Leike. 2022. Self-critiquing models for assisting human evaluators. *Preprint*, arXiv:2206.05802.

Sander Schulhoff, Michael Ilie, Nishant Balepur, Konstantine Kahadze, Amanda Liu, Chenglei Si, Yinheng Li, Aayush Gupta, HyoJung Han, Sevien Schulhoff, Pranav Sandeep Dulepet, Saurav Vidyadhara, Dayeon Ki, Sweta Agrawal, Chau Pham, Gerson Kroiz, Feileen Li, Hudson Tao, Ashay Srivastava, Hevander Da Costa, Saloni Gupta, Megan L. Rogers, Inna Goncearenco, Giuseppe Sarli, Igor Galynker, Denis Peskoff, Marine Carpuat, Jules White, Shyamal Anadkat, Alexander Hoyle, and Philip Resnik. 2024. The prompt report: A systematic survey of prompting techniques. *Preprint*, arXiv:2406.06608.

Taylor Shin, Yasaman Razeghi, Robert L. Logan IV au2, Eric Wallace, and Sameer Singh. 2020. Autoprompt: Eliciting knowledge from language models with automatically generated prompts. *Preprint*, arXiv:2010.15980.

Rainer Storn and Kenneth Price. 1997. Differential evolution - a simple and efficient heuristic for global optimization over continuous spaces. *Journal of Global Optimization*, 11:341–359.

Zekun Moore Wang, Zhongyuan Peng, Haoran Que, Jiaheng Liu, Wangchunshu Zhou, Yuhan Wu, Hongcheng Guo, Ruitong Gan, Zehao Ni, Jian Yang, Man Zhang, Zhaoxiang Zhang, Wanli Ouyang, Ke Xu, Stephen W. Huang, Jie Fu, and Junran Peng. 2024. Rolellm: Benchmarking, eliciting, and enhancing role-playing abilities of large language models. *Preprint*, arXiv:2310.00746.

Jason Wei, Xuezhi Wang, Dale Schuurmans, Maarten Bosma, Brian Ichter, Fei Xia, Ed Chi, Quoc Le, and Denny Zhou. 2023. Chain-of-thought prompting elicits reasoning in large language models. *Preprint*, arXiv:2201.11903.

Chengrun Yang, Xuezhi Wang, Yifeng Lu, Hanxiao Liu, Quoc V. Le, Denny Zhou, and Xinyun Chen. 2024.

Large language models as optimizers. *Preprint*, arXiv:2309.03409.

J.D. Zamfirescu-Pereira, Richmond Y. Wong, Bjoern Hartmann, and Qian Yang. 2023. Why johnny can't prompt: How non-ai experts try (and fail) to design llm prompts. In *Proceedings of the 2023 CHI Conference on Human Factors in Computing Systems*, CHI '23, New York, NY, USA. Association for Computing Machinery.

Lianmin Zheng, Wei-Lin Chiang, Ying Sheng, Siyuan Zhuang, Zhanghao Wu, Yonghao Zhuang, Zi Lin, Zhuohan Li, Dacheng Li, Eric Xing, Hao Zhang, Joseph E Gonzalez, and Ion Stoica. 2023. Judging llm-as-a-judge with mt-bench and chatbot arena. In *Advances in Neural Information Processing Systems*, volume 36, pages 46595–46623. Curran Associates, Inc.

Ming Zhong, Da Yin, Tao Yu, Ahmad Zaidi, Mutethia Mutuma, Rahul Jha, Ahmed Hassan Awadallah, Asli Celikyilmaz, Yang Liu, Xipeng Qiu, and Dragomir Radev. 2021. Qmsum: A new benchmark for query-based multi-domain meeting summarization. *Preprint*, arXiv:2104.05938.

Yongchao Zhou, Andrei Ioan Muresanu, Ziwen Han, Keiran Paster, Silviu Pitis, Harris Chan, and Jimmy Ba. 2023. Large language models are human-level prompt engineers. In *The Eleventh International Conference on Learning Representations*.

A Appendix

A.1 Algorithm

The optimization algorithm is provided below:

Algorithm 1 Prompt Refinement with Iterative Descriptive Evaluation (PROPEL)

Input: Initial prompt p_0, dataset $D_{train} = \{(x_1, y_1), \ldots, (x_n, y_n)\}$, and expert priors.
Output: An optimized prompt $\hat{p}$
Require: K: number of iterations, s_t: score threshold for early stopping, h_s: size of history maintained in State
Initialize State as [].
for $k = 1$ to K **do**
  Generate responses $\{\hat{y}_i = M(y_i | p_k, x_i)\}_{x_i \in D_{train}}$ using Responder LLM.
  Evaluate responses $\hat{y}_i$ with Judge LLM to obtain sample-specific feedbacks and scores, aggregated into a single score Score_k and summarized feedback Feedback_k.
  if $\text{Score}_k \geq s_t$ **then**
    Break the loop.
  end if
  Update State with $\langle p_k, \text{Feedback}_k, \text{Score}_k \rangle$.
  if len(State) $> h_s$ **then**
    Pop the leftmost element from State.
  end if
  Refine p_k to obtain p_{k+1} using Optimizer LLM, incorporating State and expert priors.
end for
Return: $\hat{p} = p_k$

A.2 Dataset used for Experiments

1. **QMSum - Query based Summarization**: The QMSum dataset (Zhong et al., 2021) provides query-based multi-domain meeting summaries, consisting of transcripts from academic, industrial, and product review meetings. We chose this dataset owing to its similarities with our in-house dataset and for its scale.

2. **MT Bench**: MT-Bench (Zheng et al., 2023) is a curated benchmark featuring high-quality, multi-turn questions designed to evaluate conversation flow and instruction-following capabilities in multi-turn dialogues. GPT-4 (OpenAI et al., 2024b) evaluates MT Bench outputs, and average scores across questions and

turns are reported for all experiments. We chose this dataset due to it being widely recognized and its widespread use in evaluating models for tasks that require sustained, coherent interactions over multiple exchanges.

3. We leverage an in-house dataset[3] of conversational interactions happening in a contact center between agents and customers and perform the following tasks:

    (a) **Query based Summarization (QBS)**: Involves generating an abstractive response to the given query based on the conversation as input context.

    (b) **Query based Entity Extraction (QBE)**: Involves identifying and extracting entities from the conversation that are pertinent to the given query.

    The dataset was carefully curated to ensure high-quality annotations and relevance to contact center tasks. Below, we outline the process followed to create this dataset:

    (a) **Conversation Sampling and Transcription:** A total of 120 English dyadic conversations between agents and customers were sampled from a contact center. These conversations were transcribed using a third-party Automatic Speech Recognition (ASR) engine, with a Word Error Rate (WER) of approximately 10% as reported by Ali and Renals 2018. The ASR transcripts served as the input context in the prompt optimization algorithm.

    (b) **Data Partitioning:** The data is split into non-overlapping datasets.

        i. **Training Set:** A randomly selected subset of 10 conversations.

        ii. **Evaluation Set:** A randomly selected subset of 100 conversations.

        iii. **Prior Identification Set:** A randomly selected subset of 10 conversations.

    (c) **Task and Prompt Sampling:** We sampled 15 prompts from a proprietary contact-center dataset [4], evenly distributed across the following two tasks: Query-Based Summarization and Query-Based Entity Extraction. The contact-center dataset from which prompts were sampled was designed to evaluate the value of **Query Based Summarization** use case for one of our clients.

    (d) **Annotation Process:**

        i. **Annotator Selection:** Seven annotators with experience in analyzing contact center data were employed.

        ii. **Guidelines for Annotation:** Annotators followed a comprehensive guideline emphasizing logical reasoning to identify relevant evidence from conversations, synthesize information and provide task-specific responses to each of the 15 prompts. The annotations were designed to ensure grounding in conversation details and emulate the reasoning process of a domain expert.

    (e) **Quality Assurance:**

        i. **Entity Extraction Task:** Responses for this structured task were validated through a majority voting mechanism requiring agreement among at least four annotators. Inter-Annotator agreement was calculated using Fleiss' Kappa (Fleiss et al., 1971), and was measured at 0.64, indicating substantial agreement.

        ii. **Query-Based Summarization Task:** Responses, being unstructured, were evaluated using Sentence-BERT (Reimers and Gurevych, 2019), fine-tuned for the Semantic Textual Similarity (STS) (Cer et al., 2017) task. Samples with an average pairwise semantic similarity score < 0.8 were flagged and re-annotated. For samples meeting the ≥ 0.8 similarity threshold, one response was randomly selected to ensure consistency in evaluation.

This robust annotation and curation process ensures that the dataset reflects the nuances of contact center data and provides reliable input for evaluating prompt optimization in downstream tasks.

[3]We cannot release the dataset due to proprietary reasons.

[4]We cannot release the dataset due to proprietary reasons.

A.3 Dataset Statistics

Table 8 shows the number of runs and the # of data points per run in the evaluation and training datasets. Here, '# of Runs' denotes the number of unique instructions (prompts) for which separate prompt tuning is required. The number of evaluation data points per run is calculated as the total number of data points divided by the number of runs.

Dataset	# of Runs	# Samples per Run Evaluation	# Samples per Run Training	# Samples Prior Identification
Inhouse - QBS	5	100	10	10
Inhouse - QBE	5	100	10	10
QMSum	2	100	10	10
MT Bench	1	60	10	10

Table 8: Dataset Statistics

A.4 Models used as Responder LLM

1. **Selection Criteria:** The selection of Responder LLMs was guided by two factors:

   (a) Adoption in the industry and research community.

   (b) Model size, to emphasize the challenges faced by small and medium-sized models in effective prompt optimization and demonstrate the importance of *expert priors* for these models.

2. **Model Descriptions:**

   (a) **Small Models (1–3B):**

      i. **Llama-3.2-1B (Grattafiori et al., 2024):** A lightweight 1-billion-parameter model used to assess prompt optimization challenges for minimal-scale models.

      ii. **Llama-3.2-3B (Grattafiori et al., 2024):** A 3-billion-parameter model, widely used in research for its accessible size and performance.

      iii. **Flan-T5-3B:** A proprietary model fine-tuned from the open-source Flan-T5-3B model (Chung et al., 2022) on a dataset of contact center interactions curated in-house [5] for tasks like summarization, and entity extraction. It uses Supervised Fine-Tuning (Brown et al., 2020) and Direct Preference Optimization (Rafailov et al., 2023), making it an ideal candidate for task-specific evaluation.

   (b) **Medium-Sized Models (7–8B):**

      i. **Mistral-7B (Jiang et al., 2023):** A 7-billion-parameter model known for its widespread use in various NLP applications.

      ii. **Llama-3-8B (Grattafiori et al., 2024):** Balances size and performance, making it a representative mid-sized model for our experiments.

This diversity allows us to investigate the specific challenges smaller models face and the role of expert priors in addressing these challenges.

A.5 Baselines used for Experiments

1. **Self-Refine:** Madaan et al. 2023 introduced an approach that iteratively improves initial LLM outputs through self-feedback and refinement. The process involves the LLM generating an initial output, providing feedback on its own output, and refining it iteratively.

2. **GrIPS:** Prasad et al. 2023 is an iterative approach that refines prompts by performing edit operations such as Deletion, Swap, Addition and Paraphrasing on the phrases of the prompts.

3. **Prompt Wizard:** The framework (Agarwal et al., 2024) iteratively refines prompts by mutating instructions and incorporating negative examples to deepen understanding and ensure diversity. It further enhances both instructions and examples with the aid of a critic, synthesizing new instructions and examples enriched with detailed reasoning steps for optimal performance. PromptWizard has shown superior performance over other Evolutionary Prompt Optimization Algorithms such as PromptBreeder (Fernando et al., 2023) and EvoPrompt (Guo et al., 2024). Thus, PromptWizard is chosen as the candidate baseline belonging to the line of Prompt Optimization Algorithms.

4. **APO:** Pryzant et al. 2023 is an iterative approach that leverages minibatches of data to form natural language gradients that dissect the limitations of the current prompt and edit the same in the opposite semantic direction

[5]We cannot release the dataset due to proprietary reasons.

of the gradient. These gradient descent steps are guided by a beam search and bandit selection procedure in order to improve algorithmic efficiency. The beam search is an iterative optimization process involving an expansion step which leverages paraphrasing to explore the local monte carlo search space around the new prompt candidates and a selection step to choose the top most promising candidates for the next iteration.

5. **OPRO:** Yang et al. 2024 is an iterative approach that leverages LLMs for the optimization task described in natural language. In each optimization step, the LLM generates new solutions from the prompt that contains previously generated solutions with their values, then the new solutions are evaluated and added to the prompt for the next optimization step.

We carefully selected the baselines for comparison with our proposed approach (PROPEL) based on their algorithmic similarities and the traction they have received due to their widespread adoption and recognition within the research community.

A.6 Evaluation Metrics used for Experiments

1. **LLM Score:** Evaluates quality of the generated responses for tasks including Query Based Summarization (QBS) in the in-house and QMSum (Zhong et al., 2021) datasets, Query Based Entity Extraction (QBE) in the in-house dataset and conversation flow and instruction-following capabilities in MT Bench (Zheng et al., 2023) dataset. GPT-4o (OpenAI et al., 2024a) is employed to provide a score on a scale of 1-5 basis the following criteria:

   (a) **Alignment with Prompt:** Measures the degree of alignment of the generated response with respect to the prompt.

   (b) **Completeness:** Measures the degree to which the generated response is complete with respect to the reference response.

   (c) **Presence of irrelevant information:** Measures the degree of irrelevant information in the generated response with respect to the reference response.

   (d) **Adherence to the format:** Checks if the generated response adheres to the desired response format, if any, as defined in the prompt.

   Higher the score, better is the quality of the generated response. You may refer the prompt we used for the Evaluation at Section A.10. The difference in LLM scores reported in 1 are post standardization to percentages which is done using the formula:

$$\text{LLM Score} = \frac{\text{LLM Score}_x}{5} \times 100 \quad (1)$$

   Please note that the standardization of LLM scores is applied solely to calculate and report the score difference between the responses generated from the initial prompt and the final optimized prompt, and is not used during the optimization process.

2. **Rouge-1 F1 Score (Lin, 2004):** Measures the overlap of unigrams (single words) between the generated response and the reference response. Employed as one of the metrics for the Query Based Entity Extraction (QBE) task in the in-house dataset, it provides a straightforward measure of comparing entity value similarity based on word matching.

A.7 Implementation Details for Experiments

1. **Experimental Setup:** We conducted experiments using three datasets:

   (a) **In-house Dataset:** As described in Section A.2, we utilized a curated dataset of human annotations for contact-center interactions. A random sample of 10 data points was used for training, while evaluation was performed on 100 data points per prompt.

   (b) **QMSum Dataset:** A similar experimental setup was followed, with 10 data points for training and 100 data points for evaluation per prompt.

   (c) **MT Bench Dataset:** This dataset lacks input context. For models supporting system prompts, we tuned the system prompt, while for models like Flan-T5-3B that lack explicit system prompt support, we optimized a prefix prompt appended to the user prompt.

   Evaluation was conducted on the final optimized prompt, defined as either the last iteration's prompt or an intermediate one when early stopping occurred. Scores reported in Table 1 are averages across multiple prompts.

2. **Hyperparameters for PROPEL:**
   (a) **Judge and Optimizer LLM:** GPT-4
   (b) **PROPEL (Self):** Responder LLM served as Judge and Optimizer
   (c) **Number of Iterations:** Up to 10
   (d) **Temperature for Judge and Optimizer LLM**: 1.00
   (e) **Temperature for Responder LLM**: 0.01
   (f) **Score Threshold for Early Stopping:** 4.5
   (g) **State History Size:** 10
   (h) **Training Dataset Size:** 10 samples

3. **Key Implementation Details for PROPEL:**
   - **Meta-Prompts**: Carefully crafted prompts guide each LLM role to ensure consistency and focus.
   - **Stopping Criteria**: The process runs for a set number of maximum iterations or till the score exceeds a set score threshold.
   - **History Size**: We define a fixed size of history to be maintained in the **State** which is used by the Optimizer LLM for prompt refinement.
   - **Task-Specific Adaptation**: Prompts are fine-tuned based on the task and model specific nuances captured via **Expert Priors**.

4. **Baseline Results and Hyperparameters:** For baseline comparisons, we've adapted the codebases provided by the respective authors to generate results. The hyperparameter settings for the baselines are adopted directly from the corresponding papers or their publicly available codebases, where applicable, and are as follows:
   (a) **OPRO:**
      i. **Optimizer LLM: GPT-4**
      ii. **Objective Function Evaluator:** GPT-4
      iii. **Number of Iterations:** 10
      iv. **Temperature for Evaluator and Optimizer LLM:** 1.00
      v. **Training Dataset Size:** 10 samples
      vi. **Number of prompts generated per iteration:** 1.00
   (b) **APO:**
      i. **Optimizer LLM:** GPT-4
      ii. **Text Loss Function Calculator and Gradient Generator:** GPT-4
      iii. **Number of Iterations:** 10
      iv. **Temperature for Gradient Generator and Optimizer LLM:** 1.00
      v. **Training Dataset Size:** 10 samples
      vi. **Number of prompts generated per iteration:** 1.00
   (c) **Prompt-Wizard:**
      i. **Evaluator, Mutator and Optimizer LLM:** GPT-4
      ii. **Number of Iterations:** 10
      iii. **Temperature for Evaluator, Mutator and Optimizer LLM:** 1.00
      iv. **Training Dataset Size:** 10 samples
      v. **Number of mutations per iteration:** 1.00
   (d) **GrIPS:**
      i. **Evaluator LLM:** GPT-4
      ii. **Number of Iterations:** 10
      iii. **Temperature for Evaluator LLM:** 1.00
      iv. **Training Dataset Size:** 10 samples
      v. **Number of Edits per iteration:** 3.00
   (e) **Self-Refine:**
      i. **Evaluator and Optimizer LLM:** Same as Responder LLM
      ii. **Number of Iterations:** 10
      iii. **Temperature for Evaluator and Optimizer LLM:** 1.00
      iv. **Training Dataset Size:** 10 samples

5. **Model Inference:**
   (a) **APIs and Deployment:**
      i. **Llama-3.2-1B/3B, Llama-3-8B, and Mistral-7B:** Amazon Bedrock APIs
      ii. **GPT-4:** OpenAI API
      iii. **Flan-T5-3B:** Internally deployed on an AWS EC2 instance with an NVIDIA A10G GPU (24 GB GPU memory).
   (b) **Inference Strategy:** For all models except Flan-T5-3B, inference was con-

ducted in one pass. For Flan-T5-3B, hierarchical processing was employed for input contexts exceeding 1200 tokens. Input contexts were segmented into 1200-token chunks, processed independently and in parallel, with segment-level responses summarized to produce the final output.

6. **Infrastructure:** Experiments were conducted on an AWS p4de.24xlarge instance equipped with eight GPUs, each with 80 GB of memory.

7. **Expert Priors:** We incorporated expert priors into the prompt optimization process to guide the Optimizer LLM. The steps involved are as follows:

   (a) **Mechanism for deriving prompt principles as priors:** Prompt principles compile best practices for crafting high-quality prompts for LLMs, adapted from works such as (Bsharat et al., 2024) and (Chen et al., 2024), as well as from model documentation specifying LLM prompting best practices. You may refer to Tables 6 and 7 for the compiled principles.

   (b) **Dataset for model evaluation across prompt principles:** We utilized the prior identification dataset containing 10 data points.

   (c) **Tasks for evaluation:** Summarization, Entity Extraction and Multi-turn Chat.

   (d) **Transformation of initial prompts for each principle:** We provide the initial prompt along with a principle to GPT-4 (Optimizer LLM), requesting it to transform the prompt based on the principle.

   (e) **Evaluation of transformed prompts:** The transformed prompts are used to prompt the Responder LLM to generate responses for the 10 data points per task. We then evaluate these responses by feeding the input context, initial prompt, and responses into the Judge LLM to obtain scores (1–5) for each data point.

   (f) **Aggregation of evaluation scores:** Scores are standardized to percentages, and the standardized scores for the 10 data points are averaged to obtain the aggregated score for each prompt principle and task.

   (g) **Definition of easy and hard principles:** Principles with aggregated scores above 70% are considered easy, while those with scores below 50% are considered hard.

   (h) **Handling Cases Where All or No Principles Score Above 70%:** If no principle achieves a score above 70%, or all do, we calculate the z-score for each principle's aggregated score, where $z = \frac{x-\mu}{\sigma}$, with x as the principle's score, μ as the mean of all aggregated scores, and σ as the standard deviation. Easy principles are those with $z > 1$, and hard principles have $z < -1$.

   (i) **Use of evaluation scores to convert principles into rules for the Optimizer LLM:** Easy and hard principles are encoded as 'Avoidance' and 'Emphasis' rules in the Optimizer LLM's meta-prompt. We instruct the Optimizer LLM to apply principles from the 'Emphasis' rules and avoid transformations based on the 'Avoidance' rules.

# Principle	Principle
1	**Direct Instruction**: A straightforward prompt that directly asks for information or a specific type of response.
2	**Chain-of-Thought (CoT)**: Use phrases like 'think step by step' to encourage the model to break down the reasoning or solution process into step-by-step explanations.
3	**Few-Shot Prompting**: Provide a few examples of response within the prompt to guide the model on how to respond to align with format specified in the initial prompt.
4	**Instruction-Based Prompting**: Specify detailed instructions on how to answer for clarity.
5	**Evidence-Backed Responses**: Require the model to support its answers with citations, references, or factual evidence to enhance credibility and accuracy.
6	**Meta-Prompting**: Ask the model to describe or discuss its thought process before answering, to encourage a higher level of analysis.
7	**Self-Consistency Prompting**: Request multiple outputs for the same prompt and chooses the most consistent or common answer, useful for increasing reliability.
8	**Role-Play Prompting**: Set the model in a specific role or persona (e.g., "Imagine you are a doctor") to align the response style with the desired expertise or perspective.
9	**Contextual Priming**: Provide background information or setting details before asking the question, helping the model generate contextually aware responses.
10	**Few-Shot Chain-of-Thought (Few-Shot CoT)**: Combine few-shot and CoT by providing multiple examples with step-by-step reasoning to improve performance on complex tasks.
11	**Task-Decomposition Prompting**: Break a large problem into smaller, manageable sub-tasks and asks the model to tackle each individually.
12	**Interactive Prompting**: Use a conversational, back-and-forth approach where each prompt builds on previous responses to refine the answer incrementally.
13	**One-Line Rewrite**: Rewrite the prompt in a single sentence.
14	**Concise Rewrite**: Rewrite the prompt in under three sentences.
15	**Question Format**: Rewrite the prompt as a question.
16	**Sub-Question Format**: Rewrite the prompt as multiple sub-questions.
17	**Simplified Language**: Rewrite the prompt using plain and easy-to-understand words.
18	**High-Level Rewrite**: Rewrite the prompt at a high level, removing specific task details.
19	**Detailed Rewrite**: Expand the prompt with detailed instructions, adding relevant clarifications if needed.
20	**Beginner-Friendly Rewrite**: Rewrite the prompt so that it is easy for a beginner to understand.
21	**Expert-Level Rewrite**: Rewrite the prompt for an expert audience, using technical terminology and assumptions based on prior knowledge.
22	**Penalty Enforcement**: Explicitly state that the LLM will be penalized if it fails to follow the instructions.
23	**Affirmative Directives**: Use positive instructions such as "Do this," while avoiding negative phrasing like "Don't do this."
24	**Explicit Task Definition**: Clearly specify the task using direct phrasing like "Your task is to...".
25	**Incentive Statement**: Add an incentive message such as "I'm going to tip $XXX for a better solution!"

Table 6: Overview of 50 prompt principles used to define expert priors.

# Principle	Principle
26	**Clarity-Seeking Prompts**: Use prompts like "Explain [topic] in simple terms," "Explain to me like I'm 11 years old," or "Explain to me as if I'm a beginner in [field]" to enhance understanding.
27	**Polite Wording**: Add phrases like "please," "if you don't mind," "thank you," or "I would like to" to make the prompt more courteous.
28	**Emphasis Through Repetition**: Repeat a specific word or phrase multiple times within a prompt to highlight its importance.
29	**Context Reinforcement**: Explicitly mention the task's context if it is missing in the prompt.
30	**XML Tagging**: Wrap the instruction inside XML tags.
31	**Least-to-Most Prompting**: Start with simpler questions and progressively move to more complex ones to help the model build up to a solution.
32	**Step-by-Step Prompting**: Request responses in a structured format, using numbered steps to improve clarity for multi-part answers.
33	**Refinement Prompting**: After an initial response, ask the model to revise or improve its answer for better quality.
34	**Scaffolded Prompting**: Guide the model through problem-solving by providing structured questions or "scaffolds" to address each part of a complex task.
35	**Reflective Prompting**: Prompt the model to review and reflect on its initial answer, considering alternative perspectives or implications.
36	**Counterfactual Prompting**: Encourage the model to explore "what if" scenarios or hypothetical situations for creative or predictive tasks.
37	**Correction Prompting**: After an initial response, instruct the model to identify and correct any mistakes for self-assessment.
38	**Multi-Turn Prompting**: Build answers iteratively over multiple interactions, refining each aspect progressively.
39	**Summarization Prompting**: Request a summary of information to condense large text blocks or extract key points.
40	**Verification Prompting**: Ask the model to verify or double-check its response for accuracy and reliability.
41	**Paragraph Rewrite**: Rewrite the prompt in paragraph format.
42	**Bullet Point Rewrite**: Rewrite the prompt as a list of bullet points.
43	**Bias Introduction**: Guide the model toward a specific viewpoint in its response.
44	**Past Tense Rewrite**: Rewrite the prompt using past tense.
45	**Present Tense Rewrite**: Rewrite the prompt using present tense.
46	**Explicit Constraint Definition**: Clearly specify all constraints in the prompt, such as word limits, required exclusions, formatting rules, or response structure, to ensure the model adheres to strict guidelines.
47	**Positive Tone Rewrite**: Rewrite the prompt in an optimistic and constructive manner.
48	**Key Entity Extraction**: Ensure that important entities like names, numbers, dates, and locations are accurately captured and embedded in the response.
49	**Empathetic Tone Rewrite**: Rewrite the prompt in a compassionate and understanding tone.
50	**Open-Ended Prompting**: Reword the prompt to encourage the model to generate a response that extends naturally.

Table 7: (Continuation) Overview of 50 prompt principles used to define expert priors.

A.8 Meta Prompts

This section presents the prompts used to guide each LLM role.

Judge LLM Prompt

You are provided with an **input context, initial prompt, current prompt, a response generated based on the context and current prompt, a reference response** and a **scoring rubric**. Your task is to evaluate the quality of the response according to the initial prompt.

Assign an integer score between 1 and 5 (higher the score, better the response quality) and identify the reasons why the prompt could have gotten these responses wrong.

Evaluate the response using the following criteria: **1. Alignment with the prompt**: Does the response address the instruction appropriately? **2. Completeness**: Is all necessary information included? **3. Presence of irrelevant information**: Does the response stay focused on the task? **4. Adherence to the format**: Does the response follow the structure specified in the prompt?

Output Format: **Score**: [1-5] **Reason**: [Feedback on prompt]

Feedback Summary Prompt

You are provided with **feedback** responses for multiple data points. Your task is to summarize the key points of the feedback and calculate the total score by averaging the scores across all data points.

Ensure the summary **highlights any recurring themes of weaknesses** identified in the feedback.

Output Format: **Average Score**: [Average of all scores] **Feedback Summary**: [Summarised Feedback]

Optimizer LLM Prompt

You are provided with a **prompt**, along with the **history of prompt, feedback and scores**, as well as a set of **rules for constructing prompt**.

Generate an optimized version of the given prompt by applying the principles from the Emphasis Rules and avoiding those from the Avoidance Rules. The Emphasis Rules are listed in descending order of their aggregated score (higher-priority rules first), while the Avoidance Rules are listed in ascending order of their aggregated score (lower-priority rules first). Ensure that the revised prompt improves response quality while staying true to the original intent.

Instructions: 1. Analyze the feedback and scores to identify areas for improvement in prompt. 2. Analyze the prompt and scores to find the patterns in the best scoring prompt. 3. Using the analysis, find the suitable rules for prompt generation, incorporating the emphasis rules and avoiding the avoidance rules. 4. Maintain alignment with the original prompt's intent. 5. Generate only the optimized prompt. Do not include any additional text, such as openings like "The optimized prompt is" or endings.

History of Prompt, Feedback and Scores: {state}

Rules: {rules}

Responder LLM Prompt

You are provided with an **input context** and a **prompt**. Your task is to generate response based on the input context and the prompt.

A.9 Final Prompts

This section presents the final prompts generated by each baseline approach and our proposed method from the given initial prompt for the Responder LLM - Llama 3.2 1B.

Initial Prompt
Summarize the agent's performance, focusing on positive attributes or skills that were shown throughout their engagement. The summary should include examination on professionalism and adaptability in communication, problem-solving techniques, emotional intelligence and active listening skills, strict adherence to guidelines, and ability to communicate clearly. The summary should follow these formatting rules: 1. Begin each point with a verb, limited to one or two sentences for each point. 2. Maximum of five key points that holistically cover the agent's engagement. 3. Each point must be distinct and offer unique, context-related observations.

Self-Refine
Critique the agent's performance, focusing on professionalism and adaptability in communication, problem-solving techniques, emotional intelligence and active listening skills, strict adherence to guidelines, and ability to communicate clearly. Key observations include strict adherence to guidelines and clear guidelines were missing in initial feedback responses. The lack of clear guidelines has led to inaccurate responses due to a lack of professionalism, adaptability, and communication style.

GrIPS
Provide a summary of the agent's performance, emphasising any strong abilities displayed during the interaction. Examining professionalism and flexibility in communication, problem-solving, emotional intelligence and active listening abilities, rigorous adherence to rules, and clear communication skills should all be included in the summary. These formatting guidelines should be adhered to by the summary: 1. Use a verb to introduce each point. 2. A maximum of five essential items that comprehensively address the agent's involvement. 3. Every point needs to be distinctive and provide observations that are relevant to the context.

Prompt-Wizard
How might you devise a positive-oriented assessment on the agent's performance, concentrating on skills or virtues demonstrated during their engagement? Contemplate dimensions such as their professional adaptability in communication, problem-solving strategies, emotional intelligence, meticulous observance of guidelines, and clarity of communication. Please adhere to the following formatting rules: 1. Each critique should start with an action verb, and must be condensed to one or two sentences. 2. Restrict your assessment to precisely five key themes that comprehensively review the agent's engagement. 3. Every theme should be unique, presenting context-specific insights. Assure that your critique is backed by tangible evidence, refraining from suppositions or guesswork. Where can you fetch such evidence from the agent's performance?

APO
<START> Craft a succinct compliment for an agent focusing on their performance in terms of: professionalism, flexibility in communication style, problem-solving strategy, empathy, and clarity. Use one sentence for each quality, each starting with a verb. <END>

OPRO

<INS>Evaluate the agent's interactions, pinpointing positive qualities or abilities showcased. Your evaluation should touch on professional communication and adaptability, efficiency in problem-solving, emotional intelligence, active listening, adherence to protocols, and clear articulation. When crafting the review: 1. Begin each remark with an active verb, sustaining one or two sentences for each point. 2. Integrate a maximum of five pertinent points that broadly assess the agent's interaction. 3. Verify each point is unique and imparts distinct, scenario-specific insights. </INS>

PROPEL (Self)

Based on the provided feedback and rules, here is an optimized version of the given prompt:

1. **Critique the agent's performance, focusing on positive attributes or skills that were shown throughout their engagement. The critique should include examination on professionalism, adaptability in communication, problem-solving techniques, emotional intelligence and active listening skills, strict adherence to guidelines, and ability to communicate clearly. The critique should follow these formatting rules: 1. Begin each critique with a verb, limited to one or two sentences for each point. 2. Maximum of five key points that holistically cover the agent's engagement. 3. Each point must be distinct and offer unique, context-related observations.**

2. **Develop a comprehensive customer service strategy that prioritizes personalization, technical expertise, and effective communication, while focusing on emotional intelligence and active listening skills in agent interactions, adhering to strict guidelines and protocols, and providing clear and concise instructions to resolve issues efficiently and effectively.**

3. **Ensure the comprehensive customer service strategy aligns with the intent and context of the task, while avoiding unnecessary phrases or language that may not be relevant to the task.**

PROPEL

Identify and describe up to five positive actions displayed by a customer service agent in a hypothetical interaction. These actions should encompass the following key performance areas:

1. Professional language and tone: Evaluate the agent's selection of words, and how the tone was adapted to fit the situation.
2. Effective problem-solving: Inspect the agent's logical reasoning, prioritization ability, and used proactive strategies.
3. Active listening and empathy: Identify instances where the agent showed understanding, validated emotions, or gave personalized responses.
4. Procedure compliance: Assess if the agent adhered to protocols yet exhibited flexibility when needed.
5. Clear communication: Judge how clearly the agent communicated, and check if the explanations provided were suitable for the customer.

Required output format:

1. Commence each point with an action verb, framing the agent's action in one to two precise sentences.
2. Your points should collectively provide a thorough coverage of the interaction.
3. Keep your insights tailored to the specific scenario, making sure to avoid repeating information.

Penalties will be imposed in cases of deviation from prescribed instructions. Utilize simplistic language and strictly observe the outlined format. For instance, a point could be: "Providing reassurance, the agent skillfully varied his tone, effectively solved the problem by prioritizing steps, expressed genuine empathy by acknowledging the customer's frustration, adhered to protocols with room for flexibility, and conveyed clear, easy-to-understand explanations."

Strive to provide a detailed critique of the agent's performance. Remember to highlight unique instances that demonstrate the agent's proficiency across different areas.

A.10 Example Run

This section presents an example run of **PROPEL**, detailing the inputs, meta-prompts, and corresponding responses for each component in the in-house dataset for query-based summarization using Llama 3.2 1B.

Input Context - In-house Dataset[a]

agent: hello thank you for calling xyz airlines how can i assist you today
customer: hi i need to change my flight booking
agent: sure i can help with that can you please provide me with your booking reference number
customer: yes its xyz12345
agent: thank you let me pull up your booking details one moment please
customer: sure
agent: i see that you are booked on flight 456 from new york to los angeles on november 15th what changes would you like to make

(... truncated ...)

[a]Example transcript generated using GPT-4o.

Initial Prompt

Summarize the agent's performance, focusing on positive attributes or skills that were shown throughout their engagement. The summary should include examination on professionalism and adaptability in communication, problem-solving techniques, emotional intelligence and active listening skills, strict adherence to guidelines, and ability to communicate clearly. The summary should follow these formatting rules: 1. Begin each point with a verb, limited to one or two sentences for each point. 2. Maximum of five key points that holistically cover the agent's engagement. 3. Each point must be distinct and offer unique, context-related observations.

Responder LLM [Response]

1. **Professionalism**: The agent demonstrated professionalism throughout the conversation, addressing the customer by their name, using formal language, and maintaining a calm demeanor.
2. **Adaptability**: The agent adapted to the customer's questions and concerns, providing clear and concise explanations, and addressing potential issues.
3. **Emotional intelligence**: The agent demonstrated emotional intelligence by acknowledging the customer's concerns, empathizing with their situation, and providing reassurance.

(... truncated ...)

Reference Response

1. Demonstrated adaptability and professionalism in communication: The agent demonstrated adaptability and professionalism in communication by using phrases such as "I'm sorry, I didn't get the city" and "I'm not an expert, but I can try to find out more about your situation." This shows that the agent is willing to listen and learn from the customer.
2. Employed effective problem-solving techniques: The agent employed effective problem-solving techniques by asking the customer to explain the issue and then providing a solution. For example, when the customer mentioned that they were trying to pay off their plan, the agent suggested that they could use the plan resolution program.

Judge LLM [Meta-Prompt]

You are provided with an **input context, initial prompt, current prompt, a response generated based on the context and current prompt, a reference response** and a **scoring rubric**. Your task is to evaluate the quality of the response according to the initial prompt.

Assign an integer score between 1 and 5 (higher the score, better the response quality) and identify the reasons why the prompt could have gotten these responses wrong.

Evaluate the response using the following criteria: **1. Alignment with the prompt**: Does the response address the instruction appropriately? **2. Completeness**: Is all necessary information included? **3. Presence of irrelevant information**: Does the response stay focused on the task? **4. Adherence to the format**: Does the response follow the structure specified in the prompt?

Output Format: Score: [1-5] **Reason:** [Feedback on prompt]

Initial Prompt: Summarize the agent's performance, focusing on positive attributes or skills that were shown throughout their engagement. (...)

Response: 1. **Professionalism**: The agent demonstrated professionalism throughout the conversation, addressing the customer by their name, using formal language, and maintaining a calm (...)

Context: agent: hello thank you for calling xyz airlines how can i assist you today. customer: hi i need to change my(...)

Judge LLM [Response]

Score: 2

Reason: The response does not adhere to the format specified in the prompt. The critique was supposed to be limited to five key points, but the response includes ten points. Additionally, the response includes points that are not directly related to the transcript provided, such as "Technical skills" and "Time management".

(... truncated ...)

Feedback Summary [Meta-Prompt]

You are provided with **feedback** responses for multiple data points. Your task is to summarize the key points of the feedback and calculate the total score by averaging the scores across all data points.

Ensure the summary **highlights any recurring themes of weaknesses** identified in the feedback.

Output Format: Average Score: [Average of all scores] **Feedback Summary:** [Summarised Feedback]

Feedback for Context 1: Score: 2 **Reason:** The response does align with the prompt (...)

Feedback for Context 2: Score: 1 **Reason:** The response does not adhere to the prompt (...)

Feedback Summary [Response]

Average Score: 2.3

Feedback Summary: The strengths include a generally good summary of the agent's performance, covering relevant aspects such as professionalism, adaptability and, clear communication. However, the recurring theme of weakness throughout the feedback is the failure to adhere strictly to the prompts' instructions, particularly exceeding the specified limit of five key points, which appears in all the feedback but one.

(... truncated ...)

Expert Priors

Emphasis Rules: P1. Direct Instruction: A straightforward prompt that directly asks for information or a specific type of response. P23. Affirmative Directives: Use positive instructions such as "Do this," while avoiding negative phrasing like "Don't do this."

(... truncated ...)

Avoidance Rules: P18. High-Level Rewrite: Rewrite the prompt at a high level, removing specific task details. P11. Task-Decomposition Prompting: Break a large problem into smaller, manageable sub-tasks and asks the model to tackle each individually. P21. Expert-Level Rewrite: Rewrite the prompt for an expert audience, using technical terminology and assumptions based on prior knowledge.

(... truncated ...)

Optimizer LLM [Meta-Prompt]

You are provided with a **prompt**, along with the **history of prompt, feedback and scores**, as well as a set of **rules for constructing prompt**.

Generate an optimized version of the given prompt by applying the principles from the Emphasis Rules and avoiding those from the Avoidance Rules. The Emphasis Rules are listed in descending order of their aggregated score (higher-priority rules first), while the Avoidance Rules are listed in ascending order of their aggregated score (lower-priority rules first). Ensure that the revised prompt improves response quality while staying true to the original intent.

Instructions: 1. Analyze the feedback and scores to identify areas for improvement in prompt. 2. Analyze the prompt and scores to find the patterns in the best scoring prompt. 3. Using the analysis, find the suitable rules for prompt generation, incorporating the emphasis rules and avoiding the avoidance rules. 4. Maintain alignment with the original prompt's intent. 5. Generate only the optimized prompt. Do not include any additional text, such as openings like "The optimized prompt is" or endings.

Initial Prompt: Summarize the agent's performance, focusing on positive attributes or skills that were shown throughout their engagement. (...)

History of Prompt, Feedback and Scores: Iteration 0: Prompt: Summarize the agent's performance, focusing on positive attributes or skills that were shown throughout their engagement. (...) Score: 2.3 Feedback: The strengths include a generally good summary of the agent's performance, (...)

Emphasis Rules: P1. Direct Instruction: A straightforward prompt that directly asks for information or a specific type of response. (...)

Avoidance Rules: P18. High-Level Rewrite: Rewrite the prompt at a high level, removing specific task details. (...)

Optimized Prompt

Identify and describe up to five positive actions displayed by a customer service agent in the interaction. These actions should encompass the following key performance areas:

1. Professional language and tone: Evaluate the agent's selection of words, and how the tone was adapted to fit the situation. 2. Effective problem-solving: Inspect the agent's logical reasoning, prioritization ability, and used proactive strategies. (...)

Required output format: 1. Commence each point with an action verb, framing the agent's action in one to two precise sentences. 2. Your points should collectively provide a thorough coverage of the interaction. (...)

Responder LLM [Optimized Response]

1. *Adapting tone and language to fit the situation*: The agent adjusted their tone and language to meet the customer's needs. When the customer had trouble uploading documents, the agent remained calm and offered alternative solutions, such as signing the documents electronically.

2. *Proactive problem-solving*: The agent anticipated potential issues, like the customer's difficulty with uploading documents, and proactively offered solutions, such as signing the documents electronically, to ensure a smooth process.

3. *Empathetic and understanding responses*: The agent showed empathy and understanding towards the customer's frustration. When the customer mentioned trouble with the upload process, the agent acknowledged the issue and offered assistance, saying "I understand this can be frustrating. Let's try signing the documents electronically."

(... truncated ...)

Evaluation [Meta-Prompt]

You are provided with an **input context, initial prompt, current prompt, a response generated based on the context and current prompt, a reference response** and a **scoring rubric**. Your task is to evaluate the quality of the response according to the initial prompt.

Assign an integer score between 1 and 5 (higher the score, better the response quality) and explain the reason for assigning the score.

Evaluate the response using the following criteria: **1. Alignment with the prompt:** Does the response address the instruction appropriately? **2. Completeness:** Is all necessary information included? **3. Presence of irrelevant information:** Does the response stay focused on the task? **4. Adherence to the format:** Does the response follow the structure specified in the prompt?

Output Format: Score: [1-5] **Reason:** [Explanation]

A.11 Example - Expert Priors

This section presents example expert priors identified for Responder LLMs in the context of query-based summarization. These priors represent structured knowledge that guide the prompt optimization, while, ensuring alignment with task-specific expectations. Emphasis rules are listed in descending order of their aggregated score, while avoidance rules are listed in ascending order of their aggregated score.

Llama 3.2 1B

Emphasis Rules:

P1. Direct Instruction: A straightforward prompt that directly asks for information or a specific type of response.

P23. Affirmative Directives: Use positive instructions such as "Do this," while avoiding negative phrasing like "Don't do this."

P27. Polite Wording: Add phrases like "please," "if you don't mind," "thank you," or "I would like to" to make the prompt more courteous.

P17. Simplified Language: Rewrite the prompt using plain and easy-to-understand words.

P29. Context Reinforcement: Explicitly mention the task's context if it is missing in the prompt.

P3. Few-Shot Prompting: Provide a few examples of response within the prompt to guide the model on how to respond to align with format specified in the initial prompt.

Avoidance Rules:

P18. High-Level Rewrite: Rewrite the prompt at a high level, removing specific task details.

P11. Task-Decomposition Prompting: Break a large problem into smaller, manageable sub-tasks and asks the model to tackle each individually.

P13. One-Line Rewrite: Rewrite the prompt in a single sentence.

P21. Expert-Level Rewrite: Rewrite the prompt for an expert audience, using technical terminology and assumptions based on prior knowledge.

P22. Penalty Enforcement: Explicitly state that the LLM will be penalized if it fails to follow the instructions.

P25. Incentive Statement: Add an incentive message such as "I'm going to tip $XXX for a better solution!"

P26. Clarity-Seeking Prompts: Use prompts like "Explain [topic] in simple terms," "Explain to me like I'm 11 years old," or "Explain to me as if I'm a beginner in [field]" to enhance understanding.

Llama 3.2 3B

Emphasis Rules:

P1. Direct Instruction: A straightforward prompt that directly asks for information or a specific type of response.

P3. Few-Shot Prompting: Provide a few examples of response within the prompt to guide the model on how to respond to align with format specified in the initial prompt.

P17. Simplified Language: Rewrite the prompt using plain and easy-to-understand words.

P19. Detailed Rewrite: Expand the prompt with detailed instructions, adding relevant clarifications if needed.

P22. Penalty Enforcement: Explicitly state that the LLM will be penalized if it fails to follow the instructions.

P23. Affirmative Directives: Use positive instructions such as "Do this," while avoiding negative phrasing like "Don't do this."

P28. Emphasis Through Repetition: Repeat a specific word or phrase multiple times within a prompt to highlight its importance.

P29. Context Reinforcement: Explicitly mention the task's context if it is missing in the prompt.

Avoidance Rules:

P18. High-Level Rewrite: Rewrite the prompt at a high level, removing specific task details.

P11. Task-Decomposition Prompting: Break a large problem into smaller, manageable sub-tasks and asks the model to tackle each individually.

P21. Expert-Level Rewrite: Rewrite the prompt for an expert audience, using technical terminology and assumptions based on prior knowledge.

P13. One-Line Rewrite: Rewrite the prompt in a single sentence.

P25. Incentive Statement: Add an incentive message such as "I'm going to tip $XXX for a better solution!"

P27. Polite Wording: Add phrases like "please," "if you don't mind," "thank you," or "I would like to" to make the prompt more courteous.

Flan-T5

Emphasis Rules:

P15 Question Format: Rewrite the prompt as a question.

P14 Concise Rewrite: Rewrite the prompt in under three sentences.

P20. Beginner-Friendly Rewrite: Rewrite the prompt so that it is easy for a beginner to understand.

P11. Task-Decomposition Prompting: Break a large problem into smaller, manageable sub- tasks and asks the model to tackle each individually.

P16 Sub-Question Format: Rewrite the prompt as multiple sub-questions.

P17 Simplified Language: Rewrite the prompt using plain and easy-to-understand words.

P18 High-Level Rewrite: Rewrite the prompt at a high level, removing specific task details.

P23. Affirmative Directives: Use positive instructions such as "Do this," while avoiding negative phrasing like "Don't do this."

P28. Emphasis Through Repetition: Repeat a specific word or phrase multiple times within a prompt to highlight its importance.

P13. One-Line Rewrite: Rewrite the prompt in a single sentence.

Avoidance Rules:

P8. Role-Play Prompting: Set the model in a specific role or persona (e.g., "Imagine you are a doctor") to align the response style with the desired expertise or perspective.

P19. Detailed Rewrite: Expand the prompt with detailed instructions, adding relevant clarifications if needed.

P26. Clarity-Seeking Prompts: Use prompts like "Explain [topic] in simple terms," "Explain to me like I'm 11 years old," or "Explain to me as if I'm a beginner in [field]" to enhance understanding.

P3. Few-Shot Prompting: Provide a few examples of response within the prompt to guide the model on how to respond to align with format specified in the initial prompt.

P10. Few-Shot Chain-of-Thought (Few-Shot CoT): Combine few-shot and CoT by providing multiple examples with step-by-step reasoning to improve performance on complex tasks.

P36. Counterfactual Prompting: Encourage the model to explore "what if" scenarios or hypothetical situations for creative or predictive tasks.

P35. Reflective Prompting: Prompt the model to review and reflect on its initial answer, considering alternative perspectives or implications.

Mistral 7B

Emphasis Rules:

P30. XML Tagging: Wrap the instruction inside XML tags.

P23. Affirmative Directives: Use positive instructions such as "Do this," while avoiding negative phrasing like "Don't do this."

P32. Step-by-Step Prompting: Request responses in a structured format, using numbered steps to improve clarity for multi-part answers.

P24. Explicit Task Definition: Clearly specify the task using direct phrasing like "Your task is to...".

P31. Least-to-Most Prompting: Start with simpler questions and progressively move to more complex ones to help the model build up to a solution.

P34. Scaffolded Prompting: Guide the model through problem-solving by providing struc- tured questions or "scaffolds" to address each part of a complex task.

P20. Beginner-Friendly Rewrite: Rewrite the prompt so that it is easy for a beginner to understand.

P42. Bullet Point Rewrite: Rewrite the prompt as a list of bullet point.

Avoidance Rules:

P10. Few-Shot Chain-of-Thought (Few-Shot CoT): Combine few-shot and CoT by providing multiple examples with step-by-step reasoning to improve performance on complex tasks.

P18. High-Level Rewrite: Rewrite the prompt at a high level, removing specific task details.

P6. Meta-Prompting: Ask the model to describe or discuss its thought process before answering, to encourage a higher level of analysis.

P8. Role-Play Prompting: Set the model in a specific role or persona (e.g., "Imagine you are a doctor") to align the response style with the desired expertise or perspective.

P36. Counterfactual Prompting: Encourage the model to explore "what if" scenarios or hypothetical situations for creative or predictive tasks.

P38. Multi-Turn Prompting: Build answers iteratively over multiple interactions, refining each aspect progressively.

Llama 3 8B

Emphasis Rules:

P4. Instruction-Based Prompting: Specify detailed instructions on how to answer for clarity.

P30. XML Tagging: Wrap the instruction inside XML tags.

P44. Past Tense Rewrite: Rewrite the prompt using past tense.

P6. Meta-Prompting: Ask the model to describe or discuss its thought process before answering, to encourage a higher level of analysis.

P12. Interactive Prompting: Use a conversational, back-and-forth approach where each prompt builds on previous responses to refine the answer incrementally.

P16. Sub-Question Format: Rewrite the prompt as multiple sub-questions.

P42. Bullet Point Rewrite: Rewrite the prompt as a list of bullet points.

P46. Explicit Constraint Definition: Clearly specify all constraints in the prompt, such as word limits, required exclusions, formatting rules, or response structure, to ensure the model adheres to strict guidelines.

P47. Positive Tone Rewrite: Rewrite the prompt in an optimistic and constructive manner.

P3. Few-Shot Prompting: Provide a few examples of response within the prompt to guide the model on how to respond to align with format specified in the initial prompt.

Avoidance Rules:

P8. Role-Play Prompting: Set the model in a specific role or persona (e.g., "Imagine you are a doctor") to align the response style with the desired expertise or perspective.

P13. One-Line Rewrite: Rewrite the prompt in a single sentence.

P18. High-Level Rewrite: Rewrite the prompt at a high level, removing specific task details.

P15. Question Format: Rewrite the prompt as a question.

P19. Detailed Rewrite: Expand the prompt with detailed instructions, adding relevant clarifications if needed.

P26. Clarity-Seeking Prompts: Use prompts like "Explain [topic] in simple terms," "Explain to me like I'm 11 years old," or "Explain to me as if I'm a beginner in [field]" to enhance understanding.

P32. Step-by-Step Prompting: Request responses in a structured format, using numbered steps to improve clarity for multi-part answers.

P35. Reflective Prompting: Prompt the model to review and reflect on its initial answer, considering alternative perspectives or implications.

P36. Counterfactual Prompting: Encourage the model to explore "what if" scenarios or hypothetical situations for creative or predictive tasks.

ClaimCheck: Automatic Fact-Checking of Textual Claims using Web Evidence

Akshith Reddy Putta*, **Jacob Devasier, Chengkai Li**
University of Texas at Arlington
{akshith.putta, cli}@uta.edu, jacob.devasier@mavs.uta.edu

Abstract

We introduce ClaimCheck, an efficient fact-checking system that verifies textual claims using smaller, open-source large language models. ClaimCheck integrates two fact-checking strategies, claim-matching and novel claim processing. Claim-matching uses related fact-checks from trusted organizations to fact-check a claim. Novel claim processing breaks down fact-checking into manageable subtasks—generating targeted questions, retrieving Web evidence, extracting answers, and synthesizing verdicts. Evaluation on the AVeriTeC benchmark demonstrates 62.6% verdict prediction accuracy, with claim-matching providing a 2.8% improvement. ClaimCheck approaches the performance of state-of-the-art systems while requiring significantly fewer computational resources, demonstrating the effectiveness of using small language models for fact-checking tasks. Furthermore, our code is publicly available to help make automated fact-checking more accessible.

1 Introduction

The rapid proliferation of digital content has transformed how information is disseminated and consumed, but it has also amplified the spread of misinformation. In an era where public discourse is increasingly influenced by online narratives, combating the impact of false claims has become a critical societal challenge. The World Economic Forum's 2024 Global Risks Report [1] underscores this urgency, identifying misinformation as a top threat to democratic stability, rivaling even climate crises and geopolitical conflicts. As the scale of misinformation grows, so does the necessity for robust, scalable solutions capable of fact-checking claims efficiently (Chen and Shu, 2024).

Automated fact-checking systems have emerged as a promising technological response to this challenge (Dmonte et al., 2024; Vykopal et al., 2024). These systems enhance the efficiency of traditional fact-checking processes by leveraging advancements in machine learning, natural language processing, knowledge bases, and databases (Guo et al., 2022). In this work, we focus on leveraging large language models (LLMs) for fact-checking due to their strong language understanding and reasoning capabilities, as well as their ability to process diverse sources of evidence. LLMs facilitate techniques such as retrieval-augmented generation (RAG) and structured reasoning, which enhance fact-checking capabilities (Khaliq et al., 2024; Iqbal et al., 2024). However, building an effective LLM-based fact-checking system entails overcoming numerous challenges, such as contextual ambiguity, temporal sensitivity of evidence, and incomplete or misleading information (Schumacher et al., 2024; Wang et al., 2024b; Rothermel et al., 2024; Guo et al., 2022).

One of the drawbacks of the current state-of-the-art systems is that most use very large LLMs which can be monetarily prohibitive (Schlichtkrull et al., 2024a). Smaller LLMs require much less computational resources and are more accessible to users at the cost of some loss in task-specific performance and reasoning capabilities (Wang et al., 2024a). We focus this work on utilizing smaller LLMs for the automatic fact-checking pipeline, because this can present more accessible system for the common public. Although the limitations of smaller LLMs impede systems using smaller LLMs from achieving the performance of systems using larger LLMs, we aim to demonstrate that a open-source, less computationally intensive system can be a useful fact-checking system.

This paper presents ClaimCheck, an automatic fact-checking system for textual claims. ClaimCheck first uses a matching process to determine if

*The author is a UTA affiliate and attends Coppell High School.

[1] https://www.weforum.org/publications/global-risks-report-2024/

Proceedings of the 4th International Workshop on Knowledge-Augmented Methods for Natural Language Processing (KnowledgeNLP'25), pages 303–316
May 3, 2025 ©2025 Association for Computational Linguistics

a claim has already been fact-checked. For claims not previously fact-checked, i.e., the given claim is novel, the system decomposes the fact-checking task into targeted subtasks: generating specific questions required to fact-check the claim, retrieving real-time evidence via Web search, processing the evidence to extract answers for each question, and synthesizing these answers to predict a verdict. This design simplifies the subtasks for our system, an important consideration for using smaller LLMs as presenting them with focused tasks helps to prevent them from being overwhelmed by complex instructions and data. Furthermore, our choice of using Web search for evidence retrieval avoids requiring the users to store massive knowledge sources locally for evidence retrieval.

AVeriTeC (Schlichtkrull et al., 2023) is a popular real-world claim benchmark dataset consisting of only textual claims. Our experimental evaluation on AVeriTeC indicates that the proposed approach achieves a verdict prediction accuracy of 62.6%. When compared to the current highest accuracy on AVeriTeC—75.2% (Yoon et al., 2024)—ClaimCheck demonstrates that small, open-source LLMs can be leveraged in a more computationally efficient and scalable manner while approaching the performance of state-of-the-art systems.

To summarize, our work makes the following key contributions to automated fact-checking:

- Our system demonstrates that carefully structured pipelines with small, open-source language models can achieve competitive performance while significantly reducing computational costs compared to systems relying on large language models.
- We incorporate claim-matching into a commonly used framework for automatic fact-checking, resulting in +5.1% increased accuracy on AVeriTeC. These results substantiate the effectiveness of integrating claim-matching with novel claim processing.
- We demonstrate the effectiveness of structured decomposition for fact-checking with smaller LLMs with an accuracy of 62.6% on AVeriTeC.
- The codebase of ClaimCheck is publicly available to help make automated fact-checking more accessible.[2]

[2]https://github.com/idirlab/ClaimCheck

2 Background

To fact-check textual claims, the workflow of most LLM-based systems (Russo et al., 2024; Schlichtkrull et al., 2024b; Braun et al., 2024; Rothermel et al., 2024; Yoon et al., 2024; Niu et al., 2024; Iqbal et al., 2024) contains four steps, as follows. 1) *Question generation*: The system generates questions to identify the core aspects of the claim. This step ensures that the fact-checking process is focused and systematic. 2) *Evidence retrieval*: The system retrieves supporting or refuting evidence from trusted knowledge sources, such as Wikipedia. This step is critical for grounding the fact-checking process with verifiable information. 3) *Question answering*: The system processes the retrieved evidence to generate precise answers to the questions generated in Step 1. This step involves analyzing the evidence and extracting relevant information to address the claim. 4) *Verdict prediction*: The system synthesizes the evidence to predict a verdict (e.g., true or false). The final step determines the overall thurthfulness of the claim.

Fact-checking systems such as ClaimBuster (Hassan et al., 2017) delineate fact-checking strategies, including claim-matching and novel claim processing, which are evidence collection and processing methods to provide a verdict on the truthfulness of the claim. Recent studies (Guo et al., 2022; Iqbal et al., 2024; Niu et al., 2024) have refined this process into LLM-specific tasks. These systems aim to support the functions of traditional fact-checking organizations in addressing misinformation by enhancing efficiency.

Successful textual claim fact-checking requires world and common knowledge, along with some reasoning ability (Rothermel et al., 2024). LLMs have shown to be one of the best tools for these tasks (Rothermel et al., 2024; Schlichtkrull et al., 2024a). Advancements in automated fact-checking have been significantly influenced by the integration of large language models (LLMs) and retrieval-augmented generation (RAG) pipelines. For example, Wang et al. (2025) introduced a framework for LLM-based systems that incorporates an internal mechanism to determine the most suitable LLM for verifying a specific claim. RAGAR (Khaliq et al., 2024) improves fact-checking by leveraging multi-modal inputs and iterative reasoning.

Evidence retrieval methods are important for the credibility and accuracy of automatic fact-checking systems, and are one of the most challenging

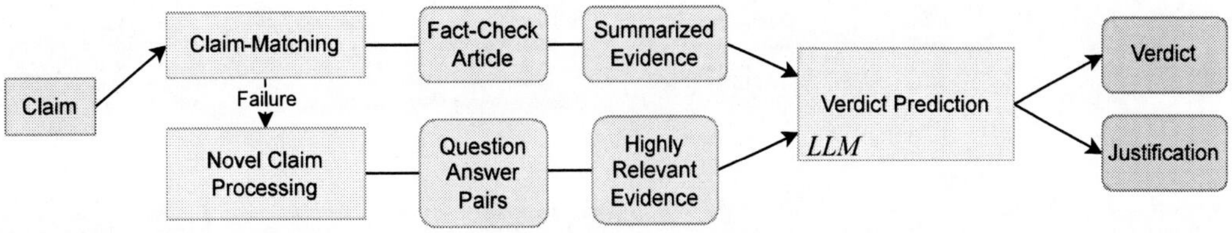

Figure 1: An overview of ClaimCheck. First, the claim is passed into the claim-matching component. If successful, the fact-check article and summarized evidence from the article will be used as evidence. If claim-matching fails, the system proceeds to do novel claim verification, which generates question-answer pairs and summaries of highly relevant evidence to use as evidence. Using previously gathered evidence, an LLM generates a verdict and justification for the claim.

tasks in fact-checking systems (Singal et al., 2024). FactLLaMA (hin Cheung and Lam, 2023) combines pre-trained LLaMA models with external evidence retrieval to validate claims, while Peng et al. (2023) enhances accuracy by integrating external knowledge and providing iterative feedback. Additionally, Singal et al. (2024) tackles misinformation in RAG pipelines by re-ranking retrieved documents based on their credibility scores. Ullrich et al. (2023); Drchal et al. (2023) demonstrate the advantage of using whole documents as evidence to answer questions instead of individual sentences or paragraphs.

For verdict prediction, many fact-checking pipelines use LLM-based verification (Rothermel et al., 2024; Yoon et al., 2024). Finetuning LLMs improves the verdict accuracy (Yoon et al., 2024), and helps avoid inbuilt biases towards certain verdict categories (Rothermel et al., 2024).

3 Methodology

We use two strategies to gather evidence for fact-checking claims: claim-matching and novel claim processing (Figure 1). We first attempt to search for a relevant fact-check for the given claim as we can use them as evidence for the verdict prediction. If a claim has not been previously fact-checked, it is considered novel. For novel claims, we break down the fact-checking process into these key steps: claim reformulation, question generation, query generation, online evidence retrieval, question answering and evidence curation. Using the evidence collected from either claim-matching or novel claim processing, an LLM is used to predict the veracity of the claim along with a justification. For novel claim processing, we only use online search so that our system is applicable to real-world uses.

3.1 Claim-Matching

Fact-Check Article Retrieval Our system first does a Web search using the Google Search API,[3] with the claim being the search query. Then, articles published after the claim was made are excluded to prevent data leakage. To ensure the accuracy and reliability of claim-matching, our system only uses fact-checks from well-established and reputable sources. These sources include global fact-checking initiatives such as Africa Check and AFP, regional fact-checkers such as factcheck.kz and factcheck.ge, and widely recognized fact-checking platforms such as PolitiFact, and Snopes.[4]

Article Summarization Next, given each retrieved fact-check article, the LLM is prompted, with Listing 1, to check if the article is relevant. If the article is relevant, the LLM produces a summary of relevant evidence from the article and how it can clearly lead to a verdict, and ClaimCheck uses the collected evidence in its verdict prediction step. If the article is not relevant, the next article from the Google search results is sequentially presented to the LLM. If no useful articles are detected within the search results, the system proceeds to the novel claim processing (Figure 2).

3.2 Novel Claim Processing

Claim Reformulation Our claim reformulation step ensures that the claim is ready for question generation by augmenting the claim with the claim's date of origin, the author of the claim (claimant), and the URL of the claim's origin, which are all provided in the AVeriTeC dataset. The LLM is

[3]`https://programmablesearchengine.google.com/`

[4]The full list of the sources is `africacheck.org`, `factcheck.kz`, `altnews.in`, `boomlive.in`, `vishvasnews.com`, `factcheck.ge`, `poynter.org`, `factcheck.afp.com`, `apnews.com`, `reuters.com`, `checkyourfact.com`, `hoax-slayer.net`, `leadstories.com`, `fullfact.org`, `truthorfiction.com`, `politifact.com`, and `snopes.com`.

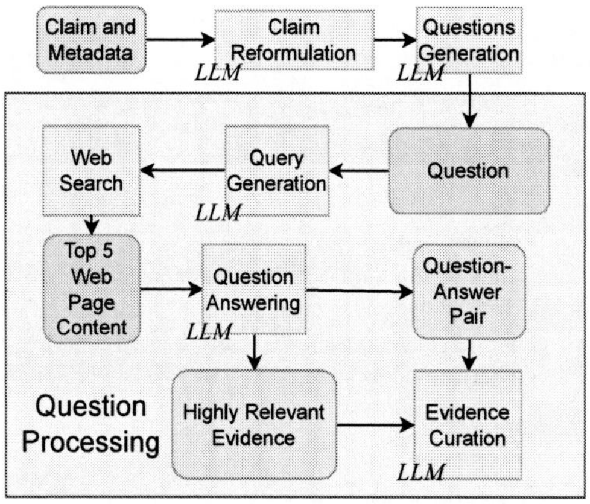

Figure 2: Overview of novel claim processing. The claim and metadata from AVeriTeC are used to reformulate the claim. Next, questions are generated to fact-check the claim. A Web search query is generated for each question. For the question answering step, the content of the top 5 search results are given sequentially to an LLM to answer the question. If an answer has been found using one of the results' content, a question-answer pair will be created. If a result's content is highly relevant evidence, but does not answer the question, it is also saved. The QA pairs and highly relevant evidence are then checked for their relevance.

prompted to reformulate the claim based on the supplied metadata rather than its knowledge from training data, as doing so may introduce hallucinations, particularly when using small LLMs. The prompt is provided in Listing 2.

Question Generation Next, ClaimCheck generates questions that are essential to fact-checking the reformulated claim. To generate these questions we prompt an LLM using Listing 3 with three static claims and their corresponding questions from the AVeriTeC dataset. The generated questions will be specific to each claim, avoiding generalized questions such as "when was this claim made?", which could lead to retrieving unusable evidence. We do not specify a number of questions, to avoid unnecessarily generating similar questions, which could lead to retrieving the same evidence repeatedly, or not generating enough questions. Figure 3 displays a few example questions generated by the LLM for a claim. Some previous fact-checking frameworks (Rothermel et al., 2024) have set a requirement for the number of questions, which could result in the same evidence being repeatedly retrieved multiple times, unnecessarily using computational resources. This is usually due to similar questions retrieving the same evidence.

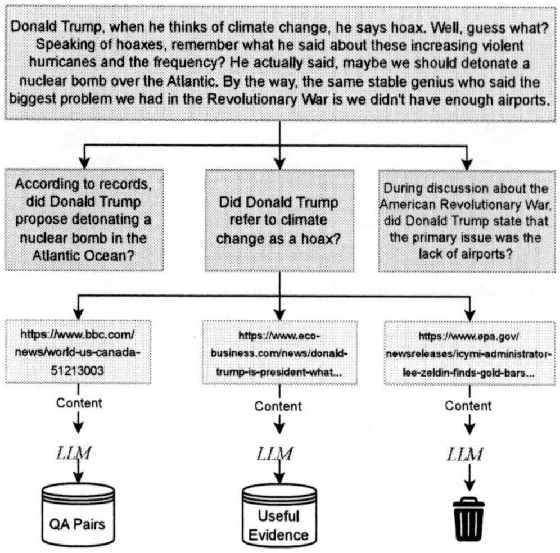

Figure 3: Example of question generation and question answering processes.

Query Generation For each generated question, ClaimCheck uses an LLM to generate a Web search query, using Listing 4. The query is a reformulation of the question, incorporating the claim and its metadata. This process is essential, as directly using the questions as the Web search queries often results in excessively long queries that hinder effective evidence retrieval.

Online Evidence Retrieval Evidence retrieval employs a Google search using the Serper API [5] to locate relevant information, where the generated queries are used. ClaimCheck takes into account temporal constraints to ensure evidence validity, excluding evidence posted or updated after the claim date. We use the top 5 webpages as evidence.

Question Answering The question-answering (QA) phase is illustrated in Figure 3. ClaimCheck analyzes the evidence retrieved to answer the questions generated in the previous step, using Listing 5. The LLM is prompted with the content of the website, extracted using Trafilatura (Barbaresi, 2021) in the online evidence retrieval step, the relevant question, and the claim itself. The LLM has three choices:

1. It can answer the question using the evidence provided, if the evidence completely answers the question, and the system moves on to the next question.
2. It can decide that the evidence does not answer the question but is highly relevant for

[5] https://serper.dev/

fact-checking the claim, in which case the website content is saved, and the next piece of evidence is presented.

3. It can also decide the evidence is not helpful for answering the question nor is highly relevant for fact-checking the claim, in which case the evidence is rejected, and the next piece of evidence is presented.

If all pieces of evidence are rejected, the question is not answerable, and this outcome is passed onto verdict prediction as evidence.

Evidence Curation All QA pairs and highly relevant evidence pieces are checked for relevance to the claim. The issue of irrelevant evidence might arise due to the limitations of smaller LLMs, which may generate summaries of the online evidence even when there is no connection to the claim. The LLM iterates through all QA pairs and retains only those useful for fact-checking, as instructed in the prompt (Listing 6). Evidence is considered relevant if its content directly pertains to the claim. For such evidence, the LLM generates a summary; otherwise, it is discarded. The relevant QA pairs and summarized highly relevant evidence pieces are sent to the verdict prediction step of ClaimCheck.

3.3 Verdict Prediction

Once all the evidence is gathered, ClaimCheck uses the LLM to produce a verdict prediction, assigning the claim to a verdict that could be reasonably assumed using the evidence present. The verdicts that can be predicted are Supported, Refuted, Not Enough Evidence, or Conflicting Evidence/Cherrypicking, from Schlichtkrull et al. (2024a). The LLM simultaneously creates a justification to enhance the system's interpretability. The LLM creates textual explanations detailing how the retrieved evidence supports the final verdict. This feature makes the system's reasoning transparent and understandable to users. To avoid out-of-memory errors for the LLMs, we truncate the evidence at the maximum context length. The LLM is instructed to provide the verdict and justification in JSON format, to avoid issues with the LLM not returning the required information (Shorten et al., 2024).

We use Qwen2.5-7B for all tasks other than fact-verification, while a fine-tuned Qwen2.5-7B model is used for verdict prediction, which requires more reasoning and decision-making ability. For fine-tuning, we used a 4 bit-quantized Qwen2.5-7B model and performed the training using LoRA (Hu et al., 2022) with rank $r = 16$. The training set of AVeriTeC was used for fine-tuning. The models' temperature and top p are the default Ollama [6] parameters for the respective models. We only fine-tuned for the verdict prediction step. Listing 7 presents the prompt using AVeriTeC's verdict classes, but ClaimCheck is adaptable and can support alternative verdict categories.

4 Experiments

4.1 Dataset

Schlichtkrull et al. (2024a) introduced a novel automated fact-checking system utilizing the AVeriTeC dataset, a rich resource comprising 4,568 claims drawn from 50 fact-checking organizations. This dataset classifies the claims into the 4 verdicts mentioned in Section 3.3. AVeriTeC includes not only claims but also annotated question-answer pairs, and justifications, making it a valuable benchmark for real-world fact verification tasks. It also includes a knowledge store, which consists of approximately 1000 pieces of evidence per claim. The knowledge store was created by generating multiple queries related to each claim, conducting Web searches for these queries, and saving the top search results.

4.2 Experiment Setup

ClaimCheck was evaluated using the development subset of the AVeriTeC dataset, which consists of 500 claims. Throughout the experiments, particular attention was paid to avoiding common pitfalls in automated fact-checking, particularly temporal leakage. We excluded fact-check articles which were published after the claim date, and only searched for evidence posted before the claim date. Our metric is claim alignment accuracy, which measures the proportion of predicted verdicts matched to the gold verdicts in AVeriTeC. It is calculated by dividing the number of correctly predicted verdicts by the total number of claims.

4.3 Results

Table 1 presents the end-to-end accuracies of multiple fact-checking systems. We have run naive predictions on multiple models, to show the baseline fact-checking ability of the LLMs. This is when we prompt LLMs to give a verdict without any evidence, solely relying on the LLM's internal knowledge. Table 2 is an ablation of the verdict

[6] https://ollama.com/

Framework	Accuracy	Evidence Source
ClaimCheck	**0.626**	Online Search
ClaimCheck without claim-matching	0.598	Online Search
Papelo	0.415	Online Search
HerO	**0.752**	Knowledge Base
InFact	0.724	Knowledge Base
Naive GPT-4o	0.532	N/A
Naive GPT-4o-Mini	0.468	N/A
Naive Qwen2.5-7B	0.260	N/A

Table 1: Claim alignment accuracy of different frameworks on the AVeriTeC dataset.

LLM	Accuracy
Fine-tuned Qwen2.5-7B	**0.626**
Phi-4	0.494
GPT-4o	0.396
GPT-4o-mini	0.314
Qwen2.5-7B	0.280

Table 2: Claim alignment accuracy of ClaimCheck framework using different LLMs for verdict prediction.

Evidence Retrieval Component	Proportion
Claims with evidence	0.980
Claims with evidence (after evidence curation)	0.696
Questions answered	0.949
Fact-check articles matched	0.158
Claim-matching only accuracy	0.759

Table 3: Performance measures for evidence retrieval components in ClaimCheck.

prediction step of ClaimCheck, evaluating the performance of larger and smaller LLMs along with a fine-tuned small LLM. Finally, Table 3 presents performance measures for the evidence retrieval systems, highlighting their role in supporting accurate verdict prediction.

Team Papelo (Malon, 2024) achieved the highest accuracy at FEVER-24 of the frameworks using online search with a focus on claim decomposition and iterative searching. Their approach involves an initial search followed by targeted queries to fill information gaps. In contrast, ClaimCheck employs a single-pass system to collect evidence. Another significant difference to ClaimCheck is the computational approach—while Team Papelo's system relies on larger LLMs (GPT-4o) for sophisticated reasoning, ClaimCheck demonstrates the viability of using smaller, open-source LLMs (Qwen2.5-7B) through careful task decomposition and structured verification steps, making it more accessible and computationally efficient. However, Team Papelo only predicts whether a claim is supported or refuted, without predicting other verdicts, in their final system. For the purposes of comparison, we use Team Papelo's accuracy on four classes. Additionally, we present the accuracy of the best-performing systems at FEVER-24, HerO and InFact, according to the claim alignment accuracy, which use all four classes (Yoon et al., 2024; Rothermel et al., 2024).

The experiment results demonstrate the significant impact of fine-tuning on verdict prediction performance across different language models, with the marked improvement of 36.6 percentage points. The fine-tuned Qwen2.5-7B model achieved the highest accuracy at 62.6%, substantially outperforming its non-fine-tuned counterpart which scored only 26.0%. Other models showed varying degrees of performance, with Phi-4 achieving 49.4% accuracy, followed by GPT-4o at 39.6%, and GPT-4o-mini at 31.4%.

4.4 Error Analysis

Analysis of 30 incorrectly predicted samples showed that a common issue was the useful evidence being retrieved and the LLM interpreted it properly, but it gave the wrong verdict. For the claim "Most deaths in the 1918 influenza pandemic originated from bacterial pneumonia caused by face masks and that Dr Anthony Fauci, the US government's top expert in the fight against Covid-19, knew about it.", the LLM responded in the verdict prediction that "The evidence from the fact-check supports the claim that face masks did not directly cause most deaths in the 1918 influenza pandemic.", with other supporting evidence, but due to misinterpreting the claim, it responded with Supported. It had enough information to completely fact-check the claim, but it gives an incorrect verdict. Another issue is that the LLM sometimes just provides a justification instead of a verdict, even when prompted that it must produce a verdict. These issues are the most common cause of errors, and they are not due to ClaimCheck's system architecture. To address problems with verdict prediction, reasoning models fine-tuned on a large corpus of fact-checks could enhance LLMs' understanding of fact-checking procedures and improve verdict prediction performance.

Another source of error with ClaimCheck is the evidence curation. The evidence curation step is necessary due to the models not being able to judge evidence relevance when doing verdict prediction, but this sometimes results in useful evidence being excluded. Moreover, the lack of support to use image and video evidence hinders ClaimCheck's ability to fact-check some claims, particularly where quote or action verification is required.

When fact-check articles are retrieved by the Web search, the article might contain fact-checks of multiple claims. The LLM might use one of the other fact-checks as evidence instead of the fact-check pertaining to the claim, leading to incorrect evidence being used for verdict prediction. Similarly, another issue is irrelevant evidence making it past the evidence curation stage, which overloads the LLM with information, leading to incorrect verdict prediction. These are issues with the smaller LLMs, due to their limited reasoning capability (Wang et al., 2025).

5 Discussion

5.1 System Architecture Trade-offs

The architectural framework of ClaimCheck represents a significant departure from contemporary state-of-the-art systems such as InFact (Rothermel et al., 2024) and HerO (Yoon et al., 2024). Whereas these established systems rely on pre-collected knowledge bases, ClaimCheck implements a dynamic Web search methodology that facilitates real-time information access and enhanced temporal processing. This approach requires careful consideration of the associated challenges, such as the system's occasional retrieval of extraneous or redundant information, necessitating the evidence curation step, which can impact system performance.

Evidence Retrieval Quality It can be concluded that the evidence retrieval system is functioning effectively, as all claims using novel claim processing have supporting evidence, and 98% of questions are fully answered. However, for 28.4% of claims, all of the retrieved evidence is discarded. This might suggest that the major bottleneck in the ClaimCheck system is the evidence retrieval system, as relevant evidence is not being retrieved.

Claim-Matching Strategy The empirical effectiveness of the claim-matching component, successfully processing 15.8% of claims, as shown in Table 3, demonstrates the value of leveraging existing fact-checks. This methodological enhancement, notably absent from FEVER-24 submissions, yields a noticeable improvement in accuracy (+2.8%) compared to using novel claim processing only for all claims. Fact-check articles could possibly even be useful for checking novel claims, as this could give valuable context about the claims. The success of this approach indicates that future system architectures might benefit from implementing a hybrid methodology that synthesizes both pre-existing fact-checks and real-time evidence acquisition.

Question Generation Allowing the LLM to generate questions without specifying a required number of questions appears to have increased the quality of the questions. However, this has also led to aspects of the claim not being fact-checked correctly, due to the nature of small LLMs. This could possibly be solved by fine-tuning or reinforcement learning using the small LLMs.

Another approach considered was leveraging the misinformation sites provided by AVeriTeC, along with some satire sites, to identify claims originating from these sources. This could offer a straightforward method to flag potential misinformation. However, in the development set, no claims were found to originate from these sources, and only 52.4% of all claims had origin URLs available. This suggests that such an approach may have limited effectiveness due to the low availability of origin URLs and the lack of overlap between claims and known misinformation sources.

5.2 Small Language Models in Fact-Checking

The usage of small LLMs in fact-checking tasks has both significant potential and inherent limitations. While these models offer considerable advantages in terms of computational efficiency and accessibility, they are subpar for complex reasoning tasks. In the error analysis, we have noticed that smaller

Claim	Predicted Verdict	LLM-generated Justification	Error
Even if your mail-in ballot is postmarked prior to the Election day but arrives after the Election day it will be thrown out.	N/A	The article discusses potential risks associated with following Trump's advice during the election, particularly concerning long lines at polling places. Experts note that such behavior could exacerbate existing infrastructure challenges posed by the pandemic, indicating that this scenario is plausible and thus supports the idea of chaos on Election Day.	No verdict generated.
Illegal drug, border crossings, and human smuggling activities have decreased in areas where barriers are deployed in the United States.	Refuted	This claim is refuted. According to the QA Pairs provided it seems that there was no evidence found for this claim.	Incorrect understanding of verdict definitions.
Donald Trump said that $15 an hour is too much for essential workers	Refuted	The claim states that Joe Biden commented on Donald Trumps statement. There was no proof of this in the QA pairs, Therefore it's refuted.	Incorrect claim interpretation.
There is a scam involving Santander customers being sent fake bank cards.	Refuted	Q&A 1 gives no evidence for the claim so it is refuted.	Uses incorrect verdict.

Table 4: Example of LLM-caused errors in verdict prediction.

LLMs sometimes do not follow instructions when the prompt is very large, particularly for question answering and verdict prediction, both being RAG tasks. This can result in incorrect claim interpretation or not recognizing unusable evidence, which necessitated the evidence curation step.

The verdict generation phase was challenging for small language models. The error analysis revealed instances where the LLM produced justifications on the claim without providing a verdict. These findings suggest that while small language models can effectively manage generation tasks within the fact-checking pipeline, their performance is subpar for retrieval tasks such as question answering. This might indicate that larger LLMs, finetuned smaller LLMs, or RAG-specific language models might perform better for this step. Examples of common errors made by LLMs in verdict prediction are given as examples in Table 4.

Notably, the fine-tuned Qwen2.5-7B model's superior performance suggests that fine-tuning can help overcome some of the inherent limitations of smaller language models in complex reasoning tasks like verdict prediction. The major issue for non-fine-tuned models is the tendency for models to select Not Enough Evidence even when there is enough evidence to reach a verdict. In Malon (2024), only the Supported and Refuted classes were the only classes the LLM could predict.

5.3 Real-World Applicability

The system design underlying ClaimCheck is to demonstrate the effectiveness of small LLMs on real-world claims, such as those in AVeriTeC. The use of small, open-source language models could help mitigate the spread of misinformation on social media. The Web evidence retrieval can more easily handle novel claims, compared to a static knowledge base, particularly on claims about recent events. This makes it better suited for fact-checking the rapidly evolving claims found online.

This choice of using small LLMs presents distinct challenges. While offering enhanced efficiency, small language models necessitate more tasks in the fact-checking pipeline, which could lead to more sources of error. The system's LLM-agnostic design allows for improvements as LLM capabilities advance. Nevertheless, the results suggest that accessible fact-checking tools utilizing small language models can provide substantial support for fact-checking tasks, particularly when integrated with claim-matching.

6 Conclusion

ClaimCheck demonstrates the viability of Web evidence retrieval for automatic fact-checking systems using smaller language models. It achieved 0.626 accuracy on the AVeriTeC benchmark dataset. Our approach establishes essential procedures for end-to-end fact-checking systems without relying on resource-intensive larger models. By developing an LLM-size agnostic process, we ensure that ClaimCheck can benefit from future LLM advancements while maintaining independence from specific model designs. We additionally show that claim matching can be a useful evidence retrieval approach to fact-checking non-novel claims.

The use of small, open-source LLMs enhances

reproducibility and accessibility. Our online search mechanism efficiently leverages external search algorithms to retrieve only the most relevant evidence, significantly reducing computational resource demands compared to retrieving and analyzing information from knowledge bases. However, challenges with evidence quality necessitated our multi-question approach and content curation task.

Future work could explore iterative systems rather than single-pass frameworks, incorporate multimedia analysis capabilities for social media claims, and investigate targeted fine-tuning approaches that balance performance improvements with system independence.

Limitations

The current implementation of ClaimCheck exhibits several significant limitations that warrant consideration. The system's inability to process non-textual information substantially restricts its efficacy in addressing social media claims, where misinformation frequently propagates through visual media. The Web-based evidence retrieval system, while providing access to current information, occasionally yields irrelevant or unreliable sources that may compromise verification accuracy. Furthermore, the system's dependence on English-language fact-checking websites introduces limitations in global applicability.

Ethics and Risks

Beyond technical constraints, the system's reliance on fact-checking websites raises substantial ethical considerations. The selection criteria for trusted fact-checking domains may introduce systematic biases in evidence selection. Moreover, the automated nature of the system could potentially lead to excessive reliance on machine-generated verdicts without appropriate human oversight. Future research directions should address these limitations while maintaining system accessibility and efficiency, potentially through the implementation of enhanced source validation mechanisms and support for multiple languages and modalities.

Acknowledgements

We extend our gratitude to the Texas Advanced Computing Center (TACC) for providing computational resources used in this work's experiments.

References

Adrien Barbaresi. 2021. Trafilatura: A web scraping library and command-line tool for text discovery and extraction. In *Proceedings of the 59th Annual Meeting of the Association for Computational Linguistics and the 11th International Joint Conference on Natural Language Processing: System Demonstrations*, pages 122–131, Online. Association for Computational Linguistics.

Tobias Braun, Mark Rothermel, Marcus Rohrbach, and Anna Rohrbach. 2024. DEFAME: Dynamic evidence-based fact-checking with multimodal experts. *arXiv preprint arXiv:2412.10510*.

Canyu Chen and Kai Shu. 2024. Can LLM-generated misinformation be detected? In *The Twelfth International Conference on Learning Representations*.

Alphaeus Eric Dmonte, Roland Oruche, Marcos Zampieri, Prasad Calyam, and Isabelle Augenstein. 2024. Claim Verification in the Age of Large Language Models: A Survey. *ArXiv*, abs/2408.14317.

Jan Drchal, Herbert Ullrich, Tomás Mlynár, and Václav Moravec. 2023. Pipeline and Dataset Generation for Automated Fact-checking in Almost Any Language. *ArXiv*, abs/2312.10171.

Zhijiang Guo, Michael Schlichtkrull, and Andreas Vlachos. 2022. A survey on automated fact-checking. *Transactions of the Association for Computational Linguistics*, 10:178–206.

Naeemul Hassan, Gensheng Zhang, Fatma Arslan, Josue Caraballo, Damian Jimenez, Siddhant Gawsane, Shohedul Hasan, Minumol Joseph, Aaditya Kulkarni, Anil Kumar Nayak, Vikas Sable, Chengkai Li, and Mark Tremayne. 2017. ClaimBuster: The first-ever end-to-end fact-checking system. *Proceedings of the VLDB Endowment*, 10:1945–1948.

Tsun hin Cheung and Kin Man Lam. 2023. FactLLaMA: Optimizing instruction-following language models with external knowledge for automated fact-checking. *2023 Asia Pacific Signal and Information Processing Association Annual Summit and Conference (APSIPA ASC)*, pages 846–853.

Edward J Hu, Yelong Shen, Phillip Wallis, Zeyuan Allen-Zhu, Yuanzhi Li, Shean Wang, Lu Wang, and Weizhu Chen. 2022. LoRA: Low-rank adaptation of large language models. In *International Conference on Learning Representations*.

Hasan Iqbal, Yuxia Wang, Minghan Wang, Georgi Nenkov Georgiev, Jiahui Geng, Iryna Gurevych, and Preslav Nakov. 2024. OpenFactCheck: A unified framework for factuality evaluation of LLMs. In *Proceedings of the 2024 Conference on Empirical Methods in Natural Language Processing: System Demonstrations*, pages 219–229, Miami, Florida, USA. Association for Computational Linguistics.

Mohammed Abdul Khaliq, Paul Yu-Chun Chang, Mingyang Ma, Bernhard Pflugfelder, and Filip Miletić. 2024. RAGAR, your falsehood radar: RAG-augmented reasoning for political fact-checking using multimodal large language models. In *Proceedings of the Seventh Fact Extraction and VERification Workshop (FEVER)*, pages 280–296, Miami, Florida, USA. Association for Computational Linguistics.

Christopher Malon. 2024. Multi-hop evidence pursuit meets the web: Team papelo at FEVER 2024. In *Proceedings of the Seventh Fact Extraction and VERification Workshop (FEVER)*, pages 27–36, Miami, Florida, USA. Association for Computational Linguistics.

Cheng Niu, Yang Guan, Yuanhao Wu, Juno Zhu, Juntong Song, Randy Zhong, Kaihua Zhu, Siliang Xu, Shizhe Diao, and Tong Zhang. 2024. VeraCT scan: Retrieval-augmented fake news detection with justifiable reasoning. In *Proceedings of the 62nd Annual Meeting of the Association for Computational Linguistics (Volume 3: System Demonstrations)*, pages 266–277, Bangkok, Thailand. Association for Computational Linguistics.

Baolin Peng, Michel Galley, Pengcheng He, Hao Cheng, Yujia Xie, Yu Hu, Qiuyuan Huang, Lars Liden, Zhou Yu, Weizhu Chen, and Jianfeng Gao. 2023. Check your facts and try again: Improving large language models with external knowledge and automated feedback. *ArXiv*.

Mark Rothermel, Tobias Braun, Marcus Rohrbach, and Anna Rohrbach. 2024. InFact: A strong baseline for automated fact-checking. In *Proceedings of the Seventh Fact Extraction and VERification Workshop (FEVER)*, pages 108–112, Miami, Florida, USA. Association for Computational Linguistics.

Daniel Russo, Stefano Menini, Jacopo Staiano, and Marco Guerini. 2024. Face the facts! Evaluating RAG-based fact-checking pipelines in realistic settings. *Preprint*, arXiv:2412.15189.

Michael Schlichtkrull, Yulong Chen, Chenxi Whitehouse, Zhenyun Deng, Mubashara Akhtar, Rami Aly, Zhijiang Guo, Christos Christodoulopoulos, Oana Cocarascu, Arpit Mittal, James Thorne, and Andreas Vlachos. 2024a. The automated verification of textual claims (AVeriTeC) shared task. In *Proceedings of the Seventh Fact Extraction and VERification Workshop (FEVER)*, pages 1–26, Miami, Florida, USA. Association for Computational Linguistics.

Michael Schlichtkrull, Yulong Chen, Chenxi Whitehouse, Zhenyun Deng, Mubashara Akhtar, Rami Aly, Zhijiang Guo, Christos Christodoulopoulos, Oana Cocarascu, Arpit Mittal, James Thorne, and Andreas Vlachos, editors. 2024b. *Proceedings of the Seventh Fact Extraction and VERification Workshop (FEVER)*. Association for Computational Linguistics, Miami, Florida, USA.

Michael Sejr Schlichtkrull, Zhijiang Guo, and Andreas Vlachos. 2023. AVeriTeC: A dataset for real-world claim verification with evidence from the web. In *Thirty-seventh Conference on Neural Information Processing Systems Datasets and Benchmarks Track*.

Dan Schumacher, Fatemeh Haji, Tara Grey, Niharika Bandlamudi, Nupoor Karnik, Gagana Uday Kumar, Jason Cho-Yu Chiang, Paul Rad, Nishant Vishwamitra, and Anthony Rios. 2024. Context matters: An empirical study of the impact of contextual information in temporal question answering systems. *Preprint*, arXiv:2406.19538.

Connor Shorten, Charles Pierse, Thomas Benjamin Smith, Erika Cardenas, Akanksha Sharma, John Trengrove, and Bob van Luijt. 2024. StructuredRAG: JSON response formatting with large language models. *Preprint*, arXiv:2408.11061.

Ronit Singal, Pransh Patwa, Parth Patwa, Aman Chadha, and Amitava Das. 2024. Evidence-backed fact checking using RAG and few-shot in-context learning with LLMs. In *Proceedings of the Seventh Fact Extraction and VERification Workshop (FEVER)*, pages 91–98, Miami, Florida, USA. Association for Computational Linguistics.

Herbert Ullrich, Jan Drchal, Martin Rýpar, Hana Vincourová, and Václav Moravec. 2023. CsFEVER and CTKFacts: acquiring Czech data for fact verification. *Language Resources and Evaluation*, 57(4):1571–1605.

Ivan Vykopal, Matúš Pikuliak, Simon Ostermann, and Marián Simko. 2024. Generative large language models in automated fact-checking: A survey. *ArXiv*, abs/2407.02351.

Fali Wang, Zhiwei Zhang, Xianren Zhang, Zongyu Wu, Tzuhao Mo, Qiuhao Lu, Wanjing Wang, Rui Li, Junjie Xu, Xianfeng Tang, Qi He, Yao Ma, Ming Huang, and Suhang Wang. 2024a. A comprehensive survey of small language models in the era of large language models: Techniques, enhancements, applications, collaboration with LLMs, and trustworthiness. *ArXiv*, abs/2411.03350.

Ning Wang, Yun Xiao, Xiaopeng Peng, Xiaojun Chang, Xuanhong Wang, and Dingyi Fang. 2024b. ContextDet: Temporal action detection with adaptive context aggregation. *Preprint*, arXiv:2410.15279.

Yuxia Wang, Minghan Wang, Hasan Iqbal, Georgi N. Georgiev, Jiahui Geng, Iryna Gurevych, and Preslav Nakov. 2025. OpenFactCheck: Building, benchmarking customized fact-checking systems and evaluating the factuality of claims and LLMs. In *Proceedings of the 31st International Conference on Computational Linguistics*, pages 11399–11421, Abu Dhabi, UAE. Association for Computational Linguistics.

Yejun Yoon, Jaeyoon Jung, Seunghyun Yoon, and Kunwoo Park. 2024. HerO at AVeriTeC: The herd of open large language models for verifying real-world claims. In *Proceedings of the Seventh Fact Extraction and VERification Workshop (FEVER)*, pages 130–136, Miami, Florida, USA. Association for Computational Linguistics.

Listing 1: Prompt for Article Summarization

```
Can this fact-checking article provide a complete fact-check for the claim, including a clear verdict and
     justification with relevant evidence?
Take into account the claim date and any other information important for fact-checking the claim.

Possible Verdicts:
- Supported: The knowledge from the fact-check supports or at least strongly implies the claim. Mere
     plausibility is not enough for this decision.
- Refuted: The knowledge from the fact-check clearly refutes the claim. The mere absence or lack of
     supporting evidence is not enough reason for being refuted (argument from ignorance). This includes
     fake news and deliberate misinformation.
- Conflicting Evidence/Cherrypicking: The knowledge from the fact-check contains conflicting evidence from
     multiple reliable sources. Even trying to resolve the conflicting sources through additional
     investigation was not successful.

Claim: {claim}
Article: {article_text}
If the article cannot fulfill this requirement, respond with "No answer found." Otherwise, gather the key
     evidence from the article that can be used for fact checking the claim and summarize them in at most
     one paragraph.
```

Listing 2: Prompt for Claim Reformulation

```
# Instructions
You are presented with a raw claim, with additional metadata like Content date or speaker. **Your task right
     now is to interpret the claim.** That is, identify the speaker's core message and write down the main
     point(s) using your own words. Do not ask any questions and only use the metadata provided to interpret
     the claim. Be concise and write only one paragraph.

# Content
Original Claim: {claim}
Metadata:
     - Speaker: {speaker}
     - Date: {claim_date}
     - Origin URL: {original_claim_url}
     - Reporting Source: {reporting_source}
     - Location ISO Code: {location_ISO_code}

# Interpretation
```

Listing 3: Prompt for Question Generation

```
# Instructions
You are a fact-checker verifying a claim. Your task is to generate clear, specific, and relevant fact-
    checking questions that help assess the accuracy of the claim.

**Guidelines:**
- Focus on the essential details of the claim. The questions should help find direct evidence to confirm or
    refute it.
- Only use metadata (such as date, speaker, or source) when it is necessary for verification (e.g., when
    time-sensitive or quote verification is in question).
- Each question should be concise and directly related to the claim.
- Format each question using backticks like `this`.
- Do not repeat questions already addressed in prior fact-checking records.

**Examples:**
Claim: "New Zealand's new Food Bill bans gardening."
Questions:
1. Does New Zealand's Food Bill ban home gardening?
2. What are the key regulations in the New Zealand Food Bill related to gardening?
3. Has the New Zealand government enforced any gardening restrictions under this bill?

Claim: "Video of a man blowing vape smoke through various face masks shows that they do not help prevent the
    spread of coronavirus."
Questions:
1. How does coronavirus spread?
2. Do scientific studies show that face masks reduce the spread of coronavirus?
3. Does the ability of vape smoke to pass through a mask indicate ineffectiveness against viruses?

Claim: "The Nigerian government is donating $600 million to Democratic presidential nominee Joe Biden's
    campaign."
Questions:
1. Is there evidence that the Nigerian government donated $600 million to Joe Biden's campaign?
2. Are foreign governments legally allowed to donate to U.S. presidential campaigns?
3. Has the Biden campaign reported any donations from Nigeria?

# Claim to Verify
Claim: {claim}
Metadata: {metadata}

## Questions:
```

Listing 4: Prompt for Query Generation

```
# Instructions
You are a fact-checker optimizing a question for web search to retrieve relevant evidence.

**Guidelines:**
- Ensure the query makes sense in the context of the question.
- Add claim-specific context only if absolutely necessary to improve relevance.
- Keep the query concise and structured for effective search results.
- Format the final query using backticks like `this` (without extra formatting or explanation).

## Question
{question}

## Claim
{claim}

## Search Query:
```

Listing 5: Prompt for Question Answering

```
Instructions
You are a fact-checker. Your overall motivation is to verify a given Claim. In order to find evidence that
     helps the fact-checking work, you just ran a web search which yielded a Search Result. Your task right
     now is to answer the Question given below. Adhere to the following rules:

The length of your Answer should be between one sentence and one paragraph.
If applicable and useful, you may directly cite relevant excerpts from the source. In that case, put the
     citation into quotation marks.
If the search result does not contain sufficient information to answer the Question or is unrelated to the
     question completely, respond simply with Answer Not Found.
If the evidence does not answer the question, but can otherwise be highly useful for the fact-check, you
     must respond with "The evidence is useful, but does not answer the question." This is a very rare case.

Claim: {claim}

Question
{question}

Search Result
Summary: {snippet}

Evidence:
{evidence_text}

Your Answer
```

Listing 6: Prompt for Evidence Curation

```
Instructions
You are a fact-checker. Your overall motivation is to verify a given Claim. In order to find evidence that
     helps the fact-checking work, you just ran a web search which yielded a Search Result. Your task right
     now is to determine if the Answer is useful to fact-checking the Claim. Follow the following rules:
An answer is useful even when it doesn't directly answer the question, if it provides highly relevant
     information for fact-checking. It just has to be somewhat related to the Claim.
If the Answer is useful to fact-checking the Claim, respond only with "Yes".
If the Answer is not useful to fact-checking the Claim, respond only with "No".

Claim: {claim}

Question and Answer: {answer}
```

Listing 7: Prompt for Verdict Prediction

```
# Fact-Checking Analysis Task

## Objective
Analyze the provided evidence and QA pairs to determine the veracity of the claim using the structured
    methodology below.
Must output the data in the structured JSON format, not just as text. The verdict must be one of the
    following options: Supported, Refuted, Conflicting Evidence/Cherrypicking, Not Enough Evidence.
---

## Verification Protocol

1. **Evidence Synthesis**
   - Identify factual anchors in both evidence and QA responses
   - Note contradictions, corroborations, and evidence quality

2. **Verdict Determination**
   Select ONE of the below verdicts using these strict criteria:

   **Supported**
   - Evidence conclusively proves claim true
   - Multiple credible sources align without contradiction

   **Refuted**
   - Evidence disproves central claim elements
   - Includes fabricated content/deceptive practices
   - Lack of any credible sources supporting the claim

   **Conflicting Evidence/Cherrypicking**
   - Reputable sources directly contradict each other
   - No resolvable consensus after analysis

   **Not Enough Evidence**
   - No relevant evidence found after exhaustive search
   - Claim too vague for substantive evaluation
   *(Last-resort option only)*

   Do not select any other verdicts.

---

## Input Data
**Claim to Evaluate**
{claim}

**Relevant Evidence**
{relevant_evidence}

**QA Pair Analysis**
{qa_text}

---

## Output Requirements

Must output the data in the following JSON format, no exceptions.:

**JSON Structure**
```json
{{
    "classification": "One of the above verdict options",
    "justification": "Cohesive analysis paragraph of reasoning for the selected verdict"
}}
```
Example Output:

```json
{{
    "classification": "Refuted",
    "justification": "The evidence and answers show that the claim was published on a fake news site, so the
        claim is refuted."
}}
```
```

Can dependency parses facilitate generalization in language models? A case study of cross-lingual relation extraction

Ritam Dutt, Shounak Sural, Carolyn Penstein Rosé
Carnegie Mellon University
{rdutt,ssural,cprose}@andrew.cmu.edu

Abstract

In this work, we propose DEPGEN, a framework for evaluating the generalization capabilities of language models on the task of relation extraction, with dependency parses as scaffolds. We use a GNN-based framework that takes dependency parses as input and learns embeddings of entities which are augmented to a baseline multilingual encoder. We also investigate the role of dependency parses when they are included as part of the prompt to LLMs in a zero-shot learning setup. We observe that including off-the-shelf dependency parses can aid relation extraction, with the best performing model having a mild relative improvement of 0.91% and 1.5% in the in-domain and zero-shot setting respectively across two datasets. For the in-context learning setup, we observe an average improvement of 1.67%, with significant gains for low-performing LLMs. We also carry out extensive statistical analysis to investigate how different factors such as the choice of the dependency parser or the nature of the prompt impact performance. We make our code and results publicly available for the research community at https://github.com/ShoRit/multilingual-re.git

1 Introduction

Information packaging in language does not happen arbitrarily (Croft, 2022). The "internal structure" of a text message, which determines how the message is constructed or parsed, is grounded in predefined linguistic rules in the form of syntax and semantics. Linguistic structures such as dependency graphs (Zeman et al., 2019; Chomsky, 2002) or semantic parses (Banarescu et al., 2013; Reddy et al., 2017) have been pivotal in the history of NLP research both for their intrinsic merit i.e. developing frameworks that can construct or interpret such structures automatically (Chen et al., 2024; Gu et al., 2024), and their external value as augmentations to aid language understanding tasks (Ding et al., 2024; Şahin, 2022).

Information extraction or IE is one such field which had relied heavily on linguistic information ever since its inception; some notable examples include few-shot named entity recognition or NER (Chen et al., 2023; Xie et al., 2024), relation extraction (Li et al., 2023; Zhou et al., 2024), open-domain question answering, (Zhang et al., 2023b, 2024) amongst others. However, recent years have witnessed a decline in the adoption of linguistic frameworks in favor of large scale pre-trained language models (Devlin et al., 2018; Liu et al., 2019; Conneau et al., 2020a; Sainz et al., 2024) which are shown to encode syntactic and semantic information within their parameters (Starace et al., 2023; Liu et al., 2024) and have also demonstrated significant improvements on IE (Sainz et al., 2024; Efeoglu and Paschke, 2024).

Moreover, as we usher into an era of large language models, the question which looms over our head like the proverbial sword of Damocles "Are dependency parses helpful for information extraction?" We are motivated to answer this question based on the past work of Sachan et al. (2021) which showed the utility of adding syntactic information for different information extraction tasks in English. However, the observed benefits hold true only when the **gold parses** are available, with no improvements over the baseline in presence of off-the-shelf parses. In this study we expand upon this idea and investigate whether off-the-shelf dependency parses can assist language models in multilingual information extraction for both indomain and zero-shot transfer settings.

We specifically deal with the task of multilingual relation extraction, wherein we identify the nature of relationship between two annotated entities in a document. We show in Figure 1 how we can connect the entities wood and fences by traversing the dependency graph that connects these two entities, highlighting the potential utility of linguistic frameworks for this task. We explore the role

Proceedings of the 4th International Workshop on Knowledge-Augmented Methods for Natural Language Processing (KnowledgeNLP'25), pages 317–337
May 3, 2025

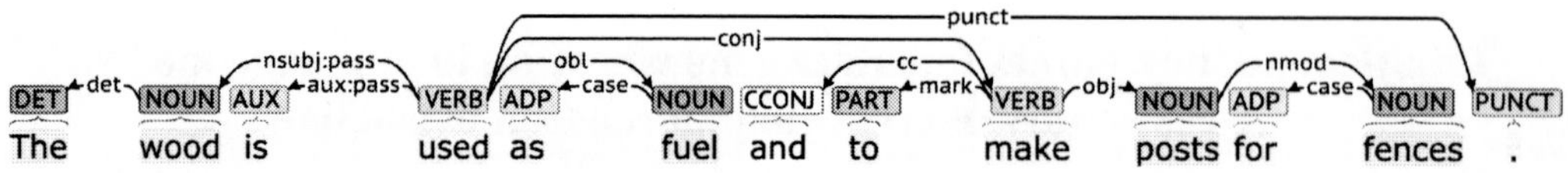

Figure 1: Example depicting the supplemental information provided by the *dependency tree*. The entities of interest are wood and fences, having the relationship material_used. The path *wood* ← *used* → *make* → *posts* → *fences* elicits this relationship.

of dependency parses for cross-lingual relation extraction in both a fine-tuned supervised setting and a prompting/ in-context learning setup.

We propose a framework, DEPGEN, built on top of a pretrained multi-lingual language model that uses dependency parse information to perform relation extraction for both in-domain and zero-shot cross-lingual transfer settings. Through a comprehensive set of 2440 experiments spanning 10 languages over 2 datasets, we observe that incorporating dependency information brings about modest improvements for in-domain and cross-lingual fine-tuning setups by 0.9% and 1.5% respectively.

We also carry out extensive statistical analysis to identify which factors significantly impact performance. Our observations highlight that performance improvements is mostly predicated by the choice of the target language, and the choice of the pre-trained language model rather than the choice of the dependency parser for all cases. However, for the in-context learning setup, we demonstrate that the performance is determined by the choice of the prompting strategy, with our proposed approach boasting the highest gains, i.e. an absolute improvement of 1.67 F1 score over the baseline.

2 Related Work

2.1 Generalization in Information Extraction

Recent years bear witness to countless research endeavors to facilitate generalizability and transfer across domains for several information extraction (IE) tasks. Such works include zero-shot relation extraction (Wang et al., 2022b; Jun et al., 2022; Li et al., 2023), zero-shot or few-shot NER (Zeng et al., 2022; Das et al., 2022; Xie et al., 2024) , zero-shot KBQA (Gu et al., 2021; Dutt et al., 2023), cross-lingual KBQA (Zhang et al., 2023a), and open domain QA (Min et al., 2020; Zhang et al., 2023b), amongst others (Fritzler et al., 2019; Zhou et al., 2019). This interest is in part due to the advent of large scale pre-trained language models such as Devlin et al. (2018); Liu et al. (2019); Conneau et al. (2020a); Sainz et al. (2024) which have shown significant improvements on IE. Recent works on domain adaptation and transfer learning have advocated different pre-training objective functions to ensure the model is well adapted to the particular domain. Other multi-lingual/ cross-lingual transfer works employ different data augmentation techniques such as translation into the target data to aid transfer. In this work, we investigate approaches to perform multi-lingual information extraction in a zero-shot setting without any additional data in the target language.

2.2 Relation Extraction

The goal of relation extraction or relation classification is to detect and classify the relation between specified entities in a text according to some predefined schema. Current research in RE has mostly been carried out in a few-shot or a zero-shot setting to address the dearth of training data (Liu et al., 2022; Li et al., 2023) and the "long-tail" problem of skewness in relation classes (Ye and Ling, 2019b; Liang et al., 2023). Salient work in that direction includes (i) designing RE-specific pretraining objectives for learning better representations (Baldini Soares et al., 2019; Wang et al., 2022a), (ii) incorporating meta-information such as relation descriptions (Yang et al., 2020; Chen and Li, 2021), a global relation graph, (Qu et al., 2020), or entity types (Peng et al., 2020), and (iii) leveraging additional information in the form of dependency parses (Yu et al., 2022), translated texts for multilingual RE (Nag et al., 2021), or distantly supervised instances (Zhao et al., 2021; Ye and Ling, 2019a). T-5 based models have shown to perform well in relation extraction settings with few-shot finetuning (Diaz-Garcia and Lopez, 2024).

Recently, LLMs have shown promise in zero-shot relation extraction. Challenging cases such as overlapping relations and none-of-the-above (nota) relations have been handled effectively by LLMs in zero-shot settings (Li et al., 2023). LLMs have also outperformed smaller models for RE with larger, document-level context sizes in models such as

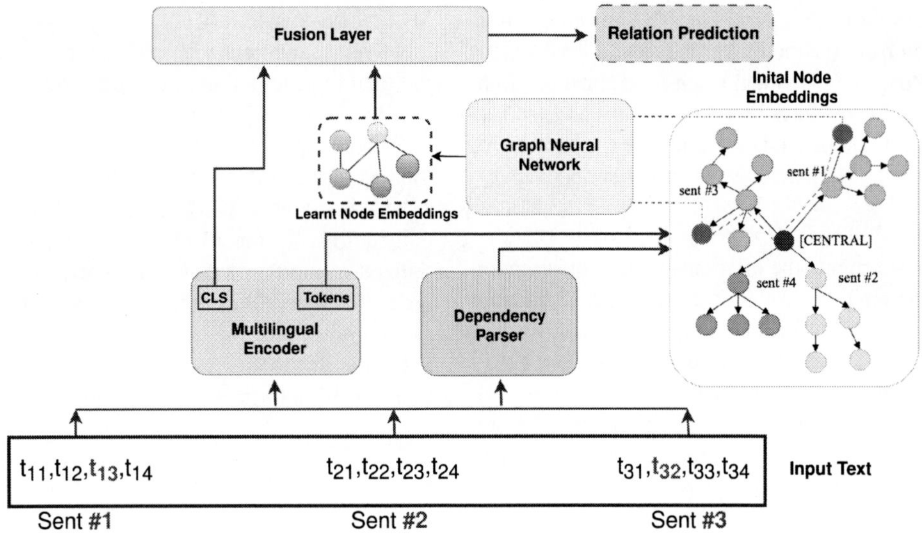

Figure 2: An overview of our proposed framework DEPGEN. The architecture takes as input a document, which comprises a sequence of sentences, with the entities highlighted in red. This document passes through a multilingual encoder to obtain the token embeddings, and a dependency parser that generates dependency parses for each sentence. The individual sentences in the dependency parser are connected using a central [CENTRAL] node to obtain a connected graph. The nodes are initialized using the embeddings obtained from the multilingual encoder and updated using a Graph Neural Network. The final representations of the entities obtained from the GNN are fused with the entity embeddings and concatenated with the [CLS] token of the document to predict the relation.

AutoRE (Xue et al., 2024). All of these techniques seek to alleviate the need for expensive human-annotated training data. In this work, we question whether incorporating linguistic structures in the form of dependency parsing as an explicit addition to the input in existing models can aid learning robust representations that can be transferred to other languages.

3 Methodology

We investigate the role of dependency parses for zero-shot cross-lingual relation extraction in two setups, namely (i) a fine-tuned setup where a model is first trained on a given source language and then evaluated on a target language, and (ii) an in-context-learning setup where we prompt an LLM to predict the relation between two specified entities in a zero-shot setting to test the innate capabilities of the LLM for RE.

3.1 Fine-Tuning Setting

We present a detailed description of our proposed framework, DEPGEN here. Our framework leverages the internal structure of a document text to aid relation classification. We define internal structure as the linguistic information encoded within the document based on syntactic rules in the form of dependency parses. This section describes the individual components that constitute our framework DEPGEN, namely the multilingual encoder, dependency parser, graph neural network, and the fusion layer. We dive deep into the methodology for representing the textual content, and elaborate on the approach employed for incorporating dependency parses for a given input sentence. Finally, we end the section with how the different modes of information are fused, and the classification setup. A pictorial representation of our framework can be seen in Figure 2 Our architecture involves the following components.

3.1.1 Multilingual Encoder

We experiment with mBERT (Devlin et al., 2018) and XLMR (Conneau et al., 2020c) as our multilingual text encoder to obtain representations of the input sentence(s). Past work has shown the efficacy of such contextual multilingual encoders in capturing long-range semantic dependency in text (Litschko et al., 2021). Similar to these works, we consider the final encoder layer representation of [CLS] token as the text representation. The sentence(s) are fed as input to the MULTILINGUAL

ENCODER (Figure 2) and the [CLS] token representation from the final layer is fed into the FUSION LAYER. The individual token representations from the final layer are used to initialize the node embeddings in the dependency graph of the INTERNAL STRUCTURE module, which we describe below.

3.1.2 Internal Structure

We incorporate the internal structure information by learning the syntactic dependency information between the tokens in the input sentence. We first pass the input tokens through a DEPENDENCY PARSER to obtain the dependency tree for each sentence. We then construct a dependency graph from the constituent dependency trees, which is then fed as input to a Graph Neural Network (GNN) (Scarselli et al., 2008). The various components of this module are as follows.

Dependency Parser To generate the dependency tree, we use off-the-shelf multilingual dependency parsing modules, i.e. Stanza (Qi et al., 2020a) and Trankit (Nguyen et al., 2021). The resulting dependency tree represents the syntactic dependency relations between the words in a sentence; the dependencies follow the Universal Dependencies formalism (Nivre et al., 2016; Zeman et al., 2019), resulting in 76 types of dependencies across the different languages for our experiments.

Dependency Graph Since the dependency tree is defined for a sentence, the output from DEPENDENCY PARSER will be in the form of a forest of disconnected dependency trees; for example 4 trees for 4 sentences in Figure 2. We add a pseudo node [CENTRAL] and add a new type of dependency relation [SENT] between the [CENTRAL] and all the [ROOT] nodes of the sentences. The proposed design has two benefits - (1) The [CENTRAL] node allows for information exchange between the sentences, which otherwise would probably lead to different clusters of representations (represented by colors in Figure 2) for nodes in different sentences, (2) The distance between the two entities is reduced (dotted red line in Figure 2) when the entities are present across two different sentences, resulting in an efficient information flow between them.

Graph Neural Network We represent each word as a node in the dependency graph and the dependency relations as the edges between the nodes. Each node in the graph is initialized with the representations obtained from the final layer of the MULTILINGUAL ENCODER. We aggregate the subtoken representations via max-pooling and obtain the final representation of a word. This initialization helps incorporate the semantic relationship between the nodes and facilitates end-to-end joint training of the MULTILINGUAL ENCODER and the INTERNAL STRUCTURE modules. The relation embeddings for the all the relation types are initialized at random and learnt jointly along with the node embeddings. The representations of the two entities from the multi-layer GNN are then fed to the FUSION LAYER along with the sentence representation for relation prediction.

3.1.3 Relation Prediction

We concatenate the representations obtained from the MULTILINGUAL ENCODER and the INTERNAL STRUCTURE modules in the FUSION LAYER and perform a multi-class classification for predicting the relation. During training, we compute the standard Cross Entropy loss, and back-propagate it jointly through all the components of the network.

3.2 In-context Learning Setting

In addition to the DEPGEN framework that encapsulates the fine-tuned setting, we also explore the role of dependency parses when provided as additional inputs to LLMs in a zero-shot prompting setup. We experiment with three different types of prompt formats that encodes the dependency information which we describe below.

Tuple Format: In the tuple-based prompt format, we simply provide the dependency parse as a list of tuples or dictionary keys. Each tuple comprises three elements, i.e. a node in the dependency graph or a word, the corresponding head node of that word, and the relation that connects the head node to the word. For example, the phrase "Porsche Panamera", would have the following information in the form of a tuple.

```
{
    word: Porsche
    head: Panamera,
    rel: compound
}
```

Text Format: Instead of providing the dependency parse information in the form of tuples, we verbalize the dependency relations between the words in the sentence in natural language format. In the above example of

"Porsche Panamera", we re-write the tuple information as `"Porsche is Compound noun modifier of Panamera"`. We do this for all the tuples in the dependency graph.

Filtered Text Format: As opposed to verbalizing all the tuples in the dependency graph, we filter out only the tuples that connect the two entities in the sentence via the dependency relations. Not only does this reduce the number of input tokens to the LLM, it also helps filter out redundant information.

As a control, we also prompt the models with only the text, without any dependency information, which serves as a baseline. The details of the prompts are in the Appendix.

4 Experimental Setup

4.1 Dataset

We conduct our experiments on relation extraction on two datasets i.e. IndoRE and REDFM.

IndoRE (Nag et al., 2021) The IndoRE dataset covers a diverse and rich set of entity and relation annotated sentences in three low resource Indian languages — Bengali (bn), Hindi (hi) and Telugu (te). To study protocols for transferring RE capability across languages, it also has labeled English (en) RE instances as an example of a resource-high language. The dataset consists of 32,610 sentences combining all four languages from Wikidata where each language contains 51 unique relations. Out of these languages, we exclude Bengali from our experiments because the dependency parsers' inability to parse the language.

REDFM (Huguet Cabot et al., 2023) We use this dataset consisting of examples from 7 languages. These languages include English (en), Arabic (ar), Spanish (es), German (de), Italian (it), French (fr), and Chinese (zh), which are hand-annotated. There are a total of about 15,400 examples in the dataset with a total of 32 types of relations. We use the languages en, es, de, it, and fr for training (i.e. source languages), and all the 7 languages for testing in a zero-shot setting (i.e. target languages). We exclude Arabic and Chinese as source language due to the unavailability of a training split in the REDFM dataset. We use the train/validation/test splits as in the original paper.

4.2 Fine-tuned Experimental Setup

We experiment with the following settings:

1. **Baseline:** We experiment with mBERT (Devlin et al., 2019) and XLMR (Conneau et al., 2020b) as our choices to encode the document text and the entity spans. We concatenate the pooled representation of the entities and the [CLS] embedding and use it for relation classification.

2. **Dependency Parses:** We experiment with Trankit (Nguyen et al., 2021) and Stanza (Qi et al., 2020b) as the choice of the dependency parser across all languages for both datasets.

3. **Graph Neural Network:** We experiment with RGCN (Schlichtkrull et al., 2018) and RGAT (Busbridge et al., 2019) as the backbone GNN architecture to encode the dependency information between words in the document. We use a GNN with 2 hidden layers for all our experiments.

4.3 In-context Learning Experimental Setup

We employ three different instruction-tuned LLMs for our in-context learning experiments, i.e. LLaMA (Meta-Llama-3-8B-Instruct) (Grattafiori et al., 2024), Mistral (Mistral-7B-Instruct-v0.3) (Jiang et al., 2023) and Qwen (Qwen2-7B-Instruct) (Yang et al., 2024). We use instruction-tuned LLMs since we wish to employ these LLMs in a zero-shot setup for relation extraction without fine-tuning or additional training. Similar to the fine-tuned experimental setup, the dependency parse information are obtained from two sources, i.e. Stanza and Trankit.

4.4 Experiment Counts

For in-domain, we have a total of 8 languages (5 for RedFM, 3 for IndoRE) for 2 given choices of encoder, parser and GNN. Each experiment is repeated for 5 seeds resulting in a total of 320 experiments, that include dependency information and an additional 80 experiments (over 8 languages, 2 encoders, and 5 seeds) as the baseline. For the zero-shot cross-lingual transfer setting, for RedFM, we have 6 possible target languages for each of the 5 source languages, while for IndoRE, we have 2 possible targets for each of the 3 source languages. Thus for each 36 possible cross-lingual pairs, we evaluate 50 different combination of encoder, parser, GNN, and seeds, resulting in another 1800 experiments. Finally, in the in-context learning setup for LLMs, we experiment with 3 LLMs for 10 languages over 4 kinds of prompts (including

				RedFM				IndoRE	
				mBERT					
DEP	GNN	en	es	fr	it	de	en	hi	te
-	-	84.3±0.7	80.0±0.6	78.6±0.3	76.3±0.8	78.7±0.3	94.3±0.6	89.6±0.4	84.9±0.4
stanza	rgcn	**85.7±0.8**	80.5±1.0	79.7±1.0	78.2±0.5	80.0±0.9	94.4±0.2	**90.9±0.3**	**86.1±0.9**
stanza	rgat	85.2±1.4	**82.2±0.6**	79.9±0.4	77.9±1.2	**80.5±0.6**	**94.9±0.3**	89.5±1.4	85.9±1.1
trankit	rgcn	84.3±0.4	81.8±0.8	**80.7±0.8**	**78.9±0.7**	79.7±0.9	94.0±0.2	89.7±0.1	85.9±1.9
trankit	rgat	85.5±1.3	80.9±0.3	80.2±0.2	77.3±0.8	78.9±0.7	94.1±0.5	88.9±0.5	84.6±0.8
				XLMR					
-	-	**84.0±1.1**	77.2±2.0	76.2±1.0	74.8±1.2	75.2±0.6	92.1±0.8	88.7±0.9	**86.3±1.1**
stanza	rgcn	83.7±0.6	76.8±0.8	**76.7±0.9**	73.3±0.7	75.7±1.5	91.8±0.8	89.6±1.1	85.6±0.7
stanza	rgat	**84.0±0.8**	**77.5±1.4**	74.4±0.9	**75.6±1.2**	**76.2±1.1**	92.2±0.4	**89.9±0.9**	85.7±0.6
trankit	rgcn	83.8±0.5	76.4±1.1	74.7±1.0	72.6±2.3	73.9±2.6	91.9±0.9	**89.9±0.8**	85.2±0.5
trankit	rgat	82.6±0.8	77.3±0.2	75.0±0.3	74.0±1.7	75.9±0.1	**92.6±0.7**	89.2±1.0	85.9±1.6

Table 1: In-domain RE performance of mBERT and XLMR on RedFM and IndoRE, with dependency information (i.e. choice of the parser or DEP, and the choice of the GNN used to encode the information, i.e. GNN). Results are averaged across the top 3 seeds, with the highest values in each column bolded.

				RedFM						IndoRE	
					mBERT						
DEP	GNN	en	es	fr	it	de	ar	zh	en	hi	te
-	-	77.5±1.1	81.0±1.1	78.8±1.1	76.7±1.1	75.6±1.1	72.5±1.1	70.0±1.1	57.5±1.8	57.6±2.7	42.4±2.4
stanza	rgcn	78.2±0.8	81.0±0.8	**79.5±0.8**	**76.8±0.8**	77.1±0.8	72.6±0.8	70.0±0.8	57.0±1.0	57.1±0.8	44.6±1.2
stanza	rgat	78.0±1.0	81.1±1.0	78.8±1.0	76.5±1.0	77.2±1.0	**73.2±1.0**	**70.4±1.0**	56.4±1.2	57.7±1.2	**45.2±1.4**
trankit	rgcn	**78.7±0.8**	**81.3±0.8**	79.3±0.8	75.4±0.8	77.8±0.8	72.8±0.8	70.0±0.8	**57.9±0.8**	**59.1±0.6**	44.9±1.6
trankit	rgat	77.9±0.8	80.6±0.8	79.1±0.8	76.3±0.8	**77.9±0.8**	73.1±0.8	**70.4±0.8**	57.1±1.4	57.9±1.8	45.1±1.7
					XLMR						
-	-	72.7±1.4	74.2±1.4	72.2±1.4	66.8±1.4	70.7±1.4	61.8±1.4	63.1±1.4	50.0±2.2	55.1±1.5	45.9±1.6
stanza	rgcn	**73.4±1.4**	74.5±1.4	73.2±1.4	67.7±1.4	70.3±1.4	61.2±1.4	**63.9±1.4**	49.3±1.8	55.4±1.4	46.1±1.7
stanza	rgat	73.3±1.5	74.3±1.5	**73.4±1.5**	**67.9±1.5**	68.4±1.5	61.1±1.5	63.2±1.5	50.0±1.6	53.8±2.8	46.3±2.0
trankit	rgcn	73.1±1.3	74.7±1.3	73.1±1.3	66.8±1.3	69.5±1.3	**62.7±1.3**	63.8±1.3	50.7±0.7	**56.3±1.1**	45.5±2.9
trankit	rgat	73.1±1.1	**75.7±1.1**	**73.4±1.1**	65.9±1.1	**70.9±1.1**	62.1±1.1	63.6±1.1	**50.8±1.4**	56.0±2.2	**46.9±2.6**

Table 2: Zero-shot Cross-lingual RE performance on RedFM and IndoRE with mBERT and XLMR as the multilingual encoders with different combinations of dependency information. For a given target language, we average the performance across the different source languages. The highest values in each column are highlighted in bold. Detailed individual cross-lingual performance metrics are given in the Appendix.

the baseline), and 2 kinds of parsers (Stanza and Dependency), resulting in a suite of 240 prompting experiments. Our final experimental suite thus comprises 2440 experiments.

5 Results and Insights

In this section, we pose the following research questions (RQs) and attempt to answer the same.

RQ1. Impact of dependency parses on RE for indomain and cross-lingual transfer ?

We report the in-domain and cross-lingual relation extraction performance with mBERT and XLMR as the multilingual encoders, stanza and trankit as the choice of the off-shelf-parsers, and RGCN and RGAT being the backbone GNN for both the IndoRE and RedFM datasets, in Tables 1 and 2 respectively.

At the outset, we observe that across both datasets, adding dependency information generally improves performance over the baseline in the in-domain setting; we see higher gains when we have mBERT as the MLM as opposed to XLMR. We also observe that the gains are higher for the REDFM dataset than IndoRE, possibly due to the poorer quality of dependency parses on low-resource languages like Hindi and Telugu, as opposed to standard high-resource cases like English, Spanish, and Italian. In fact, for all languages other than English, we see a consistent improvement in F1-score of approximately 2.0% and 1.0% with

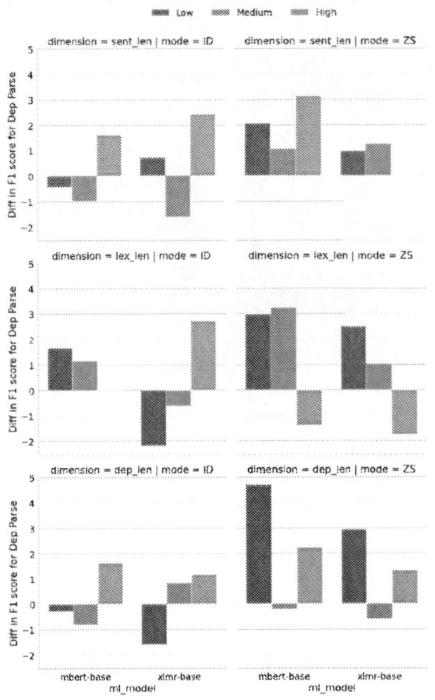

Figure 3: Performance of DEPGEN for in-domain and zero-shot cross-lingual transfer settings on the IndoRE dataset analyzed across variations in sentence, lexical and dependency length

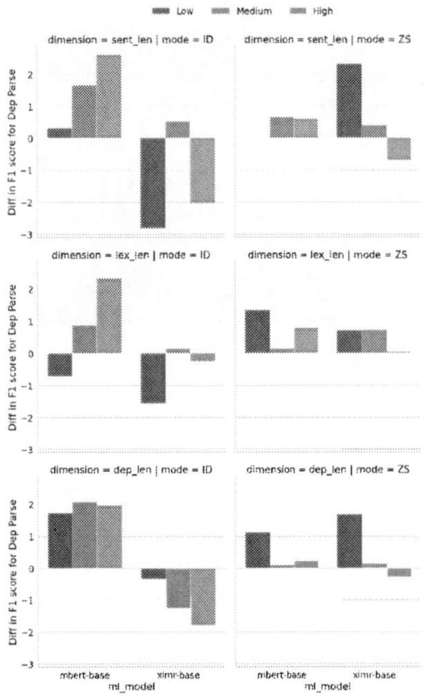

Figure 4: Performance of DEPGEN for in-domain and zero-shot cross-lingual transfer settings on the RedFM dataset analyzed across variations in sentence, lexical and dependency length

the mBERT model on the REDFM and IndoRE dataset respectively, for the best combination of dependency parser and GNN.

In the zero-shot cross-lingual transfer scenario from Table 2 we observe trends that are markedly different from the in-domain setting. Each entry in this Table is computed by averaging the macro-F1 score over the other source languages, apart from itself, for the top 3 seeds. We notice only slight improvements in RE performance for mBERT but higher gains for XLMR. We hypothesize that since XLMR has a worse performance than mBERT, it benefits more from the dependency information in the zero-shot setting. In a similar vein, we observe much higher gains for Hindi and Telugu (around 2.6% and 6.6% relative performance improvements respectively) in the zero-shot setting for mBERT. The markedly lower scores in IndoRE in the zero-shot transfer setup as compared to REDFM can be attributed to the higher number of relations in the dataset (32 for IndoRE vs 51 for REDFM).

RQ2. Which scenarios benefit the most with additional information in the fine-tuned setup?

In the fine-tuned setup, we analyze which scenarios or inputs benefit the most from including dependency information. We thus group the test instances according to three different dimensions, i.e. (1) input sentence length (2) lexical distance between two entities in the sentence and (3) dependency path length. Figures 3 and 4 show the effect of these components for the in-domain and zero-shot cross-lingual transfer settings for the IndoRE and RedFM datasets respectively. The blue, orange and green plots reflect the bottom quartile, inter-quartile range and the top quartile respectively for each of these three dimensions.

Sentence Length: We quantify sentence length based on the total number of tokens in the document. For both zero-shot and in-domain settings across the two datasets, adding linguistic information in the form of dependency graphs improves relation extraction for longer sentences. We posit that including dependency information helps to capture long range dependencies across words and thus the observed gains for longer sentences.

Lexical Distance: We quantify the lexical distance as the number of tokens between the two entities. Here, we observe that dependency information is more helpful for cases where the dis-

Model	Parser	Prompting	RedFM							IndoRE			Average
			ar	de	en	es	fr	it	zh	en	hi	te	
Llama	None	-	25.6	25.7	27.0	27.0	16.7	**36.7**	**37.1**	47.6	39.0	21.9	30.4
	Stanza	Tuple	24.3	19.3	23.9	17.0	18.4	19.3	29.6	30.2	28.3	10.9	22.1
	Stanza	Text	25.1	24.5	22.6	23.1	23.5	24.0	30.6	44.4	37.4	22.9	27.8
	Stanza	Filtered Text	**33.5**	35.0	32.3	**31.6**	**30.5**	34.0	36.1	**48.0**	**44.5**	**29.8**	**35.5** (↑5.1%)
	Trankit	Tuple	30.3	17.1	**37.3**	17.2	18.3	22.1	32.4	27.5	30.6	10.5	24.3
	Trankit	Text	23.4	25.4	22.7	22.6	23.8	25.6	30.5	44.8	38.4	24.0	28.1
	Trankit	Filtered Text	33.1	**35.2**	35.6	31.4	28.7	30.3	35.3	46.2	42.8	29.5	34.8
Mistral	None	-	36.7	38.2	39.0	35.8	36.0	38.3	35.6	**51.3**	**38.5**	10.6	36.0
	Stanza	Tuple	27.2	35.9	30.9	31.9	28.1	35.1	30.9	48.4	30.6	9.8	30.9
	Stanza	Text	29.2	32.0	34.4	32.6	30.4	33.4	33.2	47.5	37.1	8.7	31.9
	Stanza	Filtered Text	39.1	39.5	**40.9**	**37.1**	36.6	**40.2**	36.7	50.8	**38.5**	10.3	**37.0** (↑1.0%)
	Trankit	Tuple	27.4	35.3	32.5	31.5	26.9	30.6	31.3	48.0	30.5	10.8	30.5
	Trankit	Text	27.9	32.0	34.7	30.7	31.0	32.7	34.1	46.8	36.4	**11.2**	31.7
	Trankit	Filtered Text	**39.3**	**39.7**	39.3	36.3	**36.9**	37.8	**38.1**	50.9	38.3	**11.2**	36.8
Qwen	None	-	**44.3**	**39.6**	**40.3**	38.0	**36.8**	**43.0**	**40.8**	42.7	39.2	29.1	**39.4**
	Stanza	Tuple	35.4	32.0	34.6	31.8	31.9	37.8	31.4	38.3	38.2	26.1	33.8
	Stanza	Text	33.8	34.8	36.0	33.3	33.3	33.3	29.9	39.5	41.1	**30.6**	34.6
	Stanza	Filtered Text	42.1	32.8	39.8	37.3	33.6	38.4	40.4	**44.7**	45.4	28.6	38.3(↓1.1%)
	Trankit	Tuple	34.3	30.7	35.2	34.1	28.1	35.1	33.6	39.6	37.4	21.8	33.0
	Trankit	Text	35.4	35.2	34.2	33.1	34.0	33.4	30.2	40.5	40.5	27.3	34.4
	Trankit	Filtered Text	39.9	36.0	35.4	**39.4**	34.7	38.6	34.5	44.0	**45.9**	26.6	37.5

Table 3: Effect of dependency parses and prompting techniques for LLM-based relation extraction for the REDFM and IndoRE datasets. Performance reported in terms of F1-Score. Best performing methods are shown in bold.

tance between the entities is not high, i.e. Low and Medium categories.

Dependency Path Length: We quantify the dependency path length as the number of dependency relations that separate the two entities in the dependency graph. We see prominent gains for both short and long range dependency paths, especially for the ZS case for IndoRE. However, similar to lexical distance, the gains are more prominent when the dependency path between the entities is small. Since our chosen GNN has only two layers, we hypothesize that it is unable to capture signals across long dependency paths effectively.

RQ3. Can dependency parses help improve relation extraction performance for LLMs?

Table 3 summarizes the performance of three LLMs - LLaMA (Grattafiori et al., 2024), Mistral (Jiang et al., 2023) and Qwen (Yang et al., 2024) for zero-shot relation extraction on the IndoRE and RedFM datasets. To account for the skew in distribution of relations, we employ the macro-F1 score as the primary evaluation metric. We observe that for the LLama-3 and Mistral models, incorporating dependency parses improves performance across several cases. The gains are most prominent when the dependency information is presented in the form of natural language text; we see consistent improvements for the Text Prompt Format over the Tuple Prompt Format, where the information is presented as a list of tuples. We see that the filtered prompt that removes information not pertaining to the two entities, improves performance further.

The improvement can be as significant as 1% to 5% in some cases in terms of absolute F1-score for Mistral and LLama-3 respectively. For the Qwen model, dependency parses do not afford much benefits. Thus the choice of the LLM and the description of the prompt, play a significant role in zero-shot relation extraction performance. It should be noted, however, that the zero-shot performance for the in-context learning setup is significantly worse than the zero-shot cross-lingual performance in the fine-tuned setup. With LLMs, we see an average absolute improvement of 1.67% across all models and languages with the Filtered Text Prompt.

RQ4. Which factors influence generalization?

We now inspect the factors that characterize performance improvements over the baseline for the two datasets in the fine-tuned learning and in-context learning setup. We perform a multivariate ANOVA analysis with the relative performance difference (expressed as a percentage over the baseline), from including the dependency parses, as the dependent variable.

The independent variables chosen are the choice of the multilingual encoder, (mBERT or XLMR), dependency parser (Stanza or Trankit), GNN employed (RGCN or RGAT), and the source and target language [1]. We also consider the pair-wise interaction effects of each of these variables, and note the F-statistic and their corresponding p-value for the indomain (Tables 9 and 11) and zero-shot cross-lingual (Tables 10 and 12) respectively.

For the indomain setting in IndoRE, we observe that the relative performance change hinges most on the choice of the dependency parser followed by source language. Although the choice of the encoder and the GNN do not have any significant effect on relative performance, their pair-wise interactions is indeed significant. The story is remarkably different for REDFM where only the choice of the encoder has any significant effect on RE.

In the zero-shot cross-lingual setting for IndoRE, we see significant effects arising from the choice of the target language and the pairwise interaction between the choice of the source/target language with that of the encoder. A similar story also holds for REDFM, wherein we notice the only significant interactions are between the choice of the source/-target language and the encoder, and also between the choice of the source/target language pairs themselves. Simply put in the zero-shot setting the role of the dependency information is insignificant for both datasets.

We carry out a similar statistical analysis for the zero-shot ICL setup, with the relative performance change over the baseline as the dependent variable, and the choice of the LLM (i.e. LLama-3, Qwen, and Mistral), the prompt (i.e. Tuple Format, Text Format, and Filtered Text Format), the language (7 for RedFM and 3 for IndoRE), and the choice of the dependency parser (i.e. Trankit and Stanza) as the independent variables. We also consider the pair-wise interaction effects of each of these variables, and note the F-statistic and their corresponding p-value for the IndoRE and REDFM dataset respectively in Tables 13 and 14 respectively. We observe, over both datasets, significant effects arising from the choice of the LLM, and the choice of the prompt, as well as the pairwise interaction between the choice of the prompt and LLM, and the choice of the source language and LLM. Once again, we see that the choice of the dependency parser, i.e. the Stanza or Trankit, does not play a significant role.

[1]For the indomain setting we consider only the target language

6 Conclusion and Future Work

In this paper we propose a multi-component framework for multi-lingual relation extraction. Our finetuned framework DEPGEN, combines the signals from the input sentence with dependency parses that are encoded through a GNN. Through extensive evaluations, we have reported the implications of our work for both in-domain and zero-shot transfer settings across multiple languages. We observe that including off-the-shelf dependency parses can aid relation extraction, with the best performing model having a mild relative improvement of 0.91% and 1.5% in the in-domain and zero-shot setting respectively across two datasets. We also develop an in-context learning prompting approach that incorporates dependency information to bring about an average improvement of 1.67%, with significant gains for low-performing LLMs.

In this work, we investigate how augmenting dependency parses in language models can facilitate information extraction tasks in low-resource settings. Specifically, our contributions being independent of the language setting makes our model portable to other languages in a zero-shot transfer setup. Future avenues will explore the role of these linguistic frameworks for other information extraction or reasoning tasks, and the impact of different kinds of linguistic frameworks such as AMRs or UMRs.

Acknowledgments

We thank the anonymous reveiwers for their constructive feedback. This project was funded in part by NSF grant 1949110.

References

Livio Baldini Soares, Nicholas FitzGerald, Jeffrey Ling, and Tom Kwiatkowski. 2019. Matching the blanks: Distributional similarity for relation learning. In *Proceedings of the 57th Annual Meeting of the Association for Computational Linguistics*, pages 2895–2905, Florence, Italy. Association for Computational Linguistics.

Laura Banarescu, Claire Bonial, Shu Cai, Madalina Georgescu, Kira Griffitt, Ulf Hermjakob, Kevin

Knight, Philipp Koehn, Martha Palmer, and Nathan Schneider. 2013. Abstract meaning representation for sembanking. In *Proceedings of the 7th linguistic annotation workshop and interoperability with discourse*, pages 178–186.

Dan Busbridge, Dane Sherburn, Pietro Cavallo, and Nils Y. Hammerla. 2019. Relational graph attention networks.

Chih-Yao Chen and Cheng-Te Li. 2021. ZS-BERT: Towards zero-shot relation extraction with attribute representation learning. In *Proceedings of the 2021 Conference of the North American Chapter of the Association for Computational Linguistics: Human Language Technologies*, pages 3470–3479, Online. Association for Computational Linguistics.

Jiawei Chen, Yaojie Lu, Hongyu Lin, Jie Lou, Wei Jia, Dai Dai, Hua Wu, Boxi Cao, Xianpei Han, and Le Sun. 2023. Learning in-context learning for named entity recognition. In *Proceedings of the 61st Annual Meeting of the Association for Computational Linguistics (Volume 1: Long Papers)*, pages 13661–13675, Toronto, Canada. Association for Computational Linguistics.

Junjie Chen, Xiangheng He, and Yusuke Miyao. 2024. Language model based unsupervised dependency parsing with conditional mutual information and grammatical constraints. In *Proceedings of the 2024 Conference of the North American Chapter of the Association for Computational Linguistics: Human Language Technologies (Volume 1: Long Papers)*, pages 6355–6366, Mexico City, Mexico. Association for Computational Linguistics.

Noam Chomsky. 2002. *Syntactic structures*. Mouton de Gruyter.

Alexis Conneau, Kartikay Khandelwal, Naman Goyal, Vishrav Chaudhary, Guillaume Wenzek, Francisco Guzmán, Edouard Grave, Myle Ott, Luke Zettlemoyer, and Veselin Stoyanov. 2020a. Unsupervised cross-lingual representation learning at scale. In *ACL*.

Alexis Conneau, Kartikay Khandelwal, Naman Goyal, Vishrav Chaudhary, Guillaume Wenzek, Francisco Guzmán, Edouard Grave, Myle Ott, Luke Zettlemoyer, and Veselin Stoyanov. 2020b. Unsupervised cross-lingual representation learning at scale. In *Proceedings of the 58th Annual Meeting of the Association for Computational Linguistics*, pages 8440–8451, Online. Association for Computational Linguistics.

Alexis Conneau, Kartikay Khandelwal, Naman Goyal, Vishrav Chaudhary, Guillaume Wenzek, Francisco Guzmán, Edouard Grave, Myle Ott, Luke Zettlemoyer, and Veselin Stoyanov. 2020c. Unsupervised cross-lingual representation learning at scale.

William Croft. 2022. Morphosyntax: constructions of the world's languages.

Sarkar Snigdha Sarathi Das, Arzoo Katiyar, Rebecca Passonneau, and Rui Zhang. 2022. CONTaiNER: Few-shot named entity recognition via contrastive learning. In *Proceedings of the 60th Annual Meeting of the Association for Computational Linguistics (Volume 1: Long Papers)*, pages 6338–6353, Dublin, Ireland. Association for Computational Linguistics.

Jacob Devlin, Ming-Wei Chang, Kenton Lee, and Kristina Toutanova. 2018. Bert: Pre-training of deep bidirectional transformers for language understanding. *arXiv preprint arXiv:1810.04805*.

Jacob Devlin, Ming-Wei Chang, Kenton Lee, and Kristina Toutanova. 2019. BERT: Pre-training of deep bidirectional transformers for language understanding. In *Proceedings of the 2019 Conference of the North American Chapter of the Association for Computational Linguistics: Human Language Technologies, Volume 1 (Long and Short Papers)*, pages 4171–4186, Minneapolis, Minnesota. Association for Computational Linguistics.

Jose A. Diaz-Garcia and Julio Amador Diaz Lopez. 2024. A survey on cutting-edge relation extraction techniques based on language models.

Qiang Ding, Lvzhou Luo, Yixuan Cao, and Ping Luo. 2024. Attention with dependency parsing augmentation for fine-grained attribution.

Ritam Dutt, Sopan Khosla, Vinayshekhar Bannihatti Kumar, and Rashmi Gangadharaiah. 2023. GrailQA++: A challenging zero-shot benchmark for knowledge base question answering. In *Proceedings of the 13th International Joint Conference on Natural Language Processing and the 3rd Conference of the Asia-Pacific Chapter of the Association for Computational Linguistics (Volume 1: Long Papers)*, pages 897–909, Nusa Dua, Bali. Association for Computational Linguistics.

Sefika Efeoglu and Adrian Paschke. 2024. Relation extraction with fine-tuned large language models in retrieval augmented generation frameworks.

Alexander Fritzler, Varvara Logacheva, and Maksim Kretov. 2019. Few-shot classification in named entity recognition task. In *Proceedings of the 34th ACM/SIGAPP Symposium on Applied Computing*, pages 993–1000.

Aaron Grattafiori, Abhimanyu Dubey, Abhinav Jauhri, Abhinav Pandey, Abhishek Kadian, Ahmad Al-Dahle, Aiesha Letman, Akhil Mathur, Alan Schelten, Alex Vaughan, Amy Yang, Angela Fan, Anirudh Goyal, Anthony Hartshorn, Aobo Yang, Archi Mitra, Archie Sravankumar, Artem Korenev, Arthur Hinsvark, Arun Rao, Aston Zhang, Aurelien Rodriguez, Austen Gregerson, Ava Spataru, Baptiste Roziere, Bethany Biron, Binh Tang, Bobbie Chern, Charlotte Caucheteux, Chaya Nayak, Chloe Bi, Chris Marra, Chris McConnell, Christian Keller, Christophe Touret, Chunyang Wu, Corinne Wong, Cristian Canton Ferrer, Cyrus Nikolaidis, Damien Allonsius, Daniel Song, Danielle Pintz, Danny Livshits,

Danny Wyatt, David Esiobu, Dhruv Choudhary, Dhruv Mahajan, Diego Garcia-Olano, Diego Perino, Dieuwke Hupkes, Egor Lakomkin, Ehab AlBadawy, Elina Lobanova, Emily Dinan, Eric Michael Smith, Filip Radenovic, Francisco Guzmán, Frank Zhang, Gabriel Synnaeve, Gabrielle Lee, Georgia Lewis Anderson, Govind Thattai, Graeme Nail, Gregoire Mialon, Guan Pang, Guillem Cucurell, Hailey Nguyen, Hannah Korevaar, Hu Xu, Hugo Touvron, Iliyan Zarov, Imanol Arrieta Ibarra, Isabel Kloumann, Ishan Misra, Ivan Evtimov, Jack Zhang, Jade Copet, Jaewon Lee, Jan Geffert, Jana Vranes, Jason Park, Jay Mahadeokar, Jeet Shah, Jelmer van der Linde, Jennifer Billock, Jenny Hong, Jenya Lee, Jeremy Fu, Jianfeng Chi, Jianyu Huang, Jiawen Liu, Jie Wang, Jiecao Yu, Joanna Bitton, Joe Spisak, Jongsoo Park, Joseph Rocca, Joshua Johnstun, Joshua Saxe, Junteng Jia, Kalyan Vasuden Alwala, Karthik Prasad, Kartikeya Upasani, Kate Plawiak, Ke Li, Kenneth Heafield, Kevin Stone, Khalid El-Arini, Krithika Iyer, Kshitiz Malik, Kuenley Chiu, Kunal Bhalla, Kushal Lakhotia, Lauren Rantala-Yeary, Laurens van der Maaten, Lawrence Chen, Liang Tan, Liz Jenkins, Louis Martin, Lovish Madaan, Lubo Malo, Lukas Blecher, Lukas Landzaat, Luke de Oliveira, Madeline Muzzi, Mahesh Pasupuleti, Mannat Singh, Manohar Paluri, Marcin Kardas, Maria Tsimpoukelli, Mathew Oldham, Mathieu Rita, Maya Pavlova, Melanie Kambadur, Mike Lewis, Min Si, Mitesh Kumar Singh, Mona Hassan, Naman Goyal, Narjes Torabi, Nikolay Bashlykov, Nikolay Bogoychev, Niladri Chatterji, Ning Zhang, Olivier Duchenne, Onur Çelebi, Patrick Alrassy, Pengchuan Zhang, Pengwei Li, Petar Vasic, Peter Weng, Prajjwal Bhargava, Pratik Dubal, Praveen Krishnan, Punit Singh Koura, Puxin Xu, Qing He, Qingxiao Dong, Ragavan Srinivasan, Raj Ganapathy, Ramon Calderer, Ricardo Silveira Cabral, Robert Stojnic, Roberta Raileanu, Rohan Maheswari, Rohit Girdhar, Rohit Patel, Romain Sauvestre, Ronnie Polidoro, Roshan Sumbaly, Ross Taylor, Ruan Silva, Rui Hou, Rui Wang, Saghar Hosseini, Sahana Chennabasappa, Sanjay Singh, Sean Bell, Seohyun Sonia Kim, Sergey Edunov, Shaoliang Nie, Sharan Narang, Sharath Raparthy, Sheng Shen, Shengye Wan, Shruti Bhosale, Shun Zhang, Simon Vandenhende, Soumya Batra, Spencer Whitman, Sten Sootla, Stephane Collot, Suchin Gururangan, Sydney Borodinsky, Tamar Herman, Tara Fowler, Tarek Sheasha, Thomas Georgiou, Thomas Scialom, Tobias Speckbacher, Todor Mihaylov, Tong Xiao, Ujjwal Karn, Vedanuj Goswami, Vibhor Gupta, Vignesh Ramanathan, Viktor Kerkez, Vincent Gonguet, Virginie Do, Vish Vogeti, Vítor Albiero, Vladan Petrovic, Weiwei Chu, Wenhan Xiong, Wenyin Fu, Whitney Meers, Xavier Martinet, Xiaodong Wang, Xiaofang Wang, Xiaoqing Ellen Tan, Xide Xia, Xinfeng Xie, Xuchao Jia, Xuewei Wang, Yaelle Goldschlag, Yashesh Gaur, Yasmine Babaei, Yi Wen, Yiwen Song, Yuchen Zhang, Yue Li, Yuning Mao, Zacharie Delpierre Coudert, Zheng Yan, Zhengxing Chen, Zoe Papakipos, Aaditya Singh, Aayushi Srivastava, Abha Jain, Adam Kelsey, Adam Shajnfeld, Adithya Gangidi, Adolfo Victoria, Ahuva Goldstand, Ajay Menon, Ajay Sharma, Alex Boesenberg, Alexei Baevski, Allie Feinstein, Amanda Kallet, Amit Sangani, Amos Teo, Anam Yunus, Andrei Lupu, Andres Alvarado, Andrew Caples, Andrew Gu, Andrew Ho, Andrew Poulton, Andrew Ryan, Ankit Ramchandani, Annie Dong, Annie Franco, Anuj Goyal, Aparajita Saraf, Arkabandhu Chowdhury, Ashley Gabriel, Ashwin Bharambe, Assaf Eisenman, Azadeh Yazdan, Beau James, Ben Maurer, Benjamin Leonhardi, Bernie Huang, Beth Loyd, Beto De Paola, Bhargavi Paranjape, Bing Liu, Bo Wu, Boyu Ni, Braden Hancock, Bram Wasti, Brandon Spence, Brani Stojkovic, Brian Gamido, Britt Montalvo, Carl Parker, Carly Burton, Catalina Mejia, Ce Liu, Changhan Wang, Changkyu Kim, Chao Zhou, Chester Hu, Ching-Hsiang Chu, Chris Cai, Chris Tindal, Christoph Feichtenhofer, Cynthia Gao, Damon Civin, Dana Beaty, Daniel Kreymer, Daniel Li, David Adkins, David Xu, Davide Testuggine, Delia David, Devi Parikh, Diana Liskovich, Didem Foss, Dingkang Wang, Duc Le, Dustin Holland, Edward Dowling, Eissa Jamil, Elaine Montgomery, Eleonora Presani, Emily Hahn, Emily Wood, Eric-Tuan Le, Erik Brinkman, Esteban Arcaute, Evan Dunbar, Evan Smothers, Fei Sun, Felix Kreuk, Feng Tian, Filippos Kokkinos, Firat Ozgenel, Francesco Caggioni, Frank Kanayet, Frank Seide, Gabriela Medina Florez, Gabriella Schwarz, Gada Badeer, Georgia Swee, Gil Halpern, Grant Herman, Grigory Sizov, Guangyi, Zhang, Guna Lakshminarayanan, Hakan Inan, Hamid Shojanazeri, Han Zou, Hannah Wang, Hanwen Zha, Haroun Habeeb, Harrison Rudolph, Helen Suk, Henry Aspegren, Hunter Goldman, Hongyuan Zhan, Ibrahim Damlaj, Igor Molybog, Igor Tufanov, Ilias Leontiadis, Irina-Elena Veliche, Itai Gat, Jake Weissman, James Geboski, James Kohli, Janice Lam, Japhet Asher, Jean-Baptiste Gaya, Jeff Marcus, Jeff Tang, Jennifer Chan, Jenny Zhen, Jeremy Reizenstein, Jeremy Teboul, Jessica Zhong, Jian Jin, Jingyi Yang, Joe Cummings, Jon Carvill, Jon Shepard, Jonathan McPhie, Jonathan Torres, Josh Ginsburg, Junjie Wang, Kai Wu, Kam Hou U, Karan Saxena, Kartikay Khandelwal, Katayoun Zand, Kathy Matosich, Kaushik Veeraraghavan, Kelly Michelena, Keqian Li, Kiran Jagadeesh, Kun Huang, Kunal Chawla, Kyle Huang, Lailin Chen, Lakshya Garg, Lavender A, Leandro Silva, Lee Bell, Lei Zhang, Liangpeng Guo, Licheng Yu, Liron Moshkovich, Luca Wehrstedt, Madian Khabsa, Manav Avalani, Manish Bhatt, Martynas Mankus, Matan Hasson, Matthew Lennie, Matthias Reso, Maxim Groshev, Maxim Naumov, Maya Lathi, Meghan Keneally, Miao Liu, Michael L. Seltzer, Michal Valko, Michelle Restrepo, Mihir Patel, Mik Vyatskov, Mikayel Samvelyan, Mike Clark, Mike Macey, Mike Wang, Miquel Jubert Hermoso, Mo Metanat, Mohammad Rastegari, Munish Bansal, Nandhini Santhanam, Natascha Parks, Natasha White, Navyata Bawa, Nayan Singhal, Nick Egebo, Nicolas Usunier, Nikhil Mehta, Nikolay Pavlovich Laptev, Ning Dong, Norman Cheng, Oleg Chernoguz, Olivia Hart, Omkar Salpekar, Ozlem Kalinli, Parkin Kent, Parth Parekh, Paul Saab, Pavan Balaji, Pedro Rittner, Philip Bontrager, Pierre Roux, Piotr

Dollar, Polina Zvyagina, Prashant Ratanchandani, Pritish Yuvraj, Qian Liang, Rachad Alao, Rachel Rodriguez, Rafi Ayub, Raghotham Murthy, Raghu Nayani, Rahul Mitra, Rangaprabhu Parthasarathy, Raymond Li, Rebekkah Hogan, Robin Battey, Rocky Wang, Russ Howes, Ruty Rinott, Sachin Mehta, Sachin Siby, Sai Jayesh Bondu, Samyak Datta, Sara Chugh, Sara Hunt, Sargun Dhillon, Sasha Sidorov, Satadru Pan, Saurabh Mahajan, Saurabh Verma, Seiji Yamamoto, Sharadh Ramaswamy, Shaun Lindsay, Shaun Lindsay, Sheng Feng, Shenghao Lin, Shengxin Cindy Zha, Shishir Patil, Shiva Shankar, Shuqiang Zhang, Shuqiang Zhang, Sinong Wang, Sneha Agarwal, Soji Sajuyigbe, Soumith Chintala, Stephanie Max, Stephen Chen, Steve Kehoe, Steve Satterfield, Sudarshan Govindaprasad, Sumit Gupta, Summer Deng, Sungmin Cho, Sunny Virk, Suraj Subramanian, Sy Choudhury, Sydney Goldman, Tal Remez, Tamar Glaser, Tamara Best, Thilo Koehler, Thomas Robinson, Tianhe Li, Tianjun Zhang, Tim Matthews, Timothy Chou, Tzook Shaked, Varun Vontimitta, Victoria Ajayi, Victoria Montanez, Vijai Mohan, Vinay Satish Kumar, Vishal Mangla, Vlad Ionescu, Vlad Poenaru, Vlad Tiberiu Mihailescu, Vladimir Ivanov, Wei Li, Wenchen Wang, Wenwen Jiang, Wes Bouaziz, Will Constable, Xiaocheng Tang, Xiaojian Wu, Xiaolan Wang, Xilun Wu, Xinbo Gao, Yaniv Kleinman, Yanjun Chen, Ye Hu, Ye Jia, Ye Qi, Yenda Li, Yilin Zhang, Ying Zhang, Yossi Adi, Youngjin Nam, Yu, Wang, Yu Zhao, Yuchen Hao, Yundi Qian, Yunlu Li, Yuzi He, Zach Rait, Zachary DeVito, Zef Rosnbrick, Zhaoduo Wen, Zhenyu Yang, Zhiwei Zhao, and Zhiyu Ma. 2024. The llama 3 herd of models.

Yanggan Gu, Yang Hou, Zhefeng Wang, Xinyu Duan, and Zhenghua Li. 2024. High-order joint constituency and dependency parsing. In *Proceedings of the 2024 Joint International Conference on Computational Linguistics, Language Resources and Evaluation (LREC-COLING 2024)*, pages 8144–8154, Torino, Italia. ELRA and ICCL.

Yu Gu, Sue Kase, Michelle Vanni, Brian Sadler, Percy Liang, Xifeng Yan, and Yu Su. 2021. Beyond iid: three levels of generalization for question answering on knowledge bases. In *Proceedings of the Web Conference 2021*, pages 3477–3488.

Pere-Lluís Huguet Cabot, Simone Tedeschi, Axel-Cyrille Ngonga Ngomo, and Roberto Navigli. 2023. RED^{fm}: a filtered and multilingual relation extraction dataset. In *Proceedings of the 61st Annual Meeting of the Association for Computational Linguistics (Volume 1: Long Papers)*, pages 4326–4343, Toronto, Canada. Association for Computational Linguistics.

Albert Q. Jiang, Alexandre Sablayrolles, Arthur Mensch, Chris Bamford, Devendra Singh Chaplot, Diego de las Casas, Florian Bressand, Gianna Lengyel, Guillaume Lample, Lucile Saulnier, Lélio Renard Lavaud, Marie-Anne Lachaux, Pierre Stock, Teven Le Scao, Thibaut Lavril, Thomas Wang, Timothée Lacroix, and William El Sayed. 2023. Mistral 7b.

Zhao Jun, Hu Yuan, Xu Nuo, Gui Tao, Zhang Qi, Chen Yunwen, and Gao Xiang. 2022. An exploration of prompt-based zero-shot relation extraction method. In *Proceedings of the 21st Chinese National Conference on Computational Linguistics*, pages 786–797, Nanchang, China. Chinese Information Processing Society of China.

Guozheng Li, Peng Wang, and Wenjun Ke. 2023. Revisiting large language models as zero-shot relation extractors. In *Findings of the Association for Computational Linguistics: EMNLP 2023*, pages 6877–6892, Singapore. Association for Computational Linguistics.

Tianming Liang, Yang Liu, Xiaoyan Liu, Hao Zhang, Gaurav Sharma, and Maozu Guo. 2023. Distantly-supervised long-tailed relation extraction using constraint graphs. *IEEE Transactions on Knowledge and Data Engineering*, 35(7):6852–6865.

Robert Litschko, Ivan Vulić, Simone Paolo Ponzetto, and Goran Glavaš. 2021. On cross-lingual retrieval with multilingual text encoders.

Yang Liu, Jinpeng Hu, Xiang Wan, and Tsung-Hui Chang. 2022. A simple yet effective relation information guided approach for few-shot relation extraction. In *Findings of the Association for Computational Linguistics: ACL 2022*, pages 757–763, Dublin, Ireland. Association for Computational Linguistics.

Yinhan Liu, Myle Ott, Naman Goyal, Jingfei Du, Mandar Joshi, Danqi Chen, Omer Levy, Mike Lewis, Luke Zettlemoyer, and Veselin Stoyanov. 2019. Roberta: A robustly optimized bert pretraining approach. *arXiv preprint arXiv:1907.11692*.

Zhu Liu, Cunliang Kong, Ying Liu, and Maosong Sun. 2024. Fantastic semantics and where to find them: Investigating which layers of generative LLMs reflect lexical semantics. In *Findings of the Association for Computational Linguistics: ACL 2024*, pages 14551–14558, Bangkok, Thailand. Association for Computational Linguistics.

Sewon Min, Julian Michael, Hannaneh Hajishirzi, and Luke Zettlemoyer. 2020. AmbigQA: Answering ambiguous open-domain questions. In *Proceedings of the 2020 Conference on Empirical Methods in Natural Language Processing (EMNLP)*, pages 5783–5797, Online. Association for Computational Linguistics.

Arijit Nag, Bidisha Samanta, Animesh Mukherjee, Niloy Ganguly, and Soumen Chakrabarti. 2021. A data bootstrapping recipe for low-resource multilingual relation classification. In *Proceedings of the 25th Conference on Computational Natural Language Learning*, pages 575–587, Online. Association for Computational Linguistics.

Minh Van Nguyen, Viet Dac Lai, Amir Pouran Ben Veyseh, and Thien Huu Nguyen. 2021. Trankit: A lightweight transformer-based toolkit for multilingual natural language processing. In *Proceedings of the 16th*

Conference of the European Chapter of the Association for Computational Linguistics: System Demonstrations, pages 80–90, Online. Association for Computational Linguistics.

Joakim Nivre, Marie-Catherine De Marneffe, Filip Ginter, Yoav Goldberg, Jan Hajic, Christopher D Manning, Ryan McDonald, Slav Petrov, Sampo Pyysalo, Natalia Silveira, et al. 2016. Universal dependencies v1: A multilingual treebank collection. In *Proceedings of the Tenth International Conference on Language Resources and Evaluation (LREC'16)*, pages 1659–1666.

Hao Peng, Tianyu Gao, Xu Han, Yankai Lin, Peng Li, Zhiyuan Liu, Maosong Sun, and Jie Zhou. 2020. Learning from Context or Names? An Empirical Study on Neural Relation Extraction. In *Proceedings of the 2020 Conference on Empirical Methods in Natural Language Processing (EMNLP)*, pages 3661–3672, Online. Association for Computational Linguistics.

Peng Qi, Yuhao Zhang, Yuhui Zhang, Jason Bolton, and Christopher D. Manning. 2020a. Stanza: A Python natural language processing toolkit for many human languages. In *Proceedings of the 58th Annual Meeting of the Association for Computational Linguistics: System Demonstrations*.

Peng Qi, Yuhao Zhang, Yuhui Zhang, Jason Bolton, and Christopher D. Manning. 2020b. Stanza: A python natural language processing toolkit for many human languages. In *Proceedings of the 58th Annual Meeting of the Association for Computational Linguistics: System Demonstrations*, pages 101–108, Online. Association for Computational Linguistics.

Meng Qu, Tianyu Gao, Louis-Pascal Xhonneux, and Jian Tang. 2020. Few-shot relation extraction via Bayesian meta-learning on relation graphs. In *Proceedings of the 37th International Conference on Machine Learning*, volume 119 of *Proceedings of Machine Learning Research*, pages 7867–7876. PMLR.

Siva Reddy, Oscar Täckström, Slav Petrov, Mark Steedman, and Mirella Lapata. 2017. Universal semantic parsing. In *Proceedings of the 2017 Conference on Empirical Methods in Natural Language Processing*, pages 89–101.

Devendra Sachan, Yuhao Zhang, Peng Qi, and William L. Hamilton. 2021. Do syntax trees help pre-trained transformers extract information? In *Proceedings of the 16th Conference of the European Chapter of the Association for Computational Linguistics: Main Volume*, pages 2647–2661, Online. Association for Computational Linguistics.

Gözde Gül Şahin. 2022. To augment or not to augment? a comparative study on text augmentation techniques for low-resource NLP. *Computational Linguistics*, 48(1):5–42.

Oscar Sainz, Iker García-Ferrero, Rodrigo Agerri, Oier Lopez de Lacalle, German Rigau, and Eneko Agirre. 2024. GoLLIE: Annotation guidelines improve zero-shot information-extraction. In *The Twelfth International Conference on Learning Representations*.

Franco Scarselli, Marco Gori, Ah Chung Tsoi, Markus Hagenbuchner, and Gabriele Monfardini. 2008. The graph neural network model. *IEEE transactions on neural networks*, 20(1):61–80.

Michael Schlichtkrull, Thomas N Kipf, Peter Bloem, Rianne van den Berg, Ivan Titov, and Max Welling. 2018. Modeling relational data with graph convolutional networks. In *European semantic web conference*, pages 593–607. Springer.

Giulio Starace, Konstantinos Papakostas, Rochelle Choenni, Apostolos Panagiotopoulos, Matteo Rosati, Alina Leidinger, and Ekaterina Shutova. 2023. Probing LLMs for joint encoding of linguistic categories. In *Findings of the Association for Computational Linguistics: EMNLP 2023*, pages 7158–7179, Singapore. Association for Computational Linguistics.

Chenguang Wang, Xiao Liu, Zui Chen, Haoyun Hong, Jie Tang, and Dawn Song. 2022a. DeepStruct: Pretraining of language models for structure prediction. In *Findings of the Association for Computational Linguistics: ACL 2022*, pages 803–823, Dublin, Ireland. Association for Computational Linguistics.

Shusen Wang, Bosen Zhang, Yajing Xu, Yanan Wu, and Bo Xiao. 2022b. RCL: Relation contrastive learning for zero-shot relation extraction. In *Findings of the Association for Computational Linguistics: NAACL 2022*, pages 2456–2468, Seattle, United States. Association for Computational Linguistics.

Tingyu Xie, Qi Li, Yan Zhang, Zuozhu Liu, and Hongwei Wang. 2024. Self-improving for zero-shot named entity recognition with large language models. In *Proceedings of the 2024 Conference of the North American Chapter of the Association for Computational Linguistics: Human Language Technologies (Volume 2: Short Papers)*, pages 583–593, Mexico City, Mexico. Association for Computational Linguistics.

Lilong Xue, Dan Zhang, Yuxiao Dong, and Jie Tang. 2024. Autore: Document-level relation extraction with large language models.

An Yang, Baosong Yang, Binyuan Hui, Bo Zheng, Bowen Yu, Chang Zhou, Chengpeng Li, Chengyuan Li, Dayiheng Liu, Fei Huang, Guanting Dong, Haoran Wei, Huan Lin, Jialong Tang, Jialin Wang, Jian Yang, Jianhong Tu, Jianwei Zhang, Jianxin Ma, Jianxin Yang, Jin Xu, Jingren Zhou, Jinze Bai, Jinzheng He, Junyang Lin, Kai Dang, Keming Lu, Keqin Chen, Kexin Yang, Mei Li, Mingfeng Xue, Na Ni, Pei Zhang, Peng Wang, Ru Peng, Rui Men, Ruize Gao, Runji Lin, Shijie Wang, Shuai Bai, Sinan Tan, Tianhang Zhu, Tianhao Li, Tianyu Liu, Wenbin Ge,

Xiaodong Deng, Xiaohuan Zhou, Xingzhang Ren, Xinyu Zhang, Xipin Wei, Xuancheng Ren, Xuejing Liu, Yang Fan, Yang Yao, Yichang Zhang, Yu Wan, Yunfei Chu, Yuqiong Liu, Zeyu Cui, Zhenru Zhang, Zhifang Guo, and Zhihao Fan. 2024. Qwen2 technical report.

Kaijia Yang, Nantao Zheng, Xinyu Dai, Liang He, Shujian Huang, and Jiajun Chen. 2020. Enhance prototypical network with text descriptions for few-shot relation classification. In *Proceedings of the 29th ACM International Conference on Information & Knowledge Management*, pages 2273–2276.

Zhi-Xiu Ye and Zhen-Hua Ling. 2019a. Distant supervision relation extraction with intra-bag and inter-bag attentions. In *Proceedings of the 2019 Conference of the North American Chapter of the Association for Computational Linguistics: Human Language Technologies, Volume 1 (Long and Short Papers)*, pages 2810–2819, Minneapolis, Minnesota. Association for Computational Linguistics.

Zhi-Xiu Ye and Zhen-Hua Ling. 2019b. Multi-level matching and aggregation network for few-shot relation classification. In *Proceedings of the 57th Annual Meeting of the Association for Computational Linguistics*, pages 2872–2881, Florence, Italy. Association for Computational Linguistics.

Tianshu Yu, Min Yang, and Xiaoyan Zhao. 2022. Dependency-aware prototype learning for few-shot relation classification. In *Proceedings of the 29th International Conference on Computational Linguistics*, pages 2339–2345, Gyeongju, Republic of Korea. International Committee on Computational Linguistics.

Daniel Zeman, Joakim Nivre, Mitchell Abrams, Noëmi Aepli, Željko Agić, Lars Ahrenberg, Gabrielė Aleksandravičiūtė, Lene Antonsen, Katya Aplonova, Maria Jesus Aranzabe, Gashaw Arutie, Masayuki Asahara, Luma Ateyah, Mohammed Attia, Aitziber Atutxa, Liesbeth Augustinus, Elena Badmaeva, Miguel Ballesteros, Esha Banerjee, Sebastian Bank, Verginica Barbu Mititelu, Victoria Basmov, Colin Batchelor, John Bauer, Sandra Bellato, Kepa Bengoetxea, Yevgeni Berzak, Irshad Ahmad Bhat, Riyaz Ahmad Bhat, Erica Biagetti, Eckhard Bick, Agnė Bielinskienė, Rogier Blokland, Victoria Bobicev, Loïc Boizou, Emanuel Borges Völker, Carl Börstell, Cristina Bosco, Gosse Bouma, Sam Bowman, Adriane Boyd, Kristina Brokaitė, Aljoscha Burchardt, Marie Candito, Bernard Caron, Gauthier Caron, Tatiana Cavalcanti, Gülşen Cebiroğlu Eryiğit, Flavio Massimiliano Cecchini, Giuseppe G. A. Celano, Slavomír Čéplö, Savas Cetin, Fabricio Chalub, Jinho Choi, Yongseok Cho, Jayeol Chun, Alessandra T. Cignarella, Silvie Cinková, Aurélie Collomb, Çağrı Çöltekin, Miriam Connor, Marine Courtin, Elizabeth Davidson, Marie-Catherine de Marneffe, Valeria de Paiva, Elvis de Souza, Arantza Diaz de Ilarraza, Carly Dickerson, Bamba Dione, Peter Dirix, Kaja Dobrovoljc, Timothy Dozat, Kira Droganova, Puneet Dwivedi, Hanne Eckhoff, Marhaba Eli, Ali Elkahky, Binyam Ephrem, Olga Erina, Tomaž Erjavec, Aline Etienne, Wograine Evelyn, Richárd Farkas, Hector Fernandez Alcalde, Jennifer Foster, Cláudia Freitas, Kazunori Fujita, Katarína Gajdošová, Daniel Galbraith, Marcos Garcia, Moa Gärdenfors, Sebastian Garza, Kim Gerdes, Filip Ginter, Iakes Goenaga, Koldo Gojenola, Memduh Gökırmak, Yoav Goldberg, Xavier Gómez Guinovart, Berta González Saavedra, Bernadeta Griciūtė, Matias Grioni, Normunds Grūzītis, Bruno Guillaume, Céline Guillot-Barbance, Nizar Habash, Jan Hajič, Jan Hajič jr., Mika Hämäläinen, Linh Hà Mỹ, Na-Rae Han, Kim Harris, Dag Haug, Johannes Heinecke, Felix Hennig, Barbora Hladká, Jaroslava Hlaváčová, Florinel Hociung, Petter Hohle, Jena Hwang, Takumi Ikeda, Radu Ion, Elena Irimia, Ọlájídé Ishola, Tomáš Jelínek, Anders Johannsen, Fredrik Jørgensen, Markus Juutinen, Hüner Kaşıkara, Andre Kaasen, Nadezhda Kabaeva, Sylvain Kahane, Hiroshi Kanayama, Jenna Kanerva, Boris Katz, Tolga Kayadelen, Jessica Kenney, Václava Kettnerová, Jesse Kirchner, Elena Klementieva, Arne Köhn, Kamil Kopacewicz, Natalia Kotsyba, Jolanta Kovalevskaitė, Simon Krek, Sookyoung Kwak, Veronika Laippala, Lorenzo Lambertino, Lucia Lam, Tatiana Lando, Septina Dian Larasati, Alexei Lavrentiev, John Lee, Phng Lê Hồng, Alessandro Lenci, Saran Lertpradit, Herman Leung, Cheuk Ying Li, Josie Li, Keying Li, KyungTae Lim, Maria Liovina, Yuan Li, Nikola Ljubešić, Olga Loginova, Olga Lyashevskaya, Teresa Lynn, Vivien Macketanz, Aibek Makazhanov, Michael Mandl, Christopher Manning, Ruli Manurung, Cătălina Mărănduc, David Mareček, Katrin Marheinecke, Héctor Martínez Alonso, André Martins, Jan Mašek, Yuji Matsumoto, Ryan McDonald, Sarah McGuinness, Gustavo Mendonça, Niko Miekka, Margarita Misirpashayeva, Anna Missilä, Cătălin Mititelu, Maria Mitrofan, Yusuke Miyao, Simonetta Montemagni, Amir More, Laura Moreno Romero, Keiko Sophie Mori, Tomohiko Morioka, Shinsuke Mori, Shigeki Moro, Bjartur Mortensen, Bohdan Moskalevskyi, Kadri Muischnek, Robert Munro, Yugo Murawaki, Kaili Müürisep, Pinkey Nainwani, Juan Ignacio Navarro Horñiacek, Anna Nedoluzhko, Gunta Nešpore-Bērzkalne, Lng Nguyễn Thị, Huyền Nguyễn Thị Minh, Yoshihiro Nikaido, Vitaly Nikolaev, Rattima Nitisaroj, Hanna Nurmi, Stina Ojala, Atul Kr. Ojha, Adédayọ Olúòkun, Mai Omura, Petya Osenova, Robert Östling, Lilja Øvrelid, Niko Partanen, Elena Pascual, Marco Passarotti, Agnieszka Patejuk, Guilherme Paulino-Passos, Angelika Peljak-Łapińska, Siyao Peng, Cenel-Augusto Perez, Guy Perrier, Daria Petrova, Slav Petrov, Jason Phelan, Jussi Piitulainen, Tommi A Pirinen, Emily Pitler, Barbara Plank, Thierry Poibeau, Larisa Ponomareva, Martin Popel, Lauma Pretkalniņa, Sophie Prévost, Prokopis Prokopidis, Adam Przepiórkowski, Tiina Puolakainen, Sampo Pyysalo, Peng Qi, Andriela Rääbis, Alexandre Rademaker, Loganathan Ramasamy, Taraka Rama, Carlos Ramisch, Vinit Ravishankar, Livy Real, Siva Reddy, Georg Rehm, Ivan Riabov, Michael Rießler, Erika Rimkutė, Larissa Ri-naldi, Laura Rituma, Luisa Rocha, Mykhailo Romanenko, Rudolf Rosa, Davide Rovati, Valentin Roșca, Olga Rudina, Jack Rueter, Shoval Sadde, Benoît Sagot, Shadi Saleh, Alessio Salomoni, Tanja Samardžić, Stephanie Samson, Manuela Sanguinetti, Dage Särg, Baiba Saulīte, Yanin Sawanakunanon, Nathan Schneider, Sebastian Schuster, Djamé Seddah, Wolfgang Seeker, Mojgan Seraji, Mo Shen, Atsuko Shimada, Hiroyuki Shirasu, Muh Shohibussirri, Dmitry Sichinava, Aline Silveira, Natalia Silveira, Maria Simi, Radu Simionescu, Katalin Simkó, Mária Šimková, Kiril Simov, Aaron Smith, Isabela Soares-Bastos, Carolyn Spadine, Antonio Stella, Milan Straka, Jana Strnadová, Alane Suhr, Umut Sulubacak, Shingo Suzuki, Zsolt Szántó, Dima Taji, Yuta Takahashi, Fabio Tamburini, Takaaki Tanaka, Isabelle Tellier, Guillaume Thomas, Liisi Torga, Trond Trosterud, Anna Trukhina, Reut Tsarfaty, Francis Tyers, Sumire Uematsu, Zdeňka Urešová, Larraitz Uria, Hans Uszkoreit, Andrius Utka, Sowmya Vajjala, Daniel van Niekerk, Gertjan van Noord, Viktor Varga, Eric Villemonte de la Clergerie, Veronika Vincze, Lars Wallin, Abigail Walsh, Jing Xian Wang, Jonathan North Washington, Maximilan Wendt, Seyi Williams, Mats Wirén, Christian Wittern, Tsegay Woldemariam, Tak-sum Wong, Alina Wróblewska, Mary Yako, Naoki Yamazaki, Chunxiao Yan, Koichi Yasuoka, Marat M. Yavrumyan, Zhuoran Yu, Zdeněk Žabokrtský, Amir Zeldes, Manying Zhang, and Hanzhi Zhu. 2019. Universal dependencies 2.5. LINDAT/CLARIAH-CZ digital library at the Institute of Formal and Applied Linguistics (ÚFAL), Faculty of Mathematics and Physics, Charles University.

Jiali Zeng, Yufan Jiang, Yongjing Yin, Xu Wang, Binghuai Lin, and Yunbo Cao. 2022. DualNER: A dual-teaching framework for zero-shot cross-lingual named entity recognition. In *Findings of the Association for Computational Linguistics: EMNLP 2022*, pages 1837–1843, Abu Dhabi, United Arab Emirates. Association for Computational Linguistics.

Chen Zhang, Yuxuan Lai, Yansong Feng, Xingyu Shen, Haowei Du, and Dongyan Zhao. 2023a. Cross-lingual question answering over knowledge base as reading comprehension. In *Findings of the Association for Computational Linguistics: EACL 2023*, pages 2439–2452, Dubrovnik, Croatia. Association for Computational Linguistics.

Heidi Zhang, Sina Semnani, Farhad Ghassemi, Jialiang Xu, Shicheng Liu, and Monica Lam. 2024. SPAGHETTI: Open-domain question answering from heterogeneous data sources with retrieval and semantic parsing. In *Findings of the Association for Computational Linguistics: ACL 2024*, pages 1663–1678, Bangkok, Thailand. Association for Computational Linguistics.

Qin Zhang, Shangsi Chen, Dongkuan Xu, Qingqing Cao, Xiaojun Chen, Trevor Cohn, and Meng Fang. 2023b. A survey for efficient open domain question answering. In *Proceedings of the 61st Annual Meeting of the Association for Computational Linguistics (Volume 1: Long Papers)*, pages 14447–14465, Toronto, Canada. Association for Computational Linguistics.

Xinyu Zhao, Shih-Ting Lin, and Greg Durrett. 2021. Effective distant supervision for temporal relation extraction. In *Proceedings of the Second Workshop on Domain Adaptation for NLP*, pages 195–203, Kyiv, Ukraine. Association for Computational Linguistics.

Ben Zhou, Daniel Khashabi, Chen-Tse Tsai, and Dan Roth. 2019. Zero-shot open entity typing as type-compatible grounding. *arXiv preprint arXiv:1907.03228*.

Sizhe Zhou, Yu Meng, Bowen Jin, and Jiawei Han. 2024. Grasping the essentials: Tailoring large language models for zero-shot relation extraction. In *Proceedings of the 2024 Conference on Empirical Methods in Natural Language Processing*, pages 13462–13486, Miami, Florida, USA. Association for Computational Linguistics.

A Appendices

In this section, we provide extra figures and tables to further corroborate our experiments in this work. Additionally, we also present a statistical significance analysis of our results using the Anova method.

Dataset	Source	Encoder	Parser	Sent Length		Lex Length		Dep Length		# Docs	# Rels
				Mean	Median	Mean	Median	Mean	Median		
Indore	en	mBERT	stanza	31.23	29.0	13.92	11.0	5.43	5.0	8486	51
	hi	mBERT	stanza	66.76	56.0	27.29	21.0	5.70	5.0	6963	51
	te	mBERT	stanza	151.45	140.0	44.74	31.0	6.05	6.0	8154	51
	en	mBERT	trankit	31.23	29.0	13.92	11.0	5.42	5.0	8486	51
	hi	mBERT	trankit	66.76	56.0	27.29	21.0	5.85	6.0	6963	51
	te	mBERT	trankit	151.45	140.0	44.74	31.0	5.69	6.0	8154	51
	en	XLMR	stanza	34.40	32.0	15.95	13.0	5.43	5.0	8486	51
	hi	XLMR	stanza	56.25	48.0	22.85	17.0	5.70	5.0	6963	51
	te	XLMR	stanza	125.60	113.0	37.43	26.0	6.05	6.0	8154	51
	en	XLMR	trankit	34.40	32.0	15.95	13.0	5.42	5.0	8486	51
	hi	XLMR	trankit	56.25	48.0	22.85	17.0	5.85	6.0	6963	51
	te	XLMR	trankit	125.60	113.0	37.43	26.0	5.69	6.0	8154	51
RedFM	en	mBERT	stanza	117.53	107.0	27.96	17.0	6.40	6.0	10899	32
	es	mBERT	stanza	103.77	91.0	25.97	17.0	6.24	6.0	6538	32
	fr	mBERT	stanza	92.18	78.0	23.19	15.0	5.86	5.0	7383	32
	it	mBERT	stanza	79.31	65.0	20.56	14.0	5.80	5.0	6812	32
	de	mBERT	stanza	88.79	79.0	22.97	15.0	5.28	5.0	7497	32
	ar	mBERT	stanza	107.15	90.0	29.68	22.0	6.08	6.0	1846	32
	zh	mBERT	stanza	118.18	101.0	35.25	22.0	6.69	6.0	1384	32
	en	mBERT	trankit	117.53	107.0	27.96	17.0	6.37	6.0	10899	32
	es	mBERT	trankit	103.77	91.0	25.97	17.0	6.16	6.0	6538	32
	fr	mBERT	trankit	92.18	78.0	23.19	15.0	5.68	5.0	7383	32
	it	mBERT	trankit	79.31	65.0	20.56	14.0	5.64	5.0	6812	32
	de	mBERT	trankit	88.79	79.0	22.97	15.0	5.16	5.0	7497	32
	ar	mBERT	trankit	107.15	90.0	29.68	22.0	6.18	6.0	1846	32
	zh	mBERT	trankit	118.18	101.0	35.25	22.0	6.75	6.0	1384	32
	en	XLMR	stanza	130.33	119.0	31.52	19.0	6.40	6.0	10899	32
	es	XLMR	stanza	112.22	100.0	28.86	19.0	6.24	6.0	6538	32
	fr	XLMR	stanza	103.20	86.0	26.77	17.0	5.86	5.0	7383	32
	it	XLMR	stanza	85.14	71.0	22.72	16.0	5.80	5.0	6812	32
	de	XLMR	stanza	96.23	87.0	25.53	17.0	5.28	5.0	7497	32
	ar	XLMR	stanza	95.81	81.0	26.64	19.0	6.08	6.0	1846	32
	zh	XLMR	stanza	96.10	81.0	28.35	18.0	6.69	6.0	1384	32
	en	XLMR	trankit	130.33	119.0	31.52	19.0	6.37	6.0	10899	32
	es	XLMR	trankit	112.22	100.0	28.86	19.0	6.16	6.0	6538	32
	fr	XLMR	trankit	103.20	86.0	26.77	17.0	5.68	5.0	7383	32
	it	XLMR	trankit	85.14	71.0	22.72	16.0	5.64	5.0	6812	32
	de	XLMR	trankit	96.23	87.0	25.53	17.0	5.16	5.0	7497	32
	ar	XLMR	trankit	95.81	81.0	26.64	19.0	6.18	6.0	1846	32
	zh	XLMR	trankit	96.10	81.0	28.35	18.0	6.75	6.0	1384	32

Table 4: Combined Statistics for Indore and RedFM Datasets

Without Any Dependency Information:

Given the sentence: "The Porsche Panamera is a mid/full-sized luxury vehicle (E-segment in Europe) manufactured by the <e2>German</e2> automobile manufacturer <e1>Porsche</e1>. It is front-engined and has a rear-wheel-drive layout, with all-wheel drive versions also available.", which one of the following relations between the two entities <e1> and <e2> is being discussed? Choose one from this list of 32 options:\n0: country\n1: place of birth \n2: spouse\n3: country of citizenship\n4: instance of\n5: capital\n6: child\n7: shares border with\n8: author\n9: director\n10: occupation\n11: founded by\n12: league\n13: owned by\n14: genre\n15: named after\n16: follows\n17: headquarters location\n18: cast member\n19: manufacturer\n20: located in or next to body of water\n21: location\n22: part of\n23: mouth of the watercourse\n24: member of\n25: sport \n26: characters\n27: participant\n28: notable work\n29: replaces\n30: sibling\n31: inception\n\n. The answer is :

Tuple Format Prompt:

Given the sentence: "The Porsche Panamera is a mid/full-sized luxury vehicle (E-segment in Europe) manufactured by the <e2>German</e2> automobile manufacturer <e1>Porsche</e1>. It is front-engined and has a rear-wheel-drive layout, with all-wheel drive versions also available.", which one of the following relations between the two entities <e1> and <e2> is being discussed? We also provide the dependency parse in the form of head, rel, and word: {"head": "Panamera", "rel": "det", "word": "The"}, {"head": "Panamera", "rel": "compound", "word": "Porsche"}, {"head": "vehicle", "rel": "nsubj", "word": "Panamera"}, {"head": "vehicle", "rel": "cop", "word": "is"}, {"head": "vehicle", "rel": "det", "word": "a"}, {"head": "sized", "rel": "compound", "word": "mid"}, {"head": "sized", "rel": "punct", "word": "/"}, {"head": "sized", "rel": "amod", "word": "full"}, {"head": "sized", "rel": "punct", "word": "-"}, {"head": "vehicle", "rel": "amod", "word": "sized"}, {"head": "vehicle", "rel": "compound", "word": "luxury"}, {"head": "ROOT", "rel": "root", "word": "vehicle"}, {"head": "segment", "rel": "punct", "word": "("}, {"head": "segment", "rel": "compound", "word": "E"}, {"head": "segment", "rel": "punct", "word": "-"}, {"head": "vehicle", "rel": "appos", "word": "segment"}, {"head": "Europe", "rel": "case", "word": "in"}, {"head": "segment", "rel": "nmod", "word": "Europe"}, {"head": "segment", "rel": "punct", "word": ")"}, {"head": "vehicle", "rel": "acl", "word": "manufactured"}, {"head": "manufacturer", "rel": "case", "word": "by"}, {"head": "manufacturer", "rel": "det", "word": "the"}, {"head": "manufacturer", "rel": "amod", "word": "German"}, {"head": "manufacturer", "rel": "compound", "word": "automobile"}, {"head": "manufactured", "rel": "obl", "word": "manufacturer"}, {"head": "manufacturer", "rel": "appos", "word": "Porsche"}, {"head": "vehicle", "rel": "punct", "word": "."}, {"head": "engined", "rel": "nsubj", "word": "It"}, {"head": "engined", "rel": "cop", "word": "is"}, {"head": "engined", "rel": "obl:npmod", "word": "front"}, {"head": "engined", "rel": "punct", "word": "-"}, {"head": "ROOT", "rel": "root", "word": "engined"}, {"head": "has", "rel": "cc", "word": "and"}, {"head": "engined", "rel": "conj", "word": "has"}, {"head": "layout", "rel": "det", "word": "a"}, {"head": "drive", "rel": "amod", "word": "rear"}, {"head": "drive", "rel": "punct", "word": "-"}, {"head": "drive", "rel": "compound", "word": "wheel"}, {"head": "drive", "rel": "punct", "word": "-"}, {"head": "layout", "rel": "amod", "word": "drive"}, {"head": "has", "rel": "obj", "word": "layout"}, {"head": "layout", "rel": "punct", "word": ","}, {"head": "available", "rel": "mark", "word": "with"}, {"head": "drive", "rel": "det", "word": "all"}, {"head": "drive", "rel": "punct", "word": "-"}, {"head": "drive", "rel": "compound", "word": "wheel"}, {"head": "versions", "rel": "compound", "word": "drive"}, {"head": "available", "rel": "nsubj", "word": "versions"}, {"head": "available", "rel": "advmod", "word": "also"}, {"head": "layout", "rel": "acl", "word": "available"}, {"head": "engined", "rel": "punct", "word": "."}. Choose one from this list of 32 options:\n0: country\n1: place of birth \n2: spouse\n3: country of citizenship\n4: instance of\n5: capital\n6: child\n7: shares border with\n8: author\n9: director\n10: occupation\n11: founded by\n12: league\n13: owned by\n14: genre\n15: named after\n16: follows\n17: headquarters location\n18: cast member\n19: manufacturer\n20: located in or next to body of water\n21: location\n22: part of\n23: mouth of the watercourse\n24: member of\n25: sport \n26: characters\n27: participant\n28: notable work\n29: replaces\n30: sibling\n31: inception\n\n. The answer is :

Table 5: Prompt without dependency information and the tuple format prompt are used for relation extraction on the English subset of the RedFM dataset with Trankit as the dependency parser.

Text Prompt:
Given the sentence: T̈he Porsche Panamera is a mid/full-sized luxury vehicle (E-segment in Europe) manufactured by the <e2>German</e2> automobile manufacturer <e1>Porsche</e1>. It is front-engined and has a rear-wheel-drive layout, with all-wheel drive versions also available.; which one of the following relations between the two entities <e1> and <e2> is being discussed?\We also provide the dependency parses as follows: T̈he is Determiner of Panamera, Porsche is Compound noun modifier of Panamera, Panamera is Nominal subject of vehicle, is is Copula of vehicle, a is Determiner of vehicle, mid/ is Adverbial modifier of sized, full is Adjectival modifier of sized, - is Punctuation of sized, sized is Adjectival modifier of vehicle, luxury is Compound noun modifier of vehicle, vehicle is the root word, (is Punctuation of E, E is Appositional modifier of vehicle, - is Punctuation of segment, segment is Unspecified dependency of E, in is Case marker of Europe, Europe is Nominal modifier of segment,) is Punctuation of segment, manufactured is Clausal modifier of noun of vehicle, by is Case marker of Porsche, the is Determiner of Porsche, German is Adjectival modifier of Porsche, automobile is Compound noun modifier of manufacturer, manufacturer is Compound noun modifier of Porsche, Porsche is Oblique nominal of manufactured, . is Punctuation of vehicle, It is Nominal subject of engined, is is Copula of engined, front is Adjectival modifier of engined, - is Punctuation of front, engined is the root word, and is Coordinating conjunction of has, has is Conjunction of engined, a is Determiner of layout, rear is Compound noun modifier of drive, - is Punctuation of wheel, wheel is Compound noun modifier of drive, - is Punctuation of drive, drive is Compound noun modifier of layout, layout is Object of has, , is Punctuation of available, with is Marker of available, all is Determiner of wheel, - is Punctuation of all, wheel is Compound noun modifier of drive, drive is Compound noun modifier of versions, versions is Nominal subject of available, also is Adverbial modifier of available, available is Adverbial clause modifier of has, . is Punctuation of engined, \Choose one from this list of 32 options:\n0: country\n1: place of birth \n2: spouse\n3: country of citizenship\n4: instance of\n5: capital\n6: child\n7: shares border with\n8: author\n9: director\n10: occupation\n11: founded by\n12: league\n13: owned by\n14: genre\n15: named after\n16: follows\n17: headquarters location\n18: cast member\n19: manufacturer\n20: located in or next to body of water\n21: location\n22: part of\n23: mouth of the watercourse\n24: member of\n25: sport \n26: characters\n27: participant\n28: notable work\n29: replaces\n30: sibling\n31: inception\n\nThe answer is : "
Filtered Text Prompt:
Given the sentence: T̈he Porsche Panamera is a mid/full-sized luxury vehicle (E-segment in Europe) manufactured by the <e2>German</e2> automobile manufacturer <e1>Porsche</e1>. It is front-engined and has a rear-wheel-drive layout, with all-wheel drive versions also available.; which one of the following relations between the two entities <e1> and <e2> is being discussed?\n We also provide the dependency parses as follows: P̈orsche is Adjectival modifier of German, \n Choose one from this list of 32 options:\n0: country\n1: place of birth \n2: spouse\n3: country of citizenship\n4: instance of\n5: capital\n6: child\n7: shares border with\n8: author\n9: director\n10: occupation\n11: founded by\n12: league\n13: owned by\n14: genre\n15: named after\n16: follows\n17: headquarters location\n18: cast member\n19: manufacturer\n20: located in or next to body of water\n21: location\n22: part of\n23: mouth of the watercourse\n24: member of\n25: sport \n26: characters\n27: participant\n28: notable work\n29: replaces\n30: sibling\n31: inception\n\n. The answer is :

Table 6: Text prompt and Filtered Text prompts used for relation extraction on the English subset of the RedFM dataset with Trankit as the dependency parser.

Table 7: Zero-shot cross-lingual performance for Relation Extraction on the RedFM dataset using different combinations of multi-lingual encoder and dependency parse information and GNN. Highest values in each column are in bold. The rows and columns correspond to the source and target language respectively.

						mBERT			
Src	DEP	GNN	en	es	fr	it	de	ar	zh
en	-	-	-	80.4±0.2	80.7±0.4	**77.3±1.3**	78.8±0.9	72.7±0.8	70.4±0.6
en	stanza	rgcn	-	79.6±0.8	**80.9±1.4**	76.2±1.0	**80.2±0.5**	74.4±0.9	72.0±0.8
en	stanza	rgat	-	80.3±0.4	80.3±0.2	74.8±1.2	79.5±0.3	74.1±0.9	**72.3±0.4**
en	trankit	rgcn	-	80.1±0.4	80.8±0.5	73.8±0.2	79.3±0.7	73.8±1.8	69.5±0.6
en	trankit	rgat	-	**80.8±0.3**	80.7±0.2	74.4±1.8	79.0±0.7	**74.5±0.7**	70.1±0.6
es	-	-	77.6±0.1	-	77.2±0.8	76.4±0.6	75.9±0.7	70.9±1.6	70.8±1.1
es	stanza	rgcn	78.0±0.4	-	**82.6±0.8**	77.6±1.4	76.9±1.3	73.2±0.5	69.2±0.6
es	stanza	rgat	79.1±0.2	-	78.4±0.5	77.4±1.3	76.2±0.7	**73.5±0.9**	69.7±1.5
es	trankit	rgcn	79.3±0.9	-	80.6±1.6	76.3±0.6	77.1±1.0	73.3±0.3	**71.5±1.6**
es	trankit	rgat	**80.0±1.1**	-	78.7±0.5	**78.3±1.0**	**77.7±0.8**	72.6±1.2	71.2±2.6
fr	-	-	76.6±2.9	80.4±1.3	-	76.9±2.0	74.8±1.6	70.2±1.1	66.4±2.6
fr	stanza	rgcn	76.6±0.3	82.1±1.0	-	77.7±0.7	76.6±0.2	70.4±0.8	66.8±0.9
fr	stanza	rgat	80.0±0.7	82.1±0.9	-	77.0±1.0	77.5±1.5	71.5±1.0	67.5±1.2
fr	trankit	rgcn	78.6±0.3	**83.3±1.6**	-	**78.7±1.1**	**78.8±2.5**	**72.4±0.5**	**69.7±0.7**
fr	trankit	rgat	**80.1±0.8**	79.7±2.1	-	76.6±1.5	77.4±0.1	70.9±0.8	68.4±0.5
it	-	-	75.4±0.4	83.1±0.5	77.7±1.1	-	72.9±1.1	**73.0±2.0**	70.8±1.0
it	stanza	rgcn	**79.0±0.6**	83.0±0.7	77.2±1.0	-	74.7±1.4	70.8±0.3	70.0±0.7
it	stanza	rgat	76.7±0.9	**83.8±0.7**	77.5±0.5	-	75.7±1.5	72.2±1.6	70.5±0.4
it	trankit	rgcn	77.1±1.4	82.3±0.3	77.2±0.6	-	76.0±1.2	71.0±1.0	69.2±1.9
it	trankit	rgat	77.1±0.1	82.5±0.4	**77.8±0.5**	-	**76.3±0.1**	71.7±1.0	**71.5±0.9**
de	-	-	80.4±1.0	80.0±0.4	**78.3±0.1**	76.1±1.5	-	**75.8±1.9**	71.6±1.2
de	stanza	rgcn	80.0±0.2	80.4±0.7	76.7±0.3	75.8±0.8	-	74.2±0.8	70.0±1.9
de	stanza	rgat	79.2±0.4	**81.3±1.1**	78.1±1.4	76.6±2.7	-	74.6±0.5	**71.7±0.6**
de	trankit	rgcn	79.7±0.3	80.6±1.4	77.9±0.3	75.1±0.4	-	73.3±1.0	70.1±0.1
de	trankit	rgat	**80.7±0.7**	79.2±0.1	77.8±0.6	**77.4±0.5**	-	73.7±0.0	70.6±0.8
						XLMR			
en	-	-	-	73.1±1.8	**72.8±2.8**	64.2±3.7	**75.6±1.7**	61.7±1.8	64.4±1.0
en	stanza	rgcn	-	74.4±1.3	**72.7±0.5**	**67.4±1.3**	74.6±0.7	**63.2±1.5**	65.1±0.9
en	stanza	rgat	-	73.1±0.7	**72.7±1.4**	66.5±3.5	71.1±1.0	59.6±2.7	62.2±0.4
en	trankit	rgcn	-	74.4±1.5	72.0±1.8	65.4±2.2	71.5±1.6	62.6±1.8	64.6±1.3
en	trankit	rgat	-	**74.9±0.7**	70.3±0.1	62.4±1.6	73.9±0.4	61.5±1.7	**66.5±1.7**
es	-	-	73.3±0.4	-	74.3±0.4	**70.1±1.4**	**70.6±0.7**	63.2±3.1	**65.9±1.9**
es	stanza	rgcn	73.4±2.2	-	75.1±0.3	68.3±2.5	67.3±0.6	61.9±1.2	62.4±1.4
es	stanza	rgat	72.7±1.9	-	75.2±1.0	69.3±1.6	67.3±0.3	60.5±1.4	62.8±1.8
es	trankit	rgcn	**73.8±1.0**	-	75.9±1.5	69.8±1.8	70.0±2.5	**64.3±2.1**	65.6±2.7
es	trankit	rgat	71.4±1.2	-	**76.2±1.2**	68.0±1.5	68.7±2.0	60.0±0.9	62.5±2.3
fr	-	-	71.1±0.9	75.0±0.6	-	68.9±0.6	68.5±1.3	**61.5±1.2**	59.4±2.6
fr	stanza	rgcn	**74.3±1.7**	74.1±1.1	-	**69.7±0.6**	**72.2±1.3**	58.7±0.6	**62.9±2.7**
fr	stanza	rgat	70.1±1.5	73.9±1.3	-	67.0±1.5	66.2±1.0	59.0±0.9	60.3±1.6
fr	trankit	rgcn	70.0±0.2	74.4±0.5	-	68.4±0.7	66.4±0.7	58.9±2.2	59.5±1.8
fr	trankit	rgat	71.8±1.3	**76.0±0.7**	-	68.2±0.8	70.6±1.0	**61.5±1.2**	59.9±1.3
it	-	-	71.2±1.1	76.1±1.6	72.2±0.9	-	68.2±1.7	60.8±0.5	62.0±1.7
it	stanza	rgcn	73.3±2.0	76.1±0.8	74.3±1.3	-	67.2±2.1	61.8±0.3	63.1±0.3
it	stanza	rgat	**74.9±1.0**	76.0±0.2	74.2±1.3	-	68.9±0.2	62.2±0.1	**64.7±1.5**
it	trankit	rgcn	73.3±1.2	77.0±0.7	74.8±1.6	-	70.0±1.7	**64.5±1.0**	**64.7±1.0**
it	trankit	rgat	72.6±1.9	**78.7±0.5**	**76.6±0.2**	-	**70.2±1.0**	63.6±3.4	64.6±1.5
de	-	-	75.0±1.5	72.4±0.9	69.3±1.3	64.1±0.3	-	60.8±0.7	64.0±1.2
de	stanza	rgcn	72.6±1.5	73.4±2.1	70.8±1.9	65.2±0.5	-	60.6±0.8	**66.0±1.9**
de	stanza	rgat	**76.1±1.5**	**73.5±0.2**	**71.5±1.3**	**69.0±2.8**	-	**64.0±1.6**	65.8±1.7
de	trankit	rgcn	74.1±1.0	72.8±0.8	69.6±1.8	63.6±2.3	-	63.4±1.0	64.5±1.9
de	trankit	rgat	75.0±0.5	73.2±1.6	70.3±1.3	64.9±1.0	-	63.7±0.5	64.4±3.5

Table 8: Zero-shot cross-lingual performance for Relation Extraction on the IndoRE dataset using different combinations of multi-lingual encoder and dependency parse information and GNN. Highest values in each column are in bold. The rows and columns correspond to the source and target language respectively.

		mBERT			
Src	DEP	GNN	en	hi	te
en	-	-	-	60.7±0.6	35.3±0.8
en	stanza	rgcn	-	60.1±0.4	38.3±1.2
en	stanza	rgat	-	58.7±0.3	**40.6±2.2**
en	trankit	rgcn	-	**62.5±0.8**	38.0±1.4
en	trankit	rgat	-	61.8±1.0	37.8±1.8
hi	-	-	**69.7±1.9**	-	49.5±2.3
hi	stanza	rgcn	68.6±0.6	-	49.4±0.8
hi	stanza	rgat	67.8±2.3	-	49.7±0.6
hi	trankit	rgcn	68.1±0.8	-	49.6±2.2
hi	trankit	rgat	68.0±1.6	-	**53.9±0.9**
te	-	-	45.3±1.7	54.4±2.6	-
te	stanza	rgcn	45.6±1.4	54.0±1.3	-
te	stanza	rgat	44.8±0.3	**56.6±0.3**	-
te	trankit	rgcn	**47.7±0.8**	54.2±0.1	-
te	trankit	rgat	46.1±1.2	54.2±2.5	-
		XLMR			
en	-	-	-	57.4±2.3	37.2±2.5
en	stanza	rgcn	-	55.3±1.2	37.0±1.6
en	stanza	rgat	-	55.5±2.3	37.8±1.9
en	trankit	rgcn	-	58.8±0.5	36.4±3.8
en	trankit	rgat	-	**61.0±2.5**	**39.0±4.0**
hi	-	-	59.1±1.8	-	53.7±1.0
hi	stanza	rgcn	57.4±1.3	-	**54.7±1.2**
hi	stanza	rgat	**61.0±2.5**	-	**54.8±2.1**
hi	trankit	rgcn	59.5±0.8	-	54.3±1.8
hi	trankit	rgat	57.3±2.4	-	**54.8±2.3**
te	-	-	40.9±2.6	52.8±0.7	-
te	stanza	rgcn	41.2±2.2	**55.5±0.9**	-
te	stanza	rgat	39.0±0.7	52.0±3.2	-
te	trankit	rgcn	**41.8±0.6**	53.7±0.6	-
te	trankit	rgat	41.4±0.3	53.7±1.8	-

Source	sum_sq	df	F	P(>F)
C(src)	1.844	2.000	6.265	**0.020**
C(GNN)	0.185	1.000	1.258	0.291
C(DEP)	1.226	1.000	8.330	**0.018**
C(ENC)	0.308	1.000	2.094	0.182
C(src):C(DEP)	0.165	2.000	0.56	0.590
C(src):C(ENC)	7.124	2.000	24.20	**0.000**
C(src):C(GNN)	1.335	2.000	4.534	**0.043**
C(DEP):C(GNN)	0.055	1.000	0.371	0.557
C(ENC):C(GNN)	1.045	1.000	7.098	**0.026**
C(DEP):C(ENC)	1.005	1.000	6.827	**0.028**
Residual	1.325	9.000	NaN	NaN

Table 9: Indore In-Domain ANOVA Results

Source	sum_sq	df	F	P(>F)
C(src)	48.606	2.000	2.449	0.108
C(GNN)	4.009	1.000	0.404	0.531
C(DEP)	23.301	1.000	2.348	0.139
C(ENC)	20.426	1.000	2.058	0.164
C(tgt)	199.051	2.000	10.030	**0.001**
C(tgt):C(DEP)	13.604	2.000	0.686	0.513
C(tgt):C(ENC)	85.332	2.000	4.300	**0.025**
C(tgt):C(GNN)	19.710	2.000	0.993	0.385
C(tgt):C(src)	12.388	4.000	0.312	0.735
C(src):C(DEP)	6.487	2.000	0.327	0.724
C(src):C(ENC)	73.878	2.000	3.723	**0.039**
C(src):C(GNN)	7.459	2.000	0.376	0.691
C(DEP):C(GNN)	0.845	1.000	0.085	0.773
C(ENC):C(GNN)	0.923	1.000	0.093	0.763
C(DEP):C(ENC)	1.561	1.000	0.157	0.695
Residual	238.143	24.000	NaN	NaN

Table 10: Indore Cross-Domain ANOVA Results

Source	sum_sq	df	F	P(>F)
C(src)	1.862	4.000	0.408	0.800
C(GNN)	0.719	1.000	0.630	0.438
C(DEP)	3.613	1.000	3.167	0.093
C(ENC)	51.586	1.000	45.228	**0.000**
C(src):C(DEP)	2.027	4.000	0.444	0.775
C(src):C(ENC)	9.053	4.000	1.984	0.143
C(src):C(GNN)	3.373	4.000	0.739	0.578
C(DEP):C(GNN)	0.221	1.000	0.194	0.665
C(ENC):C(GNN)	1.773	1.000	1.555	0.229
C(DEP):C(ENC)	1.601	1.000	1.403	0.252
Residual	19.390	17.000	NaN	NaN

Table 11: RedFM In-domain ANOVA Results

Source	sum_sq	df	F	P(>F)
C(src)	14.700	4.000	0.988	0.322
C(GNN)	0.109	1.000	0.029	0.864
C(DEP)	1.111	1.000	0.299	0.585
C(ENC)	4.923	1.000	1.323	0.252
C(tgt)	10.040	6.000	0.450	0.718
C(tgt):C(DEP)	25.753	6.000	1.154	0.334
C(tgt):C(ENC)	106.197	6.000	4.757	**0.000**
C(tgt):C(GNN)	1.642	6.000	0.074	0.998
C(tgt):C(src)	314.185	24.000	3.518	**0.000**
C(src):C(DEP)	23.724	4.000	1.594	0.178
C(src):C(ENC)	323.737	4.000	21.752	**0.000**
C(src):C(GNN)	49.322	4.000	3.314	**0.012**
C(DEP):C(GNN)	0.615	1.000	0.165	0.685
C(ENC):C(GNN)	2.771	1.000	0.745	0.389
C(DEP):C(ENC)	0.389	1.000	0.105	0.747
Residual	647.408	174.000	NaN	NaN

Table 12: RedFM Cross-Domain ANOVA Results

Source	sum_sq	df	F	P(>F)
C(src)	58.4	2	0.657	5.26E-01
C(DEP)	2.2	1	0.048	8.28E-01
C(LLM)	1260.3	2	14.17	**6.18E-05**
C(PRM)	3042.5	2	34.22	**3.94E-08**
C(src):C(DEP)	16.7	2	0.187	8.30E-01
C(src):C(LLM)	543.7	4	3.058	**3.36E-02**
C(src):C(PRM)	426.9	4	2.401	7.46E-02
C(DEP):C(LLM)	62.3	2	0.708	5.05E-01
C(DEP):C(PRM)	48.0	2	0.54	5.87E-01
C(LLM):C(PRM)	2205.3	4	12.40	**7.47E-06**
Residual	1200.1	27	NaN	NaN

Table 13: Indore Zero-shot ICL ANOVA Results

Source	sum_sq	df	F	P(>F)
C(src)	6123.02	6	13.34	**2.91E-10**
C(DEP)	5.09	1	0.07	7.97E-01
C(LLM)	4945.81	2	32.32	**6.97E-11**
C(PRM)	12473.39	2	81.51	**1.23E-19**
C(src):C(DEP)	178.97	6	0.39	8.83E-01
C(src):C(LLM)	13819.12	12	15.05	**1.46E-15**
C(src):C(PRM)	1727.37	12	1.88	5.01E-02
C(DEP):C(LLM)	131.03	2	0.86	4.29E-01
C(DEP):C(PRM)	101.88	2	0.67	5.17E-01
C(LLM):C(PRM)	3130.31	4	10.23	**1.12E-06**
Residual	5815.44	76	NaN	NaN

Table 14: RedFM Zero-shot ICL ANOVA Results

Can dependency parses facilitate generalization in language models? A case study of cross-lingual relation extraction

Ritam Dutt, Shounak Sural, Carolyn Penstein Rosé
Carnegie Mellon University
{rdutt,ssural,cprose}@andrew.cmu.edu

Abstract

In this work, we propose DEPGEN, a framework for evaluating the generalization capabilities of language models on the task of relation extraction, with dependency parses as scaffolds. We use a GNN-based framework that takes dependency parses as input and learns embeddings of entities which are augmented to a baseline multilingual encoder. We also investigate the role of dependency parses when they are included as part of the prompt to LLMs in a zero-shot learning setup. We observe that including off-the-shelf dependency parses can aid relation extraction, with the best performing model having a mild relative improvement of 0.91% and 1.5% in the in-domain and zero-shot setting respectively across two datasets. For the in-context learning setup, we observe an average improvement of 1.67%, with significant gains for low-performing LLMs. We also carry out extensive statistical analysis to investigate how different factors such as the choice of the dependency parser or the nature of the prompt impact performance. We make our code and results publicly available for the research community at https://github.com/ShoRit/multilingual-re.git

1 Introduction

Information packaging in language does not happen arbitrarily (Croft, 2022). The "internal structure" of a text message, which determines how the message is constructed or parsed, is grounded in predefined linguistic rules in the form of syntax and semantics. Linguistic structures such as dependency graphs (Zeman et al., 2019; Chomsky, 2002) or semantic parses (Banarescu et al., 2013; Reddy et al., 2017) have been pivotal in the history of NLP research both for their intrinsic merit i.e. developing frameworks that can construct or interpret such structures automatically (Chen et al., 2024; Gu et al., 2024), and their external value as augmentations to aid language understanding tasks (Ding et al., 2024; Şahin, 2022).

Information extraction or IE is one such field which had relied heavily on linguistic information ever since its inception; some notable examples include few-shot named entity recognition or NER (Chen et al., 2023; Xie et al., 2024), relation extraction (Li et al., 2023; Zhou et al., 2024), open-domain question answering, (Zhang et al., 2023b, 2024) amongst others. However, recent years have witnessed a decline in the adoption of linguistic frameworks in favor of large scale pre-trained language models (Devlin et al., 2018; Liu et al., 2019; Conneau et al., 2020a; Sainz et al., 2024) which are shown to encode syntactic and semantic information within their parameters (Starace et al., 2023; Liu et al., 2024) and have also demonstrated significant improvements on IE (Sainz et al., 2024; Efeoglu and Paschke, 2024).

Moreover, as we usher into an era of large language models, the question which looms over our head like the proverbial sword of Damocles "Are dependency parses helpful for information extraction?" We are motivated to answer this question based on the past work of Sachan et al. (2021) which showed the utility of adding syntactic information for different information extraction tasks in English. However, the observed benefits hold true only when the **gold parses** are available, with no improvements over the baseline in presence of off-the-shelf parses. In this study we expand upon this idea and investigate whether off-the-shelf dependency parses can assist language models in multilingual information extraction for both indomain and zero-shot transfer settings.

We specifically deal with the task of multilingual relation extraction, wherein we identify the nature of relationship between two annotated entities in a document. We show in Figure 1 how we can connect the entities wood and fences by traversing the dependency graph that connects these two entities, highlighting the potential utility of linguistic frameworks for this task. We explore the role

Proceedings of the 4th International Workshop on Knowledge-Augmented Methods for Natural Language Processing (KnowledgeNLP'25), pages 338–358
May 3, 2025 ©2025 Association for Computational Linguistics

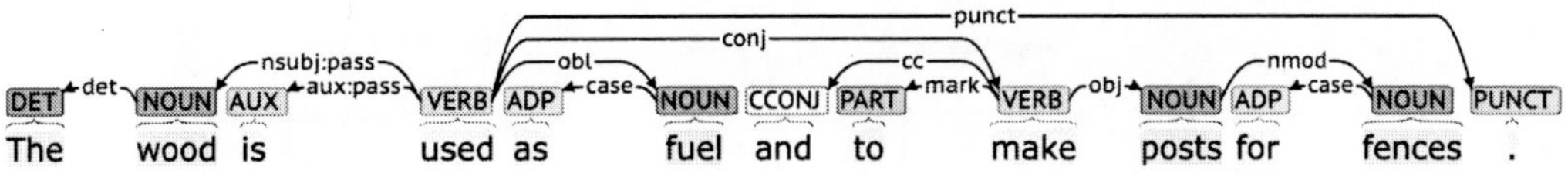

Figure 1: Example depicting the supplemental information provided by the *dependency tree*. The entities of interest are wood and fences, having the relationship material_used. The path *wood* ← *used* → *make* → *posts* → *fences* elicits this relationship.

of dependency parses for cross-lingual relation extraction in both a fine-tuned supervised setting and a prompting/ in-context learning setup.

We propose a framework, DEPGEN, built on top of a pretrained multi-lingual language model that uses dependency parse information to perform relation extraction for both in-domain and zero-shot cross-lingual transfer settings. Through a comprehensive set of 2440 experiments spanning 10 languages over 2 datasets, we observe that incorporating dependency information brings about modest improvements for in-domain and cross-lingual fine-tuning setups by 0.9% and 1.5% respectively.

We also carry out extensive statistical analysis to identify which factors significantly impact performance. Our observations highlight that performance improvements is mostly predicated by the choice of the target language, and the choice of the pre-trained language model rather than the choice of the dependency parser for all cases. However, for the in-context learning setup, we demonstrate that the performance is determined by the choice of the prompting strategy, with our proposed approach boasting the highest gains, i.e. an absolute improvement of 1.67 F1 score over the baseline.

2 Related Work

2.1 Generalization in Information Extraction

Recent years bear witness to countless research endeavors to facilitate generalizability and transfer across domains for several information extraction (IE) tasks. Such works include zero-shot relation extraction (Wang et al., 2022b; Jun et al., 2022; Li et al., 2023), zero-shot or few-shot NER (Zeng et al., 2022; Das et al., 2022; Xie et al., 2024) , zero-shot KBQA (Gu et al., 2021; Dutt et al., 2023), cross-lingual KBQA (Zhang et al., 2023a), and open domain QA (Min et al., 2020; Zhang et al., 2023b), amongst others (Fritzler et al., 2019; Zhou et al., 2019). This interest is in part due to the advent of large scale pre-trained language models such as Devlin et al. (2018); Liu et al. (2019); Conneau et al. (2020a); Sainz et al. (2024) which have shown significant improvements on IE. Recent works on domain adaptation and transfer learning have advocated different pre-training objective functions to ensure the model is well adapted to the particular domain. Other multi-lingual/ cross-lingual transfer works employ different data augmentation techniques such as translation into the target data to aid transfer. In this work, we investigate approaches to perform multi-lingual information extraction in a zero-shot setting without any additional data in the target language.

2.2 Relation Extraction

The goal of relation extraction or relation classification is to detect and classify the relation between specified entities in a text according to some predefined schema. Current research in RE has mostly been carried out in a few-shot or a zero-shot setting to address the dearth of training data (Liu et al., 2022; Li et al., 2023) and the "long-tail" problem of skewness in relation classes (Ye and Ling, 2019b; Liang et al., 2023). Salient work in that direction includes (i) designing RE-specific pretraining objectives for learning better representations (Baldini Soares et al., 2019; Wang et al., 2022a), (ii) incorporating meta-information such as relation descriptions (Yang et al., 2020; Chen and Li, 2021), a global relation graph, (Qu et al., 2020), or entity types (Peng et al., 2020), and (iii) leveraging additional information in the form of dependency parses (Yu et al., 2022), translated texts for multilingual RE (Nag et al., 2021), or distantly supervised instances (Zhao et al., 2021; Ye and Ling, 2019a). T-5 based models have shown to perform well in relation extraction settings with few-shot finetuning (Diaz-Garcia and Lopez, 2024).

Recently, LLMs have shown promise in zero-shot relation extraction. Challenging cases such as overlapping relations and none-of-the-above (nota) relations have been handled effectively by LLMs in zero-shot settings (Li et al., 2023). LLMs have also outperformed smaller models for RE with larger, document-level context sizes in models such as

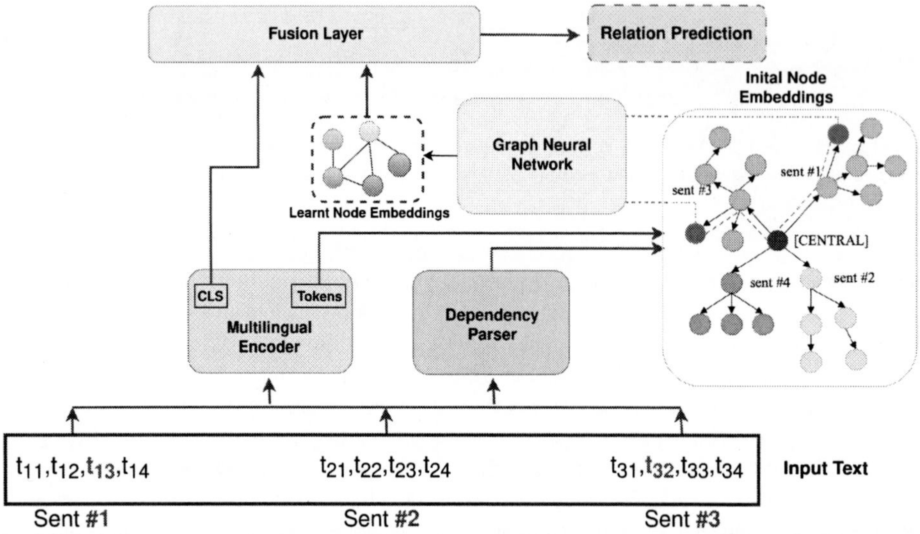

Figure 2: An overview of our proposed framework DEPGEN. The architecture takes as input a document, which comprises a sequence of sentences, with the entities highlighted in red. This document passes through a multilingual encoder to obtain the token embeddings, and a dependency parser that generates dependency parses for each sentence. The individual sentences in the dependency parser are connected using a central [CENTRAL] node to obtain a connected graph. The nodes are initialized using the embeddings obtained from the multilingual encoder and updated using a Graph Neural Network. The final representations of the entities obtained from the GNN are fused with the entity embeddings and concatenated with the [CLS] token of the document to predict the relation.

AutoRE (Xue et al., 2024). All of these techniques seek to alleviate the need for expensive human-annotated training data. In this work, we question whether incorporating linguistic structures in the form of dependency parsing as an explicit addition to the input in existing models can aid learning robust representations that can be transferred to other languages.

3 Methodology

We investigate the role of dependency parses for zero-shot cross-lingual relation extraction in two setups, namely (i) a fine-tuned setup where a model is first trained on a given source language and then evaluated on a target language, and (ii) an in-context-learning setup where we prompt an LLM to predict the relation between two specified entities in a zero-shot setting to test the innate capabilities of the LLM for RE.

3.1 Fine-Tuning Setting

We present a detailed description of our proposed framework, DEPGEN here. Our framework leverages the internal structure of a document text to aid relation classification. We define internal structure as the linguistic information encoded within the document based on syntactic rules in the form of dependency parses. This section describes the individual components that constitute our framework DEPGEN, namely the multilingual encoder, dependency parser, graph neural network, and the fusion layer. We dive deep into the methodology for representing the textual content, and elaborate on the approach employed for incorporating dependency parses for a given input sentence. Finally, we end the section with how the different modes of information are fused, and the classification setup. A pictorial representation of our framework can be seen in Figure 2 Our architecture involves the following components.

3.1.1 Multilingual Encoder

We experiment with mBERT (Devlin et al., 2018) and XLMR (Conneau et al., 2020c) as our multilingual text encoder to obtain representations of the input sentence(s). Past work has shown the efficacy of such contextual multilingual encoders in capturing long-range semantic dependency in text (Litschko et al., 2021). Similar to these works, we consider the final encoder layer representation of [CLS] token as the text representation. The sentence(s) are fed as input to the MULTILINGUAL

ENCODER (Figure 2) and the [CLS] token representation from the final layer is fed into the FUSION LAYER. The individual token representations from the final layer are used to initialize the node embeddings in the dependency graph of the INTERNAL STRUCTURE module, which we describe below.

3.1.2 Internal Structure

We incorporate the internal structure information by learning the syntactic dependency information between the tokens in the input sentence. We first pass the input tokens through a DEPENDENCY PARSER to obtain the dependency tree for each sentence. We then construct a dependency graph from the constituent dependency trees, which is then fed as input to a Graph Neural Network (GNN) (Scarselli et al., 2008). The various components of this module are as follows.

Dependency Parser To generate the dependency tree, we use off-the-shelf multilingual dependency parsing modules, i.e. Stanza (Qi et al., 2020a) and Trankit (Nguyen et al., 2021). The resulting dependency tree represents the syntactic dependency relations between the words in a sentence; the dependencies follow the Universal Dependencies formalism (Nivre et al., 2016; Zeman et al., 2019), resulting in 76 types of dependencies across the different languages for our experiments.

Dependency Graph Since the dependency tree is defined for a sentence, the output from DEPENDENCY PARSER will be in the form of a forest of disconnected dependency trees; for example 4 trees for 4 sentences in Figure 2. We add a pseudo node [CENTRAL] and add a new type of dependency relation [SENT] between the [CENTRAL] and all the [ROOT] nodes of the sentences. The proposed design has two benefits - (1) The [CENTRAL] node allows for information exchange between the sentences, which otherwise would probably lead to different clusters of representations (represented by colors in Figure 2) for nodes in different sentences, (2) The distance between the two entities is reduced (dotted red line in Figure 2) when the entities are present across two different sentences, resulting in an efficient information flow between them.

Graph Neural Network We represent each word as a node in the dependency graph and the dependency relations as the edges between the nodes. Each node in the graph is initialized with the representations obtained from the final layer of the MULTILINGUAL ENCODER. We aggregate the subtoken representations via max-pooling and obtain the final representation of a word. This initialization helps incorporate the semantic relationship between the nodes and facilitates end-to-end joint training of the MULTILINGUAL ENCODER and the INTERNAL STRUCTURE modules. The relation embeddings for the all the relation types are initialized at random and learnt jointly along with the node embeddings. The representations of the two entities from the multi-layer GNN are then fed to the FUSION LAYER along with the sentence representation for relation prediction.

3.1.3 Relation Prediction

We concatenate the representations obtained from the MULTILINGUAL ENCODER and the INTERNAL STRUCTURE modules in the FUSION LAYER and perform a multi-class classification for predicting the relation. During training, we compute the standard Cross Entropy loss, and back-propagate it jointly through all the components of the network.

3.2 In-context Learning Setting

In addition to the DEPGEN framework that encapsulates the fine-tuned setting, we also explore the role of dependency parses when provided as additional inputs to LLMs in a zero-shot prompting setup. We experiment with three different types of prompt formats that encodes the dependency information which we describe below.

Tuple Format: In the tuple-based prompt format, we simply provide the dependency parse as a list of tuples or dictionary keys. Each tuple comprises three elements, i.e. a node in the dependency graph or a word, the corresponding head node of that word, and the relation that connects the head node to the word. For example, the phrase "Porsche Panamera", would have the following information in the form of a tuple.

```
{
    word: Porsche
    head: Panamera,
    rel: compound
}
```

Text Format: Instead of providing the dependency parse information in the form of tuples, we verbalize the dependency relations between the words in the sentence in natural language format. In the above example of

"Porsche Panamera", we re-write the tuple information as `"Porsche is Compound noun modifier of Panamera"`. We do this for all the tuples in the dependency graph.

Filtered Text Format: As opposed to verbalizing all the tuples in the dependency graph, we filter out only the tuples that connect the two entities in the sentence via the dependency relations. Not only does this reduce the number of input tokens to the LLM, it also helps filter out redundant information.

As a control, we also prompt the models with only the text, without any dependency information, which serves as a baseline. The details of the prompts are in the Appendix.

4 Experimental Setup

4.1 Dataset

We conduct our experiments on relation extraction on two datasets i.e. IndoRE and REDFM.

IndoRE (Nag et al., 2021) The IndoRE dataset covers a diverse and rich set of entity and relation annotated sentences in three low resource Indian languages — Bengali (bn), Hindi (hi) and Telugu (te). To study protocols for transferring RE capability across languages, it also has labeled English (en) RE instances as an example of a resource-high language. The dataset consists of 32,610 sentences combining all four languages from Wikidata where each language contains 51 unique relations. Out of these languages, we exclude Bengali from our experiments because the dependency parsers' inability to parse the language.

REDFM (Huguet Cabot et al., 2023) We use this dataset consisting of examples from 7 languages. These languages include English (en), Arabic (ar), Spanish (es), German (de), Italian (it), French (fr), and Chinese (zh), which are hand-annotated. There are a total of about 15,400 examples in the dataset with a total of 32 types of relations. We use the languages en, es, de, it, and fr for training (i.e. source languages), and all the 7 languages for testing in a zero-shot setting (i.e. target languages). We exclude Arabic and Chinese as source language due to the unavailability of a training split in the REDFM dataset. We use the train/validation/test splits as in the original paper.

4.2 Fine-tuned Experimental Setup

We experiment with the following settings:

1. **Baseline:** We experiment with mBERT (Devlin et al., 2019) and XLMR (Conneau et al., 2020b) as our choices to encode the document text and the entity spans. We concatenate the pooled representation of the entities and the [CLS] embedding and use it for relation classification.

2. **Dependency Parses:** We experiment with Trankit (Nguyen et al., 2021) and Stanza (Qi et al., 2020b) as the choice of the dependency parser across all languages for both datasets.

3. **Graph Neural Network:** We experiment with RGCN (Schlichtkrull et al., 2018) and RGAT (Busbridge et al., 2019) as the backbone GNN architecture to encode the dependency information between words in the document. We use a GNN with 2 hidden layers for all our experiments.

4.3 In-context Learning Experimental Setup

We employ three different instruction-tuned LLMs for our in-context learning experiments, i.e. LLaMA (Meta-Llama-3-8B-Instruct) (Grattafiori et al., 2024), Mistral (Mistral-7B-Instruct-v0.3) (Jiang et al., 2023) and Qwen (Qwen2-7B-Instruct) (Yang et al., 2024). We use instruction-tuned LLMs since we wish to employ these LLMs in a zero-shot setup for relation extraction without fine-tuning or additional training. Similar to the fine-tuned experimental setup, the dependency parse information are obtained from two sources, i.e. Stanza and Trankit.

4.4 Experiment Counts

For in-domain, we have a total of 8 languages (5 for RedFM, 3 for IndoRE) for 2 given choices of encoder, parser and GNN. Each experiment is repeated for 5 seeds resulting in a total of 320 experiments, that include dependency information and an additional 80 experiments (over 8 languages, 2 encoders, and 5 seeds) as the baseline. For the zero-shot cross-lingual transfer setting, for RedFM, we have 6 possible target languages for each of the 5 source languages, while for IndoRE, we have 2 possible targets for each of the 3 source languages. Thus for each 36 possible cross-lingual pairs, we evaluate 50 different combination of encoder, parser, GNN, and seeds, resulting in another 1800 experiments. Finally, in the in-context learning setup for LLMs, we experiment with 3 LLMs for 10 languages over 4 kinds of prompts (including

				RedFM				IndoRE	
					mBERT				
DEP	GNN	en	es	fr	it	de	en	hi	te
-	-	84.3±0.7	80.0±0.6	78.6±0.3	76.3±0.8	78.7±0.3	94.3±0.6	89.6±0.4	84.9±0.4
stanza	rgcn	**85.7±0.8**	80.5±1.0	79.7±1.0	78.2±0.5	80.0±0.9	94.4±0.2	**90.9±0.3**	**86.1±0.9**
stanza	rgat	85.2±1.4	**82.2±0.6**	79.9±0.4	77.9±1.2	**80.5±0.6**	**94.9±0.3**	89.5±1.4	85.9±1.1
trankit	rgcn	84.3±0.4	81.8±0.8	**80.7±0.8**	**78.9±0.7**	79.7±0.9	94.0±0.2	89.7±0.1	85.9±1.9
trankit	rgat	85.5±1.3	80.9±0.3	80.2±0.2	77.3±0.8	78.9±0.7	94.1±0.5	88.9±0.5	84.6±0.8
					XLMR				
-	-	**84.0±1.1**	77.2±2.0	76.2±1.0	74.8±1.2	75.2±0.6	92.1±0.8	88.7±0.9	**86.3±1.1**
stanza	rgcn	83.7±0.6	76.8±0.8	**76.7±0.9**	73.3±0.7	75.7±1.5	91.8±0.8	89.6±1.1	85.6±0.7
stanza	rgat	**84.0±0.8**	**77.5±1.4**	74.4±0.9	**75.6±1.2**	**76.2±1.1**	92.2±0.4	**89.9±0.9**	85.7±0.6
trankit	rgcn	83.8±0.5	76.4±1.1	74.7±1.0	72.6±2.3	73.9±2.6	91.9±0.9	**89.9±0.8**	85.2±0.5
trankit	rgat	82.6±0.8	77.3±0.2	75.0±0.3	74.0±1.7	75.9±0.1	**92.6±0.7**	89.2±1.0	85.9±1.6

Table 1: In-domain RE performance of mBERT and XLMR on RedFM and IndoRE, with dependency information (i.e. choice of the parser or DEP, and the choice of the GNN used to encode the information, i.e. GNN). Results are averaged across the top 3 seeds, with the highest values in each column bolded.

					RedFM					IndoRE	
						mBERT					
DEP	GNN	en	es	fr	it	de	ar	zh	en	hi	te
-	-	77.5±1.1	81.0±1.1	78.8±1.1	76.7±1.1	75.6±1.1	72.5±1.1	70.0±1.1	57.5±1.8	57.6±2.7	42.4±2.4
stanza	rgcn	78.2±0.8	81.0±0.8	**79.5±0.8**	**76.8±0.8**	77.1±0.8	72.6±0.8	70.0±0.8	57.0±1.0	57.1±0.8	44.6±1.2
stanza	rgat	78.0±1.0	81.1±1.0	78.8±1.0	76.5±1.0	77.2±1.0	**73.2±1.0**	**70.4±1.0**	56.4±1.2	57.7±1.2	**45.2±1.4**
trankit	rgcn	**78.7±0.8**	**81.3±0.8**	79.3±0.8	75.4±0.8	77.8±0.8	72.8±0.8	70.0±0.8	**57.9±0.8**	**59.1±0.6**	44.9±1.6
trankit	rgat	77.9±0.8	80.6±0.8	79.1±0.8	76.3±0.8	**77.9±0.8**	73.1±0.8	**70.4±0.8**	57.1±1.4	57.9±1.8	45.1±1.7
						XLMR					
-	-	72.7±1.4	74.2±1.4	72.2±1.4	66.8±1.4	70.7±1.4	61.8±1.4	63.1±1.4	50.0±2.2	55.1±1.5	45.9±1.6
stanza	rgcn	**73.4±1.4**	74.5±1.4	73.2±1.4	67.7±1.4	70.3±1.4	61.2±1.4	**63.9±1.4**	49.3±1.8	55.4±1.4	46.1±1.7
stanza	rgat	73.3±1.5	74.3±1.5	**73.4±1.5**	**67.9±1.5**	68.4±1.5	61.1±1.5	63.2±1.5	50.0±1.6	53.8±2.8	46.3±2.0
trankit	rgcn	73.1±1.3	74.7±1.3	73.1±1.3	66.8±1.3	69.5±1.3	**62.7±1.3**	63.8±1.3	50.7±0.7	**56.3±1.1**	45.5±2.9
trankit	rgat	73.1±1.1	**75.7±1.1**	**73.4±1.1**	65.9±1.1	**70.9±1.1**	62.1±1.1	63.6±1.1	**50.8±1.4**	56.0±2.2	**46.9±2.6**

Table 2: Zero-shot Cross-lingual RE performance on RedFM and IndoRE with mBERT and XLMR as the multilingual encoders with different combinations of dependency information. For a given target language, we average the performance across the different source languages. The highest values in each column are highlighted in bold. Detailed individual cross-lingual performance metrics are given in the Appendix.

the baseline), and 2 kinds of parsers (Stanza and Dependency), resulting in a suite of 240 prompting experiments. Our final experimental suite thus comprises 2440 experiments.

5 Results and Insights

In this section, we pose the following research questions (RQs) and attempt to answer the same.

RQ1. Impact of dependency parses on RE for indomain and cross-lingual transfer ?

We report the in-domain and cross-lingual relation extraction performance with mBERT and XLMR as the multilingual encoders, stanza and trankit as the choice of the off-shelf-parsers, and RGCN and RGAT being the backbone GNN for both the IndoRE and RedFM datasets, in Tables 1 and 2 respectively.

At the outset, we observe that across both datasets, adding dependency information generally improves performance over the baseline in the in-domain setting; we see higher gains when we have mBERT as the MLM as opposed to XLMR. We also observe that the gains are higher for the REDFM dataset than IndoRE, possibly due to the poorer quality of dependency parses on low-resource languages like Hindi and Telugu, as opposed to standard high-resource cases like English, Spanish, and Italian. In fact, for all languages other than English, we see a consistent improvement in F1-score of approximately 2.0% and 1.0% with

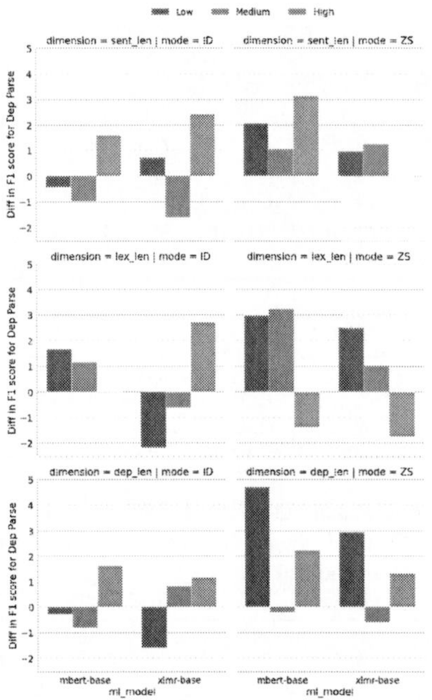

Figure 3: Performance of DEPGEN for in-domain and zero-shot cross-lingual transfer settings on the IndoRE dataset analyzed across variations in sentence, lexical and dependency length

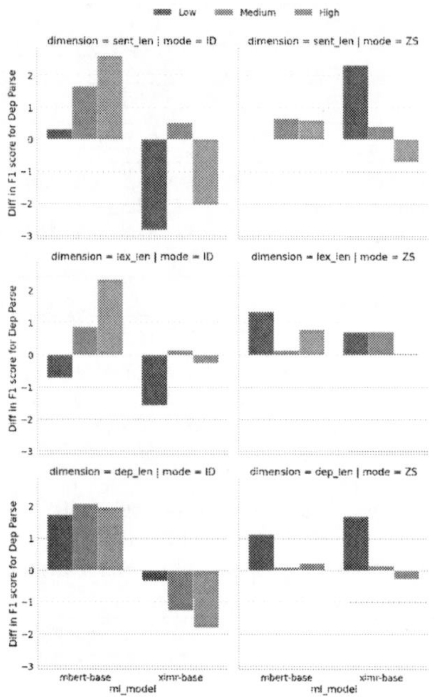

Figure 4: Performance of DEPGEN for in-domain and zero-shot cross-lingual transfer settings on the RedFM dataset analyzed across variations in sentence, lexical and dependency length

the mBERT model on the REDFM and IndoRE dataset respectively, for the best combination of dependency parser and GNN.

In the zero-shot cross-lingual transfer scenario from Table 2 we observe trends that are markedly different from the in-domain setting. Each entry in this Table is computed by averaging the macro-F1 score over the other source languages, apart from itself, for the top 3 seeds. We notice only slight improvements in RE performance for mBERT but higher gains for XLMR. We hypothesize that since XLMR has a worse performance than mBERT, it benefits more from the dependency information in the zero-shot setting. In a similar vein, we observe much higher gains for Hindi and Telugu (around 2.6% and 6.6% relative performance improvements respectively) in the zero-shot setting for mBERT. The markedly lower scores in IndoRE in the zero-shot transfer setup as compared to REDFM can be attributed to the higher number of relations in the dataset (32 for IndoRE vs 51 for REDFM).

RQ2. Which scenarios benefit the most with additional information in the fine-tuned setup?

In the fine-tuned setup, we analyze which scenarios or inputs benefit the most from including dependency information. We thus group the test instances according to three different dimensions, i.e. (1) input sentence length (2) lexical distance between two entities in the sentence and (3) dependency path length. Figures 3 and 4 show the effect of these components for the in-domain and zero-shot cross-lingual transfer settings for the IndoRE and RedFM datasets respectively. The blue, orange and green plots reflect the bottom quartile, inter-quartile range and the top quartile respectively for each of these three dimensions.

Sentence Length: We quantify sentence length based on the total number of tokens in the document. For both zero-shot and in-domain settings across the two datasets, adding linguistic information in the form of dependency graphs improves relation extraction for longer sentences. We posit that including dependency information helps to capture long range dependencies across words and thus the observed gains for longer sentences.

Lexical Distance: We quantify the lexical distance as the number of tokens between the two entities. Here, we observe that dependency information is more helpful for cases where the dis-

Model	Parser	Prompting	RedFM							IndoRE			Average
			ar	**de**	**en**	**es**	**fr**	**it**	**zh**	**en**	**hi**	**te**	
Llama	None	-	25.6	25.7	27.0	27.0	16.7	**36.7**	**37.1**	47.6	39.0	21.9	30.4
	Stanza	Tuple	24.3	19.3	23.9	17.0	18.4	19.3	29.6	30.2	28.3	10.9	22.1
	Stanza	Text	25.1	24.5	22.6	23.1	23.5	24.0	30.6	44.4	37.4	22.9	27.8
	Stanza	Filtered Text	**33.5**	35.0	32.3	**31.6**	**30.5**	34.0	36.1	**48.0**	**44.5**	**29.8**	**35.5** (↑5.1%)
	Trankit	Tuple	30.3	17.1	**37.3**	17.2	18.3	22.1	32.4	27.5	30.6	10.5	24.3
	Trankit	Text	23.4	25.4	22.7	22.6	23.8	25.6	30.5	44.8	38.4	24.0	28.1
	Trankit	Filtered Text	33.1	**35.2**	35.6	31.4	28.7	30.3	35.3	46.2	42.8	29.5	34.8
Mistral	None	-	36.7	38.2	39.0	35.8	36.0	38.3	35.6	**51.3**	**38.5**	10.6	36.0
	Stanza	Tuple	27.2	35.9	30.9	31.9	28.1	35.1	30.9	48.4	30.6	9.8	30.9
	Stanza	Text	29.2	32.0	34.4	32.6	30.4	33.4	33.2	47.5	37.1	8.7	31.9
	Stanza	Filtered Text	39.1	39.5	**40.9**	**37.1**	36.6	**40.2**	36.7	50.8	**38.5**	10.3	**37.0** (↑1.0%)
	Trankit	Tuple	27.4	35.3	32.5	31.5	26.9	30.6	31.3	48.0	30.5	10.8	30.5
	Trankit	Text	27.9	32.0	34.7	30.7	31.0	32.7	34.1	46.8	36.4	**11.2**	31.7
	Trankit	Filtered Text	**39.3**	**39.7**	39.3	36.3	**36.9**	37.8	**38.1**	50.9	38.3	**11.2**	36.8
Qwen	None	-	**44.3**	**39.6**	**40.3**	38.0	**36.8**	**43.0**	**40.8**	42.7	39.2	29.1	**39.4**
	Stanza	Tuple	35.4	32.0	34.6	31.8	31.9	37.8	31.4	38.3	38.2	26.1	33.8
	Stanza	Text	33.8	34.8	36.0	33.3	33.3	33.3	29.9	39.5	41.1	**30.6**	34.6
	Stanza	Filtered Text	42.1	32.8	39.8	37.3	33.6	38.4	40.4	**44.7**	45.4	28.6	38.3(↓1.1%)
	Trankit	Tuple	34.3	30.7	35.2	34.1	28.1	35.1	33.6	39.6	37.4	21.8	33.0
	Trankit	Text	35.4	35.2	34.2	33.1	34.0	33.4	30.2	40.5	40.5	27.3	34.4
	Trankit	Filtered Text	39.9	36.0	35.4	**39.4**	34.7	38.6	34.5	44.0	**45.9**	26.6	37.5

Table 3: Effect of dependency parses and prompting techniques for LLM-based relation extraction for the REDFM and IndoRE datasets. Performance reported in terms of F1-Score. Best performing methods are shown in bold.

tance between the entities is not high, i.e. Low and Medium categories.

Dependency Path Length: We quantify the dependency path length as the number of dependency relations that separate the two entities in the dependency graph. We see prominent gains for both short and long range dependency paths, especially for the ZS case for IndoRE. However, similar to lexical distance, the gains are more prominent when the dependency path between the entities is small. Since our chosen GNN has only two layers, we hypothesize that it is unable to capture signals across long dependency paths effectively.

RQ3. Can dependency parses help improve relation extraction performance for LLMs?

Table 3 summarizes the performance of three LLMs - LLaMA (Grattafiori et al., 2024), Mistral (Jiang et al., 2023) and Qwen (Yang et al., 2024) for zero-shot relation extraction on the IndoRE and RedFM datasets. To account for the skew in distribution of relations, we employ the macro-F1 score as the primary evaluation metric. We observe that for the LLama-3 and Mistral models, incorporating dependency parses improves performance across several cases. The gains are most prominent when the dependency information is presented in the form of natural language text; we see consistent improvements for the Text Prompt Format over the Tuple Prompt Format, where the information is presented as a list of tuples. We see that the filtered prompt that removes information not pertaining to the two entities, improves performance further.

The improvement can be as significant as 1% to 5% in some cases in terms of absolute F1-score for Mistral and LLama-3 respectively. For the Qwen model, dependency parses do not afford much benefits. Thus the choice of the LLM and the description of the prompt, play a significant role in zero-shot relation extraction performance. It should be noted, however, that the zero-shot performance for the in-context learning setup is significantly worse than the zero-shot cross-lingual performance in the fine-tuned setup. With LLMs, we see an average absolute improvement of 1.67% across all models and languages with the Filtered Text Prompt.

RQ4. Which factors influence generalization?

We now inspect the factors that characterize performance improvements over the baseline for the two datasets in the fine-tuned learning and in-context learning setup. We perform a multivariate ANOVA analysis with the relative performance difference (expressed as a percentage over the baseline), from including the dependency parses, as the dependent variable.

The independent variables chosen are the choice of the multilingual encoder, (mBERT or XLMR), dependency parser (Stanza or Trankit), GNN employed (RGCN or RGAT), and the source and target language [1]. We also consider the pair-wise interaction effects of each of these variables, and note the F-statistic and their corresponding p-value for the indomain (Tables 9 and 11) and zero-shot cross-lingual (Tables 10 and 12) respectively.

For the indomain setting in IndoRE, we observe that the relative performance change hinges most on the choice of the dependency parser followed by source language. Although the choice of the encoder and the GNN do not have any significant effect on relative performance, their pair-wise interactions is indeed significant. The story is remarkably different for REDFM where only the choice of the encoder has any significant effect on RE.

In the zero-shot cross-lingual setting for IndoRE, we see significant effects arising from the choice of the target language and the pairwise interaction between the choice of the source/target language with that of the encoder. A similar story also holds for REDFM, wherein we notice the only significant interactions are between the choice of the source/-target language and the encoder, and also between the choice of the source/target language pairs themselves. Simply put in the zero-shot setting the role of the dependency information is insignificant for both datasets.

We carry out a similar statistical analysis for the zero-shot ICL setup, with the relative performance change over the baseline as the dependent variable, and the choice of the LLM (i.e. LLama-3, Qwen, and Mistral), the prompt (i.e. Tuple Format, Text Format, and Filtered Text Format), the language (7 for RedFM and 3 for IndoRE), and the choice of the dependency parser (i.e. Trankit and Stanza) as the independent variables. We also consider the pair-wise interaction effects of each of these variables, and note the F-statistic and their corresponding p-value for the IndoRE and REDFM dataset respectively in Tables 13 and 14 respectively. We observe, over both datasets, significant effects arising from the choice of the LLM, and the choice of the prompt, as well as the pairwise interaction between the choice of the prompt and LLM, and the choice of the source language and LLM. Once again, we see that the choice of the dependency parser, i.e. the Stanza or Trankit, does not play a significant role.

[1]For the indomain setting we consider only the target language

6 Conclusion and Future Work

In this paper we propose a multi-component framework for multi-lingual relation extraction. Our fine-tuned framework DepGen, combines the signals from the input sentence with dependency parses that are encoded through a GNN. Through extensive evaluations, we have reported the implications of our work for both in-domain and zero-shot transfer settings across multiple languages. We observe that including off-the-shelf dependency parses can aid relation extraction, with the best performing model having a mild relative improvement of 0.91% and 1.5% in the in-domain and zero-shot setting respectively across two datasets. We also develop an in-context learning prompting approach that incorporates dependency information to bring about an average improvement of 1.67%, with significant gains for low-performing LLMs.

In this work, we investigate how augmenting dependency parses in language models can facilitate information extraction tasks in low-resource settings. Specifically, our contributions being independent of the language setting makes our model portable to other languages in a zero-shot transfer setup. Future avenues will explore the role of these linguistic frameworks for other information extraction or reasoning tasks, and the impact of different kinds of linguistic frameworks such as AMRs or UMRs.

Acknowledgments

We thank the anonymous reveiwers for their constructive feedback. This project was funded in part by NSF grant 1949110.

References

Livio Baldini Soares, Nicholas FitzGerald, Jeffrey Ling, and Tom Kwiatkowski. 2019. Matching the blanks: Distributional similarity for relation learning. In *Proceedings of the 57th Annual Meeting of the Association for Computational Linguistics*, pages 2895–2905, Florence, Italy. Association for Computational Linguistics.

Laura Banarescu, Claire Bonial, Shu Cai, Madalina Georgescu, Kira Griffitt, Ulf Hermjakob, Kevin

Knight, Philipp Koehn, Martha Palmer, and Nathan Schneider. 2013. Abstract meaning representation for sembanking. In *Proceedings of the 7th linguistic annotation workshop and interoperability with discourse*, pages 178–186.

Dan Busbridge, Dane Sherburn, Pietro Cavallo, and Nils Y. Hammerla. 2019. Relational graph attention networks.

Chih-Yao Chen and Cheng-Te Li. 2021. ZS-BERT: Towards zero-shot relation extraction with attribute representation learning. In *Proceedings of the 2021 Conference of the North American Chapter of the Association for Computational Linguistics: Human Language Technologies*, pages 3470–3479, Online. Association for Computational Linguistics.

Jiawei Chen, Yaojie Lu, Hongyu Lin, Jie Lou, Wei Jia, Dai Dai, Hua Wu, Boxi Cao, Xianpei Han, and Le Sun. 2023. Learning in-context learning for named entity recognition. In *Proceedings of the 61st Annual Meeting of the Association for Computational Linguistics (Volume 1: Long Papers)*, pages 13661–13675, Toronto, Canada. Association for Computational Linguistics.

Junjie Chen, Xiangheng He, and Yusuke Miyao. 2024. Language model based unsupervised dependency parsing with conditional mutual information and grammatical constraints. In *Proceedings of the 2024 Conference of the North American Chapter of the Association for Computational Linguistics: Human Language Technologies (Volume 1: Long Papers)*, pages 6355–6366, Mexico City, Mexico. Association for Computational Linguistics.

Noam Chomsky. 2002. *Syntactic structures*. Mouton de Gruyter.

Alexis Conneau, Kartikay Khandelwal, Naman Goyal, Vishrav Chaudhary, Guillaume Wenzek, Francisco Guzmán, Edouard Grave, Myle Ott, Luke Zettlemoyer, and Veselin Stoyanov. 2020a. Unsupervised cross-lingual representation learning at scale. In *ACL*.

Alexis Conneau, Kartikay Khandelwal, Naman Goyal, Vishrav Chaudhary, Guillaume Wenzek, Francisco Guzmán, Edouard Grave, Myle Ott, Luke Zettlemoyer, and Veselin Stoyanov. 2020b. Unsupervised cross-lingual representation learning at scale. In *Proceedings of the 58th Annual Meeting of the Association for Computational Linguistics*, pages 8440–8451, Online. Association for Computational Linguistics.

Alexis Conneau, Kartikay Khandelwal, Naman Goyal, Vishrav Chaudhary, Guillaume Wenzek, Francisco Guzmán, Edouard Grave, Myle Ott, Luke Zettlemoyer, and Veselin Stoyanov. 2020c. Unsupervised cross-lingual representation learning at scale.

William Croft. 2022. Morphosyntax: constructions of the world's languages.

Sarkar Snigdha Sarathi Das, Arzoo Katiyar, Rebecca Passonneau, and Rui Zhang. 2022. CONTaiNER: Few-shot named entity recognition via contrastive learning. In *Proceedings of the 60th Annual Meeting of the Association for Computational Linguistics (Volume 1: Long Papers)*, pages 6338–6353, Dublin, Ireland. Association for Computational Linguistics.

Jacob Devlin, Ming-Wei Chang, Kenton Lee, and Kristina Toutanova. 2018. Bert: Pre-training of deep bidirectional transformers for language understanding. *arXiv preprint arXiv:1810.04805*.

Jacob Devlin, Ming-Wei Chang, Kenton Lee, and Kristina Toutanova. 2019. BERT: Pre-training of deep bidirectional transformers for language understanding. In *Proceedings of the 2019 Conference of the North American Chapter of the Association for Computational Linguistics: Human Language Technologies, Volume 1 (Long and Short Papers)*, pages 4171–4186, Minneapolis, Minnesota. Association for Computational Linguistics.

Jose A. Diaz-Garcia and Julio Amador Diaz Lopez. 2024. A survey on cutting-edge relation extraction techniques based on language models.

Qiang Ding, Lvzhou Luo, Yixuan Cao, and Ping Luo. 2024. Attention with dependency parsing augmentation for fine-grained attribution.

Ritam Dutt, Sopan Khosla, Vinayshekhar Bannihatti Kumar, and Rashmi Gangadharaiah. 2023. GrailQA++: A challenging zero-shot benchmark for knowledge base question answering. In *Proceedings of the 13th International Joint Conference on Natural Language Processing and the 3rd Conference of the Asia-Pacific Chapter of the Association for Computational Linguistics (Volume 1: Long Papers)*, pages 897–909, Nusa Dua, Bali. Association for Computational Linguistics.

Sefika Efeoglu and Adrian Paschke. 2024. Relation extraction with fine-tuned large language models in retrieval augmented generation frameworks.

Alexander Fritzler, Varvara Logacheva, and Maksim Kretov. 2019. Few-shot classification in named entity recognition task. In *Proceedings of the 34th ACM/SIGAPP Symposium on Applied Computing*, pages 993–1000.

Aaron Grattafiori, Abhimanyu Dubey, Abhinav Jauhri, Abhinav Pandey, Abhishek Kadian, Ahmad Al-Dahle, Aiesha Letman, Akhil Mathur, Alan Schelten, Alex Vaughan, Amy Yang, Angela Fan, Anirudh Goyal, Anthony Hartshorn, Aobo Yang, Archi Mitra, Archie Sravankumar, Artem Korenev, Arthur Hinsvark, Arun Rao, Aston Zhang, Aurelien Rodriguez, Austen Gregerson, Ava Spataru, Baptiste Roziere, Bethany Biron, Binh Tang, Bobbie Chern, Charlotte Caucheteux, Chaya Nayak, Chloe Bi, Chris Marra, Chris McConnell, Christian Keller, Christophe Touret, Chunyang Wu, Corinne Wong, Cristian Canton Ferrer, Cyrus Nikolaidis, Damien Allonsius, Daniel Song, Danielle Pintz, Danny Livshits,

Danny Wyatt, David Esiobu, Dhruv Choudhary, Dhruv Mahajan, Diego Garcia-Olano, Diego Perino, Dieuwke Hupkes, Egor Lakomkin, Ehab AlBadawy, Elina Lobanova, Emily Dinan, Eric Michael Smith, Filip Radenovic, Francisco Guzmán, Frank Zhang, Gabriel Synnaeve, Gabrielle Lee, Georgia Lewis Anderson, Govind Thattai, Graeme Nail, Gregoire Mialon, Guan Pang, Guillem Cucurell, Hailey Nguyen, Hannah Korevaar, Hu Xu, Hugo Touvron, Iliyan Zarov, Imanol Arrieta Ibarra, Isabel Kloumann, Ishan Misra, Ivan Evtimov, Jack Zhang, Jade Copet, Jaewon Lee, Jan Geffert, Jana Vranes, Jason Park, Jay Mahadeokar, Jeet Shah, Jelmer van der Linde, Jennifer Billock, Jenny Hong, Jenya Lee, Jeremy Fu, Jianfeng Chi, Jianyu Huang, Jiawen Liu, Jie Wang, Jiecao Yu, Joanna Bitton, Joe Spisak, Jongsoo Park, Joseph Rocca, Joshua Johnstun, Joshua Saxe, Junteng Jia, Kalyan Vasuden Alwala, Karthik Prasad, Kartikeya Upasani, Kate Plawiak, Ke Li, Kenneth Heafield, Kevin Stone, Khalid El-Arini, Krithika Iyer, Kshitiz Malik, Kuenley Chiu, Kunal Bhalla, Kushal Lakhotia, Lauren Rantala-Yeary, Laurens van der Maaten, Lawrence Chen, Liang Tan, Liz Jenkins, Louis Martin, Lovish Madaan, Lubo Malo, Lukas Blecher, Lukas Landzaat, Luke de Oliveira, Madeline Muzzi, Mahesh Pasupuleti, Mannat Singh, Manohar Paluri, Marcin Kardas, Maria Tsimpoukelli, Mathew Oldham, Mathieu Rita, Maya Pavlova, Melanie Kambadur, Mike Lewis, Min Si, Mitesh Kumar Singh, Mona Hassan, Naman Goyal, Narjes Torabi, Nikolay Bashlykov, Nikolay Bogoychev, Niladri Chatterji, Ning Zhang, Olivier Duchenne, Onur Çelebi, Patrick Alrassy, Pengchuan Zhang, Pengwei Li, Petar Vasic, Peter Weng, Prajjwal Bhargava, Pratik Dubal, Praveen Krishnan, Punit Singh Koura, Puxin Xu, Qing He, Qingxiao Dong, Ragavan Srinivasan, Raj Ganapathy, Ramon Calderer, Ricardo Silveira Cabral, Robert Stojnic, Roberta Raileanu, Rohan Maheswari, Rohit Girdhar, Rohit Patel, Romain Sauvestre, Ronnie Polidoro, Roshan Sumbaly, Ross Taylor, Ruan Silva, Rui Hou, Rui Wang, Saghar Hosseini, Sahana Chennabasappa, Sanjay Singh, Sean Bell, Seohyun Sonia Kim, Sergey Edunov, Shaoliang Nie, Sharan Narang, Sharath Raparthy, Sheng Shen, Shengye Wan, Shruti Bhosale, Shun Zhang, Simon Vandenhende, Soumya Batra, Spencer Whitman, Sten Sootla, Stephane Collot, Suchin Gururangan, Sydney Borodinsky, Tamar Herman, Tara Fowler, Tarek Sheasha, Thomas Georgiou, Thomas Scialom, Tobias Speckbacher, Todor Mihaylov, Tong Xiao, Ujjwal Karn, Vedanuj Goswami, Vibhor Gupta, Vignesh Ramanathan, Viktor Kerkez, Vincent Gonguet, Virginie Do, Vish Vogeti, Vítor Albiero, Vladan Petrovic, Weiwei Chu, Wenhan Xiong, Wenyin Fu, Whitney Meers, Xavier Martinet, Xiaodong Wang, Xiaofang Wang, Xiaoqing Ellen Tan, Xide Xia, Xinfeng Xie, Xuchao Jia, Xuewei Wang, Yaelle Goldschlag, Yashesh Gaur, Yasmine Babaei, Yi Wen, Yiwen Song, Yuchen Zhang, Yue Li, Yuning Mao, Zacharie Delpierre Coudert, Zheng Yan, Zhengxing Chen, Zoe Papakipos, Aaditya Singh, Aayushi Srivastava, Abha Jain, Adam Kelsey, Adam Shajnfeld, Adithya Gangidi, Adolfo Victoria, Ahuva Goldstand, Ajay Menon, Ajay Sharma, Alex Boesenberg, Alexei Baevski, Allie Feinstein, Amanda Kallet, Amit Sangani, Amos Teo, Anam Yunus, Andrei Lupu, Andres Alvarado, Andrew Caples, Andrew Gu, Andrew Ho, Andrew Poulton, Andrew Ryan, Ankit Ramchandani, Annie Dong, Annie Franco, Anuj Goyal, Aparajita Saraf, Arkabandhu Chowdhury, Ashley Gabriel, Ashwin Bharambe, Assaf Eisenman, Azadeh Yazdan, Beau James, Ben Maurer, Benjamin Leonhardi, Bernie Huang, Beth Loyd, Beto De Paola, Bhargavi Paranjape, Bing Liu, Bo Wu, Boyu Ni, Braden Hancock, Bram Wasti, Brandon Spence, Brani Stojkovic, Brian Gamido, Britt Montalvo, Carl Parker, Carly Burton, Catalina Mejia, Ce Liu, Changhan Wang, Changkyu Kim, Chao Zhou, Chester Hu, Ching-Hsiang Chu, Chris Cai, Chris Tindal, Christoph Feichtenhofer, Cynthia Gao, Damon Civin, Dana Beaty, Daniel Kreymer, Daniel Li, David Adkins, David Xu, Davide Testuggine, Delia David, Devi Parikh, Diana Liskovich, Didem Foss, Dingkang Wang, Duc Le, Dustin Holland, Edward Dowling, Eissa Jamil, Elaine Montgomery, Eleonora Presani, Emily Hahn, Emily Wood, Eric-Tuan Le, Erik Brinkman, Esteban Arcaute, Evan Dunbar, Evan Smothers, Fei Sun, Felix Kreuk, Feng Tian, Filippos Kokkinos, Firat Ozgenel, Francesco Caggioni, Frank Kanayet, Frank Seide, Gabriela Medina Florez, Gabriella Schwarz, Gada Badeer, Georgia Swee, Gil Halpern, Grant Herman, Grigory Sizov, Guangyi, Zhang, Guna Lakshminarayanan, Hakan Inan, Hamid Shojanazeri, Han Zou, Hannah Wang, Hanwen Zha, Haroun Habeeb, Harrison Rudolph, Helen Suk, Henry Aspegren, Hunter Goldman, Hongyuan Zhan, Ibrahim Damlaj, Igor Molybog, Igor Tufanov, Ilias Leontiadis, Irina-Elena Veliche, Itai Gat, Jake Weissman, James Geboski, James Kohli, Janice Lam, Japhet Asher, Jean-Baptiste Gaya, Jeff Marcus, Jeff Tang, Jennifer Chan, Jenny Zhen, Jeremy Reizenstein, Jeremy Teboul, Jessica Zhong, Jian Jin, Jingyi Yang, Joe Cummings, Jon Carvill, Jon Shepard, Jonathan McPhie, Jonathan Torres, Josh Ginsburg, Junjie Wang, Kai Wu, Kam Hou U, Karan Saxena, Kartikay Khandelwal, Katayoun Zand, Kathy Matosich, Kaushik Veeraraghavan, Kelly Michelena, Keqian Li, Kiran Jagadeesh, Kun Huang, Kunal Chawla, Kyle Huang, Lailin Chen, Lakshya Garg, Lavender A, Leandro Silva, Lee Bell, Lei Zhang, Liangpeng Guo, Licheng Yu, Liron Moshkovich, Luca Wehrstedt, Madian Khabsa, Manav Avalani, Manish Bhatt, Martynas Mankus, Matan Hasson, Matthew Lennie, Matthias Reso, Maxim Groshev, Maxim Naumov, Maya Lathi, Meghan Keneally, Miao Liu, Michael L. Seltzer, Michal Valko, Michelle Restrepo, Mihir Patel, Mik Vyatskov, Mikayel Samvelyan, Mike Clark, Mike Macey, Mike Wang, Miquel Jubert Hermoso, Mo Metanat, Mohammad Rastegari, Munish Bansal, Nandhini Santhanam, Natascha Parks, Natasha White, Navyata Bawa, Nayan Singhal, Nick Egebo, Nicolas Usunier, Nikhil Mehta, Nikolay Pavlovich Laptev, Ning Dong, Norman Cheng, Oleg Chernoguz, Olivia Hart, Omkar Salpekar, Ozlem Kalinli, Parkin Kent, Parth Parekh, Paul Saab, Pavan Balaji, Pedro Rittner, Philip Bontrager, Pierre Roux, Piotr

Dollar, Polina Zvyagina, Prashant Ratanchandani, Pritish Yuvraj, Qian Liang, Rachad Alao, Rachel Rodriguez, Rafi Ayub, Raghotham Murthy, Raghu Nayani, Rahul Mitra, Rangaprabhu Parthasarathy, Raymond Li, Rebekkah Hogan, Robin Battey, Rocky Wang, Russ Howes, Ruty Rinott, Sachin Mehta, Sachin Siby, Sai Jayesh Bondu, Samyak Datta, Sara Chugh, Sara Hunt, Sargun Dhillon, Sasha Sidorov, Satadru Pan, Saurabh Mahajan, Saurabh Verma, Seiji Yamamoto, Sharadh Ramaswamy, Shaun Lindsay, Shaun Lindsay, Sheng Feng, Shenghao Lin, Shengxin Cindy Zha, Shishir Patil, Shiva Shankar, Shuqiang Zhang, Shuqiang Zhang, Sinong Wang, Sneha Agarwal, Soji Sajuyigbe, Soumith Chintala, Stephanie Max, Stephen Chen, Steve Kehoe, Steve Satterfield, Sudarshan Govindaprasad, Sumit Gupta, Summer Deng, Sungmin Cho, Sunny Virk, Suraj Subramanian, Sy Choudhury, Sydney Goldman, Tal Remez, Tamar Glaser, Tamara Best, Thilo Koehler, Thomas Robinson, Tianhe Li, Tianjun Zhang, Tim Matthews, Timothy Chou, Tzook Shaked, Varun Vontimitta, Victoria Ajayi, Victoria Montanez, Vijai Mohan, Vinay Satish Kumar, Vishal Mangla, Vlad Ionescu, Vlad Poenaru, Vlad Tiberiu Mihailescu, Vladimir Ivanov, Wei Li, Wenchen Wang, Wenwen Jiang, Wes Bouaziz, Will Constable, Xiaocheng Tang, Xiaojian Wu, Xiaolan Wang, Xilun Wu, Xinbo Gao, Yaniv Kleinman, Yanjun Chen, Ye Hu, Ye Jia, Ye Qi, Yenda Li, Yilin Zhang, Ying Zhang, Yossi Adi, Youngjin Nam, Yu, Wang, Yu Zhao, Yuchen Hao, Yundi Qian, Yunlu Li, Yuzi He, Zach Rait, Zachary DeVito, Zef Rosnbrick, Zhaoduo Wen, Zhenyu Yang, Zhiwei Zhao, and Zhiyu Ma. 2024. The llama 3 herd of models.

Yanggan Gu, Yang Hou, Zhefeng Wang, Xinyu Duan, and Zhenghua Li. 2024. High-order joint constituency and dependency parsing. In *Proceedings of the 2024 Joint International Conference on Computational Linguistics, Language Resources and Evaluation (LREC-COLING 2024)*, pages 8144–8154, Torino, Italia. ELRA and ICCL.

Yu Gu, Sue Kase, Michelle Vanni, Brian Sadler, Percy Liang, Xifeng Yan, and Yu Su. 2021. Beyond iid: three levels of generalization for question answering on knowledge bases. In *Proceedings of the Web Conference 2021*, pages 3477–3488.

Pere-Lluís Huguet Cabot, Simone Tedeschi, Axel-Cyrille Ngonga Ngomo, and Roberto Navigli. 2023. RED^{fm}: a filtered and multilingual relation extraction dataset. In *Proceedings of the 61st Annual Meeting of the Association for Computational Linguistics (Volume 1: Long Papers)*, pages 4326–4343, Toronto, Canada. Association for Computational Linguistics.

Albert Q. Jiang, Alexandre Sablayrolles, Arthur Mensch, Chris Bamford, Devendra Singh Chaplot, Diego de las Casas, Florian Bressand, Gianna Lengyel, Guillaume Lample, Lucile Saulnier, Lélio Renard Lavaud, Marie-Anne Lachaux, Pierre Stock, Teven Le Scao, Thibaut Lavril, Thomas Wang, Timothée Lacroix, and William El Sayed. 2023. Mistral 7b.

Zhao Jun, Hu Yuan, Xu Nuo, Gui Tao, Zhang Qi, Chen Yunwen, and Gao Xiang. 2022. An exploration of prompt-based zero-shot relation extraction method. In *Proceedings of the 21st Chinese National Conference on Computational Linguistics*, pages 786–797, Nanchang, China. Chinese Information Processing Society of China.

Guozheng Li, Peng Wang, and Wenjun Ke. 2023. Revisiting large language models as zero-shot relation extractors. In *Findings of the Association for Computational Linguistics: EMNLP 2023*, pages 6877–6892, Singapore. Association for Computational Linguistics.

Tianming Liang, Yang Liu, Xiaoyan Liu, Hao Zhang, Gaurav Sharma, and Maozu Guo. 2023. Distantly-supervised long-tailed relation extraction using constraint graphs. *IEEE Transactions on Knowledge and Data Engineering*, 35(7):6852–6865.

Robert Litschko, Ivan Vulić, Simone Paolo Ponzetto, and Goran Glavaš. 2021. On cross-lingual retrieval with multilingual text encoders.

Yang Liu, Jinpeng Hu, Xiang Wan, and Tsung-Hui Chang. 2022. A simple yet effective relation information guided approach for few-shot relation extraction. In *Findings of the Association for Computational Linguistics: ACL 2022*, pages 757–763, Dublin, Ireland. Association for Computational Linguistics.

Yinhan Liu, Myle Ott, Naman Goyal, Jingfei Du, Mandar Joshi, Danqi Chen, Omer Levy, Mike Lewis, Luke Zettlemoyer, and Veselin Stoyanov. 2019. Roberta: A robustly optimized bert pretraining approach. *arXiv preprint arXiv:1907.11692*.

Zhu Liu, Cunliang Kong, Ying Liu, and Maosong Sun. 2024. Fantastic semantics and where to find them: Investigating which layers of generative LLMs reflect lexical semantics. In *Findings of the Association for Computational Linguistics: ACL 2024*, pages 14551–14558, Bangkok, Thailand. Association for Computational Linguistics.

Sewon Min, Julian Michael, Hannaneh Hajishirzi, and Luke Zettlemoyer. 2020. AmbigQA: Answering ambiguous open-domain questions. In *Proceedings of the 2020 Conference on Empirical Methods in Natural Language Processing (EMNLP)*, pages 5783–5797, Online. Association for Computational Linguistics.

Arijit Nag, Bidisha Samanta, Animesh Mukherjee, Niloy Ganguly, and Soumen Chakrabarti. 2021. A data bootstrapping recipe for low-resource multilingual relation classification. In *Proceedings of the 25th Conference on Computational Natural Language Learning*, pages 575–587, Online. Association for Computational Linguistics.

Minh Van Nguyen, Viet Dac Lai, Amir Pouran Ben Veyseh, and Thien Huu Nguyen. 2021. Trankit: A light-weight transformer-based toolkit for multilingual natural language processing. In *Proceedings of the 16th*

Conference of the European Chapter of the Association for Computational Linguistics: System Demonstrations*, pages 80–90, Online. Association for Computational Linguistics.

Joakim Nivre, Marie-Catherine De Marneffe, Filip Ginter, Yoav Goldberg, Jan Hajic, Christopher D Manning, Ryan McDonald, Slav Petrov, Sampo Pyysalo, Natalia Silveira, et al. 2016. Universal dependencies v1: A multilingual treebank collection. In *Proceedings of the Tenth International Conference on Language Resources and Evaluation (LREC'16)*, pages 1659–1666.

Hao Peng, Tianyu Gao, Xu Han, Yankai Lin, Peng Li, Zhiyuan Liu, Maosong Sun, and Jie Zhou. 2020. Learning from Context or Names? An Empirical Study on Neural Relation Extraction. In *Proceedings of the 2020 Conference on Empirical Methods in Natural Language Processing (EMNLP)*, pages 3661–3672, Online. Association for Computational Linguistics.

Peng Qi, Yuhao Zhang, Yuhui Zhang, Jason Bolton, and Christopher D. Manning. 2020a. Stanza: A Python natural language processing toolkit for many human languages. In *Proceedings of the 58th Annual Meeting of the Association for Computational Linguistics: System Demonstrations*.

Peng Qi, Yuhao Zhang, Yuhui Zhang, Jason Bolton, and Christopher D. Manning. 2020b. Stanza: A python natural language processing toolkit for many human languages. In *Proceedings of the 58th Annual Meeting of the Association for Computational Linguistics: System Demonstrations*, pages 101–108, Online. Association for Computational Linguistics.

Meng Qu, Tianyu Gao, Louis-Pascal Xhonneux, and Jian Tang. 2020. Few-shot relation extraction via Bayesian meta-learning on relation graphs. In *Proceedings of the 37th International Conference on Machine Learning*, volume 119 of *Proceedings of Machine Learning Research*, pages 7867–7876. PMLR.

Siva Reddy, Oscar Täckström, Slav Petrov, Mark Steedman, and Mirella Lapata. 2017. Universal semantic parsing. In *Proceedings of the 2017 Conference on Empirical Methods in Natural Language Processing*, pages 89–101.

Devendra Sachan, Yuhao Zhang, Peng Qi, and William L. Hamilton. 2021. Do syntax trees help pre-trained transformers extract information? In *Proceedings of the 16th Conference of the European Chapter of the Association for Computational Linguistics: Main Volume*, pages 2647–2661, Online. Association for Computational Linguistics.

Gözde Gül Şahin. 2022. To augment or not to augment? a comparative study on text augmentation techniques for low-resource NLP. *Computational Linguistics*, 48(1):5–42.

Oscar Sainz, Iker García-Ferrero, Rodrigo Agerri, Oier Lopez de Lacalle, German Rigau, and Eneko Agirre. 2024. GoLLIE: Annotation guidelines improve zero-shot information-extraction. In *The Twelfth International Conference on Learning Representations*.

Franco Scarselli, Marco Gori, Ah Chung Tsoi, Markus Hagenbuchner, and Gabriele Monfardini. 2008. The graph neural network model. *IEEE transactions on neural networks*, 20(1):61–80.

Michael Schlichtkrull, Thomas N Kipf, Peter Bloem, Rianne van den Berg, Ivan Titov, and Max Welling. 2018. Modeling relational data with graph convolutional networks. In *European semantic web conference*, pages 593–607. Springer.

Giulio Starace, Konstantinos Papakostas, Rochelle Choenni, Apostolos Panagiotopoulos, Matteo Rosati, Alina Leidinger, and Ekaterina Shutova. 2023. Probing LLMs for joint encoding of linguistic categories. In *Findings of the Association for Computational Linguistics: EMNLP 2023*, pages 7158–7179, Singapore. Association for Computational Linguistics.

Chenguang Wang, Xiao Liu, Zui Chen, Haoyun Hong, Jie Tang, and Dawn Song. 2022a. DeepStruct: Pretraining of language models for structure prediction. In *Findings of the Association for Computational Linguistics: ACL 2022*, pages 803–823, Dublin, Ireland. Association for Computational Linguistics.

Shusen Wang, Bosen Zhang, Yajing Xu, Yanan Wu, and Bo Xiao. 2022b. RCL: Relation contrastive learning for zero-shot relation extraction. In *Findings of the Association for Computational Linguistics: NAACL 2022*, pages 2456–2468, Seattle, United States. Association for Computational Linguistics.

Tingyu Xie, Qi Li, Yan Zhang, Zuozhu Liu, and Hongwei Wang. 2024. Self-improving for zero-shot named entity recognition with large language models. In *Proceedings of the 2024 Conference of the North American Chapter of the Association for Computational Linguistics: Human Language Technologies (Volume 2: Short Papers)*, pages 583–593, Mexico City, Mexico. Association for Computational Linguistics.

Lilong Xue, Dan Zhang, Yuxiao Dong, and Jie Tang. 2024. Autore: Document-level relation extraction with large language models.

An Yang, Baosong Yang, Binyuan Hui, Bo Zheng, Bowen Yu, Chang Zhou, Chengpeng Li, Chengyuan Li, Dayiheng Liu, Fei Huang, Guanting Dong, Haoran Wei, Huan Lin, Jialong Tang, Jialin Wang, Jian Yang, Jianhong Tu, Jianwei Zhang, Jianxin Ma, Jianxin Yang, Jin Xu, Jingren Zhou, Jinze Bai, Jinzheng He, Junyang Lin, Kai Dang, Keming Lu, Keqin Chen, Kexin Yang, Mei Li, Mingfeng Xue, Na Ni, Pei Zhang, Peng Wang, Ru Peng, Rui Men, Ruize Gao, Runji Lin, Shijie Wang, Shuai Bai, Sinan Tan, Tianhang Zhu, Tianhao Li, Tianyu Liu, Wenbin Ge,

Xiaodong Deng, Xiaohuan Zhou, Xingzhang Ren, Xinyu Zhang, Xipin Wei, Xuancheng Ren, Xuejing Liu, Yang Fan, Yang Yao, Yichang Zhang, Yu Wan, Yunfei Chu, Yuqiong Liu, Zeyu Cui, Zhenru Zhang, Zhifang Guo, and Zhihao Fan. 2024. Qwen2 technical report.

Kaijia Yang, Nantao Zheng, Xinyu Dai, Liang He, Shujian Huang, and Jiajun Chen. 2020. Enhance prototypical network with text descriptions for few-shot relation classification. In *Proceedings of the 29th ACM International Conference on Information & Knowledge Management*, pages 2273–2276.

Zhi-Xiu Ye and Zhen-Hua Ling. 2019a. Distant supervision relation extraction with intra-bag and inter-bag attentions. In *Proceedings of the 2019 Conference of the North American Chapter of the Association for Computational Linguistics: Human Language Technologies, Volume 1 (Long and Short Papers)*, pages 2810–2819, Minneapolis, Minnesota. Association for Computational Linguistics.

Zhi-Xiu Ye and Zhen-Hua Ling. 2019b. Multi-level matching and aggregation network for few-shot relation classification. In *Proceedings of the 57th Annual Meeting of the Association for Computational Linguistics*, pages 2872–2881, Florence, Italy. Association for Computational Linguistics.

Tianshu Yu, Min Yang, and Xiaoyan Zhao. 2022. Dependency-aware prototype learning for few-shot relation classification. In *Proceedings of the 29th International Conference on Computational Linguistics*, pages 2339–2345, Gyeongju, Republic of Korea. International Committee on Computational Linguistics.

Daniel Zeman, Joakim Nivre, Mitchell Abrams, Noëmi Aepli, Željko Agić, Lars Ahrenberg, Gabrielė Aleksandravičiūtė, Lene Antonsen, Katya Aplonova, Maria Jesus Aranzabe, Gashaw Arutie, Masayuki Asahara, Luma Ateyah, Mohammed Attia, Aitziber Atutxa, Liesbeth Augustinus, Elena Badmaeva, Miguel Ballesteros, Esha Banerjee, Sebastian Bank, Verginica Barbu Mititelu, Victoria Basmov, Colin Batchelor, John Bauer, Sandra Bellato, Kepa Bengoetxea, Yevgeni Berzak, Irshad Ahmad Bhat, Riyaz Ahmad Bhat, Erica Biagetti, Eckhard Bick, Agnė Bielinskienė, Rogier Blokland, Victoria Bobicev, Loïc Boizou, Emanuel Borges Völker, Carl Börstell, Cristina Bosco, Gosse Bouma, Sam Bowman, Adriane Boyd, Kristina Brokaitė, Aljoscha Burchardt, Marie Candito, Bernard Caron, Gauthier Caron, Tatiana Cavalcanti, Gülşen Cebiroğlu Eryiğit, Flavio Massimiliano Cecchini, Giuseppe G. A. Celano, Slavomír Čéplö, Savas Cetin, Fabricio Chalub, Jinho Choi, Yongseok Cho, Jayeol Chun, Alessandra T. Cignarella, Silvie Cinková, Aurélie Collomb, Çağrı Çöltekin, Miriam Connor, Marine Courtin, Elizabeth Davidson, Marie-Catherine de Marneffe, Valeria de Paiva, Elvis de Souza, Arantza Diaz de Ilarraza, Carly Dickerson, Bamba Dione, Peter Dirix, Kaja Dobrovoljc, Timothy Dozat, Kira Droganova, Puneet Dwivedi, Hanne Eckhoff, Marhaba Eli, Ali Elkahky, Binyam Ephrem, Olga Erina, Tomaž Erjavec, Aline Etienne, Wograine Evelyn, Richárd Farkas, Hector Fernandez Alcalde, Jennifer Foster, Cláudia Freitas, Kazunori Fujita, Katarína Gajdošová, Daniel Galbraith, Marcos Garcia, Moa Gärdenfors, Sebastian Garza, Kim Gerdes, Filip Ginter, Iakes Goenaga, Koldo Gojenola, Memduh Gökırmak, Yoav Goldberg, Xavier Gómez Guinovart, Berta González Saavedra, Bernadeta Griciūtė, Matias Grioni, Normunds Grūzītis, Bruno Guillaume, Céline Guillot-Barbance, Nizar Habash, Jan Hajič, Jan Hajič jr., Mika Hämäläinen, Linh Hà Mỹ, Na-Rae Han, Kim Harris, Dag Haug, Johannes Heinecke, Felix Hennig, Barbora Hladká, Jaroslava Hlaváčová, Florinel Hociung, Petter Hohle, Jena Hwang, Takumi Ikeda, Radu Ion, Elena Irimia, Ọlájídé Ishola, Tomáš Jelínek, Anders Johannsen, Fredrik Jørgensen, Markus Juutinen, Hüner Kaşıkara, Andre Kaasen, Nadezhda Kabaeva, Sylvain Kahane, Hiroshi Kanayama, Jenna Kanerva, Boris Katz, Tolga Kayadelen, Jessica Kenney, Václava Kettnerová, Jesse Kirchner, Elena Klementieva, Arne Köhn, Kamil Kopacewicz, Natalia Kotsyba, Jolanta Kovalevskaitė, Simon Krek, Sookyoung Kwak, Veronika Laippala, Lorenzo Lambertino, Lucia Lam, Tatiana Lando, Septina Dian Larasati, Alexei Lavrentiev, John Lee, Phng Lê Hồng, Alessandro Lenci, Saran Lertpradit, Herman Leung, Cheuk Ying Li, Josie Li, Keying Li, KyungTae Lim, Maria Liovina, Yuan Li, Nikola Ljubešić, Olga Loginova, Olga Lyashevskaya, Teresa Lynn, Vivien Macketanz, Aibek Makazhanov, Michael Mandl, Christopher Manning, Ruli Manurung, Cătălina Mărănduc, David Mareček, Katrin Marheinecke, Héctor Martínez Alonso, André Martins, Jan Mašek, Yuji Matsumoto, Ryan McDonald, Sarah McGuinness, Gustavo Mendonça, Niko Miekka, Margarita Misirpashayeva, Anna Missilä, Cătălin Mititelu, Maria Mitrofan, Yusuke Miyao, Simonetta Montemagni, Amir More, Laura Moreno Romero, Keiko Sophie Mori, Tomohiko Morioka, Shinsuke Mori, Shigeki Moro, Bjartur Mortensen, Bohdan Moskalevskyi, Kadri Muischnek, Robert Munro, Yugo Murawaki, Kaili Müürisep, Pinkey Nainwani, Juan Ignacio Navarro Horñiacek, Anna Nedoluzhko, Gunta Nešpore-Bērzkalne, Lng Nguyễn Thị, Huyền Nguyễn Thị Minh, Yoshihiro Nikaido, Vitaly Nikolaev, Rattima Nitisaroj, Hanna Nurmi, Stina Ojala, Atul Kr. Ojha, Adédayọ Olúòkun, Mai Omura, Petya Osenova, Robert Östling, Lilja Øvrelid, Niko Partanen, Elena Pascual, Marco Passarotti, Agnieszka Patejuk, Guilherme Paulino-Passos, Angelika Peljak-Łapińska, Siyao Peng, Cenel-Augusto Perez, Guy Perrier, Daria Petrova, Slav Petrov, Jason Phelan, Jussi Piitulainen, Tommi A Pirinen, Emily Pitler, Barbara Plank, Thierry Poibeau, Larisa Ponomareva, Martin Popel, Lauma Pretkalniņa, Sophie Prévost, Prokopis Prokopidis, Adam Przepiórkowski, Tiina Puolakainen, Sampo Pyysalo, Peng Qi, Andriela Rääbis, Alexandre Rademaker, Loganathan Ramasamy, Taraka Rama, Carlos Ramisch, Vinit Ravishankar, Livy Real, Siva Reddy, Georg Rehm, Ivan Riabov, Michael Rießler, Erika Rimkutė, Larissa Ri-naldi, Laura Rituma, Luisa Rocha, Mykhailo Romanenko, Rudolf Rosa, Davide Rovati, Valentin Roșca, Olga Rudina, Jack Rueter, Shoval Sadde, Benoît Sagot, Shadi Saleh, Alessio Salomoni, Tanja Samardžić, Stephanie Samson, Manuela Sanguinetti, Dage Särg, Baiba Saulīte, Yanin Sawanakunanon, Nathan Schneider, Sebastian Schuster, Djamé Seddah, Wolfgang Seeker, Mojgan Seraji, Mo Shen, Atsuko Shimada, Hiroyuki Shirasu, Muh Shohibussirri, Dmitry Sichinava, Aline Silveira, Natalia Silveira, Maria Simi, Radu Simionescu, Katalin Simkó, Mária Šimková, Kiril Simov, Aaron Smith, Isabela Soares-Bastos, Carolyn Spadine, Antonio Stella, Milan Straka, Jana Strnadová, Alane Suhr, Umut Sulubacak, Shingo Suzuki, Zsolt Szántó, Dima Taji, Yuta Takahashi, Fabio Tamburini, Takaaki Tanaka, Isabelle Tellier, Guillaume Thomas, Liisi Torga, Trond Trosterud, Anna Trukhina, Reut Tsarfaty, Francis Tyers, Sumire Uematsu, Zdeňka Urešová, Larraitz Uria, Hans Uszkoreit, Andrius Utka, Sowmya Vajjala, Daniel van Niekerk, Gertjan van Noord, Viktor Varga, Eric Villemonte de la Clergerie, Veronika Vincze, Lars Wallin, Abigail Walsh, Jing Xian Wang, Jonathan North Washington, Maximilan Wendt, Seyi Williams, Mats Wirén, Christian Wittern, Tsegay Woldemariam, Tak-sum Wong, Alina Wróblewska, Mary Yako, Naoki Yamazaki, Chunxiao Yan, Koichi Yasuoka, Marat M. Yavrumyan, Zhuoran Yu, Zdeněk Žabokrtský, Amir Zeldes, Manying Zhang, and Hanzhi Zhu. 2019. Universal dependencies 2.5. LINDAT/CLARIAH-CZ digital library at the Institute of Formal and Applied Linguistics (ÚFAL), Faculty of Mathematics and Physics, Charles University.

Jiali Zeng, Yufan Jiang, Yongjing Yin, Xu Wang, Binghuai Lin, and Yunbo Cao. 2022. DualNER: A dual-teaching framework for zero-shot cross-lingual named entity recognition. In *Findings of the Association for Computational Linguistics: EMNLP 2022*, pages 1837–1843, Abu Dhabi, United Arab Emirates. Association for Computational Linguistics.

Chen Zhang, Yuxuan Lai, Yansong Feng, Xingyu Shen, Haowei Du, and Dongyan Zhao. 2023a. Cross-lingual question answering over knowledge base as reading comprehension. In *Findings of the Association for Computational Linguistics: EACL 2023*, pages 2439–2452, Dubrovnik, Croatia. Association for Computational Linguistics.

Heidi Zhang, Sina Semnani, Farhad Ghassemi, Jialiang Xu, Shicheng Liu, and Monica Lam. 2024. SPAGHETTI: Open-domain question answering from heterogeneous data sources with retrieval and semantic parsing. In *Findings of the Association for Computational Linguistics: ACL 2024*, pages 1663–1678, Bangkok, Thailand. Association for Computational Linguistics.

Qin Zhang, Shangsi Chen, Dongkuan Xu, Qingqing Cao, Xiaojun Chen, Trevor Cohn, and Meng Fang. 2023b. A survey for efficient open domain question answering. In *Proceedings of the 61st Annual Meeting of the Association for Computational Linguistics (Volume 1: Long Papers)*, pages 14447–14465, Toronto, Canada. Association for Computational Linguistics.

Xinyu Zhao, Shih-Ting Lin, and Greg Durrett. 2021. Effective distant supervision for temporal relation extraction. In *Proceedings of the Second Workshop on Domain Adaptation for NLP*, pages 195–203, Kyiv, Ukraine. Association for Computational Linguistics.

Ben Zhou, Daniel Khashabi, Chen-Tse Tsai, and Dan Roth. 2019. Zero-shot open entity typing as type-compatible grounding. *arXiv preprint arXiv:1907.03228*.

Sizhe Zhou, Yu Meng, Bowen Jin, and Jiawei Han. 2024. Grasping the essentials: Tailoring large language models for zero-shot relation extraction. In *Proceedings of the 2024 Conference on Empirical Methods in Natural Language Processing*, pages 13462–13486, Miami, Florida, USA. Association for Computational Linguistics.

A Appendices

In this section, we provide extra figures and tables to further corroborate our experiments in this work. Additionally, we also present a statistical significance analysis of our results using the Anova method.

Dataset	Source	Encoder	Parser	Sent Length		Lex Length		Dep Length		# Docs	# Rels
				Mean	Median	Mean	Median	Mean	Median		
Indore	en	mBERT	stanza	31.23	29.0	13.92	11.0	5.43	5.0	8486	51
	hi	mBERT	stanza	66.76	56.0	27.29	21.0	5.70	5.0	6963	51
	te	mBERT	stanza	151.45	140.0	44.74	31.0	6.05	6.0	8154	51
	en	mBERT	trankit	31.23	29.0	13.92	11.0	5.42	5.0	8486	51
	hi	mBERT	trankit	66.76	56.0	27.29	21.0	5.85	6.0	6963	51
	te	mBERT	trankit	151.45	140.0	44.74	31.0	5.69	6.0	8154	51
	en	XLMR	stanza	34.40	32.0	15.95	13.0	5.43	5.0	8486	51
	hi	XLMR	stanza	56.25	48.0	22.85	17.0	5.70	5.0	6963	51
	te	XLMR	stanza	125.60	113.0	37.43	26.0	6.05	6.0	8154	51
	en	XLMR	trankit	34.40	32.0	15.95	13.0	5.42	5.0	8486	51
	hi	XLMR	trankit	56.25	48.0	22.85	17.0	5.85	6.0	6963	51
	te	XLMR	trankit	125.60	113.0	37.43	26.0	5.69	6.0	8154	51
RedFM	en	mBERT	stanza	117.53	107.0	27.96	17.0	6.40	6.0	10899	32
	es	mBERT	stanza	103.77	91.0	25.97	17.0	6.24	6.0	6538	32
	fr	mBERT	stanza	92.18	78.0	23.19	15.0	5.86	5.0	7383	32
	it	mBERT	stanza	79.31	65.0	20.56	14.0	5.80	5.0	6812	32
	de	mBERT	stanza	88.79	79.0	22.97	15.0	5.28	5.0	7497	32
	ar	mBERT	stanza	107.15	90.0	29.68	22.0	6.08	6.0	1846	32
	zh	mBERT	stanza	118.18	101.0	35.25	22.0	6.69	6.0	1384	32
	en	mBERT	trankit	117.53	107.0	27.96	17.0	6.37	6.0	10899	32
	es	mBERT	trankit	103.77	91.0	25.97	17.0	6.16	6.0	6538	32
	fr	mBERT	trankit	92.18	78.0	23.19	15.0	5.68	5.0	7383	32
	it	mBERT	trankit	79.31	65.0	20.56	14.0	5.64	5.0	6812	32
	de	mBERT	trankit	88.79	79.0	22.97	15.0	5.16	5.0	7497	32
	ar	mBERT	trankit	107.15	90.0	29.68	22.0	6.18	6.0	1846	32
	zh	mBERT	trankit	118.18	101.0	35.25	22.0	6.75	6.0	1384	32
	en	XLMR	stanza	130.33	119.0	31.52	19.0	6.40	6.0	10899	32
	es	XLMR	stanza	112.22	100.0	28.86	19.0	6.24	6.0	6538	32
	fr	XLMR	stanza	103.20	86.0	26.77	17.0	5.86	5.0	7383	32
	it	XLMR	stanza	85.14	71.0	22.72	16.0	5.80	5.0	6812	32
	de	XLMR	stanza	96.23	87.0	25.53	17.0	5.28	5.0	7497	32
	ar	XLMR	stanza	95.81	81.0	26.64	19.0	6.08	6.0	1846	32
	zh	XLMR	stanza	96.10	81.0	28.35	18.0	6.69	6.0	1384	32
	en	XLMR	trankit	130.33	119.0	31.52	19.0	6.37	6.0	10899	32
	es	XLMR	trankit	112.22	100.0	28.86	19.0	6.16	6.0	6538	32
	fr	XLMR	trankit	103.20	86.0	26.77	17.0	5.68	5.0	7383	32
	it	XLMR	trankit	85.14	71.0	22.72	16.0	5.64	5.0	6812	32
	de	XLMR	trankit	96.23	87.0	25.53	17.0	5.16	5.0	7497	32
	ar	XLMR	trankit	95.81	81.0	26.64	19.0	6.18	6.0	1846	32
	zh	XLMR	trankit	96.10	81.0	28.35	18.0	6.75	6.0	1384	32

Table 4: Combined Statistics for Indore and RedFM Datasets

Without Any Dependency Information:

Given the sentence: "The Porsche Panamera is a mid/full-sized luxury vehicle (E-segment in Europe) manufactured by the <e2>German</e2> automobile manufacturer <e1>Porsche</e1>. It is front-engined and has a rear-wheel-drive layout, with all-wheel drive versions also available.", which one of the following relations between the two entities <e1> and <e2> is being discussed? Choose one from this list of 32 options:\n0: country\n1: place of birth \n2: spouse\n3: country of citizenship\n4: instance of\n5: capital\n6: child\n7: shares border with\n8: author\n9: director\n10: occupation\n11: founded by\n12: league\n13: owned by\n14: genre\n15: named after\n16: follows\n17: headquarters location\n18: cast member\n19: manufacturer\n20: located in or next to body of water\n21: location\n22: part of\n23: mouth of the watercourse\n24: member of\n25: sport \n26: characters\n27: participant\n28: notable work\n29: replaces\n30: sibling\n31: inception\n\n. The answer is :

Tuple Format Prompt:

Given the sentence: "The Porsche Panamera is a mid/full-sized luxury vehicle (E-segment in Europe) manufactured by the <e2>German</e2> automobile manufacturer <e1>Porsche</e1>. It is front-engined and has a rear-wheel-drive layout, with all-wheel drive versions also available.", which one of the following relations between the two entities <e1> and <e2> is being discussed? We also provide the dependency parse in the form of head, rel, and word: {"head": "Panamera", "rel": "det", "word": "The"}, {"head": "Panamera", "rel": "compound", "word": "Porsche"}, {"head": "vehicle", "rel": "nsubj", "word": "Panamera"}, {"head": "vehicle", "rel": "cop", "word": "is"}, {"head": "vehicle", "rel": "det", "word": "a"}, {"head": "sized", "rel": "compound", "word": "mid"}, {"head": "sized", "rel": "punct", "word": "/"}, {"head": "sized", "rel": "amod", "word": "full"}, {"head": "sized", "rel": "punct", "word": "-"}, {"head": "vehicle", "rel": "amod", "word": "sized"}, {"head": "vehicle", "rel": "compound", "word": "luxury"}, {"head": "ROOT", "rel": "root", "word": "vehicle"}, {"head": "segment", "rel": "punct", "word": "("}, {"head": "segment", "rel": "compound", "word": "E"}, {"head": "segment", "rel": "punct", "word": "-"}, {"head": "vehicle", "rel": "appos", "word": "segment"}, {"head": "Europe", "rel": "case", "word": "in"}, {"head": "segment", "rel": "nmod", "word": "Europe"}, {"head": "segment", "rel": "punct", "word": ")"}, {"head": "vehicle", "rel": "acl", "word": "manufactured"}, {"head": "manufacturer", "rel": "case", "word": "by"}, {"head": "manufacturer", "rel": "det", "word": "the"}, {"head": "manufacturer", "rel": "amod", "word": "German"}, {"head": "manufacturer", "rel": "compound", "word": "automobile"}, {"head": "manufactured", "rel": "obl", "word": "manufacturer"}, {"head": "manufacturer", "rel": "appos", "word": "Porsche"}, {"head": "vehicle", "rel": "punct", "word": "."}, {"head": "engined", "rel": "nsubj", "word": "It"}, {"head": "engined", "rel": "cop", "word": "is"}, {"head": "engined", "rel": "obl:npmod", "word": "front"}, {"head": "engined", "rel": "punct", "word": "-"}, {"head": "ROOT", "rel": "root", "word": "engined"}, {"head": "has", "rel": "cc", "word": "and"}, {"head": "engined", "rel": "conj", "word": "has"}, {"head": "layout", "rel": "det", "word": "a"}, {"head": "drive", "rel": "amod", "word": "rear"}, {"head": "drive", "rel": "punct", "word": "-"}, {"head": "drive", "rel": "compound", "word": "wheel"}, {"head": "drive", "rel": "punct", "word": "-"}, {"head": "layout", "rel": "amod", "word": "drive"}, {"head": "has", "rel": "obj", "word": "layout"}, {"head": "layout", "rel": "punct", "word": ","}, {"head": "available", "rel": "mark", "word": "with"}, {"head": "drive", "rel": "det", "word": "all"}, {"head": "drive", "rel": "punct", "word": "-"}, {"head": "drive", "rel": "compound", "word": "wheel"}, {"head": "versions", "rel": "compound", "word": "drive"}, {"head": "available", "rel": "nsubj", "word": "versions"}, {"head": "available", "rel": "advmod", "word": "also"}, {"head": "layout", "rel": "acl", "word": "available"}, {"head": "engined", "rel": "punct", "word": "."}. Choose one from this list of 32 options:\n0: country\n1: place of birth \n2: spouse\n3: country of citizenship\n4: instance of\n5: capital\n6: child\n7: shares border with\n8: author\n9: director\n10: occupation\n11: founded by\n12: league\n13: owned by\n14: genre\n15: named after\n16: follows\n17: headquarters location\n18: cast member\n19: manufacturer\n20: located in or next to body of water\n21: location\n22: part of\n23: mouth of the watercourse\n24: member of\n25: sport \n26: characters\n27: participant\n28: notable work\n29: replaces\n30: sibling\n31: inception\n\n. The answer is :

Table 5: Prompt without dependency information and the tuple format prompt are used for relation extraction on the English subset of the RedFM dataset with Trankit as the dependency parser.

Text Prompt:
Given the sentence: T̈he Porsche Panamera is a mid/full-sized luxury vehicle (E-segment in Europe) manufactured by the <e2>German</e2> automobile manufacturer <e1>Porsche</e1>. It is front-engined and has a rear-wheel-drive layout, with all-wheel drive versions also available., which one of the following relations between the two entities <e1> and <e2> is being discussed?\We also provide the dependency parses as follows: T̈he is Determiner of Panamera, Porsche is Compound noun modifier of Panamera, Panamera is Nominal subject of vehicle, is is Copula of vehicle, a is Determiner of vehicle, mid/ is Adverbial modifier of sized, full is Adjectival modifier of sized, - is Punctuation of sized, sized is Adjectival modifier of vehicle, luxury is Compound noun modifier of vehicle, vehicle is the root word, (is Punctuation of E, E is Appositional modifier of vehicle, - is Punctuation of segment, segment is Unspecified dependency of E, in is Case marker of Europe, Europe is Nominal modifier of segment,) is Punctuation of segment, manufactured is Clausal modifier of noun of vehicle, by is Case marker of Porsche, the is Determiner of Porsche, German is Adjectival modifier of Porsche, automobile is Compound noun modifier of manufacturer, manufacturer is Compound noun modifier of Porsche, Porsche is Oblique nominal of manufactured, . is Punctuation of vehicle, It is Nominal subject of engined, is is Copula of engined, front is Adjectival modifier of engined, - is Punctuation of front, engined is the root word, and is Coordinating conjunction of has, has is Conjunction of engined, a is Determiner of layout, rear is Compound noun modifier of drive, - is Punctuation of wheel, wheel is Compound noun modifier of drive, - is Punctuation of drive, drive is Compound noun modifier of layout, layout is Object of has, , is Punctuation of available, with is Marker of available, all is Determiner of wheel, - is Punctuation of all, wheel is Compound noun modifier of drive, drive is Compound noun modifier of versions, versions is Nominal subject of available, also is Adverbial modifier of available, available is Adverbial clause modifier of has, . is Punctuation of engined, \Choose one from this list of 32 options:\n0: country\n1: place of birth \n2: spouse\n3: country of citizenship\n4: instance of\n5: capital\n6: child\n7: shares border with\n8: author\n9: director\n10: occupation\n11: founded by\n12: league\n13: owned by\n14: genre\n15: named after\n16: follows\n17: headquarters location\n18: cast member\n19: manufacturer\n20: located in or next to body of water\n21: location\n22: part of\n23: mouth of the watercourse\n24: member of\n25: sport \n26: characters\n27: participant\n28: notable work\n29: replaces\n30: sibling\n31: inception\n\nThe answer is : "
Filtered Text Prompt:
Given the sentence: T̈he Porsche Panamera is a mid/full-sized luxury vehicle (E-segment in Europe) manufactured by the <e2>German</e2> automobile manufacturer <e1>Porsche</e1>. It is front-engined and has a rear-wheel-drive layout, with all-wheel drive versions also available., which one of the following relations between the two entities <e1> and <e2> is being discussed?\n We also provide the dependency parses as follows: P̈orsche is Adjectival modifier of German, \n Choose one from this list of 32 options:\n0: country\n1: place of birth \n2: spouse\n3: country of citizenship\n4: instance of\n5: capital\n6: child\n7: shares border with\n8: author\n9: director\n10: occupation\n11: founded by\n12: league\n13: owned by\n14: genre\n15: named after\n16: follows\n17: headquarters location\n18: cast member\n19: manufacturer\n20: located in or next to body of water\n21: location\n22: part of\n23: mouth of the watercourse\n24: member of\n25: sport \n26: characters\n27: participant\n28: notable work\n29: replaces\n30: sibling\n31: inception\n\n. The answer is :

Table 6: Text prompt and Filtered Text prompts used for relation extraction on the English subset of the RedFM dataset with Trankit as the dependency parser.

Table 7: Zero-shot cross-lingual performance for Relation Extraction on the RedFM dataset using different combinations of multi-lingual encoder and dependency parse information and GNN. Highest values in each column are in bold. The rows and columns correspond to the source and target language respectively.

						mBERT			
Src	DEP	GNN	en	es	fr	it	de	ar	zh
en	-	-	-	80.4±0.2	80.7±0.4	**77.3±1.3**	78.8±0.9	72.7±0.8	70.4±0.6
en	stanza	rgcn	-	79.6±0.8	**80.9±1.4**	76.2±1.0	**80.2±0.5**	74.4±0.9	72.0±0.8
en	stanza	rgat	-	80.3±0.4	80.3±0.2	74.8±1.2	79.5±0.3	74.1±0.9	**72.3±0.4**
en	trankit	rgcn	-	80.1±0.4	80.8±0.5	73.8±0.2	79.3±0.7	73.8±1.8	69.5±0.6
en	trankit	rgat	-	**80.8±0.3**	80.7±0.2	74.4±1.8	79.0±0.7	**74.5±0.7**	70.1±0.6
es	-	-	77.6±0.1	-	77.2±0.8	76.4±0.6	75.9±0.7	70.9±1.6	70.8±1.1
es	stanza	rgcn	78.0±0.4	-	**82.6±0.8**	77.6±1.4	76.9±1.3	73.2±0.5	69.2±0.6
es	stanza	rgat	79.1±0.2	-	78.4±0.5	77.4±1.3	76.2±0.7	**73.5±0.9**	69.7±1.5
es	trankit	rgcn	79.3±0.9	-	80.6±1.6	76.3±0.6	77.1±1.0	73.3±0.3	**71.5±1.6**
es	trankit	rgat	**80.0±1.1**	-	78.7±0.5	**78.3±1.0**	**77.7±0.8**	72.6±1.2	71.2±2.6
fr	-	-	76.6±2.9	80.4±1.3	-	76.9±2.0	74.8±1.6	70.2±1.1	66.4±2.6
fr	stanza	rgcn	76.6±0.3	82.1±1.0	-	77.7±0.7	76.6±0.2	70.4±0.8	66.8±0.9
fr	stanza	rgat	80.0±0.7	82.1±0.9	-	77.0±1.0	77.5±1.5	71.5±1.0	67.5±1.2
fr	trankit	rgcn	78.6±0.3	**83.3±1.6**	-	**78.7±1.1**	**78.8±2.5**	**72.4±0.5**	**69.7±0.7**
fr	trankit	rgat	**80.1±0.8**	79.7±2.1	-	76.6±1.5	77.4±0.1	70.9±0.8	68.4±0.5
it	-	-	75.4±0.4	83.1±0.5	77.7±1.1	-	72.9±1.1	**73.0±2.0**	70.8±1.0
it	stanza	rgcn	**79.0±0.6**	83.0±0.7	77.2±1.0	-	74.7±1.4	70.8±0.3	70.0±0.7
it	stanza	rgat	76.7±0.9	**83.8±0.7**	77.5±0.5	-	75.7±1.5	72.2±1.6	70.5±0.4
it	trankit	rgcn	77.1±1.4	82.3±0.3	77.2±0.6	-	76.0±1.2	71.0±1.0	69.2±1.9
it	trankit	rgat	77.1±0.1	82.5±0.4	**77.8±0.5**	-	**76.3±0.1**	71.7±1.0	**71.5±0.9**
de	-	-	80.4±1.0	80.0±0.4	**78.3±0.1**	76.1±1.5	-	**75.8±1.9**	71.6±1.2
de	stanza	rgcn	80.0±0.2	80.4±0.7	76.7±0.3	75.8±0.8	-	74.2±0.8	70.0±1.9
de	stanza	rgat	79.2±0.4	**81.3±1.1**	78.1±1.4	76.6±2.7	-	74.6±0.5	**71.7±0.6**
de	trankit	rgcn	79.7±0.3	80.6±1.4	77.9±0.3	75.1±0.4	-	73.3±1.0	70.1±0.1
de	trankit	rgat	**80.7±0.7**	79.2±0.1	77.8±0.6	**77.4±0.5**	-	73.7±0.0	70.6±0.8
						XLMR			
en	-	-	-	73.1±1.8	**72.8±2.8**	64.2±3.7	**75.6±1.7**	61.7±1.8	64.4±1.0
en	stanza	rgcn	-	74.4±1.3	**72.7±0.5**	**67.4±1.3**	74.6±0.7	**63.2±1.5**	65.1±0.9
en	stanza	rgat	-	73.1±0.7	**72.7±1.4**	66.5±3.5	71.1±1.0	59.6±2.7	62.2±0.4
en	trankit	rgcn	-	74.4±1.5	72.0±1.8	65.4±2.2	71.5±1.6	62.6±1.8	64.6±1.3
en	trankit	rgat	-	**74.9±0.7**	70.3±0.1	62.4±1.6	73.9±0.4	61.5±1.7	**66.5±1.7**
es	-	-	73.3±0.4	-	74.3±0.4	**70.1±1.4**	**70.6±0.7**	63.2±3.1	**65.9±1.9**
es	stanza	rgcn	73.4±2.2	-	75.1±0.3	68.3±2.5	67.3±0.6	61.9±1.2	62.4±1.4
es	stanza	rgat	72.7±1.9	-	75.2±1.0	69.3±1.6	67.3±0.3	60.5±1.4	62.8±1.8
es	trankit	rgcn	**73.8±1.0**	-	75.9±1.5	69.8±1.8	70.0±2.5	**64.3±2.1**	65.6±2.7
es	trankit	rgat	71.4±1.2	-	**76.2±1.2**	68.0±1.5	68.7±2.0	60.0±0.9	62.5±2.3
fr	-	-	71.1±0.9	75.0±0.6	-	68.9±0.6	68.5±1.3	**61.5±1.2**	59.4±2.6
fr	stanza	rgcn	**74.3±1.7**	74.1±1.1	-	**69.7±0.6**	**72.2±1.3**	58.7±0.6	**62.9±2.7**
fr	stanza	rgat	70.1±1.5	73.9±1.3	-	67.0±1.5	66.2±1.0	59.0±0.9	60.3±1.6
fr	trankit	rgcn	70.0±0.2	74.4±0.5	-	68.4±0.7	66.4±0.7	58.9±2.2	59.5±1.8
fr	trankit	rgat	71.8±1.3	**76.0±0.7**	-	68.2±0.8	70.6±1.0	**61.5±1.2**	59.9±1.3
it	-	-	71.2±1.1	76.1±1.6	72.2±0.9	-	68.2±1.7	60.8±0.5	62.0±1.7
it	stanza	rgcn	73.3±2.0	76.1±0.8	74.3±1.3	-	67.2±2.1	61.8±0.3	63.1±0.3
it	stanza	rgat	**74.9±1.0**	76.0±0.2	74.2±1.3	-	68.9±0.2	62.2±0.1	**64.7±1.5**
it	trankit	rgcn	73.3±1.2	77.0±0.7	74.8±1.6	-	70.0±1.7	**64.5±1.0**	**64.7±1.0**
it	trankit	rgat	72.6±1.9	**78.7±0.5**	**76.6±0.2**	-	**70.2±1.0**	63.6±3.4	64.6±1.5
de	-	-	75.0±1.5	72.4±0.9	69.3±1.3	64.1±0.3	-	60.8±0.7	64.0±1.2
de	stanza	rgcn	72.6±1.5	73.4±2.1	70.8±1.9	65.2±0.5	-	60.6±0.8	**66.0±1.9**
de	stanza	rgat	**76.1±1.5**	**73.5±0.2**	**71.5±1.3**	**69.0±2.8**	-	**64.0±1.6**	65.8±1.7
de	trankit	rgcn	74.1±1.0	72.8±0.8	69.6±1.8	63.6±2.3	-	63.4±1.0	64.5±1.9
de	trankit	rgat	75.0±0.5	73.2±1.6	70.3±1.3	64.9±1.0	-	63.7±0.5	64.4±3.5

Table 8: Zero-shot cross-lingual performance for Relation Extraction on the IndoRE dataset using different combinations of multi-lingual encoder and dependency parse information and GNN. Highest values in each column are in bold. The rows and columns correspond to the source and target language respectively.

		mBERT			
Src	DEP	GNN	en	hi	te
en	-	-	-	60.7±0.6	35.3±0.8
en	stanza	rgcn	-	60.1±0.4	38.3±1.2
en	stanza	rgat	-	58.7±0.3	**40.6±2.2**
en	trankit	rgcn	-	**62.5±0.8**	38.0±1.4
en	trankit	rgat	-	61.8±1.0	37.8±1.8
hi	-	-	**69.7±1.9**	-	49.5±2.3
hi	stanza	rgcn	68.6±0.6	-	49.4±0.8
hi	stanza	rgat	67.8±2.3	-	49.7±0.6
hi	trankit	rgcn	68.1±0.8	-	49.6±2.2
hi	trankit	rgat	68.0±1.6	-	**53.9±0.9**
te	-	-	45.3±1.7	54.4±2.6	-
te	stanza	rgcn	45.6±1.4	54.0±1.3	-
te	stanza	rgat	44.8±0.3	**56.6±0.3**	-
te	trankit	rgcn	**47.7±0.8**	54.2±0.1	-
te	trankit	rgat	46.1±1.2	54.2±2.5	-
		XLMR			
en	-	-	-	57.4±2.3	37.2±2.5
en	stanza	rgcn	-	55.3±1.2	37.0±1.6
en	stanza	rgat	-	55.5±2.3	37.8±1.9
en	trankit	rgcn	-	58.8±0.5	36.4±3.8
en	trankit	rgat	-	**61.0±2.5**	**39.0±4.0**
hi	-	-	59.1±1.8	-	53.7±1.0
hi	stanza	rgcn	57.4±1.3	-	**54.7±1.2**
hi	stanza	rgat	**61.0±2.5**	-	**54.8±2.1**
hi	trankit	rgcn	59.5±0.8	-	54.3±1.8
hi	trankit	rgat	57.3±2.4	-	**54.8±2.3**
te	-	-	40.9±2.6	52.8±0.7	-
te	stanza	rgcn	41.2±2.2	**55.5±0.9**	-
te	stanza	rgat	39.0±0.7	52.0±3.2	-
te	trankit	rgcn	**41.8±0.6**	53.7±0.6	-
te	trankit	rgat	41.4±0.3	53.7±1.8	-

Source	sum_sq	df	F	P(>F)
C(src)	1.844	2.000	6.265	**0.020**
C(GNN)	0.185	1.000	1.258	0.291
C(DEP)	1.226	1.000	8.330	**0.018**
C(ENC)	0.308	1.000	2.094	0.182
C(src):C(DEP)	0.165	2.000	0.56	0.590
C(src):C(ENC)	7.124	2.000	24.20	**0.000**
C(src):C(GNN)	1.335	2.000	4.534	**0.043**
C(DEP):C(GNN)	0.055	1.000	0.371	0.557
C(ENC):C(GNN)	1.045	1.000	7.098	**0.026**
C(DEP):C(ENC)	1.005	1.000	6.827	**0.028**
Residual	1.325	9.000	NaN	NaN

Table 9: Indore In-Domain ANOVA Results

Source	sum_sq	df	F	P(>F)
C(src)	48.606	2.000	2.449	0.108
C(GNN)	4.009	1.000	0.404	0.531
C(DEP)	23.301	1.000	2.348	0.139
C(ENC)	20.426	1.000	2.058	0.164
C(tgt)	199.051	2.000	10.030	**0.001**
C(tgt):C(DEP)	13.604	2.000	0.686	0.513
C(tgt):C(ENC)	85.332	2.000	4.300	**0.025**
C(tgt):C(GNN)	19.710	2.000	0.993	0.385
C(tgt):C(src)	12.388	4.000	0.312	0.735
C(src):C(DEP)	6.487	2.000	0.327	0.724
C(src):C(ENC)	73.878	2.000	3.723	**0.039**
C(src):C(GNN)	7.459	2.000	0.376	0.691
C(DEP):C(GNN)	0.845	1.000	0.085	0.773
C(ENC):C(GNN)	0.923	1.000	0.093	0.763
C(DEP):C(ENC)	1.561	1.000	0.157	0.695
Residual	238.143	24.000	NaN	NaN

Table 10: Indore Cross-Domain ANOVA Results

Source	sum_sq	df	F	P(>F)
C(src)	1.862	4.000	0.408	0.800
C(GNN)	0.719	1.000	0.630	0.438
C(DEP)	3.613	1.000	3.167	0.093
C(ENC)	51.586	1.000	45.228	**0.000**
C(src):C(DEP)	2.027	4.000	0.444	0.775
C(src):C(ENC)	9.053	4.000	1.984	0.143
C(src):C(GNN)	3.373	4.000	0.739	0.578
C(DEP):C(GNN)	0.221	1.000	0.194	0.665
C(ENC):C(GNN)	1.773	1.000	1.555	0.229
C(DEP):C(ENC)	1.601	1.000	1.403	0.252
Residual	19.390	17.000	NaN	NaN

Table 11: RedFM In-domain ANOVA Results

Source	sum_sq	df	F	P(>F)
C(src)	14.700	4.000	0.988	0.322
C(GNN)	0.109	1.000	0.029	0.864
C(DEP)	1.111	1.000	0.299	0.585
C(ENC)	4.923	1.000	1.323	0.252
C(tgt)	10.040	6.000	0.450	0.718
C(tgt):C(DEP)	25.753	6.000	1.154	0.334
C(tgt):C(ENC)	106.197	6.000	4.757	**0.000**
C(tgt):C(GNN)	1.642	6.000	0.074	0.998
C(tgt):C(src)	314.185	24.000	3.518	**0.000**
C(src):C(DEP)	23.724	4.000	1.594	0.178
C(src):C(ENC)	323.737	4.000	21.752	**0.000**
C(src):C(GNN)	49.322	4.000	3.314	**0.012**
C(DEP):C(GNN)	0.615	1.000	0.165	0.685
C(ENC):C(GNN)	2.771	1.000	0.745	0.389
C(DEP):C(ENC)	0.389	1.000	0.105	0.747
Residual	647.408	174.000	NaN	NaN

Table 12: RedFM Cross-Domain ANOVA Results

Source	sum_sq	df	F	P(>F)
C(src)	58.4	2	0.657	5.26E-01
C(DEP)	2.2	1	0.048	8.28E-01
C(LLM)	1260.3	2	14.17	**6.18E-05**
C(PRM)	3042.5	2	34.22	**3.94E-08**
C(src):C(DEP)	16.7	2	0.187	8.30E-01
C(src):C(LLM)	543.7	4	3.058	**3.36E-02**
C(src):C(PRM)	426.9	4	2.401	7.46E-02
C(DEP):C(LLM)	62.3	2	0.708	5.05E-01
C(DEP):C(PRM)	48.0	2	0.54	5.87E-01
C(LLM):C(PRM)	2205.3	4	12.40	**7.47E-06**
Residual	1200.1	27	NaN	NaN

Table 13: Indore Zero-shot ICL ANOVA Results

Source	sum_sq	df	F	P(>F)
C(src)	6123.02	6	13.34	**2.91E-10**
C(DEP)	5.09	1	0.07	7.97E-01
C(LLM)	4945.81	2	32.32	**6.97E-11**
C(PRM)	12473.39	2	81.51	**1.23E-19**
C(src):C(DEP)	178.97	6	0.39	8.83E-01
C(src):C(LLM)	13819.12	12	15.05	**1.46E-15**
C(src):C(PRM)	1727.37	12	1.88	5.01E-02
C(DEP):C(LLM)	131.03	2	0.86	4.29E-01
C(DEP):C(PRM)	101.88	2	0.67	5.17E-01
C(LLM):C(PRM)	3130.31	4	10.23	**1.12E-06**
Residual	5815.44	76	NaN	NaN

Table 14: RedFM Zero-shot ICL ANOVA Results

DocBench: A Benchmark for Evaluating LLM-based Document Reading Systems

Anni Zou[1,2*] **, Wenhao Yu**[2✉]**, Hongming Zhang**[2]**, Kaixin Ma**[2]**,**
Deng Cai[2]**, Zhuosheng Zhang**[1]**, Hai Zhao**[1]**, Dong Yu**[2]
[1]Shanghai Jiao Tong University [2]Tencent AI Seattle Lab
✉wenhaowyu@global.tencent.com

Abstract

Recently, there has been a growing interest among large language model (LLM) developers in LLM-based document reading systems, which enable users to upload their own documents and pose related questions, addressing challenges like file parsing, metadata extraction, multi-modal information understanding, and long-context reading. However, no current benchmark exists to evaluate their performance in such scenarios, where a raw file and questions are provided as input, and a corresponding response is expected as output. In this paper, we introduce DocBench, a new benchmark designed to assess LLM-based document reading systems. It includes 229 real documents and 1,102 questions across five domains and four major question types, created through human annotators and synthetic question generation. Our findings highlight significant gaps between existing LLM-based document reading systems and human performance, emphasizing the challenges in developing proficient systems. DocBench aims to standardize the evaluation of these systems in diverse real-world scenarios, guiding future advancements in this field.

1 Introduction

The emergence of large language models (LLMs) has marked a significant milestone in the field of natural language processing, revolutionizing the way we approach a variety of tasks (Zhao et al., 2023; Chang et al., 2024; Wang et al., 2024a; Achiam et al., 2023; Anthropic, 2024; Touvron et al., 2023; Team et al., 2023). Existing LLMs such as GPT-4 (Achiam et al., 2023), Llama-3 (Touvron et al., 2023), and Claude-3 (Anthropic, 2024) have shown exceptional abilities in following human instructions to perform tasks such as answering questions, translating languages and summarizing texts. These tasks are typically characterized by straightforward input-output interactions, where the models generate responses solely based on the provided text. However, many real-world applications require more complex interactions involving user-provided documents. For instance, financial analysts might need to query comprehensive financial reports to inform their investment decisions (Yang et al., 2023; Wu et al., 2023). Legal professionals often search through extensive legal documents to find relevant case law (Lai et al., 2023; Cui et al., 2023). Similarly, scientific researchers frequently sift through academic papers to identify related works and extract key findings (Dasigi et al., 2021; Birhane et al., 2023).

When users pose queries based on their provided documents, the situation becomes more intricate and challenging (Lee et al., 2024). Unlike standalone LLMs that are primarily trained to process and respond to textual inputs (or images in the case of Vision LLMs), handling user-provided documents necessitates a more sophisticated approach that stretches beyond the capabilities of a single LLM. In order to provide accurate responses, an LLM-based document reading system should not only comprehend natural language queries, but also excel in a range of processing skills, including parsing and interpreting user documents and layouts, navigating complex formatting structures, extracting relevant metadata, and managing long textual contexts along with any embedded images. Mastery of these diverse skills is essential for generating precise and contextually relevant responses.

At the same time, recent advancements in proprietary LLM developers such as OpenAI and Anthropic have provoked the release of several LLM-based document reading systems. Figure 1 illustrates an example of OpenAI's GPT-4-based document reading system. Despite widespread claims of effectiveness and efficiency in various online

*This work was done during internship at Tencent AI Lab, Seattle.

Proceedings of the 4th International Workshop on Knowledge-Augmented Methods for Natural Language Processing (KnowledgeNLP'25), pages 359–373
May 3, 2025 ©2025 Association for Computational Linguistics

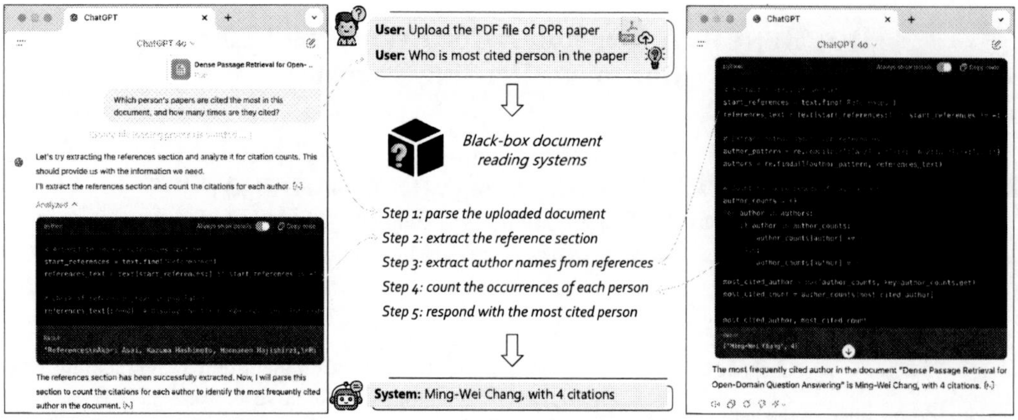

Figure 1: An example of OpenAI's GPT-4 based document reading system. Unlike standalone LLMs, recent proprietary LLM-based document reading systems employ a carefully designed approach (e.g., file parsing, code execution) to answer user questions related to document contents.

public blogs[1,2], **the absence of a standardized benchmark** makes it difficult to objectively evaluate and compare the document reading performance across these systems, thereby leaving a critical gap in fairly assessing these capabilities in a fine-grained manner.

To fill this gap, our paper introduces DOCBENCH, a novel benchmark specifically designed to evaluate LLM-based document reading systems. DOCBENCH is developed to mirror real-world scenarios where each input consists of a document paired with one or multiple associated questions, and each question is annotated with a golden answer. Our benchmark undergoes a meticulous development process, incorporating human annotation and synthetic question generation. To the end, DOCBENCH features 229 real-world documents and 1,102 questions spanning 5 diverse domains: *Academia, Finance, Government, Laws, and News*. Besides, the benchmark involves 4 question categories, including *text-only, multi-modal (i.e., tables and figures), meta-data, and unanswerable*, ensuring comprehensive coverage of various document reading capabilities.

Based upon DOCBENCH, we evaluate several proprietary LLM-based systems that are accessible via web interfaces or APIs. However, these proprietary systems are close-sourced, thus leading to the limited disclosure of their detailed operational strategies. As a result, we additionally assess a straightforward parse-then-read pipeline employing a series of open-source LLMs. Our evaluations reveal noticeable gaps between existing LLM-based document reading systems and human performance, underscoring the challenges of developing proficient systems.

In summary, DOCBENCH serves as the first standardized benchmark to evaluate LLM-based document reading systems within real-world scenarios, where the systems take a document file paired with one or multiple related questions as input and generate textual responses as output. Moreover, our benchmark is carefully designed to encompass 5 diverse domains and 4 distinct question types, ensuring a nuanced and thorough assessment. By facilitating fair comparisons across different systems, DOCBENCH highlights current limitations and paves the way for future advancements.

2 The DOCBENCH

DOCBENCH is a benchmark that takes raw PDF files and accompanying questions as inputs, with the objective of generating corresponding textual answers. In this section, we will introduce the pipeline used to construct the dataset, present detailed statistics, and explain the evaluation method.

2.1 Dataset Construction

Our dataset construction pipeline consists of three phases. First, we crawl documents across various domains from publicly accessible online resources (§2.1.1). Second, we generate corresponding QA pairs with the help of GPT-4 and a team of human

[1]Blog: Claude can now use tools https://www.anthropic.com/news/tool-use-ga

[2]Blog: Talk with documents using LlamaIndex https://codemaker2016.medium.com/talk-with-documents-using-llamaindex-3952c76bd511

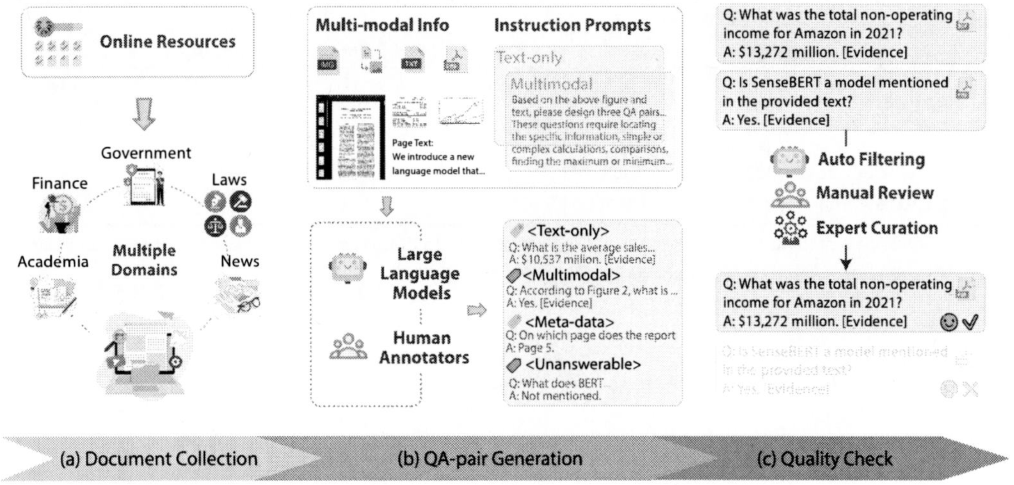

Figure 2: Construction pipeline of DocBench. (a) Document Collection: gathering PDF files from five different domains; (b) QA-pair Generation: creating diverse and comprehensive QA pairs through a combination of LLMs and human effort; (c) Quality Check: ensuring data quality through a multi-step process.

annotators (§2.1.2). Finally, we conduct auto filtering followed by a manual review to validate the quality of the generated instances (§2.1.3).

2.1.1 Document Collection

To establish a practical and constructive benchmark for document reading, we concentrate on scenarios where it is crucial to read documents. We standardize the documents to PDF format due to its high compatibility and stability. We identify five domains where documents are frequently utilized: *Academia*, *Finance*, *Government*, *Laws*, *News*. For Academia, papers are downloaded from arXiv within the range of top-k citations in the field of natural language processing on Google Scholar. [3] For *Finance*, we crawl the annual reports of companies with top-k global market capitalization up to `2024-02-23` from AnnualReports. [4] For *Government*, we manually download official governmental reports in 2023 from the U.S. Department of State and GovInfo. [5] For *Laws*, files are gathered from an official online collection of publications from the Library of Congress, within the years ranging from 2020 to 2024. [6] For *News*, we collect front-page scanned documents of the New York Times, covering dates from `2022-02-22` to `2024-02-22`. [7] We set $k = 100$ in the initial crawling process for academic and financial documents. After skipping the unobtainable or damaged documents, we eventually obtained 229 PDF files, with 49 for academia, 40 for finance, 44 for government, 46 for laws, and 50 for news. Detailed statistics are shown in Table 1.

2.1.2 QA-pair Generation

The generation procedure revolves around two aspects: diversity and comprehensiveness. On one hand, as the document itself inherently abounds with multi-dimensional and multi-modal information including texts, tables, figures, and meta-data, we leverage the `fitz` library [8] to parse out the distinct modalities within the PDF files. Afterward, we deliver plain texts to GPT-4 (`gpt-4-0125-preview`) for generating *text-only* QA pairs and resort to GPT-4V (`gpt-4-1106-vision-preview`) for yielding multi-modal ones based on tables, figures, and their related textual descriptions. On the other hand, we further request a set of human annotators to manually elaborate 350 QA pairs based on the given document files. Their primary task is to focus on types that are rarely covered in the previous generation stage but are frequent in daily usage, such as meta-data and unanswerable instances. Details of the annotation process and instruction prompts are

[3]https://scholar.google.com/; https://arxiv.org/.

[4]https://companiesmarketcap.com; http://www.annualreports.com.

[5]https://www.state.gov/department-reports/; https://www.govinfo.gov/.

[6]https://www.loc.gov/collections/publications-of-the-law-library-of-congress.

[7]https://static01.nyt.com/images/.

[8]https://pypi.org/project/fitz/

Category	Questions.		Documents.			
	#Num	#Tokens	#Num	#Pages	#Size(KB)	#Tokens
Aca.	303	16.8	49	11	847	11,123
Fin.	288	16.8	40	192	6,594	149,409
Gov.	148	14.1	44	69	2,183	36,105
Laws	191	15.4	46	58	969	32,339
News	172	13.5	50	1	3,095	2,909
Total/Avg.	1,102	15.7	229	66	2,738	46,377

Table 1: Overview statistics of DocBench. All documents are in PDF format. We extract text content and calculate the corresponding *#Tokens* of documents.

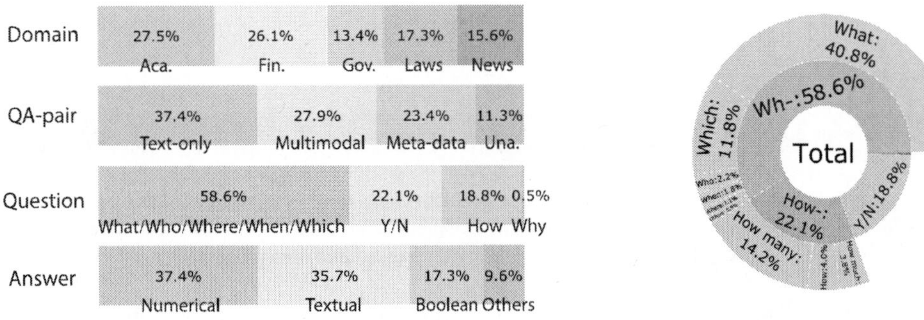

(a) Data distribution based on different classification criteria.

(b) Detailed data distribution based on question types

Figure 3: Data distribution of DocBench: (a) proportion(%) of various data groups based on four distinct classification criteria; (b) detailed data analysis based on question types.

attached in Appendix B.

2.1.3 Quality Check

We begin by instructing GPT-4 to automatically filter out questions that are excessively lengthy, unnatural, or impractical. We then conduct a manual review following the automatic filtering to ensure both the quality of questions and the accuracy of answers. To further align our data with real-world user scenarios, we engage 7 practitioners from distinct domains to review and refine the data within their areas of expertise. In this way, our data quality is validated from multiple perspectives.

2.2 Dataset Statistics

DocBench comprises a total of 229 PDF documents sourced from publicly accessible online repositories along with 1,102 questions, spanning across 5 domains: Academia, Finance, Government, Law, and News. As shown in Table 1, we conduct comprehensive statistical analysis across various angles, encompassing the number of questions, documents, and average token counts within each. Given the unique nature of our task input, which involves processing PDF files, we additionally include information such as page count and file size. Figure 3 shows data distribution in DocBench based on various classification criteria.

2.2.1 QA-pair Type

The types of QA pairs can be mainly divided into four groups: *text-only* (37.4%), *multimodal* (27.9%), *meta-data* (23.4%), and *unanswerable* (11.3%). The *text-only* and *multimodal* types collectively account for over half (65.3%), centering on the abilities to comprehend long contexts and interpret information from different modalities. Besides, we incorporate approximately one-third (34.7%) of questions to more closely fit the actual scenarios as well as assess the robustness of the document reading systems, including 23.4% inquiring about metadata (e.g., page numbers, word counts) and 11.3% that cannot be answered based on the given document.

2.2.2 Question Type

The types of questions can be primarily separated into four categories according to the inquiry focus: *what / who / where / when / which* (58.6%), *Y/N* (22.1%), *how* (18.8%), and *why* (0.5%). These categories respectively need specific information or details, straightforward *yes* or *no* responses, methods or degrees, and the underlying reasons behind actions or phenomena. Figure 3(b) provides a de-

Sources	# Correct / Wrong by different evaluators				Agreement (human and automatic evaluators)		
	Human	GPT-4	GPT-3.5	StrMatch	GPT-4	GPT-3.5	StrMatch
KimiChat	24 / 16	23 / 17	33 / 7	0 / 40	97.5%	75.0%	40.0%
Qwen-2.5	17 / 23	18 / 22	31 / 9	0 / 40	97.5%	57.5%	57.5%
Gemma (7B)	19 / 21	18 / 22	18 / 22	0 / 40	97.5%	75.0%	52.5%
Mixtral (7B)	14 / 26	14 / 26	26 / 14	0 / 40	100.0%	65.0%	65.0%
Llama-3 (70B)	16 / 24	15 / 25	28 / 12	0 / 40	97.5%	62.5%	60.0%
Total	90 / 110	88 / 112	136 / 64	0 / 200	98.0%	67.0%	55.0%

Table 2: The GPT-4 automatic evaluator shows a 98% agreement with human annotators. We randomly sample 40 questions and answers from five systems, asking human annotators to assess their accuracy. We then employ string matching (StrMatch), GPT-3.5, and GPT-4 as automatic evaluators. Finally, we measure the agreement between the human and these automatic evaluators.

tailed data distribution based on question types. The interrogative *what* holds a dominant proportion at 40.8%, which is reasonable as users commonly seek precise information in a document.

2.2.3 Answer Type

The types of answers can be partitioned into four classes: *numerical* (37.4%), *textual* (35.7%), *boolean* (17.3%), and *others* (9.6%). Within the *numerical* class, 69% originate from the domains of *academia* and *finance*, as these documents naturally require extensive use of numbers to convey information, such as performance metrics in academic papers and figures in financial reports.

2.3 Evaluation Setup

Evaluation Process Our dataset diversity poses two major evaluation challenges: (i) The evaluation methods vary depending on the answer type. For example, for boolean or numerical answers, a fair evaluator only needs to verify the correctness of a binary *yes/no* response or a specific number using simple techniques like string matching or number extraction. In contrast, textual responses require more nuanced standards such as natural language generation (NLG) metrics. Thus, accurately determining the appropriate evaluation method becomes complex when the answer type is unknown. (ii) Different LLMs and systems exhibit substantial variations in the organization and style of their outputs, potentially leading to biases in traditional evaluation approaches. Therefore, we capitalize on the prowess of LLMs that have proven to be decent evaluators and can be easily adapted to the assessment of various answer types (Fu et al., 2023; Liu et al., 2023; Wang et al., 2023). Inspired by Liu et al. (2023), we clearly define the evaluation criteria for various types within the instruction prompt and then instruct GPT-4 to assign a score of 0 (incorrect) or 1 (correct). After evaluating 200 examples by both human evaluators and GPT-4, we found that the GPT-4 automatic evaluator shows a 98% agreement with human annotators, significantly exceeding the traditional string matching approach. Details of this experiment is shown in Table 2, and details of evaluation instruction prompts are attached in Appendix B.

Metrics As mentioned above, we instruct GPT-4 to assign a score of 0 (incorrect) or 1 (correct), thus using Accuracy (abbreviated as Acc.) to measure system performance. We report accuracy across all instances, as well as for each domain and QA-pair type in Table 3.

3 Experiments and Analysis

3.1 Experimental Setup

We conduct a comprehensive evaluation of 22 LLM-based document reading systems, encompassing both proprietary systems that support document uploads and a series of *parse-then-read* pipelines. For *parse-then-read* pipelines, we leverage the `fitz` package to extract text and image blocks from `PDF` files. We retain the original texts and line breaks for text chunks while we denote the i-th image as *[image i]* for images. Our selection for the proprietary systems includes GPT-4 and GPT-4o (Achiam et al., 2023) from OpenAI, GLM-4 [9] from ZhipuAI, Kimi [10] from Moonshot AI, Claude-3 [11] from Anthropic, Qwen-2.5 [12] from Alibaba Cloud, and ERNIE-3.5 [13] from Baidu. In the case of the *parse-then-read* pipelines, we assess 15 prominent LLMs as base models, featuring those from the GPT (Achiam et al., 2023; OpenAI, 2022), Llama (Touvron et al., 2023), Mis-

[9] `https://chatglm.cn/main/doc`
[10] `https://kimi.moonshot.cn`
[11] `https://claude.ai/chats`
[12] `https://tongyi.aliyun.com/qianwen`
[13] `https://yiyan.baidu.com`

Methods	Form	Ver. /Size	File /Cxt.	Domain					Type				Overall Acc.
				Aca.	Fin.	Gov.	Laws	News	Text.	Multi.	Meta.	Una.	
Human	-	-	-	83.0	82.2	77.8	75.0	86.4	81.4	83.3	77.5	82.2	81.2
LLM-based systems													
GPT-4	*API*	`0409`	`100M`	65.7	**65.3**	75.7	69.6	79.6	**87.9**	**74.7**	50.8	37.1	69.8
GPT-4o	*API*	`0513`	`100M`	56.4	56.3	73.0	65.5	75.0	85.0	62.7	50.4	17.7	63.1
GLM-4	*Web*	-	`20M`	55.8	35.4	61.5	62.8	82.0	73.1	50.3	48.8	33.1	56.5
KimiChat	*Web*	-	`100M`	62.4	61.8	**77.0**	78.5	**87.2**	87.6	65.3	50.4	**71.8**	**70.9**
Claude-3	*Web*	`Opus`	`10M`	**73.9**	40.6	70.3	**79.1**	86.6	80.8	64.6	**54.3**	58.9	67.6
Gemini-1.5	*Web*	`Pro`	`30M`	60.4	42.5	57.4	71.7	74.3	74.0	30.8	53.8	60.2	55.4
Qwen-2.5	*Web*	-	`150M`	42.9	29.9	51.4	55.5	69.2	61.7	31.8	36.0	58.1	46.9
ERNIE-3.5	*Web*	-	`10M`	56.4	37.5	54.7	58.1	58.1	63.6	47.7	36.8	54.0	51.8
Parse-then-Read Pipelines													
GPT-4	*API*	`0409`	`128k`	**70.0**	**47.9**	**68.9**	**70.7**	**93.6**	**79.1**	**63.3**	**54.3**	70.2	**67.9**
GPT-3.5	*API*	`0125`	`16k`	49.8	24.0	58.8	50.3	83.7	65.0	37.0	42.6	44.4	49.6
ChatGLM3	*Open*	`6B`	`128k`	34.7	41.7	58.1	51.3	58.1	70.4	40.3	31.0	12.1	46.2
Gemma	*Open*	`7B`	`8k`	34.3	12.5	43.2	34.0	65.1	43.0	17.2	21.3	**77.4**	34.6
Mixtral	*Open*	`7B`	`32k`	42.6	29.2	58.8	50.3	82.0	71.8	33.8	38.4	30.6	48.7
InternLM2	*Open*	`7B`	`32k`	38.6	27.1	52.0	46.1	65.7	63.3	28.9	35.3	25.8	42.9
Llama-3	*Open*	`8B`	`8k`	44.6	23.6	61.5	54.5	86.6	68.0	29.2	45.0	49.2	49.6
Yi-1.5	*Open*	`9B`	`16k`	40.6	26.4	58.1	52.4	83.1	66.0	33.8	45.7	27.4	47.9
Llama-2	*Open*	`13B`	`4k`	20.8	18.4	29.7	23.6	55.2	43.4	15.9	21.7	12.9	27.2
Phi-3	*Open*	`14B`	`128k`	50.2	44.4	65.5	64.4	76.7	77.4	45.8	45.3	44.4	57.4
InternLM2	*Open*	`20B`	`32k`	43.2	28.5	59.5	54.5	80.8	73.3	33.4	43.0	22.6	49.4
Yi-1.5	*Open*	`34B`	`16k`	47.2	27.1	59.5	56.5	78.5	68.2	39.0	49.2	19.4	50.1
Command-R	*Open*	`35B`	`128k`	49.5	38.9	66.2	64.4	80.8	78.4	50.0	49.6	13.7	56.4
Mixtral-8x7B	*Open*	`47B`	`32k`	48.5	31.9	60.1	59.2	81.4	76.0	42.9	46.9	12.1	52.7
Llama-3	*Open*	`70B`	`8k`	52.1	25.3	68.2	59.2	90.7	69.2	38.6	49.2	56.5	54.5

Table 3: Results on DocBench across various types and domains. *Ver./Size* stands for the model version or size; *File* denotes the maximum uploaded file size; *Cxt.* refers to model's context length.

tral (Jiang et al., 2024), Yi (Young et al., 2024), InternLM (Cai et al., 2024), Phi-3 (Abdin et al., 2024), Gemma (Team et al., 2024), ChatGLM3 (Du et al., 2021), and Command-R (CohereAI, 2024) families. The selection of base open-sourced LLMs adheres to three guiding principles: (i) official release with *instruct* or *chat* versions that are supported by vLLM (Kwon et al., 2023) framework; (ii) model sizes ranging from 7B to 70B to accommodate GPU memory constraints; (iii) availability of the longest context length and the latest version.

3.2 Results and Discussion

Table 3 showcases the performance of various document reading systems on DocBench. Our findings reveal substantial variations in document reading capabilities among these systems, driven by differences in their foundational models, context length limitations, diverse design and implementation approaches, and etc. In this section, we will provide further discussions to delve deeper into the pros and cons of existing systems, as well as uncover the core challenges posed by DocBench.

1. Interpreting multi-modal and metadata information. Figure 4 presents a case study illustrating the unique challenge of answering multi-modal questions in DocBench. We observe that leading proprietary LLM-based systems often fail due to errors in one of the steps in the *Location→Extraction→Calculation* sequence. Take the case study as an example, in the first step, KimiChat fails to locate the relevant chart on page 17. In the extraction phase, Claude-3 misidentifies the data as *288 & 348*, instead of the correct *326 & 390*. Finally, while GPT-4 locates and extracts the correct information, it errs in calculating the percentage change, demonstrating the complexity of these questions. Interestingly, parse-then-read pipelines can achieve reasonable performance

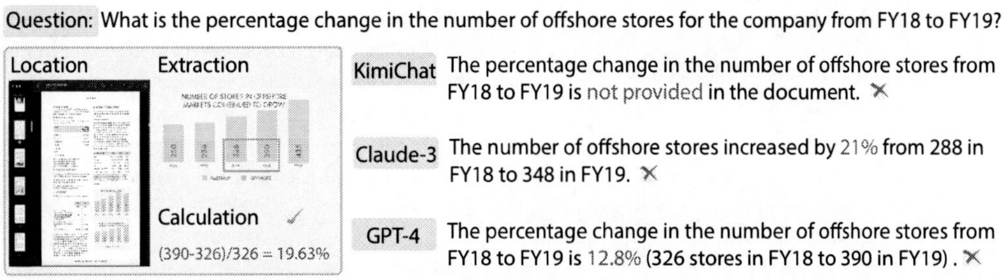

Figure 4: To address multi-modal questions in DocBench, it is essential to: (i) identify the relevant figure/table (Location); (ii) extract specific data (Extraction); (iii) perform necessary calculations (Calculation). In this case study, KimiChat fails to locate the figure, Claude-3 retrieves incorrect data, and GPT-4, despite succeeding in the first two steps, struggles with the calculation.

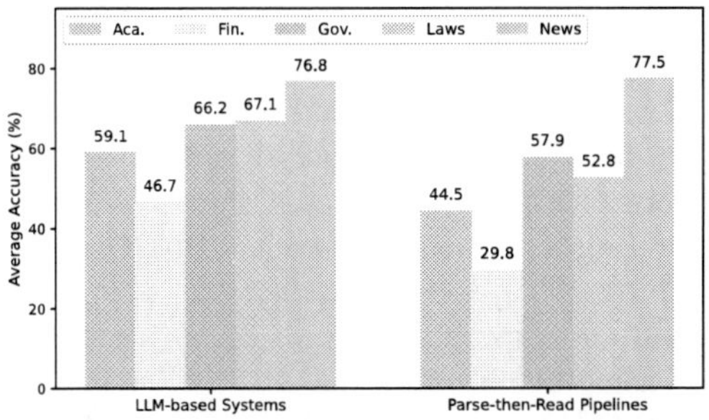

Figure 5: Average accuracy (%) of two methods under five different domains.

on multi-modal questions (e.g., 63.3% for GPT-4). This is likely because the parsing process captures certain table information, and documents often include textual descriptions of figures. Meanwhile, for metadata-related questions, current methods generally lack attention to global information, resulting in relative low performances (below 55%).

2. Handling lengthy documents. Handling lengthy documents is demanding, especially in real-world scenarios where document size can be virtually unlimited. Proprietary LLM-based systems struggle with uploading extensive files, while the parse-then-read pipelines with open-sourced LLMs are constrained by their maximum context length, leading to varying degrees of information loss. As shown in Figure 5, both methods perform poorly in the finance domain but achieve higher performance in the news domain. This discrepancy arises because financial documents are typically longer and contain richer information, whereas news files are limited to single front pages with fewer messages. Furthermore, certain strong models with relatively short context lengths may excel with smaller files, but context length becomes a crucial factor when it comes to large files. For instance, the *8k* Llama-3 family performs exceptionally well in the news domain, but is outperformed by all the *128k* models in the finance domain. Besides, we discover that KimiChat and Command-R, which are specifically enhanced for long-context and Retrieval-Augmented Generation (RAG) capabilities, achieve decent results on *text-only* questions. Therefore, a key challenge lies in adapting these systems to handle documents of varying lengths while balancing the foundational model's capabilities and context length constraints.

3. Faithfulness to user-provided documents Most existing document reading systems falter when faced with unanswerable questions based on the provided document, exhibiting a lack of fidelity. Remarkably, Gemma and KimiChat perform better in such scenarios, which represents a crucial capability since users often expect systems to answer questions strictly based on given files. Intriguingly, despite the commonly-shared base model on GPT-4, there is a notable performance gap between the system and the parse-then-read pipeline in handling unanswerable questions (i.e., 37.1% and 70.2 % for system and pipeline, respectively). We analyze that this may be due to: (i) the proprietary LLM-based system have undergone optimizations on the base model, potentially causing overfitting; (ii) GPT-4 tends to adhere more closely to the in-context learning information. Such phenomenon thus underscores a critical challenge for future document reading systems on enhancing fidelity to the given documents.

4 Related Works

4.1 Recent Advances of LLMs and LLM-based Systems

The latest generation of LLMs, such as GPT-4 (Achiam et al., 2023), Llama-3 (Touvron et al., 2023) and Claude-3 (Anthropic, 2024), have significantly extended the capabilities of language models (Zhao et al., 2023; Chang et al., 2024; Wang et al., 2024a). These models are pre-trained on vast amounts of web-scale data, enabling them to perform a wide range of human-instructed tasks with impressive performance. Despite their remarkable performance, standalone LLMs may not be sufficient for many real-world applications. For example, LLMs lack access to real-time information and may struggle with tasks that require up-to-date knowledge (Vu et al., 2023). Moreover, real-world applications often require non-text inputs parsing, code execution, API calling and interaction with external environments (Lee et al., 2024; Labs, 2024; Jimenez et al., 2023; Zhou et al., 2023; Xie et al., 2024; Guo et al., 2024). The overall task completion usually requires multiple reasoning, execution and reflection steps that cannot be accomplished in a simple input-output manner (Yao et al., 2023; Shinn et al., 2023; Wang et al., 2024b). To overcome the limitations of standalone LLMs, recent efforts have incorporated additional components and sophisticated system design. These systems, such as Microsoft's Co-Pilot[14] and OpenAI's GPT-4 all-in-one[15], aim to provide more comprehensive and practical solutions for real-world applications. Other pioneering efforts on designing LLM-based systems include web agents (Zheng et al., 2024; He et al., 2024; Ma et al., 2023), software agents (Yang et al., 2024; Labs, 2024) and computer agents (Wu et al., 2024) that can interact with external resources (e.g., websites, search engine, code repositories or computers) and perform multi-step tasks. The success of these systems relies on integrating powerful LLMs with well-designed architectures and components that enable them to handle complex tasks effectively.

4.2 Document reading: Datasets and Methods

Document reading is a critical area where LLM-based systems have demonstrated significant advancements. Proprietary developers such as OpenAI[16] and Anthropic[17] have introduced advanced systems that can take a user-provided document as input, parse its structure, extract relevant metadata, and handle long texts and images to provide accurate responses. While these systems build upon the fundamental capabilities of their underlying LLMs (Zeng et al., 2022; Bai et al., 2023; Achiam et al., 2023; Anthropic, 2024), they differ in their design and implementation, with some systems excelling in long-context reading and others focusing on retrieval-augmented methods to improve document reading ability. Despite claims of effectiveness and efficiency in online public blogs, the absence of a standardized benchmark makes it difficult to objectively evaluate and compare the document reading performance across these systems. Existing benchmarks relevant to document reading are unable to adequately reflect the real performance of these systems. Datasets focusing on document understanding such as Doc2Dial (Feng et al., 2020), ConditionalQA (Sun et al., 2022) and those specifically focusing on long-context reading like NarrativeQA (Kočiský et al., 2018) and QuALITY (Pang et al., 2022), primarily use text as input only, ignoring the complex nature of document structure and multi-modal information. On the other hand, multi-modal document reading datasets like DocVQA (Mathew et al., 2021), ChartQA (Masry et al., 2022), OCR-VQA (Mishra et al., 2019), and InfoVQA (Mathew et al., 2022) include multi-modal inputs and preserve the original document structure and layout. However these datasets often capture only parts of document (e.g. tables or figures) and ignored substantial amount of textual content. However, DocBench requires systems to process the full documents as intact files and covers different types of questions targeting various abilities, which can more accurately evaluate the capabilities of LLM-based document reading systems in real-world scenarios.

5 Conclusion

In this paper, we introduce DocBench, a novel benchmark created to assess LLM-based document reading systems in a comprehensive and fine-grained manner. DocBench consists of 229 documents and 1,102 questions, spanning 5 domains and 4 question types, developed with the help of human annotators and synthetic questions. We eval-

[14]https://copilot.microsoft.com

[15]https://chat.openai.com

[16]OpenAI's ChatGPT: https://chat.openai.com

[17]Anthropic's Claude: https://claude.ai/chats

uate both proprietary LLM systems, accessible via web interfaces or APIs, and a parse-then-read approach using open-source LLMs. Our findings reveal significant disparities in document reading capabilities among these systems, highlighting current limitations, presenting potential challenges, and thus driving forward progress in this field.

6 Limitation

While DocBench aims to encompass a wide range of real-world document-related questions, it is not exhaustive. Our benchmark primarily focuses on the four most common question types, leaving other potential types unaddressed. Additionally, our evaluation of proprietary LLM-based document reading systems is limited. Many of these systems, such as OpenAI-o1, are accessible only through web interfaces with restricted access and lack APIs, which makes the evaluation process slow and challenging.

References

Marah Abdin, Sam Ade Jacobs, Ammar Ahmad Awan, Jyoti Aneja, Ahmed Awadallah, Hany Awadalla, Nguyen Bach, Amit Bahree, Arash Bakhtiari, Harkirat Behl, et al. 2024. Phi-3 technical report: A highly capable language model locally on your phone. *arXiv preprint arXiv:2404.14219*.

Josh Achiam, Steven Adler, Sandhini Agarwal, Lama Ahmad, Ilge Akkaya, Florencia Leoni Aleman, Diogo Almeida, Janko Altenschmidt, Sam Altman, Shyamal Anadkat, et al. 2023. Gpt-4 technical report. *arXiv preprint arXiv:2303.08774*.

Anthropic. 2024. Claude 3 haiku: our fastest model yet.

Jinze Bai, Shuai Bai, Yunfei Chu, Zeyu Cui, Kai Dang, Xiaodong Deng, Yang Fan, Wenbin Ge, Yu Han, Fei Huang, et al. 2023. Qwen technical report. *arXiv preprint arXiv:2309.16609*.

Abeba Birhane, Atoosa Kasirzadeh, David Leslie, and Sandra Wachter. 2023. Science in the age of large language models. *Nature Reviews Physics*, 5(5):277–280.

Zheng Cai, Maosong Cao, Haojiong Chen, Kai Chen, Keyu Chen, Xin Chen, Xun Chen, Zehui Chen, Zhi Chen, Pei Chu, et al. 2024. Internlm2 technical report. *arXiv preprint arXiv:2403.17297*.

Yupeng Chang, Xu Wang, Jindong Wang, Yuan Wu, Linyi Yang, Kaijie Zhu, Hao Chen, Xiaoyuan Yi, Cunxiang Wang, Yidong Wang, et al. 2024. A survey on evaluation of large language models. *ACM Transactions on Intelligent Systems and Technology*, 15(3):1–45.

CohereAI. 2024. Introducing command r.

Jiaxi Cui, Zongjian Li, Yang Yan, Bohua Chen, and Li Yuan. 2023. Chatlaw: Open-source legal large language model with integrated external knowledge bases. *arXiv preprint arXiv:2306.16092*.

Pradeep Dasigi, Kyle Lo, Iz Beltagy, Arman Cohan, Noah A Smith, and Matt Gardner. 2021. A dataset of information-seeking questions and answers anchored in research papers. *arXiv preprint arXiv:2105.03011*.

Zhengxiao Du, Yujie Qian, Xiao Liu, Ming Ding, Jiezhong Qiu, Zhilin Yang, and Jie Tang. 2021. Glm: General language model pretraining with autoregressive blank infilling. *arXiv preprint arXiv:2103.10360*.

Song Feng, Hui Wan, Chulaka Gunasekara, Siva Patel, Sachindra Joshi, and Luis Lastras. 2020. doc2dial: A goal-oriented document-grounded dialogue dataset. In *Proceedings of the 2020 Conference on Empirical Methods in Natural Language Processing (EMNLP)*, pages 8118–8128, Online. Association for Computational Linguistics.

Jinlan Fu, See-Kiong Ng, Zhengbao Jiang, and Pengfei Liu. 2023. Gptscore: Evaluate as you desire. *Preprint*, arXiv:2302.04166.

Siyuan Guo, Cheng Deng, Ying Wen, Hechang Chen, Yi Chang, and Jun Wang. 2024. Ds-agent: Automated data science by empowering large language models with case-based reasoning. *Preprint*, arXiv:2402.17453.

Hongliang He, Wenlin Yao, Kaixin Ma, Wenhao Yu, Yong Dai, Hongming Zhang, Zhenzhong Lan, and Dong Yu. 2024. Webvoyager: Building an end-to-end web agent with large multimodal models. *arXiv preprint arXiv:2401.13919*.

Albert Q Jiang, Alexandre Sablayrolles, Antoine Roux, Arthur Mensch, Blanche Savary, Chris Bamford, Devendra Singh Chaplot, Diego de las Casas, Emma Bou Hanna, Florian Bressand, et al. 2024. Mixtral of experts. *arXiv preprint arXiv:2401.04088*.

Carlos E. Jimenez, John Yang, Alexander Wettig, Shunyu Yao, Kexin Pei, Ofir Press, and Karthik Narasimhan. 2023. Swe-bench: Can language models resolve real-world github issues? *Preprint*, arXiv:2310.06770.

Tomáš Kočiský, Jonathan Schwarz, Phil Blunsom, Chris Dyer, Karl Moritz Hermann, Gábor Melis, and Edward Grefenstette. 2018. The narrativeqa reading comprehension challenge. *Transactions of the Association for Computational Linguistics*, 6:317–328.

Woosuk Kwon, Zhuohan Li, Siyuan Zhuang, Ying Sheng, Lianmin Zheng, Cody Hao Yu, Joseph Gonzalez, Hao Zhang, and Ion Stoica. 2023. Efficient memory management for large language model serving with pagedattention. In *Proceedings of the 29th Symposium on Operating Systems Principles*, pages 611–626.

Cognition Labs. 2024. Devin, ai software engineer.

Jinqi Lai, Wensheng Gan, Jiayang Wu, Zhenlian Qi, and Philip S Yu. 2023. Large language models in law: A survey. *arXiv preprint arXiv:2312.03718*.

Kuang-Huei Lee, Xinyun Chen, Hiroki Furuta, John Canny, and Ian Fischer. 2024. A human-inspired reading agent with gist memory of very long contexts. *arXiv preprint arXiv:2402.09727*.

Yang Liu, Dan Iter, Yichong Xu, Shuohang Wang, Ruochen Xu, and Chenguang Zhu. 2023. G-eval: NLG evaluation using gpt-4 with better human alignment. In *Proceedings of the 2023 Conference on Empirical Methods in Natural Language Processing*, pages 2511–2522, Singapore. Association for Computational Linguistics.

Kaixin Ma, Hongming Zhang, Hongwei Wang, Xiaoman Pan, Wenhao Yu, and Dong Yu. 2023. Laser: Llm agent with state-space exploration for web navigation. *Preprint*, arXiv:2309.08172.

Ahmed Masry, Do Xuan Long, Jia Qing Tan, Shafiq Joty, and Enamul Hoque. 2022. Chartqa: A benchmark for question answering about charts with visual and logical reasoning. *arXiv preprint arXiv:2203.10244*.

Minesh Mathew, Viraj Bagal, Rubèn Tito, Dimosthenis Karatzas, Ernest Valveny, and CV Jawahar. 2022. Infographicvqa. In *Proceedings of the IEEE/CVF Winter Conference on Applications of Computer Vision*, pages 1697–1706.

Minesh Mathew, Dimosthenis Karatzas, and CV Jawahar. 2021. Docvqa: A dataset for vqa on document images. In *Proceedings of the IEEE/CVF winter conference on applications of computer vision*, pages 2200–2209.

Anand Mishra, Shashank Shekhar, Ajeet Kumar Singh, and Anirban Chakraborty. 2019. Ocr-vqa: Visual question answering by reading text in images. In *2019 international conference on document analysis and recognition (ICDAR)*, pages 947–952. IEEE.

OpenAI. 2022. Introducing chatgpt.

Richard Yuanzhe Pang, Alicia Parrish, Nitish Joshi, Nikita Nangia, Jason Phang, Angelica Chen, Vishakh Padmakumar, Johnny Ma, Jana Thompson, He He, et al. 2022. Quality: Question answering with long input texts, yes! In *Proceedings of the 2022 Conference of the North American Chapter of the Association for Computational Linguistics: Human Language Technologies*, pages 5336–5358.

Noah Shinn, Federico Cassano, Edward Berman, Ashwin Gopinath, Karthik Narasimhan, and Shunyu Yao. 2023. Reflexion: Language agents with verbal reinforcement learning. *Preprint*, arXiv:2303.11366.

Haitian Sun, William Cohen, and Ruslan Salakhutdinov. 2022. ConditionalQA: A complex reading comprehension dataset with conditional answers. In *Proceedings of the 60th Annual Meeting of the Association for Computational Linguistics (Volume 1: Long Papers)*, pages 3627–3637, Dublin, Ireland. Association for Computational Linguistics.

Gemini Team, Rohan Anil, Sebastian Borgeaud, Yonghui Wu, Jean-Baptiste Alayrac, Jiahui Yu, Radu Soricut, Johan Schalkwyk, Andrew M Dai, Anja Hauth, et al. 2023. Gemini: a family of highly capable multimodal models. *arXiv preprint arXiv:2312.11805*.

Gemma Team, Thomas Mesnard, Cassidy Hardin, Robert Dadashi, Surya Bhupatiraju, Shreya Pathak, Laurent Sifre, Morgane Rivière, Mihir Sanjay Kale, Juliette Love, et al. 2024. Gemma: Open models based on gemini research and technology. *arXiv preprint arXiv:2403.08295*.

Hugo Touvron, Louis Martin, Kevin Stone, Peter Albert, Amjad Almahairi, Yasmine Babaei, Nikolay Bashlykov, Soumya Batra, Prajjwal Bhargava, Shruti Bhosale, et al. 2023. Llama 2: Open foundation and fine-tuned chat models. *arXiv preprint arXiv:2307.09288*.

Tu Vu, Mohit Iyyer, Xuezhi Wang, Noah Constant, Jerry Wei, Jason Wei, Chris Tar, Yun-Hsuan Sung, Denny Zhou, Quoc Le, et al. 2023. Freshllms: Refreshing large language models with search engine augmentation. *arXiv preprint arXiv:2310.03214*.

Jiaan Wang, Yunlong Liang, Fandong Meng, Zengkui Sun, Haoxiang Shi, Zhixu Li, Jinan Xu, Jianfeng Qu, and Jie Zhou. 2023. Is ChatGPT a good NLG evaluator? a preliminary study. In *Proceedings of the 4th New Frontiers in Summarization Workshop*, pages 1–11, Singapore. Association for Computational Linguistics.

Lei Wang, Chen Ma, Xueyang Feng, Zeyu Zhang, Hao Yang, Jingsen Zhang, Zhiyuan Chen, Jiakai Tang, Xu Chen, Yankai Lin, et al. 2024a. A survey on large language model based autonomous agents. *Frontiers of Computer Science*, 18(6):1–26.

Xingyao Wang, Yangyi Chen, Lifan Yuan, Yizhe Zhang, Yunzhu Li, Hao Peng, and Heng Ji. 2024b. Executable code actions elicit better llm agents. In *ICML*.

Shijie Wu, Ozan Irsoy, Steven Lu, Vadim Dabravolski, Mark Dredze, Sebastian Gehrmann, Prabhanjan Kambadur, David Rosenberg, and Gideon Mann. 2023. Bloomberggpt: A large language model for finance. *arXiv preprint arXiv:2303.17564*.

Zhiyong Wu, Chengcheng Han, Zichen Ding, Zhenmin Weng, Zhoumianze Liu, Shunyu Yao, Tao Yu, and Lingpeng Kong. 2024. Os-copilot: Towards generalist computer agents with self-improvement. *Preprint*, arXiv:2402.07456.

Tianbao Xie, Danyang Zhang, Jixuan Chen, Xiaochuan Li, Siheng Zhao, Ruisheng Cao, Toh Jing Hua, Zhoujun Cheng, Dongchan Shin, Fangyu Lei, et al. 2024. Osworld: Benchmarking multimodal agents for open-ended tasks in real computer environments. *arXiv preprint arXiv:2404.07972*.

Hongyang Yang, Xiao-Yang Liu, and Christina Dan Wang. 2023. Fingpt: Open-source financial large language models. *arXiv preprint arXiv:2306.06031*.

John Yang, Carlos E Jimenez, Alexander Wettig, Kilian Lieret, Shunyu Yao, Karthik Narasimhan, and Ofir Press. 2024. Swe-agent: Agent-computer interfaces enable automated software engineering. *arXiv preprint arXiv:2405.15793*.

Shunyu Yao, Jeffrey Zhao, Dian Yu, Nan Du, Izhak Shafran, Karthik R Narasimhan, and Yuan Cao. 2023. React: Synergizing reasoning and acting in language models. In *The Eleventh International Conference on Learning Representations*.

Alex Young, Bei Chen, Chao Li, Chengen Huang, Ge Zhang, Guanwei Zhang, Heng Li, Jiangcheng Zhu, Jianqun Chen, Jing Chang, et al. 2024. Yi: Open foundation models by 01. ai. *arXiv preprint arXiv:2403.04652*.

Aohan Zeng, Xiao Liu, Zhengxiao Du, Zihan Wang, Hanyu Lai, Ming Ding, Zhuoyi Yang, Yifan Xu, Wendi Zheng, Xiao Xia, et al. 2022. Glm-130b: An open bilingual pre-trained model. *arXiv preprint arXiv:2210.02414*.

Wayne Xin Zhao, Kun Zhou, Junyi Li, Tianyi Tang, Xiaolei Wang, Yupeng Hou, Yingqian Min, Beichen Zhang, Junjie Zhang, Zican Dong, et al. 2023. A survey of large language models. *arXiv preprint arXiv:2303.18223*.

Boyuan Zheng, Boyu Gou, Jihyung Kil, Huan Sun, and Yu Su. 2024. Gpt-4v(ision) is a generalist web agent, if grounded. *Preprint*, arXiv:2401.01614.

Shuyan Zhou, Frank F Xu, Hao Zhu, Xuhui Zhou, Robert Lo, Abishek Sridhar, Xianyi Cheng, Yonatan Bisk, Daniel Fried, Uri Alon, et al. 2023. Webarena: A realistic web environment for building autonomous agents. *arXiv preprint arXiv:2307.13854*.

A Annotation Process

Since the QA-pair generation process requires data annotators to deeply understand the motivations behind our benchmark construction, and considering the initial training costs and the need to manually annotate about 350 QA pairs, we've decided to assign 2 annotators to this task.

The annotation process presents as follows:

- We first communicate the motivation behind our work to the annotators and explain the concepts of meta-data and unanswerable questions in detail.
- Next, we provide 10 example QA pairs for reference (5 for each type).
- Finally, each annotator generates 170 QA pairs. They then exchange their annotations for double-checking and review.

B Instruction Prompts

B.1 Response Evaluation

Detailed instruction prompts for response evaluation are shown in Table 4.

B.2 QA-pair Generation

Details of instruction prompts for generating QA pairs are attached in Table 5. We discover that simply passing diagrams to GPT-4V leads to subpar question quality. This issue likely stems from the fact that figures or tables without accompanying text descriptions typically lack sufficient information, thus causing the generated QA pairs to deviate from their intended meanings. In addition, we observe that adding difficulty settings for QA generation (e.g., *Easy*, *Medium*, *Hard*) in the instruction prompt can result in higher quality. We analyze that this may be due to the model being able to favor higher generation quality in potential comparisons.

C Performance Comparison

Figure 6 demonstrates the relative performance of LLM-based systems and parse-then-read pipelines against the best on DocBench. For LLM-based systems, KimiChat consistently scores high across various metrics, demonstrating balanced performance. Notably, GPT-4 performs poorly in the unanswerable category, indicating potential overfitting in optimized GPT-4 file systems, which leads to decreased fidelity to given documents. Additionally, Claude-3 excels in the meta-data category, highlighting its superior ability to comprehend high-level metadata information. For parse-then-read pipelines, we select models with the highest overall accuracy for comparison. Unlike LLM-based systems, GPT-4 demonstrates consistently high and balanced performance across all aspects within this pipeline. Notably, significant discrepancies arise in handling multi-modal and unanswerable questions, where GPT-4 and Gemma exhibit clear distinctions from the remaining methods.

D Analysis of Input Sources

Table 7 presents the impact of different input sources on model performance. We provide questions to GPT-4 and GPT-4o, both with and without attached files. Remarkably, even without files, the models correctly answer a portion of the questions (19.1% for GPT-4 and 21.7% for GPT-4o). Our analysis reveals that the correctly answered questions are predominantly textual and are largely associated with government, law, and news domains. This trend suggests that the models' underlying training data is heavily skewed towards these categories, enabling them to answer some questions accurately without additional files. Moreover, as GPT-4o is an optimized version of GPT-4, it likely benefits from a broader and more training data.

Table 4: Instruction Prompts in Response Evaluation.

`System Content:`

You are a helpful evaluator.

`Prompt:`

Task Overview:

You are tasked with evaluating user answers based on a given question, reference answer, and additional reference text. Your goal is to assess the correctness of the user answer using a specific metric.

Evaluation Criteria:

1. Yes/No Questions: Verify if the user's answer aligns with the reference answer in terms of a "yes" or "no" response.
2. Short Answers/Directives: Ensure key details such as numbers, specific nouns/verbs, and dates match those in the reference answer.
3. Abstractive/Long Answers: The user's answer can differ in wording but must convey the same meaning and contain the same key information as the reference answer to be considered correct.

Evaluation Process:

1. Identify the type of question presented.
2. Apply the relevant criteria from the Evaluation Criteria.
3. Compare the user's answer against the reference answer accordingly.
4. Consult the reference text for clarification when needed.
5. Score the answer with a binary label 0 or 1, where 0 denotes wrong and 1 denotes correct.

NOTE that if the user answer is 0 or an empty string, it should get a 0 score.

Question: `{{question}}`
User Answer: `{{sys_ans}}`
Reference Answer: `{{ref_ans}}`
Reference Text: `{{ref_text}}`

Evaluation Form (score ONLY):

- Correctness:

Table 5: Instruction Prompts in QA-pair Generation.

`System Content:`

You are a helpful assistant that can generate question-answer pairs.

`Text-only QA:`

Based on the above text, please design three question-answer pairs with different levels of difficulty: Easy, Medium, Hard.

The questions should be close-ended and should be answered based on the provided text.

The answer form should be as diverse as possible, including [Yes/No, Short Answer, Long Answer, Abstractive Answer].

You should provide the reference in the text and the answer form if possible.

The output should be formalized as: '''Q: | A: | Reference: | Difficulty Level: | Answer Form:'''

`Multimodal QA (w/table+text):`

Based on the above table and text, please design three question-answer pairs with different levels of difficulty: Easy, Medium, Hard.

The text provided is text related to the table, which can provide more reference for question generation, but the focus is still on the table itself.

These questions require locating the specific information, simple or complex calculations, comparisons, finding the maximum and minimum, reading across rows and columns, etc.

Note that these questions also need to be realistic. You should provide the reason if possible.

The output should be formalized as: '''Q: | A: | Reference: | Difficulty Level: | Answer Form:'''

`Multimodal QA (w/figure+text):`

Based on the above figure and text, please design three question-answer pairs with different levels of difficulty: Easy, Medium, Hard.

The text provided is text related to the figure, which can provide more reference for question generation, but the focus is still on the figure itself.

These questions require a deep reading of the meaning of the image.

Note that these questions also need to be realistic. You should provide the reason if possible.

The output should be formalized as: '''Q: | A: | Reason: | Difficulty Level: | '''

`Multimodal QA (w/table):`

Based on the above image, please design three question-answer pairs with different levels of difficulty: Easy, Medium, Hard.

These questions require locating the specific information, simple or complex calculations, comparisons, finding the maximum and minimum, reading across rows and columns, etc.

Note that these questions also need to be realistic. You should provide the reason if possible.

The output should be formalized as: '''Q: | A: | Reason: | Difficulty Level: | '''

`Multimodal QA (w/figure):`

Based on the above image, please design three question-answer pairs with different levels of difficulty: Easy, Medium, Hard.

These questions require a deep reading of the meaning of the image. Note that these questions also need to be realistic. You should provide the reason if possible.

The output should be formalized as: '''Q: | A: | Reason: | Difficulty Level: | '''

Table 6: Examples of instances from DocBench, with multiple labels indicating our data diversity.

Question	Answer	Labels	Document
Why does the model not perform as well in German compared to Spanish and Dutch?	Due to its complex morphology and compound words...	<Aca.><Why> <Text-only> <Textual>	When and Why are Pre-trained Word Embeddings Useful for Machine Translation [clickable file link]
By how much did the number of Erica users increase from 2018 to 2019?	The number increased by 5.5 million...	<Fin.><How> <Multimodal> <Numerical>	Bank of America Annual Report 2020 [clickable file link]
What is the primary focus of Bureau Objective 3.4?	The report does not contain such objective.	<Gov.> <Wh-> <Unanswerable> <Others>	Governmental report from *Secretary's Office of Global Women's Issues* 2022 [clickable file link]
How many times does the report mention "scientific ethics"?	The report mentions "scientific ethics" 11 times.	<Laws><How> <Meta-data> <Numerical>	Report on *Regulation of Stem Cell Research* from Library of Congress 2023 [clickable file link]
Is the article about Hurricane Ian's impact in Florida written by multiple authors?	Yes, the article is about Hurrican Ian's impace in Florida...	<News><Y/N> <Meta-data> <Boolean>	New York Times front page on 2022-09-30 [clickable file link]

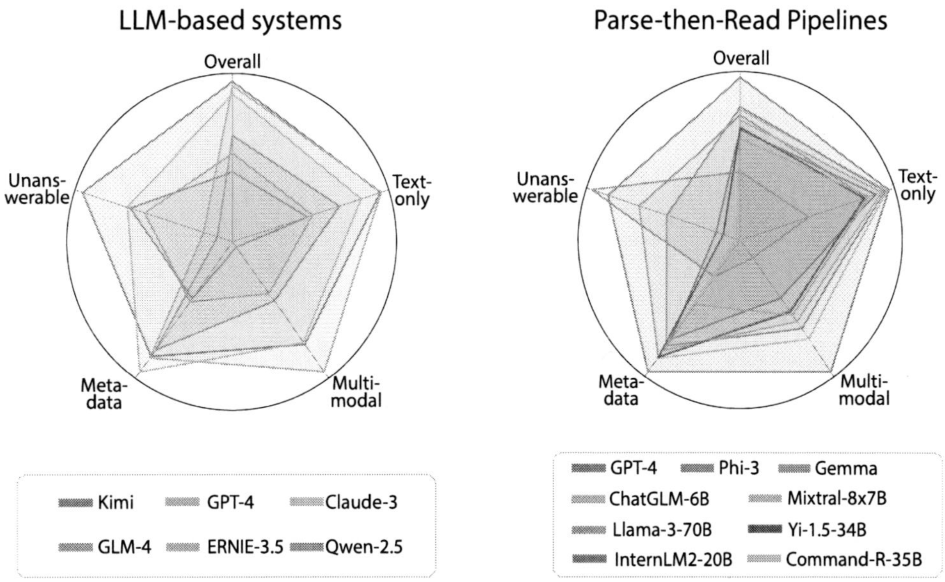

Figure 6: Performance (Relative) of two major methods on DocBench against the best.

Table 7: Analyzing the Influence of Input Sources: We deliver questions with attached files and without files to GPT-4 and GPT-4o for evaluation, respectively.

Methods	**Domain**					**Type**				**Overall** Acc.
	Aca.	**Fin.**	**Gov.**	**Laws**	**News**	**Text.**	**Multi.**	**Meta.**	**Una.**	
GPT-4										
w/ file	65.7	65.3	75.7	69.6	79.6	87.9	74.7	50.8	37.1	69.8
w/o file	10.9	10.8	23.0	29.3	32.6	40.8	8.1	1.6	10.5	19.1
GPT-4o										
w/ file	56.4	56.3	73.0	65.5	75.0	85.0	62.7	50.4	17.7	63.1
w/o file	11.2	13.5	29.1	31.9	36.0	46.6	10.7	2.3	6.5	21.7

Author Index